DEFINING DOCUMENTS IN AMERICAN HISTORY

The 1900s
(1900-1909)

DEFINING DOCUMENTS
IN AMERICAN HISTORY

The 1900s (1900-1909)

Editor

Michael Shally-Jensen, PhD

SALEM PRESS
A Division of EBSCO Information Services
Ipswich, Massachusetts

GREY HOUSE PUBLISHING

Copyright ©2016, by Salem Press, A Division of EBSCO Information Services, Inc., and Grey House Publishing, Inc.

All rights reserved. No part of this work may be used or reproduced in any manner whatsoever or transmitted in any form or by any means, electronic or mechanical, including photocopy, recording, or any information storage and retrieval system, without written permission from the copyright owner. For permissions requests, contact proprietarypublishing@ebsco.com.

∞ The paper used in these volumes conforms to the American National Standard for Permanence of Paper for Printed Library Materials, Z39.48 1992 (R2009).

Publisher's Cataloging-In-Publication Data
(Prepared by The Donohue Group, Inc.)

Names: Shally-Jensen, Michael, editor.
Title: The 1900s (1900-1909) / editor, Michael Shally-Jensen, PhD.
Other Titles: Nineteen hundreds (1900-1909) | Defining documents in American history (Salem Press)
Description: [First edition]. | Ipswich, Massachusetts : Salem Press, a division of EBSCO Information Services ; [Amenia, New York] : Grey House Publishing, [2016] | Includes bibliographical references and index.
Identifiers: ISBN 978-1-68217-185-1 (hardcover)
Subjects: LCSH: United States--History--1901-1909--Sources. | United States--Politics and government--1897-1901--Sources. | United States--Politics and government--1901-1909--Sources. | United States--Social conditions--1865-1918--Sources. | United States--Economic conditions--1865-1918--Sources. | Nineteen hundreds (Decade)
Classification: LCC E756 .A19 2016 | DDC 973.911--dc23

FIRST PRINTING ·
PRINTED IN THE UNITED STATES OF AMERICA

Table of Contents

Publisher's Note vii
Editor's Introduction. ix
Contributors xiii

POLITICS AND REFORM

William McKinley: Last Speech 3
Eugene V. Debs: "How I Became a Socialist". 8
Lincoln Steffens: "The Shame of Minneapolis" 13
Anna Howard Shaw: Address on the Place of Women in Industry and Address on the Condition of Women in Industry. 26
American Antiquities Act 32
Pure Food and Drug Act 35
Jane Addams: "Passing of the War Virtues" 43
Muller v. Oregon 49
Robert La Follette: Speech on the Amendment of National Banking Laws 58
Samuel Gompers: Editorial on the Supreme Court Ruling in the Danbury Hatters' Case. 64

FOREIGN CHALLENGES

Henry Cabot Lodge: Speech on the Retention of the Philippine Islands 73
The Insular Cases: *Downes v. Bidwell* 79
Boxer Protocol 94
Vladimir Lenin: *What Is to Be Done?* 103
Panama Canal Treaty 117
Roosevelt Corollary to the Monroe Doctrine 127
The Treaty of Portsmouth. 134
John Kenneth Turner: *Barbarous Mexico* 142

AFRICAN AMERICAN DEBATES

Ida B. Wells: "Lynch Law in America". 155
George H. White: Farewell Address to Congress. 166
Booker T. Washington: "Statement on Suffrage" 176

W. E. B. Du Bois: *The Souls of Black Folk* 184
W. E. B. Du Bois: "The Parting of the Ways" 200
Ida B. Wells: "Booker T. Washington and His Critics" 206
Niagara Movement Declaration of Principles 213
Theodore Roosevelt: Brownsville Legacy Special Message to the Senate 223

NATIVE AMERICAN LIFE

Charles Eastman: *Indian Boyhood* 239
Edward S. Curtis: Introduction to *The North American Indian* 247

RELIGION AND PHILOSOPHY

Rufus M. Jones: "Essential Truths" 257
Rudolf Steiner: *Theosophy* 266

APPENDIXES

Chronological List 279
Web Resources 280
Bibliography 282
Index 289

Publisher's Note

Defining Documents in American History series, produced by Salem Press, consists of a collection of essays on important historical documents by a diverse range of writers on a broad range of subjects in American history. This established series offers twenty-one titles ranging from Colonial America to the 1970s.

This volume, *Defining Documents in American History: The 1900s (1900-1909)*, offers in-depth analysis of a broad range of historical documents and historic events that shaped first decade of the twentieth century in American history. This text closely studies thirty primary source documents and delivers a thorough examination of events and movements in the U.S. from 1900 to 1909. The material is organized under five broad categories:

- Politics and Reform
- Foreign Challenges
- African American Debates
- Native American Life
- Religion and Philosophy

Historical documents provide a compelling view of these important aspects of American history. Designed for high school and college students, the aim of the series is to advance historical document studies as an important activity in learning about history.

Essay Format
The 1900s contains 30 primary source documents—many in their entirety. Each document is supported by a critical essay, written by historians and teachers, that includes a Summary Overview, Defining Moment, Author Biography, Document Analysis, and Essential Themes. Readers will appreciate the diversity of the collected texts, including journal entries from James Audubon, pamphlets from political leaders such as Eugene V. Debs and Vladimir Lenin, speeches from activists such as W. E. B. Du Bois and Booker T. Washington, religious and philosophical tracts from Rudolf Steiner and Rufus Jones, laws such as the American Antiquities Act and the Pure Food and Drug Act, editorials from writers such as Samuel Gompers, trial notes relating to decisions that pertained to labor laws and sex discrimination, and a turn-of-the-century photograph by Edward Curtis, among other genres. An important feature of each essay is a close reading of the primary source that develops evidence of broader themes, such as the author's rhetorical purpose, social or class position, point of view, and other relevant issues. In addition, essays are organized by section themes, listed above, highlighting major issues of the period, many of which extend across eras and continue to shape life as we know it around the world. Each section begins with a brief introduction that defines questions and problems underlying the subjects in the historical documents. Each essay also includes a Bibliography and Additional Reading section for further research.

Appendixes
- **Chronological List** arranges all documents by year.
- **Web Resources** is an annotated list of websites that offer valuable supplemental resources.
- **Bibliography** lists helpful articles and books for further study.

Contributors
Salem Press would like to extend its appreciation to all involved in the development and production of this work. The essays have been written and signed by scholars of history, humanities, and other disciplines related to the essays' topics. Without these expert contributions, a project of this nature would not be possible. A full list of contributor's names and affiliations appears in the front matter of this volume.

Editor's Introduction

The 20th century in the United States opened under both auspicious and inauspicious circumstances. On the positive side, a sustained period of relative economic prosperity was in place under Republican leadership (in both executive and legislative branches of government). Part of that stability, though, was attributable to artificial trade protection measures (the Dingley Tariff), which raised rates on imported goods up to 57 percent. The Gold Standard Act of 1900, arguably, also played a role; it made paper money redeemable only in gold (not silver), helping to rationalize industrial capitalism but favoring bankers and the investor class. Contributing to the positive economic picture, too, was the fact that the Sherman Antitrust Act and the Interstate Commerce Act had both been severely weakened by the courts, thus fostering an amalgamation of business (and political) interests.

On the negative side, there was increasing unrest among the laboring classes at the start of the decade over the conditions and terms of workers' employment. A growing recognition among political reformers that practices like child labor were intolerable led to significant changes yet alarmed business owners and many working families that traditionally relied on that source of income. In the presidential election of 1900, the Democrats, led by William Jennings Bryan, predictably denounced monopolies, industry-friendly tariffs, the gold standard (proclaiming the benefits of "free silver" instead), unjust labor practices, and, above all, militarism and imperialism in the aftermath of the Spanish-American War (1898). Republicans, on the other hand, were content to "stand pat" with President William McKinley for a second term; McKinley had proved himself to be a friend to business expansion, even if meant exploiting labor at home and capturing new markets abroad, sometimes forcefully. McKinley chose Theodore Roosevelt, the "hero of San Juan Hill," as his vice presidential candidate. The 1900 election results endorsed McKinley and Roosevelt by a margin of about 3 to 2 over Bryan and his running mate, Adlai Stevenson I.

Change was soon at hand, however. During a visit to the Pan American Exposition in Buffalo, New York, in the early fall of 1901, McKinley was shot by an anarchist. He died eight days later and Roosevelt acceded to the presidency. "TR," as he was informally known, would have a lasting impact on the office.

Progressive Social and Political Reforms

The period between the start of the Roosevelt administration and the entry of the United States into World War I is known as the Progressive Era. Progressive reformers during this period sought an end to political corruption and greater protections for workers and the American public from the worst ravages of unbridled capitalism. One may recall that the Gilded Age—the time of the great robber barons—had been around for some three decades prior to the rise of the Progressive movement in the early 20th century. Progressives sought to change the dynamics of political power—no more political bosses or corporate cabals—and give voice to workers, farmers, and women who had been left behind by the dominant business and political class. They wanted to replace laissez-faire capitalism with a regulatory welfare state. Immigrants, too, came in for modest upgrades to their status as urban dwellers, even as they continued to be feared by the majority of (white) Americans. To a far less degree, Progressives attended to the rights of communities of color.

Although Theodore Roosevelt believed in business and understood its value to society, he knew as well that, given free reign, corporations sometimes engaged in practices that tended to harm the general welfare. The problem was compounded when business interests consolidated in the form of a "trust," or monopoly, and colluded in order to reap increased profits and eliminate any market competition. Despite his own claims to the contrary, Roosevelt became known as a "trust buster," beginning with the creation of the Bureau of Corporations in 1903 to monitor business methods. All told, the Roosevelt administration brought some 45 suits against suspect companies under the newly revived Sherman Antitrust Act. Combinations in restraint of trade faced dissolution under the act—except after 1911, when antitrust laws were once again drained of their force by the Supreme Court.

Roosevelt also appreciated the government's role in resolving labor disputes. For example, a coal miners' strike in 1902 saw Roosevelt bringing together mine owners and mine workers to arrange a settlement—under the threat of having the mine seized by the federal government. The president felt that maintaining an adequate coal supply was in the public interest and therefore mining operations must go on. Other gains during the Progressive Era similarly aided labor, such as state laws against child labor and for workmen's compensation. Nevertheless, in the same years, businesses maintained their traditional strength, supported by the courts and by organizations such as the National Association of Manufacturers. The economy in general was thriving, but the distribution of wealth was anything but equal during this period. The "middle class" was barely even a concept, so extreme was the difference between the haves and the have-nots.

By the end of his first term Roosevelt was popular enough to easily win the nomination of the Republican Party for a second term, even though the old guard of his party was not pleased with the direction he was taking. In the 1904 general election Roosevelt made quick work of the Democratic challenger, the little-known Alton B. Parker. For the first time, too, the Socialist Party fielded a candidate in a presidential election, the laborite Eugene Debs. Although not finding much success in electoral politics, the Socialists became increasingly important in the labor movement, founding the Industrial Workers of the World in Chicago in 1905 with the aim of dismantling capitalism. Anarchists were on the rise too. Meanwhile, Roosevelt was content to closely regulate industry, always holding the public trust above any other interest group or organization. Near the end of his second term, in 1908, Roosevelt yielded to his friend and colleague William H. Taft for the Republican nomination. Taft won the election, yet a split soon developed between the two leaders, resulting in Roosevelt running again in 1912 on the independent "Bull Moose" ticket.

Key to the Progressives' reform activities was information put out by a new brand of investigative journalism undertaken by writers known as muckrakers. Theirs was the "literature of exposure," a genre concerned with revealing any and all varieties of unsavory business and political conduct wherever it was present. The leading talent here included such figures as Lincoln Steffens, Ida Tarbell, Ray Stannard Baker, Jacob Riis, and Upton Sinclair. Steffens wrote of graft and corruption, Tarbell of corporate perfidy, Baker of racial injustice, Riis of labor excesses, and so on. In some cases the muckrakers' accounts led directly to legislative action. Sinclair's *The Jungle,* for example, documented the grim conditions in the meat-packing industry and prompted the subsequent Meat Inspection and Pure Food and Drug acts of 1906.

The campaign to gain the vote for women and to broaden women's roles in society saw progress in the decade, but no concrete results were forthcoming. That women were entering the workforce in unprecedented numbers was obvious, and this trend was paralleled to a lesser degree by increased enrollments among women in higher education and the professions. The main focus of women's political activism, however, remained the suffrage movement, led by a group of upper-class feminists who had the education and leisure time to enable them to pursue the cause. Although some advances were made at the state level, it would not be until the end of the next decade that women would finally win the vote nationwide. Other reform efforts led by or involving women were the temperance movement, which sought to prohibit alcoholic beverages; the sanitation movement, which aimed to improve public hygiene; the settlement movement, which designed to bring volunteers to poor urban neighborhoods to alleviate poverty; and the campaign to end child labor, particularly in the mining and manufacturing industries. Most such efforts gained ground in the 1900s but did not reach their peak until the following decade or later.

Minority communities continued to face grave struggles between 1900 and 1910. Even as the Progressives provided uplift to some, they allowed the exclusion of others. The courts, in particular, were a barrier, denying the rights of African Americans, Native Americans, Latinos, and others in the name of economic progress for property owners and the moneyed class. Racism was, as always, embedded in the American psyche. It would not be until the Civil Rights movement of the 1950s and 1960s that things would start to change in that regard.

The United States as a World Power

With the emergence of a modern, industrial America came the rise, too, of the United States as a global force and an imperial power. A vast new "white navy," made possible by new types of hardened steel and government investment in military materiel, served to project the Roosevelt administration's aggressive aims abroad. The military had authority under the Monroe Doctrine to police the waters and territories of the Caribbean and South America to preserve US strength in the hemisphere. The same doctrine had been applied in 1895 by President Grover Cleveland to ward off Britain in a boundary dispute between it and Venezuela, which was regarded as within the US sphere of interest. "Monroe" was applied once again in Venezuela in 1902 by Theodore Roosevelt, when a German naval blockade sought to punish the Venezuelan government for defaulting on its debts. In that situation, Admiral George Dewey—another Spanish-American War hero—threatened war if Germany pursued the matter militarily. A corollary to the doctrine was subsequently added by Roosevelt in 1904, when his administration took over the financial affairs of a failing Dominican Republic. The new "Roosevelt Corollary" stated that although European powers must not intervene in the affairs of the Americas (per the Monroe Doctrine), and although generally it was not the policy of the United States to intervene in a nation's domestic affairs, in circumstances such as those surrounding the Dominican Republic, where US interests were involved, intervention by the United States was deemed acceptable, even necessary. In later years, American presidents would cite the Roosevelt Corollary in intervening in Cuba, Nicaragua, Haiti, and elsewhere.

After the Spanish-American War, Cuba had been made essentially a US protectorate. Although the island nation was formally granted the right to self-government, the United States was not averse to intervening in Cuban affairs. Similarly, Puerto Rico and the Philippines were made colonial territories, with the American president appointing their governors and state councils. Although in subsequent years the two states were allowed to exercise greater administrative independence, the Supreme Court ruled in 1901 (in the Insular Cases) that island residents were not entitled to the full array of rights and privileges embedded in the US Constitution. In the case of the Philippines, a war took place 1899-1902 between the self-proclaimed Philippine Republic and the United States over the status of that nation, with sporadic fighting afterward.

China was by the turn of the century being divided up by European powers and Japan into trade spheres. Secretary of State John Hay proposed, in 1899, maintaining an Open Door policy under which existing port treaties would remain in force. In early 1900, Hay announced that the various powers had agreed to continue the Open Door policy and, moreover, would respect a Chinese sphere of influence. The reaction in China was not universally positive, however. In June 1900, an anti-foreign militia known in English as the Boxers occupied Beijing and attacked foreign diplomatic and religious missions. A coalition of British, French, Russian, German, Japanese, and American forces formed to combat the uprising, moving inland from Tientsin to Beijing. With the suppression of the Boxer Rebellion, the United States and its partners re-affirmed the equal-trade agreements and, after extracting a variety of humiliating obligations from China, allowed it to pay a war indemnity in cash rather than in territory.

East Asia, in fact, was a politically volatile region in the decade of the 1900s. At the start of the Russo-Japanese War in 1904, which was fought over territorial disputes in Manchuria and Korea, President Roosevelt cautioned that support of Russia by any European nation would cause the United States to intervene on the side of Japan. After over a year of conflict, the two belligerents were persuaded by Roosevelt to convene in Portsmouth, New Hampshire, to discuss a settlement. A deal was signed in September 1905.

Another signal foreign policy achievement by the Roosevelt administration was the creation of the Panama Canal Zone. In 1903 the United States paid $40 million to take over the works of a failed canal project begun by a French firm; it also obtained rights from Columbia to operate in its Panama province. A separatist effort was then under way on the isthmus, however, and by November 1903 its leaders had declared an independent Panama. Roosevelt effectively blocked the Columbian military from retaking the area by posting US naval vessels offshore and by refusing Columbia's use of the US-owned Panama Railroad. Consequently, Panama granted the United States rights in perpetuity with respect to the Canal Zone. Construction of the shipping passage was begun later in the decade, and it was opened in 1914.

—*Michael Shally-Jensen, PhD*

Bibliography

Chambers, John Whiteclay. *The Tyranny of Change: America in the Progressive Era, 1890-1920.* New Brunswick, NJ: Rutgers University Press, 2000.

Lears, Jackson. *Rebirth of a Nation: The Making of Modern America, 1877-1920.* New York: HarperCollins, 2009.

McGerr, Michael. *A Fierce Discontent: The Rise and Fall of the Progressive Movement in America, 1870-1920.* New York: Oxford University Press, 2005.

Painter, Nell Irvin. *Standing at Armageddon: A Grassroots History of the Progressive Era.* New York: W.W. Norton, 2008.

Wolraich, Michael. *Unreasonable Men: Theodore Roosevelt and the Republican Rebels Who Created Progressive Politics.* New York: St. Martin's, 2014.

Contributors

Brian Bonhomme, PhD
Youngstown State University

Ron Briley, PhD
Sandia Preparatory School

Garna L. Christian, PhD
University of Houston--Downtown

Allan L. Damon, MA
Horace Greeley High School (Ret.)

Steven L. Danver, PhD
Walden University

Adam W. Darlage, PhD
Oakton Community College, Des Plaines

K. P. Dawes, MA
Chicago, IL

Amber R. Dickinson, PhD
Oklahoma State University

Justus D. Doenecke, PhD
New College of Florida

Mark Elliott, PhD
University of North Carolina, Greensboro

Ashleigh Fata, MA
University of California, Los Angeles

Gerald F. Goodwin, PhD
Bloomington, IN

Lewis L. Gould, PhD
University of Texas, Austin

Aaron Gulyas, MA
Mott Community College

Mark Joy, PhD
University of Jamestown

Scott C. Monje, PhD
Tarrytown, NY

Michael J. O'Neal, PhD
Moscow, Idaho

Steven L. Piott, PhD
Clarion University

Luca Prono, PhD
Bologna, Italy

Jonathan Reese, PhD
Colorado State University, Pueblo

Bartholomew H. Sparrow, PhD
University of Texas, Austin

Randy Wagner, JD, PhD
University of Denver Sturm College of Law

Leland Ware, JD
University of Delaware

Cary D. Wintz, PhD
Texas Southern University

DEFINING DOCUMENTS
IN AMERICAN HISTORY

The 1900s (1900-1909)

POLITICS AND REFORM

The assassination of President William McKinley in September 1901 seemed to herald the end of one era and the beginning of another. McKinley, a Republican who enjoyed the support of both houses of Congress, was of a type that understood the presidency as a reflection of the will of the people rather than as an office from which one might lead the nation down new paths. Not that the United States under the McKinley administration did not take some unexpected turns, such as when it sought, in 1898, to "free Cuba" from Spanish brutality—and in the course of that struggle also captured Puerto Rico, Guam, and the Philippines from Spain. The Republican leadership (and much of the public) saw the Spanish-American War as a great victory and regarded the overseas colonies created in its wake as just spoils. Democrats, on the other hand, construed the whole matter as a form of unwanted imperialism that went against the grain of domestic interests. In any case, McKinley was not the hero of the Spanish-American War; rather, that title belonged to his soon-to-be vice president, Colonel Theodore Roosevelt. Thus, when an anarchist's bullet felled McKinley, "Teddy" Roosevelt moved into the White House and made the office of the president very much his own.

Under Roosevelt, a variety of progressive reforms would take place—so much so that the era became known as the Progressive Era. His administration supported, to one degree or another, the breakup of monopolies (or "trusts"), the ending of political corruption, the increased participation of citizen-voters (not just elites) in governmental affairs, greater legal protections for workers and farmers, the expansion of educational opportunities, infrastructural improvements in the cities and beyond, better health and sanitation measures, consumer protections, and the creation of national parks, among other things. To the old guard of his party, Roosevelt was something a turncoat. To most of the rest of the nation, however, he was a revelation.

In truth, many of the reforms—and the problems they addressed—unfolded not at the federal but at the state and municipal level. Nevertheless, the federal government played a significant role in setting the agenda, passing needed legislation and giving Progressive groups a national stage on which to operate. The US Supreme Court, too, weighed in on a variety of measures, although the justices' rulings usually reflected a more conservative philosophy than that held by Roosevelt and other Progressives.

Politics and Reform

William McKinley: Last Speech

Date: 1901
Author: William McKinley
Genre: speech

Summary Overview

William McKinley was president of the United States during the period of overseas expansion that grew out of the war with Spain in 1898. A popular speaker as a campaigner, McKinley wrote presidential messages and delivered addresses that proved significant in persuading Americans to adopt this expanded world role at the end of the nineteenth century. At a time when radio did not yet exist, the president had to make his case through the prose that his constituents read in their newspapers or in pamphlet form. McKinley proved quite adept at framing arguments that would convince citizens of the wisdom of the course he was proposing. On the day before he was shot by an assassin, McKinley delivered his Last Speech in Buffalo, New York. In it, he encouraged reciprocal trade arrangements with foreign countries and emphasized the need to put aside attitudes of isolationism.

Author Biography

William McKinley was born in Ohio in 1843. He fought in the Civil War and then was elected to the House of Representatives, where he served from 1876 to 1890. From 1892 to 1896 he was governor of Ohio. Nominated by the Republicans for the presidency in 1896, McKinley was elected and served from 1897 until he was assassinated in 1901. During his four and a half years in office, a dispute with Spain over the rebellion of Cuba against the Spanish led to war in 1898. That conflict, in turn, resulted in an American victory and the negotiation of a peace treaty in Paris. The outcome of the war led to America's acquisition of Guam, the Philippines, and Puerto Rico. McKinley was reelected to the presidency in 1900. He was shot by an anarchist sympathizer on September 6, 1901, and died on September 14, 1901.

Defining Moment

McKinley was the first modern president. Although he had been elected largely on domestic issues in the campaign of 1896, he became a significant chief executive in the area of foreign policy. During his administration the United States fought the Spanish-American War over the fate of the island of Cuba. McKinley used his power as commander in chief to direct the war effort, govern the possessions that were added from the peace treaty with Spain, and prosecute a war in the Philippines. The administration also sought to penetrate the Far East for American trade through the policy of the Open Door with China, a concept developed in the mid-nineteenth century and stating that all nations, in principle, should have equal trading rights in China. These developments accelerated the process by which the United States became a world power.

HISTORICAL DOCUMENT

I am glad again to be in the city of Buffalo and exchange greetings with her people, to whose generous hospitality I am not a stranger, and with whose good will I have been repeatedly and signally honored. To-day I have additional satisfaction in meeting and giving welcome to the foreign representatives assembled here, whose presence and participation in this Exposition have contributed in so marked a degree to its interest and success....

Expositions are the timekeepers of progress. They record the world's advancement. They stimulate the energy, enterprise and intellect of the people, and quicken human genius. They go into the home. They broaden and brighten the daily life of the people. They open mighty storehouses of information to the student. Every exposition, great or small, has helped to some onward step.

Comparison of ideas is always educational and, as such, instructs the brain and hand of man. Friendly rivalry follows, which is the spur to industrial improvement, the inspiration to useful invention and to high endeavor in all departments of human activity. It exacts a study of the wants, comforts, and even the whims of the people, and recognizes the efficacy of high quality and low prices to win their favor. The quest for trade is an incentive to men of business to devise, invent, improve and economize in the cost of production. Business life, whether among ourselves, or with other peoples, is ever a sharp struggle for success. It will be none the less in the future.

Without competition we would be clinging to the clumsy and antiquated process of farming and manufacture and the methods of business of long ago, and the twentieth would be no further advanced than the eighteenth century. But though commercial competitors we are, commercial enemies we must not be. The Pan-American Exposition has done its work thoroughly, presenting in its exhibits evidences of the highest skill and illustrating the progress of the human family in the Western Hemisphere. This portion of the earth has no cause for humiliation for the part it has performed in the march of civilization. It has not accomplished everything; far from it. It has simply done its best, and without vanity or boastfulness, and recognizing the manifold achievements of others it invites the friendly rivalry of all the powers in the peaceful pursuits of trade and commerce, and will cooperate with all in advancing the highest and best interests of humanity. The wisdom and energy of all the nations are none too great for the world work. The success of art, science, industry and invention is an international asset and a common glory.

After all, how near one to the other is every part of the world. Modern inventions have brought into close relation widely separated peoples and make them better acquainted. Geographic and political divisions will continue to exist, but distances have been effaced. Swift ships and fast trains are becoming cosmopolitan. They invade fields which a few years ago were impenetrable. The world's products are exchanged as never before and with increasing transportation facilities come increasing knowledge and larger trade. Prices are fixed with mathematical precision by supply and demand. The world's selling prices are regulated by market and crop reports. We travel greater distances in a shorter space of time and with more ease than was ever dreamed of by the fathers. Isolation is no longer possible or desirable. The same important news is read, though in different languages, the same day in all Christendom.

The telegraph keeps us advised of what is occurring everywhere, and the Press foreshadows, with more or less accuracy, the plans and purposes of the nations. Market prices of products and of securities are hourly known in every commercial mart, and the investments of the people extend beyond their own national boundaries into the remotest parts of the earth. Vast transactions are conducted and international exchanges are made by the tick of the cable. Every event of interest is immediately bulletined. The quick gathering and transmission of news, like rapid transit, are of recent origin, and are only made possible by the genius of the inventor and the courage of the investor. It took a special messenger of the government, with every facility known at the time for rapid travel, nineteen days to go from the City of Washington to New Orleans with a message to General Jackson that the war with England had ceased and a treaty of peace had been signed. How different now!...

At the beginning of the nineteenth century there was not a mile of steam railroad on the globe; now there are enough miles to make its circuit many times. Then there was not a line of electric telegraph; now we have a vast mileage traversing all lands and seas. God and man have linked the nations together. No nation can longer be indifferent to any other. And as we are brought more and more in touch with each other, the less occasion is there for misunderstandings, and the stronger the disposition, when we have differences, to adjust them in the court of arbitration, which is the noblest forum for the settlement of international disputes....

We have a vast and intricate business, built up

through years of toil and struggle in which every part of the country has its stake, which will not permit of either neglect or of undue selfishness. No narrow, sordid policy will subserve it. The greatest skill and wisdom on the part of manufacturers and producers will be required to hold and increase it. Our industrial enterprises, which have grown to such great proportions, affect the homes and occupations of the people and the welfare of the country. Our capacity to produce has developed so enormously and our products have so multiplied that the problem of more markets requires our urgent and immediate attention. Only a broad and enlightened policy will keep what we have. No other policy will get more. In these times of marvelous business energy and gain we ought to be looking to the future, strengthening the weak places in our industrial and commercial systems, that we may be ready for any storm or strain.

By sensible trade arrangements which will not interrupt our home production we shall extend the outlets for our increasing surplus. A system which provides a mutual exchange of commodities is manifestly essential to the continued and healthful growth of our export trade. We must not repose in the fancied security that we can for ever sell everything and buy little or nothing. If such a thing were possible it would not be best for us or for those with whom we deal. We should take from our customers such of their products as we can use without harm to our industries and labor. Reciprocity is the natural outgrowth of our wonderful industrial development under the domestic policy now firmly established.

What we produce beyond our domestic consumption must have a vent abroad. The excess must be relieved through a foreign outlet, and we should sell everywhere we can and buy wherever the buying will enlarge our sales and productions, and thereby make a greater demand for home labor.

The period of exclusiveness is past. The expansion of our trade and commerce is the pressing problem. Commercial wars are unprofitable. A policy of good will and friendly trade relations will prevent reprisals. Reciprocity treaties are in harmony with the spirit of the times; measures of retaliation are not....

Who can tell the new thoughts that have been awakened, the ambitions fired and the high achievements that will be wrought through this Exposition?

Gentlemen, let us ever remember that our interest is in concord, not conflict; and that our real eminence rests in the victories of peace, not those of war. We hope that all who are represented here may be moved to higher and nobler efforts for their own and the world's good, and that out of this city may come not only greater commerce and trade for us all, but, more essential than these, relations of mutual respect, confidence and friendship which will deepen and endure. Our earnest prayer is that God will graciously vouchsafe prosperity, happiness and peace to all our neighbors, and like blessings to all the peoples and powers of earth.

GLOSSARY

bulletined: recorded in written form

Christendom: the entire Christianized world, comprising primarily Europe and nations founded elsewhere by descendants of Europeans

Exposition: a public exhibition, displaying technological and other achievements of a given place and time

quicken: encourage

reciprocity treaties: agreements beneficial to all participants

tick of the cable: the transmission of messages in Morse code over telegraph wires

Document Analysis

The last speech that McKinley ever delivered came on September 5, 1901, at the Pan-American Exposition in Buffalo, New York. For that reason, it has become known as "McKinley's Last Speech" and copies of the address usually carry that title. Of course, McKinley did not know at that time that he would be shot the next day. His comments were part of a campaign he was launching as he began his second term. He had been reelected in November 1900 over William Jennings Bryan and believed that his policies had been endorsed as well. Although McKinley had been identified with the doctrine of the protective tariff from the start of his political career, he had come to think that it was time for the United States to liberalize its trade relations with other countries. His administration had negotiated reciprocal trade agreements with several countries, and the United States Senate was to take those up when Congress met for its regular session in December 1901.

The Republicans in the Senate did not share McKinley's view of trade policy, and so the president intended to build public support for his new program through a series of speeches during the fall of 1901. After McKinley's death, Theodore Roosevelt as his successor abandoned the trade treaties and pursued attacks on large corporations or "trusts" instead. McKinley's speech at Buffalo thus represented not the start of a presidential campaign for his program but a punctuation point for McKinley's life and presidency. Read in the context of what he hoped to accomplish during his second term, it is a document that says much about McKinley's vision of the future for the United States. In his remarks, for example, he notes in the third paragraph that "isolation is no longer possible or desirable." His comments in the third and fourth paragraphs describe a crude form of early-twentieth-century globalization and the changes that technology was making in people's lives. For that reason, the president adds, "no nation can longer be indifferent to any other." Having outlined these elements, McKinley then comes to the point of his address. "By sensible trade arrangements which will not interrupt our home production, we shall extend the outlets for our increasing surplus" of products.

The message of trade reciprocity then becomes clear: "We must not repose in fancied security that we can forever sell everything and buy little or nothing." As a result, "reciprocity is the natural outgrowth of our wonderful industrial development under the domestic policy now firmly established." McKinley argues that "reciprocity treaties are in harmony with the spirit of the times; measures of retaliation are not." He then lists the policies that the nation should follow—promotion of the merchant marine, the building of a canal across Central America, and telegraph cable service to the Pacific. Praise came in the newspaper accounts the next day (September 6) for what McKinley had said. That same afternoon, McKinley was shot; he died eight days later. People remembered his speech for a time. As the dynamic personality of Theodore Roosevelt took over the presidency, the import of McKinley's words receded, however, and his themes became indistinct and eventually disappeared.

Essential Themes

McKinley's importance stemmed from his impact on the office of the presidency itself. In forging closer relationships with the press, traveling extensively to promote his programs, and working closely with Congress, McKinley set precedents that subsequent executives emulated during the twentieth century. By the start of his second term, there were complaints in some quarters that McKinley had accumulated too much power and was stretching the authority of the presidency in directions the framers of the Constitution had not anticipated. Such criticisms attest to the significant impact McKinley's policies and his public articulation of the goals of his administration had in reshaping the way Americans saw their presidents.

In domestic affairs, McKinley's presidency witnessed an economic rebound from the depression of the 1890s. The enactment of the Dingley Act (1897) and the Gold Standard Act (1900) were key elements in the Republican program of a protective tariff and a sound, reliable currency, respectively. As businesses consolidated during the years of returning prosperity, the issue of "the trusts" (monopolies) became an important one in American politics. McKinley was assassinated before he could fully engage the issue, but there were indications as his second term began that he intended to regulate the trusts along the lines that Theodore Roosevelt later followed in his first term as president. Even though he had been an advocate of a protective tariff early in his career, McKinley endorsed liberalizing of American trade and planned to make that a hallmark of his second term. His last speech, delivered in September 1901 in Buffalo, New York, was a significant indication of the direction in which he, as president, wanted to take the country.

——*Lewis L. Gould, University of Texas at Austin*

Bibliography and Further Reading

McKinley, William, John S. Olgilvie, and Stewart L. Woodford. *Life and Speeches of William Mckinley: Containing a Sketch of His Eventful Life ... Proceedings of National Convention, St. Louis, Platform of the Republican Party, Sketch of the Candidate for Vice-President, and Other Valuable Information for Every Citizen.* New York: J.S. Ogilvie Pub. Co, 1981. Print.

McKinley, William. *Speeches and Addresses of William Mckinley: From March 1, 1897 to May 30, 1900.* New York: Doubleday & McClure Co, 1900. Print.

Eugene V. Debs: "How I Became a Socialist"

Date: 1902
Author: Eugene V. Debs
Genre: article

Summary Overview

The American trade union leader, orator, and Socialist Party activist Eugene Debs was a master at making what might look today like radical political ideas seem as American as apple pie. A student of history as well as politics, Debs regularly invoked the memory of the Founding Fathers to make his policy suggestions seem more acceptable. Motivated by an unyielding sense of justice, he often tried to shame authorities to do what he thought was right. Whether addressing audiences at a labor rally or on the campaign trail, Debs invariably came back to a sharp critique of the American political system, touting the virtues of his brand of Socialism. His goal as a politician was not necessarily to win elections but instead to inspire listeners by his own example and to win converts to the Socialist cause. In a country with no Socialist legacy—unlike many European countries where Socialism was established—it is really quite remarkable that Debs had any success at all as a politician. That success was due in no small part to the power of Debs's oratory and prose. In his 1902 article "How I Became a Socialist," Debs traces his path toward growing class consciousness and final embrace of Socialism.

Defining Moment

Debs' greatest struggle throughout his life was trying to realign perceptions of Socialism in American society. In this article and others throughout his life, Debs tried to move people toward a political viewpoint that he believed was more in sync with their best interests. It was only through an embrace of Socialism, Debs believed, could American workers achieve the sort of equality and justice that they deserved. His target for these speeches were chiefly American industrial workers, the men and women toiling in factories, in mines, and, perhaps above all else, laboring on the railroads. Working under hazardous conditions, long hours, and for little pay, American workers were ripe for recruitment into Debs' movement. By documenting his journey to Socialism, Debs hoped to inspire others in similar conditions, and in so doing call them to action.

Author Biography

Eugene Victor Debs was a trade union leader, orator, and frequent Socialist Party candidate for the presidency of the United States. He was born in Terre Haute, Indiana, in 1855. While working his way up through the hierarchy of the Brotherhood of Locomotive Firemen, an important railroad union, he was elected city clerk in Terre Haute in 1879. He also served one term in the Indiana state legislature in 1885. In 1893 Debs cofounded the American Railway Union (ARU), an industrial union that, unlike most exclusive railroad brotherhoods of the era, admitted railroad workers of all skill levels. As the leader of that organization, Debs led the infamous Pullman strike of 1894.

The Pullman strike was an effort to organize workers at the Pullman Palace Car Company of Pullman, Illinois. As part of the strike, ARU members nationwide decided to boycott all trains that carried the company's famous sleeping cars in an effort to force them to recognize the union. As a result, rail traffic stopped nationwide. In response, railroad companies deliberately placed mail cars on trains with Pullman Palace Cars in order to encourage government intervention in the dispute. The legal injunction issued by a federal judge in response to the boycott essentially shut down the strike and destroyed the union. In 1895 Debs was convicted of interfering with the mail as a result of his refusal to abide by that injunction. Debs's political views were greatly affected by the Socialist literature he read during his short stay in jail. Indeed, this incarceration would prove to be the pivotal point of his entire life.

Upon his release Debs announced his conversion to Socialism. He also changed career paths from being a trade union leader to being a political leader. Debs would serve as a Socialist Party presidential candidate five times: 1900, 1904, 1908, 1912, and 1920. His best showing occurred in 1912 when he came close to garnering a million votes. That was 6 percent of the total votes cast in that election. In 1918 Debs was convicted of sedition for a speech he had given in Canton, Ohio, earlier that year. Debs had to run his final campaign for president as a protest candidate from his jail cell. A famous campaign button from 1920 read "For President—Convict No. 9653." Between elections Debs toured the country giving speeches and writing articles that critiqued the American capitalist system and championed the cause of Socialism. Debs died in 1926 at the age of seventy.

Debs represented a vision of Socialism in America that got lost in the anti-Communist hysteria of the cold war era. His political beliefs, though Socialist, were grounded in American ideals like justice, equal rights, and Christianity. Debs's willingness to go to prison for the causes he championed greatly increased his appeal and the popularity of his ideas. While many other figures in American Socialism were immigrants from European countries like Germany, where Socialism was more in the mainstream, Debs attracted native-born Americans to the Socialist cause. His success as a politician came as the result of hundreds of thousands of Americans entertaining the possibility of radical change in American life in an era when the adverse effects of industrialization had made them unhappy with the existing political system.

HISTORICAL DOCUMENT

On the evening of February 27, 1875, the local lodge of the Brotherhood of Locomotive Firemen was organized at Terre Haute, Ind., by Joshua A. Leach, then grand master, and I was admitted as a charter member and at once chosen secretary. "Old Josh Leach" as he was affectionately called, a typical locomotive fireman of his day, was the founder of the brotherhood, and I was instantly attracted by his rugged honesty, simple manner and homely speech. How well I remember feeling his large, rough hand on my shoulder, the kindly eye of an elder brother searching my own as he gently said, "My boy, you're a little young, but I believe you're in earnest and will make your mark in the brotherhood." Of course, I assured him that I would do my best....

My first step was thus taken in organized labor and a new influence fired my ambition and changed the whole current of my career. I was filled with enthusiasm and my blood fairly leaped in my veins. Day and night I worked for the brotherhood. To see its watchfires glow and observe the increase of its sturdy members were the sunshine and shower of my life. To attend the "meeting" was my supreme joy, and for ten years I was not once absent when the faithful assembled....

Through all these years I was nourished at Fountain Proletaire. I drank deeply of its waters and every particle of my tissue became saturated with the spirit of the working class. I had fired an engine and been stung by the exposure and hardship of the rail. I was with the boys in their weary watches, at the broken engine's side and often helped to bear their bruised and bleeding bodies back to wife and child again. How could I but feel the burden of their wrongs? How the seed of agitation fail to take deep root in my heart?

And so I was spurred on in the work of organizing, not the firemen merely, but the brakemen, switchmen, telegraphers, shopmen, track-hands, all of them in fact, and as I had now become known as an organizer, the call came from all sides and there are but few trades I have not helped to organize and less still in whose strikes I have not at some time had a hand.

In 1894 the American Railway Union was organized and a braver body of men never fought the battle of the working class.

Up to this time I had heard but little of Socialism, knew practically nothing about the movement, and what little I did know was not calculated to impress me in its favor. I was bent on thorough and complete organization of the railroad men and ultimately the whole working class, and all my time and energy were given to that end. My supreme conviction was that if they were only organized in every branch of the service and all acted together in concert they could redress their wrongs and regulate the conditions of their employment. The stockholders of the corporation acted as one, why not the men? It was such a plain proposition—simply to follow the example set before their eyes by their masters—surely they could not fail to see it, act as one, and solve the problem....

The skirmish lines of the A. R. U. were well advanced. A series of small battles were fought and won without the loss of a man. A number of concessions were made by the corporations rather than risk an encounter. Then came the fight on the Great Northern, short, sharp, and decisive. The victory was complete—the only railroad strike of magnitude ever won by an organization in America.

Next followed the final shock—the Pullman strike—and the American Railway Union again won, clear and complete. The combined corporations were paralyzed and helpless. At this juncture there were delivered, from wholly unexpected quarters, a swift succession of blows that blinded me for an instant and then opened wide my eyes—and in the gleam of every bayonet and the flash of every rifle *the class struggle was revealed*. This was my first practical lesson in Socialism, though wholly unaware that it was called by that name.

An army of detectives, thugs and murderers were equipped with badge and beer and bludgeon and turned loose; old hulks of cars were fired; the alarm bells tolled; the people were terrified; the most startling rumors were set afloat; the press volleyed and thundered, and over all the wires sped the news that Chicago's white throat was in the clutch of a red mob; injunctions flew thick and fast, arrests followed, and our office and headquarters, the heart of the strike, was sacked, torn out and nailed up by the "lawful" authorities of the federal government; and when in company with my loyal comrades I found myself in Cook County jail at Chicago with the... press screaming conspiracy, treason and murder, and by some fateful coincidence I was given the cell occupied just previous to his execution by the assassin of Mayor Carter Harrison, Sr., overlooking the spot, a few feet distant, where the anarchists were hanged a few years before, I had another exceedingly practical and impressive lesson in Socialism....

The Chicago jail sentences were followed by six months at Woodstock and it was here that Socialism gradually laid hold of me in its own irresistible fashion. Books and pamphlets and letters from socialists came by every mail and I began to read and think and dissect the anatomy of the system in which workingmen, however organized, could be shattered and battered and splintered at a single stroke....

The American Railway Union was defeated but not conquered—overwhelmed but not destroyed. It lives and pulsates in the Socialist movement, and its defeat but blazed the way to economic freedom and hastened the dawn of human brotherhood.

GLOSSARY

Chicago's white throat was in the clutch of a red mob: sarcastic comparison of the city to a woman (white, at that) in danger from "reds," or Socialists

class struggle: fundamental conflict between the workers (proletariat) and business owners (capitalists)

Fountain Proletaire: an expression, apparently of Debs's own coinage, that used the French adjectival format (noun followed by adjective) and presented the struggle of industrial workers as an opportunity to gain wisdom and grow

grand master: a master craftsman, a leading figure in many local union bodies

Great Northern: the Great Northern Railway

homely: down home

watches: shifts at work

where the anarchists were hanged a few years before: a reference to the place of execution of four men out of eight charged for their alleged roles in the Haymarket riot in Chicago on May 4, 1886

Document Analysis

In his article "How I Became a Socialist" Debs does his best to convey that he had always been a kind of Socialist, even though he had explicitly rejected that label for his political ideas before his imprisonment in 1895. His goal in this piece is to suggest that people like him who saw aspects of class conflict all around them but did not understand Socialism would come to embrace the movement once Socialists like Debs taught them to understand the world. Here he describes his own education in the hope that others might follow along his same path.

In the early sections of the essay, Debs conveys his enthusiasm for organizing his fellow members of the working class as a sign of his growing class consciousness. At that point in his life, he thought organization alone was enough to redress the many wrongs that management inflicted upon labor. Debs explains that unlike other labor leaders of that era, he helped organize the ARU because he thought that all railroad men would do best standing together rather than separated into unions organized by skill. This is an implied contrast to the American Federation of Labor, an umbrella organization for unions that was just getting started around the time that Debs first gained prominence in the labor movement. Despite his comparatively broad view of organized labor's potential base, Debs's vision remained limited to what he could do in support of the trade union movement.

Then came the Pullman strike. "In the gleam of every bayonet and the flash of every rifle" Debs writes, "*the class struggle was revealed.*" This justifiably famous line not only supports the idea that the Pullman strike converted Debs to Socialism but also helps explain his reasons for supporting Socialism. Since the federal army kept the exploitation of Pullman workers going, ordinary people had to be able to control the state so that it could support their cause rather than the goals of giant corporations. To Debs, then, labor and politics were inseparable. He could not help the working class without entering politics.

This philosophy is in sharp contrast to the predominant labor union philosophy of that era. The American Federation of Labor, led by Samuel Gompers, believed in what Gompers called "pure and simple unionism." This meant that trade unions should worry about raising the wages and improving the working conditions of their members, and absolutely nothing else. Unions that followed this philosophy ignored politics because politics took time and resources away from their core purpose—helping their members. This debate was sometimes referred to as the "political question" within union circles. However, by the time of his death in 1924, Gompers came around to Debs's point of view on this issue even if he never adopted Debs's radical positions.

Essential Themes

The industrial revolution completely transformed not just how products were made but also the relationship between labor and capital. Whereas before products were handcrafter, requiring specialized skill, the industrial revolution allowed, and in fact demanded, large numbers of unskilled workers. To the men who owned the factories, labor became just another resource, on the same order as coal or oil. As need for labor increased, workers began to make demands on owners, including higher pay, shorter hours, and higher safety standards. When owners refused, the clashes often became violent. One industry especially fraught with conflict were the railroads, run with an iron fist by industrialists such as Jay Gould and Cornelius Vanderbilt. These robber barons continuously fought against the rise of unions and bettering conditions for their workers, even going so far as to employ private police to put down work stoppage and protest, violently, if need be. By the 1880s several unions had formed as a counter measure to the power of the industrialists, among them Eugene V. Deb' American Railway Union. Tensions erupted in 1893. When after a panic in the market, George Pullman began to lay off employees and cut wages. Pullman, owner of the Pullman Palace Car Company, required workers to live in a planned community he designed on the south side of Chicago, but despite firing workers and cutting wages, he did not cut the already steep rents he forced his employees to pay. The following year, the ARU organized a mass boycott, in which 125,000 Pullman employees walked off the job at over two dozen railroads. The boycott, along with sympathy strikes launched by other unions, halted railroad transportation across the country. When the railroads responded by hiring strikebreakers, the strikes became violent. In response President Grover Cleveland sent in the army, leading to clashes between armed troops and strikers, resulting in 30 deaths. Ultimately the boycott was a failure with much of the nation against the unions, the press blaming the action on immigrants. Although the government tried to extend an olive branch by making

Labor Day a federal holiday, the Pullman strikes had the effect of radicalizing much of the union movement and its leadership, much of whom, Debs among them, were jailed after the boycott. As tensions continued to grow, labor, heavily influenced by the ideas of German philosopher Karl Marx, began to organize around the idea of socialism. In fact, by 1901, following Debs' release from prison, the disparate far left groups came together as a unified Socialist Party of America, setting the stage for a multi-pronged conflict between capital and labor that would dominate industrial relations for the next century. The challenge for union leaders such as Debs was to drive up recruitment for what they saw as a full scale war between capital and labor, especially as an increasingly vocal segment of the population viewed socialism as a threat to the natural order, with the federal government even considering groups such as the Socialist Party as potentially treasonous.

The efforts of Eugene Debs to recruit people into socialism yielded mixed results. Despite his impassioned writing, speaking, and organizing, despite several failed presidential bids, one of them from prison, socialism generally, and the Socialist Party of America specifically, never gained much of a following. Some of this had to do with the rigidity of the far left, as the Socialist Party and its affiliate groups would not form coalitions with other parties or even allow members to vote for other candidates. Another factor was the fact that the United States at the turn of the century had already embarrassed left-leaning policy, with both major parties representing progressive ideas in their platforms, most prominently on display during the 1912 election between Howard Taft, Woodrow Wilson, and Theodore Roosevelt. Finally, the rise of Russian Communism in 1917, had the effect of turning much of public opinion against socialism, as average Americans equated the political ideas of Karl Marx with the authoritarianism of the Soviet Union. Red Scares became a common tactic of the political right to galvanize support against the socialist agenda. However, Debs and his Socialist Party did have a profound effect on organized labor and the form of the liberal agenda in the mainstream parties. Debs won converts across organized labor who then helped shape and influence the political discourse across the nation. Debs' tireless advocacy for the workers and the poor helped normalize concepts such as socialized medical and retirement benefits, in fact, many of the ideas first espoused by Debs later became the basis for Franklin Roosevelt's New Deal, which in turn became the structure on which the Democratic party is built upon today. Debs continues to be a major influence on liberals and progressives, with many prominent members of the left, including Senator Bernie Sanders of Vermont, claiming Debs as a personal hero. Although in life Eugene V. Debs never achieved the kind of social changed he dreamed of, his ideas continue to resonate to this day, influencing public debate and the ongoing relationship between capital and labor.

—*Jonathan Rees, PhD and KP Dawes, MA*

Bibliography and Further Reading

Chace, James. *Wilson, Roosevelt, Taft and Debs -The Election that Changed the Country*. Simon and Schuster, 2009.

Debs, Eugene V. *Writings of Eugene V Debs: A Collection of Essays by America's Most Famous Socialist*. Red and Black Publishers, 2009.

Debs, Eugene V. *Gentle Rebel: Letters of Eugene V. Debs*. University of Illinois Press, 1995.

Freeberg, Ernest. *Democracy's Prisoner*. Harvard University Press, 2009.

Ginger, Ray. *The Bending Cross: A Biography of Eugene Victor Debs*. Haymarket Books, 2007.

Salvatore, Nick. *Eugene V. Debs: Citizen and Socialist*. University of Illinois Press, 1984.

■ Lincoln Steffens: "The Shame of Minneapolis"

Date: 1903
Author: Lincoln Steffens
Genre: magazine article

Summary Overview

Lincoln Steffens (1866–1936) was a New York City journalist whose name is often associated with early-twentieth-century "muckraking"—investigative journalism, often sensational, that exposed scandal and corruption. "The Shame of Minneapolis" was an exposé published in *McClure's Magazine* in January 1903, but the title does not give the full story of the article, for its subtitle reads "The Rescue and Redemption of a City That Was Sold Out." Essentially, the article tells the story of corruption, bribery, cronyism, graft, and a host of other political ills that beset the city of Minneapolis, Minnesota, under its mayor, Albert Alonzo "Doc" Ames, who served four terms (not always consecutively) beginning in 1876. Steffens also details the work of a grand jury leader, Hovey C. Clarke, who brought to light evidence that led to Ames resigning from office and actually fleeing the city, and the work of city council president D. Percy Jones, who became acting mayor, to clean up city government in Minneapolis. This article appeared in an issue of *McClure's* that also had articles by the muckrakers Ida Tarbell (on Standard Oil) and Ray Baker (on corruption among union leaders); this issue sold out in three days and helped establish *McClure's* as one of the leading organs of the muckraking movement. The article was later published in a 1904 collection of similar pieces, *The Shame of the Cities*, but by that time Ames had been driven from office.

Defining Moment

In an attempt to expose political corruption and prompt reforms, Steffens no doubt hoped for as broad an audience as possible. In reality, however, the readership of magazines like *McClure's* was mostly a body of white, middle class Americans—virtually the same demographic that formed the heart of the Progressive movement. Progressivism and "muckrakers" like Steffens went hand in hand—Progressive politicians and activists used the writings of the muckrakers as evidence of the problems that existed and needed reform. The muckrakers, in turn, were often closely associated with the leaders of the Progressive movement. Steffens, for example had been a friend and confidant of Theodore Roosevelt since the days when Steffens was a New York police reporter and Roosevelt chaired the city's Board of Police Commissioners.

The working poor, whose votes and tax dollars were manipulated by political machines like those Steffens attacked, were not a major part of the audience he reached. Many were recent immigrants who read English with difficulty, or not at all. But one of the ironies of Progressive attempts to reform city government is that the urban poor often thought the machine "worked" for them, since it bought their votes patronage and favors—therefore they often resented the Progressive's reform agenda.

Author Biography

Joseph Lincoln Steffens was born in San Francisco, California, on April 6, 1866. His father, Joseph Steffens, was a prosperous businessman. In 1870, the family moved to Sacramento, California.

Steffens attended the University of California at Berkeley, graduating in 1889. His father financed some travel and further study in Europe. Steffens studied a variety of subjects at the universities in Berlin, Heidelberg, and Leipzig in Germany, and at the Sorbonne in Paris. In 1891, he married Josephine Bontecou, an American student he met in Leipzig. They moved to New York City in 1892. Steffens became a reporter for the *New York Evening Post*. He covered a number of different news beats, but eventually became the first police reporter for the *Post*.

In 1897, Steffens became the city editor of the *New York Commercial Advertiser* and gathered round him a staff of talented writers. In 1901, S. S. McClure offered the Steffens the job of managing editor of *McClure's* magazine. Many of the writers that Steffens recruited became prominent examples of the "muckraker" genre. Steffens left *McClure's* in 1906, when he and several other writers bought *The American Magazine*. In 1909, however, he sold his share in the magazine as a result of disagreements with some of the other owners over editorial policy. He spent the rest of his life as a freelance writer, and also travelled widely, speaking in support of liberal political causes and the labor movement. In 1931, he published his autobiography, which was a financial success, and revived interest in some of his earlier work. Steffens's first wife, Josephine, died in 1911. In 1924, he married Ella Winter. They settled in Carmel, CA, and had one son, Steffens's only offspring.

While on a speaking tour in Chicago in 1933, Steffens had a heart attack. It did not totally disable him, but ended his public touring and speaking. He worked from his home in Carmel for the rest of his life, and died there on August 9, 1936.

HISTORICAL DOCUMENT

Whenever anything extraordinary is done in American municipal politics, whether for good or for evil, you can trace it almost invariably to one man. The people do not do it. Neither do the "gangs" "combines" or political parties. These are but instruments by which bosses (not leaders; we Americans are not led, but driven) rule the people, and commonly sell them out. But there are at least two forms of the autocracy which has supplanted the democracy here as it has everywhere it has been tried. One is that of the organized majority by which, as in Tammany Hall in New York and the Republican machine in Philadelphia, the boss has normal control of more than half the voters. The other is that of the adroitly managed minority. The "good people" are herded into parties and stupefied with convictions and a name, Republican or Democrat; while the "bad people" are so organized or interested by the boss that he can wield their votes to enforce terms with party managers and decide elections. St. Louis is a conspicuous example of this form. Minneapolis is another. Colonel Ed. Butler is the unscrupulous opportunist who handled the non-partisan minority which turned St. Louis into a "boodle town." In Minneapolis "Doc" Ames was the man.

Minneapolis is a New England town on the upper Mississippi. The metropolis of the Northwest, it is the metropolis also of Norway and Sweden in America. Indeed, it is the second largest Scandinavian city in the world. But Yankees, straight from Down East, settled the town, and their New England spirit predominates. They had Bayard Taylor lecture there in the early days of the settlement; they made it the seat of the University of Minnesota. Yet even now, when the town has grown to a population of more than 200,000, you feel that there is something Western about it too—a Yankee with a small Puritan head, an open prairie heart, and a great, big Scandinavian body. The Roundhead takes the Swede and Norwegian bone out into the woods, and they cut lumber by forests, or they go out on the prairies and raise wheat and mill it into fleet-cargoes of flour. They work hard, they make money, they are sober, satisfied, busy with their own affairs. There isn't much time for public business. Taken together, Miles, Hans, and Ole are very American. Miles insists upon strict laws, Ole and Hans want one or two Scandinavians on their ticket. These things granted, they go off on raft or reaper, leaving whoso will to enforce the laws and run the city.

The people who were left to govern the city hated above all things strict laws. They were the loafers, saloon keepers, gamblers, criminals, and the thriftless poor of all nationalities. Resenting the sobriety of a staid, industrious community, and having no Irish to boss them, they delighted to follow the jovial pioneer doctor, Albert Alonzo Ames. He was the "good fellow"—a genial, generous reprobate. Devery, Tweed, and many more have exposed in vain this amiable type. "Doc" Ames, tall, straight, and cheerful, attracted men, and they gave him votes for his smiles. He stood for license. There was nothing of the Puritan about him. His father, the sturdy old pioneer, Dr. Alfred Elisha Ames, had a strong strain of it in him, but he moved on with his family of six sons from Garden Prairie, Ill., to Fort Snelling reservation, in 1851, before Minneapolis was founded, and young Albert Alonzo, who then was ten years old, grew up free, easy, and tolerant. He was sent to school, then to college in Chicago, and he returned home a doctor of medicine before he was twenty-one. As the town waxed soberer and richer, "Doc" grew gayer and more and more generous. Skillful as a surgeon, devoted as a physician, and as a man kindly, he increased his practice till he was the best-loved man in the community. He was especially good to the poor. Anybody could summon "Doc" Ames at any hour to any distance. He went, and he gave not only his professional service, but sympathy, and often charity. "Richer men than you will pay your bill" he told the destitute. So there was a basis for his "good-fellowship." There always is; these good fellows are not frauds—not in the beginning.

But there is another side to them sometimes. Ames was sunshine not to the sick and destitute only. To the vicious and the depraved also he was a comfort. If a man was a hard drinker, the good Doctor cheered him with another drink; if he had stolen something, the Doctor helped to get him off. He was naturally vain; popularity developed his love of approbation. His loose life brought disapproval only from the good people, so gradually the Doctor came to enjoy best the society of the barroom and the streets. This society, flattered in turn, worshipped the good Doctor, and, active in politics always, put its physician into the arena.

Had he been wise, or even shrewd, he might have made himself a real power. But he wasn't calculating, only light and frivolous, so he did not organize his forces and run men for office. He sought office himself from the start, and he got most of the small places he wanted by changing his party to seize the opportunity. His floating minority, added to the regular partisan vote, was sufficient ordinarily for his useless victories. As time went on he rose from smaller offices to be a Republican mayor, then twice at intervals to be a Democratic mayor. He was a candidate once for Congress; he stood for governor once on a sort of Populist-Democrat ticket. Ames could not get anything outside of his own town, and after his third term as mayor it was thought he was out of politics altogether. He was getting old, and he was getting worse.

Like many a "good fellow" with hosts of miscellaneous friends down town to whom he was devoted, the good Doctor neglected his own family. From neglect he went on openly to separation from his wife and a second establishment. The climax came not long before the election of 1900. His wife was dying, and his daughter wrote to her father a note saying that her mother wished to see and forgive him. The messenger found him in a saloon. The Doctor read the note, laid it on the bar, and scribbled across it a sentence incredibly obscene. His wife died. The outraged family would not have the father at the funeral, but he appeared, not at the house, but in a carriage on the street. He sat across the way, with his feet up and a cigar in his mouth, till the funeral moved; then he circled around, crossing it and meeting it, and making altogether a scene which might well close any man's career.

It didn't end his. The people had just secured the passage of a new primary law to establish direct popular government. There were to be no more nominations by convention. The voters were to ballot for their party candidates. By a slip of some sort, the laws did not specify that Republicans only should vote for Republican candidates, and only Democrats for Democratic candidates. Any voter could vote at either primary. Ames, in disrepute with his own party, the Democratic, bade his followers vote for his nomination for mayor on the Republican ticket. They all voted; not all the Republicans did. He was nominated. Nomination is far from election, and you would say that the trick would not help him. But that was a Presidential year, so the people of Minneapolis had to vote for Ames, the Republican candidate for Mayor. Besides, Ames said he was going to reform; that he was getting old, and wanted to close his career with a good administration. The effective argument, however, was that, since McKinley had to be elected to save the country, Ames must be supported for Mayor of Minneapolis. Why? The great American people cannot be trusted to scratch a ticket.

Well, Minneapolis got its old mayor back, and he was reformed. Up to this time Ames had not been very venal personally. He was a "spender" not a "grafter" and he was guilty of corruption chiefly by proxy; he took the honors and left the spoils to his followers. His administrations were no worse than the worst. Now, however, he set out upon a career of corruption which for deliberateness, invention, and avarice has never been equalled. It was as if he had made up his mind that he had been careless long enough, and meant to enrich his last years. He began early.

Immediately upon his election, before he took office (on January 7th), he organized a cabinet and laid plans to turn the city over to outlaws who were to work under police direction for the profit of his administration. He chose for chief his brother, Colonel Fred W. Ames, who had recently returned under a cloud from service in the Philippines. The Colonel had commanded a Minnesota regiment out there till he proved a coward under fire; he escaped court-martial only on the understanding that he should resign on reaching San Francisco, whither he was immediately shipped. This he did not do, and his brother's influence at Washington saved him to be mustered out with the regiment. But he was a weak vessel for chief of police, and the mayor picked for chief of detectives an abler man, who was to direct the more difficult operations. This was Norman W. King, a former gambler, who knew the criminals needed in the business ahead. King was to invite to Minneapolis thieves, confidence men, pickpockets, and gamblers, and release some that were in the local jail. They were to be organized into groups, according to their profession, and detectives were assigned to assist and direct them. The head of the gambling syndicate was to have charge of the gambling, making the terms and collecting the "graft" just as King and a Captain Hill were to collect from the thieves. The collector for women of the town was to be Irwin A. Gardner, a medical student in the Doctor's office, who was made a special policeman for the purpose. These men looked over the force, selected those men who could be trusted, charged them a price for their retention, and marked for dismissal 107 men out of 225, the 107 being the best policemen in the department from the point of view of the citizens who afterward reorganized the force. John Fitchette, better known as "Coffee John" a Virginian (who served on the Jeff Davis jury), the keeper of a notorious coffee-house, was to be a captain of police, with no duties except to sell places on the police force.

And they did these things that they planned—all and more. The administration opened with the revolution on the police force. They liberated the thieves in the local jail, and made known to the Under World generally that "things were doing" in Minneapolis. The incoming swindlers reported to King or his staff for instructions, and went to work, turning the "swag" over to the detectives in charge. Gambling went on openly, and disorderly houses multiplied under the fostering care of Gardner, the medical student. But all this was not enough. Ames dared to break openly into the municipal system of vice protection.

There was such a thing. Minneapolis, strict in its laws, forbade vices which are inevitable, then regularly permitted them under certain conditions. Legal limits, called "patrol lines" were prescribed, within which saloons might be opened. These ran along the river front, out through part of the business section, with long arms reaching into the Scandinavian quarters, north and south. Gambling also was confined, but more narrowly. And there were limits, also arbitrary, but not always identical with those for gambling, within which the social evil was allowed. But the novel feature of this scheme was that disorderly houses were practically licensed by the city, the women appearing before the clerk of the Municipal Court each month to pay a "fine" of $100. Unable at first to get this "graft" Ames's man Gardner persuaded women to start houses, apartments, and, of all things, candy stores, which sold sweets to children and tobacco to the "lumber Jacks" in front, while a nefarious traffic was carried on in the rear. But they paid Ames, not the city, and that was all the reform administration cared about.

The revenue from all these sources must have been enormous. It only whetted the avarice of the mayor and his Cabinet. They let gambling privileges without restriction to location or "squareness"; the syndicate could cheat and rob as it would. Peddlers and pawnbrokers, formerly licensed by the city, bought permits now instead from "Gardner's father" A. L. Gardner, who was the mayor's agent in this field. Some two hundred slot machines were installed in various parts of the town, with owner's agent and mayor's agent watching and collecting from them enough to pay the mayor $15,000 a year as his share. Auction frauds were instituted. Opium joints and unlicensed saloons, called "blind pigs" were protected. Gardner even had a police baseball team, for whose games tickets were sold to people who had to buy them. But the women were the easiest "graft." They were compelled to buy illustrated biographies of the city officials; they had to give presents of money, jewelry, and gold stars to police officers. But the money they still paid direct to the city in fines, some $35,000 a year, fretted the mayor, and at last he reached for it. He came out with a declaration, in his old character as friend of the oppressed, that $100 a month was too much for these women to pay. They should be required to pay the city fine only once in two months. This puzzled the town till it became generally known that Gardner collected the other month for the mayor. The final outrage in this department, however, was an order of the mayor for the periodic visits to disorderly houses, by the city's physicians, at from $5 to $20 per visit. The two physicians he appointed called when they willed, and more and more frequently, till toward the end the calls became a pure formality, with the collections as the one and only object.

In a general way all this business was known. It did not arouse the citizens, but it did attract criminals, and more and more thieves and swindlers came hurrying to Minneapolis. Some of them saw the police, and made terms. Some were seen by the police and invited to go to work. There was room for all. This astonishing fact that the government of a city asked criminals to rob the people is fully established. The police and the criminals have confessed it separately. Their statements agree in detail. Detective Norbeck made the arrangement, and introduced the swindlers to Gardner, who, over King's head, took the money from them. Here is the story "Billy" Edwards, a "big mitt" man, told under oath of his reception in Minneapolis:

"I had been out to the coast, and hadn't seen Norbeck for some time. After I returned I boarded a Minneapolis car one evening to go down to South Minneapolis to visit a friend. Norbeck and Detective DeLaittre were on the car. When Norbeck saw me he came up and shook hands, and said, 'Hullo, Billy, how goes it?' I said, 'Not very well.' Then he says, 'Things have changed since you went away. Me and Gardner are the whole thing now. Before you left they thought I didn't know anything, but I turned a few tricks, and now I'm It.' 'I'm glad of that, Chris,' I said. He says, 'I've got great things for you. I'm going to fix up a joint for you.' 'That's good,' I said, 'but I don't believe you can do it.' 'Oh, yes, I can,' he replied. 'I'm It now—Gardner and me.' 'Well, if you can do it,' says I, 'there's money in it.' 'How much can you pay?' he asked. 'Oh, $150 or $200 a week,' says I. 'That settles it,' he said; 'I'll take you down to see Gardner, and we'll fix it up.' Then he made an appointment to meet me the next night, and we went down to Gardner's house together."

There Gardner talked business in general, showed his drawer full of bills, and jokingly asked how Edwards would like to have them. Edwards says:

"I said, 'That looks pretty good to me,' and Gardner told us that he had 'collected' the money from the women he had on his staff, and that he was going to pay it over to the 'old man' when he got back from his hunting trip next morning. Afterward he told me that the mayor had been much pleased with our $500, and that he said everything was all right, and for us to go ahead."

"Link" Crossman, another confidence man who was with Edwards, said that Gardner demanded $1,000 at first, but compromised on $500 for the mayor, $50 for Gardner, and $50 for Norbeck. To the chief, Fred Ames, they gave tips now and then of $25 or $50. "The first week we ran" said Crossman, "I gave Fred $15. Norbeck took me down there. We shook hands, and I handed him an envelope with $15. He pulled out a list of steerers we had sent him, and said he wanted to go over them with me. He asked where the joint was located. At another time I slipped $25 into his hand as he was standing in the hallway of City Hall." But these smaller payments, after the first "opening, $500" are all down on the pages of the "big mitt" ledger, photographs of which illuminate this article. This notorious book, which was kept by Charlie Howard, one of the "big mitt" men, was much talked of at the subsequent trials, but was kept hidden to await the trial of the mayor himself.

The "big mitt" game was swindling by means of a stacked hand at stud poker. "Steerers" and "boosters" met "suckers" on the street, at hotels, and railway stations, won their confidence, and led them to the "joint." Usually the "sucker" was called, by the amount of his loss, "the $102 man" or "the $35 man." Roman Meix alone had the distinction among all the Minneapolis victims of going by his own name. Having lost $775, he became known for his persistent complainings. But they all "kicked" some. To Norbeck at the street door was assigned the duty of hearing their complaints, and "throwing a scare into them." "Oh, so you've been gambling" he would say. "Have you got a license? Well, then, you better get right out of this town." Sometimes he accompanied them to the station and saw them off. If they were not to be put off thus, he directed them to the chief of police. Fred Ames tried to wear them out by keeping them waiting in the anteroom. If they outlasted him, he saw them and frightened them with threats of all sorts of trouble for gambling without a license. Meix wanted to have payment on his check stopped. Ames, who had been a bank clerk, told him so, and then had the effrontery to say that payment on such a check could not be stopped.

Burglaries were common. How many the police planned may never be known. Charles F. Brackett and Fred Malone, police captains and detectives, were active, and one well-established crime of theirs is the robbery of the Pabst Brewing Company office. They persuaded two men, one an employee, to learn the combination of the safe, open and clean it out one night, while the two officers stood guard outside.

The excesses of the municipal administration became so notorious that some of the members of it remonstrated with the others, and certain county officers were genuinely alarmed. No restraint followed their warnings. Sheriff Megaarden, no Puritan himself, felt constrained to interfere, and he made some arrests of gamblers. The Ames people turned upon him in a fury; they accused him of making overcharges in his accounts with the county for fees, and laying the evidence before Governor Van Sant, they had Megaarden removed from office. Ames offered bribes to two county commissioners to appoint Gardner sheriff, so as to be sure of no more trouble in that quarter. This move failed, but the lesson taught Megaarden served to clear the atmosphere, and the spoliation went on as recklessly as ever. It became impossible.

Even lawlessness must be regulated. Dr. Ames, never an organizer, attempted no control, and his followers began to quarrel among themselves. They deceived one another; they robbed the thieves; they robbed Ames himself. His brother became dissatisfied with his share of the spoils, and formed cabals with captains who plotted against the administration and set up disorderly houses, "panel games" and all sorts of "grafts" of their own. The one man loyal to the mayor was Gardner, and Fred Ames, Captain King, and their pals, plotted the fall of the favorite. Now anybody could get anything from the Doctor, if he could have him alone. The Fred Ames clique chose a time when the mayor was at West Baden; they filled him with suspicion of Gardner and the fear of exposure, and induced him to let a creature named "Reddy" Cohen, instead of Gardner, do the collecting, and pay over all the moneys, not directly, but through Fred. Gardner made a touching appeal. "I have been honest. I have paid you all" he said to the mayor. "Fred and the rest will rob you." This was true, but it was of no avail.

Fred Ames was in charge at last, and he himself went about giving notice of the change. Three detectives were with him when he visited the women, and here is the women's story, in the words of one, as it was told again and again in court: "Colonel Ames came in with the detectives. He stepped into a side room and asked me if I had been paying Gardner. I told him I had, and he told me not to pay no more, but to come to his office later, and he would let me know what to do. I went to the City Hall in about three weeks, after Cohen had called and said he was 'the party.' I asked the chief if it was all right to pay

Cohen, and he said it was."

The new arrangement did not work so smoothly as the old. Cohen was an oppressive collector, and Fred Ames, appealed to, was weak and lenient. He had no sure hold on the force. His captains, free of Gardner, were undermining the chief. They increased their private operations. Some of the detectives began to drink hard and neglect their work. Norbeck so worried the "big mitt" men by staying away from the joint, that they complained to Fred about him. The chief rebuked Norbeck, and he promised to "do better" but thereafter he was paid, not by the week, but by piece work—so much for each "trimmed sucker" that he ran out of town. Protected swindlers were arrested for operating in the street by "Coffee John's" new policemen who took the places of the negligent detectives. Fred let the indignant prisoners go when they were brought before him, but the arrests were annoying, inconvenient, and disturbed business. The whole system became so demoralized that every man was for himself. There was not left even the traditional honor among thieves.

It was at this juncture, in April, 1902, that the grand jury for the summer term was drawn. An ordinary body of unselected citizens, it received no special instructions from the bench; the county prosecutor offered it only routine work to do. But there was a man among them who was a fighter—the foreman, Hovey C. Clarke. He was of an old New England family. Coming to Minneapolis when a young man, seventeen years before, he had fought for employment, fought with his employers for position, fought with his employees, the lumber-Jacks, for command, fought for his company against competitors; and he had won always, till now he had the habit of command, the impatient, imperious manner of the master, and the assurance of success which begets it. He did not want to be a grand juryman, he did not want to be a foreman; but since he was both, he wanted to accomplish something.

Why not rip up the Ames gang? Heads shook, hands went up; it was useless to try. The discouragement fired Clarke. That was just what he would do, he said, and he took stock of his jury. Two or three were men with backbone; that he knew, and he quickly had them with him. The rest were all sorts of men. Mr. Clarke won over each man to himself, and interested them all. Then he called for the county prosecutor. The prosecutor was a politician; he knew the Ames crowd; they were too powerful to attack.

"You are excused" said the foreman.

There was a scene; the prosecutor knew his rights.

"Do you think, Mr. Clarke" he cried, "that you can run the grand jury and my office, too?"

"Yes" said Clarke, "I will run your office if I want to; and I want to. You're excused."

Mr. Clarke does not talk much about his doings last summer; he isn't the talking sort. But he does say that all he did was to apply simple business methods to his problem. In action, however, these turned out to be the most approved police methods. He hired a lot of local detectives who, he knew, would talk about what they were doing, and thus would be watched by the police. Having thus thrown a false scent, he hired some other detectives whom nobody knew about. This was expensive; so were many of the other things he did; but he was bound to win, so he paid the price, drawing freely on his own and his colleagues' pockets. (The total cost to the county for a long summer's work by this grand jury was $259.) With his detectives out, he himself went to the jail to get tips from the inside, from criminals who, being there, must have grievances. He made the acquaintance of the jailor, Captain Alexander, and Alexander was a friend of Sheriff Megaarden. Yes, he had some men there who were "sore" and might want to get even.

Now two of these were "big mitt" men who had worked for Gardner. One was "Billy" Edwards, the other "Cheerful Charlie" Howard. I heard too many explanations of their plight to choose any one; this general account will cover the ground: In the Ames mêlée, either by mistake, neglect, or for spite growing out of the network of conflicting interests and gangs, they were arrested, arraigned, not before Fred Ames, but a judge, and held in bail too high for them to furnish. They had paid for an unexpired period of protection, yet could get neither protection nor bail. They were forgotten. "We got the double cross all right" they said, and they bled with their grievance; but squeal, no, sir! — that was "another deal."

But Mr. Clarke had their story, and he was bound to force them to tell it under oath on the stand. If they did, Gardner and Norbeck would be indicted, tried, and probably convicted. In themselves, these men were of no great importance; but they were the key to the situation, and a way up to the mayor. It was worth trying. Mr. Clarke went into the jail with Messrs. Lester Elwood and Willard J. Hield, grand jurors on whom he relied most for delicate work. They stood by while the foreman talked. And the foreman's way of talking was to smile, swear, threaten, and cajole. "Billy" Edwards told me afterwards that he and Howard were finally persuaded to turn state's evidence, because they believed that Mr. Clarke was the kind of a man to keep his promises and fulfil his threats, "We" he said, meaning criminals generally, "are always stacking up against juries and lawyers who want us to holler. We don't, because we see they ain't wise, and won't get there. They're quitters; they can be pulled off. Clarke has a hard eye. I know men. It's my business to size 'em up, and I took him for a winner, and I played in with him against that whole big bunch of easy things that was running things on the bum." The grand jury was ready at the end of three weeks of hard work to find bills. A prosecutor was needed. The public prosecutor was being ignored, but his first assistant and friend, Al. J. Smith, was taken in hand by Mr. Clarke. Smith hesitated; he knew better even than the foreman the power and resources of the Ames gang. But he came to believe in Mr. Clarke, just as Edwards had; he was sure the foreman would win; so he went over to his side, and, having once decided, he led the open fighting, and, alone in court, won cases against men who had the best lawyers in the State to defend them. His court record is extraordinary. Moreover, he took over the negotiations with criminals for evidence, Messrs. Clarke, Hield, Elwood, and the other jurors providing means and moral support. These were needed. Bribes were offered to Smith; he was threatened; he was called a fool. But so was Clarke, to whom $28,000 was offered to quit, and for whose slaughter a slugger was hired to come from Chicago. What startled the jury most, however, was the character of the citizens who were sent to them to dissuade them from their course. No reform I ever studied has failed to bring out this phenomenon of virtuous cowardice, the baseness of the decent citizen.

Nothing stopped this jury, however. They had courage. They indicted Gardner, Norbeck, Fred Ames, and many lesser persons. But the gang had courage, too, and raised a defence fund to fight Clarke. Mayor Ames was defiant. Once, when Mr. Clarke called at the City Hall, the mayor met and challenged him. The mayor's heelers were all about him, but Clarke faced him.

"Yes, Doc. Ames, I'm after you" he said. "I've been in this town for seventeen years, and all that time you've been a moral leper. I hear you were rotten during the ten years before that. Now I'm going to put you where all contagious things are put—where you cannot contaminate anybody else."

The trial of Gardner came on. Efforts had been made to persuade him to surrender the mayor, but the young man was paid $15,000 "to stand pat" and he went to trial and conviction silent. Other trials followed fast—Norbeck's, Fred Ames's, Chief of Detectives King's. Witnesses who were out of the State were needed, and true testimony from women. There was no county money for extradition, so the grand jurors paid these costs also. They had Meix followed from Michigan down to Mexico and back to Idaho, where they got him, and he was presented in court one day at the trial of Norbeck, who had "steered" him out of town. Norbeck thought Meix was a thousand miles away, and had been bold before. At the sight of him in court he started to his feet, and that night ran away. The jury spent more money in his pursuit, and they caught him. He confessed, but his evidence was not accepted. He was sentenced to three years in state's prison. Men caved all around, but the women were firm, and the first trial of Fred Ames failed. To break the women's faith in the ring, Mayor Ames was indicted for offering the bribe to have Gardner made sheriff—a genuine, but not the best case against him. It brought the women down to the truth, and Fred Ames, retried, was convicted and sentenced to six and a half years in state's prison. King was tried for accessory to felony (helping in the theft of a diamond, which he afterward stole from the thieves), and sentenced to three and a half years in prison. And still the indictments came, with trials following fast. Al. Smith resigned with the consent and thanks of the grand jury; his chief, who was to run for the same office again, wanted to try the rest of the cases, and he did very well.

All men were now on the side of law and order. The panic among the "grafters" was laughable, in spite of its hideous significance. Two heads of departments against whom nothing had been shown suddenly ran away, and thus suggested to the grand jury an in-inquiry which revealed another source of "graft" in the sale of supplies to public institutions and the diversion of great quantities of provisions to the private residences of the mayor and other officials. Mayor Ames, under indictment and heavy bonds for extortion, conspiracy, and bribe-offering, left the State on a night train; a gentleman who knew him by sight saw him sitting up at eleven o'clock in the smoking-room of the sleeping-car, an unlighted cigar in his mouth, his face ashen and drawn, and at six o'clock the next morning he still was sitting there, his cigar still unlighted. He went to West Baden, a health resort in Indiana, a sick and broken man, aging years in a month. The city was without a mayor, the ring was without a leader; cliques ruled, and they pictured one another hanging about the grand-jury room begging leave to turn state's evidence. Tom Brown, the mayor's secretary, was in the mayor's chair; across the hall sat Fred Ames, the chief of police, balancing Brown's light weight. Both were busy forming cliques within the ring. Brown had on his side Coffee John and Police Captain Hill. Ames had Captain "Norm" King (though he had been convicted and had resigned), Captain Krumweide, and Ernest Wheelock, the chief's secretary. Alderman D. Percy Jones, the president of the council, an honorable man, should have taken the chair, but he was in the East; so this unstable equilibrium was all the city had by way of a government.

Then Fred Ames disappeared. The Tom Brown clique had full sway, and took over the police department. This was a shock to everybody, to none more than to the King clique, which joined in the search for Ames. An alderman, Fred M. Powers, who was to run for mayor on the Republican ticket, took charge of the mayor's office, but he was not sure of his authority or clear as to his policy. The grand jury was the real power behind him, and the foreman was telegraphing for Alderman Jones. Meanwhile the cliques were making appeals to Mayor Ames, in West Baden, and each side that saw him received authority to do its will. The Coffee John clique, denied admission to the grand-jury room, turned to Alderman Powers, and were beginning to feel secure, when they heard that Fred Ames was coming back. They rushed around, and obtained an assurance from the exiled mayor that Fred was returning only to resign. Fred—now under conviction—returned, but he did not resign; supported by his friends, he took charge again of the police force. Coffee John besought Alderman Powers to remove the chief, and when the acting mayor proved himself too timid, Coffee John, Tom Brown, and Captain Hill laid a deep plot. They would ask Mayor Ames to remove his brother. This they felt sure they could persuade the "old man" to do. The difficulty was to keep him from changing his mind when the other side should reach his ear. They hit upon a bold expedient. They would urge the "old man" to remove Fred, and then resign himself, so that he could not undo the deed that they wanted done. Coffee John and Captain Hill slipped out of town one night; they reached West Baden on one train and they left for home on the next, with a demand for Fred's resignation in one hand and the mayor's own in the other. Fred Ames did resign, and though the mayor's resignation was laid aside for a while, to avoid the expense of a special election, all looked well for Coffee John and his clique. They had Fred out, and Alderman Powers was to make them great. But Mr. Powers wobbled. No doubt the grand jury spoke to him.

At any rate he turned most unexpectedly on both cliques together. He turned out Tom Brown, but he turned out also Coffee John, and he did not make their man chief of police, but another of some one else's selection. A number of resignations was the result, and these the acting mayor accepted, making a clearing of astonished rascals which was very gratifying to the grand jury and to the nervous citizens of Minneapolis.

But the town was not yet easy. The grand jury, which was the actual head of the government, was about to be discharged, and, besides, their work was destructive. A constructive force was now needed, and Alderman Jones was pelted with telegrams from home bidding him hurry back. He did hurry, and when he arrived, the situation was instantly in control. The grand jury prepared to report, for the city had a mind and a will of its own once more. The criminals found it out last.

Percy Jones, as his friends call him, is of the second generation of his family in Minneapolis. His father started him well-to-do, and he went on from where he was started. College graduate and business man, he has a conscience which, however, he has brains enough to question. He is not the fighter, but the slow, sure executive. As an alderman he is the result of a movement begun several years ago by some young men who were convinced by an exposure of a corrupt municipal council that they should go into politics. A few did go in; Jones was one of these few.

The acting mayor was confronted at once with all the hardest problems of municipal government. Vice rose right up to tempt or to fight him. He studied the situation deliberately, and by and by began to settle it point by point, slowly but finally, against all sorts of opposition. One of his first acts was to remove all the proved rascals on the force, putting in their places men who had been removed by Mayor Ames. Another important step was the appointment of a church deacon and personal friend to be chief of police, this on the theory that he wanted at the head of his police a man who could have no sympathy with crime, a man whom he could implicitly trust. Disorderly houses, forbidden by law, were permitted, but only within certain patrol lines, and they were to pay nothing, in either blackmail or "fines." The number and the standing and the point of view of the "good people" who opposed this order was a lesson to Mr. Jones in practical government. One very prominent citizen and church member threatened him for driving women out of two flats owned by him; the rent was the surest means of "support for his wife and children." Mr. Jones enforced his order.

Other interests—saloon-keepers, brewers, etc.—gave him trouble enough, but all these were trifles in comparison with his experience with the gamblers. They represented organized crime, and they asked for a hearing. Mr. Jones gave them some six weeks for negotiations. They proposed a solution. They said that if he would let them (a syndicate) open four gambling places down town, they would see that no others ran in any part of the city. Mr. Jones pondered and shook his head, drawing them on. They went away, and came back with a better promise. Though they were not the associates of criminals, they knew that class and their plans. No honest police force, unaided, could deal with crime. Thieves would soon be at work again, and what could Mr. Jones do against them with a police force headed by a church deacon? The gamblers offered to control the criminals for the city.

Mr. Jones, deeply interested, declared he did not believe there was any danger of fresh crimes. The gamblers smiled and went away. By an odd coincidence there happened just after that what the papers called "an epidemic of crime." They were petty thefts, but they occupied the mind of the acting mayor. He wondered at their opportuneness. He wondered how the news of them got out.

The gamblers soon reappeared. Hadn't they told Mr. Jones crime would soon be prevalent in town again? They had, indeed, but the mayor was unmoved; "porch climbers" could not frighten him. But this was only the beginning, the gamblers said: the larger crimes would come next. And they went away again. Sure enough, the large crimes came. One, two, three burglaries of jewelry in the houses of well-known people occurred; then there was a fourth, and the fourth was in the house of a relative of the acting mayor. He was seriously amused. The papers had the news promptly, and not from the police.

The gamblers called again. If they could have the exclusive control of gambling in Minneapolis, they would do all that they had promised before, and, if any large burglaries occurred, they would undertake to recover the "swag" and sometimes catch the thief. Mr. Jones was sceptical of their ability to do all this. The gamblers offered to prove it. How? They would get back for Mr. Jones the jewelry recently reported stolen from four houses in town. Mr. Jones expressed a curiosity to see this done, and the gamblers went away. After a few days the stolen jewelry, parcel by parcel, began to return; with all due police-criminal mystery it was delivered to the chief of police.

When the gamblers called again, they found the acting mayor ready to give his decision on their propositions. It was this: There should be no gambling, with police connivance, in the city of Minneapolis during his term of office.

Mr. Jones told me that if he had before him a long term, he certainly would reconsider this answer. He believed he would decide again as he had already, but he would at least give studious reflection to the question—Can a city be governed without any alliance with crime? It was an open question. He had closed it only for the four months of his emergency administration. Minneapolis should be clean and sweet for a little while at least, and the new administration should begin with a clear deck.

GLOSSARY

Autocracy: literally rule by elites or aristocrats; Steffens uses it in the context of rule by the powerful, whose power was often gained by illicit means

boodle town: boodle refers to money gained or used illegally; a "boodle town" would be a city where it was easy to do so, because of government corruption

bosses: the "boss" of a political machine controlled an organization intended to keep a particular party or faction of a party in power

disorderly houses: bordellos or houses of prostitution

Ft. Snelling Reservation: the twin cities of St. Paul and Minneapolis grew up around what was at first the Ft. Snelling military base or "military reservation"

Document Analysis

"The Shame of Minneapolis" is a narrative of the career of "Doc" Ames, who began as a frontier physician but wound up entering politics in Minneapolis, and the efforts eventually undertaken by reformers to break Ames's power. At the time, Minneapolis was a city of about 200,000 dominated by hardworking people of Scandinavian descent who minded their own business and were content to leave the running of the city to others. This was a pattern that Steffen's publisher, S. S. McClure, believed existed in many cities—people generally ignored city and local government, which opened the door for bosses and political machines to take control behind the scenes. Ames controlled what would be called a political machine, although Steffens does not use that term. A political machine, ran by a "boss," was an unofficial political organization that existed to keep one party or a faction of a party in power. Machines often did this by controlling the vote of the poor and recent immigrants; they offered patronage to the poor in return for their votes. The favors and gifts they granted to voters were paid for from the money the machine raised through graft and corruption. Much of the corruption involved in Ames control of Minneapolis was typical of machine politics, but there also were some unusual features there. Many political bosses did hold elected office like Ames did, but others worked as "the power behind the throne," and dictated policy to whoever happened to hold office. Ames switched from the Democratic to Republican parties when the political situation favored such a move; this is unusual for a machine politician, who usually had firm loyalties to the group that put him in power. Also, the extent to which the police in Minneapolis were complicit in "ordinary" criminal activity was somewhat rare. In many cities controlled by a machine, the police took bribes to turn a blind eye to crime, especially to "vices" such as gambling, prostitution, or illegal liquor sales. But for the police to actually encourage petty crime like burglaries, and even to put the word out to invite criminals to their city, was not typical.

When Ames was elected mayor, at first he turned a blind eye to the corruption of others in city government, although he benefited from that corruption. As Steffens writes, "He was a 'spender,' not a 'grafter,' and he was guilty of corruption chiefly by proxy; he took the honors and left the spoils to his followers." But when he was reelected as mayor in 1900, it seemed as though he was determined to enrich himself from his office. The result was "a career of corruption which for deliberateness, invention, and avarice has never been equalled."

Ames gathered around him a gang of corrupt officials, including his brother, and under this phase of his administration, gamblers, unlicensed saloon keepers, thieves, prostitutes, and opium dealers operated openly with police connivance, all the while sharing their spoils with city officials in exchange for impunity. This was "the shame of Minneapolis." But the city's "rescue and redemption" began in 1902 under the leadership of a grand jury foreman, Hovey C. Clarke, who was determined to use his position to end the corruption. Employing a team of investigators, he gathered information; he and other grand jurors often paid the investigators out of their own pockets. In time, numerous city officials were indicted, tried, and convicted. As the pressure on Ames mounted, he resigned and fled the city. In the power vacuum that followed, city council president D. Percy Jones assumed control and functioned as acting mayor. He replaced the "rascals" in city government and stood up to the criminal elements, determined that "Minneapolis should be clean and sweet for a little while at least, and the new administration should begin with a clear deck." In Steffens's telling, good eventually triumphed over evil.

In his autobiography, Steffens devoted a chapter to the writing of this article, which established his credentials as a "muckraker." Many of the facts he used had been public knowledge for years before he began his research. Steffens was also successful in getting much information from those who were directly involved in the graft and corruption. He found that if he could plant the suggestion that he already knew everything, even the guilty would open up to him, as they believed there was no danger is discussing things he already knew.

The work of Hovey C. Clarke and D. Percy Jones did clean up Minneapolis for a time. But, as in many cities, corruption re-emerged over time. Steffens eventually lost confidence in the idea that reform could be brought about simply by replacing bad men with good men. He believed more systematic changes had to be sought, and this led him to move more and more to the left politically as he got older.

Essential Themes

Three trends converged to give rise to the type of article Steffens wrote. The first was improvements in printing technology, which fostered the publication of a large number of relatively inexpensive magazines, like *McClure's*, that kept people abreast of current affairs. *McClure's* became known as one of the leading journals publishing the muckrakers, and the popularity of some of the writers whose works were featured there led other magazines to also provide outlets for muckraking journalists.

The second trend was the rise of Progressive politics under the presidential administration of Theodore Roosevelt; in fact, Roosevelt is credited with coining the term *muckraking* when he referred in a speech to the "Muck-Rake" in John Bunyan's classic novel *Pilgrim's Progress*—a character who was so busy raking in the muck that he would not lift up his eyes to see the glory of heaven. In this climate, muckraking journalists exposed all manner of social ills in their articles: child labor, political corruption, prison conditions, conditions in the meatpacking industry, scandals involving corporations, and the like—often leading to legislation to correct the ills. Steffens became widely known as a muckraker, and was generally thought to be one of the earliest and one of the best practitioners of this genre of investigation and exposure of corruption.

The third trend was the prevalence of political "machines" in urban centers. Bosses like "Doc" Ames controlled cities by using patronage to attract and keep supporters. They ran a highly efficient system that had power over a political party, elections, and the city's purse strings, granting favors in exchange for support and political contributions. Although these machines in some cases functioned for the good—for example, they often provided recent immigrants from a favored ethnic group with a toehold in their new country—they were just as often corrupt. Machines in some simple form had existed since the late 1700s, but they grew to their greatest power as cities grew tremendously in the late nineteenth and early twentieth cities. As cities grew, people in new neighborhoods often lacked the infrastructure needed like sewer lines, water lines, or convenient access to electricity. Also, there usually was no "welfare safety net" to care for people who were truly in need. Machines often worked to meet these needs, but at the price of demanding the vote of the working class poor and recent immigrants. One of the best known of these machines was Tammany Hall, or the Society of Saint Tammany, which began as a New York City fraternal organization but in the nineteenth century evolved under William March "Boss" Tweed into a machine that often relied on corruption to control the city's politics until the mid-1930s. Steffens wrote articles for *McClure's* on similar machines in several other cities, including Pittsburg, Philadelphia, Chicago, and New York City, and two articles on St. Louis. In 1904, these articles were put together as a book entitled, *The Shame of the Cities*, which sold widely.

An immediate impact of "The Shame of Minneapolis" was the establishment of Steffens as a major writer in the genre of exposé journalism that would be termed "muckraking" a few years later. In the same issue of *McClure's* in which Steffens's article appeared (January 1903), two other writers who would also become prominent muckrakers also had important piece—Ida Tarbell published some of her research on Standard Oil's questionable business practices, and Ray Baker wrote about corruption among union officials. The issue sold faster than any previous issue of *McClure's*, and was entirely sold out in three days. The success of *McClure's* stable of muckrakers prompted similar articles in other leading magazines of the time.

Of course, the fact that there was corruption in many city governments was not a groundbreaking revelation. But what Steffens and others did was provide detailed evidence and specific naming of names. The work of the muckrakers did lead to reforms in several cities around the nation aimed at limiting the power of political machines. One such reform was the creation of a city council or commission. In this system, most real power in city government was put in the hands of an elected council or commission; the mayor was only an administrator or figurehead. The theory was that a group of commissioners would be harder for machine politicians to control than a single mayor. A further development of this plan was the commission-city manager form, where citizens elect the commission, and the commission then hires a city manager. This was an example of the Progressive era's belief in efficiency and expertise—the city manager would usually be a person with a graduate degree in urban administration or some related field. The Progressives believed the people, through their vote, should decide the goals or ends of public policy, and expert, trained professionals, would figure out how to implement these goals.

City government reform did clean up machine politics in many cities, at least temporarily. But machines had a nagging habit of coming back, eventually, or a new machine would replace the old one. Steffens himself, in his later years, lost faith in such modest efforts at reform and came to believe that revolutionary change was needed.

—Mark S. Joy, Ph.D. and Michael J. O'Neal, Ph.D.

Bibliography and Further Reading

Brasch, Walter M. *Forerunners of the Revolution: Muckrakers and the American Social Conscience.* Lanham, MD: University Press of America, 1990.

Goodwin, Doris Kearns. *The Bully Pulpit: Theodore Roosevelt, William Howard Taft, and the Golden Age of Journalism.* New York: Simon and Schuster, 2013.

Graham, Jr., Otis L. *An Encore for Reform: The Old Progressives and the New Deal.* New York: Oxford University Press, 1967.

Hartshorn, Peter. *I Have Seen the Future: A Life of Lincoln Steffens.* Berkeley, CA: Counterpoint, 2011.

Hofstadter, Richard. *The Age of Reform; From Bryan to F.D.R.* New York: Vintage Books, 1955

Steffens, Lincoln. *The Autobiography of Lincoln Steffens.* New York: Harcourt, Brace, and World, 1931.

Wilson, Harold. *McClure's Magazine and the Muckrakers.* Princeton, NJ: Princeton University Press, 1970.

Anna Howard Shaw: Address on the Place of Women in Industry *and* Address on the Condition of Women in Industry

Date: 1905 and 1906
Author: Anna Howard Shaw
Genre: speeches

Summary Overview

By the turn of the century Anna Howard Shaw was already a seismic figure in the surging progressive movement. A champion of suffrage, temperance, and reform, she was, beginning in 1904, the president of the National American Woman Suffrage Association, the largest suffrage group, and in fact, the largest voluntary organization in the country. A lifelong activist, brought out of a reform Christian background, Shaw represented the culmination of over a century of struggle and served in many ways as the embodiment of the feminine gender paradigm crafted as a counter argument against the dominance of men over the public sphere. Her ideas, built out of Enlightenment feminist theory, but shaped by a modern, industrialized world in open class conflict, represent a shift from one generation to the next. The passing of the old guard, in favor of the new. This convergence of traditions and ideas set amidst the backdrop of a growing movement focused on the passage of the Nineteenth Amendment, is well exemplified in Shaw's 1905 "Address on the Place of Women in Society," in which she combines old notions of social degeneration and femininity with new notions of class reform and feminist empowerment. The speech, directed at both the women entering the suffrage movement and the men who opposed it, was an attempt to both call attention to the problems of society in need of reform, and also the unique qualities of women which might be harnessed to fix them, while all the while asking the gender in power why they would work against their own interests. Her 1906 speech concerning the condition of women in industry addresses fears--irrational fears in her estimation--that allowing women to participate in the public sphere will undermine the sanctity of the family or a woman's ability to care for her children. Shaw's view is of a society on the verge of collapse, in desperate need of women's care of protection, only made possible by a leveling of political power.

Defining Moment

In her speeches and in her writing, Anna Howard Shaw focused on two primary audiences: women who might be enticed into the suffrage movement, and the men who opposed it. Walking a razor's edge Shaw wanted to argue for her movement while also shifting male attitudes on women, in some ways by reinforcing established roles. Her arguments helped shaped the national dialogue on women's place in society, and provided rhetorical and philosophical framework for the broader suffrage movement. Although much of the credit for the ultimate passage of the Nineteenth Amendment went to the next generation of suffragists, such as Alice Paul, it was primarily the gender and reform arguments advanced by activists like Shaw that laid the foundations for the Amendment in the first place.

Author Biography

Anna Howard Shaw was born in Newcastle-upon-Tyne in the United Kingdom on February 14, 1847. Her father, a budding homesteader, moved the family first to Massachusetts and eventually the American frontier, establishing a farm in northern Michigan. Life was hard in rural Antebellum America, and Shaw, grown resentful of her father for forcing them into a survivalist lifestyle, began to assert herself, doing much of the work in and around the farm. After the Civil War and the death of two siblings, Shaw first went into teaching and then later preaching for a Methodist congregation in the town of Big Rapids. Despite success at preaching, Shaw was all but abandoned by her family, angered by her conversion, and struck out on her own, attending first Albion College and then Boston University, from which she earned a medical degree. A lifelong supporter of women's suffrage, Shaw joined the Women's Christian Temperance Union in 1880s, and after meeting Susan B. Anthony in 1887, became an officer in the National Woman Suffrage Association, later merged with the American Woman Suffrage Association suffrage group to become the National American Woman Suffrage Association. In 1904 Shaw became the president of NAWSA, giving tepid, support to the efforts of Alice Paul and Lucy Burns for more militant action. She received a Distinguished Service Medal for her work on the Council of National Defense during World War I, and after the war continued to be a vocal proponent of suffrage. She died of pneumonia on July 2, 1919, only months before the ratification of the Nineteenth Amendment.

HISTORICAL DOCUMENT

Address on the Place of Women in Industry

When the cry of race-suicide is heard, and men arraign women for race decadence, it would be well for them to examine conditions and causes, and base their attacks upon firmer foundations of fact. Instead of attacking women for their interest in public affairs and relegating them to their children, their kitchen, and their church, they will learn that the kitchen is in politics; that the children's physical, intellectual, and moral well-being is controlled and regulated by law; that the real cause of race decadence is not the fact that fewer children are born, but to the more fearful fact that, of those born, but to the more fearful fact that, of those born, so few live, not primarily because of the neglect of the mother, but because men themselves neglect their duty as citizens and public officials. If men honestly desire to prevent the causes of race decadence, let them examine the accounts of food adulteration, and learn that from the effect of impure milk alone, in one city 56,000 babies died in a single year. Let them examine the water supply, so impregnated with disease that in some cities there is continual epidemic of typhoid fever. Let them gaze upon the filthy streets, from which perpetually arises contagion of scarlet fever and diphtheria. Let them examine the plots of our great cities, and find city after city with no play places for children, except the streets, alleys, and lanes. Let them examine the school buildings, many of them badly lighted, unsanitary, and without yards. Let them turn to the same cities, and learn that from five to a score or thousand children secure only half-day tuition because there are not adequate schoolhouse facilities. Let them watch these half-day children playing in the streets and alleys and viler places, until they have learned the lessons which take them to ever-growing numbers of reformatories, whose inmates are increasing four times as rapidly as the population. Let them follow the children who survive all these ills of early childhood, until they enter the sweat-shops and factories, and behold there the maimed, dwarfed, and blighted little ones, 500,000 of whom under 14 years of age are employed in these pestilential places. Let them behold the legalized saloons and the dens of iniquity where so many of the voting population spend the money that should be used in feeding, housing, and caring for their children. Then, if these mentors of women's clubs and mothers' meetings do not find sufficient cause for race degeneracy where they have power to control conditions, let them turn to lecturing women. It is infinitely more important that a child shall be well born and well reared than that more children shall be born. It is better that one well-born child shall live than that two shall be born and one die in infancy. That which is desirable is not that the greatest possible number of children should be born into the world; the need is for more intelligent motherhood and fatherhood, and for better born and better educated children....

The great fear that the participation of women in public affairs will impair the quality and character of home service is irrational and contrary to the tests of experience. Does an intelligent interest in the education of a child render a woman less a mother? Does the housekeeping instinct of woman, manifested in a desire for clean street, pure water, and unadulterated food, destroy her efficiency as a home-maker? Does a desire for an environment of moral and civic purity show neglect of the highest good of the family? It is the "men must fight and women must week" theory of life which makes men fear that the larger services of women will impair the high ideal of home. The newer ideal, that men must cease fighting and thus remove one prolific cause for women's weeping, and that they shall together build up a more perfect home and a more ideal government, is infinitely more sane and desirable. Participation in the larger and broader concerns of the State, will increase instead of decreasing the efficiency of motherhood, and tend to develop that self-control, that more perfect judgment which is wanting in much of the home training of to-day.

Address on the Condition of Women in Industry

In his annual address to Congress, under the heading "Labor," President Roosevelt recommends the Department of Commerce and Labor to make a thorough investigation of the condition of women in industry.

This recommendation will meet with the hearty approval of suffragists everywhere. Realizing as we do its importance to women and to the nation, our Association has been urging it for years, but hitherto our efforts have been futile to direct the attention of the government to it.

The variety of claims and counter-claims which have been made by those interested in the subject of woman's industrial condition and its effect upon the character and the life of the nation, has so confused the ordinary mind that there is little rational thinking upon the subject. It is impossible to draw any definite conclusions, for, as the President points out, "There is an almost complete dearth of data upon which to base any trustworthy conclusion as regards a subject as important as it is complicated." There is need of full knowledge on which to base action looking toward "State and municipal legislation for the protection of working women," and he [Roosevelt] might have justly added, the right of women to work cannot be denied, when one reads the following statement in the President's message:

The introduction of women into industry is working change and disturbance in the domestic and social life of the nation. The decrease in marriage, and especially in the birth rate, have been coincident with it.

This is unquestionably true, but it is also true that this has been coincident with the discovery of gold and the applicant of steam and electricity to mechanics; and in the last analysis it will be discovered that the latter facts that have had more to do with the present condition of the home and the birth-rate than has any unreasonable desire on the part of women to escape from the responsibility of family life or from the joys of domestic felicity.

To draw sweeping and universal conclusions in regard to a matter upon which there is an "almost complete dearth of date" is never wise. While it is true that marriage and the birth-rate have decreased within recent years, before the results are charged to the participation of women in industry, one must answer many questions.

Is it true that there is more "domestic infelicity" to-day than in times past? Is it true that there is greater "domestic infelicity" in homes where women are engaged in gainful pursuits than in those homes in which the strength of women is never taxed by toil, even to the extent of self-service? Is it true that there is a lower birth-rate among working women than among those of the wealthy class? Are not the effects of over-work and long hours in the household as great as are those of the factory or of the office?

Another point of inquiry would lead the Committee to ask: Is the birth-rate less among women who are engaged in the new pursuits or occupations unknown to women of the past? Or is it the decline alike marked among those who are pursuing the ancient occupations which women have followed from time immemorial, but under different conditions?

As a matter of fact, it is no new thing for women to be engaged in industrial pursuits. From primitive times women have been great industrial factors, and modern economic conditions, instead of introducing them to industries, have introduced to the world's markets the multiform industries in which women from the earliest times have engaged, with ever widening circles of activity, as inventive genius has developed and civilization progressed.

Woman as an industrial factor and wage-earner is not new. But woman as an industrial competitor and wage-collector with man is new, not because of woman's revolt against her own industrial slavery, but because changed economic conditions through the inventive genius and industrial centralization have laid their hands upon the isolated labors and products of woman's toil, and brought them forth from the tent, the cottage, and the farm house, to the shop, the factory, and the marketplace.

If conditions surrounding their employment are such as to make it a "social question of the first importance" it is unfortunate the President had not seen that women, the most deeply interested factor in the problem, should constitute at least a part of any commission authorized to investigate it. No body of men, unaided by women, can be qualified to do so "in a sane and scientific spirit." Such a commission lacks the essential quality of being able to put itself in the position and to understand the character of the very people and conditions is seeks to investigate.

I trust that a resolution will be passed by this convention petitioning the government of the United States to place women upon every commission that investigates the conditions which so deeply affect their lives and the lives of their children.

But if the required investigations were made, even with women upon the committee, what power would the five millions of disfranchised women possess to enact beneficent laws or enforce needed reform?

One can not but wish that with this recognized desire for "fair play" and his policy of "a square deal," it had occurred to the President that, if five millions of American women are employed in gainful occupations, every principle of justice known to a Republic would demand that these five millions of toiling women should be enfranchised to enable them to secure enforced legislation for their own protection.

In all governments, a subject class is always at a disadvantage and at the mercy of the ruling class. It matters not whether its name be Empire, Kingdom, or Republic, whether the rules are one or many; and in a democracy there is no way known among men for any class to protect its interests or to be secure in its most sacred rights, except through the power of the ballot.

GLOSSARY

adulteration: to corrupt, debase, or make impure by the addition of a foreign or inferior substance or element; especially, to prepare for sale by replacing more valuable with less valuable or inert ingredients.

pestilential: harmful or destructive, or to cause disease.

race decadence/degeneration: based on notions founded in Social Darwinism, the idea that a race is in decline and, or, near collapse due to social failings.

race-suicide: the gradual extinction of a people or racial strain through a tendency to restrict voluntarily the rate of reproduction.

Document Analysis

Colored in the language of race-based social theory such as Social Darwinism, Anna Howard Shaw describes a civilization on the brink of collapse. Children are neglected, and go without food, disease and moral decrepitude are spreading. But although her warnings are rooted in nineteenth century concerns over what is referred to here as race degeneration, she levels the blame for the current state not on immigrants or minorities, but instead on men who would relegate women to the private sphere, that is, to the house and tending of children. Shaw argues, that it is the very same qualities that make women the masters of the home, that would make women agents of change and reform in the broader world. Men, according to Shaw, have done next to nothing to combat the dark forces unleashed by modernity, and it is only by empowering women, by allowing them to drive policy, could the path be corrected before it is too late. This notion that women should be allowed to moderate society by virtue of their femininity was not new. The idea of feminine purity serving as a counterbalance to corruption had been in vogue for the previous century, but Shaw ties this concept to that of Republican Motherhood, that is the idea that maternal instinct natural to all women is inherently linked to the interests of the state. Or, to put it another way, for Shaw, women's influence over society would not only safeguard western civilization but the very institutions that govern the nation. She writes: "Instead of attacking women for their interest in public affairs and relegating them to their children, their kitchen, and their church, they will learn that the kitchen is in politics; that the children's physical, intellectual, and moral well-being is controlled and regulated by law; that the real cause of race decadence is not the fact that fewer children are born, but to the more fearful fact that, of those born, so few live, not primarily because of the neglect of the mother, but because men themselves neglect their duty as citizens and public officials." The men who run society simply do not possess the nurturing instincts of women, and thus do not know how to act, or even they that they should act, in the face of collapse. Shaw gives plenty of examples of the many ills plaguing society. She speaks of adulteration of food, typhoid fever in the water supply, filthy living conditions, lack of recreational areas, rundown and inadequate schools, and child labor. And after listing the various failures of law to protect future generations she announces: "It is infinitely more important that a child shall be well born and well reared than that more children shall be born." This point is an important departure from prevailing attitudes and a central point of Shaw's speech who was accused of promoting what was called "race-suicide." America, recently come down from the fervent settlement of the West, still put value on population quantity, but Shaw was turning against this notion and putting highest value on quality. Quality of life in a modern world of near limitless possibility. To Shaw, the great wealth of the robber barons and the wonders of the nineteenth century must have been signs that life needed to be lived, that opportunity must be afforded to all. She concludes with a simple argument: women, by virtue of being caretakers of the home, should be given the power to serve as caretakers of the nation. Motherhood, the moral purity of femininity, will better the country by cleaning the streets, feeding the hungry, and restoring moral decency. In Shaw's own words: "Participation in the larger and broader concerns of the State, will increase instead of decreasing the efficiency of motherhood, and tend to develop that self-control, that more perfect judgment which is wanting in much of the home training of to-day."

Essential Themes

Women had been fighting for equality in the United States since before the American Revolution, but it wasn't until the early nineteenth century that the movement for universal suffrage slowly began to gain steam. Prevailing notions in the nation held that women were too pure and delicate to survive in the rough and tumble world of politics. Motherhood, planted firmly in the private sphere of the home, should not be defiled by the corruption of the street, whether that be in the factory or Congress. But with the coming of the Second Great Awakening and the Industrial Revolution, women began to argue that feminine morality was a vital countermeasure to the degradations of modernity. While industry was offering millions of people new opportunities, it was also creating countless new problems for which society had no easy solution. The demand for labor was driving rapid urbanization, leading to problems of urban poverty, crime, and pollution. As more men entered the workforce new industries devoted to drink and vice began to emerge, increasing crime and rates of domestic violence. As populations swelled so did disease. As the need for labor increased a growing number of children took their place on the line. To the educated men and women of America, it must have seemed like civilization was nearing collapse. Only women, early suffragists argued, could bring to bear the power of motherhood to fix society's many ills. In July, 1848 several hundred women, mainly Christian abolitionists influenced by the salons of intellectual luminaries like Margaret Fuller, met in Seneca Falls, New York for what became the first women's rights convention. There the attendees signed a declaration of women's rights and committed to holding similar meetings throughout the country. Over the next decade women's groups sprang up across the states and territories combining in a reform effort galvanized around abolition, temperance, and suffrage. With the Civil War millions of women faced the hardships of having to fend for themselves and their families when their husbands went to war. But the sacrifices of women were not ignored, and women, mothers especially, were increasingly identified as the caretakers of the union. With experience gained in organizing from the war, women launched the first national suffrage organizations, most notably the National Woman Suffrage Association and the rival American Woman Suffrage Association. With slavery ended with the Thirteenth Amendment women focused on the right to vote and the prohibition of alcohol, which many argued, destabilized family life. As suffragists argued for the closure of prohibition of vice, they began taking on other causes across America's rapidly industrializing landscape. Women became champions of what collectively became known as the reform movement. A concentrated effort to reshape the social contract of the United States. As a mother tends to her children, the government should tend to its citizens. It was up to the state to provide protection, to regulate food safety, to supply clean water, spaces for recreation, and nurture new generations. In 1890 the two leading suffrage organizations merged into the National American Woman Suffrage Association of which in 1904, Anna Howard Shaw was elected president, with an eye to secure a Constitutional Amendment. The stage was set for a major political clash. On the one hand was the old guard of party bosses and brewers, and on the other a collection of reform minded Victorian suffragists and a younger cadre of European-inspired militants.

Although Anna Howard Shaw died before the passage of the Nineteenth Amendment to the Constitution, one cannot overstate her importance to its success. A major figure in the national suffrage movement, Shaw helped shape the argument that won the vote. By presenting women as the moral core of the nation, the only ones possessing the natural gifts of tenderness and nurturing, so vital to keep civilization from suffering collapse in the most classical sense of the term, suffragists such as Shaw were able to cast themselves as the only force able to push against the darkness, and violence of the modern machine world. All that is worst in society could be made better, but only with the vote. These sentiments along with real reform work helped shift perceptions across the country. As another war came and women were once again asked to make sacrifices with no real gain, protests, marches, and other acts of civil disobedience pushed things over the top. With universal suffrage also came prohibition and a host of other reforms. Cities across the nation began offering public education to the young. Unions saw major concessions from industry. Better safety standards were introduced. The foundations of the social safety net began to be laid, reflective in Roosevelt's New Deal, Johnson's Great Society, and even Barack Obama's Affordable Care Act. But while notions of pure femininity allowed women to gain the vote, they also limited their choices and freedoms. And so, within fifty years of the Nineteenth Amendment a second women's movement would be formed, this one, calling itself feminism, would challenge the nation not only to give women even greater political power, but full social equality outside and inside the home. It is a struggle that continues until this day.

—K.P. Dawes, MA

Bibliography and Further Reading

Baker, Jean H. *Sisters: The Lives of America's Suffragists*. Hill and Wang, 2005.

Bausum, Ann. *With Courage and Cloth: Winning the Fight for a Woman's Right to Vote*. National Geographic, 2004

Bederman, Gail. *Manliness and Civilization: A Cultural History of Gender and Race in the United States, 1880-1917 (Women in Culture and Society)*. University of Chicago Press, 1995.

Dubois, Ellen Carol. *Feminism and Suffrage: The Emergence of an Independent Women's Movement in America, 1848-1869*. Cornell University Press, 1999.

Franzen, Trisha. *Anna Howard Shaw: The Work of Woman Suffrage (Women in American History)*. University of Illinois Press, 2014.

Friedan, Betty. *The Feminine Mystique (50th Anniversary Edition)*. Norton Press, 2001.

American Antiquities Act

Date: 1906
Author: U.S. Congress
Genre: legislation

Summary Overview

On June 8, 1906, President Theodore Roosevelt signed into law the American Antiquities Act—or more formally, An Act for the Preservation of American Antiquities. This law gave the president the authority to issue executive orders to restrict the use of public lands owned by the federal government, primarily with the purpose of protecting these lands from "pot hunters" or private collectors who were looting public lands of prehistoric Indian ruins and artifacts. Throughout the late nineteenth century, archeologists and historians were becoming increasingly concerned about looting and vandalism at these sites. The more immediate impetus behind the act was a study conducted by Iowa congressman John F. Lacey and the renowned anthropologist Edgar Lee Hewett, who traveled to the American Southwest to study the archeological resources of the region and the extent of the problem caused by pot hunters. Hewett issued his report in 1904.

Defining Moment

Enactment of the Antiquities Act involved the work of many individuals and organization over the course of about 25 years of work. Americans' interest in preserving the archeological remains of the United States grew throughout the nineteenth century with much of the interest focused on the archeological sites of the Southwest. The act drew the interest of both those who plundered the prehistoric ruins for ancient artifacts or even building materials such as stone and roof beams that could be put to modern use as well as museums and other archeological organizations eager to examine and study the ruins, and to curate collections for their institutions and the public.

Investigators charged with reporting on the condition of these sites could not help but report on destruction that was occurring, which inspired early advocates to call for government action to protect the sites. One notable success included setting aside the Casa Grande Ruin as the first national archeological reservation in 1892. Exhibitions at events including the 1893 World's Columbian Exposition in Chicago and the 1904 Louisiana Purchase Exposition in St. Louis increased the American public's awareness of their country's irreplaceable antiquities. Visitors to municipal and university museums in large cities throughout the country saw displays of American Indian antiquities. Explorers and investigators published popular accounts of ruins in the Southwestern and archeological sites in throughout the country and the hemisphere.

As American artifacts became increasing popular, and as the demand for authentic antiquities to populate not only museums but personal collections, looting at archeological sites continued to rise. This was especially true of areas throughout the Southwest, where such sites were easy to access and difficult to protect, until efforts to improve protections finally culminated in President Theodore Roosevelt signature on the Antiquities Act, making it the law of the land on June 8, 1906.

Author Biography

The 59th Congress of the United States met between 1905 and 1907 during President Roosevelt's fifth and sixth year in office. After sweeping the elections, the Republican majority in the House increased and the Senate maintained a firm Republican hold. Reforms were a major focus of this particular Congress, with a strong emphasis on creating regulatory policy impacting a variety of interests- including an effort to provide general protection for any general kind of cultural or natural resource. The 59th Congress' choice to enact the Pure Food and Drug Act reversed an almost thirty year tradition of congressional failure to pass meaningful regulation of the food and drug industry. The bill originated in the Senate, and after a three month delay in a House committee was passed by the House with just 17 members in opposition of the legislation. The House and Senate worked together to reconcile their difference on the act to ultimately provide the public with the type of major consumer protection law the public was demanding. President Roosevelt signed the bill into law the day after the bill was passed by Congress. Passage of this important legislation led to the eventual creation of the Food and Drug Administration, which was tasked by the 59th Congress to protect the American consumer from ingesting and using harmful materials.

HISTORICAL DOCUMENT

Be it enacted by the Senate and House of Representatives of the United States of America in Congress assembled, That any person who shall appropriate, excavate, injure, or destroy any historic or prehistoric ruin or monument, or any object of antiquity, situated on lands owned or controlled by the Government of the United States, without the permission of the Secretary of the Department of the Government having jurisdiction over the lands on which said antiquities are situated, shall, upon conviction, be fined in a sum of not more than five hundred dollars or be imprisoned for a period of not more than ninety days, or shall suffer both fine and imprisonment, in the discretion of the court.

Sec. 2. That the President of the United States is hereby authorized, in his discretion, to declare by public proclamation historic landmarks, historic and prehistoric structures, and other objects of historic or scientific interest that are situated upon the lands owned or controlled by the Government of the United States to be national monuments, and may reserve as a part thereof parcels of land, the limits of which in all cases shall be confined to the smallest area compatible with proper care and management of the objects to be protected: Provided, That when such objects are situated upon a tract covered by a bona fide unperfected claim or held in private ownership, the tract, or so much thereof as may be necessary for the proper care and management of the object, may be relinquished to the Government, and the Secretary of the Interior is hereby authorized to accept the relinquishment of such tracts in behalf of the Government of the United States.

Sec. 3. That permits for the examination of ruins, the excavation of archaeological sites, and the gathering of objects of antiquity upon the lands under their respective jurisdictions may be granted by the Secretaries of the Interior, Agriculture, and War to institutions which they may deem properly qualified to conduct such examination, excavation, or gathering, subject to such rules and regulation as they may prescribe: Provided, That the examinations, excavations, and gatherings are undertaken for the benefit of reputable museums, universities, colleges, or other recognized scientific or educational institutions, with a view to increasing the knowledge of such objects, and that the gatherings shall be made for permanent preservation in public museums.

Sec. 4. That the Secretaries of the Departments aforesaid shall make and publish from time to time uniform rules and regulations for the purpose of carrying out the provisions of this Act.

Approved, June 8, 1906

Document Analysis

The act itself is relatively simple and brief. Section 1 makes it against the law for any person to "appropriate, excavate, injure, or destroy any historic or prehistoric ruin or monument, or any object of antiquity, situated on lands owned or controlled by the Government of the United States." This section does, however, allow for the possibility that the government agency in charge of the land can grant permission for individuals to presumably excavate ruins and artifacts for purposes of scientific and historical study.

Section 2 grants the president executive authority to "declare by public proclamation historic landmarks, historic and prehistoric structures, and other objects of historic or scientific interest that are situated upon the lands owned or controlled by the Government of the United States to be national monuments." This section specifies that the amount of land held in reserve has to be the smallest amount of land consistent with the care and protection of antiquities—a provision of the act that has often been ignored. It also states that any privately held land that contains such antiquities can be relinquished to the government.

Section 3 provides details about the conditions under which such antiquities can be excavated or examine, and by whom. It grants the secretaries of the interior, agriculture, and war the authority to authorize "the examination of ruins, the excavation of archaeological sites, and the gathering of objects of antiquity" provided that these activities are "undertaken for the benefit of reputable museums, universities, colleges, or other recognized scientific or educational institutions." Section 4 is a boilerplate statement that the secretaries of the interior, agriculture, and war can issue rules and regulations for the enforcement of the act.

Essential Themes
The purpose of the act was to enable the president to designate natural public lands of historic and scientific interest as national monuments. This was perceived as a way to protect such a piece of land that was more efficient than turning it into a national park. The first president to invoke the act and the executive authority it granted was Roosevelt himself, who used it to create the Devils Tower National Monument in Wyoming—a site familiar to movie fans, for it played a major role in *Close Encounters of the Third Kind* in 1977. Roosevelt also invoked the act to create the Grand Canyon National Monument. The act was also used to create the Jackson Hole National Monument in Wyoming in 1943.

The Antiquities Act is important for many reasons, both specific and general. It asserted wide and general public interest in and control over archeological resources on federal and Indian lands. This assertion remains the basis for the federal government's efforts to protect archeological sites as well as preserve areas important for their historical, and scientific resources. Just as importantly, the Antiquities Act made it abundantly clear to the American people that their historic and prehistoric artifacts were of enormous value. The act made it possible to create and safeguard a number of national monuments, develop significant educational programs for visitors, and ultimately salvage archaeological objects threatened by public works such as dams.

One controversial use of the act occurred in 1978 when President Jimmy Carter issued an executive order designating some 56 million acres of land in Alaska as national monuments—and thus placing those lands off limits to development, particularly oil drilling. In response to Carter's action, the Alaska National Interest Lands Conservation Act imposed limits on executive authority by stating that Congress had to ratify any use of the Antiquities Act for any parcel of land larger than five thousand acres.

The Antiquities Act has not always able to prevent deliberate acts of looting. In fact, in the 1970s, attempts to prosecute looters under Antiquities Act resulted in court decisions that were disastrous to the cause of preservation. As a result, a coalition of archeologists, the law enforcement community, and supporters in Congress worked to pass a new statute, the Archaeological Resources Protection Act of 1979, rather simply amend the existing Antiquities Act.

——*Michael J. O'Neal, Ph.D.*

Bibliography and Further Reading
American Antiquities Act of 1906. , n.d.. Internet resource.
Centennial of the American Antiquities Act of 1906: 100 Years of Preservation. Salem, Or.: Oregon State Parks and Recreation Dept., Heritage Programs Division, State Historic Preservation Office, 2006. Internet resource.
Harmon, David, Francis P. McManamon, and Dwight T. Pitcaithley. The Antiquities Act: A Century of American Archaeology, Historic Preservation, and Nature Conservation. Tucson: University of Arizona Press, 2006. Print.

■ Pure Food and Drug Act

Date: 1906
Author: U.S. Congress
Genre: Legislation

Summary Overview

On June 30, 1906, the U.S. Congress passed the Pure Food and Drug Act, which took effect on January 1, 1907. The Food and Drug Act is sometimes called the Wiley Act after Harvey Washington Wiley (1844–1930), the director of the Bureau of Chemistry, who had long lobbied for food and drug regulation. The act, signed by President Theodore Roosevelt, was one of the federal government's first comprehensive efforts to impose regulation on the products that the public ingested, principally meats and other food products, along with patent medicines—so called because their manufacturers misled the public into thinking their compounds were patented by the U.S. government. The 1906 act was replaced in 1938 by the more comprehensive Food, Drug, and Cosmetic Act. It remains significant, however, because it was passed during the Progressive era, when numerous reforms were implemented to protect the public from unscrupulous business practices.

Behind many of these reforms were writers and journalists who were often referred to as "muckrakers." Although the term itself has unsavory connotations, the muckraking press tended to publish largely accurate reports about corruption, fraud, and scandal. These journalists focused on a range of social issues, including child labor, monopolistic business practices, adulterated food products and medicines, dangerous labor conditions, and poor conditions in hospitals and mental asylums. The term is attributed to Roosevelt, although he never specifically used the word *muckraker*; rather, in a speech he referred to the "Muck-rake" mentioned in John Bunyan's seventeenth-century classic *Pilgrim's Progress*—a forklike tool used for cleaning up manure. As a result of the efforts of the muckraking press, public outcry for reforms swelled, and the government responded.

Two writers played a major role in the passage of the Food and Drug Act. One was the writer Upton Sinclair (1878–1968), whose 1906 novel *The Jungle* (first published serially in 1905) was an exposé of the evils of the meatpacking industry, where workers face dangerous and filthy conditions, inspectors are paid off, and the American dream pursued by immigrant workers turns into a nightmare. His novel led to the passage of a companion bill to the Pure Food and Drug Act, the Meat Inspection Act, which Congress passed on the same day. The other writer was Samuel Hopkins Adams (1871–1958), who took on the patent medicine industry. In a series of articles for *Collier's Weekly* in 1905, he exposed the false claims of drug manufacturers, who used ingredients in their medicines that were at best ineffective and at worst dangerous. Indeed, narcotics made up as much as 50 percent of the ingredients of many patent medicines, including those for children.

Defining Moment

The Pure Food and Drug Act was developed and implemented to protect Americans from consuming both food and medicine that could be harmful to their health. As such, this legislation was well-received by the American public who was in large part at least somewhat educated on the dangers of harmful food and medicine exposure. Through industry professional's willingness to expose these problems, the powerful and insightful writing of Upton Sinclair, and muckraking journalists' heightened-focus on the food and medicine industry, the public was aware of the dangers they were encountering in food and medicine consumption. Passage of the Pure Food and Drug Act was a relief to many who were genuinely concerned for their health and believed they had a right to consume safer products. Congress received tremendous support for this legislation from American citizens who were thankful to see the federal government taking steps to provide access to safer foods and more truth in food and medicine labeling.

Author Biography

The 59th Congress of the United States met between 1905 and 1907 during President Roosevelt's fifth and sixth year in office. After sweeping the elections, the Republican majority in the House increased and the Senate maintained a firm Republican hold. Reforms were a major focus of this particular Congress, with a strong emphasis on creating regulatory policy impacting a variety of interests- including the food and drug industry. The 59th Congress' choice to enact the Pure Food and Drug Act reversed an almost thirty year tradition of congressional failure to pass meaningful regulation of the food and drug industry. The bill originated in the Senate, and after a three month delay in a House committee was passed by the House with just 17 members in opposition of the legislation. The House and Senate worked together to reconcile their difference on the act to ultimately provide the public with the type of major consumer protection law the public was demanding. President Roosevelt signed the bill into law the day after the bill was passed by Congress. Passage of this important legislation led to the eventual creation of the Food and Drug Administration, which was tasked by the 59th Congress to protect the American consumer from ingesting and using harmful materials.

HISTORICAL DOCUMENT

An Act for preventing the manufacture, sale, or transportation of adulterated or misbranded or poisonous or deleterious foods, drugs, medicines, and liquors, and for regulating traffic therein, and for other purposes.

Be it enacted by the Senate and House of Representatives of the United States of America in Congress assembled, That it shall be unlawful for any person to manufacture within any Territory or the District of Columbia any article of food or drug which is adulterated or misbranded, within the meaning of this Act; and any person who shall violate any of the provisions of this section shall be guilty of a misdemeanor, and for each offense shall, upon conviction thereof, be fined not to exceed five hundred dollars, or shall be sentenced to one year's imprisonment, for each subsequent offense and conviction thereof shall be fined not less than one thousand dollars or sentenced to one year's imprisonment, or both such fine and imprisonment, in the discretion of the court.

SEC. 2

That the introduction into any State or Territory or the District of Columbia from any other State or Territory or the District of Columbia, from any other State or Territory or the District of Columbia, or form any foreign country, or shipment to any foreign country of any article of food or drugs which is adulterated or misbranded, within the meaning of this Act, is hereby prohibited; and any person who shall ship or deliver for shipment from any State or Territory or the District of Columbia to any other State or Territory or the District of Columbia, or to a foreign country, or who shall receive in any State or Territory or the District of Columbia, or foreign country, and having so received, shall deliver, in original unbroken packages, for pay or otherwise, or offer to deliver to any other person, any such article so adulterated or misbranded within the meaning of this Act, or any person who shall sell or offer for sale in the District of Columbia or the Territories of the United States any such adulterated or misbranded foods or drugs, or export or offer to export the same to any foreign country, shall be guilty of a misdemeanor, and for such offense be fined not exceeding two hundred dollars for the first offense, and upon conviction for each subsequent offense not exceeding three hundred dollars or be imprisoned not exceeding one year, or both, in the discretion of the court: Provided, That no article shall be deemed misbranded or adulterated within the provisions of this Act when intended for export to any foreign country and prepared or packed according to the specifications or directions of the foreign purchaser when no substance is used in the preparation or packing thereof in conflict with the laws of the foreign country to which said article is intended to be shipped; but if said article shall be in fact sold or offered for sale for domestic use or consumption, then this proviso shall not exempt said article from the operation of any of the other provisions of this Act.

SEC. 3

That the Secretary of the Treasury, the Secretary of Agriculture, and the Secretary of Commerce and Labor shall make uniform rules and regulations for carrying out the provisions of this Act, including the collection and examination of specimens of foods and drugs manufactured or offered for sale in the District of Columbia, or in any Territory of the United States, or which shall be offered for sale in unbroken packages in any State other than that in which they shall have been respectively manufactured or produced, or which shall be received from any foreign country, or intended for shipment to any foreign country, which may be submitted for examination by the chief health, food, or drug officer of any State, Territory, or the District of Columbia, or at any domestic or foreign port through which such product is offered for interstate commerce, or for export or import between the United States and any foreign port or country.

SEC. 4

That the examinations of specimens of foods and drugs shall be made in the Bureau of chemistry of the Department of Agriculture, or under the direction and supervision of such Bureau, for the purpose of determining from such examinations whether such articles are adulterated or misbranded within the meaning of this Act; and if it shall appear from any such examination that any of such specimens is adulterated or misbranded within the meaning of this act, the Secretary of Agriculture shall cause notice thereof to be given to the party from whom such sample was obtained. Any party so notified shall be given an opportunity to be heard, under such rules and regulations as may be prescribed as aforesaid, and if it appears that any of the provisions of this act have been violated by such party, then the Secretary of Agriculture shall at once certify the facts to the proper United States district attorney, with a copy of the results of the analysis or the examination of such article duly authenticated by the analyst or officer making such examination, under the oath of such officer. After judgment of the court, notice shall be given by publication in such manner as may be prescribed by the rules and regulations aforesaid.

SEC. 5

That it shall be the duty of each district attorney to whom the Secretary of Agriculture shall report any violation of this Act, or to whom any health or food or drug officer or agent of any State, Territory, or the District of Columbia shall present satisfactory evidence of any such violation, to cause appropriate proceedings to be commenced and prosecuted in the proper courts of the United States, without delay, for the enforcement of the penalties as in such case herein provided.

SEC. 6

That the term "drug" as used in this Act, shall include all medicines and preparations recognized in the United States Pharmacopoeia or National Formulary for internal or external use, and any substance or mixture of substances intended to be used for the cure, mitigation, or prevention of disease of either man or other animals. The term "food" as used herein, shall include all articles used for food, drink, confectionery, or condiment by man or other animals, whether simple, mixed, or compound.

SEC. 7

That for the purposes of this Act an article shall be deemed to be adulterated:
In case of drugs:
First. If, when a drug is sold under or by a name recognized in the United States Pharmacopoeia or National formulary, it differs from the standard of strength, quality, or purity, as determined by the test laid down in the United States Pharmacopoeia or National Formulary official at the time of investigation: *Provided*, That no drug defined in the United States Pharmacopoeia or National Formulary shall be deemed to be adulterated under this provision if the standard of strength, quality, or purity be plain-

ly stated upon the bottle, box, or other container thereof although the standard may differ from that determined by the test laid down in the United States Pharmacopoeia or National Formulary.

Second. If its strength or purity fall below the professed standard or quality under which it is sold.

In the case of confectionery:

If it contains terra alba, barites, talc, chrome yellow, or other mineral substance or poisonous color or flavor, or other ingredient deleterious or detrimental to health, or any vinous, malt or spirituous liquor or compound or narcotic drug.

In the case of food:

First. If any substance has been mixed and packed with it so as to reduce or lower or injuriously affect its quality or strength.

Second. If any substance has been substituted wholly or in part for the article.

Third. If any valuable constituent of the article has been wholly or in part abstracted.

Fourth. If it be mixed, colored powdered, coated, or stained in a manner whereby damage or inferiority is concealed.

Fifth. If it contain any added poisonous or other added deleterious ingredient which may render such article injurious to health: Provided, That when in the preparation of food products for shipment they are preserved by any external application applied in such manner that the preservative is necessarily removed mechanically, or by maceration in water, or otherwise, and directions for the removal of said preservative shall be printed on the covering or the package, the provisions of this act shall be construed as applying only when said products are ready for consumption.

Sixth. If it consists in whole or in part of a filthy, decomposed, or putrid animal or vegetable substance, or any portion of an animal unfit for food, whether manufactured or not, or if it is the product of a diseased animal, or one that has died otherwise than by slaughter.

SEC. 8

That the term "misbranded" as used herein, shall apply to all drugs, or articles of food, or articles which enter into the composition of food, the package or label of which shall bear any statement, design, or device regarding such article, or the ingredients or substances contained therein which shall be false or misleading in any particular, and to any food or drug product which is falsely branded as the State, territory, or country in which it is manufactured or produced.

That for the purposes of this Act an article shall also be deemed to be misbranded:

In the case of Drugs:

First. If it be an imitation of or offered for sale under the name of another article.

Second. If the contents of the package as originally put up shall have been removed, in whole or in part, and other contents shall have been placed in such package, or if the package fail to bear a statement on the label of the quantity or proportion of any alcohol, morphine, opium, cocaine, heroin, alpha or beta eucaine, chloroform, cannabis indica, chloral hydrate, or acetanilide, or any derivative or preparation of any such substances contained therein.

Third. If in package form, and the contents are stated in terms of weight or measure, they are not plainly and correctly stated on the outside of the package.

Fourth. If the package containing it or its label shall bear any statement, design, or device regarding the ingredients or the substances contained therein, which statement, design, or device shall be false or misleading in any particular: Provided, That an article of food which does not contain any added poisonous or deleterious ingredients shall not be deemed to be adulterated or misbranded in the following cases:

First. In the case of mixtures or compounds which may be now or from time to time hereafter known as articles of food, under their own distinctive names, and not an imitation of or offered for sale under the distinctive name of another article, if the name be accompanied on the same label or brand with a statement of the place where said article has been manufactured or produced.

Second. In the case of articles labeled, branded, or tagged so as to plainly indicate that they are compounds, imitations, or blends, and the word "compound" "imitation" or "blend" as the case may be is plainly stated on the package in which it is offered for sale: Provided, That the term blend as used herein shall be construed to mean a mixture of like substances, not excluding harmless coloring or flavoring ingredients used for the purpose of coloring and flavoring only: And provided further, That nothing in this Act shall be construed as requiring or compelling proprietors or manufacturers of proprietary foods which contain no unwholesome added ingredients to disclose their trade formulas, except in so far as the provisions of this Act may require to secure freedom from adulteration or misbranding.

SEC. 9

That no dealer shall be prosecuted under the provisions of this Act when he can establish a guaranty signed by the wholesaler, jobber, manufacturer, or other party residing in the united States, from whom he purchases such articles to the effect that the same is not adulterated or misbranded within the meaning of this Act, designating it.

Said guaranty, to afford protection, shall contain the name and address of the party or parties making the sale of such articles to such dealer, and such case said party or parties shall be amenable to the prosecutions, fines, and other penalties which would attach, in due course, to the dealer under the provisions of this Act.

SEC. 10

That any article of food, drug, or liquor that is adulterated or misbranded within the meaning of this Act, and is being transported from one State, Territory, District, or insular possession to another for sale, or, having been transported, remains unloaded, unsold, or in original unbroken packages, or if it be sold or offered for sale in the District of Columbia or the Territories, or insular possessions of the United States, or if it be imported from a foreign country for sale, or if it is intended for export to a foreign country shall be liable to be proceeded against in any district court of the United States within the district where the same is found, and seized for confiscation by a process of libel for condemnation. And if such article is condemned as being adulterated or misbranded, or of a poisonous or deleterious character, within the meaning of this Act, the same shall be disposed of by destruction or sale, as the said court may direct, and the proceeds thereof, if sold, less the legal costs and charges shall be paid into the Treasury of the United States, but such goods shall not be sold in any jurisdiction contrary to the provisions of this Act or the laws of that jurisdiction: Provided, however, That upon the payment of the costs of such libel proceedings and the execution and delivery of a good and sufficient bond to the effect that such articles shall not be sold or otherwise disposed of contrary to the provisions of this Act, or the laws of any State, Territory, District, or insular possession, the court may by order direct that such articles be delivered to the owner thereof. The proceedings of such libel cases shall conform, as near as may be, to the proceedings in admiralty, except that either party may demand trial by jury of any issue of fact joined in any such case, and all such proceedings shall be at the suit of and in the name of the United States.

SEC. 11

The Secretary of the Treasury shall deliver to the Secretary of Agriculture, upon his request from time to time, samples of foods and drugs which are being imported into the United States or offered for import, giving notice thereof to the owner or consignee, who may appear before the Secretary of Agriculture, and have the right to introduce testimony, and if it appear from the examination of such samples that any article of food or drug offered to be imported into the United States is adulterated or misbranded within the meaning of this Act, or is otherwise dangerous to the health of the people of the United States, or is of a kind forbidden entry into, or forbidden to be sold or restricted in sale in the country in which it is made or from which it is exported, or is otherwise falsely labeled in any respect, the said article shall be refused admission, and the Secretary of the Treasury shall refuse delivery to the consignee and shall cause the destruction of any goods refused delivery which shall not be exported by the consignee within three months from the date of notice of such refusal under such regulations as the Secretary of the Treasury may prescribe: Provided, That the Secretary of the Treasury may deliver to the consignee such goods pending examination and decision in the matter on execution of a penal bond for the amount of the full invoice value of such goods, together with the duty thereon, and on refusal to return such goods for any cause to the custody of the Secretary of the Treasury, when demanded, for the purpose of excluding them from the country, or for any other purpose, said consignee shall forfeit the full amount of the bond: And provided further, That all charges for storage, cartage, and labor on goods which are refused admission or delivery shall be paid by the owner or consignee, and in default of such payment shall constitute a lien against any future importation made by such owner or consignee.

SEC. 12

That the term "Territory" as used in this Act shall include the insular possessions of the United States. The word "person" as used in this Act shall be construed to import both the plural and the singular, as the case demands, and shall include corporations, companies, societies and associations. When construing and enforcing the provisions of this Act, the act, omission, or failure of any officer, agent, or other person acting for or employed by any corporation, company, society, or association, within the scope of his employment or office, shall in every case be also deemed to be the act, omission, or failure of such corporation, company, society, or association as well as that of the person.

SEC. 13

That this Act shall be in force and effect from and after the first day of January, nineteen hundred and seven. Approved, June 30, 1906.

Document Analysis

A major focus of the Food and Drug Act is adulterated food, defined as food that is combined with another substance that affects its quality or strength. Also considered adulterated were foods in which a key ingredient is replaced with another substance, foods from which an essential substance is removed (for instance, the cream from milk), or foods that are blended, coated, or dyed to conceal inferiority or damage. Most important, the law defined adulterated foods as those that contain poisonous or harmful additives, are made of decomposed or dirty vegetable or animal products, or come from diseased animals or those that died other than by slaughtering.

Another focus of the bill was accurate product labeling. The law outlawed "misbranded" foods and required manufacturers to indicate on labels the presence of admixtures or impurities. These provisions also applied to drugs, so pharmaceutical companies had to inform consumers if their products contained such substances as morphine, heroin, cocaine, or cannabis. At this time these substances could be legally purchased as long as the products' labels accurately described their contents; it was not until the passage of the Harrison Narcotics Tax Act of 1914 that possession of such drugs as heroin and morphine became essentially illegal. Meanwhile, the Pure Food and Drug Act required that drugs listed in the *United States Pharmacopoeia* and the *National Formulary* conform to the standards of these publications.

Initially, the responsibility for enforcing the act fell to the Bureau of Chemistry, a division of the U.S. Department of Agriculture. In 1927 this bureau would be renamed the Food, Drug, and Insecticide Administration; in 1931 the name was shortened to Food and Drug Administration (FDA). In 1940 the FDA was made part of the Federal Security Agency, which was folded into the newly formed Department of Health, Education and Welfare in 1953. The FDA remains the chief federal agency that oversees the nation's food products and pharmaceuticals.

Essential Themes
In the late 1800's, chemical preservatives were starting to be added to food in order to ensure long-term storage. Some members of the food industry; driven by ethical principles, were concerned some corporate manufacturers were motivated to cut standards in order to keep up with industry competition. Additionally, there was concern certain medicines were not being labeled in a way that would allow the average consumer to understand what exactly they were consuming. Finally, profound writings like Sinclair's *The Jungle* highlighted sub-standard conditions within the meat industry. Concern over the potential harm these low-quality and harmful chemical preservatives and medicines could cause to American consumers, and disgust with meat industry practices, pushed some members of the food and medical industry to call for a change in food and medicine regulation. While laws were being enacted at the state level to address the growing concern over some of these issues, those laws proved inadequate in addressing the growing problem of food and medicine safety. The Chief Chemist of the USDA, Harvey Wiley, felt compelled to expose the issue of chemical preservatives and mislabeling to Congress and the American people, and his efforts were successful in raising public concern over the issue.

Wiley's sensationalized use of a "poison squad"; a group of people willing to eat chemical preservatives to expose the negative health effects caused by consumption of these substances, was successful in captivating the attention of the American public. The public's attentiveness to the issue combined with the writings of muckraking journalists highlighting food and medicine safety concerns, compelled Congress to begin paying serious attention to the growing concerns over food and medicine safety. While many in the food industry were actively lobbying Congress for change, not all were supportive of the request for more regulation within the industry, In particular, the meat industry proved to be unsupportive of the tighter inspection process being called for. President Roosevelt exposed the meat industry's pushback and the public, encouraged by Sinclair's *The Jungle,* were outraged. Meat sales were cut by almost half in the United States, causing members of the meat industry to change their stance and support the efforts of Congress. Fueled by the pressure from industry professionals, media focus, and the public's demand for meaningful legislation, Congress felt compelled to act. The combined efforts of food and medicine industry workers, the general public, journalists and authors, and Congress, resulted in the passage of the Pure Food and Drug Act in 1906.

The Pure Food and Drug Act of 1906 had a tremendous impact on the American public's ability to access information regarding the types of substances they consume, and allowed the public to access safer foods and medicines. This legislation sought out to successfully remedy some of the major problems running rampant within the food and medical industry, and was successful in alleviating problems such as helping consumers avoid products that contained harmful ingredients like cocaine, morphine, and other chemical additives. Because of this legislation, a precedent was established and companies were obligated to meet legally-defined standards of quality in the manufacturing and labeling of food and medicines. Over time, the law was amended to continue the pattern of enforcing higher standards of governmental regulation of food and medicine. Additionally, this law led to the creation of the Food and Drug Administration, tasked with the responsibility of assuring high-quality food and medicines and truthful labeling for products consumed by the American public. The Pure Food and Drug Act was effectively replaced by the Food, Drug, and Cosmetic act of 1938, but continues to serve as the foundation for which food and medicine standards have been built upon. Without this legislation, American consumers could have been exposed to extremely harmful chemicals for an indefinite amount of time without their knowledge or consent.

—*Amber R. Dickinson, Ph.D. and Michael J. O'Neal, Ph.D.*

Bibliography and Further Reading

"Congress Profiles | US House of Representatives: History, Art & Archives." *Congressional Profiles*. N.p., n.d. Web. 25 July 2016.

Barkan, I.D. 1985. "Industry Invites Regulation: The Passage of the Pure Food and Drug Act of 1906." *American Journal of Public Health*. Vol. 75, No. 1, pp. 18-26.

Johnson, Dennis R. 1982. "The History of the 1906 Pure Food and Drug Act and the Meat Inspection Act." *Food Drug Cosmetic Law Journal*. Vol. 37, pp. 5-9.

Lerner, Adrienne. 2011. "Pure Food and Drug Act of 1906". *Food: In Context*. Vol. 2.

Jane Addams: "Passing of the War Virtues"

Date: 1907
Author: Jane Addams
Genre: Essay

Summary Overview

Jane Addams was part of the Progressive movement, a broad and diverse middle-class coalition that, at the turn of the twentieth century, tried to reform American society and reconcile democracy with capitalism. The steady industrialization and urbanization of the 1880s and 1890s had deeply transformed American society, spurring harsh conflicts between labor and management. The middle class had supported the process of industrialization by espousing the Victorian values of laissez-faire individualism, domesticity, and self-control. Yet by the 1890s it was apparent that these values had trapped the middle class between the warring demands of big business and the working classes. Growing consumerism, a new wave of immigration, and tensions between the sexes further challenged bourgeois existence. In the face of these confrontations, the Progressives tried to reform the American capitalist system and its institutions from within, seeking to strike a compromise between radical demands and the preservation of established interests. Addams's concern with the major issues of Progressivism and her own agenda for social reform clearly emerge in a variety of her essays and speeches. In chapter 8 of her book *Newer Ideals of Peace* (1907), entitled "Passing of the War Virtues" she makes clear, for example, her condemnation of military ideals in the conception of an effective model of social control and efficient management of economic and political institutions.

Defining Moment

In the essay titled "Passing of the War Virtues" Addams was reaching out to like-minded Progressive thinkers who were already sympathetic to the movement. Individuals who favored social change, particularly in terms of equality for women, and pacifists were likely a targeted audience. However, in a fashion that was typical of Addams, she was also attempting to reach out to more conservative members of society who might be persuaded to consider her point of view on the issue of progressive social change. Addams realized in order to see true change in the nation there had to be constructive action that could only be achieved through the coming together of individuals who did not necessarily share the same world view. Therefore, this essay was an attempt to appeal to a base of supporters already in place while recruiting new members to the Progressive movement.

Author Biography

Jane Addams, the eighth of nine children, was born on September 6, 1860, in Cedarville, Illinois, into a wealthy family of Quaker background. Addams was a member of the first generation of American women to attend college. She graduated in 1881 from Rockford Female Seminary, in Illinois, which the following year became Rockford College for Women, allowing Addams to obtain her bachelor's degree. In the 1880s Addams began studying medicine at the Women's Medical College of Philadelphia, but she had to suspend her studies because of poor health. Throughout the decade Addams also suffered from depression owing to her father's sudden death in 1881. Her physical and mental conditions, however, did not prevent her from traveling extensively in Europe. During one of her voyages, Addams visited London's original settlement house of Toynbee Hall, established in 1884, with her companion, Ellen Gates Starr. The visit led the two women to establish the Chicago settlement house of Hull House in 1889, the second such house to be established in America. (Dr. Stanton Coit and Charles B. Stover had founded the first American settlement house, the Neighborhood Guild of New York City, in 1886.) Through Hull House, Addams found a vocation for her adult life, overcoming the sense of uselessness that had besieged her for most of the 1880s.

Addams campaigned for every major reform issue of her era, such as fairer workplace conditions for men and women, tenement regulation, juvenile-court law, women's suffrage, and women's rights. She worked closely with social workers, politicians, and labor and immigrant groups to achieve her purposes, and she was not afraid to take controversial stances, as when she decided to campaign against U.S. entry into World War I. While in the first part of her life Addams was mainly involved in social work in Hull House, in the twentieth century she used her notoriety to advance political causes and became a well-known public figure. In 1910 she was the first woman president of the National Conference of Social Work, and in 1912 she actively campaigned for the Progressive presidential candidate, Theodore Roosevelt, becoming the first woman to give a nominating speech at a party convention. Addams was also a founding member of the National Association for the Advancement of Colored People.

In conjunction with her antiwar efforts, she became the president of the Woman's Peace Party in 1915 and chaired the International Women's Congress for Peace and Freedom at The Hague, Netherlands. That congress led to the foundation of the Women's International League for Peace and Freedom, which Addams chaired until 1929, when she was made honorary president for the remainder of her life. Americans were not unanimous in their praise for Addams's campaigning for peace. On the contrary, she was bitterly attacked by the press and was expelled from the Daughters of the American Revolution. In 1931, however, Addams's antiwar efforts won her the Nobel Peace Prize, which she shared with Nicholas Murray Butler. Because of her declining health, she was unable to collect the prize in person. Addams died in Chicago on May 21, 1935, three days after being diagnosed with cancer.

Addams's life, speeches, and writings are typical of middle-class reformers at the turn of the century. She was widely acknowledged as a pioneer social worker, and she spoke vigorously in favor of social reform. Her addresses and public interventions show her to have been idealistic yet committed to concrete action. Like other Progressive thinkers, such as John Dewey, Herbert Croly, Walter Lippmann, and Charlotte Perkins Gilman, Addams was deeply concerned with the changing nature of human ties and the meaning of community in an increasingly industrialized and urbanized world. Taking a critical stance toward the laissez-faire capitalism that had characterized the Gilded Age, a period of excessive displays of wealth in the late nineteenth century, Progressives like Addams expanded the authority to solve private and public problems to include not only the individual but also the government. They charged the state with the task of intervening in social and economic matters when appropriate, to defeat self-interest in the name of the common good.

HISTORICAL DOCUMENT

Let us by all means acknowledge and preserve that which has been good in warfare and in the spirit of warfare; let us gather it together and incorporate it in our national fibre. Let us, however, not be guilty for a moment of shutting our eyes to that which for many centuries must have been disquieting to the moral sense, but which is gradually becoming impossible, not only because of our increasing sensibilities, but because great constructive plans and humanized interests have captured our hopes and we are finding that war is an implement too clumsy and barbaric to subserve our purpose. We have come to realize that the great task of pushing forward social justice could be enormously accelerated if primitive methods as well as primitive weapons were once for all abolished....

Warfare in the past has done much to bring men together. A sense of common anger and the stirring appeal to action for a common purpose, easily open the channels of sympathy through which we partake of the life about us. But there are certainly other methods of opening those channels. A social life to be healthy must be consciously and fully adjusted to the march of social needs, and as we may easily make a mistake by forgetting that enlarged opportunities are ever demanding an enlarged morality, so we will fail in the task of substitution if we do not demand social sympathy in a larger measure and of a quality better adapted to the contemporaneous situation. Perhaps the one point at which this undertaking is most needed is in regard to our conception of patriotism, which, although as genuine as ever before, is too much dressed in the trappings of the past and continually carries us back to its beginnings in military prowess and defence....

Unless our conception of patriotism is progressive, it cannot hope to embody the real affection and the real interest of the nation. We know full well that the patriotism of common descent is the mere patriotism of the clan—the early patriotism of the tribe—and that, while the possession of a like territory is an advance upon that first conception, both of them are unworthy to be the patriotism of a great cosmopolitan nation. We shall not have made any genuine advance until we have grown impatient of a patriotism founded upon military prowess and defence, because this really gets in the way and prevents the growth of that beneficent and progressive patriotism which we need for the understanding and healing of our current national difficulties....

We come at last to the practical question as to how these substitutes for the war virtues may be found. How may we, the children of an industrial and commercial age, find the courage and sacrifice which belong to our industrialism. We may begin with August Comte's assertion that man seeks to improve his position...by the destruction of obstacles and by the construction of means, or, designated by their most obvious social results, if his contention is correct, by military action and by industrial action....

Then we find ourselves asking what may be done to make more picturesque those lives which are spent in a monotonous and wearing toil, compared to which the camp is exciting and the barracks comfortable. How shall it be made to seem as magnificent patiently to correct the wrongs of industrialism as to do battle for the rights of the nation? This transition ought not to be so difficult in America, for to begin with, our national life in America has been largely founded upon our success in invention and engineering, in manufacturing and commerce. Our prosperity has rested upon constructive labor and material progress, both of them in striking contrast to warfare....

We ignore the fact that war so readily throws back the ideals which the young are nourishing into the mold of those which the old should be outgrowing. It lures young men not to develop, but to exploit; it turns them from the courage and toil of industry to the bravery and endurance of war, and leads them to forget that civilization is the substitution of law for war....

It remains to be seen whether or not democratic rule will diminish war. Immoderate and uncontrolled desires are at the root of most national as well as of most individual crimes, and a large number of persons may be moved by unworthy ambitions quite as easily as a few. If the electorate of a democracy accustom themselves to take the commercial view of life, to consider the extension of trade as the test of a national prosperity, it becomes comparatively easy for mere extension of commercial opportunity to assume a moral aspect and to receive the moral sanction. Unrestricted commercialism is an excellent preparation for governmental aggression. The nation which is accustomed to condone the questionable business methods of a rich man because of his success, will find no difficulty in obscuring the moral issues involved in any undertaking that is successful. It becomes easy to deny the moral basis of self-government and to substitute militarism....

The advance of constructive labor and the subsidence and disappearance of destructive warfare is a genuine line of progression....

To some of us it seems clear that marked manifestations of [the] movement [for world peace] are found in the immigrant quarters of American cities. The...survey of the immigrant situation would indicate that all the peoples of the world have become part of the American tribunal, and that their sense of pity, their clamor for personal kindness, their insistence upon the right to join in our progress, can no longer be disregarded. The burdens and sorrows of men have unexpectedly become intelligent and urgent to this nation, and it is only by accepting them with some magnanimità that we can develop the larger sense of justice which is becoming worldwide and is lying in ambush, as it were, to manifest itself in governmental relations. Men of all nations are determining upon the abolition of degrading poverty, disease, and intellectual weakness, with their resulting industrial inefficiency, and are making a determined effort to conserve even the feeblest citizen to the State. To join in this determined effort is to break through national bonds and to unlock the latent fellowship between man and man....It is but necessary to make this fellowship wider, to extend its scope without lowering its intensity. Those emotions which stir the spirit to deeds of self-surrender and to high enthusiasm, are among the world's most precious assets. That this emotion has so often become associated with war, by no means proves that it cannot be used for other ends. There is something active and tangible in this new internationalism, although it is difficult to make it clear, and in our striving for a new word with which to express this new and important sentiment, we are driven to the rather absurd phrase of "cosmic patriotism." Whatever it may be called, it may yet be strong enough to move masses of men out of their narrow national considerations and cautions into new reaches of human effort and affection....

The International Peace Conference held in Boston in 1904 was opened by a huge meeting in which men of influence and modern thought from four continents, gave reasons for their belief in the passing of war. But none was so modern, so fundamental and so trenchant, as the address which was read from the prophet Isaiah....He contended that peace could be secured only as men abstained from the gains of oppression and responded to the cause of the poor; that swords would finally be beaten into plowshares and pruning-hooks, not because men resolved to be peaceful, but because all the metal of the earth would be turned to its proper use when the poor and their children should be abundantly fed. It was as if the ancient prophet foresaw that under an enlightened industrialism peace would no longer be an absence of war, but the unfolding of worldwide processes making for the nurture of human life. He predicted the moment which has come to us now that peace is no longer an abstract dogma but has become a rising tide of moral enthusiasm slowly engulfing all pride of conquest and making war impossible.

GLOSSARY

American tribunal: a court of law, but here suggesting a larger and more informal community of shared ideals

camp: the military life

Comte, Auguste: French social philosopher and reformer (1798–1857)

conserve: preserve the existence of

enlarged morality: a matured and maturing sense of right and wrong

intelligent: understood

Isaiah: Israelite prophet of the 700s B.C.E for whom one of the most significant books in the Old Testament is named

magnanimità: Italian version of the word magnanimity, meaning generosity of spirit

march: changing nature

patriotism of common descent: loyalty to one's nation that comes simply from having been born there, as opposed to loyalty based on principles

Document Analysis

One of the chief concerns of Progressives was the establishment of effective institutions that could replace the notions of individualism and unrestrained commercialism that had characterized the Gilded Age. In chapter 8 of her book *Newer Ideals of Peace* (1907), entitled "Passing of the War Virtues" Addams claims that a fairer society can be achieved only if the older military values that are considered founding virtues of the American social order are replaced by "the growth of that beneficent and progressive patriotism which we need for the understanding and healing of our current national difficulties." The chapter is a logical anticipation of Addams's involvement in the movement against U.S. entry into World War I. Although Addams credits the war spirit of the past with having brought men together, she claims that the changing times require a new type of spirit, one that seeks "the construction of means" by "industrial action" rather than "the destruction of obstacles" by "military action."

In an effort to appeal also to the most conservative sector of American society, Addams states that the quintessentially American faith in material progress itself discords with military virtues. American prosperity, she asserts, rests on "constructive labor and material progress, both of them in striking contrast to warfare." Military values lead to the establishment of an exploitative society and encourage younger people to "forget that civilization is the substitution of law for war." Addams is careful not to espouse a vision of society based merely on the accumulation of wealth, however. Consistent with the Progressive tenets that the government should intervene in social and economic affairs and that forms of social control are needed to protect the common good, Addams claims that one should be wary of "unrestricted commercialism" which is "an excellent preparation for governmental aggression." This line of thought is typical of Addams's strategy to mediate between those with more radical demands and those who want to preserve society as is. She begins by expressing her faith in the American ideal of material progress, yet she leads the reader to question the individualistic notions that hard work necessarily translates into economic success and that the poor have only themselves to blame.

Addams cites the urban poor and the immigrant as examples of citizens who are helping to develop the world peace movement: "Their sense of pity, their clamor for personal kindness, their insistence upon the right to join in our progress, can no longer be disregarded." The fight against poverty can stimulate "the latent fellowship between man and man"; thus, the quest for a fairer society can replace the war virtues to unite human beings across national borders. Like other Progressive reformers, Addams also stresses the importance of efficient industrial management. She holds that the fight against "degrading poverty, disease and intellectual weakness" will result in the improvement of industrial efficiency. Addams thus frames the replacement of military values and the fight against poverty within the Progressives' quest for proficient administration in economic, social, and political institutions. "Passing of the War Virtues" is revealing of Addams's beliefs that the present system of government was inadequate in a complex industrial age and that public officials should eliminate inefficiency and exploitation.

Another important dimension of the fight against poverty in this era was its international significance. Addams clearly emphasizes the importance of extending human fellowship beyond national interests, stating that the fight against social injustices can become a common element for nations. In accordance with its international dimension, the chapter ends with a description of the International Peace Conference held in Boston in 1904. Addams refers to it as a "huge meeting" at which influential thinkers from all over the world "gave reasons for their belief in the passing of war." Citing "the address which was read from the prophet Isaiah" Addams speaks of the prophet's vision of peace as being attainable only if men forsake "the gains of oppression" and respond "to the cause of the poor." She ends her chapter affirming that "an enlightened industrialism" would help to define peace not only in negative terms as "an absence of war" but also as "the unfolding of worldwide processes making for the nurture of human life." Once again Addams tries to strike a compromise between the demands of labor and management; the phrase "enlightened industrialism" positions the author, like the majority of the Progressives, as functioning within the capitalist economy. Addams's reformist creed did not target the system to overthrow it; on the contrary, it sought to prevent conflicts and promote a more harmonious society.

Essential Themes

Around the time Addams' essay was written women were engaged in the struggle for equal rights, and even though some states had granted women the right to vote by 1907 there were still significant barriers in place preventing women from being equal to men in society and under the law. Regardless of the progress some states were seeing in terms of women's suffrage, some powerful political forces and certain portions of the male population were not in favor of the advancement of women in society. Because of this, attempts to become more civically engaged were becoming a top priority for many women. Due to industrialization, men were more frequently drawn away from the home for work, and women began to focus on public welfare and improving their own position within society. Many women believed their job was to take care of the home, and for these women home referred to the surrounding communities in which they lived. These women believed they had an obligation to not only make advancements for themselves both socially and politically, but many felt they had a responsibility to look out for the welfare of children and poverty-stricken individuals in society. Women in this time period were in need of a role model and leader, many of whom looked to Jane Addams to fill this role.

Jane Addams was viewed as a charismatic leader of the Progressive party, and was nationally revered as a woman to be respected. Her social work was highly regarded, and her dedication to women's equality was unquestionable. In this period of time when men were dominant in politics and some of these men were dedicated to keeping women oppressed and unequal, Addams' focus never faltered. Addams managed to become a prominent fixture in the political realm, as evidenced by her 1912 endorsement of Roosevelt's presidential nomination on behalf of all American women. While her political agenda was evident, her focus extended well beyond the scope of electoral politics, as she wrote prolifically about issues such as peace, education, faith, and prostitution. She was involved with the peace movement during World War I, and encouraged others to embrace a pacifist ideology. Her tireless efforts to aid the plight of women, children, and those in need, as well as her work towards causing social change and encouraging peace positioned Addams to become a heroine to many.

The work of Jane Addams had a tremendously positive impact on the fight for women's equality, and the promotion of Progressive ideals and values. While Addams was certainly not the only women fighting for these principles, she was successful in capturing the nation's attention, which proved to be a valuable resource in the struggle for social change. By gaining national attention and earning the support and respect of those who also wished to see social change, many found themselves in improved social, economic, and political situations. Addams and those who agreed with, and supported her efforts, found themselves able to influence the government to intervene in the lives of individuals to make positive changes. While it will never be completely possible to know exactly the degree to which Addams influenced societal change, it is clear that her efforts helped many embrace the idea of Progressive reforms in this country.

—*Luca Prono, Ph.D. and Amber R. Dickinson, Ph.D.*

Bibliography and Further Reading

Conway, Jill. 1964. "Jane Addams: An American Heroine." *Daedalus*. Vol. 93, No. 2, pp. 761-780.

Miller, Grant. 2008. "Women's Suffrage, Political Responsiveness, and Child Survival in American History." *The Quarterly Journal of Economics*. Vol. 123, No. 3, pp. 1287-1327.

Seigfried, Charlene Haddock. 2013. "The Social Self in Jane Addams' Prefaces and Introductions." *Transactions of the Charles S. Peirce Society: A Quarterly Journal in American Philosophy*. Vol. 49, No. 2, pp. 127-156.

Muller v. Oregon

Date: 1908
Author: David J. Brewer
Genre: Court Decision

Summary Overview

In 1908, in *Muller v. Oregon*, the U.S. Supreme Court upheld a state law that regulated the employment of women. The Court's decision in *Muller v. Oregon* gave rise to many questions about the progressive agenda and how its goals might best be achieved. In the late 1800s and early 1900s, political progressives pursued economic and political reforms. Many pushed hard to improve working conditions for men, women, and children laboring in shops and factories. The women's movement was pressing for the right to vote and the right to exercise autonomy in legal and economic affairs.

The case of *Muller v. Oregon* arose when the owner of a laundry in Portland, Oregon, violated a state law limiting the number of hours a woman could work in his shop. The man challenged the constitutionality of this protective legislation; the direction the Supreme Court was taking in cases of this sort at the time portended a victory for the laundry owner. However, the Court, presented with a mountain of evidence demonstrating the danger to women workers of industrial practices left unregulated, unanimously upheld Oregon's law. This victory for progressives supporting worker protections thus came at a cost, as the Court's decision upholding protective legislation undermined women's rights.

Defining Moment

The significance of the case is that Oregon's law stands, along with Muller's conviction and fine. Progressives supporting protective regulations could take from this decision a victory for the present on the road to greater protection in the future. In their view, the decision to uphold Oregon's law protecting women who worked in laundries amounted to a wedge prying open possibilities for more comprehensive protective measures. One example among many such measures was a law passed by the Oregon legislature in 1913 setting maximum workday hours for all manufacturing employees (men and women) and providing for overtime pay when that maximum was exceeded.

At the same time, supporters of the right to contract in a free market where labor is exchanged for pay could take heart in the way the Court, in the decision's final paragraph, phrased its holding narrowly and endorsed *Lochner*'s principles. After *Muller*, until 1937, the Court continued to strike down legislative measures protecting workers for unconstitutionally violating the right to contract, not every time but often.

Author Biography

The decision in *Muller v. Oregon* was unanimous, with Justice David J. Brewer writing the opinion for the Court. Born in 1837 in what is now the nation of Turkey to missionary parents, Brewer was a member of a family prominent in U.S. legal history. His uncle Stephen J. Field served on the Court from 1863 to 1897; Field's final years on the bench overlapped with Brewer's early years there. David Dudley Field, another uncle, was the driving force behind the development of the code of civil procedure, a major contribution to U.S. law. In 1890, President Benjamin Harrison appointed Brewer to the Supreme Court, where he served for 20 years. His votes consistently supported a free-market economy.

Louis D. Brandeis was not an author of the decision, but on behalf of the defendant he contributed the "Brandeis brief" for which the *Muller* case is known. Brandeis was a prominent attorney in Boston and was deeply involved in progressive and public-interest causes. When *Muller* was appealed to the Supreme Court, the National Consumers League, a pro-worker group advocating protective regulation, asked Brandeis to prepare a brief supporting Oregon's limit on working hours. Brandeis agreed on the condition that he would be the lead attorney for the Supreme Court appeal. Working closely with officials from the National Consumers League, Brandeis prepared the brief submitted to support Oregon's case. In its decision, the Court famously refers to the Brandeis brief. In 1916, President Woodrow Wilson appointed Brandeis to the Supreme Court; he served there until 1939.

HISTORICAL DOCUMENT

Messrs. William D. Fenton and Henry H. Gilfry for plaintiff in error.

Messrs. H. B. Adams, Louis Brandeis, John Manning, A. M. Crawford, and B. E. Haney for defendant in error.

Mr. Justice Brewer Delivered the Opinion of the Court

On February 19, 1903, the legislature of the state of Oregon passed an act (Session Laws 1903, p. 148) the first section of which is in these words:

Sec. 1. That no female (shall) be employed in any mechanical establishment, or factory, or laundry in this state more than ten hours during any one day. The hours of work may be so arranged as to permit the employment of females at any time so that they shall not work more than ten hours during the twenty-four hours of any one day.

Sec. 3 made a violation of the provisions of the prior sections a misdemeanor subject to a fine of not less than $10 nor more than $25. On September 18, 1905, an information was filed in the circuit court of the state for the county of Multnomah, charging that the defendant "on the 4th day of September, A. D. 1905, in the county of Multnomah and state of Oregon, then and there being the owner of a laundry, known as the Grand Laundry, in the city of Portland, and the employer of females therein, did then and there unlawfully permit and suffer one Joe Haselbock, he, the said Joe Haselbock, then and there being an overseer, superintendent, and agent of said Curt Muller, in the said Grand Laundry, to require a female, to wit, one Mrs. E. Gotcher, to work more than ten hours in said laundry on said 4th day of September, A. D. 1905, contrary to the statutes in such cases made and provided, and against the peace and dignity of the state of Oregon."

A trial resulted in a verdict against the defendant, who was sentenced to pay a fine of $10. The supreme court of the state affirmed the conviction (48 Or. 252, 85 Pac. 855), whereupon the case was brought here on writ of error.

The single question is the constitutionality of the statute under which the defendant was convicted, so far as it affects the work of a female in a laundry. That it does not conflict with any provisions of the state Constitution is settled by the decision of the supreme court of the state. The contentions of the defendant, now plaintiff in error, are thus stated in his brief:

(1) Because the statute attempts to prevent persons sui juris from making their own contracts, and thus violates the provisions of the 14th Amendment, as follows:

No state shall make or enforce any law which shall abridge the privileges or immunities of citizens of the United States; nor shall any state deprive any person of life, liberty, or property, without due process of law; nor deny to any person within its jurisdiction the equal protection of the laws.

(2) Because the statute does not apply equally to all persons similarly situated, and is class legislation.

(3) The statute is not a valid exercise of the police power. The kinds of work prescribed are not unlawful, nor are they declared to be

immoral or dangerous to the public health; nor can such a law be sustained on the ground that it is designed to protect women on account of their sex. There is no necessary or reasonable connection between the limitation prescribed by the act and the public health, safety, or welfare.

It is the law of Oregon that women, whether married or single, have equal contractual and personal rights with men. As said by Chief Justice Wolverton, in *First Nat. Bank v. Leonard*, 36 Or. 390, 396, 59 Pac. 873, 874, after a review of the various statutes of the state upon the subject:

We may therefore say with perfect confidence that, with these three sections upon the statute book, the wife can deal, not only with her separate property, acquired from whatever source, in the same manner as her husband can with property belonging to him, but that she may make contracts and incur liabilities, and the same may be enforced against her, the same as if she were a feme sole. There is now no residuum of civil disability resting upon her which is not recognized as existing against the husband. The current runs steadily and strongly in the direction of the emancipation of the wife, and the policy, as disclosed by all recent legislation upon the subject in this state, is to place her upon the same footing as if she were a *feme sole*, not only with respect to her separate property, but as it affects her right to make binding contracts; and the most natural corollary to the situation is that the remedies for the enforcement of liabilities incurred are made coextensive and coequal with such enlarged conditions.

It thus appears that, putting to one side the elective franchise, in the matter of personal and contractual rights they stand on the same plane as the other sex. Their rights in these respects can no more be infringed than the equal rights of their brothers. We held in *Lochner v. New York*, 198 U.S. 45, 49 L. ed. 937, 25 Sup. Ct. Rep. 539, that a law providing that no laborer shall be required or permitted to work in bakeries more than sixty hours in a week or ten hours in a day was not as to men a legitimate exercise of the police power of the state, but an unreasonable, unnecessary, and arbitrary interference with the right and liberty of the individual to contract in relation to his labor, and as such was in conflict with, and void under, the Federal Constitution. That decision is invoked by plaintiff in error as decisive of the question before us. But this assumes that the difference between the sexes does not justify a different rule respecting a restriction of the hours of labor.

In patent cases counsel are apt to open the argument with a discussion of the state of the art. It may not be amiss, in the present case, before examining the constitutional question, to notice the course of legislation, as well as expressions of opinion from other than judicial sources. In the brief filed by Mr. Louis D. Brandeis for the defendant in error is a very copious collection of all these matters, an epitome of which is found in the margin. While there have been but few decisions bearing directly upon the question, the following sustain the constitutionality of such legislation: *Com. v. Hamilton Mfg. Co.* 120 Mass. 383; *Wenham v. State*, 65 Neb. 394, 400, 406, 58 L.R.A. 825, 91 N. W. 421; *State v. Buchanan*, 29 Wash. 602, 59 L.R.A. 342, 92 Am. St. Rep. 930, 70 Pac. 52; *Com. v. Beatty*, 15 Pa. Super. Ct. 5, 17; against them is the case of *Ritchie v. People*, 155 Ill. 98, 29 L.R.A. 79, 46 Am. St. Rep. 315, 40 N. E. 454.

The legislation and opinions referred to in the margin may not be, technically speaking, authorities, and in them is little or no discussion of the constitutional question presented to us for determination, yet they are significant of a widespread belief that woman's physical structure, and the functions she performs in consequence thereof, justify special legislation restricting or qualifying the conditions under which she should be permitted to toil. Constitutional questions, it is true, are not settled by even a consensus of present public opinion, for it is the peculiar value of a written constitution that it places in unchanging form limitations upon legislative action, and thus gives a permanence and stability to popular government which otherwise would be lacking. At the same time, when a question of fact is debated and debatable, and the extent to which a special constitutional limitation goes is affected by the truth in respect to that fact, a widespread and long continued belief concerning it is worthy of consideration. We take judicial cognizance of all matters of general knowledge.

It is undoubtedly true, as more than once declared by this court, that the general right to contract in relation to one's business is part of the liberty of the individual, protected by the 14th Amendment to the Federal Constitution; yet it is equally well settled that this liberty is not absolute and extending to all contracts, and that a state may, without conflicting with the provisions of the 14th Amendment, restrict in many respects the individual's power of contract. Without stopping to discuss at length the extent to which a state may act in this respect, we refer to the following cases in which the question has been considered: *Allgeyer v. Louisiana*, 165 U.S. 578, 41 L. ed. 832, 17 Sup. Ct. Rep. 427; *Holden v. Hardy*, 169 U.S. 366, 42 L. ed. 780,

18 Sup. Ct. Rep. 383; *Lochner v. New York*, supra.

That woman's physical structure and the performance of maternal functions place her at a disadvantage in the struggle for subsistence is obvious. This is especially true when the burdens of motherhood are upon her. Even when they are not, by abundant testimony of the medical fraternity continuance for a long time on her feet at work, repeating this from day to day, tends to injurious effects upon the body, and, as healthy mothers are essential to vigorous offspring, the physical well-being of woman becomes an object of public interest and care in order to preserve the strength and vigor of the race.

Still again, history discloses the fact that woman has always been dependent upon man. He established his control at the outset by superior physical strength, may, without conflicting with the provisions and this control in various forms, with diminishing intensity, has continued to the present. As minors, thought not to the same extent, she has been looked upon in the courts as needing especial care that her rights may be preserved. Education was long denied her, and while now the doors of the schoolroom are opened and her opportunities for acquiring knowledge are great, yet even with that and the consequent increase of capacity for business affairs it is still true that in the struggle for subsistence she is not an equal competitor with her brother. Though limitations upon personal and contractual rights may be removed by legislation, there is that in her disposition and habits of life which will operate against a full assertion of those rights. She will still be where some legislation to protect her seems necessary to secure a real equality of right. Doubtless there are individual exceptions, and there are many respects in which she has an advantage over him; but looking at it from the viewpoint of the effort to maintain an independent position in life, she is not upon an equality. Differentiated by these matters from the other sex, she is properly placed in a class by herself, and legislation designed for her protection may be sustained, even when like legislation is not necessary for men, and could not be sustained. It is impossible to close one's eyes to the fact that she still looks to her brother and depends upon him. Even though all restrictions on political, personal, and contractual rights were taken away, and she stood, so far as statutes are concerned, upon an absolutely equal plane with him, it would still be true that she is so constituted that she will rest upon and look to him for protection; that her physical structure and a proper discharge of her maternal functions—having in view not merely her own health, but the well-being of the race—justify legislation to protect her from the greed as well as the passion of man. The limitations which this statute places upon her contractual powers, upon her right to agree with her employer as to the time she shall labor, are not imposed solely for her benefit, but also largely for the benefit of all. Many words cannot make this plainer. The two sexes differ in structure of body, in the functions to be performed by each, in the amount of physical strength, in the capacity for long continued labor, particularly when done standing, the influence of vigorous health upon the future well-being of the race, the self-reliance which enables one to assert full rights, and in the capacity to maintain the struggle for subsistence. This difference justifies a difference in legislation, and upholds that which is designed to compensate for some of the burdens which rest upon her.

We have not referred in this discussion to the denial of the elective franchise in the state of Oregon, for while that may disclose a lack of political equality in all things with her brother, that is not of itself decisive. The reason runs deeper, and rests in the inherent difference between the two sexes, and in the different functions in life which they perform.

For these reasons, and without questioning in any respect the decision in *Lochner v. New York*, we are of the opinion that it cannot be adjudged that the act in question is in conflict with the Federal Constitution, so far as it respects the work of a female in a laundry, and the judgment of the Supreme Court of Oregon is affirmed.

GLOSSARY

epitome: an abstract account of a longer text

***feme sole*:** in the English-American common law tradition, an unmarried woman in charge of her separate estate and against whom legal obligations are enforceable; the term is of French origin

sui juris: of age and capacity to take full possession of one's rights

Document Analysis

The first party, Curt Muller, is the "plaintiff in error"; the Oregon Supreme Court decided against Muller, and in this case he appealed that decision to the U.S. Supreme Court. The second party is the State of Oregon, which convicted and fined Muller for violating the state law that set a limit on work hours. William D. Fenton, the lead attorney for Muller, was a member of a prominent Portland law firm. His regular clients included large corporate interests. For the State of Oregon, Louis Brandeis took charge of the case upon its appeal to the U.S. Supreme Court.

The Court begins by citing the Oregon law that Muller violated. An example of protective legislation, it is quite focused. It applies only to females and only to females working in particular places of employment. It sets maximum hours for any one day but does not restrict the number of days per week a woman might work. Moreover, this law does not limit the particular time during the day when a woman may work. Some protective laws, by contrast, set maximum working hours per week and prohibited women from working at nighttime.

The Court proceeds in paragraphs 2 and 3 to cite the enforcement mechanism contained in the law. This case arose from a complaint lodged by an employee of the Portland Grand Laundry, Emma Gotcher, who stated that her supervisor had forced her to work past the ten-hour daily limit. The laundry owner, Muller, was charged, found guilty by the circuit-court judge, and fined $10, the minimum penalty. Upon appeal, the Oregon Supreme Court upheld the conviction.

Much is implied by the Court in the first sentence of paragraph 4, which begins, "The single question." The issue in this case is whether Oregon's law is consistent with the U.S. Constitution, "so far as it affects the work of a female in a laundry." The Court signals that it will construct a holding that applies only to women workers engaged in a particular kind of labor. The ruling will not go beyond the facts of the case. In the next sentence, the Court, as is customary, accepts as authority the state supreme court's ruling that the law in question is consistent with the state's constitution. In the third sentence, the Court lists the arguments underlying the appeal by Muller. His "brief" consists of the written arguments prepared by his attorneys, setting out the facts and the legal issues as perceived by them in support of their side.

The Court lists three arguments brought by Muller, each grounded in the U.S. Constitution: First, Muller argues that Oregon's statute violates the Constitution by preventing persons (women working in laundries) who are sui juris (of age and of capacity to exercise their rights) from making their own contracts (deciding on their own how many hours in a day they wish to work). The right to contract, Muller argues, is protected by the Fourteenth Amendment. The text of the Fourteenth Amendment, quoted here, does not specifically mention a "right to contract" but the Court states that the amendment's due process clause included that right in 1905 in *Lochner v. New York*. (The "right to contract" established in *Lochner* is an example of a substantive due process right.)

Second, Muller argues that Oregon's statute violates the Fourteenth Amendment's equal protection clause: "No state shall...deny to any person within its jurisdiction the equal protection of the laws." The class of people treated differently by the state's legislation is women, in that it restricts their right to contract.

Third, Muller argues that "the statute is not a valid exercise of the police power" retained by the states under the Constitution, permitting them to protect the health, safety, morals, and general welfare of their citizens. *Lochner* set this standard: The state may use its police powers to restrict the right to contract, but the restriction must be fair, reasonable, and appropriate; it may not be unreasonable, unnecessary, or arbitrary. Muller argues that the legitimate goals of public health, safety, and welfare are not advanced by Oregon's restriction. The state's use of its police powers, Muller posits, is unconstitutional.

The Court proceeds to recognize that Oregon law establishes legal status for women equal to men's. Common law tradition merged a woman's legal status with her husband's, effectively making her a dependent in the eyes of the law. Statutes passed by Oregon in the late 1800s extended to women legal rights denied them under common law, including, as held by the state supreme court, the right to make binding contracts.

At issue in *Muller* was whether Oregon's law limiting daily work hours for a woman employed by a laundry was consistent with the U.S. Constitution; therefore, a woman's legal equality under Oregon law did not determine the decision in this case. (Even so, the state's supreme court, which recognized that a state law insured a woman's equal right to make a binding contract, had also ruled that the maximum-hours law for women under review in this case did not violate the state's constitution.)

Paragraph 6 contains the point upon which the case turned. In Oregon, the Court writes, women are equal to men regarding the right to contract, "putting to one side the elective franchise." (The state's woman suffrage proclamation would not be signed until 1912.) In *Lochner*, a law for maximum work hours applied to men was unconstitutional. Muller urges the Court to reach the same finding here. "But this" writes the Court, "assumes that the difference between the sexes does not justify a different rule respecting a restriction of the hours of labor." The direction the Court is taking is clear: Women in Oregon have an equal right to contract, but a state's police powers may apply different protections to womenthan to men.

In paragraph 7 the Court states that it will note "the course of legislation, as well as expressions of opinion from other than judicial sources." The nonjudicial information taken note of by the Court is abridged in the first footnote and famously includes over one hundred pages of "facts"—including laws passed in other jurisdictions protecting women employees and the opinions of government, medical, and social work experts who, based on their observations of modern industry, concluded that long hours of labor are dangerous for women.

This "very copious collection" of facts was compiled by Louis Brandeis, attorney for Oregon, and his collaborator, Josephine Goldmark, an official with the National Consumers League. That organization was lobbying hard around the nation for protective legislation advancing the cause of workers. The regulatory laws and expert opinions that Brandeis and Goldmark assembled and submitted as a brief, intending to overwhelm the Court with facts supporting a law protecting women workers, became known as the "Brandeis brief." It won acclaim as an early and auspicious demonstration of a realist style of argument bringing to bear on judicial reasoning the real-world causes and consequences of laws and of decisions made by courts.

In paragraph 8 the Court acknowledges and tries to explain its reliance on the nontraditional sources contained in the Brandeis brief, which "may not be, technically speaking, authorities." Here, the term *authorities* refers to the established sources relied on by the Court to arrive at decisions, a venerable example being precedent established in prior cases. Though technically not authorities, says the Court, the state laws and opinions contained in the Brandeis brief "are significant of a widespread belief" that a woman's physical structure and the functions she performs justify protective legislation that restricts "the conditions under which she should be permitted to toil." The Constitution places limits on legislative action "in unchanging form"; nevertheless, a "widespread and long continued belief"—here, regarding how a woman's physical nature affects her ability to work—may influence the extent to which a constitutional limitation is applied.

The Court next states the principles of *Lochner*: The right to contract is protected by the Fourteenth Amendment, but, consistent with the Constitution, a state may restrict that right, to an extent. The question begged is, of course, to what extent may that right be restricted? The answer, the Court asserts, can be found in three prior cases: *Allgeyer v. Louisiana* (1897), in which the Court struck down a state law prohibiting the purchase of insurance from companies outside the state because the law violated the Fourteenth Amendment rights of individuals; *Holden v. Hardy* (1898), in which the Court upheld a state law setting maximum work hours for coal miners owing to the dangers of exposure to coal dust; and *Lochner v. New York* (1905), in which the Court struck down a state law setting maximum work hours for bakery employees because the restriction was unreasonable and arbitrary.

In paragraphs 10 and 11 the Court states two findings that, as of 1908, added shape to the body of constitutional law then developing around the issues of right to contract and the government's power to regulate economic activity: Equal protection is not violated by Oregon's laws treating women differently than men, and women's physical nature and maternal functions permit states to restrict their right to contract in the way Oregon has done here. The Court surrounds these holdings with extensive commentary on the limitations placed on women by their physical nature and societal role.

Women, the Court states, have a particular physical structure, and they also perform maternal functions. Up to this point, nothing about Oregon's law or its application has been associated with "maternal functions." In fact, the generalization drawn by the Court ignores the truths that all women do not have the same "physical structure" and that not all women are mothers. Nonetheless, the opinion holds that these characteristics "place her at a disadvantage in the struggle for subsistence." The Court knows that, at this time in history, most women who work are paid low wages; but the law under review is not about pay—it is about maximum-hour regulations.

The Court sharpens its portrait of women by drawing comparisons to men. Women are held to be dependent on men, who are stronger. As such, courts have always made compensations for women. Although they have gained equal rights, their dispositions and habits of life keep them from asserting those rights. The opinion reads, "She is properly placed in a class by herself, and legislation designed for her protection may be sustained, even when like legislation is not necessary for men, and could not be sustained." The Court is rejecting Muller's second argument, that Oregon's maximum-hours law for women workers denies women the equal protection of the law. A woman may be singled out by legislation, the Court holds, for the sake of her own health and for the sake of the race, which depends on the "proper discharge of her maternal functions." The Court thus cements the connection it requires between the state's power to protect the health and safety of its citizens and its restriction on the number of hours women may work.

In paragraph 12 the Court notes for the second time that women are not able to vote in Oregon. Women's suffrage was a hotly debated issue throughout the country and would result four years later in the establishment of woman's right to vote in Oregon and a dozen years later in the Nineteenth Amendment to the U.S. Constitution, which nationalized suffrage for women. The Court states that its decision that Oregon may restrict working hours for women, even when a restriction on men would not stand, does not depend on Oregon's denial to women of the right to vote. "The reason runs deeper" the Court states, "and rests in the inherent difference between the two sexes."

In closing, the Court confirms that its decision in *Muller* is not to be extended past the facts of the case: Oregon's protective legislation does not violate the Constitution "so far as it respects the work of a female in a laundry." The decision in *Muller* does not challenge "in any respect" the decision in *Lochner*.

Essential Themes

Rapid industrialization and increased urbanization in the United States in the late nineteenth century inspired reform campaigns associated with the progressive movement. In the early 1900s, progressives worked to secure the health of citizens, to address the plights of workers, and to win rights for women. While many tactics were employed and many roads taken, an especially successful, if often arduous, route lay in persuading legislatures to pass laws supporting the progressive agenda. Even after legislative victory, however, a formidable obstacle remained—the U.S. Supreme Court.

A conservative majority sat on the Court during the time of this progressive movement. When called on to determine the constitutionality of laws intended to alter social conditions and economic relations, this bloc of justices consistently struck down government regulation. The Court protected the private sector and enforced its own preferred system of economic relations, the laissez-faire doctrine. The prime case in which government regulation was defeated and individual economic liberty supported was *Lochner v. New York*, decided in 1905.

In *Lochner*, the Supreme Court considered New York's law restricting bakery employees to a sixty-hour workweek. The state argued that its law was a legitimate exercise of its police power, which included the authority to protect the health, safety, and welfare of its citizens. The Court thought otherwise, however, asserting that no reasonable foundation existed for the contention that the maximum-hours regulation was necessary or appropriate for the safeguarding of the health of the bakery employees or the public. The regulation was held to interfere with the right of individuals to contract in the labor market, which the Court identified as a liberty interest protected by the Fourteenth Amendment. The Court declared New York's law unconstitutional.

In cases that followed, the Court employed the principles put forth in *Lochner* to strike down state and federal legislation that regulated economic activity. Critics of these results argued that the Supreme Court was prioritizing abstract principles and was taking no account at all of the real-world conditions, social and economic, to which regulatory legislation was responding. The Court was failing, the critics contended, to consider the impact its decisions had on society. These arguments informed the supporters of government regulation who participated in the 1908 constitutional challenge to Oregon's law restricting the number of hours women could work in a laundry.

The Court cabined, or kept narrow, its holding in *Muller*, but the long-term impacts of the decision were profound and far reaching. These effects traveled in two distinct directions. Along one path, *Muller* legitimated consideration by the Supreme Court of real-world conditions, as demonstrated in facts supplied by experts and scientists, when giving shape to the law. Along another path, *Muller* legitimated a view of women that supported sex discrimination, thus blocking or hindering the campaign for gender equality far into the twentieth century.

Predictably, the persuasive power of the Brandeis brief in *Muller* generated reliance on the same strategy in later cases. In state and federal courts alike, lawyers defending protective restrictions on economic activity compiled studies and statistics to bolster their cases. A high mark for sheer volume was achieved with the brief of over 1,000 pages prepared, again by Brandeis and Goldmark, to support a maximum-working-hours law for manufacturing employees, which was passed by the Oregon legislature in 1913 and promptly challenged in court. By 1917, when *Bunting v. Oregon* reached the Supreme Court, Brandeis had been appointed to a seat there. He recused himself from the case, which resulted in a 5–3 decision to uphold Oregon's restriction on the right to contract. Brandeis's selection to the Court signaled the respect given to the idea that factual studies of real-world conditions merited consideration by courts. The approach has played a role in many cases since, including the landmark decision in *Brown v. Board of Education* (1954). There, the Court struck down separate-but-equal educational facilities for different racial groups, stating its reliance on "modern authority" including psychological and sociological studies (*Brown v. Board of Education*, 47 U.S. 483).

In *Muller*, the Court justified Oregon's restriction on the right to contract by linking the state's protective regulation to cited characteristics of women workers emphasizing their relative weakness and their difference from men workers. Much of the Court's description of women in this vein was gratuitous. Observations on the weakness of women were iterated and then reiterated. A woman's "physical structure" and her "maternal functions" it was argued, justify the diminishing of her rights. The Court's view of women in the workplace did not arise solely from the Brandeis brief. The historian Nancy Woloch remarks, "Leaving the 'facts' of the Brandeis brief behind, [Justice] Brewer presented a timeless portrait of the 'dependent women'" (p. 38). One might easily imagine that the Brandeis brief supplied the Court (particularly Brewer, who wrote for the Court) with facts used to support opinions about women already held.

The decision in *Muller* marked an important step in the evolution of the law during the first four decades of the twentieth century regarding when government regulation may interfere with the right to contract. The case also stitched into the law a retro-view of women, as embodied in prior legal discourse, that equal rights advocates were fighting to change at the time the decision was announced. With respect to the decision in *Muller*, Kirp, Yudof, and Franks write, "This description of 'dependent' woman has its obvious antecedents in rationales for earlier common law paternalism. Women won their maximum-hours laws, but only because they could be described in a way which rendered such special treatment permissible, even laudable" (p. 38). Thus, the *Muller* decision and the Court's recognition of the Brandeis brief—victories for progressives campaigning for protective workplace measures—were at the same time defeats for progressives campaigning for women's equal rights. The view adopted in *Muller* that a particular characterization of women could form the basis for laws treating them unequally survived a long time. "For more than sixty years" writes political scientist Judith Baer, "courts upheld nearly all cases of sex discrimination, citing this case as binding precedent, following its lead in emphasizing permanent rather than temporary, physical rather than economic or social, aspects of women's condition.".

——*Randy Wagner, JD, PhD*

Bibliography and Further Reading

Baer, Judith A. *The Chains of Protection: The Judicial Response to Women's Labor Legislation*. Westport, Conn.: Greenwood Press, 1978.

Erickson, Nancy S. "*Muller v. Oregon* Reconsidered: The Origins of a Sex-Based Doctrine of Liberty of Contract." *Labor History* 30, no. 2 (1989): 228–250.

Kirp, David L., Mark G. Yudof, and Marlene Strong Franks. *Gender Justice*. Chicago: University of Chicago Press, 1986.

Mason, Alpheus Thomas. "The Case of the Overworked Laundress." In *Quarrels That Have Shaped the Constitution*, ed. John A. Garraty. New York: Harper & Row, 1964.

"Muller v. Oregon (Supreme Court upholds maximum hour law), February 24, 1908." *Women Working, 1800–1930*, Harvard University Library Web site. http://ocp.hul.harvard.edu/ww/events_muller.html. Accessed on October 15, 2007.

Rhode, Deborah L. *Justice and Gender: Sex Discrimination and the Law*. Cambridge, Mass.: Harvard University Press, 1989.

Sklar, Kathryn Kish. "Why Were Most Politically Active Women Opposed to the ERA in the 1920s?" In *Rights of Passage: The Past and Future of the ERA*, ed. Joan Hoff-Wilson. Bloomington: Indiana University Press, 1986.

Urofsky, Melvin I. *Louis D. Brandeis and the Progressive Tradition*. Boston: Little, Brown, 1981.

Woloch, Nancy. Muller v. Oregon: *A Brief History with Documents*. Boston: Bedford Books of St. Martin's Press, 1996.

Zimmerman, Joan G. "The Jurisprudence of Equality: The Women's Minimum Wage, the First Equal Rights Amendment, and *Adkins v. Children's Hospital*, 1905–1923." *Journal of American History* 78, no. 1 (1991): 188–225.

Robert La Follette: Speech on the Amendment of National Banking Laws

Date: 1908
Author: Robert Marion La Follette
Genre: speech

Summary Overview

Throughout much of his adult life, Robert M. La Follette was known as "Fighting Bob," and the appellation was most apt. He was admittedly by nature combative and suspicious. At the same time, he was an indefatigable researcher who could often intimidate opponents with mounds of supporting data. He always characterized himself as a spokesman for a public trampled by predatory capitalists and Wall Street speculators. In 1908, in his Speech on the Amendment of National Banking Laws, La Follette indicted the entire financial system, which he believed was grinding down the true producers of the nation. He saw the marriage of investment banks with corporations as creating what he termed a "money trust" of groups lining their pockets and putting at peril smaller institutions and businesses.

Author Biography

Robert Marion La Follette, a son of farmers, was born on June 14, 1855, in Primrose, Wisconsin. At age twenty he entered the University of Wisconsin, graduating in 1879. In 1880, after briefly attending law school, he was elected district attorney of Dane County, where Madison, the capital of Wisconsin, is located. In 1884 he was elected as the youngest member of U.S. House of Representatives, where he was so orthodox in his Republicanism that he ardently supported the high rates of the McKinley Tariff. The victim of a Democratic landslide in 1890, he resumed his law practice in Madison. An attempted bribe by the Wisconsin senator Philetus Sawyer, who asked La Follette to intervene in a case in which his brother-in-law was judge, radicalized the young attorney, who henceforth became a strong foe of entrenched interests.

After two abortive bids for Wisconsin's governorship, La Follette won the race in 1900 and was reelected in both 1902 and 1904. He pushed through a battery of reform measures, including conservation acts, antilobbying laws, regulation of telephone and telegraph companies, educational expansion, public utility controls, consumer protection, tax and civil service legislation, a direct primary, and railroad and industrial commissions. He also pioneered what was called the "Wisconsin idea" by which university experts aided in drafting significant legislation. While still governor, he was chosen in January 1905 by the state legislature to represent Wisconsin in the U.S. Senate, where he would serve until his death in 1925.

In the Senate, La Follette was one of the more vocal members, focusing in particular on giant business, which he saw as an evil in itself. In 1906, breaking the unwritten rule that freshman senators should not speak, he delivered an address on strengthening the pending Hepburn Act, a railroad regulation bill that was so detailed that it filled 148 pages of the Congressional Record. He produced similar documentation in advocating the direct election of senators, more powerful antitrust legislation, income redistribution, lower tariffs, and protection for American workers. He led the attack against the Aldrich-Vreeland bill in 1908, a measure to allow banks to issue emergency currency against securities and bonds. In his presentation, he claimed that fewer than a hundred men dominated and controlled business and industry in America. Although he was nominally a Republican, he broke with the presidency of William Howard Taft over the high Payne-Aldrich Tariff and over alleged corruption in the Department of the Interior. He sought to gain the Republican presidential nomination of 1912, but his major supporters abandoned him once former President Theodore Roosevelt entered the race.

When Woodrow Wilson became president in 1913, La Follette backed such "New Freedom" proposals as the Underwood Tariff and the Federal Reserve System. La Follette authored only one major bill, the Seamen's Act, legislation that abrogated one-year contracts and mandated safety measures for passengers and crew. Always a foe of military intervention, he spoke forcefully against armed involvement in Mexico and the Caribbean. In March 1917 he led a filibuster against Wilson's proposal to arm American merchant ships in the aftermath of Germany's declaration of unrestricted submarine warfare, at which point the president snapped, "A little group of willful men, representing no opinion but their own, have rendered the great Government of the United States helpless and contemptible" (Link, p. 362). La Follette was equally outspoken in his opposition to American entrance into World War I, conscription, the curbing of the freedoms of speech and the press, the Treaty of Versailles, and entry into the League of Nations. In 1924 he ran for president on an independent Progressive Party ticket, gaining 4.8 million votes. His platform included collective bargaining, public ownership of water power and railroads, aid to farmers, a ban on child labor, and the recall of federal judges. On June 18, 1925, he died of heart failure in Washington, D.C.

HISTORICAL DOCUMENT

Eighteen hundred and ninety-eight was the beginning of great industrial reorganization. Men directly engaged in production brought about in the first instance an association of the independent concerns which they had built up. These reorganizations were at the outset limited to those turning out finished products similar in kind. Within a period of three years following, 149 such reorganizations were effected with a total stock and bond capitalization of $3,784,000,000. In making these reorganizations, the opportunity for a large paper capitalization offered too great a temptation to be resisted. This was but the first stage in the creation of fictitious wealth. The success of these organizations led quickly on to a consolidation of combined industries, until a mere handful of men controlled the industrial production of the country.

The opportunity to associate the reorganization of the industrial institutions of the country with banking capital presented itself. Such connections were a powerful aid to reorganization, and reorganization offered an unlimited field for speculation....

I have compiled a list of about one hundred men with their directorships in the great corporate business enterprises of the United States. It furnishes indisputable proof of the community of interest that controls the industrial life of the country....

It discloses their connections with the transportation, the industrial, and the commercial life of the American people. This exhibit will make it clear to anyone that a small group of men hold in their hands the business of this country.

No student of the economic changes in recent years can escape the conclusion that the railroads, telegraph, shipping, cable, telephone, traction, express, mining, iron, steel, coal, oil, gas, electric light, cotton, copper, sugar, tobacco, agricultural implements, and the food products are completely controlled and mainly owned by these hundred men; that they have through reorganization multiplied their wealth almost beyond their own ability to know its amount with accuracy....

But the country seems not to understand how completely great banking institutions in the principal money centers have become bound up with the control of industrial institutions, nor the logical connection of this relationship to the financial depression which we have so recently suffered, nor the dangers which threaten us from this source in the future....

The closeness of business association between Wall Street and the centralized banking power of New York can, unfortunately, be but imperfectly traced through the official reports. It would seem that the radical changes taking place in the banking business of the country, suggesting to the conservative, economic, and financial authorities the gravest possible dangers to our industrial and commercial integrity, might well have caused the Treasury Department to recognize the necessity of so directing its investigations of the national banks in the greater cities which are centers of speculation and to so classify their returns as to inform itself and the country definitely respecting such changes. This has not been done....

It is, however, possible to find evidence which establishes the diversion of a large volume of the bank resources to securities which are the subject of speculative operation in the stock exchange....

Official figures do not show the real condition.

The reports from banks upon which statistics are based fail to make clear the actual investment in speculative securities....These banks have either established connections with trust companies or have organized inside trust companies as a protection and convenience....These companies afford a convenient cover for the banks....Their securities can be borrowed and shuffled back and forth to make a good showing. The trust companies can handle securities which the banks can not touch. They can underwrite bonds and float loans for which the banks could not openly stand sponsor. They can deal with themselves in innumerable ways to their own benefit and the detriment of the public....

The effect of the proposed legislation becomes more apparent as we investigate the grouping together of the great financial institutions holding these railroad bonds and other special securities and then trace their connection with the companies issuing these bonds....

The twenty-three directors of the National City Bank, the head of the Standard Oil group, and the directors of the National Bank of Commerce, thirty-nine in number, hold 1,007 directorships on the great transportation, industrial, and commercial institutions of this country....

Fourteen of the directors of the National City Bank are at the head of fourteen great combinations representing 38 per cent of the capitalization of all the industrial trusts of the country.

The railroad lines represented on the board of this one bank cover the country like a network....These same twenty-three directors, through their various connections, represent more than 350 other banks, trust companies, railroads, and industrial corporations, with an aggregate capitalization of more than twelve thousand million dollars....

It was inevitable that this massing of banking power should attract to itself the resources of other banks throughout the country. Capital attracts capital. It inspires confidence. It appeals to the imagination....

The law providing that 15 per cent of the deposits of a country bank should be held for the protection of its depositors conveniently permits three-fifths of the amount to be deposited in reserve city banks, and of the 25 per cent of reserve for the protection of depositors in reserve city banks one-half may be deposited with central reserve city banks. As there are but three central reserve cities, one of which, of course, is New York City, the alluring interest rates which these all-powerful groups could offer inevitably tended to draw the great proportion of lawful reserves subject to transfer from the country and reserve banks....

The power which the New York banks derive through these vast accumulations of the resources of other national banks strengthen their position so that they could draw in the surplus money of all the other financial institutions of the country, State, private, and savings banks and trust companies....

The ability of these group banks of New York through their connected interests to engage in underwriting, to finance promotion schemes, where the profits resulting from overcapitalization represent hundreds of millions of dollars, places them beyond let or hindrance from competitors elsewhere in the country. Their ability to take advantage of conditions in Wall Street...would enable them to command, almost at will, the capital of the country for these speculative purposes.

But one result could follow. Floating the stocks and bonds in overcapitalized transportation, traction, mining, and industrial organizations does not create wealth, but it does absorb capital. Through the agency of these great groups hundreds of millions of dollars of the wealth of the country have been tied up....

The plain truth is that legitimate commercial banking is being eaten up by financial banking. The greatest banks of the financial center of the country have ceased to be agents of commerce and have become primarily agencies of promotion and speculation....Trained men, who a dozen years ago stood first among the bankers of the world as heads of the greatest banks of New York City, are, in the main, either displaced or do the bidding of men who are not bankers, but masters of organization....

Sir, can any sane man doubt the power of a little group of men in whose hands are lodged the control of the railroads and the industries, outside of agriculture, as well as the great banks, insurance, and trust companies of the principal money center of the country, to give commercial banking and general business a shock at will?...

Taking the general conditions of the country, it is difficult to find any sufficient reason outside of manipulation for the extraordinary panic of October, 1907....

The panic came. It had been scheduled to arrive. The way had been prepared. Those who were directing it were not the men to miss anything in their way as it advanced....

The panic was working well. The stock market had gone to smash. Harriman was buying back Union Pacific shorts, but still smashing the market. Morgan was buying in short steel stocks and bonds, but still smashing the market....The country banks were begging for their balances. Business was being held up....On the street and in the brokers' offices the strain of apprehension was intense. In the midst of a Wall Street fight, when fear supersedes reason, it is difficult for those who are in it, but not directing it, to determine how much is real, how much is sham. Some of the guns are loaded only with blank cartridges to alarm; some are loaded with powder and ball to kill....

The floor of the stock exchange was chosen as the scene for the closing act, October 24 the time.

The men who had created the money stringency, who had absorbed the surplus capital of the country with promotions and reorganization schemes, who had deliberately forced a panic and frightened many innocent depositors to aid them by hoarding, who had held up the country banks by lawlessly refusing to return their deposits, never lost sight of one of the chief objects to be attained. The cause of currency revision was not neglected for one moment. It was printed day by day in their press; it passed from mouth to mouth....High interest rates should be made to plead for emergency money through the telegraph dispatches of October 24 in every countinghouse, factory, and shop in America. The banks refused credit to old customers—all business to new customers. Call loans for money were at last denied at any price....It spelled ruin....

How perfect the stage setting! How real it all seemed! But back of the scenes Morgan and Stillman were in conference. They had made their representations at Washington. They knew when the next installment of aid would reach New York.... They awaited its arrival and deposit. Thereupon they pooled an equal amount. But they held it....Interest rates soared. Wall street was driven to a frenzy.... The smashing of the market became terrific. Still they waited....Men looked into each other's ghastly faces. Then, at precisely 2.15, the curtain went up with Morgan and Standard Oil in the center of the stage with money—real money, twenty-five millions of money—giving it away at 10 per cent....

And so ended the panic.

How beautifully it all worked out. They had the whole country terrorized. They had the money of the deposits of the banks of every State in the Union to the amount of five hundred million, nearly all of which was in the vaults of the big group banks. This served two purposes—it made the country banks join in the cry for currency revision and it supplied the big operators with money to squeeze out investors and speculators at the very bottom of the decline, taking in the stock at an enormous profit.... The operations of Morgan and the Standard Oil furnish additional evidence of the character of this panic. We have record proof of their utter contempt for commercial interests....Did they give aid and support to the distressed merchant and manufacturer?...Alas, no. They pursued the course of the speculating banker....They let great commercial houses, great manufacturing concerns,...down to ruin and dishonor, while they protected their speculative patrons. No better evidence could be asked to establish the character of this panic or the character of the men who were in command. By their fruits ye shall know them!

GLOSSARY

capitalization: the total value of a company, based usually on the total value of the company's shares of stock

Harriman: E. H. Harriman, father of W. Averell Harriman and director of the Union Pacific Railroad

Morgan: James Pierpont Morgan, American financier in the steel industry

shorts: also called "short sales," an investment technique that involves first selling a stock one does not own with the expectation of later buying the stock back at a lower price when its value falls, thus realizing a profit in a falling market

speculative securities: investments that are highly risky but hold the potential for large profits

Stillman: James Stillman, American financier and banker

trust companies: combinations of companies, usually formed with the purpose of driving out competition

underwrite: to guarantee financial support; to finance stocks or bonds and sell them to the public

Wall Street: the street in Lower Manhattan where the New York Stock Exchange is located; as a figure of speech, the financial sector of the economy

Document Analysis

By the beginning of the twentieth century, the corporation became the linchpin of the American economy. Moreover, thanks to such devices as the trust and the holding company, many of these enterprises became increasingly concentrated in fewer hands. By 1904 two-fifths of all manufacturing was controlled by 305 industrial combinations possessing an aggregate capital of $7 billion. The epitome of such consolidation of power was John D. Rockefeller's Standard Oil Company, a firm that by 1900 dominated the petroleum industry. The imbalanced situation was fostered by Wall Street investment banks, particularly J. P. Morgan & Company. These banks would raise needed capital for new corporations by selling their stocks and bonds and would, at the same time, police these new ventures by placing their own representatives on the boards of directors and by controlling sources of credit. Critics of this new centralization, such as La Follette, referred to the phenomenon as the "money trust."

On March 17, 1908, La Follette began a series of speeches attacking the money trust. This first speech was triggered by the Aldrich currency bill, proposed in the aftermath of the Panic of 1907. Nelson Aldrich, the powerful chairman of the Senate Finance Committee, proposed the issue of $500 million in emergency currency that would be backed by state, municipal, and private railroad bonds. Edward B. Vreeland of New York offered a similar bill in the House. Aldrich soon renounced the clause involving railroad bonds, acting out of the fear that the proposal would injure the Finance Committee members William B. Allison of Iowa and Chester I. Long of Kansas in their forthcoming races for reelection. La Follette had intended to blast Aldrich's original proposal, but he hastily rewrote his speech, with the result containing some of the most sensationalist charges ever made on the floor of Congress.

In his Senate speech of March 17, 1908, La Follette begins with the accusation that about a hundred men "hold in their hands the business of the country." He lists the enterprises they controlled, ranging from railroads to mining, from cotton to food. He then points to the domination of American banking by Wall Street, which he found to be involved in destructive speculation. The Wisconsin senator refers to a special committee, established in 1905 by the New York State Legislature and headed by the state senator William M. Armstrong, which investigated the corrupt use of life insurance funds. Wall Street banks either established connections with trust companies or organized such firms themselves so as to sell securities, underwrite bonds, and float loans that ordinary banks could not openly sponsor. La Follette then produces a massive "List of Men Who Control Industrial, Franchise, Transportation, and Financial Business of the United States, with Their Directorships and Offices in Various Corporations." This document covered ten pages of fine print in the Congressional Record. Here, La Follette argues, was firm evidence showing the control exercised by Morgan and Standard Oil at the expense of ordinary Americans.

In the last part of his speech, La Follette accuses the Morgan and Standard Oil banks of creating the Panic of 1907 so as to line their own pockets. During the October panic, the great New York financial institutions were unable to supply funds to needy banks in the interior of the country. Therefore, bankruptcies took place among several large industrial corporations and many small western and southern banks as well. Only intervention by J. P. Morgan himself, who switched funds from one bank to another as well as to securities markets, could save the day. La Follette, however, does not see Morgan as a redeemer but as one who profited unjustly from the crisis. He quotes predictions of impending disaster made that summer by James J. Hill, chairman of the Great Northern Railway Company, and Edward Payson Ripley, president of the Atchison, Topeka and Santa Fe Railway. He also notes warnings of banking concentration made by Thomas F. Woodlock, former editor of the Wall Street Journal; Charles J. Bullock, an economist at Williams College; and the commercial expert Edward E. Pratt.

It was Morgan's effort to squeeze out a conglomeration centering on the Heinze United Copper Company that created the panic. Only after it became obvious that "every countinghouse, factory, and shop in America" might be affected did J.P. Morgan and James Stillman, board chairman of the Rockefeller-controlled National City Bank of New York, meet on October 24 to end the crisis. La Follette concludes by denouncing the Morgan and Rockefeller interests for sacrificing "the distressed merchant and manufacturer" to the interests of "the speculating banker." His final remark, "By their fruits ye shall know them!" was taken from Jesus' Sermon on the Mount (Matthew 7:20).

Essential Themes

La Follette's claims concerning the panic of 1907 were widely publicized. Not surprisingly, he was immediately challenged. The president of the First National Bank of Chicago, one of the men on the senator's list, called the speech "worse than rot" and said that it was "a deliberate stirring up of passion and rage among people who have no facility for acquiring knowledge at first hand and are dependent upon men whom they trust" (New York Times, March 19, 1908). Such attacks did not faze La Follette, who concluded his series of addresses on March 24. On this occasion he denied that he was attacking such figures as Rockefeller, Morgan, and E. H. Harriman, of the Union Pacific Railroad, as individuals, remarking that they were merely types, the embodiment of an evil. It was what drove them that had to be destroyed in order to safeguard America's free institutions.

Some business interests backed La Follette, among them the New York Board of Trade, which distributed copies of the speech among its most active members. Indeed, in contrast to earlier requests, this time it was companies in the Northeast, not the Midwest, that sought many reprints. Aldrich accepted a La Follette amendment prohibiting banks from investing in the securities of other firms in which they had interlocking directorates. However, defeated by a vote of thirty-seven to thirteen was a La Follette proposal to forbid banks from making loans to people who were officers of the same banks. On May 29, La Follette proved furious enough to start a filibuster of the Aldrich-Vreeland bill. Battling a cold and addressing his Senate colleagues in ninety-degree heat, La Follette spoke for a record nineteen hours, but parliamentary blundering by allies led to the bill's adoption, by a vote of forty-three to twenty-two. Only with the adoption of the Federal Reserve System in 1913 were genuine reforms made to the nation's banking and credit system.

———*Justus D. Doenecke, New College of Florida*

Bibliography and Further Reading

La, Follette R. M, and Matthew Rothschild. *La Follette's Autobiography: A Personal Narrative of Political Experiences*. Madison, Wisconsin: University of Wisconsin Press, 2013. Print.

Unger, Nancy C. Fighting Bob La Follette: The Righteous Reformer. Chapel Hill: University of North Carolina Press, 2000. Print.

Samuel Gompers: Editorial on the Supreme Court Ruling in the Danbury Hatters' Case

Date: 1908
Author: Samuel Gompers
Genre: Editorial

Summary Overview

After flirting with Marxism in his youth, Samuel Gompers played a leading role in developing craft trade unionism, serving as president of the American Federation of Labor for all but one year from its founding in 1886 until his death in 1924. An opponent of Socialism, Gompers advocated in his speeches and writings for the AFL a faith in voluntarism—a philosophy by which craft unions enjoyed considerable local autonomy. He also believed that better conditions for workers could be obtained through collective bargaining rather than legislative action. The nonpartisanship of Gompers and the AFL, however, was abandoned in 1912 with the endorsement of Woodrow Wilson. Labor's alliance with Wilson's Democratic administration, as well as co-operation with the National Civic Federation, provided Gompers with considerable influence on the national stage, although Gompers and labor played less of a role in the Republican administrations of the 1920s. Although he was not a fiery orator, Gompers was an effective speaker and writer who worked tirelessly on behalf of labor during the late nineteenth and early twentieth centuries, establishing the AFL as an important national organization. In reaction to the Supreme Court decision in the 1908 Danbury Hatters' Case, which placed labor under the restrictions of the Sherman Antitrust Act, Gompers penned an angry response—Editorial on the Supreme Court Ruling in the Danbury Hatters' Case—urging labor to seek relief through congressional action. This tactic was rewarded with the passage of the Clayton Act (1914), which exempted labor unions from the restraint of trade provisions contained in the Sherman Antitrust Act.

Defining Moment

Gompers editorial was specifically addressed to those individuals who were a part of the organized labor effort, and those who considered themselves to be friends of labor interests. The editorial reflected Gompers' genuine concern over the Danbury Hatters' opinion; with Gompers calling into question the decision's potential to threaten the very existence of trade unions. Futhermore, the editorial expressed fear that labor unions could in fact be denied the right to organize as a result of the Supreme Court's actions. These concerns, as well as the concern over the potential for the formation of monopolies, were wide-spread among the labor community, and Gompers' appeal to Congress through the editorial was well supported by the labor unions and those sympathetic to the plight of labor workers. The editorial was key in influencing the creation and passage of the Clayton Act of 1914, a bill that more clearly addressed concerns regarding the creation of monopolies and the infringement on union members' rights. Gompers believed The Clayton Act was the most important act of the government since the abolishment of slavery. This enthusiasm for the Clayton Act was shared among members of the labor community, and Gompers' effort in encouraging the legislature to take action in response to the Supreme Court's decision in Danbury Hatters was significantly praised.

Author Biography

Samuel Gompers was born on January 27, 1850, in London, England. In July 1863, his family immigrated to the United States, where Gompers and his father found employment in New York City as skilled cigar rollers. Although Gompers lacked formal education, he was introduced to the ideas of the political economists Karl Marx and Ferdinand Lassalle through the working-class self-education practiced by cigar makers, who hired a fellow worker to read aloud to those rolling cigars. This education helped convince Gompers of the necessity for trade unionism, and he became active in the Cigar Makers' International Union. Along with his friend Adolph Strasser, who assumed the presidency of the union in 1877, Gompers fostered a more centralized union model for skilled craft workers in response to the fragility of the labor movement during such troubled economic times as the Panic of 1873—a financial depression that led to losses of jobs.

As a trade unionist, Gompers believed that political

action was premature prior to workers' forming a sense of class consciousness. Accordingly, he opposed political alignments with the Democrats and Republicans or parties of the left, such as the Socialists, in favor of direct action that would increase a sense of labor solidarity. Driven by these ideas, Gompers helped found the Federation of Organized Trades and Labor Unions in 1881. Although the federation was underfunded and organizationally weak, Gompers was successful in opposing the political orientation and influence of the Knights of Labor among the unions. In 1886, Gompers and supporters among organized skilled workers formed the American Federation of Labor (AFL), and Gompers was elected president. The AFL supported the independence of autonomous trade unions in the ordering of their internal affairs. Gompers and the AFL believed in voluntarism, rejecting an active role for the state in the regulation of industrial relations. In fact, with court decisions often overturning pro-labor legislation, Gompers was convinced that only collective action by workers, the essence of labor voluntarism, could protect the interests of labor and achieve such goals as the eight-hour workday. Gompers addressed workers across the nation to rally American workers to the forefront of an international campaign to allow labor more dignity by providing time for workers to cultivate their minds.

During the 1880s and 1890s Gompers worked tirelessly to establish the AFL's influence over skilled workers. Although he was often accused of fostering elitism within the labor movement, Gompers was a critic of the International Association of Machinists, which opposed black membership. Rejecting the Marxism and radicalism of his youth, Gompers attempted to distance himself from the influence of the Socialist and Populist parties. In an August 1894 editorial for the *American Federationist*, the newspaper organ of the AFL, Gompers opposed the actions of Eugene Debs and the American Railway Union (ARU) during the 1894 strike against the Pullman Palace Car Company. Debs, who would emerge as the leader of the Socialist Party of America in the early twentieth century, and the ARU were supporting striking workers at the Pullman company factory town where railroad sleeping cars were produced. Although Gompers condemned George Pullman's wage cuts for initiating the labor stoppage, he failed to support the call by Debs for a general strike by American labor. This stance led to Gompers's failure to win reelection as AFL president in 1895.

Regaining the presidency of the AFL the following year, Gompers soon attempted to offset employer opposition to unionization by cooperating with the National Civic Federation, a reform group composed of the nation's corporate leadership. Although this alliance produced few tangible benefits for the AFL, the organization's membership continued to grow, numbering nearly two million workers by 1904. Nevertheless, Gompers was troubled by the actions of the Supreme Court in the 1908 *Loewe v. Lawlor* decision, also referred to as the Danbury Hatters' Case. In a March 1908 editorial for the *American Federationist*, Gompers criticized the Court's declaration of the AFL's boycott against the hat manufacturer Dietrich Lowe, for its refusal to recognize the hatters' union, as an unlawful restraint of trade under the Sherman Antitrust Act (1890). In his editorial, Gompers displays frustration with the legal system, but his more conservative nature is apparent in his conclusion that the AFL must bow to the Court's ruling.

Gompers also came to rethink his organization's avoidance of political entanglements, and in 1906 he presented labor's Bill of Grievances to President Theodore Roosevelt and Congress. As the ruling Republican Party proved unsympathetic to Gompers, in 1912 the AFL executive abandoned nonpartisanship, supporting the presidential candidacy of the Democrat Woodrow Wilson, who prevailed. The Wilson administration honored labor's support by appointing a former coal miner, William B. Wilson, to head the Department of Labor and enacting legislation beneficial to labor. The 1914 Clayton Act, further antitrust legislation, was proclaimed by Gompers as labor's Magna Carta for exempting unions from the restraint of trade provisions of the Sherman Antitrust Act. Gompers's enthusiasm for both the Clayton Act and the Wilson administration is apparent in his 1915 circular letter dispatched to AFL organizers. Gompers concludes in that letter that working within the political system allowed labor to legislatively address the inequities of the Supreme Court decision in the 1908 Danbury Hatters' Case.

As the United States struggled with maintaining Wilson's policy of neutrality during World War I, Gompers spoke before the 1916 annual meeting of the National Civic Federation, asserting that labor would support national preparedness but needed to be a full participant in any plans for the nation to move to war footing. When the United States entered World War I in April 1917, Gompers supported the nation's effort, breaking with Eugene Debs and the Socialists, who opposed U.S. participation. Gompers also endorsed the National War Labor Board, which encouraged the cooperation of business and labor in the war effort, a relationship Gompers had advocated in his 1916 address before the National Civic Federation. Gompers also served the Wilson administration as an adviser on the labor sections of the Versailles Treaty. His influence waned with Wilson's failing health and the election of the Republican Warren G. Harding to the presidency in 1920. In December 1924, Gompers collapsed while participating in a meeting of the Pan-American Federation of Labor; he died a week later, on December 13, in San Antonio, Texas. While labor was on the defensive in the 1920s, Gompers's leadership of the AFL from 1886 until his death established a strong foundation for craft unionism in the United States.

HISTORICAL DOCUMENT

TO ORGANIZED LABOR AND FRIENDS.

It has seldom occurred that I have found it necessary to use the first person in addressing my fellow-workers and the people through the editorial columns of the *American Federationist*. What follows here refers to such an extraordinary circumstance and affects the labor organizations, their members and our friends so fundamentally, that I am impelled to address them in the most direct manner. The Supreme Court of the United States on February 3, 1908, rendered a decision in the case of the hat manufacturer Loewe against the United Hatters of North America, and decreed that the Loewe suit for threefold damages can be maintained under the Sherman anti-trust law. The Supreme Court holds that the action of the hatters, as described in the complaint, is a combination "in restraint of trade or commerce among the several states" in the sense in which those words are used in the Sherman law.

A decision by the Supreme Court, the highest tribunal of the country, is law and must be obeyed, regardless of whether or not we believe the decision to be a just one.

We protest that the trade unions of the country should not be penalized under the provisions of the Sherman anti-trust law. In fact, I know that Congress never intended the law to apply to the labor unions, but the Supreme Court rules that it shall apply to them; therefore, pending action by Congress to define our status and restore our rights by modifying or amending the Sherman law, there is no alternative for labor but to obey the mandate of the court....

I have no words adequate to express the regret I feel at being obliged to take this action, especially as in the opinion of competent lawyers—and their opinion is shared by many other laymen as well as myself—this decision by the Supreme Court is unwarranted and unjust, but until Congressional relief can be obtained it must undoubtedly be binding upon us all. Were it only myself personally who might suffer, for conscience sake I should not hesitate to risk every penalty, even unto the extreme, in defense of what I believe to be labor's rights. In this case of the adverse court decision, and indeed in every other circumstance which may arise, I think those who know me do not question my loyalty, devotion, and willingness to bear fully any responsibility involved in the forwarding of the cause to which my life is pledged; but unfortunately the terms of the decision are such that no one person, even though president of the American Federation of Labor and willing to assume entire responsibility, will be permitted to take upon himself the sole penalty of protest against what I and every member of every organization affiliated to the American Federation of Labor, and indeed every patriotic citizen, must feel to be a most sweeping drag-net decision making the natural and rational voluntary action of workmen unlawful and punishable by fine and imprisonment....

Under the court's construction of the Sherman law the voluntary and peaceful associations of labor that are organized for the uplifting of the workers, these unions I say, are made the greatest offenders under the anti-trust law. It is almost unbelievable that our unions which perform so important a service in the interest of civilization and moral and material progress are to be accorded the treatment of malefactors. Yet the more carefully this decision is read the more absolutely clear does it become that our unions are to be penalized by it, as the most vicious of trusts were intended to be, yet the trusts still go unpunished.

I have a strong hope that Congress will promptly take heed of the injustice that has been done the workers, and will so amend or modify the Sherman anti-trust law, that the labor unions will be restored to the exercise of the powers and rights guaranteed to all our citizens under the constitution.

It is not conceivable that Congress will turn a deaf ear to the rightful demand of the workers of the country for relief from this most amazing decision, but until such time as relief is assured, I am compelled, for the safety of our men of labor, to obey literally the decision of the Supreme Court; but this situation created by the court must be met. It will be met.

While abiding by this decision, I urge most strongly upon my fellow unionists everywhere to be more energetic than ever before in organizing the yet unorganized, in standing together, in uniting and federating for the common good. Be more active than ever before in using every lawful and honorable means, not only to secure relief from the present situation at the hands of Congress, but in the doing of everything which may promote the uplifting and noble work of our great cause of humanity. Like all great causes it must meet temporary opposition, but in the end it will accomplish all the more on account of the trials endured.

GLOSSARY

Danbury Hatters' Case: *Loewe v. Lawlor*, a 1908 ruling in which the Supreme Court held that the boycott of D. E. Loewe & Company by the United Hatters of North America constituted a conspiracy in restraint of trade, a violation of the Sherman Antitrust Act

hat manufacturer: Dietrich Loewe, whose refusal to allow unions to organize in his Danbury, Connecticut–based firm, D. E. Loewe & Company, resulted in a strike and boycott

laymen: nonprofessionals

met: dealt with

Sherman anti-trust law: an 1890 act of Congress, the first such law to limit the power of monopolies

Document Analysis

On February 3, 1908, the Supreme Court of the United States delivered its decision in the Danbury Hatters' Case. According to the Court, the boycott by the United Hatters of North America was an unlawful restraint of trade, and the manufacturer was entitled to triple damages under the Sherman Antitrust Act. In his *American Federationist* editorial of March 1908, Gompers asserts his opposition to the Court's ruling, although he concludes that the decision must be obeyed until Congress is able to bestow legislative relief for labor. In his advice to AFL organizers, Gompers makes it clear that as union president he is willing to accept the legal burdens that defiance of the Supreme Court's decision would entail. Nevertheless, he concludes that such a course of action would do little to avoid coercive actions by the state against other union officials and members. Gompers concludes that under the court's ruling all union officers would be liable for any violations committed by any AFL official or member. Thus, any individual action taken by Gompers would endanger the entire organization. Gompers goes on to argue that is almost inconceivable that the Court would make such a draconian decision. considering the services rendered by the AFL and labor movement to the economy and American civilization, but the Court is punishing labor while allowing big business, whose monopolistic policies the Sherman Act was passed to regulate, to remain unpunished.

Indeed, while finding the decision unjust, Gompers insists that labor must work within the system. He indicates, however, that he is willing to somewhat abandon his principles of voluntarism on this occasion, arguing that direct congressional action is necessary to protect organized labor, for the Court made the "natural and rational voluntary action of workmen unlawful and punishable by fine and imprisonment." Gompers recognizes the dangers of legislation generally in asserting that Congress did not intend that the Sherman Antitrust Act be applied to labor organizations. Nevertheless, the Court's ruling means that labor must seek relief from the legislative branch. Gompers concludes his editorial with a traditional call for continued organization to "promote the uplifting and noble work of our great cause of humanity."

Essential Themes

In protest of the D.E. Loewe & Company who refused to recognize the hatters' union, the United Hatters of North America, aided by the American Federation of Labor, were on strike and actively pushing for consumers and manufacturers to make union-only purchases. The boycott was met with success, and Loewe's business was suffering as a result. Traditionally, labor organizations are guaranteed to right to organize and strike as they see fit. However, in this particular instance, the unions were categorized as having an impact on interstate commerce and therefore the actions violated certain provisions in the Sherman Anti-Trust Act. While the government interpreted the actions of the unions as a clear violation of established legislation, the unions interpreted the Supreme Court's decision in the case to mean they were no longer allowed to organize. Gompers, as President of the AFL, took to the editorial page to express his sincere concerns regarding the Court's decision and the impact it could have on unions in the future.

Gompers had previously been successful in shifting the focus of labor unions and their members away from social issues to issues more concerned with things like wages and working conditions. The focus on such issues and subsequent victories for unions under Gompers' leadership earned him great favor within the labor community. So, it would stand to reason his editorial would prove to be persuasive with people either in unions or in support of labor interests due to his established credibility. Gompers used his position to emphasize the significance of the Supreme Court's decision, and because of his positive record for success, his editorial did not go unnoticed by the public or Congress.

Gompers pointed out the fact the Danbury Hatters' ruling could threaten labor's ability to organize, or worse, threaten to end unions completely. With over two million working members of the American Federation of Labor, and many more in support of union workers, this group had the power to have their voices heard when motivated. Due to the nature of politics, holding favor with voters traditionally results in the ability to persuade members of Congress who have an interest in being re-elected. Therefore, had Congress ignored the passionate editorial and the laborer's response, voters—particularly those sympathetic to labor concerns—would have noticed and been unlikely to support re-election efforts of those in office. Gompers' choice to appeal to Congress through a powerful editorial, knowing he was popular within the large labor community, was a smart political move that led to yet another victory for the American Federation of Labor under the direction of Gompers.

It is clear Gompers' position as the leader of the AFL, a well-organized group with high membership, gave him the opportunity to yield influence over Congress. Had Gompers chosen not to publish the editorial that effectively put public pressure on Congress, one could speculate as to whether or not passage of the Clayton Act would have ever happened. As history would reflect, The Clayton Act was passed as a result of Gompers' influence over Congress, members of the AFL, and labor supporters. Labor workers ability to organize was left intact, and anticompetitive practices harmful to a competitive market were prevented through this important legislation. The attempt to ensure protection from the creation of monopolies in the Sherman Antitrust Act was given a more concrete definition in the Clayton Act. From Gompers perspective, the Clayton Act was a more efficient and effective piece of legislation for protecting the interest of labor unions and their members. Without this legislation, it could be said that labor unions throughout history would have suffered tremendously. Issues such as wages and working conditions could have worsened, and as a result many workers could have been treated unfairly or forced to work in dangerous work environments. By preventing the formation of unstoppable monopolies, Congress protect workers' interests and promoted a more competitive market.

—*Ron Briley, Ph.D. and Amber R. Dickinson, Ph.D.*

Bibliography and Further Reading
Harvey, Roland Hill. 1935. *Samuel Gompers, Champion of the Toiling Masses.* Stanford University Press.
Mason, Alpheus T. 1924. "The Labor Clauses of the Clayton Act." *The American Political Science Review.* Vol. 18, No. 3, pp. 498-512.
Merritt, Walter Gordon. 1910. "The Law of the Danbury Hatters' Case." *The Annals of the American Academy of Political and Social Science.* Vol. 36, No. 2, pp 11-22.

FOREIGN CHALLENGES

Typically, any ten-year span in US history bears the marks of challenges facing the nation from abroad, and the period 1900-1909 was no exception. It may not have been the most riotous decade in American foreign affairs, but neither was it the quietest. Whereas McKinley was somewhat cautious in his approach to foreign policy, Roosevelt came to be known for his "big stick" diplomacy (after the saying "Speak softly but carry a big stick"). The latter figure not only applied the Monroe Doctrine to the affairs of Latin America but expanded it, with his "Roosevelt Corollary," to include greater scope for US intervention. A string of international treaties, along with Roosevelt's own strategic maneuvering in the region, cleared the way for the building of the Panama Canal, among other things. Indeed, the United States maintained control over the Canal Zone until very recently.

One key area of focus for the McKinley and Roosevelt administrations was East Asia and the Pacific. First, there was the Philippines to deal with—a consequence of the Spanish-American War (1898). An anti-American insurrection there had developed after the United States failed to grant the Philippines independence in the wake of the war with Spain. A US fact-finding mission found that the Filipinos were "not ready" for self-government. After over two years of intermittent fighting and a continued expansion of the US presence in the islands, the insurrection collapsed and the Philippines became an overseas territory of the United States.

Meanwhile, in China a trade dispute erupted into fighting as part of the Boxer Rebellion (1898-1900). A coalition of forces, including the United States, Japan, and European nations, moved from the port city of Tientsin to Beijing to put down the rebellion and force a settlement. (China was compelled to pay an indemnity of $333 million and agree to a number of other concessions.) Elsewhere in the region, war broke out (1904) between Japan and Russia over territorial claims. Roosevelt played a key role in bringing the parties together under the Treaty of Portsmouth (1905). Japan and the United States faced problems in their own relationship over both territory in the western Pacific and Japanese immigration in the United States. Diplomatic agreements settled the main points involved, but Roosevelt was still happy to send his Great White Fleet to the Sea of Japan and adjacent waters to project US power.

To the south of the US mainland, in Mexico, the dictator Porfirio Díaz benefitted from US capital flowing into the country. It fueled resentments that eventually burst forth in the Mexican Revolution (1910-1917) in the following decade. Included in this section is a scathing look at Mexico under Díaz.

Henry Cabot Lodge: Speech on the Retention of the Philippine Islands

Date: 1900
Author: Henry Cabot Lodge
Genre: Speech

Summary Overview

Henry Cabot Lodge's speech on the retention of the Philippine Islands was an argument in favor of imperialism in the aftermath of the Spanish-American War (1898). The expression "Manifest Destiny" had been used since 1845 to argue that the United States should expand across the North American continent until it stretched from coast to coast. After that had been achieved, some began to argue that it was only natural for U.S. expansion to continue beyond the natural borders of the continent and that U.S. rule would be a blessing for many foreign peoples. Also, the rapid expansion of Europe's colonial empires in Africa and Asia in the late 1800s raised concerns that the European powers would divide the world among themselves and then exclude American commerce from their possessions.

The Imperialist and Anti-Imperialist tendencies in the United States had at various times crossed party lines. An early focus of overseas expansion was Cuba, a Spanish colony where slavery was practiced until 1886. Southern Democrats saw it as a potential slave state until the U.S. Civil War made that issue irrelevant. Then Northern Republicans looked upon it as a possible base for commercial expansion. What would later become the Spanish-American War began in 1895 as a Cuban rebellion against Spanish rule. Imperialist voices in the United States soon advocated intervening on behalf of the Cuban rebels, sometimes basing their arguments on the oppressive nature of Spanish colonialism and sometimes stressing the commercial opportunities. That intervention, and the official start of the Spanish-American War, came in 1898, but not before the Anti-Imperialists had made their move. Congress passed a war resolution but included the Teller Amendment, which prohibited the annexation of Cuba. As a result, Cuba was occupied temporarily, but it was not annexed (although the later Platt Amendment assured the United States a major role in the politics of independent Cuba for years). Other Spanish territories, however, were treated as fair game. Quick victory over Spain led to the occupation and annexation of Puerto Rico, Guam, and the Philippines. (In its war-fired enthusiasm, the United States also annexed Hawaii, where American plantation owners—with the unauthorized connivance of U.S. Navy and State Department personnel—had overthrown the government of Queen Lili'uokalani five years earlier).

Defending the Philippines in 1898 was an obsolete and ill-supplied Spanish flotilla, which was quickly defeated by the American Asiatic Squadron under Commodore George Dewey in the Battle of Manila Bay (May 1). (Dewey was promoted to rear admiral 11 days later.) Then troops under Major General Wesley Merritt and Brigadier General Arthur MacArthur (later military governor of the Philippines and the father of Douglas MacArthur) accepted the surrender of the Spanish garrison ashore after a mock battle on August 13. Under a prearranged agreement between the Spanish governor and Dewey, the doomed garrison capitulated after giving the token resistance that the governor considered necessary to preserve the honor of Spain. The governor's main condition in this arrangement was that the Americans keep the Filipino rebels (*insurrectos*) led by Emilio Aguinaldo out of Manila because he feared they would massacre his troops. Thus the Spanish administration in the Philippines collapsed and the archipelago fell into the hands of the United States before most of the troops sailing from San Francisco had even arrived. The *insurrectos*, who had been actively assisting the Americans until then, felt bitterly betrayed. Although Aguinaldo had declared independence on June 12, 1898, the Imperialists now insisted that the United States had to annex the otherwise ungoverned islands for their own good. (The Imperialists were also concerned about the intentions of rival powers. By the summer of 1898, warships from Britain, France, Germany, and Japan were actively scouting the islands as potential colonies, with U.S. and German ships nearly coming to open combat.) After U.S. troops occupied the islands, fighting broke out between them and the *insurrectos,* triggering the Philippine-American War

(1899–1902; a conventional war from February to November 1899, a guerrilla war from then until spring 1902).

The Treaty of Paris, ending the Spanish-American War, gave the United States possession of the Philippines. Insurgency among the Filipinos grew, and American legislators were soon at odds over how to address the problem. As chairman of the Standing Committee on the Philippines and a member of the Senate Committee on Foreign Relations, Henry Cabot Lodge advocated a militant foreign policy, one based on the premise that the United States was a great power and should always act as such. In his 1900 Speech on the Retention of the Philippine Islands, he portrayed an American destiny that would soon encompass mastery of the entire Pacific.

The immediate audience for Lodge's speech, of course, was the combination of Imperialists and Anti-Imperialists in the Senate debating a proposal by Senator John C. Spooner regarding the fate of the Philippines. At the same time, Lodge was addressing a larger audience, the whole of the politically engaged public in the United States, which he hoped to turn to the cause of Imperialism. In his view, the American public was generally too disengaged to pursue such a policy with the necessary consistency.

Defining Moment

Since the presidency of George Washington, the United States had primarily followed a policy of isolation in foreign affairs. For Lodge, however, isolation was not so much a policy as a habit born of a lack of reasonable alternatives. He, like the other Imperialists, believed that a great nation had to have an expansive foreign policy in order to remain great, if only the public would support it. The Imperialists had no trouble convincing themselves that colonial rule by the United States would have positive consequences for "lesser" peoples, thus viewing imperialism simultaneously as a power-politics objective and a humanitarian objective. For them, American imperialism would be a model imperialism, an agent of international reform. At home, Lodge said, imperialism would "elevate and enlarge the whole tone and scope of our politics."

Lodge was not known to have ever uttered the name of the Philippine Islands, publicly or privately, prior to the outbreak of the Spanish-American War. With the conquest of the Philippines, he believed that fate had dealt the United States a new hand. The victory in the Spanish-American War and the retention of the Philippines would be an opportunity to achieve "the abandonment of isolation" and to build popular support for a more expansive foreign policy.

Author Biography

Henry Cabot Lodge (1850–1924), as a Republican U.S. senator (1893–1924) from Massachusetts, was a somewhat hesitant Progressive in domestic affairs and a convinced Imperialist in foreign affairs. He had a significant influence on U.S. foreign policy. An admirer of Rear Admiral Alfred Thayer Mahan (ret.), Lodge believed that a strong navy and domination of the Caribbean Sea and Pacific Ocean were vital to U.S. national security. He favored entry into the Spanish-American War and World War I, although he is best remembered for leading the Senate opposition to the League of Nations.

Among his numerous positions in the Senate, Lodge chaired (1899–1911) the Committee on the Philippines. He was also a member of the Committee on Foreign Relations, which he chaired in 1919–24. He was a long-time associate of Theodore Roosevelt, breaking with him temporarily only when Roosevelt ran for president as a third-party candidate in 1912.

In addition to a law degree (1874), Lodge earned one of Harvard University's first Ph.D.s in history and government (1876). His grandson, also Henry Cabot Lodge (1902–85), was a prominent Republican senator and a diplomat.

HISTORICAL DOCUMENT

One of the great political parties of the country has seen fit to make what is called "an issue" of the Philippines. They have no alternative policy to propose which does not fall to pieces as soon as it is stated. A large and important part of their membership, North and South, is heartily in favor of expansion, because they are Americans, and have not only patriotism but an intelligent perception of their own interests. They are the traditional party of expansion, the party which first went beyond seas and tried to annex Hawaii, which plotted for years to annex Cuba, which have in our past acquisitions of territory their one great and enduring monument. In their new wanderings they have developed a highly commendable, if somewhat hysterical, tenderness for the rights of men with dark skins dwelling in the islands of the Pacific, in pleasing contrast to the harsh indifference which they have always manifested toward those American citizens who "wear the shadowed livery of the burnished sun" within the boundaries of the United States. The Democratic party has for years been the advocate of free trade and increased exports, but now they shudder at our gaining control of the Pacific and developing our commerce with the East....

Once more our opponents insist that we shall be the only political party devoted to American policies. As the standard of expansion once so strongly held by their great predecessors drops from their nerveless hands we take it up and invite the American people to march with it. We offer our policy to the American people, to Democrats and to Republicans, as an American policy, alike in duty and honor, in morals and in interest, as one not of skepticism and doubt, but of hope and faith in ourselves and in the future, as becomes a great young nation which has not yet learned to use the art of retreat or to speak with the accents of despair....

The next argument of the opponents of the Republican policy is that we are denying self-government to the Filipinos. Our reply is that to give independent self-government at once, as we understand it, to a people who have no just conception of it and no fitness for it, is to dower them with a curse instead of a blessing. To do this would be to entirely arrest their progress instead of advancing them on the road to the liberty and free government which we wish them to achieve and enjoy. This contention rests, of course, on the proposition that the Filipinos are not to-day in the least fitted for self-government, as we understand it....

They think that we should abandon the Philippines because they are not fit for self-government. I believe that for that very reason we should retain them and lead them along the path of freedom until they are able to be self-governing, so far, at least, as all their own affairs are concerned....

We are also told that the possession of these islands brings a great responsibility upon us. This, Mr. President, I freely admit. A great nation must have great responsibilities. It is one of the penalties of greatness. But the benefit of responsibilities goes hand in hand with the burdens they bring....

Men who have done great things are those who have never shrunk from trial or adventure. If a man has the right qualities in him, responsibility sobers, strengthens, and develops him. The same is true of nations. The nation which fearlessly meets its responsibilities rises to the task when the pressure is upon it. I believe that these new possessions and these new questions, this necessity for watching over the welfare of another people, will improve our civil service, raise the tone of public life, and make broader and better all our politics and the subjects of political discussion. My faith in the American people is such that I have no misgiving as to their power to meet these responsibilities and to come out stronger and better for the test, doing full justice to others as well as to themselves....

Thus, Mr. President, I have shown that duty and interest alike, duty of the highest kind and interest of the highest and best kind, impose upon us the retention of the Philippines, the development of the islands, and the expansion of our Eastern commerce. All these things, in my belief, will come to pass, whatever the divisions of the present moment, for no people who have come under our flag have ever sought to leave it, and there is no territory which we have acquired that any one would dream of giving up....

Even now we can abandon the Monroe doctrine, we can reject the Pacific....Or we may follow the true laws of our being, the laws in obedience to which we have come to be what we are, and then we shall stretch out into the Pacific; we shall stand in the front rank of the world powers....

I do not believe that this nation was raised up for nothing. I do not believe that it is the creation of blind chance. I have faith that it has a great mission in the world—a mission of good, a mission of freedom. I believe that it can live up to that mission; therefore I want to see it step forward boldly and take its place at the head of the nations. I wish to see it master of the Pacific. I would have it fulfill what I think is its manifest destiny if it is not false to the laws which govern it. I am not dreaming of a primrose path....

Onward and forward it will still be, despite stumblings and mistakes as before, while we are true to ourselves and obedient to the laws which have ruled our past and will still govern our future....

I have unbounded faith and pride in my country. I am proud of her past, and in that past I read her future. I do not read it in any vain or boastful temper, but with a spirit of reverence and gratitude for all that has gone, and with a very humble prayer that we may make the present and future worthy of the past, and that, in the old Latin words —

Sicut patribus sit Deus nobis.

GLOSSARY

dower: to bequeath, provide, endow

"shadowed livery of the burnished sun": dark-complexioned skin (quotation adapted from William Shakespeare's *Merchant of Venice*, act 2, scene 1)

Sicut patribus sit Deus nobis: As to our fathers, may God be to us. (Latin)

Document Analysis

On December 10, 1898, the Treaty of Paris was signed, formally ending the Spanish-American War. During the negotiations, President William McKinley had demanded cession of the Philippines, which were transferred to the United States for $20 million. Eleven days after the peace was signed, McKinley issued a presidential proclamation, in which he pledged the "benevolent assimilation" of the Filipinos. By February 1899, however, a national rebellion was taking place, led by the guerrilla leader Emilio Aguinaldo. As American occupation forces were becoming increasingly enmeshed in ruthless suppression of the Filipino insurgents, Senator John C. Spooner sought to give the president personal authority to govern the islands until the Congress should decide otherwise—in reality, until the insurrection had been suppressed. Conversely the Democrats sought to make their opposition to imperialism and, in particular, to the Philippine conflict a major issue in the coming presidential campaign.

On March 7, 1900, Lodge defended the Spooner bill, and with it McKinley's Philippine policy, for three hours. Serving both as chairman of the Standing Committee on the Philippines and a member of the Senate's Committee on Foreign Relations, Lodge discusses all aspects of island policy, ranging from the character of Aguinaldo to the commercial potential of the islands. His address ably articulates the imperialism proclaimed by defenders of the "large policy" that found the nation's welfare integrally tied to overseas expansion.

Lodge attacks the Democratic Party for betraying its own heritage of expansionism, which could be traced to Thomas Jefferson's Louisiana Purchase and to later demands for annexing Hawaii and Cuba. By engaging in partisan opposition for its own sake, Democrats were spurning a prosperous trade with all of Asia. Conscious that much of the Democratic Party's strength was rooted in the American South, Lodge finds that southern "tenderness for the rights of men with dark skins" living in the Pacific stands in sharp contrast with southerners' treatment of African Americans at home.

In contrast to arguments made by Anti-Imperialists, the Massachusetts senator denies that the Filipinos are ready for self-government. Within the past two months, he notes, the Democratic Party leader William Jennings Bryan had acknowledged their limitations. Indeed, Lodge claims, Bryan really wanted to abandon this people, whereas he—Lodge—would "lead them along the path of freedom." Using Haiti and Santo Domingo as negative examples, Lodge warns that continued anarchy and native dictatorship on the islands would lead to European intervention. Sounding a bit like Rudyard Kipling's poem "The White Man's Burden," which itself was originally subtitled "The United States and the Philippine Islands," the senator denies that Americans are grasping new powers. Rather, they are assuming fresh and essential responsibilities.

While not oblivious to the new market that the Philippines might provide, Lodge stresses their role as a stepping-stone to far more significant trade with China. It was Admiral George Dewey's capture of Manila in May 1898, he maintains, that made the United States an Eastern power, one that could now gain the commerce needed to assure prosperity to American farmers and laborers. In the last part of his speech, Lodge offers an updated version of "Manifest Destiny" the slogan of the 1840s. He points as well to the "hands off" warnings to Europe embodied in the Monroe Doctrine. Instead of limiting himself to the matter of continental expansion, however, he invokes "the true laws of our being" which—he asserts—involve mastery of the Pacific. To violate such laws would only lead to national ruin and disgrace. Reflecting his learning, he concludes his address with a selection from William Ernest Henley's poem "Invictus" and offers a Latin quotation invoking divine protection.

Lodge's Philippine committee reported the bill, but the Republican majority decided to delay any vote until after the 1900 election. In that election, Bryan, who spoke for Filipino rights, was defeated in his second bid for the presidency. Only on February 28, 1901, did Spooner's proposal pass Congress, in the form of an amendment to an army appropriation bill. Lodge's hopes for a thriving China market remained unfulfilled for close to a century. In the short term, however, his immediate imperialist aims were gratified. By mid-1902 the Filipino resistance had ended. That year Congress declared the islands an unorganized territory in which an American commission, headed by William Howard Taft, then a federal circuit court judge, would establish a civil government.

Essential Themes

The overall context related to the struggle within U.S. politics between Imperialist and Anti-Imperialist tendencies. The Imperialists were represented by people like Lodge, Sen. John Spooner, and Sen. Albert Beveridge. In discussing the prospect of independence for the Philippines, for instance, Beveridge—who referred to the Filipinos as "a barbarous race," "savages" and "deluded children,"—commented, "It is barely possible that 1,000 men in all the archipelago are capable of self-government in the Anglo-Saxon sense." In general they viewed the Filipinos as they had the American Indians, as a backward people who stood in the way of American progress. Americans, the Imperialists believed, had a duty to "civilize" them, for their own good and for the good of the United States.

Arrayed against them were the Anti-Imperialists, who originally consisted of northeastern reformers and mavericks. The Anti-Imperialist League had been formed expressly to prevent the annexation of Cuba, which its members saw as the Imperialists' ultimate objective for the Spanish-American War. The Anti-Imperialists argued that Americans should apply the same constitutional principles abroad that they abided by at home, that Cuba, for example, should be governed only by the Cubans. Some of them opposed the Imperialists simply out of opposition to the McKinley administration or out of fear that non-white Filipinos might one day gain a say in the American government. Among the Anti-Imperialists were Sen. John Teller and Sen. George Hoar, Lodge's colleague from Massachusetts.

Cuba had been the focus of debate in the run-up to the war, and no plans had been developed regarding the Spanish possessions that were actually annexed: Puerto Rico, Guam, and the Philippines. Nevertheless, one prominent figure had at least had his eye on the islands for some time, Assistant Secretary of the Navy Theodore Roosevelt. (From 1897 to 1901, Roosevelt's career progressed from assistant secretary of the navy, to acting secretary of the navy, to colonel in charge of the 1st U.S. Volunteer Cavalry [the "Rough Riders"] in Cuba, to governor of New York, to vice president of the United States, to president of the United States [following the assassination of McKinley].) From Roosevelt's point of view, the acquisition of the Philippine Islands as a U.S. colony would serve two purposes. First, a colony so close to the Asian mainland would open up Asian markets to U.S. commerce. Second, the Philippines would have to be defended, and the defense of a colony so far from the United States would require the development of a larger and stronger navy, which he saw as a necessity for any great nation. As soon as the battleship U.S.S. *Maine* exploded in Havana Harbor, the event that eventually triggered the Spanish-American War, Roosevelt instructed Commodore Dewey to prepare plans for an invasion of the Philippines.

The Spooner bill did not come to a vote in 1900, but the United States ultimately decided to keep the Philippines as an overseas territory. In 1901 the Supreme Court determined that the Constitution and citizenship rights did not extend automatically to newly annexed territories. In the same year, Lodge maneuvered the passage of the contents of the Spooner bill as an amendment to a war appropriations bill, the Spooner Amendment. It transferred "all military, civil, and judicial powers necessary to govern the Philippine Islands" to the president. Lodge, himself, was wary of it, but only as a derogation of legislative powers. He satisfied himself with some adjustments to Spooner's wording, making the measure temporary pending final action by Congress and limiting the disposition of public lands and franchises.

In keeping with the Imperialists' theme, when President McKinley declared U.S. sovereignty over the archipelago, he asserted that the country's purpose was not conquest, but rather the "benevolent assimilation" of the Filipino people. Nevertheless, press reports accused U.S. troops of brutality during the Philippine-American War. In 1902 Lodge, as chairman of the Senate Committee on the Philippines, was compelled to conduct a five-month investigation of military practices. Despite his best efforts to put a positive face on it, the investigation revealed tales of torture, reprisals, and concentration camps. General Jacob "Hell-roaring Jake" Smith, who freely admitted to having advised troops on Samar Island to kill all persons above the age of 10 capable of bearing arms, was court-martialed and found guilty. As punishment, however, he was simply admonished for his behavior. In May 1902 Lodge argued that the American tactics, while regrettable, were a natural response to brutalities inflicted by Filipino *insurrectos*.

Once the Filipino insurrection was put down (officially on July 4, 1902, although sporadic resistance persisted), the military occupation authorities were replaced with a civilian administration, initially led by future president William Howard Taft. Nevertheless, the Anti-Imperialist trend in U.S. politics did not die out. Many Americans were uncomfortable with the idea of a colonial empire (or, in the view of the Imperialists, lacked the necessary "duty-loving spirit" to put up with the fuss and expense of ruling other peoples), and the Filipinos continued to press for full independence. In 1935 Congress granted the islands internal self-government in and set July 4, 1945, as a target date for full independence. World War II delayed by a year, and the Philippines became an independent republic on July 4, 1946. In 1962 the Philippines changed its national holiday from July 4 to June 12 in honor of Aguinaldo's original declaration of independence.

——*Justus D. Doenecke, PhD and Scott C. Monje, PhD*

Bibliography and Additional Reading

Garraty, John A. *Henry Cabot Lodge: A Biography*. New York: Alfred A. Knopf, 1953.

Jones, Gregg. *Honor in the Dust: Theodore Roosevelt, War in the Philippines, and the Rise and Fall of America's Imperial Dream*. New York: New American Library, 2012.

Linn, Brian McAllister. *The Philippine War, 1899–1902*. Lawrence: University Press of Kansas, 2000.

Miller, Stuart Creighton. *Benevolent Assimilation: The American Conquest of the Philippines, 1899–1903*. New Haven, Conn.: Yale University Press, 1982.

Silbey, David J. *A War of Frontier and Empire: The Philippine-American War, 1899–1902*. New York: Hill and Wang, 2007.

Widenor, William C. *Henry Cabot Lodge and the Search for an American Foreign Policy*. Berkeley: University of California Press, 1980.

Zimmermann, Warren. *First Great Triumph: How Five Americans Made Their Country a World Power*. New York: Farrar, Straus, and Giroux, 2002

The Insular Cases: *Downes v. Bidwell*

Date: 1901
Author: Henry Billings Brown
Genre: court ruling

Summary Overview

Downes v. Bidwell is one of a handful of U.S. Supreme Court cases that together make up what are called the Insular Cases. Decided in the first several years of the twentieth century, these cases determined that full constitutional rights were not necessarily granted to people living in American territories. In one of the most important of the Insular Cases, *Downes v. Bidwell*, the Supreme Court established that the United States was not just a nation of states and temporary territories; it was a nation of states and potentially permanent territories. Although the United States had always possessed territories, they were assumed to be transitional phases for areas under U.S. sovereignty. They were to be administered from the nation's capital until they had reached sufficient population size and had written constitutions establishing republican government, following the blueprint of the 1787 Northwest Ordinance. Congress could then annex U.S. territories as new states into the Union, which it ultimately did for thirty-one of the fifty states.

Justice Edward White's concurring opinion in *Downes v. Bidwell*, however, introduced a novel doctrine that distinguished between the United States's "incorporated" territories, those of continental North America as well as, later, Hawaii and Alaska, and its new, not-to-be-incorporated territories of Puerto Rico, the Philippines, and Guam. The United States acquired all three of those territories from Spain in the 1898 Treaty of Paris. The United States would also add American Samoa in 1899 in a tripartite arrangement with Great Britain and Germany and would annex the U.S. Virgin Islands in 1917 and the Northern Mariana Islands in 1976. Under Justice White's incorporation doctrine, the island territories could remain indefinitely outside of the American polity without needing to be on the road to statehood.

Defining Moment

Downes v. Bidwell was, like other Supreme Court rulings, written for other judges, members of Congress, government officials, lawyers, and future members of the U.S. Supreme Court. Distinguishing the opinions in *Downes v. Bidwell*, however, is the sweep of American history and the scale of the issue—the political identity of the United States—discussed by the several justices. Indeed, politicians, judges, journalists, lawyers, and members of the public closely followed the decisions in *Downes v. Bidwell* and the other Insular Cases of 1901, since the Court's decisions were to greatly affect the nature of the nation that the United States would be—ethnically and racially (as to which peoples were "American"), economically (as to whether tariff laws and other economic policies applied to the territories), politically (as to which branch of government was to determine the political status of territories), and, not least, strategically (as to whether the United States could have sovereignty over areas that did not come under all of the protections of the Constitution).

Author Biography

Henry Billings Brown, who wrote the lead opinion in *Downes v. Bidwell* and six other Insular Cases decided on May 27, 1901, grew up in South Lee, Massachusetts, in an upper-middle-class, Puritan, and Republican household. Brown attended Yale, Yale Law School, and Harvard Law School. He then moved west to Detroit, where he was appointed deputy U.S. marshal for Detroit and became an expert in admiralty law. Later, as district judge for the Eastern District of Michigan, Brown became renowned nationally for his mastery of admiralty law. President Benjamin Harrison appointed Brown to the Supreme Court in 1891, following Justice Samuel Miller's death.

Brown, who is best known for his lead opinion in *Plessy v. Ferguson* (1896), did not believe that the Constitution applied to Puerto Rico, the Philippines, or any other territory belonging to the United States in the absence of Congress's expressed extension of the Constitution. Brown was the swing judge for six of the seven Insular Cases decided in May 1901 and for the two cases of December 1901—all of which were decided by 5–4 margins. Whereas Brown upheld the constitutionality of the tariff in question, along with Justice White and the other justices in the *Downes* and *Dooley II* majorities, Brown joined Chief Justice Fuller and the *Downes* dissenters in the other Insular Cases of 1901.

Edward Douglass White, who wrote the concurring opinion in *Downes*, was born in 1845 near Thibodaux, Louisiana, to a former governor of Louisiana and sugar-plantation owner. White left college at the age of sixteen to serve in the Confederate army and returned to New Orleans after the Civil War. After studying law at what is now Tulane University, White became a leading lawyer in New Orleans and Louisiana and a successful Democratic politician. He was later appointed as a U.S. senator from Louisiana, serving for three years. In that period, he worked to uphold the gold standard, the interests of southern states, and other policies of the administration of Grover Cleveland. In 1894 President Cleveland chose White for the U.S. Supreme Court, acknowledging White's credentials as a conservative Democrat. White was later appointed chief justice of the United States in 1910—the first associate justice ever to be appointed chief justice—serving in that capacity until 1921. White argued that territories could be either fully included under the Constitution or subject to only some constitutional provisions, depending on the conditions specified by treaty or congressional legislation. He held that territories could even be divested by the United States, if Congress so chose.

Melville Weston Fuller, the author of one of the dissenting opinions in *Downes v. Bidwell*, grew up in an upper-class Maine family as the son of a lawyer and state politician. Fuller attended Bowdoin College and Harvard Law School. He left law school before graduating to work in his uncle's private practice, but at the age of twenty-three he left for Chicago. There, he became a successful Democratic politician, a member of the state legislature, and, at length, a leader of the Democrats in the Illinois House of Representatives. After the Civil War, he became a prominent corporate lawyer and real estate investor. When Chief Justice Morrison Waite died, President Cleveland turned to Fuller to replace him; Fuller served as chief justice from 1888 to 1910. The Fuller Court is known for its conservative and pro-business rulings, such as its decisions in *Plessy v. Ferguson*, *Lochner v. New York*, *United States v. E. C. Knight Co.* (the Sugar Trust Case), and *In Re Debs*. Fuller himself is known for his antiregulatory and laissez-faire positions, per his opinions in *Pollock v. Farmers' Loan and Trust Co.* (the Income Tax Case), the Sugar Trust Case, and *Champion v. Ames* (the Lottery Case, in which he dissented). Fuller's antipathy toward government interference in commerce led him to oppose the majority opinion in *Downes*.

HISTORICAL DOCUMENT

Statement by Mr. Justice Brown

This case involves the question whether merchandise brought into the port of New York from Porto Rico since the passage of the Foraker act is exempt from duty, notwithstanding the 3d section of that act which requires the payment of "15 per centum of the duties which are required to be levied, collected, and paid upon like articles of merchandise imported from foreign countries."

1. The exception to the jurisdiction of the court is not well taken. By Rev. Stat. 629, subd. 4, the circuit courts are vested with jurisdiction "of all suits at law or in equity arising under any act providing for revenue from imports or tonnage" irrespective of the amount involved. This section should be construed in connection with 643, which provides for the removal from state courts to circuit courts of the United States of suits against revenue officers "on account of any act done under color of his office, or of any such [revenue] law, or on account of any right, title, or authority claimed by such officer or other person under any such law." Both these sections are taken from the act of March 2, 1833... commonly known as the force bill, and are evidently intended to include all actions against customs officers acting under color of their office. While, as we have held in *De Lima v. Bidwell*,...actions against the collector to recover back duties assessed upon

non-importable property are not "customs cases" in the sense of the administrative act, they are, nevertheless, actions arising under an act to provide for a revenue from imports, in the sense of 629, since they are for acts done by a collector under color of his office. This subdivision of 629 was not repealed by the jurisdictional act of 1875, or the subsequent act of August 13, 1888, since these acts were "not intended to interfere with the prior statutes conferring jurisdiction upon the circuit or district courts in special cases and over particular subjects."...As the case "involves the construction or application of the Constitution" as well as the constitutionality of a law of the United States, the writ of error was properly sued out from this court.

2. In the case of *De Lima v. Bidwell* just decided,...we held that, upon the ratification of the treaty of peace with Spain, Porto Rico ceased to be a foreign country, and became a territory of the United States, and that duties were no longer collectible upon merchandise brought from that island. We are now asked to hold that it became a part of the United States within that provision of the Constitution which declares that "all duties, imposts, and excises shall be uniform throughout the United States." Art. 1, 8. If Porto Rico be a part of the United States, the Foraker act imposing duties upon its products is unconstitutional, not only by reason of a violation of the uniformity clause, but because by 9 "vessels bound to or from one state" cannot "be obliged to enter, clear, or pay duties in another."

The case also involves the broader question whether the revenue clauses of the Constitution extend of their own force to our newly acquired territories. The Constitution itself does not answer the question. Its solution must be found in the nature of the government created by that instrument, in the opinion of its contemporaries, in the practical construction put upon it by Congress, and in the decisions of this court.

The Federal government was created in 1777 by the union of thirteen colonies of Great Britain in "certain articles of confederation and perpetual union" the first one of which declared that "the stile of this confederacy shall be the United States of America."

***

The confederacy, owing to well-known historical reasons, having proven a failure, a new Constitution was formed in 1787 by "the people of the United States" "for the United States of America" as its preamble declares. All legislative powers were vested in a Congress consisting of representatives from the several states, but no provision was made for the admission of delegates from the territories, and no mention was made of territories as separate portions of the Union, except that Congress was empowered "to dispose of and make all needful rules and regulations respecting the territory or other property belonging to the United States." At this time all of the states had ceded their unappropriated lands except North Carolina and Georgia. It was thought by Chief Justice Taney in the Dred Scott Case,...that the sole object of the territorial clause was "to transfer to the new government the property then held in common by the states, and to give to that government power to apply it to the objects for which it had been destined by mutual agreement among the states before their league was dissolved;" that the power "to make needful rules and regulations" was not intended to give the powers of sovereignty, or to authorize the establishment of territorial governments—in short, that these words were used in a proprietary, and not in a political, sense. But, as we observed in *De Lima v. Bidwell*, the power to establish territorial governments has been too long exercised by Congress and acquiesced in by this court to be deemed an unsettled question. Indeed, in the Dred Scott Case it was admitted to be the inevitable consequence of the right to acquire territory.

It is sufficient to observe in relation to these three fundamental instruments, that it can nowhere be inferred that the territories were considered a part of the United States. The Constitution was created by the people of the United States, as a union of states, to be governed solely by representatives of the states; and even the provision relied upon here, that all duties, imposts, and excises shall be uniform "throughout the United States" is explained by subsequent provisions of the Constitution, that "no tax or duty shall be laid on articles exported from any state" and "no preference shall be given by any regulation of commerce or revenue to the ports of one state over those of another; nor shall vessels bound to or from one state be obliged to enter, clear, or pay duties in another." In short, the Constitution deals with states, their people, and their representatives.

***

The question of the legal relations between the states and the newly acquired territories first became the subject of public discussion in connection with the purchase of Louisiana in 1803....

To cover the questions raised by this purchase Mr. Jefferson prepared two amendments to the Constitution, the first of which declared that "the province of Louisiana is incorporated with the United States and made part thereof;" and the second of which was couched in a little different language, viz.: "Louisiana, as ceded by France to the United States, is made a part of the United States. Its white inhabitants shall be citizens, and stand, as to their rights and obligations, on the same footing as other citizens in analogous situations." But by the time Congress assembled, October 17, 1803, either the argument of his friends or the pressing necessity of the situation seems to have dispelled his doubts regarding his power under the Constitution, since in his message to Congress he referred the whole matter to that body, saying that "with the wisdom of Congress it will rest to take those ulterior measures which may be necessary for the immediate occupation and temporary government of the country; for its incorporation into the Union."...

As a sequence to this debate two bills were passed, one October 31, 1803..., authorizing the President to take possession of the territory and to continue the existing government, and the other November 10, 1803..., making provision for the payment of the purchase price. These acts continued in force until March 26, 1804, when a new act was passed providing for a temporary government..., and vesting all legislative powers in a governor and legislative council, to be appointed by the President. These statutes may be taken as expressing the views of Congress, first, that territory may be lawfully acquired by treaty, with a provision for its ultimate incorporation into the Union; and, second, that a discrimination in favor of certain foreign vessels trading with the ports of a newly acquired territory is no violation of that clause of the Constitution (art. 1, 9) that declares that no preference shall be given to the ports of one state over those of another. It is evident that the constitutionality of this discrimination can only be supported upon the theory that ports of territories are not ports of state within the meaning of the Constitution. The same construction was adhered to in the treaty with Spain for the purchase of Florida...the 6th article of which provided that the inhabitants should "be incorporated into the Union of the United States, as soon as may be consistent with the principles of the Federal Constitution;" and the 15th article of which agreed that Spanish vessels coming directly from Spanish ports and laden with productions of Spanish growth or manufacture should be admitted, for the term of twelve years, to the ports of Pensacola and St. Augustine "without paying other or higher duties on their cargoes, or of tonnage, than will be paid by the vessels of the United States" and that "during the said term no other nation shall enjoy the same privileges within the ceded territories."

So, too, in the act annexing the Republic of Hawaii, there was a provision continuing in effect the customs relations of the Hawaiian islands with the United States and other countries, the effect of which was to compel the collection in those islands of a duty upon certain articles, whether coming from the United States or other countries, much greater than the duty provided by the general tariff law then in force. This was a discrimination against the Hawaiian ports wholly inconsistent with the revenue clauses of the Constitution, if such clauses were there operative.

***

Notwithstanding these provisions for the incorporation of territories into the Union, Congress, not only in organizing the territory of Louisiana by act of March 26, 1804, but all other territories carved out of this vast inheritance, has assumed that the Constitution did not extend to them of its own force, and has in each case made special provision, either that their legislatures shall pass no law inconsistent with the Constitution of the United States, or that the Constitution or laws of the United States shall be the supreme law of such territories....

The researches of counsel have collated a large number of other instances in which Congress has in its enactments recognized the fact that provisions intended for the states did not embrace the territories, unless specially mentioned. These are found in the laws prohibiting the slave trade with "the United States or territories thereof;" or equipping ships "in any port or place within the jurisdiction of the United States;" in the internal revenue laws, in the early ones of which no provision was made for the collection of taxes in the territory not included within the boundaries of the existing states, and others of which extended them expressly to the territories, or "within the exterior boundaries of the United States;" and in the acts extending the internal revenue laws to the territories of Alaska and Oklahoma. It would prolong this opinion unnecessarily to set forth the provisions of these acts in detail. It is sufficient to say that Congress has or has not applied the revenue laws to the territories, as the circumstances of each case seemed to require, and has specifically legislated for the territories whenever it was its intention to execute laws beyond the limits of the states....

Eliminating, then, from the opinions of this court all expressions unnecessary to the disposition of the particular case, and gleaning therefrom the exact point decided in each, the following propositions may be considered as established:

1. That the District of Columbia and the territories are not states within the judicial clause of the Constitution giving jurisdiction in cases between citizens of different states;

2. That territories are not states within the meaning of Rev. Stat. 709, permitting writs of error from this court in cases where the validity of a state statute is drawn in question;

3. That the District of Columbia and the territories are states as that word is used in treaties with foreign powers, with respect to the ownership, disposition, and inheritance of property;

4. That the territories are not within the clause of the Constitution providing for the creation of a supreme court and such inferior courts as Congress may see fit to establish;

5. That the Constitution does not apply to foreign countries or to trials therein conducted, and that Congress may lawfully provide for such trials before consular tribunals, without the intervention of a grand or petit jury;

6. That where the Constitution has been once formally extended by Congress to territories, neither Congress nor the territorial legislature can enact laws inconsistent therewith.

***

To sustain the judgment in the case under consideration, it by no means becomes necessary to show that none of the articles of the Constitution apply to the island of Porto Rico. There is a clear distinction between such prohibitions as go to the very root of the power of Congress to act at all, irrespective of time of place, and such as are operative only "throughout the United States" or among the several states.

Thus, when the Constitution declares that "no bill of attainder or ex post facto law shall be passed" and that "no title of nobility shall be granted by the United States" it goes to the competency of Congress to pass a bill of that description. Perhaps the same remark may apply to the 1st Amendment, that "Congress shall make no law respecting an establishment of religion, or prohibiting the free exercise thereof; or abridging the freedom of speech, or of the press; or the right of the people to peacefully assemble and to petition the government for a redress of grievances." We do not wish, however, to be understood as expressing an opinion how far the bill of rights contained in the first eight amendments is of general and how far of local application.

Upon the other hand, when the Constitution declares that all duties shall be uniform "throughout the United States" it becomes necessary to inquire whether there be any territory over which Congress has jurisdiction which is not a part of the "United States" by which term we understand the states whose people united to form the Constitution, and such as have since been admitted to the Union upon an equality with them. Not only did the people in adopting the 13th Amendment thus recognize a distinction between the United States and "any place subject to their jurisdiction" but Congress itself, in the act of March 27, 1804,…providing for the proof of public records, applied the provisions of the act, not only to "every court and office within the United States" but to the "courts and offices of the respective territories of the United States and countries subject to the jurisdiction of the United States" as to the courts and offices of the several states. This classification, adopted by the Eighth Congress, is carried into the Revised Statutes as follows:

"Sec. 905. The acts of the legislature of any state or territory, or of any country subject to the jurisdiction of the United States, shall be authenticated" etc.

"Sec. 906. All records and exemplifications of books which may be kept in any public office of and state or territory, or of any country subject to the jurisdiction of the United States" etc.

Unless these words are to be rejected as meaningless, we must treat them as a recognition by Congress of the fact that there may be territories subject to the jurisdiction of the United States, which are not of the United States.

In determining the meaning of the words of article 1, section 8, "uniform throughout the United States" we are bound to consider, not only the provisions forbidding preference being given to the ports of one state over those of another (to which attention has already been called), but the other clauses declaring that no tax or duty shall be laid on articles exported from any state, and that no state shall, without the consent of Congress, lay any imposts or duties upon imports or exports, nor any duty on tonnage. The object of all of these was to protect the states which united in forming the Constitution from discriminations by Congress, which would operate unfairly or injuriously upon some states and not equally upon others. The opinion of Mr. Justice White in *Knowlton v. Moore*…contains an elaborate historical review of the proceedings in the convention, which resulted in the adoption of these different clauses and their arrangement, and he there comes to the conclusion…that "although the provision as to preference between ports and that regarding uniformity of duties, imposts, and excises were one in purpose, one in their adoption" they were originally placed together, and "became separated only in arranging the Constitution for the purpose of style." Thus construed together, the purpose is irresistible that the words "throughout the United States" are indistinguishable from the words "among or between the several states" and that these prohibitions were intended to apply only to commerce between ports of the several states as they then existed or should thereafter be admitted to the Union.

Indeed, the practical interpretation put by Congress upon the Constitution has been long continued and uniform to the effect that the Constitution is applicable to territories acquired by purchase or conquest, only when and so far as Congress shall so direct. Notwithstanding its duty to "guarantee to every state in this Union a republican form of government" (art. 4, 4), by which we understand, according to the definition of Webster, "a government in which the supreme power resides in the whole body of the people, and is exercised by representatives elected by them" Congress did not hesitate, in the original organization of the territories of Louisiana, Florida, the Northwest Territory, and its subdivisions of Ohio, Indiana, Michigan, Illinois, and Wisconsin and still more recently in the case of Alaska, to establish a form of government bearing a much greater analogy to a British Crown colony than a republican state of America, and to vest the legislative power either in a governor and council, or a governor and judges, to be appointed by the President. It was not until they had attained a certain population that power was given them to organize a legislature by vote of the people. In all these cases, as well as in territories subsequently organized west of the Mississippi, Congress thought it necessary either to extend to Constitution and laws of the United States over them, or to declare that the inhabitants should be entitled to enjoy the right of trial by jury, of bail, and of the privilege of the writ of habeas corpus, as well as other privileges of the bill of rights.

We are also of opinion that the power to acquire territory by treaty implies, not only the power to govern such territory, but to prescribe upon what terms the United States will receive its inhabitants, and what their status shall be in what Chief Justice Marshall termed the "American empire." There seems to be no middle ground between this position and the doctrine that if their inhabitants do not become, immediately upon annexation, citizens of the United States, their children thereafter born, whether savages or civilized, are such, and entitled to all the rights, privileges and immunities of citizens. If such be their status, the consequences will be extremely serious. Indeed, it is doubtful if Congress would ever assent to the annexation of territory upon the condition that its inhabitants, however foreign they may be to our habits, traditions, and modes of life, shall become at once citizens of the United States. In all its treaties hitherto the treaty-making power has made special provision for this subject; in the cases of Louisiana and Florida, by stipulating that "the inhabitants shall be incorporated into the Union of the United States and admitted as soon as possible...to the enjoyment of all the rights, advantages, and immunities of citizens of the United States;" in the case of Mexico, that they should "be incorporated into the Union, and be admitted at the proper time (to be judged of by the Congress of the United States) to the enjoyment of all the rights of citizens of the United States;" in the case of Alaska, that the inhabitants who remained three years, "with the exception of uncivilized native tribes, shall be admitted to the enjoyment of all the rights" etc; and in the case of Porto Rico and the Philippines, "that the civil rights and political status of the native inhabitants...shall be determined by Congress." In all these cases there is an implied denial of the right of the inhabitants to American citizenship until Congress by further action shall signify its assent thereto.

Grave apprehensions of danger are felt by many eminent men—a fear lest an unrestrained possession of power on the part of Congress may lead to unjust and oppressive legislation in which the natural rights of territories, or their inhabitants, may be engulfed in a centralized despotism. These fears, however, find no justification in the action of Congress in the past century, nor in the conduct of the British Parliament towards its outlying possessions since the American Revolution. Indeed, in the only instance in which this court has declared an act of Congress unconstitutional as trespassing upon the rights of territories (the Missouri Compromise), such action was dictated by motives of humanity and justice, and so far commanded popular approval as to be embodied in the 13th Amendment to the Constitution. There are certain principles of natural justice inherent in the Anglo-Saxon character, which need no expression in constitutions or statutes to give them effect or to secure dependencies against legislation manifestly hostile to their real interests. Even in the Foraker act itself, the constitutionality of which is so vigorously assailed, power was given to the legislative assembly of Porto Rico to repeal the very tariff in question in this case, a power it has not seen fit to exercise. The words of Chief Justice Marshall in *Gibbons v. Ogden*...with respect to the power of Congress to regulate commerce, are pertinent in this connection: "This power" said he, "like all others vested in Congress, is complete in itself, may be exercised to its utmost extent, and acknowledges no limitations other than are prescribed in the Constitution....The wisdom and discretion of Congress, their identity with the people, and the influence which their constituents possess at elections, are in this, as in many other instances—as that, for example, of declaring war—the sole restraints on which they have relied to secure them from its abuse. They are the restraints on which the people must often rely solely in all representative governments."

***

It is obvious that in the annexation of outlying and distant possessions grave questions will arise from differences of race, habits, laws, and customs of the people, and from differences of soil, climate, and production, which may require action on the part of Congress that would be quite unnecessary in the annexation of contiguous territory inhabited only by people of the same race, or by scattered bodies of native Indians.

We suggest, without intending to decide, that there may be a distinction between certain natural rights enforced in the Constitution by prohibitions against interference with them, and what may be termed artificial or remedial rights which are peculiar to our own system of jurisprudence. Of the former class are the rights to one's own religious opinions and to a public expression of them, or, as sometimes said, to worship God according to the dictates of one's own conscience; the right to personal liberty and individual property; to freedom of speech and of the press; to free access to courts of justice, to due process of law, and to an equal protection of the laws; to immunities from unreasonable searches and seizures, as well as cruel and unusual punishments; and to such other immunities as are indispensable to a free government. Of the latter class are the rights to citizenship, to suffrage (*Minor v. Happersett*...), and to the particular methods of procedure pointed out in the Constitution, which are peculiar to Anglo-Saxon jurisprudence, and some of which have already been held by the states to be unnecessary to the proper protection of individuals.

Whatever may be finally decided by the American people as to the status of these islands and their inhabitants—whether they shall be introduced into the sisterhood of states or be permitted to form independent governments—it does not follow that in the meantime, awaiting that decision, the people are in the matter of personal rights unprotected by the provisions of our Constitution and subject to the merely arbitrary control of Congress. Even if regarded as aliens, they are entitled under the principles of the Constitution to be protected in life, liberty, and property. This has been frequently held by this court in respect to the Chinese, even when aliens, not possessed of the political rights of citizens of the United States. *Yick Wo v. Hopkins*,...*Fong Yue Ting v. United States*,...Lem Moon Sing,...*Wong Wing v. United States*,.... We do not desire, however, to anticipate the difficulties which would naturally arise in this connection, but merely to disclaim any intention to hold that the inhabitants of these territories are subject to an unrestrained power on the part of Congress to deal with them upon the theory that they have no rights which it is bound to respect.

Large powers must necessarily be entrusted to Congress in dealing with these problems, and we are bound to assume that they will be judiciously exercised. That these powers may be abused is possible. But the same may be said of its powers under the Constitution as well as outside of it. Human wisdom has never devised a form of government so perfect that it may not be perverted to bad purposes. It is never conclusive to argue against the possession of certain powers from possible abuses of them. It is safe to say that if Congress should venture upon legislation manifestly dictated by selfish interests, it would receive quick rebuke at the hands of the people. Indeed, it is scarcely possible that Congress could do a greater injustice to these islands than would be involved in holding that it could not impose upon the states taxes and excises without extending the same taxes to them. Such requirement would bring them at once within our internal revenue system, including stamps, licenses, excises, and all the paraphernalia of that system, and apply it to territories which have had no experience of this kind, and where it would prove an intolerable burden.

This subject was carefully considered by the Senate committee in charge of the Foraker bill, which found, after an examination of the facts, that property in Porto Rico was already burdened with a private debt amounting probably to $30,000,000; that no system of property taxation was or ever had been in force in the island, and that it probably would require two years to inaugurate one and secure returns from it; that the revenues had always been chiefly raised by duties on imports and exports, and that our internal revenue laws, if applied in that island, would prove oppressive and ruinous to many people and interests; that to undertake to collect our heavy internal revenue tax, far heavier than Spain ever imposed upon their products and vocations, would be to invite violations of the law so innumerable as to make prosecutions impossible, and to almost certainly alienate and destroy the friendship and good will of that people for the United States.

In passing upon the questions involved in this and kindred cases, we ought not to overlook the fact that, while the Constitution was intended to establish a permanent form of government for the states which should elect to take advantage of its conditions, and continue for an indefinite future, the vast possibilities of that future could never have entered the minds of its framers. The states had but recently emerged from a war with one of the most powerful nations of Europe, were disheartened by the failure of the confederacy, and were doubtful as to the feasibility of a stronger union. Their territory was confined to a narrow strip of land on the Atlantic coast from Canada to Florida, with a somewhat indefinite claim to territory beyond the Alleghenies, where their sovereignty was disputed by tribes of hostile Indians supported, as was popularly believed, by the British, who had never formally delivered possession under the treaty of peace. The vast territory beyond the Mississippi, which formerly had been claimed by France, since 1762 had belonged to Spain, still a powerful nation and the owner of a great part of the Western Hemisphere. Under these circumstances it is little wonder that the question of annexing these territories was not made a subject of debate. The difficulties of bringing about a union of the states were so great, the objections to it seemed so formidable, that the whole thought of the convention centered upon surmounting these obstacles. The question of territories was dismissed with a single clause, apparently applicable only to the territories then existing, giving Congress the power to govern and dispose of them.

Had the acquisition of other territories been contemplated as a possibility, could it have been foreseen that, within little more than one hundred years, we were destined to acquire, not only the whole vast region between the Atlantic and Pacific Oceans, but the Russian possessions in America and distant islands in the Pacific, it is incredible that no provision should have been made for them, and the question whether the Constitution should or should not extend to them have been definitely settled. If it be once conceded that we are at liberty to acquire foreign territory, a presumption arises that our power with respect to such territories is the same power which other nations have been accustomed to exercise with respect to territories acquired by them. If, in limiting the power which Congress was to exercise within the United States, it was also intended to limit it with regard to such territories as the people of the United States should thereafter acquire, such limitations should have been expressed. Instead of that, we find the Constitution speaking only to states, except in the territorial clause, which is absolute in its terms, and suggestive of no limitations upon the power of Congress in dealing with them. The states could only delegate to Congress such powers as they themselves possessed, and as they had no power to acquire new territory they had none to delegate in that connection. The logical inference from this is that if Congress had power to acquire new territory, which is conceded, that power was not hampered by the constitutional provisions. If, upon the other hand, we assume that the territorial clause of the Constitution was not intended to be restricted to such territory as the United States then possessed, there is nothing in the Constitution to indicate that the power of Congress in dealing with them was intended to be restricted by any of the other provisions.

There is a provision that "new states may be admitted by the Congress into this Union." These words, of course, carry the Constitution with them, but nothing is said regarding the acquisition of new territories or the extension of the Constitution over them. The liberality of Congress in legislating the Constitution into all our contiguous territories has undoubtedly fostered the impression that it went there by its own force, but there is nothing in the Constitution itself, and little in the interpretation put upon it, to confirm that impression. There is not even an analogy to the provisions of an ordinary mortgage, for its attachment to after-acquired property, without which it covers only property existing at the date of the mortgage. In short, there is absolute silence upon the subject. The executive and legislative departments of the government have for more than a century interpreted this silence as precluding the idea that the Constitution attached to these territories as soon as acquired, and unless such interpretation be manifestly contrary to the letter or spirit of the Constitution, it should be followed by the judicial department. Cooley, Const. Lim. 81-85. *Burrow-Giles Lithographic Co. v. Sarony,...Marshall Field & Co. v. Clark....*

Patriotic and intelligent men may differ widely as to the desirableness of this or that acquisition, but this is solely a political question. We can only consider this aspect of the case so far as to say that no construction of the Constitution should be adopted which would prevent Congress from considering each case upon its merits, unless the language of the instrument imperatively demand it. A false step at this time might be fatal to the development of what Chief Justice Marshall called the American empire. Choice in some cases, the natural gravitation of small bodies towards large ones in others, the result of a successful war in still others, may bring about conditions which would render the annexation of distant possessions desirable. If those possessions are inhabited by alien races, differing from us in religion, customs, laws, methods of taxation, and modes of thought, the administration of government and justice, according to Anglo-Saxon principles, may for a time be impossible; and the question at once arises whether large concessions ought not to be made for a time, that ultimately our own theories may be carried out, and the blessings of a free government under the Constitution extended to them. We decline to hold that there is anything in the Constitution to forbid such action.

We are therefore of opinion that the island of Porto Rico is a territory appurtenant and belonging to the United States, but not a part of the United States within the revenue clauses of the Constitution; that the Foraker act is constitutional, so far as it imposes duties upon imports from such island, and that the plaintiff cannot recover back the duties exacted in this case.

The judgment of the Circuit Court is therefore affirmed.

GLOSSARY

appurtenant: annexed to a more important thing; a property considered incident to the principal property

tariff: a tax on trade

territorial clause: Article IV, Section 3, Clause 2, of the U.S. Constitution, which reads, "Congress shall have Power to dispose of and make all needful Rules and Regulations respecting the Territory or other Property belonging to the United States"

uniformity clause: Article I, Section 8, Clause 1, of the U.S. Constitution, which reads, "all Duties, Imposts and Excises shall be uniform throughout the United States"

Document Analysis

Justice Brown accepts the argument made by the War Department's Division of Insular Affairs, the U.S. solicitor general John K. Richards, and the U.S. attorney general John Griggs that Puerto Ricans should be considered subject to the complete sovereignty of the U.S. government. Specifically, Brown asserts that Puerto Ricans have no legal rights except those contained in the treaty with Spain. Since the U.S. government has full authority over its territories, the U.S. Constitution applies only when Congress extends its provisions. In Brown's view, Chief Justice Taney's argument in the *Dred Scott* case does not apply either. Taney's argument held that the Constitution applied throughout the U.S.

territories (and states) dictum, but the Supreme Court had effectively overturned Taney's decision in the Mormon Church Case (*Late Corporation of the Church of Jesus Christ of Latter-Day Saints v. United States*, 1890), which held that the United States consisted of the states, and the states alone. Brown concedes that territorial residents are entitled to the "natural rights" of religious freedom, property, contract, free speech, and equal protection under the laws, among other rights. However, they are not entitled to the "rights of citizenship, to suffrage, and to the particular methods of procedure pointed out in the Constitution." These were "political rights" that Congress had to deliberately apply to territorial inhabitants.

Notwithstanding the fact that the leading lawyers of the McKinley administration also argued that the United States was composed only of the states, no other justices joined Brown's lead opinion. Instead, Justices Shiras and McKenna sided with Justice White, who argues in his opinion that the Constitution *does* apply to the U.S. territories. Still, he argues, the only constitutional provisions that apply are those that Congress itself decides to grant, given Congress's plenary authority under the territory clause. Since neither the Treaty of Paris nor the Foraker Act—nor any other legislation—explicitly incorporated the new territories of Puerto Rico and the Philippines into the United States, these were to be considered unincorporated territories, which Congress could govern as it chose. That is, in White's opinion, the new island territories are not a part of the United States for the purposes of the tariff.

Chief Justice Fuller agrees with the plaintiff's lawyers, holding that taxes, imposts, and duties have to be uniform throughout the United States, whether in the states themselves, the District of Columbia, or "territory west of the Missouri." The chief justice argues in his dissent that the Constitution should apply wherever the United States exerts its sovereignty and that neither acts of Congress nor treaties with foreign nations could be in violation of the Constitution. The Constitution, in turn, could not be changed without a duly ratified amendment. Joining Fuller in his dissenting opinion were Justices Rufus Wheeler Peckham, the author of the "substantive due process" doctrine; David Brewer, an economic libertarian and the nephew of the former justice Stephen Field; and John Marshall Harlan, the "Great Dissenter" and grandfather of the later Supreme Court justice of the same name. Harlan also wrote a more pointed dissent responding to Justice Brown's and Justice White's opinions.

The other Insular Cases decided on May 27, 1901—*De Lima v. Bidwell*, *Goetze v. United States*, *Crossman v. United States*, *Dooley v. United States I*, and *Armstrong v. United States*—differed from *Downes v. Bidwell* insofar as the Supreme Court was in these other cases addressing the constitutionality of the Foraker Act in the period *before* it went into effect. These other cases were heard both before and after the ratification of the 1898 Treaty of Paris. During this earlier period, before Congress had enacted the tariff on island trade, the Court ruled that the island territories (including Hawaii) were a part of the United States for the purposes of the uniformity clause. This holding applied not just with respect to the tariffs paid on goods imported from the new territories into the states (*De Lima v. Bidwell* and *Goetze v. United States*) but also in cases where goods were taxed upon being imported into Puerto Rico from the states (*Armstrong v. United States* and *Dooley v. United States*).

In two cases from the first set of Insular Cases the Court delayed its decisions until December 1901. In *Fourteen Diamond Rings v. United States*, known as the Philippine Case, the Supreme Court established that the rulings with respect to Puerto Rico also held for the Philippines—even though government lawyers argued otherwise because of the continuation of military conflict in the Philippines. Justice Brown was again the swing judge, and in the case of diamonds being brought into Chicago by a returning serviceman, he argued that they were exempt from U.S. customs duties. In *Dooley v. United States II*, however, the Court ruled as it did in *Downes* (although with respect to goods being imported into Puerto Rico from the states, the Court ruled as in *Dooley I* and *Armstrong*). Furthermore, the prohibitions in the Constitution on imposing taxes on exports from the United States (the export clause) and on granting preferences among ports of the United States (the preference clause) were held not to restrict Congress's authority to set territorial policies under the territory clause. Again, since neither Puerto Rico nor the Philippines had been made a part of the United States for the purposes of the Constitution's provisions relating to taxes and commerce, the tariff was thus deemed constitutional. In this case, the chief justice dissented vigorously once more on the ground that the tariff was unconstitutional: If the tariffs did not violate the export clause in imposing taxes on foreign trade, he argued, then they necessarily violated the uniformity clause's mandate that trade be uniform throughout the United

States.

The decisions in *Downes v. Bidwell* and the other Insular Cases of 1901 rested on fragile ground. Eight of these cases were decided by one-vote margins, such that each could be overturned by the death or retirement of a single Supreme Court justice. Furthermore, the Court had yet to address nontariff issues apart from extradition (considered in *Neely v. Henkel*, a case that involved a crime committed in Cuba) and admiralty law (touched upon in *Huus v. New York*, a case that concerned "coastwise shipping" rules). The Court ruled unanimously in both cases: Neely could be extradited even though Cuba was a foreign country, and Puerto Rico was part of the United States for the purposes of U.S. shipping regulations.

In the post-1901 Insular Cases, the Court clarified its positions regarding which constitutional provisions applied to the island territories. In the 1903 decision in *Hawaii v. Mankichi*, Justice Brown—joined by Justices Oliver Wendell Holmes, Jr., and William R. Day, the new appointees—held that the Hawaiian Supreme Court was not bound by the constitutional guarantees of a jury trial or of indictment by a grand jury in cases of felony. Justices White and McKenna concurred with this opinion, though on different grounds; White argued that since Hawaii had not been incorporated into the Union, neither the Fifth nor the Sixth Amendments applied. Chief Justice Fuller and Justices Harlan, Brewer, and Peckham dissented.

A case decided a year later, *Dorr v. United States*, permanently tipped the balance on the Court in favor of the incorporation doctrine and against the Constitution applying *ex proprio vigore*. Therein, Justice Day's lead opinion held that the defendant, Fred Dorr, was not guaranteed a jury trial and indictment by a grand jury. Since the Philippines were not incorporated, per Justice White's opinion in *Downes v. Bidwell*, Congress could "make laws for such territories, and subject [them] to such constitutional restrictions" as it thought suitable (195 U.S. 38). In this particular case, now, Justices Peckham and Brewer and Chief Justice Fuller concurred with Day's opinion (Day was joined by Justices White, Brown, McKenna, and Holmes), for the reason that Day's opinion took pains to distinguish the application of the Constitution to criminal law from its application to the regulation of commerce. The result was an 8–1 decision in favor of the U.S. and Philippine governments. Less than a year later, in *Rasmussen v. United States*, the Court explicitly and almost unanimously endorsed the incorporation doctrine: Justice White's lead opinion was based solely on the incorporation doctrine and was joined not only by his ally McKenna but also by the two recent appointees, Holmes and Day, along with three of the four dissenters in the Insular Cases of 1901 and in *Hawaii v. Mankichi*—Chief Justice Fuller, Brewer, and Peckham. Brown and Harlan wrote separate concurring opinions.

The Supreme Court used the incorporation doctrine to deny territorial citizens the right to jury trial and other guarantees of the Fifth and Sixth Amendments. In *Hawaii v. Mankichi*, *Dorr v. United States*, *Balzac v. Porto Rico* (the last of the Insular Cases), and other cases, the Court denied territorial citizens the right to a jury trial by peers; rejected their right to grand jury indictment in felony cases; refused the right of the accused to protection against self-incrimination; disallowed defendants the right to "speedy and public trial" (*Hawaii v. Mankichi*, 190 U.S. 197); and did not protect the right of the accused "to be confronted with witnesses against him" (*Dowdell v. United States*, 221 U.S. 325). As a general rule, the Supreme Court upheld the right of the territorial governments, created by the U.S. Congress, to prosecute crimes—political crimes in particular—by the terms of their own laws and by those of the U.S. Congress. In contrast, the Court ruled in Insular Cases concerning issues of commerce and property that territories and their citizens were indeed to be protected under the U.S. Constitution. The uniformity clause, due process in the taking of property (the takings clause), and other commercial rights were protected in the territories unless Congress explicitly legislated otherwise.

The incorporation doctrine enabled the United States to divest itself of unincorporated territories, as it would do with the Philippines in 1946. The U.S. assistant attorney general, the U.S. solicitor general, the Philippine governor-general William Howard Taft, the president of the University of Chicago, and other legal experts agreed that the new island territories could be held in trust by the United States and then eventually divested if in the United States' best interest. That is, unlike states, unincorporated territories could be removed from the United States. As Justice White wrote in *Downes v. Bidwell*, a country conquered and occupied by the United States could be held "for an indefinite period" and then, as Congress wished, "either released or retained because it was apt for incorporation into the United States." If a territory was "unfit" to be a part of the United States, White stated, the United

States could "terminate" its occupation.

The incorporation doctrine left important issues unsettled. One is that the doctrine by no means makes clear how territories are to be incorporated. In his concurring opinion in *Downes*, Justice White quoted from the 1898 Treaty of Paris to point out that the treaty did not contain the term *incorporation*, in contrast to the text of Article III of the 1803 treaty that annexed the Louisiana Territory and to that of the 1848 Treaty of Guadalupe Hidalgo, which annexed the northern portion of Mexico, the "Mexican Cession" constituting the southwestern United States. On the other hand, the language adding Alaska in 1867 also lacked reference to incorporation, yet the Court nevertheless decided that Alaska was an incorporated territory. A distinction between organized territories and unorganized governments also failed to decide matters, as incorporated territories could be organized (Hawaii) or unorganized (Alaska), and unincorporated territories, too, could be either organized (Puerto Rico) or unorganized (Guam).

Also left unresolved by the incorporation doctrine is the constitutional principle upon which territories can be kept as "unincorporated" territories. Chief Justice Taft's opinion in the capstone case *Balzac v. Porto Rico* (258 U.S. 298) rests on a hazy results-oriented argument: that "locality" determines whether the Constitution applies or not. Even though neither Puerto Rico nor Alaska were annexed with explicit language of incorporation, the opinion holds, "Alaska was a very different case...an enormous territory, very sparsely settled, and offering opportunity and settlement by American citizens." The right to jury trial could not be granted, Taft quoted from *Dorr v. United States*, "no matter the needs or capacities of the people." For Taft and other Americans of the period, Puerto Rico, like the Philippines and other island territories, was one of a handful of "distant ocean communities of different origin and language from those of our continental people." In the multicultural and ethnically diverse United States of the twenty-first century, however, Taft's argument would seem to lose its force.

Essential Themes

The United States seized control of Cuba and Puerto Rico during the Spanish-American War of 1898, acquiring the Philippines and Guam afterward in the peace settlement with Spain. Three days after that war ended, the United States annexed Hawaii through a joint congressional resolution, the Newlands Resolution. Expansionists in the administrations of William McKinley and Theodore Roosevelt and in the Republican Party sought to annex these islands for their strategic value as naval stations and coaling stations. The new bases in the Pacific Ocean and the Caribbean Sea would allow the U.S. Navy to protect American trade with the Far East and to guard the entrance to the planned isthmian canal connecting the Atlantic and Pacific oceans. American politicians, government officials, political writers, and others wished for the United States to emulate the other great world powers—Great Britain, France, Germany, and others—through the establishment of colonies and overseas empires. At the same time, the business allies of the McKinley and Roosevelt administrations were very aware of the economic potential, in sugar production especially, of the newly annexed islands.

Even if most Americans agreed that these islands should come under U.S. sovereignty, few wanted hundreds of thousands of Puerto Ricans and millions of Filipinos to become fellow citizens, equals in the American polity. In fact, just eight days after the signing of the 1898 Treaty of Paris, the Senate passed a resolution not to incorporate Filipinos as U.S. citizens and not to annex the Philippines. Just before the Spanish-American War, Congress had passed the Teller Amendment, which prohibited the United States from annexing Cuba. After the war, Congress passed the Platt Amendment, which guaranteed Cuba's independence under the conditions, among others, that the United States could intervene militarily in Cuba if need be and that the U.S. Navy could lease Guantánamo Bay and other naval bases. The Platt Amendment later became a part of the new Cuban constitution.

When Congress passed the Foraker Act in 1900, a tariff on trade between Puerto Rico and the mainland states was included; funds collected from the tariff were to be used for the administration of Puerto Rico, given the island's low tax base. The tariff, set at 15 percent of the existing Dingley Act tariff rates, was challenged by lawyers from Coudert Brothers, the international law firm that represented Samuel B. Downes & Co. and other trading firms, as a violation of the Constitution's uniformity clause, which stipulates that "all Duties, Imposts, and Excises" must "be uniform throughout the United States."

The attorneys for Downes & Co. argued that the duties imposed by the U.S. government on the oranges shipped from Puerto Rico to New York were uncon-

Boxer Protocol

Date: 1901
Author: Eight-Nation Alliance; Qing Empire
Genre: treaty; charter

Summary Overview

Signed on September 7, 1901, the Boxer Protocol was an agreement between China's ruling Qing Dynasty and the coalition of nations that had been affected by the Boxer Rebellion of 1900. This uprising had targeted both foreign nationals and Chinese subjects who had, for example, converted to Christianity. Although the Boxer Rebellion had been initiated by a mystical group called the Society of Righteous and Harmonious Fists, it had received support from the royal court. A multinational military force succeeded in suppressing the uprising.

One of a long series of "unequal treaties" between China and Western powers, the Boxer Protocol had three broad goals: to humiliate China, to financially punish China, and to strengthen the position of the powers that had established economic footholds in China. The Boxer Protocol required that China erect monuments at the sites of the legations that had been attacked in the uprising as well as a monument to Clemens von Ketteler, the German minister who had been assassinated by the Boxers. This symbolic humiliation was compounded by the condition that China try to execute a number of the high-ranking officials implicated in the Boxer Rebellion. This effort to dictate policy to the Chinese also extended to suspending the traditional and long-standing civil service exams in locales that had been party to the uprising. The protocol also obliged China to pay an enormous indemnity to the victorious nations, spread out over nearly four decades.

Several requirements of the Boxer Protocol served to strengthen the position of the protocol powers within China. Among them was the granting to these foreign powers exclusive use rights of the legation areas in the capital city, including the right to fortify and defend these areas. The Boxer Protocol also required China to abandon several military positions between the sea and Beijing. Ostensibly this was to improve "communication" but was designed to remove possible points of Chinese resistance in the event of another invasion by the powers of the Boxer Protocol.

Defining Moment

The Boxer Protocol was a truly international treaty. The nations involved spanned Europe, North America, and Asia. The message behind the document, however, was aimed squarely at the Chinese: any attempt to assert China's power or deny foreign influence was disastrous. The humiliating terms of the protocol did not convince China to embrace submission, but compelled renewed calls for change that cumulated in the dissolution of the Qing Empire in 1911. Among the Western nations, the Boxer Protocol seemed to exact righteous retributions—except in the eyes of a few, including Mark Twain. The aging American author took to newspapers and magazines to lambast imperialism and especially the role of missionaries in implementing imperialism's terms.

Author Biography

The major authors of this document included representatives from the Eight-Nation Alliance (Great Britain, Germany, the United States, Russia, Japan, France, Italy, and Austria). These nations represented the chief imperialist forces in the world at the time; they all were part of the "scramble for concessions" from China and the main countries colonizing Africa and Asia. Among the plenipotentiaries, the British Empire was at its height of power, and forces from British-controlled India and Australia participated in the multinational expedition to China during the Boxer Rebellion. Germany and Russia were also at the height of colonizing, and, although they would begin losing territory in the twentieth century, their participation in the Boxer expedition was part of the two nation's increasing efforts to expand their hegemony and source of later conflicts. The United States, too, was not immune to imperializing pressure: around the same time as the Boxer Protocol, the Americans were involved in the Philippine-American War.

On the opposite side of the bargaining table, the Qing Empire's representative was the elderly Li Hongzhang, who died shortly following the signing of the Boxer Protocol. Empress Dowager Cixi and her court, fearing any attempts by the Western nations in Beijing to control them, remained in Xi'an during the protocol's composition. Li was a well-known negotiator for the Qing Empire, though, and he often defended China's interests during a century of unequal treaties.

HISTORICAL DOCUMENT

THE PLENIPOTENTIARIES...[ambassadors from nine European powers, the United States, and Japan together with Chinese representatives Li Hongzhang and Yikuang] have met for the purpose of declaring that China has complied with the conditions laid down in the note of the 22nd December, 1900, and which were accepted in their entirety by His Majesty the Emperor of China in a Decree dated the 27th December, 1900.

ARTICLE 1.

1) By an Imperial Edict of the 9th June last, Prince of the First Rank, Chun, was appointed Ambassador of His Majesty the Emperor of China, and directed in that capacity to convey to His Majesty the German Emperor the expression of the regrets of His Majesty the Emperor of China and of the Chinese Government at the assassination of his Excellency the late Baron von Ketteler, German Minister. Prince Chun left Peking on the 12th July last to carry out the orders which had been given him.

2) The Chinese Government has stated that it will erect on the spot of the assassination of his Excellency the late Baron von Ketteler, commemorative monument worthy of the rank of the deceased, and bearing an inscription in the Latin, German, and Chinese languages which shall express the regrets of His Majesty the Emperor of China for the murder committed. The Chinese Plenipotentiaries have informed his Excellency the German Plenipotentiary, in a letter dated the 22nd July last, that an arch of the whole width of the street would be erected on the said spot, and that work on it was begun on the 25th June last.

ARTICLE II.

1) Imperial Edicts of the 13th and 21st February, 1901, inflicted the following punishments on the principal authors of the attempts and of the crimes committed against the foreign Governments and their nationals: Tsa-Ii, Prince Tuan, and Tsai-Lan, Duke Fu-kuo, were sentenced to be brought before the Autumnal Court of Assize for execution, and it was agreed that if the Emperor saw fit to grant them their lives, they should be exiled to Turkestan, and there imprisoned for life, without the possibility of commutation of these punishments. Tsai Hsun, Prince Chuang, Ying-Nien, President of the Court of Censors, and Chao Shu-chiao, President of the Board of Punishments, were condemned to commit suicide. Yu Hsun, Governor of Shansi, Chi Hsiu, President of the Board of Rites, and Hsu Cheng-yu, formerly Senior Vice-President of the Board of Punishments, were condemned to death. Posthumous degradation was inflicted on Kang Yi, Assistant Grand Secretary, President of the Board of Works, Hsu Tung, Grand Secretary, and Li Ping-heng, former Governor-General of Szu-chuan. Imperial Edict of the 13th February last rehabilitated the memories of Hsu Yung-yi, President of the Board of War; Li Shan, President of the Board of Works; Hsu Ching Cheng, Senior Vice President of the Board of Civil Office; Lien Yuan, Vice-Chancellor of the Grand Council; and Yuan Chang, Vice-President of the Court of Sacrifices, who had been put to death for having protested against the outrageous breaches of international law of last year. Prince Chuang committed suicide on the 21st February last; Ying Nien and Chao Shu-chiao on the 24th February; Yu Hsien was executed on the 22nd February; Chi Hsiu and Hsu Cheng-yu on the 26th February; Tung Fu-hsiang, General in Kan-su, has been deprived of his office by Imperial Edict of the 13th February last, pending the determination of the final punishment to be inflicted on him. Imperial Edicts, dated

the 29th April and 19th August, 1901, have inflicted various punishments on the provincial officials convicted of the crimes and outrages of last summer.

2) An Imperial Edict, promulgated the 19th August, 1901, ordered the suspension of official examinations for five years in all cities where foreigners were massacred or submitted to cruel treatment.

ARTICLE III.

So as to make honourable reparation for the assassination of Mr. Sugiyama, Chancellor of the Japanese Legation, His Majesty the Emperor of China, by an Imperial Edict of the 18th June, 1901, appointed Na T'ung, Vice-President of the Board of Finances, to be his Envoy Extraordinary, and specially directed him to convey to His Majesty the Emperor of Japan the expression of the regrets of His Majesty the Emperor of China and of his Government at the assassination of Mr. Sugiyama.

ARTICLE IV.

The Chinese Government has agreed to erect an expiatory monument in each of the foreign or international cemeteries which were desecrated, and in which the tombs were destroyed. It has been agreed with the Representatives of the Powers that the Legations interested shall settle the details for the erection of these monuments, China bearing all the expenses thereof, estimated at 10,000 taels, for the cemeteries at Peking and in its neighbourhood, and at 5,000 taels for the cemeteries in the provinces. The amounts have been paid, and the list of these cemeteries is inclosed herewith.

ARTICLE V.

China has agreed to prohibit the importation into its territory of arms and ammunition, as well as of materials exclusively used for the manufacture of arms and ammunition. An Imperial Edict has been issued on the 25th August, forbidding said importation for a term of two years. New Edicts may be issued subsequently extending this by other successive terms of two years in case of necessity recognized by the Powers.

ARTICLE VI.

By an Imperial Edict dated the 29th May, 1901, His Majesty the Emperor of China agreed to pay the Powers an indemnity of 450,000,000 of Haikwan taels. This sum represents the total amount of the indemnities for States, Companies, or Societies, private individuals and Chinese, referred to in Article 6 of the note of the 22nd December, 1900.

1) These 450,000,000 constitute a gold debt calculated at the rate of the Haikwan tael to the gold currency of each country [the equivalent of $330 million]....

This sum in gold shall bear interest at 4 per cent per annum, and the capital shall be reimbursed by China in thirty-nine years in the manner indicated in the annexed plan of amortization. Capital and interest shall be payable in gold or at the rates of exchange corresponding to the dates at which the different payments fall due. The amortization shall commence the 1st January, 1902, and shall finish at the end of the year 1940. The amortizations are payable annually, the first payment being fixed on the 1st January, 1903. Interest shall run from the 1st July, 1901, but the Chinese Government shall have the right to pay off within a term of three years, beginning January 1902, the arrears of the first six months ending the 31st December, 1901, on condition, however, that it pays compound interest at the rate of 4 per cent a year on the sums the payment of which shall have been thus deferred. Interest shall be payable semi-annually, the first payment being fixed on the 1st July, 1902.

2) The service of the debt shall take place in Shanghai in the following manner: Each Power shall be represented by a Delegate on a Commission of bankers authorized to receive the amount of interest and amortization which shall be paid to it by the Chinese authorities designated for that purpose, to divide it among the interested parties, and to give a receipt for the same.

3) The Chinese Government shall deliver to the Doyen [i.e., the senior member] of the Diplomatic Corps at Peking a bond for the lump sum, which shall subsequently be converted into fractional bonds bearing the signature of the Delegates of the Chinese Government designated for that purpose. This operation and all those relating to issuing of the bonds shall be performed by the above-mentioned Commission, in accordance with the instructions which the Powers shall send their Delegates.

4) The proceeds of the revenues assigned to the payment of the bonds shall be paid monthly to the Commission.

5) The seven assigned as security for the bonds are the following: a) The balance of the revenues of the Imperial Maritime Customs, after payment of the interest and amortization of preceding loans secured on these revenues, plus the proceeds of the raising to 5 per cent effective of the present tariff of maritime imports, including articles until now on the free list, but exempting rice, foreign cereals, and flour, gold and silver bullion and coin. b) The revenues of the native Customs, administered in the open ports by the Imperial Maritime Customs. c) The total revenues of the salt gabelle, exclusive of the fraction previously set aside for other foreign loans.

6) The raising of the present tariff on imports to 5 per cent effective is agreed to on the conditions mentioned below. It shall be put in force two months after the signing of the present Protocol, and no exceptions shall be made except for merchandize in transit not more than ten days after the said signing....b) The beds of the Rivers Whangpoo and Peiho shall be improved with the financial participation of China.

ARTICLE VII.

The Chinese Government has agreed that the quarter occupied by the Legations shall be considered as one specially reserved for their use and placed under their exclusive control, in which Chinese shall not have the right to reside, and which may be made defensible....In the Protocol annexed to the letter of the 16th January, 1901, China recognized the right of each Power to maintain a permanent guard in the said quarter for the defence of its Legation.

ARTICLE VIII.

The Chinese Government has consented to raze the forts of Taku, and those which might impede free communication between Peking and the sea. Steps have been taken for carrying this out.

ARTICLE IX.

The Chinese Government conceded the right to the Powers in the Protocol annexed to the letter of the 16th January, 1901, to occupy certain points, to be determined by an Agreement between them for the maintenance of open communication between the capital and the sea. The points occupied by the Powers are: Huang-tsun, Lang-fang, Yang-tsun, Tien-tsin, Chun-liang-Cheng, Tong-ku, Lu-tai, Tong-shan, Lan-chou, Chang-li, Chin-wang Tao, Shan-hai Kuan.

ARTICLE X.

The Chinese Government has agreed to post and to have published during two years in all district cities the following Imperial Edicts:

1) Edict of the 1st February, 1901, prohibiting for ever under pain of death, membership in any anti-foreign society.

2) Edicts of the 13th and 21st February, 29th April and 19th August, 1901, enumerating the punishments inflicted on the guilty.

3) Edict of the 19th August, 1901, prohibiting examinations in all cities where foreigners were massacred or subjected to cruel treatment.

4) Edicts of the 1st February, 1901, declaring all Governors General, Governors, and provincial or local officials responsible for order in their respective districts, and that in case of new anti-foreign troubles or other infractions of the Treaties which shall not be immediately repressed and the authors of which shall not have been punished, these officials shall be immediately dismissed without possibility of being given new functions or new honours. The posting of these Edicts is being carried on throughout the Empire.

ARTICLE XI.

The Chinese Government has agreed to negotiate the amendments deemed necessary by the foreign Governments to the Treaties of Commerce and Navigation and the other subjects concerning commercial relations with the object of facilitating them. At present, and as a result of the stipulation contained in Article 6 concerning the indemnity, the Chinese Government agrees to assist in the improvement of the courses of the Rivers Peiho and Whangpoo, as stated below.

1) The works for the improvement of the navigability of the Peiho, begun in 1898 with the co-operation of the Chinese Government, have been resumed under the direction of an International Commission. As soon as the Administration of Tientsin shall have been handed back to the Chinese Government it will be in a position to be represented on this Commission, and will pay each year a sum of 60,000 Haikwan taels for maintaining the works.

2) A Conservancy Board, charged with the management and control of the works for straightening the Whangpoo and the improvement of the course of that river, is hereby created. The Board shall consist of members representing the interests of the Chinese Government and those of foreigners in the shipping trade of Shanghai. The expenses incurred for the works and the general management of the undertaking are estimated at the annual sum of 460,000 Haikwan taels for the first twenty years. This sum shall be supplied in equal portions by the Chinese Government and the foreign interests concerned.

ARTICLE XII.

An Imperial Edict of the 24th July, 1901, reformed the Office of Foreign Affairs, Tsung-li Yamen, on the lines indicated by the Powers, that is to say, transformed it into a Ministry of Foreign Affairs, Wai Wu Pu, which takes precedence over the six other Ministries of State; the same Edict appointed the principal Members of this Ministry. An agreement has also been reached concerning the modification of Court ceremonial as regards the reception of foreign Representatives, and has been the subject of several notes from the Chinese Plenipotentiaries, the substance of which is embodied in a Memorandum herewith annexed. Finally, it is expressly understood that as regards the declarations specified above and the annexed documents originating with the foreign Plenipotentiaries, the French text only is authoritative. The Chinese Government having thus complied to the satisfaction of the Powers with the conditions laid down in the above-mentioned note of the 22nd December, 1900, the Powers have agreed to accede to the wish of China to terminate the situation created by the disorders of the summer of 1900. In consequence thereof, the foreign Plenipotentiaries are authorized to declare in the names of their Governments that, with the exception of the Legation guards mentioned in Article VII, the international troops will completely evacuate the city of Peking on the 7th September, 1901, and, with the exception of the localities mentioned in Article IX, will withdraw from the Province of Chihli on the 22nd September, 1901. The present final Protocol has been drawn up in twelve identical copies, and signed by all the Plenipotentiaries of the contracting countries.

GLOSSARY

Tsungli Yamen: Zongli Yamen (alternate spelling), a Qing foreign affairs office

Document Analysis

The plenipotentiaries systematically arranged the terms of the Boxer Protocol to humiliate and disable Qing authority. They accomplished this in the terms of the agreement by both insisting on the construction of visual markers in Beijing that would reinforce foreign power and undercut any ability of the Qing court to assert centralized political and economic power.

To start, one of the very first requirements of the protocol illustrates how the Eight-Nation Alliance were determined to use visual reminders in the city of Beijing to reinforce Qing weakness before the foreign coalition. In Article I, it says that the Qing are to erect a "commemorative monument worthy of the rank of the deceased" to Baron von Ketteler. The German diplomat was no innocent, however. The insistence on his memorialization in the treaty belies the true motives of the protocol: to humiliate China. Ketteler achieved notoriety for his bellicosity: he caned Chinese on the street and took aggressive action against Boxers training below the Tartar Wall in a move that drew criticism from his fellow diplomats. After the Qing ultimatum to the legations to leave, Ketteler's rash decision not to await deliberations with the other diplomats and to leave the legation compound likely resulted in his death on the dangerous streets. As a "martyr" for resistance to the Boxer Rebellion, there was surely a better choice for the plenipotentiaries than Baron von Ketteler, if they had pure intentions. The insistence on a visual reminder of the death of a belligerent foreign diplomat reinforces what the Boxer Protocol actually wanted: to humiliate the Qing.

However, the monument to Baron von Ketteler was not the only term in the Boxer Protocol dedicated to reinforcing foreign superiority over the Qing Empire. The protocol also insisted on "an expiatory monument in each of the foreign or international cemeteries which were desecrated," fully-funded by the Qing. The word "expiatory" implicated the Qing in wrongdoing, and like the formal apologies Qing diplomats had to give in person to foreign governments, it automatically placed China in a subservient role. Monuments as opposed to verbal apologies have the benefit of reminding people from all social backgrounds visually for many years that the foreign nations battled down not just a peasant rebellion, but also the imperial military. Additionally, the protocol also stipulates a term that affects the visual landscape of Beijing: no Chinese could occupy land within the foreign legations quarter, the legations were permitted to construct defenses, and the legations were outside of any Chinese control. This term especially would reinforce foreign control in the visual landscape of Beijing. The foreign legations and the "Tartar Wall" were at the center of the armed conflict in June 1900. It was, after all, in this region that Baron von Ketteler was killed. The Boxer Protocol mandates that a part of Beijing be officially recognized as not Chinese nor belonging in any way to China.

This agreement that the Qing had no power over the foreign legations quarter also illustrates how the plenipotentiaries aimed to disable Qing political and economic authority. By stipulating that the foreign legations had the right to construct defenses, like the Tartar Wall, the protocol was also asserting that the Qing had no sovereignty or recourse over those legations activities. Article VIII also strips the Qing of authority because it mandates the destruction of Dagu fortress and the concession of certain other points to foreign powers. Without the ability to man its own defensive positions, the protocol stripped the Qing of any protective power: China was open, whether it wanted to be or not.

This term in the protocol also reinforced the regionalism that had already plagued the Qing Dynasty in the nineteenth century. The foreign powers' intervention widened the gap between the central government and local governors. The concession of certain defensive points to foreign powers meant that there were fewer places for the imperial military to assert Qing authority; furthermore, the prohibition of civil service examinations in places that had were the source of uprisings meant that those places would then be divorced from a very important tradition linking men in the provinces to the central government. The requirements in Article II for the execution or exile of a number of high-ranking members of the Qing court compounded this issue of banning civil service examinations: after depopulating the Qing court of a number of high-ranking imperial members, it would then be difficult to recoup those losses.

Finally, the plenipotentiaries also exacted enormous indemnities from the Qing in a calculated move to disable imperial power. The Qing Empire was already suffering economically; the enormous fines now imposed would not help the situation that contributed to the Boxer Rebellion in the first place. These fines, however, meant that the Qing would not be able for at least forty years to sustain any resistance against foreign militaries or businesses. Although many of the nations which received payments from China returned the money into Chinese infrastructure by building schools, railways, and bridges, the effect of the indemnities was clear: to damage the Qing as administrators of their own nation's affairs.

Clearly, the Boxer Protocol is a paradigmatic example of a series of unequal treaties between Western nations and China. It demanded the creation of external monuments to China's subservience and required the internal disabling of China's political and economic authority. It is no wonder that soon after the Qing Dynasty fell and the European countries began to attack each other, China successfully negotiated for the redirection of payments to Chinese interests and renamed the von Ketteler monument so that it would no longer reflect a demeaning period in the nation's history.

Essential Themes

The Boxer Rebellion started with isolated acts of brutality in the coastal province of Shandong and exploded into an international debacle. This local uprising that swelled into a global military expedition was not the first of China's peasant rebellions, nor would it be the last. The Boxers and their defeat were the product of centuries of tumultuous Chinese domestic history and invasive Western imperialism.

As a domestic affair, the Boxer Rebellion was one of many peasant rebellions against the dynastic system just in the nineteenth century. Civil examinations, feudalism, and regionalism mired the Qing Empire in varying degrees of stagnation by 1900. To begin, the tradition of civil examinations was meant to encourage meritocracy, but often it favored those individuals who came from wealth, reinforced the feudal social strata, and encouraged corruption. Even for those who were able to achieve the highest degree, a degree did not guarantee a job as there were more degree holders than offices. Additionally, the exams favored classical and literary knowledge, not technical skill or science, which some attributed to the fact that China was not modernizing at the same pace as other nations.

Finally, as a large country with a diverse populace, the central imperial government was often distant; governing became an ad hoc process that relied on local administrators. The regionalism of the late imperial system meant that the imperial court often relied on often-corrupt local officials to keep order and their militias to put down uprisings. These uprisings were aggravated by local economic concerns and the imperial court often had difficulty quelling the rebellions. The White Lotus Rebellion (1796-1804) only ended with difficulty primarily by the local militias and the Chinese military. Half a century later, it took the Chinese military over a decade with the help of local forces to end the Taiping Rebellion (1850-1864). The Boxer Rebellion mirrored these two earlier uprisings in both its conception and its defeat.

These initially local peasant uprisings were not just a response to decades of an intransigent political system. Demographic changes and Western interference aggravated an economic system that was already suffering from bad harvests. First, the Opium Wars 1839-42, 1850-64) and the Sino-Japanese War (1894-5) taught the Chinese a costly lesson, that they had failed to modernize efficiently and were at the mercy of the European powers and Japan. An enormous population growth in China over the eighteenth and nineteenth century meant that there was less land available for development and more people resorting to cheap labor, migratory work, and banditry. A terrible drought in 1899 destroyed crops and left a number of ordinary Chinese with a lot of time to contemplate the privileges they did not receive, but foreigners and Chinese Christians did.

At the center of the Boxer Rebellion were the foreign missionaries. These Christian groups from the Western nations had aggressively made their presence recognized in the Chinese landscape for decades. These foreign missionaries were, on the one hand, responsible for buildings churches, schools, and hospitals that offered many services to marginalized members in Chinese society; on the other hand, these missionaries were often exempt from national law and caused resentment because Chinese Christians often benefited from their association to these missions in local courts, too. For this reason, the Boxers targeted Chinese Christians first in Shandong. The Boxers began murdering Chinese Christians in the late spring of 1900 and their attacks increased into June.

As more adherents joined the Boxers, the fire spread from Chinese Christians to the missions themselves. This growing movement force and the Western powers arrayed against them forced the Qing to make a show of allegiance: to the Chinese people or their Western business interests. On June 11th, the Japanese chancellor Sugiyama Akira was killed; on June 13th, the foreign delegations in Beijing began to fortify themselves with the "Tartar Wall." Finally on June 20th, while the foreign delegations waited for a response from the Zongli Yamen (a Qing foreign affairs office) about an ultimatum to leave, Baron von Ketteler was killed. As the same time, a multinational military expedition, which was sent to China to relieve their delegations from the Boxer threat, was battling Boxers and imperial troops on the coast at the Dagu fortress. In particular, the foreign assault on Dagu culminated in the Qing finally throwing their support behind the Boxers officially and declaring war on the Western powers on June 21, 1900.

The Boxer Protocol document reified the declining power of the Qing Dynasty. Foreign interference and governmental infighting aggravated this decline throughout the nineteenth century, but by 1912, the imperial system would be replaced by a republic and decades of further national turmoil. The terms of the Boxer Protocol, although they were similar to other agreements forced upon China in defeat earlier in the nineteenth century, signaled that China needed to change. The Chinese interpreted change in two different, not mutually exclusive ways, however. One camp saw change as the need to modernize, to adopt Western customs and schools of thoughts in order to meet the nations that continued to defeat themselves with more equal capabilities. The other camp saw the Boxers as an example and an inspiration for changing China's continued subservience to foreign powers. Both camps were Chinese nationalists and part of a global movement towards nationalism and away from the imperialism of the nineteenth century.

For those part of the first group, Japan's great advancement during the Meiji Restoration and participation in crushing the Boxer Rebellion was proof of China's need to modernize. The Self-Strengthening Movement in the second half of the nineteenth century improved China's military somewhat, but ultimately the change was not enough or fast enough compared to the staggering pace of development in other nations vying for influence in China. Modernization efforts were equally not helped by the fact that for years the dowager empress Cixi and conservative Qing court members had stymied efforts to modernize. The most devastating assault on modernization efforts was Cixi's coup d'etat against the Guangxu Emperor and his attempted Hundred Days of Reform in 1898. Eventually, after the Qing Empire disintegrated in 1911, a group of reformers such as Chen Duxiu and the students involved in the May Fourth Movement would be inspired to action over foreign influence in Shandong province, just like the Boxers. Unlike the Boxers, these reformers believed that Confucianism was responsible for many of China's problems and advocated science, an end to feudalism, egalitarian values, and a critique of the past.

The May Fourth Movement and the wider New Culture Movement of the 1910s and 1920s began the process of questioning China's history that would lead to Mao Zedong and the Chinese Communist Revolution in 1949. For Mao Zedong and others, the Boxers were one of the great peasant movements that resisted and attacked foreign capitalism. Instead of the Boxers as the symptom of a reactionary broken system, they became the first modern Chinese patriots. Especially during the traumatic Cultural Revolution in the 1960s, the Red Guard drew explicit parallels between themselves and the Boxers and their anti-foreign and anti-imperialist messages.

As crushing as the Boxer Protocol was, the divisive Boxers remained for decades behind the process of China loosening itself from the bonds of imperialism and the development of the modern Chinese nation.

———*Ashleigh Fata, MA and Aaron Gulyas, MA*

Bibliography and Additional Reading

Bickers, Robert and R. G. Tiedemann, eds. *The Boxers, China, and the World*. New York: Rowman & Littlefield, 2007. Print.

Cohen, Paul A. *History in Three Keys: the Boxers as Event, Experience, and Myth*. New York: Columbia UP, 1997. Print.

Esherick, Joseph. *The Origins of the Boxer Uprising*. Berkeley: UC Press, 1987. Print.

O'Connor, Richard. *The Boxer Rebellion*. London: Robert Hale, 1973. Print.

Silbey, David J. *The Boxer Rebellion and the Great Game in China*. New York: Hill and Wang, 2012. Print.

Smith, Richard. *China's Cultural Heritage: the Qing Dynasty*, 1644-1912. Boulder, CO: Westview Press, 1994. Print.

Vladimir Lenin: *What Is to Be Done?*

Date: 1902
Author: Vladimir Lenin
Genre: political tract

Summary Overview

What Is to Be Done? is a political pamphlet written by Vladimir Ilich Lenin, the architect of the 1917 Bolshevik Revolution in Russia and one of the chief founders of the Soviet Union. Lenin's real last name was Ulyanov (sometimes spelled Ulianov). He began writing *What Is to Be Done?* in 1901, and it was published in 1902 under the name "N. Lenin." Although it is only a single document in the large corpus of Lenin's writings, it is often considered his most important. This is because it appears to provide a blueprint for the final form of the Bolshevik Party and therefore also for the revolutionary regime that the party established after seizing power in Russia on November 7–8, 1917 (October 25–26, according to the Russian calendar still in use at that time). In *What Is to Be Done?* Lenin focuses on questions of political agitation and proper revolutionary organization. In particular, he rejects open mass membership in the Russian Social Democratic Labor Party (RSDLP), also called the Russian Social Democratic Workers Party. The RSDLP had been founded in Minsk in 1898 to unite the movement for "social democracy" which at the time was represented by various Russian revolutionary Socialist organizations. Instead, he emphasizes the need for a highly organized, "centralized" "secret" and "conspiratorial" party composed of "professional revolutionaries" who would direct to a successful conclusion the much larger workers' movement in Russia.

Defining Moment

Despite his view that social democrats must propagandize as widely as possible, Lenin wrote *What Is to Be Done?* with a narrow audience in mind. It was aimed first and foremost at certain Socialists and pro-worker groups then active in Russia or as émigrés (some of whom are explicitly named in the excerpts presented here). It was intended to convince as many of these people as possible of the correctness of Lenin's ideas—and of the wrongheadedness of alternatives—specifically on questions of party organization and activity in Russia at that time. More broadly, but certainly secondarily, it was written for the wider international Socialist movement of the day. The pamphlet was, of course, read somewhat beyond these circles as well, including by the czarist authorities. Lenin had only recently adopted his famous pseudonym at this point, and his identity was not well known.

The pamphlet's real rise to fame came after 1917, once Lenin had established himself as the founder of a new and hugely controversial state. Whereas in the Soviet Union the *whole body* of Lenin's work quickly became a kind of secular scripture (especially after his death in 1924), in the West only *What Is to Be Done?* began to attract particular attention. Beginning in the late 1920s, Stalin, Lenin's successor, took the Soviet Union off in bold and terrible new directions. His first Five-Year Plan (1928–1932) forced breakneck industrialization on the country, and agriculture was brutally collectivized with disastrous results. At the same time, Lenin's works became increasingly available in translation abroad. Of all his writings, *What Is to Be Done?* seemed to offer Western observers the clearest insights into the roots and real nature of the Soviet system that Lenin had created and Stalin later dominated. This opinion, although not unchallenged, is still largely accepted today.

Author Biography

Like many champions of the working poor, Lenin was not of them. He was born into a prosperous family in Simbirsk (known as Ulyanovsk from 1924 to 1991) on the Volga River. His father was an inspector of schools and a ranking noble. Lenin was of mixed ancestry, including Russian, Swedish, German, Jewish, Kalmyk, and Mordvinian. Like most Russians, he was raised in the Orthodox Christian tradition. He was baptized as a sixteen-year-old in 1886. Lenin's "baptism" into the world of radical politics came the following year, when his older brother, Alexander, was arrested and executed for involvement in a plot to assassinate Alexander III, a very repressive czar. Lenin's sister was also implicated and sentenced to house arrest. Lenin soon enrolled in Kazan University but was subsequently expelled for his radical ideals. He studied independently for a time, focusing on Marxism, law, history, and languages, and he later enrolled in the University of Saint Petersburg, from which he graduated with a law degree in 1892.

After a short legal career, Lenin, already a convinced Marxist, turned increasingly to revolutionary propaganda and organization. He was arrested in late 1895 and sent to Siberia, where he shared company with other exiled Marxists, including Nadezhda Konstantinovna Krupskaya, who became his wife in 1898. Lenin's first major publication, *The Development of Capitalism in Russia*, appeared in 1899. This began a prolific writing career. After his release in 1900, Lenin traveled widely in Western Europe. He came into contact with most of the leading left-wing thinkers and activists of the day, joined the RSDLP, and cofounded its official paper, *Iskra* ("The Spark"). It was at this time that Lenin began to regularly use his pseudonym—which means "man from the Lena river"—instead of his real name. (The Lena River actually is thousands of miles east of Lenin's birthplace.) Lenin's ideas on capitalism, revolution, and Communism had already begun to develop beyond their Marxist origins into a somewhat altered theory known subsequently as Marxism-Leninism (or just Leninism). Some of its most characteristic innovations, which focused on questions of organization, can be seen in *What Is to Be Done?*

HISTORICAL DOCUMENT

II: The Spontaneity of the Masses and the Consciousness of Social Democracy

...The [main] strength of the current movement [for worker liberation] is the awakening of the masses (primarily the industrial proletariat), while its [main] weakness is the insufficiency of consciousness and initiative among revolutionary leaders.... The relationship between consciousness and spontaneity is of enormous general interest and must be treated in detail....

The Beginning of the Spontaneous Upsurge

We noted in the previous chapter the [great] general interest shown by educated Russian youth in the theory of Marxism during the mid-1890s. At around the same time, the labor strikes that followed the famous Saint Petersburg industrial war of 1896 showed a similar general character. Their spread across all of Russia clearly testifies to the depth of the newly awakened popular movement, and if we are speaking of a "spontaneous element" then, of course, it is precisely this strike movement that must be recognized above all as spontaneous. But there are different levels of spontaneity. There were strikes in Russia during the seventies and sixties...accompanied by the "spontaneous" destruction of machinery and so on. Compared with these "riots" the strikes of the nineties could even be called "conscious"—so significant was the progress the workers' movement had made during that time. This shows that the "spontaneous element" is, in essence, nothing other than consciousness in *embryonic form*. Even primitive riots represent a certain degree of awakening of consciousness: the workers were beginning to lose their age-old faith in the permanence of the system of their oppression, and [they] began...I shan't say to understand, but to feel the need for collective resistance, and decisively broke from slavish submission toward the bosses. But this was still more a case of despair and revenge than of [genuine class] *struggle*. The strikes of the 1890s show us much more significant flashes of consciousness: specific demands were voiced; advance thought was given to picking the best moment [to act]; there was discussion of well-known events and examples from other places. If the riots [of the 1860s–1870s] were simply uprisings of oppressed people, then the systematic strikes [of the 1890s] represented class struggle in embryo, but only in embryo. In and of themselves these strikes were [only] trade unionist struggles, and not yet social democratic struggles; they marked the awakening of antagonism between the workers and owners, but the workers did not have—indeed they could not have—[true] consciousness of the irreconcilable opposition of their interests to the current political and social structure; in other words, [they did not have] social democratic consciousness. In this sense, the strikes of the 1890s, regardless of the great progress made in comparison with the "riots" [of the 1860s–1870s], remained purely an expression of spontaneity.

We have said there *could not have been* social democratic consciousness among the workers. It could be brought [to them] only from outside. The history of all countries demonstrates that exclusively by its own efforts the working class is capable only of working out trade union consciousness—that is, the conviction that it is necessary to combine into unions [in order to] carry on a struggle with the owners, win from the authorities passage of this or that vital law, and so on. The teachings of socialism grew out of philosophical, historical, and economic theories worked out by educated representatives of the propertied classes, [that is, by] intellectuals. The founders of modern scientific socialism, Marx and Engels, themselves belonged—by their social status—to the bourgeois intelligentsia. In just the same way, here in Russia the theoretical teachings of social democracy also arose as a natural and inevitable result of the development of thought among the revolutionary socialist intelligentsia—that is, completely independently of the spontaneous growth of the workers' movement.

Bowing Down to Spontaneity: *Rabochaia mysl'*

...There can be no talk of an independent ideology worked out by the working masses themselves within the process of their own movement. There are only two choices: bourgeois ideology or socialist ideology. There is no middle path (for humankind has not worked out any 'third' ideology; moreover, in a society torn by class conflict there cannot be any kind of ideology that is non-class or above-class). Thus, *any* belittlement of socialist ideology, *any deviation* from it at all strengthens bourgeois ideology. People talk about spontaneity. But the *spontaneous* development of the workers' movement leads precisely toward its subordination to bourgeois ideology...for the spontaneous workers' movement is trade unionism...and trade unionism means the ideological enslavement of the workers to the bourgeoisie. Therefore, our task, the task of social democracy, is to *battle spontaneity*, to *divert* the workers' movement away from these spontaneous trade unionist strivings that lead it under the wing of the bourgeoisie, and to [instead] attract [the workers' movement] under the wing of revolutionary social democracy....

But why—the reader asks—does the spontaneous movement, a movement along the line of least resistance, lead in fact to domination by bourgeois ideology? For the simple reason that bourgeois ideology...is much older than socialist ideology, because [therefore] it has been worked out from all angles, because it has at its disposal *immeasurably* greater resources for its dissemination. The younger the socialist movement is in any given country, the more energetically must the struggle be waged against all attempts to strengthen non-socialist ideology, the more necessary does it become to warn the workers against the bad counsel of those whose cry out against "the exaggerations of the conscious element."

III: Trade Unionist and Social Democratic Politics

...We have already demonstrated how the "economists" while they do not completely reject "politics" instead simply and consistently stray away from a social democratic conception of politics into a trade-unionist one....

Political Agitation and Its Narrowing by the Economists

...Social democracy leads the working class struggle not just for improvement of the conditions under which [the workers] sell their labor, but also for the destruction of the social conditions that force the have-nots to sell themselves to the rich. Social democracy conceives of the working class not just in terms of its relationship to a given group of entrepreneurs, but in its relationship to all classes of modern society and to the government—and as an organized political force. Thus, social democrats must not limit themselves only to the economic struggle; and they must not allow themselves to be dragged into an almost exclusive focus on exposing economic [exploitation of the workers]. We must actively take up the political education of the working class and the development of its political awareness....

The question arises, what should the political education [of the masses] consist of? Is it enough to limit ourselves to propagandizing the idea of the hostility of the working class to the autocracy? Of course not. It is not sufficient merely to *explain* the political oppression of the workers (just as it is not sufficient merely to explain to the workers the irreconcilable nature of their interests and those of the owners). It is necessary [also] to carry out agitation in connection with every concrete example of [the workers'] oppression (just as we have begun to do with regard to concrete examples of economic oppression). Since *this* oppression [political rather than economic] falls upon the greatest diversity of social classes, and since it is apparent in the most varied areas of life and activity—professional, civic, private, family, religious, scientific, and so on—is it not evident that *we shall not be carrying out our mission* to develop the political consciousness of the workers if we do not *take upon ourselves* the organization of [efforts to] *expose all aspects of the political* [oppressiveness] of the autocracy? After all, in order to carry out agitation in response to concrete examples of oppression, it is necessary to [clearly] expose these examples (just as it was necessary to expose factory abuses in order to carry on economic agitation)....

The Working Class as the Vanguard Fighter for Democracy

...Class political consciousness may be brought to the workers *only from outside*—that is, from outside the economic struggle, outside the sphere of relations between workers and owners. The only place from which this knowledge can come is from the sphere of relations of *all* classes and [social] layers to the state and government, [from] the nexus of interrelations among *all* classes. Therefore, when one is asked what is to be done in order to bring political knowledge to the workers, the answer cannot be... [simply] "Go among the workers." To bring political knowledge *to the workers* the social democrats must *go among all classes of the population*, must send detachments...to all *sides*....

IV: The Amateurishness of the Economists and the Organization of Revolutionaries

Organization of Workers and Organization of Revolutionaries

A social democrat who understands the political struggle as simply an "economic struggle with the owners and the government" will, naturally enough, conceive of the "organization of revolutionaries" as—more or less—an "organization of workers." And this is what actually happens, so that when speaking about [questions of] organization we are literally speaking different languages. In fact, I can recall a conversation with a reasonably consistent Economist whom I had not known previously. We were talking about a pamphlet entitled "Who Will Carry Out the Political Revolution? [*Kto sovershit politicheskuiu revoliutsiiu?*]." We quickly agreed that the pamphlet's main deficiency was that it ignored the question of organization. It seemed that we were firmly of one mind, but as the conversation progressed it became clear that we were talking about different things entirely. [The Economist started] accusing me of ignoring strike funds, mutual aid societies, and the like, but I had in mind the organization of revolutionaries—[which is] absolutely necessary for "accomplishing" the political revolution. And as soon as our differences became apparent I don't think there was a single thing at all about which I was in agreement with this "economist."

What was the source of our disagreement? It was precisely this: regardless of whether we are talking about organizational issues or political ones, the "economists" are always slipping away from social democracy and into trade unionism. The political struggle of social democracy is much broader and more complex than the economic struggle that pits the workers against their bosses and the authorities. In just the same way (indeed, because of this), the organization of the revolutionary Social Democratic Party must also be of a *different sort* than the organization of workers. First of all, the workers must be organized by trade; second, their organizations must be as broad as possible; third, they must be as unconspiratorial as possible (I am speaking here and elsewhere, of course, only about autocratic Russia). In contrast, the organization of revolutionaries must encompass first and foremost people who are revolutionary activists by trade (which is why I speak of an organization of *revolutionaries*, meaning revolutionary social democrats). Given that all members of the organization will share this general characteristic, *we must completely erase all distinction among them as to which is a worker and which an intellectual*, not to mention distinctions of trade among them. This organization definitely must not be very broad, and it must be as secret as possible....

In countries with political freedom, the distinction between a trade organization and a political one is perfectly clear, as is the distinction between trade unionism and social democracy. Of course, the relationship of the latter to the former will inevitably take different forms in different countries, depending on [relevant] historical, legal, and other conditions. They might be more or less close or complex....But in free countries there is never any conversation about them being basically the same thing. However, in Russia the oppressiveness of the autocracy immediately wipes out all distinctions between social democratic organization and labor unions, because any and all labor unions and any and all [organized] circles are forbidden, for the primary manifestation and weapon of the workers' economic struggle—the strike—is a criminal (and sometimes even a political) act! Thus, our circumstances, on the one hand, very much "push" those workers leading the economic struggle into political issues while, on the other hand, they "push" social democrats to mix trade unionism with social democratism....

The moral to be drawn here is simple: if we start by firmly establishing a strong organization of revolutionaries, then we can guarantee the stability of the movement overall and bring to fruition the goals both of social democracy and of the trade union movement. But if we start with a broader worker movement, one that is supposedly more "accessible" to the masses (but, in fact, just more accessible to the gendarmes, thereby making revolutionaries more accessible to the police), then we shall realize neither of these goals...and, because of the fragmented nature [of our movement] we will only be giving the masses over to trade unions of the Zubatov and Ozerov type....

...I affirm: 1) That no revolutionary organization can be durable without a stable organization of leaders to preserve continuity; 2) That the greater the number of the masses who are attracted in spontaneous fashion to the struggle—who form the basis of the movement and who participate in it—then the more urgent does the need become for such an organization and the more solid must such an organization be (for it also becomes easier for the demagogues to attract the undeveloped stratum of the masses); 3) That such an organization must consist chiefly of persons engaged in revolutionary activity as their profession; 4) That in an autocratic country, the more we *narrow* the membership of such an organization to the participation only of persons for whom revolutionary activity is their profession and who have received professional training in the art of struggle against the political police, then the harder will it be [for the authorities] "to fish out" such an organization; and 5) The *broader* will the roster become of persons both from the working class and other social classes who are participating in the movement and actively working for it.

...If we rely on a broad organization we shall never be able to achieve the necessary level of conspiratorial work; and without this one cannot even talk about waging a solid and continuous struggle against the government. But the concentration of all conspiratorial functions in the hands of the smallest possible number of professional revolutionaries does not at all mean that these few will "think for everyone" or that the crowd will not take part in *the movement*. Quite the opposite, the crowd will itself produce these professional revolutionaries—and in ever-increasing numbers—because the crowd will realize that it is not sufficient to simply have a few students or working men—veterans of the economic struggle—come together in a "committee"; [they will understand instead] that it takes years to turn oneself into a professional revolutionary; and so the crowd will start to think not only of amateurish methods, but of this kind of training instead. The centralization of the conspiratorial functions *of the organization* does not at all mean the centralization of all functions *of the movement*. The active participation by the very widest number of the masses in illegal literature will not diminish, but will *increase* tenfold because a dozen or so professional revolutionaries will centralize the conspiratorial functions of this enterprise. Only in this way shall we get to a point where the reading of illegal literature, contributing to it, and even distributing it *will all cease to be conspiratorial work*, for the police will soon realize the absurdity and the impossibility of pursuing through legal and administrative channels every publication of which there will be thousands of copies. And this concerns not only the press, but every function of the movement, even demonstrations.... The centralization of the conspiratorial functions of the organization of revolutionaries will not weaken but will enrich the breadth and content of the activity of a whole mass of other organizations that are geared toward the general public and are therefore much less formalized and less conspiratorial: including workers' trade unions, workers' circles for self-education and the reading of illegal literature, socialist circles, and also democratic circles in *all* other strata of the population, and so on. These kinds of circles, unions, and organizations are necessary everywhere and in the *absolute greatest* numbers, with the greatest diversity of functions; but it would be absurd and dangerous to *mingle* them with the organizations of revolutionaries, to destroy the barrier between them, to extinguish in the [minds of] the masses their already incredibly faint awareness that in order to "serve" the mass movement we need people who specially and wholly devote themselves to social democratic activity—and that to make a professional revolutionary of oneself takes patience and persistence.

Yes, this awareness is indeed incredibly faint. Our primary sin in terms of organization is that *with our amateurishness we have denigrated the prestige of the revolutionary* in [Russia]. Limp and shaky on questions of theory; with a narrow viewpoint; reliant on the spontaneity of the masses to justify his own apathy; more resembling a trade-union secretary than a tribune of the people; incapable of putting forward a broad and bold plan, one that would earn the respect even of our opponents; inexperienced and clumsy in practicing his trade—the struggle with the political police: Excuse me! Such a person is not a revolutionary, but just some kind of miserable amateur.

Nobody [within our movement] should take offense at my sharp comments, for when I speak of a lack of preparedness, I speak most of all about myself. I worked in a circle that undertook very broad, all-encompassing tasks—and all us, the members of this circle, suffered to the point of illness because we knew we were showing ourselves to be amateurs at that very historical moment when it could have been said—to adapt a well-known saying: give us an organization of revolutionaries and we will turn Russia upside down! And the more I have since thought about the burning shame I felt at that time, the angrier I have become with these pseudo social democrats who by their teachings bring disgrace to the rank of the revolutionary, who do not understand that our task is not to help lower the revolutionary to the rank of an amateur but to *elevate* the amateurs to [the rank of] revolutionaries....

"Conspiratorial" Organization and "Democratism"

...The objection will be raised that such a powerful and strictly secret organization, one that concentrates in its hands all the threads of conspiratorial activity, one that is highly centralized...may too easily throw itself into a premature attack, may carelessly push the movement [to act] before [the necessary wider levels of] political discontent [have been reached], before the ferment and anger of the working class [has matured]. We reply: abstractly speaking, it cannot be denied, of course, that a militant organization *could* throw itself into an ill-conceived battle that *could* end in a defeat—one that might have been avoided in different circumstances. But we cannot limit ourselves to abstract reasoning when looking at this issue. It is possible, speaking abstractly, for any battle at all to end in defeat, and there is no way to *reduce* this possibility except through organized preparation for battle. If we [avoid abstractions and] deal instead with the concrete realities of the current Russian situation, then one has to come to the more optimistic conclusion that a solid revolutionary organization is absolutely indispensable [both] for giving stability to the movement and to *prevent* it from carrying out ill-conceived attacks. Precisely now, when there is no such organization, and when the revolutionary movement is growing rapidly and spontaneously *we already see* two opposite extremes (which, not surprisingly, "meet"). [These are] the completely ill-founded "economism" with its doctrine of moderation; and the equally ill-founded "excitative terror" which strives "to create artificially the symptoms of the end-stages of a [revolution] that is currently developing and becoming stronger, [but which is still] nearer its beginnings than its end" ([Vera Zasulich] in "Zaria")....*Already there exist* social democrats who fail to resist these extremes. This is hardly surprising, because—among other reasons—the "economic struggle against the owners and the government" will *never* be enough for a revolutionary, and opposite extremes will always appear here and there. Only a centralized and militant organization—one that persistently follows social democratic policies and satisfies, so to speak, all revolutionary instincts and strivings—is capable of protecting the movement from wrong-headed attacks and also of preparing an attack that promises success.

We face yet another criticism—that our views on organization contradict "the democratic principle."...Let us look more closely at this "principle" put forward by the "economists." Everyone will agree, no doubt, that "the principle of broad democracy" requires the two following conditions: first, complete openness, and, second, that all [offices and] functions be decided by election. Without openness it would be silly to talk about democracy at all, and we mean openness that is not limited just to the members of the organization. We call the organization of the German Social Democratic Party democratic because everything in it is done openly, even the sessions of the Party Congress. But no one will call an organization democratic when it is [necessarily] sealed off from all non-members by a cloak of secrecy. So let us ask—what sense is there in promoting the "principle of broad democracy" when the basic condition underlying this principle [that of openness] *is impossible* for a secret organization *to fulfill?* The "principle of broad [democracy]" thus turns out to be simply a resonant but empty phrase....

Things are no better when we look at the second condition of democratism—elections. In countries with political freedom this condition makes perfect sense. "Everyone who accepts the principles of the Party program and supports the Party as best he can is considered a member" says the first paragraph of the organizational by-laws of the German Social Democratic Party. And since the whole political arena is open for all to see—just like the stage before a theater audience—so can everyone see how someone accepts, rejects, supports, or opposes [a given position]. All such things are well-known to all and sundry simply by reading the papers or by [attending] popular assemblies. Everyone knows that a given political figure started out from such-and-such a position, went through whatever changes, responded in this way or that to a difficult situation, and distinguishes himself by this or that set of qualities. And so it is only natural that *all* members of the Party may make an informed choice and elect or not elect a particular person to a particular post. [Similarly, the fact that] anyone...can oversee every step taken by a Party member...creates a self-mechanism akin to that which in biology is called "survival of the fittest." The "natural selection" provided by complete openness, the electoral process, and general public oversight guarantees that every activist finds his appropriate place in the end, gets the most suitable role based on his strengths and abilities, suffers all the consequences of his own mistakes, and demonstrates publicly his ability to realize these mistakes and to correct them in the future.

Now try putting this picture into the frame of our [Russian] autocracy! Is it conceivable that [here] everyone "who accepts the principles of the Party program and supports the Party as best he can" could remain informed about every step taken by a revolutionary conspirator? That they could all elect this or that revolutionary—when the revolutionary is *obliged* in the interests of work to hide his very identity from 90 percent of the people? Think for just a moment...and you will see that "broad democratism" of Party organization in the darkness of the autocracy, under the "[artificial] selection" of the gendarmes is nothing other than an *empty and dangerous toy*. I say "empty" because, in fact, no revolutionary organization of any sort has ever put this *broad* democratism into practice [under the conditions of autocracy] and never could, no matter how much it wished to. I say "dangerous" because any attempt to put "broad democratism" into practice would only help the police to expose [us]; would prolong indefinitely the current amateurishness [of the movement]; would distract...[revolutionary activists] from the serious, urgent work involved in transforming themselves into professional revolutionaries and [would burden them instead] with the "paperwork" involved in setting up elections. This "game of democratism" can develop only abroad—among people who are unable to find themselves real and vital work, in [their] various little groups.

...The single serious organizational principle for activists in our movement must be the strictest [level of] conspiracy, the strictest selection of members, [and] the preparation of professional revolutionaries. Once these qualities are achieved then we are assured of something greater than "democratism"—namely: complete comradely confidence among revolutionaries. And this is even more absolutely necessary among us [than in other countries] for in Russia there can be no question at all of replacing this [loyalty] with any general public oversight. But it would be a great mistake to assume that the impossibility of actual "democratic" oversight thereby renders the members of revolutionary organization beyond any accountability at all ....[On the contrary, these revolutionaries will] feel their *responsibility* vividly, knowing by their own experience that an organization of genuine revolutionaries will stop at nothing to rid itself of a substandard member. Moreover, there is a well-developed and time-honored system of thinking among Russian (and international) revolutionary circles that mercilessly punishes any and all slacking-off from the responsibilities of comradeship (indeed, "democratism"—real, not toy democratism—is a constituent part of this larger system of comradeship). Take all of this under consideration, and you will understand that all these conversations and resolutions about our [supposed] "anti-democratic tendencies" reek with the musty odor of outsiders playing at being generals.

Local and All-Russian Work

...There is one more question that is frequently raised and deserves examining in detail. This concerns the relationship between local and all-Russian work. Some have voiced a worry that the formation of a centralized organization might shift the center of gravity towards all-Russian work in general, and away from local control; [and they worry] that this may threaten, in turn, to undermine the [the movement's] connection with the mass of workers and generally weaken the solidity of local agitation. We answer that our movement has suffered in recent years precisely because of the fact that local activists are totally swamped by local work and that it is therefore necessary to shift the center of gravity towards all-Russian work. Such a shift will not weaken but will strengthen our ties with [the working mass] as well as the stability of local agitation.

> **GLOSSARY**
>
> **Saint Petersburg industrial war of 1896:** Lenin's name for a textile workers' strike that lasted more than three weeks and was suppressed by the government of Czar Nicholas II
>
> **Vera Zasulich:** Russian revolutionary (1849–1919), who contributed to the publication "Zaria" (sunrise, or morning star; sometimes Mother Russia)

Document Analysis

The full Russian version of *What Is to Be Done?* runs to about 150 pages arranged in five sections, all of which treat in one way or another the question of how best to organize for a successful Socialist revolution in Russia (as opposed to in other countries). It was written in dialog with other Socialist pamphleteers of the time—that is, with other would-be leaders or spokespersons for working-class movements, both Russian and foreign. Writing in a fairly polemical style, and often naming names, Lenin takes his opponents to task for one or another fault in their basic approach and lays out what he believes is the one proper path forward. The excerpts presented here represent the heart of Lenin's arguments and are drawn from sections 2–4. Sections 1 and 5 deal, respectively, with trends in Marxist criticism and ideas for establishing an all-Russian political newspaper.

"The Spontaneity of the Masses and the Consciousness of Social Democracy" proposes and analyzes a critical distinction between two aspects of the overall struggle for worker liberation: "spontaneity" and "consciousness." Scholars have debated how best to translate and understand these and other key Russian terms—and by extension how best to understand Lenin himself. In general as well as in the context of Lenin's analysis, "spontaneity" connotes actions carried out without forethought or planning—emotional responses, gut reactions, and the like. They are often exhibited by crowds or unorganized groups. The reactions of masses of workers to everyday problems and oppressions are often spontaneous, as in a demonstration, riot, or act of sabotage carried out by workers against their employers and under the influence of anger and raised emotions. "Consciousness" on the other hand, connotes clarity and purposiveness, and it is accompanied and informed by a proper understanding of the whole structure of forces and circumstances at play. "Conscious" actions are carefully planned and done with a specific, achievable end result in mind. Lenin's twin goals in *What Is to Be Done?* are to define the two tendencies in all their details, varieties, and ramifications, and then to promote the idea that only through conscious action and proper organization could the goal of worker liberation be achieved. Spontaneity is presented more negatively. At times it is an indispensable but volatile force—something that, when properly controlled and directed, can achieve important results. More often, Lenin views spontaneity as a blind alley and critical weakness in the movement.

In "The Beginning of the Spontaneous Upsurge," Lenin begins with a few examples of "spontaneity" and "consciousness." He notes that workers' own actions are usually spontaneous, but at the same time he suggests that spontaneous actions can develop eventually into at least the "embryo" of conscious ones. Thus, workers might be expected eventually to achieve a level of consciousness themselves. However, Lenin also seems to reject this thought, stating instead that workers' actions ultimately remain spontaneous. For example, in the last paragraph of this section, Lenin asserts that true social democratic consciousness can be brought to the workers only "from outside"—that is, from dedicated revolutionary intellectuals—and that it can never develop out of workers' own experiences. This ambiguity in Lenin's thinking provides material for those who see him as an elitist and would-be tyrant as well as for those who see him instead as genuine supporter of the interests of the working masses.

In this same section, Lenin makes the first of numerous contrasts between "trade unionist struggles" and "social democratic" ones. Shortly thereafter, he compares "trade union consciousness" with "social democratic consciousness." In each case, social democratic consciousness is presented as the higher form. Roughly speaking, trade union consciousness corresponds to spontaneous movements. Trade union consciousness focuses on the (spontaneous) short-term economic concerns of workers, such as pay and working conditions. The ultimate purpose of trade unions is to negotiate with—and within—the capitalist system, not to overthrow it. Trade union goals are thus inherently nonrevolutionary. They are also economic, not political. It was Lenin's conviction as a Marxist that true worker liberation required not only the economic adjustments that workers wanted (such as pay raises or shorter hours) but also a worldwide political revolution that would usher in a total transformation of the economic system by abolishing private ownership of the means of production.

Since Lenin viewed most workers as "capable only of working out trade union consciousness" he identified a compelling need for the input of revolutionary intellectuals. Around 1900 these men and women had typically come *not* from the working class but, like Lenin, from the property-owning class (the bourgeoisie). Lenin calls these revolutionary intellectuals the "social democrats" and he sees them as the only bearers of true political consciousness. Without them, the workers remain stuck forever either at trade union consciousness or mere "embryonic" forms of social democratic class consciousness. With them, however, real change is possible, even inevitable. The question remains, however, what is to be the form and organization of the merging of these two elements? Should the revolutionary social democrats lead the workers? Or was this to be a more equal partnership? What would the roles of each be? Lenin returns to these questions throughout *What Is to Be Done?*

Rabochaia mysl', translated as *The Workers' Thought*, was the name of a radical newspaper of the time, and Lenin critiques its stance in this subsection. Lenin again shoots down any questions about the workers' developing an "independent ideology" for their own liberation. There are, he asserts, only two possible ideologies: bourgeois and Socialist. The first leads to oppression of the workers, the second to their liberation. Any effort by the workers to find their own "middle path" simply plays into the hands of autocracy and the employers. Statements like these have convinced many observers that from the start Lenin was completely dismissive of the workers and ready to use them as a means to his ends; that he was at heart undemocratic, paternalistic, and even dictatorial—characteristics that would later describe the Soviet regime.

Lenin defends himself from these charges at several points. In a lengthy footnote to this section (not reproduced), he argues that the workers *can and will* play a vital role in their liberation, but not *as* workers. Rather, he places his hopes on individual members of the working class who—through experience, hard work, and persistent study—will gain a sufficient level of education and themselves become revolutionary intellectuals and true social democrats. He cites as examples the French Socialist Pierre-Joseph Proudhon (a former print worker) and the German Socialist Wilhelm Weitling (a former tailor). Lenin returns to this theme later in the excerpts provided here.

In the section titled "Trade Unionist and Social Democratic Politics," Lenin again contrasts the two aspects of the workers' struggle. By "economists" Lenin does not mean what is now commonly understood by the term but rather a group of moderate Marxists, including Russian social democrats then living in exile in Europe. The term *economists* derives from the group's preference for focusing on precisely those same worker economic demands and concerns that Lenin criticizes as "spontaneous." Unlike Lenin, the "economists" believed that spontaneous worker action could grow into a genuine revolutionary movement that would sweep away the Russian autocracy and usher in a period of liberal bourgeois capitalism that would itself eventually sow the seeds of Socialist revolution. In comparison with Lenin, the economists generally took a longer-term view of the revolutionary movement and placed greater emphasis on following and supporting, rather than controlling and leading, the spontaneous actions of the workers. Lenin too, like any Marxist, accepted that the coming of Socialism would have to be preceded by a period of capitalism. But to a greater degree than many of his contemporaries, he maintained that capitalism had already taken hold in Russia, and he had already argued that point in detail in *The Development of Capitalism in Russia*.

In the subsection, Political Agitation and Its Narrowing by the Economists, Lenin continues to distinguish between social democracy as he understands it and economism. Economism has a "narrow" viewpoint focused on workers' day-to-day economic struggles, while social democracy assumes a broader and more commanding perspective. Social democracy takes into account the full range and structure of class relations, and it emphasizes the importance of the political struggle against the Russian autocracy. Lenin urges social democrats not to lapse into economism. He calls for specific forms of propaganda and education aimed at opening workers' eyes to the larger issues and ideas of social democracy.

By calling the working class the "vanguard" Lenin emphasizes the critical role the workers themselves will play in their own liberation. But then he restates that the workers cannot develop "class political consciousness" by themselves or from within the sphere of their own economic interests and struggles. They must see their struggle in the much larger context of class relations; that is, from the viewpoint of intellectual Marxists or social democrats.

In the critically important subsection, Organization of Workers and Organization of Revolutionaries, Lenin further pursues his division of revolutionary activity into two camps: the conscious "political struggle of social democracy" versus the spontaneous and trade unionist "economic struggle that pits the workers against their bosses and the authorities." Thereafter, he arrives at the heart of his argument, or at least the part that has attracted the greatest attention. This is the question of how best to *organize* revolutionary activity.

Lenin makes two points. First, he argues that both camps have an important role to play, although he clearly considers the "political struggle of social democracy" to be the primary one. Second, he argues that because the roles are *different*, each must be *differently organized*. Workers' organizations should be "by trade" "broad" and "un-conspiratorial" meaning that they should operate openly. But the organization of revolutionaries, he asserts, must be very different. It must "not be very broad" and it should be "as secret as possible." The organization must comprise "first and foremost people who are revolutionary activists by trade"— that is, persons engaged full-time in revolution. Later in the same section and then repeatedly throughout much of the document, Lenin refers to these persons as "professional revolutionaries." This term has become almost iconic in the literature about Lenin and *What Is to Be Done?*

"Professional revolutionaries" as Lenin explains, are more than mere full-time activists. They are also revolutionary intellectuals; they are men and women from any background, including the working masses, who have by experience and study made themselves experts in class theory and Socialist literature. Some scholars have argued that the word and concept of a "professional" does not translate perfectly from Russian to English and that this should be noted particularly in regard to Lenin's famous phrase. In English, the word generally refers to persons engaged in certain fields of work, such as law, medicine, or higher education. In Russian, it can sometimes be used more broadly in the sense of a trade or skill. An alternative translation, "revolutionary by trade" has recently been offered.

For critics of Lenin and of the Soviet system more generally, the seeds of future tyranny may be found exactly here in Lenin's organizational blueprint for a small, compact, secretive party of "professional revolutionaries"—a party that is closed off to the broad mass of workers and certain of its own status as the correct and politically conscious leader of a wider spontaneous movement. Add to this Lenin's conviction that the spontaneous workers' movement, if left to its own devices, would head into defeat and disaster. In light of Lenin's biases, many of his critics have identified in *What Is to Be Done?* a formula destined to eventuate in a highly undemocratic system of leaders (the Bolsheviks) and followers (the workers).

Lenin does not see it this way, however. Much of the rest of *What Is to Be Done?* counters arguments of this sort, which had been leveled at him already from various quarters. In this section he takes on some of these criticisms. In the paragraph beginning "in countries with political freedom" Lenin argues that while an open party organization might be appropriate in other places, in the autocratic Russia of 1902 it is not. Openness would simply make it easier for the police to infiltrate and break up social democratic circles, dooming the movement to failure. Moreover, unlike the situation in western Europe, in Russia most public expressions of the workers' spontaneous and economic struggles (such as strikes and demonstrations) were illegal, as was also true for "conscious" political revolutionary activity. Thus, the two struggles tended to be easily confused with each other. Lenin maintains they need to be kept separate, both conceptually and organizationally. Leadership by conscious and conspiratorial social democrats is also necessary to thwart the drift into spontaneity, which Lenin asserts would "only be giving the masses over to trade unions of the Zubatov and Ozerov type."

After restating his convictions about party organization in five short statements of principle, Lenin attends to another criticism: that his plan to concentrate "all conspiratorial functions in the hands of the smallest possible number of professional revolutionaries" will mean that "these few 'will think for everyone'" and take over the entire movement. Lenin counters that without a stable and professional organization to guide it, the movement will inevitably fail. Moreover, the masses will, in fact, participate more, not less, because the "professional revolutionary" will provide a kind of highly respected role model that ever-increasing numbers of ordinary workers will emulate. He continues, however, to speak of the need for a barrier between the mass movement and the organization of professional social democrats.

Lenin rejects two further criticisms. The first is that the organization he envisions—one that is "powerful and strictly secret" and "concentrates in its hands all the threads of conspiratorial activity" and "is highly centralized"—may ruin the revolution by acting before the masses of workers are sufficiently ready to back them up. The danger, he says, is the reverse. By acting without proper organizational leadership, the working masses themselves risk a devastating loss. He condemns the economists again and also "excitative" terrorists—groups who resort to spontaneous acts of violence and terror intended to bring about revolution before the objective conditions for it were ready.

Lenin then returns to charges that he is being antidemocratic. He expands on his ideas about the unsuitability of open and democratic practices in the context of the autocratic political climate of czarist Russia. How, he asks, can social democrats talk and vote openly, even among themselves, when everything they do is illegal and they must hide their very identities from the czarist authorities?

In the subsection concerning Local and All-Russian Work, Lenin deflects the concern that centralization of social democratic organization will undermine local control and activity and thus place excessive power in the hands of professional revolutionaries. He answers that centralization will instead free up local activists for more productive work and improve the effectiveness of local agitation.

Essential Themes
What Is to Be Done? appeared at a critical moment in the history of the Russian labor movement as well as in the history of the RSDLP. In the very early 1900s the conditions for social revolution in Russia were developing rapidly. Industrialization, although it was still nascent, had expanded significantly, especially under the influence of the Russian minister of finance, Count Sergey Yulyevich Witte, who had pursued a major expansion of railroads and other industries. Foreign investment capital had begun to pour into the country. The number of industrial workers, or urban proletarians, in Russia had reached two to three million (out of a total population of about 160 million). Most of these workers were concentrated in the few large cities, including Moscow and Saint Petersburg, where conditions were particularly oppressive and exploitative. Worker unrest festered, and workers began to organize. The government responded only with minor concessions, such as an 1897 law that established a maximum 11 1/2-hour workday in larger factories. Meanwhile, worker discontent and demands continued to rise.

Beginning in the 1880s, a growing number of Russian intellectuals had begun to look at these developments through the lens of Marxist philosophy, which initially had been expounded abroad. The explosive pamphlet *The Communist Manifesto*, by the German thinkers Karl Marx and Friedrich Engels, had been published in 1848. Marxism—soon dubbed "scientific Socialism"—viewed all history as a struggle between economic classes, primarily between those who owned the means of production and those who did not. Developed further in Marx's other writings, the theory offered a grand analysis of industrial capitalism and predicted its inevitable demise at the hands of class-conscious proletarians who would destroy the very foundation of the system that oppressed them.

Convinced that the march of history was on their side, Lenin and other members of the RSDLP sought to introduce into the broad workers' movement the concepts and ideals of Marxism, but they did not all agree on the appropriate methods for doing so. By far the largest and leading Socialist party in Europe at the time was the German Social Democratic Party, which in most respects provided a model for the much smaller Russian group. Matters were complicated, however, by the differences between the German and Russian political environments. German intellectual Socialists benefited from relatively advanced political freedoms that allowed the Social Democratic Party to participate openly in the political process. German industrial workers could legally unionize, demonstrate, and read and share ideas without necessarily bringing on government reprisal.

None of this was true in autocratic czarist Russia when Lenin wrote *What Is to Be Done?* All political power emanated from the czar. At least prior to 1905, Russia had neither a parliament nor a constitution. Political parties were illegal, and their members faced harassment and arrest at every turn; moreover, the legal system did not recognize basic civil rights. Workers could not legally organize, demonstrate, or strike. Between 1898 and 1903, Russia experimented briefly with so-called "police unions" which were groups of workers authorized by the state and under police control. The intent behind allowing these unions was to undermine or control working-class movements rather than to achieve significant change, however. To Lenin, all of these circumstances meant that social democracy would have to work very differently in Russia than elsewhere. In particular, it would have to be differently organized, which is the main theme of *What Is to Be Done?*

The title of Lenin's work is borrowed from the identically titled 1863 novel by Nikolay Gavrilovich Chernyshevsky. A leading radical thinker in his own right, Chernyshevsky wrote in the immediate aftermath of the epochal 1861 emancipation of Russia's serfs by Czar Alexander II. This event—and the difficulties and discontent it engendered among the newly liberated peasants—provided the context within which a generation of pre-Marxist Russian radicals wrote and worked. Chernyshevsky was one of the founders of an unsuccessful Russian revolutionary movement known as Populism or Narodism, which advocated agitation among the peasants in order to weld them into a revolutionary force for the overthrow of the czarist regime and its replacement with a decentralized system based on peasant communes. The movement largely burned out in the summer of 1874. Although Lenin later criticized Narodism as utopian and unachievable, he was greatly impressed with Chernyshevsky's depiction of the revolutionary hero as a practical and utterly dedicated individual who through immense personal effort could affect the course of history.

The ideas put forth in *What Is to Be Done?* split the RSDLP into two factions (effectively in 1903 and finally and officially in 1912). Those who rejected Lenin's ideas—preferring instead a broader and more open movement and a more orthodox interpretation of Marxism—became known as Mensheviks ("minoritarians"), while Lenin's supporters became the Bolsheviks ("majoritarians"). *What Is To Be Done?* also helped shape the subsequent form and function of the Bolshevik Party itself, thus laying at least some of the groundwork for the Bolshevik seizure of power in 1917.

Beyond this effect, however, historians are not of one mind when assessing the document's overall importance and impact. While many argue that it remains the single clearest expression of Lenin's basic political ideology and also serves as a key for understanding the eventual Soviet system he founded, others have pointed out that Lenin himself rarely, if ever, referred back to this work after about 1907; that his thought underwent significant modifications thereafter; that many aspects of subsequent Bolshevik Party practice and organization are not covered here; and that the pamphlet in general should be seen as a specific response to particular debates and circumstances current only in 1901–1902 and not as a timeless and essential statement of Bolshevik ideology.

—Brian Bonhomme, PhD

Bibliography and Further Reading

Haimson, Leopold H. *The Russian Marxists and the Origins of Bolshevism*. Cambridge, Mass.: Harvard University Press, 1955.

———. "Russian Workers' Political and Social Identities: The Role of Social Representations in the Interaction between Members of the Labor Movement and the Social Democratic Intelligentsia." In *Workers and Intelligentsia in Late Imperial Russia: Realities, Representations, Reflections*, ed. Reginald Zelnik. Berkeley: University of California Press, 1999.

Harding, Neil. *Lenin's Political Thought: Theory and Practice in the Democratic Revolution*. London: Macmillan, 1977.

Lih, Lars T. *Lenin Rediscovered: What Is to Be Done? in Context*. Boston: Brill Academic Publishers, 2005.

"Marxism and Workers' Organisation: Writings of Marxists on Trade Unions, the General Strike, Soviets and Working Class Organisation." Marxists Internet Archive Web site. http://marxists.org/subject/workers/index.htm.

Mayer, Robert. "Lenin and the Concept of the Professional Revolutionary." *History of Political Thought* 14, no. 2 (1993): 249–263.

Service, Robert. *Lenin: A Biography.* Cambridge, Mass.: Harvard University Press, 2000.

Schapiro, Leonard. "Lenin's Intellectual Formation and the Russian Revolutionary Background." In his *Russian Studies.* New York: Viking, 1987.

"Vladimir Lenin Works Index." Lenin Internet Archive Web site. http://marxists.org/archive/lenin/works/index.htm.

Panama Canal Treaty

Date: 1903
Authors: John Hay and Philippe-Jean Bunau-Varilla
Genre: Treaty

Summary Overview

Westerners had dreamed of building an interoceanic passage across the Isthmus of Panama ever since Vasco Núñez de Balboa crossed it in 1513. The emergence of the United States as an imperial power brought new urgency to the problem: the United States needed to protect its coastlines, and also needed a fast passage to allow its navy to move freely between the Atlantic and Pacific. In 1903, Theodore Roosevelt's administration offered the Colombian government $10 million in cash and an annual payment of $250,000 for a six-mile-wide strip across the Colombian province of Panama. The Colombian senate refused to ratify the treaty, believing that the payment was not high enough. Instead, Panamanian rebels conveniently proclaimed their independence from Colombia in the same year; the presence of ten U.S. warships offshore from Panama City prevented Colombia from sending in troops to put down the revolt. The United States immediately recognized the independent Republic of Panama, and what is commonly known as the Panama Canal Treaty was quickly ratified by the U.S. Senate.

The primary treaty negotiators were U.S. Secretary of State John Hay and a Frenchman, Philippe Bunau-Varilla, for Panama. Thus the treaty is sometimes called the Hay–Bunau-Varilla Treaty. It is worth noting that Bunau-Varilla owned most of the shares in an old French company that had bought the land coveted by the United States but had failed to build the canal. In other words, the signer of the treaty for Panama did not live there and would never set foot there again once the treaty was signed.

Defining Moment

American "gunboat diplomacy" in the affair was blatant, and Roosevelt faced a great deal of criticism. As his own Secretary of War Elihu Root joked, "Mr. President,…you [have been] accused of seduction…and proved that you were guilty of rape." In most respects, considering the poverty of an independent Panama, the treaty rendered Panama a de facto colony of the United States. This naturally created conflict; after riots in 1964, successive U.S. governments surrendered sovereignty over the Canal Zone. Panama has owned the canal and has controlled its profits since January 1, 2000.

Being a treaty, the document in question is not formally addressed to a particular audience. Figuratively speaking, the audiences are the governments of the United States and Panama and the businesses that were to operate in the Panama Canal Zone, as the treaty regulates the relations among them.

About the Authors

John Hay (1838–1905), the U.S. secretary of state, had been a private secretary to Abraham Lincoln and then pursued careers as a diplomat, writer, and businessman. Having supported the 1896 presidential campaign of William McKinley, he was appointed ambassador to the United Kingdom (1897) and then secretary of state (1898–1905). He generally had a freer rein in foreign policy under McKinley than under Theodore Roosevelt, who succeeded upon McKinley's assassination in 1901. In addition to the Panama Canal Treaty, he is known for the Hay Notes, calling for free trade with China (the Open Door policy), rather than its division into colonies. Hay initiated the custom of regular press conferences.

Philippe-Jean Bunau-Varilla (1859–1940), a French engineer, had been assigned by Ferdinand de Lesseps to lead the French project to build a canal across the Isthmus of Panama. After the project was canceled, in 1888, he spent 15 years trying to revive it in some form, seeking the assistance of France, Russia, and then the United States, in the hope of making good on the investors' lost investments. He ultimately convinced the United States to build a canal in Panama instead of Nicaragua, encouraged Panamanian revolutionaries to secede from Colombia, and negotiated the Panama Canal Treaty as the official envoy of the newly formed Republic of Panama. Bunau-Varilla was the principal author of the treaty.

HISTORICAL DOCUMENT

The United States of America and the Republic of Panama being desirous to insure the construction of a ship canal across the Isthmus of Panama to connect the Atlantic and Pacific oceans, and the Congress of the United States of America having passed an act approved June 28, 1902, in furtherance of that object, by which the President of the United States is authorized to acquire within a reasonable time the control of the necessary territory of the Republic of Colombia, and the sovereignty of such territory being actually vested in the Republic of Panama, the high contracting parties have resolved for that purpose to conclude a convention and have accordingly appointed as their plenipotentiaries,—

The President of the United States of America, John Hay, Secretary of State, and

The Government of the Republic of Panama, Philippe Bunau-Varilla, Envoy Extraordinary and Minister Plenipotentiary of the Republic of Panama, thereunto specially empowered by said government, who after communicating with each other their respective full powers, found to be in good and due form, have agreed upon and concluded the following articles:

ARTICLE I

The United States guarantees and will maintain the independence of the Republic of Panama.

ARTICLE II

The Republic of Panama grants to the United States in perpetuity the use, occupation and control of a zone of land and land under water for the construction maintenance, operation, sanitation and protection of said Canal of the width of ten miles extending to the distance of five miles on each side of the center line of the route of the Canal to be constructed; the said zone beginning in the Caribbean Sea three marine miles from mean low water mark and extending to and across the Isthmus of Panama into the Pacific ocean to a distance of three marine miles from mean low water mark with the proviso that the cities of Panama and Colón and the harbors adjacent to said cities, which are included within the boundaries of the zone above described, shall not be included within this grant. The Republic of Panama further grants to the United States in perpetuity the use, occupation and control of any other lands and waters outside of the zone above described which may be necessary and convenient for the construction, maintenance, operation, sanitation and protection of the said Canal or of any auxiliary canals or other works necessary and convenient for the construction, maintenance, operation, sanitation and protection of the said enterprise.

The Republic of Panama further grants in like manner to the United States in perpetuity all islands within the limits of the zone above described and in addition thereto the group of small islands in the Bay of Panama, named, Perico, Naos, Culebra and Flamenco.

ARTICLE III

The Republic of Panama grants to the United States all the rights, power and authority within the zone mentioned and described in Article II of this agreement and within the limits of all auxiliary lands and waters mentioned and described in said Article II which the United States would possess and exercise if it were the sovereign of the territory within which said lands and waters are located to the entire exclusion of the exercise by the Republic of Panama of any such sovereign rights, power or authority.

ARTICLE IV

As rights subsidiary to the above grants the Republic of Panama grants in perpetuity to the United States the right to use the rivers, streams, lakes and other bodies of water within its limits for navigation, the supply of water or water-power or other purposes, so far as the use of said rivers, streams, lakes and bodies of water and the waters thereof may be necessary and convenient for the construction, maintenance, operation, sanitation and protection of the said Canal.

ARTICLE V

The Republic of Panama grants to the United States in perpetuity a monopoly for the construction, maintenance and operation of any system of communication by means of canal or railroad across its territory between the Caribbean Sea and the Pacific Ocean.

ARTICLE VI

The grants herein contained shall in no manner invalidate the titles or rights of private land holders or owners of private property in the said zone or in or to any of the lands or waters granted to the United States by the provisions of any Article of this treaty, nor shall they interfere with the rights of way over the public roads passing through the said zone or over any of the said lands or waters unless said rights of way or private rights shall conflict with rights herein granted to the United States in which case. The rights of the United States shall be superior. All damages caused to the owners of private lands or private property of any kind by reason of the grants contained in this treaty or by reason of the operations of the United States, its agents or employees, or by reason of the construction, maintenance, operation, sanitation and protection of the said Canal or of the works of sanitation and protection herein provided for, shall be appraised and settled by a joint Commission appointed by the Governments of the United States and the Republic of Panama, whose decisions as to such damages shall be final and whose awards as to such damages shall be paid solely by the United States. No part of the work on said Canal or the Panama railroad or on any auxiliary works relating thereto and authorized by the terms of this treaty shall be prevented, delayed or impeded by or pending such proceedings to ascertain such damages. The appraisal of said private lands and private property and the assessment of damages to them shall be based upon their value before the date of this convention.

ARTICLE VII

The Republic of Panama grants to the United States within the limits of the cities of Panama and Colón and their adjacent harbors and within the territory adjacent thereto the right to acquire by purchase or by the exercise of the right of eminent domain, any lands, buildings, water rights or other properties necessary and convenient for the construction, maintenance, operation and protection of the Canal and of any works of sanitation, such as the collection and disposition of sewage and the distribution of water in the said cities of Panama and Colón, which in the discretion of the United States may be necessary and convenient for the construction, maintenance, operation, sanitation and protection of the said Canal and railroad. All such works of sanitation, collection and disposition of sewage and distribution of water in the cities of Panama and Colón shall be made at the expense of the United States, and the Government of the United States, its agents or nominees shall be authorized to impose and collect water rates and sewerage rates which shall be sufficient to provide for the payment of interest and the amortization of the principal of the cost of said works within a period of fifty years and upon the expiration of said term of fifty years the system of sewers and water works shall revert to and become the properties of the cities of Panama and Colón, respectively, and the use of the water shall be free to the inhabitants of Panama and Colón, except to the extent that water rates may be necessary for the operation and maintenance of said system of sewers and water.

The Republic of Panama agrees that the cities of Panama and Colón shall comply in perpetuity with the sanitary ordinances whether of a preventive or curative character prescribed by the United States and in case the Government of Panama is unable or fails in its duty to enforce this compliance by the cities of Panama and Colón with the sanitary ordinances of the United States the Republic of Panama grants to the United States the right and authority to enforce the same.

The same right and authority are granted to the United States for the maintenance of public order in the cities of Panama and Colón and the territories and harbors adjacent thereto in case the Republic of Panama should not be, in the judgment of the United States, able to maintain such order.

ARTICLE VIII

The Republic of Panama grants to the United States all rights which it now has or hereafter may acquire to the property of the New Panama Canal Company and the Panama Railroad Company as a result of the transfer of sovereignty from the Republic of Colombia to the Republic of Panama over the Isthmus of Panama and authorizes the New Panama Canal Company to sell and transfer to the United States its rights, privileges, properties and concessions as well as the Panama Railroad and all the shares or part of the shares of that company; lot the public lands situated outside of the zone described in Article II of this treaty now included in the concessions to both said enterprises and not required in the construction or operation of the Canal shall revert to the Republic of Panama except any property now owned by or in the possession of said companies within Panama or Colón or the ports or terminals thereof.

ARTICLE IX

The United States agrees that the ports at either entrance of the Canal and the waters thereof, and the Republic of Panama agrees that the towns of Panama and Colón shall be free for all time so that there shall not be imposed or collected custom house tolls, tonnage, anchorage, lighthouse, wharf, pilot, or quarantine dues or any other charges or taxes of any kind upon any vessel using or passing through the Canal or belonging to or employed by the United States, directly or indirectly, in connection with the construction, maintenance, operation, sanitation and protection of the main Canal, or auxiliary works, or upon the cargo, officers, crew, or passengers of any such vessels, except such tolls and charges as may be imposed by the United States for the use of the Canal and other works, and except tolls and charges imposed by the Republic of Panama upon merchandise destined to be introduced for the consumption of the rest of the Republic of Panama, and upon vessels touching at the ports of Colón and Panama and which do not cross the Canal.

The Government of the Republic of Panama shall have the right to establish in such ports and in the towns of Panama and Colón such houses and guards as it may deem necessary to collect duties on importations destined to other portions of Panama and to prevent contraband trade. The United States shall have the right to make use of the towns and harbors of Panama and Colón as places of anchorage, and for making repairs, for loading, unloading, depositing, or transshipping cargoes either in transit or destined for the service of the Canal and for other works pertaining to the Canal.

ARTICLE X

The Republic of Panama agrees that there shall not be imposed any taxes, national, municipal, departmental, or of any other class, upon the Canal, the railways and auxiliary works, tugs and other vessels employed in bye service of the Canal, store houses, work shops, offices, quarters for laborers, factories of all kinds, warehouses, wharves, machinery and other works, property, and effects appertaining to the Canal or railroad and auxiliary works, or their officers or employees, situated within the cities of Panama and Colón, and that there shall not be imposed contributions or charges of a personal character of any kind upon officers, employees, laborers, and other individuals in the service of the Canal and railroad and auxiliary works.

ARTICLE XI

The United States agrees that the official dispatches of the Government of the Republic of Panama shall be transmitted over any telegraph and telephone lines established for canal purposes and used for public and private business at rates not higher than those required from officials in the service of the United States.

ARTICLE XII

The Government of the Republic of Panama shall permit the immigration and free access to the lands and workshops of the Canal and its auxiliary works of all employees and workmen of whatever nationality under contract to work upon or seeking employment upon or in any wise connected with the said Canal and its auxiliary works, with their respective families, and all such persons shall be free and exempt from the military service of the Republic of Panama.

ARTICLE XIII

The United States may import at any time into the said zone and auxiliary lands, free of custom duties, imposts, taxes, or other charges, and without any restrictions, any and all vessels, dredges, engines, cars, machinery, tools, explosives, materials, supplies, and other articles necessary and convenient in the construction, maintenance, operation, sanitation and protection of the Canal and auxiliary works, and all provisions, medicines, clothing, supplies and other things necessary and convenient for the officers, employees, workmen and laborers in the service and employ of the United States and for their families. If any such articles are disposed of for use outside of the zone and auxiliary lands granted to the United States and within the territory of the Republic, they shall be subject to the same import or other duties as like articles imported under the laws of the Republic of Panama.

ARTICLE XIV

As the price or compensation for the rights, powers and privileges granted in this convention by the Republic of Panama to the United States, the Government of the United States agrees to pay to the Republic of Panama the sum of ten million dollars ($10,000,000) in gold coin of the United States on the exchange of the ratification of this convention and also an annual payment during the life of this convention of two hundred and fifty thousand dollars ($250,000) in like gold coin, beginning nine years after the date aforesaid.

The provisions of this Article shall be in addition to all other benefits assured to the Republic of Panama under this convention.

But no delay or difference of opinion under this Article or any other provisions of this treaty shall affect or interrupt the full operation and effect of this convention in all other respects.

ARTICLE XV

The joint commission referred to in Article VI shall be established as follows:

The President of the United States shall nominate two persons and the President of the Republic of Panama shall nominate two persons and they shall proceed to a decision; but in case of disagreement of the Commission (by reason of their being equally divided in conclusion) an umpire shall be appointed by the two Governments who shall render the decision. In the event of the death, absence, or incapacity of a Commissioner or Umpire, or of his omitting, declining or ceasing to act, his place shall be filled by the appointment of another person in the manner above indicated. All decisions by a majority of the Commission or by the Umpire shall be final.

ARTICLE XVI

The two Governments shall make adequate provision by future agreement for the pursuit, capture, imprisonment, detention and delivery within said zone and auxiliary lands to the authorities of the Republic of Panama of persons charged with the commitment of crimes, felonies or misdemeanors without said zone and for the pursuit, capture, imprisonment, detention and delivery without said zone to the authorities of the United States of persons charged with the commitment of crimes, felonies and misdemeanors within said zone and auxiliary lands.

ARTICLE XVII

The Republic of Panama grants to the United States the use of all the ports of the Republic open to commerce as places of refuge for any vessels employed in the Canal enterprise, and for all vessels passing or bound to pass through the Canal which may be in distress and be driven to seek refuge in said ports. Such vessels shall be exempt from anchorage and tonnage dues on the part of the Republic of Panama.

ARTICLE XVIII

The Canal, when constructed, and the entrances thereto shall be neutral in perpetuity, and shall be opened upon the terms provided for by Section I of Article three of, and in conformity with all the stipulations of, the treaty entered into by the Governments of the United States and Great Britain on November 18, 1901.

ARTICLE XIX

The Government of the Republic of Panama shall have the right to transport over the Canal its vessels and its troops and munitions of war in such vessels at all times without paying charges of any kind. The exemption is to be extended to the auxiliary railway for the transportation of persons in the service of the Republic of Panama, or of the police force charged with the preservation of public order outside of said zone, as well as to their baggage, munitions of war and supplies.

ARTICLE XX

If by virtue of any existing treaty in relation to the territory of the Isthmus of Panama, whereof the obligations shall descend or be assumed by the Republic of Panama, there may be any privilege or concession in favor the Government or the citizens and subjects of a third power relative to an interoceanic means of communication which in any of its terms may be incompatible with the terms of the present convention, the Republic of Panama agrees to cancel or modify such treaty in due form, for which purpose it shall give to the said third power the requisite notification within the term of four months from the date of the present convention, and in case the existing treaty contains no clause permitting its modification or annulment, the Republic of Panama agrees to procure its modification or annulment in such form that there shall not exist any conflict with the stipulations of the present convention.

ARTICLE XXI

The rights and privileges granted by the Republic of Panama to the United States in the preceding Articles are understood to be free of all anterior debts, liens, trusts, or liabilities, or concessions or privileges to other Governments, corporations, syndicates or individuals, and consequently, if there should arise any claims on account of the present concessions and privileges or otherwise, the claimants shall resort to the Government of the Republic of Panama and not to the United States for any indemnity or compromise which may be required.

ARTICLE XXII

The Republic of Panama renounces and grants to the United States the participation to which it might be entitled in the future earnings of the Canal under Article XV of the concessionary contract with Lucien N. B. Wyse now owned by the New Panama Canal Company and any and all other rights or claims of a pecuniary nature arising under or relating to said concession, or arising under or relating to the concessions to the Panama Railroad Company or any extension or modification thereof; and it likewise renounces, confirms and grants to the United States, now and hereafter, all the rights and property reserved in the said concessions which otherwise would belong to Panama at or before the expiration of the terms of ninety-nine years of the concessions granted to or held by the above mentioned party and companies, and all right, title and interest which it now has or many hereafter have, in and to the lands, canal, works, property and rights held by the said companies under said concessions or otherwise, and acquired or to be acquired by the United States from or through the New Panama Canal Company, including any property and rights which might or may in the future either by lapse of time, forfeiture or otherwise, revert to the Republic of Panama, under any contracts or concessions, with said Wyse, the Universal Panama Canal Company, the Panama Railroad Company and the New Panama Canal Company.

The aforesaid rights and property shall be and are free and released from any present or reversionary interest in or claims of Panama and the title of the United States thereto upon consummation of the contemplated purchase by the United States from the New Panama Canal (company, shall be absolute, so far as concerns the Republic of Panama, excepting always the rights of the Republic specifically secured under this treaty.

ARTICLE XXIII

If it should become necessary at any time to employ armed forces for the safety or protection of the Canal, or of the ships that make use of the same, or the railways and auxiliary works, the United States shall have the right, at all times and in its discretion, to use its police and its land and naval forces or to establish fortifications for these purposes.

ARTICLE XXIV

No change either in the Government or in the laws and treaties of the Republic of Panama shall, without the consent of the United States, affect any right of the United States under the present convention, or under any treaty stipulation between the two countries that now exists or may hereafter exist touching the subject matter of this convention.

If the Republic of Panama shall hereafter enter as a constituent into any other Government or into any union or confederation of states, so as to merge her sovereignty or independence in such Government, union or confederation, the rights of the United States under this convention shall not be in any respect lessened or impaired.

ARTICLE XXV

For the better performance of the engagements of this convention and to the end of the efficient protection of the Canal and the preservation of its neutrality, the Government of the Republic of Panama will sell or lease to the United States lands adequate and necessary for naval or coaling stations on the Pacific coast and on the western Caribbean coast of the Republic at certain points to be agreed upon with the President of the United States.

ARTICLE XXVI

This convention when signed by the Plenipotentiaries of the Contracting Parties shall be ratified by the respective Governments and the ratifications shall be exchanged at Washington at the earliest date possible.

In faith whereof the respective Plenipotentiaries have signed the present convention in duplicate and have hereunto affixed their respective seals.

Done at the City of Washington the 18th day of November in the year of our Lord nineteen hundred and three.

JOHN HAY [SEAL]
P. BUNAU VARILLA [SEAL]

GLOSSARY

plenipotentiary: a diplomatic agent or representative of a government

Document Analysis

Known variously as the Panama Canal Treaty and the Hay-Bunau-Varilla Treaty, the document's official title was "Convention for the Construction of a Ship Canal." The treaty reflects Bunau-Varilla's eagerness to draw up a document that so closely reflected American interests that it would be certain to gain the necessary approval of two-thirds of the Senate.

In the treaty's first article, the United States guaranteed the independence of Panama, presumably against attempts by Colombia to take it back as well as other outside powers. This was the key concession sought by Panama and the reason that the weak new republic agreed to the otherwise unequal terms of the treaty.

Key provisions sought by the United States come in the following articles. Panama granted to the United States "in perpetuity the use, occupation and control" of the Canal Zone as well as "all the rights, power and authority within the zone" that the United States would possess if it were sovereign over the territory "to the entire exclusion of the Republic of Panama of any such sovereign rights, power or authority." The United States also acquired rights to use Panamanian waterways outside the Canal Zone if their use was needed for the construction or operation of the canal and a monopoly on the construction, maintenance, and operation of any means of transportation connecting the Caribbean Sea and the Pacific Ocean across Panama. It could also expropriate other lands, outside the Canal Zone, that were "necessary and convenient" for the construction, operation, and defense of the canal.

A later article (Art. XXIII) granted the United States the right to use its police or land or naval forces or to build fortifications to assure the safety and protection of the canal, the ships using it or auxiliary works or railroads. To further assure the protection of the canal, Panama (Art. XXV) will supply land on both its coasts for U.S. naval stations.

Many subordinate provisions followed. The cities of Colón and Panama City, situated at the two ends of the canal, were expressly excluded from the Canal Zone, despite their location. Nevertheless, the treaty gave the United States the right of eminent domain within the cities, to build sanitary works and establish sanitary rules and regulations (a major concern owing to the prevalence of yellow fever and malaria), and to maintain public order there if the government of Panama failed to do so.

Panama also expressed its agreement to the transfer to the United States of the property and rights of the New Panama Canal Company (Compagnie Nouvelle du Canal de Panama), the legal successor to de Lesseps's company (Compagnie Universelle du Canal Interocéanique de Panama) and of the Panama Railroad Company. The railroad, built in the 1850s by a U.S. firm, had been acquired by de Lesseps in 1881. Panama gave up any claim to revenues from them. Any debts, liens, or other obligations associated with property transferred from Panama to the United States remained the responsibility of Panama.

Panama gave up the right to charge customs or other fees for ships using the canal or for U.S. ships involved in the construction or operation of the canal, or to tax the canal or it associated works or the equipment imported for the canal or for the employees and their families, whereas the United States could charge tolls for the use of the canal. Panama shall not charge fees for ships in distress belonging to the canal enterprise or headed for the canal if they seek refuge in Panamanian ports. Panama cannot restrict the immigration of canal employees or draft them into the military. Official Panamanian dispatches using U.S. telephone and telegraph lines will be charged at the same rate as official U.S. messages.

The United States agreed to pay a lump sum and an annual fee to Panama, but even after 100 years of payments the accumulated sum would be less than the $40 million paid to the New Panama Canal Company. Disputes about payments to Panama will not delay fulfillment of other aspects of the treaty.

Any fugitive of the law who commits a crime in Panama and flees to the Canal Zone, or who commits a crime in the Canal Zone and flees to Panama, shall be turned over to the respective legal authorities.

The canal and access to it shall be neutral and open to all ships in perpetuity. The Panamanian military and police may use the canal and railroad without charge.

Panama agreed to cancel or amend any treaty it had that contravened the terms of the present treaty. The terms of the present treaty will not be affected by any Panamanian law or treaty or by any change of government in Panama or by the merger of Panama into another country.

Essential Themes

The world's leading maritime nations had long considered the possibility of building a canal linking the Atlantic and Pacific Oceans. For the United States, in particular, an interoceanic canal would greatly shorten the route linking the country's east and west coasts. Lacking such a route, the migration set off by the Gold Rush of 1849 had to travel the long and dangerous route around Cape Horn or by sea to Central America (usually Nicaragua or Panama, which was then a province of Colombia), then over land to the Pacific coast, and then by sea again to California. (Either of these routes was quicker than traveling directly by land across the continent, especially after U.S. entrepreneurs built a railroad across the Isthmus of Panama.)

The expanding U.S. role in the region in the mid-19th century, and efforts to acquire canal rights at all the narrowest points, came into conflict with the British, who had been a predominant presence there. Benjamin Bidlack, for instance, had negotiated the Bidlack-Mallarino Treaty with Colombia in 1846 (ratified in 1848), which gave the United States an exclusive right-of-way across the Isthmus of Panama for any existing or future mode of transportation (e.g., railroad or canal) as well as the right to intervene militarily to guarantee Colombia's sovereignty over the area or in the event of disorders that threatened transit. Yet the desire to avoid a conflict with the British pressed in the opposite direction. Thus the United States and Britain negotiated the Clayton-Bulwer Treaty in 1850, which stipulated the joint U.S.-British construction and operation of any transisthmian canal, although Nicaragua was the route most in mind at the time. The vague terms of the treaty, however, created new disputes, and each country eventually lost interest in building a canal that it would not control. In the United States, the opinion persisted that Britain ought to stay in its own hemisphere. Concern grew in the 1880s as Nicaragua sought to interest the British in building a canal and Colombia contracted with Ferdinand de Lesseps, the French engineer who had built the Suez Canal, to build a canal in Panama. Retired Civil War general Ambrose Burnside declared a French-built canal "dangerous to our peace and safety." President Rutherford B. Hayes declared the policy of the United States to be "either a canal under American control, or no canal," but he did nothing about it other than elicit a French promise that it was a purely private venture. The de Lesseps project failed because it was impossible to build a Suez-style sea-level canal, as he intended, across the hilly spine of Panama and because of rampant disease that cost the lives of 25,000 workers over the course of nine years, but not because of Great Power interference.

After the Spanish-American War (1898), the need to defend the newly acquired Philippine and Hawaiian Islands highlighted the strategic importance of being able to move ships quickly between oceans. (During the war, the U.S.S. *Oregon* had needed more than two months to steam from San Francisco around South America to Florida, and it was incommunicado for weeks at a time.) The United States thus pressed Britain to renegotiate the Clayton-Bulwer Treaty, which the British—tied down in the Boer War and losing interest in Central America—agreed to do. It was replaced with the Hay-Pauncefote Treaty in November 1901. Now, as far as London was concerned, the United States had the exclusive right to build, operate, and fortify a transisthmian canal.

Philippe-Jean Bunau-Varilla, the French engineer who had been in charge of de Lesseps's failed canal project, successfully lobbied the U.S. Congress to give up plans to build a canal across Nicaragua and to pay his company for the rights to the Panama route instead, finally convincing them in June 1902 that Nicaragua's volcanoes and earthquakes would be a constant threat to the canal and its traffic (and reportedly paying lots of bribes). With that decided, only the agreement of Colombia was needed. Colombia, however, balked at accepting the offer of a 100-year lease ceding a six-mile-wide right-of-way to the United States. Although Colombia, bankrupt after a civil war, may have just been holding out for higher compensation, Bunau-Varilla encouraged Panamanian secessionists to start another in a long series of uprisings, and provided financing. President Theodore Roosevelt and Secretary of State John Hay discreetly relayed to Bunau-Varilla that the United States would not stand in the way of a revolt. The U.S. Navy dispatched ships to the scene, cynically invoking the Bidlack-Mallarino Treaty of 1846, which in effect prevented the Colombian army from moving troops to Panama to put down the revolt. (Thick rain forests, swamps, and mountains made the land route from Colombia to Panama nearly impassable.) Panama declared its independence on November 3, 1903, and Roosevelt recognized it ten days later, before anyone from Panama had arrived.

The new Panamanian government had appointed Bunau-Varilla (who was not Panamanian and had not been in Panama for 17 years) as its envoy to the United States, after his assurances that he could secure a U.S. guarantee of Panama's independence. Bunau-Varilla wrote the treaty, with only the briefest of changes by

Hay. Panama ratified it after Bunau-Varilla alleged that failure to do so would prompt the United States to abandon its guarantee of Panama and go back to negotiating with Colombia, although the U.S. government had not indicated this. Indeed, Panama telegraphed its intention to ratify the treaty before the text had arrived there.

The treaty granted the United States complete sovereignty in perpetuity over a 10-mile-wide zone stretching across the width of Panama in return for a modest annual stipend. The rest of the country, on both sides of the Canal Zone, retained its sovereignty, but deeply dependent on the United States. The treaty granted the United States the right to intervene militarily to guarantee Panamanian sovereignty or to assure order, and these provisions were carried over into the Panamanian constitution of 1904. The canal, completed in 1914, was indeed a strategic advantage for the U.S. Navy, which had priority over other shipping waiting to use the passage, and a boon to commerce. In return, the United States paid Panama a lump sum of $10 million plus an annual sum of $250,000 starting nine years after ratification of the treaty. The United States paid the French canal company $40 million for its rights and properties in Panama. The United States paid Colombia an indemnity of $25 million in 1921, after years of dispute.

In the United States the press complained about the high-handed process by which Panama had gained independence and the United States had gained the Canal Zone. The debate in the Senate was highly contentious, but in the end even the administration's opponents acknowledged that the treaty came "more liberal in its concessions to us and giving us more than anybody in this Chamber ever dreamed of having." The treaty passed on February 23, 1904, by a vote of 66 to 14. Most Americans eventually came to the conclusion that the Panama Canal was a noble cause, promoting both U.S. security (indeed, hemispheric security) and international commerce, and that Panama was better off for the experience.

The attitude in Panama was different. The Hay–Bunau-Varilla Treaty of 1903 essentially made Panama a U.S. protectorate, a status that roiled Panamanian politics for decades. Many Panamanian citizens agreed that the treaty had given the United States the right to build, operate, and defend a canal but denied that it had granted de facto sovereignty over the Canal Zone, despite the wording to that effect. Anti-American riots in 1964 led to a slow reconsideration of the status of the Canal Zone and the ownership of the canal. President Jimmy Carter accelerated that process. He signed a new treaty (the Carter-Torrijos Treaty) with Panama in 1977, abrogating the Hay–Bunau-Varilla Treaty and providing for the transfer of sovereignty over the Canal Zone to Panama in 1979, the establishment of a joint U.S.-Panamanian commission to operate the canal from then until the end of 1999, and the final transfer of ownership of the canal itself on December 31, 1999. The canal has been owned and operated by Panama since that time.

———*Scott C. Monje, PhD and David Simonelli, PhD*

Bibliography and Further Reading

Anguizola, Gustave. *Philippe Bunau-Varilla: The Man behind the Panama Canal.* Chicago: Nelson-Hall, 1980.

Bunau-Varilla, Philippe. *From Panama to Verdun.* Philadelphia: Dorrance and Co., 1940; <http://www.columbia.edu/cu/lweb/digital/collections/cul/texts/ldpd_6345181_000/index.html>.

Carlisle, J. M. *The Cowboy and the Canal: How Theodore Roosevelt Cheated Colombia, Stole Panama, and Bamboozled America.* Tucson, Ariz.: Tangent Publishers, 2014.

LaFeber, Walter. *The Panama Canal: The Crisis in Historical Perspective,* updated ed. New York: Oxford University Press, 1989.

Leonard, Thomas M. *The United States and Central America: The Search for Stability.* Athens: University of Georgia Press, 1991.

McCullough, David. *The Path between the Seas: The Creation of the Panama Canal, 1870–1914.* New York: Simon & Schuster, 1977.

Morris, Edmund. *Theodore Rex.* New York: Random House, 2001.

Taliaferro, John. *All the Great Prizes: The Life of John Hay, from Lincoln to Roosevelt.* New York: Simon & Schuster, 2003.

Roosevelt Corollary to the Monroe Doctrine

Date: 1904
Author: Theodore Roosevelt
Genre: policy statement; political doctrine

Summary Overview

On December 6, 1904, President Theodore Roosevelt submitted, in written form, his annual message to the Congress of the United States, which contained what came to be called the Roosevelt Corollary to the Monroe Doctrine. In that document Roosevelt wrote at length about many national problems, from railroad regulation to conservation of natural resources. When it came to foreign policy, however, he wrote several long paragraphs about the relations between the United States and its neighbors in Latin America. In one key paragraph, the president modified the diplomatic policy that had come to be known as the Monroe Doctrine. The Monroe Doctrine had been put forward by President James Monroe in December 1823, in his seventh annual message to Congress. That doctrine set out several propositions governing American relations with European countries relative to the Western Hemisphere. The main point Monroe made was that North and South America were not to be seen as areas for further European colonization. If the nations of Europe made such steps, the United States would take appropriate action. In his corollary, Roosevelt asserted new American rights relative to other countries in the region and proclaimed a broad ability to set the rules for the Caribbean Sea and countries that surrounded it.

Defining Moment

The language in Roosevelt's annual message was aimed at two constituencies. First, he was preparing the American people for the potential need for further interventions in Latin America. His main targets, however, were the nations of the Western Hemisphere themselves and the European powers that might be tempted to establish a presence in the Caribbean. The Latin American countries resented American assertiveness but could do little at that time to resist the power of the United States in a direct way. At the same time, the European nations were mindful of the power of the navy of Great Britain, when combined with that of the United States, to exert power in the Caribbean. While Germany, in particular, chafed at the way in which Roosevelt wielded his power over the next several years, there was little disposition in Berlin to provide a direct challenge to the United States. As long as American dominance of the region continued, the response in Europe and Latin America to the Roosevelt Corollary was one of grudging acquiescence.

Author Biography

Theodore Roosevelt was forty-six in December 1904. He was born in New York City in 1858, and he entered politics in 1881 after graduation from Harvard University. During the next twenty years, he became one of the rising stars of the Republican Party. He served in the New York legislature, spent six years on the United States Civil Service Commission, and was a New York Police Commissioner in the mid-1890s. President William McKinley appointed him as assistant secretary of the navy in 1897, a post he held until the outbreak of the war with Spain in 1898. He raised a regiment called the "Rough Riders" and fought in Cuba at the battle of San Juan Hill. The Republicans nominated him for governor of New York in the fall of 1898, and he won a narrow victory. In 1900 the Republican National Convention selected him as McKinley's vice presidential candidate, and the ticket won the general election in November 1900. Following McKinley's assassination in 1901, Roosevelt assumed the presidency. He won the 1904 presidential election, serving until 1909. He died in 1919.

In foreign policy, Roosevelt operated from a number of well-defined ideas. He believed that power politics determined how a nation fared in the world. As a result, the United States must have a strong army and navy to defend itself. He quoted an African phrase that his country must "speak softly and carry a big stick" (Roosevelt, 1904, p. 121). At the same time, he knew that American public opinion did not want overseas adventures. Despite his reputation for warlike rhetoric, Roosevelt was not reckless in seeking intervention abroad in the affairs of other nations.

As far as Latin America was concerned, however, Roosevelt believed that the United States had a responsibility to guide and tutor the unruly countries south of the border. Elements of racism entered his thinking on such issues. In his mind, peoples of Latin blood and temperament lacked the stability and sense of law and order that the Anglo-Saxons possessed. It was, therefore, the duty of civilized peoples to set a good example that Hispanic countries might follow. That the objects of his solicitude might resent his condescension never entered Roosevelt's thinking.

Believing, as he did, that the presidency offered him a platform for moral instruction, Roosevelt saw his annual message in 1904 as an excellent time to enunciate the principles of foreign policy that should govern American relations with Latin America. He framed several paragraphs that addressed the issues of national responsibility that the conduct of the Dominican Republic had raised. One paragraph, in particular, set forth the president's elaboration of the meaning of the Monroe Doctrine.

HISTORICAL DOCUMENT

It is not true that the United States feels any land hunger or entertains any projects as regards the other nations of the Western Hemisphere save such as are for their welfare. All that this country desires is to see the neighboring countries stable, orderly, and prosperous. Any country whose people conduct themselves well can count upon our hearty friendship. If a nation shows that it knows how to act with reasonable efficiency and decency in social and political matters, if it keeps order and pays its obligations, it need fear no interference from the United States. Chronic wrong-doing, or an impotence which results in a general loosening of the ties of civilized society, may in America, as elsewhere, ultimately require intervention by some civilized nation, and in the Western Hemisphere the adherence of the United States to the Monroe Doctrine may force the United States, however reluctantly, in flagrant cases of such wrongdoing or impotence, to the exercise of an international police power. If every country washed by the Caribbean Sea would show the progress in stable and just civilization which with the aid of the Platt Amendment Cuba has shown since our troops left the island, and which so many of the republics in both Americas are constantly and brilliantly showing, all question of interference by this Nation with their affairs would be at an end. Our interests and those of our southern neighbors are in reality identical. They have great natural riches, and if within their borders the reign of law and justice obtains, prosperity is sure to come to them. While they thus obey the primary laws of civilized society they may rest assured that they will be treated by us in a spirit of cordial and helpful sympathy. We would interfere with them only in the last resort, and then only if it became evident that their inability or unwillingness to do justice at home and abroad had violated the rights of the United States or had invited foreign aggression to the detriment of the entire body of American nations. It is a mere truism to say that every nation, whether in America or anywhere else, which desires to maintain its freedom, its independence, must ultimately realize that the right of such independence can not be separated from the responsibility of making good use of it.

In asserting the Monroe Doctrine, in taking such steps as we have taken in regard to Cuba, Venezuela, and Panama, and in endeavoring to circumscribe the theater of war in the Far East, and to secure the open door in China, we have acted in our own interest as well as in the interest of humanity at large. There are, however, cases in which, while our own interests are not greatly involved, strong appeal is made to our sympathies. Ordinarily it is very much wiser and more useful for us to concern ourselves with striving for our own moral and material betterment here at home than to concern ourselves with trying to better the condition of things in other nations. We have plenty of sins of our own to war against, and under ordinary circumstances we can do more for the general uplifting of humanity by striving with heart and soul to put a stop to civic corruption, to brutal lawlessness and violent race prejudices here at home than by passing resolutions and wrongdoing elsewhere. Nevertheless there are occasional crimes committed on so vast a scale and of such peculiar horror as to make us doubt whether it is not our manifest duty to endeavor at least to show our disapproval of the deed and our sympathy with those who have suffered by it. The cases must be extreme in which such a course is justifiable. There must be no effort made to remove the mote from our brother's eye if we refuse to remove the beam from our own. But in extreme cases action may be justifiable and proper. What form the action shall take must depend upon the circumstances of the case; that is, upon the degree of the atrocity and upon our power to remedy it. The cases in which we could interfere by force of arms as we interfered to put a stop to intolerable conditions in Cuba are necessarily very few. Yet it is not to be expected that a people like ours, which in spite of certain very obvious shortcomings, nevertheless as a whole shows by its consistent practice its belief in the principles of civil and religious liberty and of orderly freedom, a people among whom even the worst crime, like the crime of lynching, is never more than sporadic, so that individuals and not classes are molested in their fundamental rights—it is inevitable that such a nation should desire eagerly to give expression to its horror on an occasion like that of the massacre of the Jews in Kishenef, or when it witnesses such systematic and long-extended cruelty and oppression as the cruelty and oppression of which the Armenians have been the victims, and which have won for them the indignant pity of the civilized world.

GLOSSARY

chronic: recurring often

detriment: damage or harm

flagrant: outrageous or notorious

impotence: in diplomacy, lacking in power or strength

land hunger: desire to expand national territory

Monroe Doctrine: a policy asserted by Monroe in 1823 that the United States would regard an expansion of European influence in the Western Hemisphere as an unfriendly act

obligations: responsibilities

Platt Amendment: an amendment adopted in 1901 that gave the United States a veto over the foreign policy of the Republic of Cuba

truism: obvious statement

wrongdoing: transgression

Document Analysis

The heart of the Roosevelt Corollary occupies as a main subject a single paragraph in Roosevelt's annual message. He begins in his first sentence by disclaiming "any land hunger" or other designs on the countries of the Western Hemisphere "save such as are for their welfare." The American goal is to see to it that "the neighboring countries" are "stable, orderly, and prosperous." The president then adds that any country "whose people conduct themselves well can count upon our hearty friendship." This type of language from the government was customary in approaching Latin American nations.

Roosevelt then sets up the problem that he hopes to resolve with his new approach to the Monroe Doctrine. For a nation that behaves "with reasonable efficiency and decency in social and political matters, if it keeps order and pays its obligations" the United States will not be a large element in its international relations. Then, Roosevelt comes to the core of his argument. He cites "chronic wrongdoing" and "an impotence which results in a general loosening of the ties of civilized society" as a cause for American concern. The Dominican Republic, of course, is on his mind, but he refers also to events with Colombia and Venezuela as examples of his argument.

In the remainder of this key sentence, Roosevelt notes that if the misbehavior he has mentioned necessitates intervention by some civilized nation, it might trigger the Monroe Doctrine and require the United States to exercise "an international police power." The civilized nations he alludes to are Great Britain, Italy, and Germany, which recently had used their naval power to compel Venezuela to pay its debts. Since the U.S. government is not pleased with the prospect of European countries wielding military force in the Western Hemisphere, the only alternative to Roosevelt's way of thinking is for the United States to compel correct policies through the application of diplomacy and, if necessary, force.

The president then cites the example of the island of Cuba, which had been liberated from Spanish rule during the war with Spain in 1898. Out of that process had come a new Cuban Republic, of which Americans during the Roosevelt era were very proud. To ensure that Cuba would not become the pawn of a European country, however, in 1901 the United States insisted that the new nation adhere to the terms of the Platt Amendment. That document, named after the Republican senator Orville H. Platt of Connecticut, was part of congressional action related to Cuba. The United States required that Cuba agree to the amendment's terms. The language included the right of the United States to intervene in Cuba to prevent dominance by a foreign power. The United States also received a perpetual lease on the naval base at Guantanamo Bay on the island. The Cuban Republic had regained its sovereignty but under terms that limited its autonomy to what the American government would accept. Roosevelt concludes in his address, "If every country washed by the Caribbean Sea would show the progress in stable and just civilization which with the aid of the Platt Amendment Cuba has shown since our troops left the island, and which so many of the republics in both Americas are constantly and brilliantly showing" there would be no need for the United States to intervene.

The president asserts that the United States and its southern neighbors have identical interests. If they follow the rules of civilized society, they have nothing to fear. Roosevelt promises in the next sentence that any intervention would be "only in the last resort" if the country in question "violated" American rights or "invited foreign aggression to the detriment of the entire body of American nations." The president, in closing his main discussion of affairs in Latin America, maintains that independence and international responsibility are inseparable. As he writes, "The right of such independence can not be separated from the responsibility of making good use of it."

In his next paragraph, Roosevelt discusses when the United States should be involved beyond its borders. He claims, "The cases in which we could interfere by force of arms as we interfered to put a stop to intolerable conditions in Cuba are necessarily very few." But it is in the national character for Americans to protest against atrocities that befall Jews in Russia or Armenians in the Ottoman Empire. The president then passes on to subjects relating to these problems.

Essential Themes

The Monroe Doctrine had first been enunciated by President James Monroe in his annual message to Congress in December 1823. The doctrine, the brainchild of his secretary of state, John Quincy Adams, set out several propositions governing American relations with European countries relative to the Western Hemisphere. North and South America, said Monroe, were not areas where European nations should look for further colonization. If they did so, the United States would take appropriate action (though they would have to depend on the fleet of Great Britain to make such moves stick). Over the rest of the nineteenth century, the Monroe Doctrine came up on occasion, as when the French set up a puppet regime in Mexico during the mid-1860s and in the Venezuelan crisis with Great Britain in 1895 and 1896, when the U.S. demanded that Britain submit its boundary dispute with Venezuela for arbitration.

By the early twentieth century, the Monroe Doctrine was a well-established precept of American foreign policy. When Roosevelt took over the presidency after the death of William McKinley in September 1901, the United States faced new challenges in Latin America that went beyond the limits of the Monroe Doctrine. For Roosevelt, the essential priorities, taken over from McKinley, were to build a canal across Central America and to make the Caribbean basin an area of clear United States dominance.

In the case of the canal, Roosevelt proceeded to do that through the process of first negotiating with Colombia for a canal across Panama, which was then part of the Colombian nation. When the government in Bogotá declined to accept Roosevelt's terms in the treaty the two countries had negotiated, he encouraged a revolution in Panama that would see that country secede from Colombia. Once that was accomplished in late 1903, Roosevelt and his secretary of state, John Hay, worked out a treaty with the new Panamanian government that gave the United States the canal zone and the right to construct a canal.

The experience of working with the politicians in Colombia on this matter did not instill confidence in their ability as far as Roosevelt was concerned. Believing that the United States had the superior political system and culture, he looked down on the abilities and honesty of Latin American officials. Like so many in the United States, he believed that Americans were more intelligent, further advanced, and more responsible than their neighbors to the South. As a result, in Roosevelt's mind it was acceptable for the government to impose discipline and order on peoples who lacked those qualities on their own. Racism and ethnocentrism would play a large part in Roosevelt's approach to foreign relations during his presidency.

The president and his advisers also were aware of what they perceived to be a renewed threat from European nations to test the limits of the Monroe Doctrine. Latin American countries had borrowed funds from investors in Europe to finance economic development within their impoverished territories. When corruption, a lack of skill, or bad luck saw these investments go sour, Great Britain, Germany, and other powers asserted their right to compel the Latin American nations to pay their debts. On some occasions, these demands were backed up with gunboat diplomacy and naval blockades. The presence of foreign vessels in the Caribbean for such purposes disturbed Roosevelt and the American military.

One nation that caused special concern was the Germany of Kaiser Wilhelm II. The U.S. government watched with unease the penetration of the Germans into the Caribbean, a process that began during the McKinley administration. German trade with the region was growing, and German settlers were making homes in South American nations. Was Berlin endeavoring to create a permanent presence in the region? The United States could not be sure of German intentions. These developments prompted American policy makers to consider what would happen if the Germans sought a naval base near the Caribbean. As a result, the United States and Great Britain drew closer together, and U.S. relations with Berlin grew less amicable.

An episode in 1902 underscored the American suspicion about the Germans and provided background for the Roosevelt statement in 1904. Germany had made extensive loans to the dictator of Venezuela, Cipriano Castro, reaching some seventy million marks. Castro did not pay any interest on these loans and in 1901 indicated that he did not plan to repay the money either. Great Britain went through a comparable experience with the Venezuelan ruler. The only feasible solution in the minds of Kaiser Wilhelm and his advisers was a blockade of Venezuela to collect the money that was owed.

This course raised questions for the U.S. government. The Germans told the Americans that they had no plans to establish permanent bases in Venezuela. They did concede, however, that they might have to occupy on a temporary basis some harbors in Venezuela where they could collect duties from foreign ships trading in those waters. Those assertions troubled Roosevelt, who worried that temporary occupations had a way of turning into more permanent arrangements. The Germans were reminded that a permanent base of any kind would be a violation of the Monroe Doctrine and traditional American foreign policy.

A year later, at the end of 1902, Great Britain, Germany, and Italy decided to blockade Castro's regime. The dictator rejected a European ultimatum, and the powers acted to compel him to give in. Faced with overwhelming power, Castro agreed to have the dispute submitted to international arbitration. Negotiations then broke down, and the European fleets remained in place. Shelling of Venezuelan installations took place in January 1903. Through all of these events, the United States kept its fleet on alert and ready to act if matters should get out of hand. For Roosevelt and the navy, there were some suggestions that the United States might not prevail in the event of a confrontation with Germany. The experience compelled Roosevelt to think about the Monroe Doctrine and his attitude toward protecting Latin American governments from the consequences of their own mistakes. He would later observe that his relations with Berlin and its attitude toward Latin America played a large part in shaping how he formulated the Roosevelt Corollary.

With the Panamanian and Venezuelan episodes in mind, Roosevelt took steps in the spring of 1904 to articulate the views that would find expression in his annual message. He asked his former secretary of war, Elihu Root, to read a letter at a dinner in May celebrating the second anniversary of the founding of the Cuban Republic following the war with Spain. In this document, Roosevelt said, "All we desire is to see all neighboring countries stable, orderly and prosperous." The president then went on to say, however, that "brutal wrongdoing, or an impotence which results in a general loosening of the ties of civilized society, may finally require intervention by some civilized nation, and in the western hemisphere the United States cannot ignore this duty." He added that all he and his country asked of his Latin American neighbors was that "they shall govern themselves well, and be prosperous and orderly" (Roosevelt to Root, May 20, 1904; qtd. in Roosevelt, 1951–1954, vol. 4, p. 801). Roosevelt put it with more candor in a letter to Root a month later. If the United States was saying "'hands off' to the powers of Europe, then sooner or later, we must keep order ourselves" (Roosevelt to Root, June 7, 1904; qtd. in Roosevelt, 1951–1954, vol. 4, pp. 821–822).

The nation that seemed to Roosevelt incapable of managing its own affairs at this time was the Dominican Republic. The government of that country had run up some $32 million in debts, most of them with European investors. By the opening months of 1904, reports reached Washington, D.C., that the Dominican economy was deteriorating. There were disclosures of apparent German interest in the area. The government of the island dispatched its foreign minister to request American aid. Roosevelt decided to be cautious in making a commitment. As he wrote in February 1904, "I want to do nothing but what a policeman has to do in Santo Domingo. As for annexing the island, I have about the same desire to annex it as a gorged boa constrictor might have to swallow a…porcupine wrong-end-to" (Roosevelt to Joseph Bucklin Bishop, February 23, 1904; qtd. in Roosevelt, 1951–1954, vol. 4, p. 734).

With the impending election of 1904, Roosevelt concluded that his best strategy was to see what would happen in the Dominican crisis. As he did so, the financial condition of that country further worsened. Following his victory in the presidential election of November 1904, Roosevelt confronted complaints from European countries about the failure of the Dominican government to meet its claims. It was in this context that Roosevelt considered what to do in terms of asserting his view of the responsibilities of the governments in Latin America. The annual message, when he spoke to the whole nation and the world, seemed an ideal moment to set forth his ideas about the role of the United States relative to its neighbors.

The Roosevelt Corollary to the Monroe Doctrine, as it soon came to be known, was much discussed during 1905 as the president sought Senate approval of his arrangements with Santo Domingo. Since Democratic opposition persisted, Roosevelt elaborated on his views about the Monroe Doctrine in his annual message of December 5, 1905. "It must be understood" he wrote in that message, "that under no circumstances will the United States use the Monroe Doctrine as a cloak for territorial aggression." To further reassure his critics, the president added that any action to enforce the Roosevelt Corollary "will be taken at all only with extreme reluctance and when it has become evident that every other resource has been exhausted."

Despite these assurances of discretion in its use, the Roosevelt Corollary was implemented at various times by Roosevelt himself in the case of Cuba in 1906 and by Woodrow Wilson during his presidency in Nicaragua and Haiti. The public appetite for these adventures receded after World War I. By the late 1920s the Roosevelt Corollary seemed like a diplomatic relic, and President Calvin Coolidge repudiated it in 1928. Herbert Hoover and Franklin D. Roosevelt instituted the good neighbor policy, which no longer claimed the authority to have the United States supervise the political behavior of countries in the Western Hemisphere. Thus, the corollary came to be seen as an example of how the United States exercised its military and diplomatic supremacy at the turn of the twentieth century in a manner that a century later seemed unwise and inappropriate.

———*Lewis L. Gould, PhD*

Bibliography and Further Reading

Beale, Howard K. *Theodore Roosevelt and the Rise of America to World Power.* Baltimore, Md.: Johns Hopkins University Press, 1959.

Brands, H. W. *T.R.: The Last Romantic.* New York: Basic Books, 1997.

Collin, Richard H. *Theodore Roosevelt's Caribbean: The Panama Canal, the Monroe Doctrine, and the Latin American Context.* Baton Rouge: Louisiana State University Press, 1990.

Dalton, Kathleen. *Theodore Roosevelt: A Strenuous Life.* New York: Alfred A. Knopf, 2002.

Gould, Lewis L. *The Presidency of Theodore Roosevelt.* Lawrence: University Press of Kansas, 1991.

Morris, Edmund. *Theodore Rex.* New York: Random House, 2001.

Munro, Dana G. *Intervention and Dollar Diplomacy in the Caribbean, 1900–1921.* Princeton, N.J.: Princeton University Press, 1964.

Rippy, J. Fred. "The British Bondholders and the Roosevelt Corollary of the Monroe Doctrine." *Political Science Quarterly* 49 (June 1934): 195–206.

———. "Antecedents of the Roosevelt Corollary of the Monroe Doctrine." *Pacific Historical Review* 9 (September 1940): 267–279.

Roosevelt, Theodore. *Addresses and Presidential Addresses by Theodore Roosevelt, 1902–1904.* New York: G. P. Putnam's Sons, 1904.

"Theodore Roosevelt Speeches: Fifth Annual Message (December 5, 1905)." Miller Center of Public Affairs Web site. http://www.millercenter.virginia.edu/scripps/digitalarchive/speeches/spe_1 905_1205_roosevelt. Accessed on February 11, 2008.

"Theodore Roosevelt Speeches: First Annual Message (December 3, 1901)." Miller Center of Public Affairs Web site. http://millercenter.org/president/speeches/detail/3777. Accessed on February 11, 2008.

Vesser, Cyrus. *A World Safe for Capitalism: Dollar Diplomacy and America's Rise to Global Power.* New York: Columbia University Press, 2002.

———. "Inventing Dollar Diplomacy: The Gilded Age Origins of the Roosevelt Corollary to the Monroe Doctrine." *Diplomatic History* 27 (June 2003): 301–326.

■ The Treaty of Portsmouth

Date: 1905
Author: Japanese delegation; Russian delegation; American mediators
Genre: treaty

Summary Overview

The Treaty of Portsmouth officially ended the Russo-Japanese War when it was signed on September 5, 1905. In the years following the Sino-Japanese War in 1894-5 and Boxer Rebellion of 1900, tensions between Russia and Japan over territorial gains had increased. Japan was particularly worried about how Russian expansion in Manchuria would affect Japanese hegemony in Korea. Neither Russia nor Japan were prepared for a protracted war; nevertheless, Japan finally decided to cut off diplomatic relations with Russia and attack the fleet at Port Arthur on February 6, 1904. After Russia's devastating defeat at the Battle of Tsushima, Tsar Nicholas II was ready to discuss peace terms.

Acting as arbitrator, United States President Theodore Roosevelt offered Portsmouth, New Hampshire as the site to conduct peace talks. The Japanese delegation accomplished in the first days of the talks their three "absolutely indispensible" conditions for peace: Russia must acknowledge Japan's rights in Korea, both sides must evacuate Manchuria, and Russia must cede Port Arthur and control of the Southern Manchuria Railway to Japan. The issue of financial reparations and control of Sakhalin were more difficult for the two countries to agree on. Ultimately, Russia held firm on not paying any indemnities and the two countries agreed on Roosevelt's suggestion to divide control over Sakhalin.

Japan could not have sustained a longer war and had accomplished many of its goals in the negotiations, but many Japanese were dissatisfied with the treaty. Japan's victory in the Russo-Japanese War reinforced a growing national pride in Japanese military prowess. The victory also marked a new stage in Japanese imperialism that would find itself unrestricted in East Asia as the European powers turned to domestic issues like political revolutions in the 1910s and on.

Defining Moment

The first two groups of people to whom the Treaty of Portsmouth obviously concerned were the Russians and the Japanese. In Russia, the people were largely indifferent to the news of the treaty. Some Russians, however, had anticipated Russia's defeat and the war's resolution. Revolutionaries, like Lenin, hoped that the breakdown of Russian imperial power would create a situation ripe for new government. Russian dissatisfaction with the imperial government was growing at the same time as the Russo-Japanese War, and Russia's ultimate failure would assist in spreading lack of confidence in the Tsar.

In Japan, the reaction to the treaty was quite different. Many were dissatisfied with the terms and believed that Japan could have pushed for more from Russia. An anti-peace rally in Hibiya Park escalated into a riot that only ended because of the institution of martial law. Japan's victory in the war became a mark of glory for the people and increased national pride. Until 1945, the anniversary of the occupation at Mukden was celebrated as Army Day.

Others saw Japan's victory in the peace terms with new hope. The Americans thought that the Japanese would support American interests in Asia in return for the Americans recognizing Japanese influence. The larger Asian community viewed the results of the peace process as the beginning of the end of European power in the region, only to find that the promise of Japan as savior was not to be.

Author Biography

The Treaty of Portsmouth resulted from work of three principal parties: the Russians, the Japanese, and the American mediators. Sergei Witte led the Russian delegation. A minister of finance under Tsars Alexander III and Nicholas II, Witte had the reputation of being the "main architect" of Russian policy in East Asia. Witte presided over the industrialization and expansion of the railways from Odessa to Manchuria, and he especially hoped to exploit connections in northern China to improve the Russian economy. This Russian expansion and control of Manchuria, of course, contributed to hostilities with Japan in 1904. On the Japanese side, Foreign Minister Komura Jutarō led the delegation. Before the Russo-Japanese War, Komura was one of the key Japanese diplomats involved in the negotiations to end the First Sino-Japanese War and the Boxer Protocol; Komura would ply his skills at drafting treaties again at Portsmouth, where he secured Russian recognition of Japanese rights to Korea and Manchuria.

President Theodore Roosevelt initiated the peace talks in Portsmouth at the secret request of the Japanese. An ardent imperialist, Roosevelt defended the United States' acquisition of the Philippines; he also focused American ambitions on the Caribbean: it was during Roosevelt's presidency that the United States took over the Panama Canal project in 1904. For his efforts in arbitrating the Russo-Japanese conflict President Roosevelt received the Nobel Peace Prize in 1906, although he was motivated to arbitrate the conflict less because of a desire to see peace and more because he wanted to see Russia and Japan thwarted in total domination in Manchuria.

HISTORICAL DOCUMENT

The Emperor of Japan on the one part, and the Emperor of all the Russias, on the other part, animated by a desire to restore the blessings of peace, have resolved to conclude a treaty of peace, and have for this purpose named their plenipotentiaries, that is to say, for his Majesty the Emperor of Japan, Baron Komura Jutaro, Jusami, Grand Cordon of the Imperial Order of the Rising Sun, his Minister for Foreign Affairs, and his Excellency Takahira Kogoro, Imperial Order of the Sacred Treasure, his Minister to the United States, and his Majesty the Emperor of all the Russias, his Excellency Sergius Witte, his Secretary of State and President of the Committee of Ministers of the Empire of Russia, and his Excellency Baron Roman Rosen, Master of the Imperial Court of Russia, his Majesty's Ambassador to the United States, who, after having exchanged their full powers, which were found to be in good and due form, and concluded the following articles:

ARTICLE I.

There shall henceforth be peace and amity between their Majesties the Emperor of Japan and the Emperor of all the Russias, and between their respective States and subjects.

ARTICLE II.

The Imperial Russian Government, acknowledging that Japan possesses in Korea paramount political, military and economical interests engages neither to obstruct nor interfere with measures for guidance, protection and control which the Imperial Government of Japan may find necessary to take in Korea. It is understood that Russian subjects in Korea shall be treated in exactly the same manner as the subjects and citizens of other foreign Powers; that is to say, they shall be placed on the same footing as the subjects and citizens of the most favored nation. It is also agreed that, in order to avoid causes of misunderstanding, the two high contracting parties will abstain on the Russian-Korean frontier from taking any military measure which may menace the security of Russian or Korean territory.

ARTICLE III.

Japan and Russia mutually engage:

First.--To evacuate completely and simultaneously Manchuria, except the territory affected by the lease of the Liaotung Peninsula, in conformity with the provisions of the additional article I annexed to this treaty, and,

Second.--To restore entirely and completely to the exclusive administration of China all portions of Manchuria now in occupation, or under the control of the Japanese or Russian troops, with the exception of the territory above mentioned.

The Imperial Government of Russia declares that it has not in Manchuria any territorial advantages or preferential or exclusive concessions in the impairment of Chinese sovereignty, or inconsistent with the principle of equal opportunity.

ARTICLE IV.

Japan and Russia reciprocally engage not to obstruct any general measures common to all countries which China may take for the development of the commerce or industry of Manchuria.

ARTICLE V.

The Imperial Russian Government transfers and assigns to the Imperial Government of Japan, with the consent of the Government of China, the lease of Port Arthur, Talien and the adjacent territorial waters, and all rights, privileges and concessions connected with or forming part of such lease, and it also transfers and assigns to the Imperial government of Japan all public works and properties in the territory affected by the above-mentioned lease.

The two contracting parties mutually engage to obtain the consent of the Chinese Government mentioned in the foregoing stipulation.

The Imperial Government of Japan, on its part, undertakes that the proprietary rights of Russian subjects in the territory above referred to shall be perfectly respected.

ARTICLE VI.

The Imperial Russian Government engages to transfer and assign to the Imperial Government of Japan, without compensation and with the consent of the Chinese Government, the railway between Chang-chunfu and Kuanchangtsu and Port Arthur, and all the branches, together with all the rights, privileges and properties appertaining thereto in that region, as well as all the coal mines in said region belonging to or worked for the benefit of the railway. The two high contracting parties mutually engage to obtain the consent of the Government of China mentioned in the foregoing stipulation.

ARTICLE VII.

Japan and Russia engage to exploit their respective railways in Manchuria exclusively for commercial and industrial purposes and nowise for strategic purposes. It is understood that this restriction does not apply to the railway in the territory affected by the lease of the Liaotung Peninsula.

ARTICLE VIII.

The imperial Governments of Japan and Russia with the view to promote and facilitate intercourse and traffic will as soon as possible conclude a separate convention for the regulation of their connecting railway services in Manchuria.

ARTICLE IX.

The Imperial Russian Government cedes to the Imperial Government of Japan in perpetuity and full sovereignty the southern portion of the Island of Saghalin and all the islands adjacent thereto and the public works and properties thereon. The fiftieth degree of north latitude is adopted as the northern boundary of the ceded territory. The exact alignment of such territory shall be determined in accordance with the provisions of the additional article II annexed to this treaty.

Japan and Russia mutually agree not to construct in their respective possessions on the Island of Saghalin or the adjacent islands any fortification or other similar military works. They also respectively engage not to take any military measures which may impede the free navigation of the Strait of La Perouse and the Strait of Tartary.

ARTICLE X.

It is reserved to Russian subjects, inhabitants of the territory ceded to Japan, to sell their real property and retire to their country, but if they prefer to remain in the ceded territory they will be maintained protected in the full exercise of their industries and rights of property on condition of submitting to the Japanese laws and jurisdiction. Japan shall have full liberty to withdraw the right of residence in or to deport from such territory of any inhabitants who labor under political or administrative disability. She engages, however, that the proprietary rights of such inhabitants shall be fully respected.

ARTICLE XI.

Russia engages to arrange with Japan for granting to Japanese subjects rights of fishery along the coasts of the Russian possession in the Japan, Okhotsk and Bering Seas.

It is agreed that the foregoing engagement shall not affect rights already belonging to Russian or foreign subjects in those regions.

ARTICLE XII.

The treaty of commerce and navigation between Japan and Russia having been annulled by the war the Imperial Governments of Japan and Russia engage to adopt as a basis for their commercial relations pending the conclusion of a new treaty of commerce and navigation the basis of the treaty which was in force previous to the present war, the system of reciprocal treatment on the footing of the most favored nation, in which are included import and export duties, customs formalities, transit and tonnage dues and the admission and treatment of agents, subjects and vessels of one country in the territories of the other.

ARTICLE XIII.

As soon as possible after the present treaty comes in force all prisoners of war shall be reciprocally restored. The Imperial Governments of Japan and Russia shall each appoint a special commissioner to take charge of the prisoners. All prisoners in the hands of one Government shall be delivered to and be received by the commissioner of the other Government or by his duly authorized representative in such convenient numbers and at such convenient ports of the delivering State as such delivering State shall notify in advance to the commissioner of the receiving State.

The Governments of Japan and Russia shall present each other as soon as possible after the delivery of the prisoners is completed with a statement of the direct expenditures respectively incurred by them for the care and maintenance of the prisoner from the date of capture or surrender and up to the time of death or delivery. Russia engages to repay as soon as possible after the exchange of statement as above provided the difference between the actual amount so expended by Japan and the actual amount similarly disbursed by Russia.

ARTICLE XIV.

The present treaty shall be ratified by their Majesties the Emperor of Japan and the Emperor of all the Russias. Such ratification shall be with as little delay as possible, and in any case no later than fifty days from the date of the signature of the treaty, to be announced to the Imperial Governments of Japan and Russia respectively through the French Minister at Tokio and the Ambassador of the United States at St. Petersburg, and from the date of the latter of such announcements shall in all its parts come into full force. The formal exchange of ratifications shall take place at Washington as soon as possible.

ARTICLE XV.

The present treaty shall be signed in duplicate in both the English and French languages. The texts are in absolute conformity, but in case of a discrepancy in the interpretation the French text shall prevail.

SUB-ARTICLES

In conformity with the provisions of articles 3 and 9 of the treaty of the peace between Japan and Russia of this date the undersigned plenipotentiaries have concluded the following additional articles:

SUB-ARTICLE TO ARTICLE III.

The Imperial Governments of Japan and Russia mutually engage to commence the withdrawal of their military forces from the territory of Manchuria simultaneously and immediately after the treaty of peace comes into operation, and within a period of eighteen months after that date the armies of the two countries shall be completely withdrawn from Manchuria, except from the leased territory of the Liaotung Peninsula. The forces of the two countries occupying the front positions shall first be withdrawn.

The high contracting parties reserve to themselves the right to maintain guards to protect their respective railway lines in Manchuria. The number of such guards shall not exceed fifteen per kilometre and within that maximum number the commanders of the Japanese and Russian armies shall by common accord fix the number of such guards to be employed as small as possible while having in view the actual requirements.

The commanders of the Japanese and Russian forces in Manchuria shall agree upon the details of the evacuation in conformity with the above principles and shall take by common accord the measures necessary to carry out the evacuation as soon as possible, and in any case not later than the period of eighteen months.

SUB-ARTICLE TO ARTICLE IX.

As soon as possible after the present treaty comes into force a committee of delimitation composed of an equal number of members is to be appointed by the two high contracting parties which shall on the spot mark in a permanent manner the exact boundary between the Japanese and Russian possessions on the Island of Saghalin. The commission shall be bound so far as topographical considerations permit to follow the fiftieth parallel of north latitude as the boundary line, and in case any deflections from that line at any points are found to be necessary compensation will be made by correlative deflections at other points. It shall also be the duty of the said commission to prepare a list and a description of the adjacent islands included in the cession, and finally the commission shall prepare and sign maps showing the boundaries of the ceded territory. The work of the commission shall be subject to the approval of the high contracting parties.

The foregoing additional articles are to be considered ratified with the ratification of the treaty of peace to which they are annexed.

In witness whereof the respective plenipotentiaries have signed and affixed seals to the present treaty of peace.

Done at Portsmouth, New Hampshire, this fifth day of the ninth month of the thirty-eighth year of the Meijei, corresponding to the twenty-third day of August, one thousand nine hundred and five, (September 5, 1905.)

GLOSSARY

Saghalin: Sakhlain (alternate spelling)

Document Analysis

The careful wording of the Treaty of Portsmouth reflects the precarious global situation caused by massive military and economic expansion. At the beginning of the twentieth century, the major world powers worked to keep a careful equilibrium in the "Great Game" of political and economic expansion. Any territorial gains by one country could endanger this equilibrium: The cautious language of the Treaty of Portsmouth illustrates this concern for equilibrium in both the rights of Russian and Japanese nationals under the other country's hegemony and economic rights in occupied lands. Altogether, the language of the treaty attempts to portray a new balance between Japan and Russia that will ameliorate the previous conditions leading to war instead of exacting any punishment for perceived wrongdoing.

Following the first article of the treaty, which merely states that there shall be war between the two countries, he second article of the treaty addresses the concern of lasting enmity between Russian and Japanese nationals living abroad in newly demarcated lands. The treaty says: "it is understood that Russian subjects in Korea shall be treated in exactly the same manner as the subjects and citizens of other foreign Powers; that is to say, they shall be placed on the same footing as the subjects and citizens of the most favored nation." This term of the treaty impresses that Russians will be held with the same respect as other imperialist powers: the Japanese will still accord the Russians a greater standing in Japanese territories than the natives. This was similar practice among foreign powers in China and helped maintain an exclusive group of foreign powers with high standing. Later in Article V, the Japanese must concede "the proprietary rights of Russian subjects in the territory above [i.e., Port Arthur and surrounding areas] referred to shall be perfectly respected." The treaty reiterates similar stipulations in Articles X and XI, continuing to maintain that "the foregoing engagement shall not affect rights already belonging to Russian or foreign subjects in those regions." Rather than insist on the removal of Russian subjects or hampering former Japanese maritime rights, the Treaty of Portsmouth attempts to maintain a status quo among imperial powers in East Asia. Any destabilization of this carefully composed status quo could result in more hostilities between the two nations or worse, the participation of other imperial powers in warfare.

Furthermore, the treaty maintains this language of equality between Russia and Japan when it addresses economic and territorial concerns. The word "mutually" is used throughout the treaty, even when at the two countries must agree on an undesired term, such as the unilateral withdrawal of troops from Manchuria in Article III. The division of Sakhalin in Article IX, the compromise suggested by President Roosevelt, particularly illustrates the emphasis on equilibrium between the two imperial powers. In Article IX, Russia and Japan "mutually agree" and "respectively engage" to respect the other's rights in their regions of the large contested island; in the sub-article to this section, Russia and Japan agree to form a commission on the division of Sakhalin composed of "an equal number of members." This treaty sets terms which should create more cooperation between Russia and Japan instead of subordinating one country to the other. The stipulations in the treaty regarding fishing rights even compel the same level of regard. Russia and Japan are equals in this treaty: it does not convey a tone asserting Japanese superiority over Russia.

To conclude, the emphasis on equilibrium attempts to create the impression of a balanced imperial game. Although Japan's victory upset the traditional narrative of white supremacy in the imperial "Great Game," the Treaty of Portsmouth does not hint to the significance of the Russo-Japanese War's result. This shows that John Hays' Open Door Note, which called for keeping any one nation from gaining total control in China, had influence in other parts of Asia. The Treaty of Portsmouth delineates compromises not "inconsistent with the principle of equal opportunity" for Russia and Japan: clearly, this 1905 treaty was an optimistic attempt to return the state of foreign intervention in East Asia to one of peace between imperialists. In such a system, the imperial powers would be free to focus on insurgencies in occupied countries instead of fighting with each other. However, the insistence on maintaining equilibrium did not appeal to the Japanese public, which had been looking for more recognition of Japan's political and martial capabilities among the already-ruling European powers. Instead of dampening pride, the results of the Treaty of Portsmouth only encouraged the development of a proud national character founded on the legendary wins in the Russo-Japanese War.

Essential Themes

It was only in 1852 that Commodore Perry's expedition resulted in the opening of Japan to American and European trade. After this, the formerly-isolationist Japan would have to endure the ambitions of old European powers conflicting with its own ambitions for growth. The Meiji Restoration in 1868 was a reaction to the influx of foreign ships and modern technology. Japan realized that in order to be taken seriously by these groups, the country needed to be able to compete on an equal technological and political level. At the same time as Japan was modernizing, it also faced competition in acquiring advantageous territory from China and Korea.

The beginning of the tensions between Japan and Russia that resulted in war can be traced to the middle of the nineteenth century. The border between Russia and Japan shifted around a few islands until Japan grew fearful that Russia would attempt to question Japanese authority in Korea. Starting in 1855, the Russo-Japanese Treaty of Amity opened ports to Russia in Japan, delineated the frontier between the two countries, and arranged for joint occupation of Sakhalin. Joint control over Sakhalin increased conflict between Russia and Japan; eventually Japan agreed to Russia's control over Sakhalin in return for the Kurile Islands. The peace terms of the Sino-Japanese War of 1894-5 also contributed to rising Russian and Japanese tensions. This war was fought mostly in Manchuria and Korea: it eliminated China as a rival for Japan in Korea and granted Taiwan and the Liaotung Peninsula to Japan. The "Triple Intervention" of European powers forced Japan to give up the Liaotung Peninsula "for the sake of peace;" this acquisition of this peninsula would again be important in the peace terms in the Treaty of Portsmouth. Finally, Russia and Japan were part of the multinational expedition to quell the Boxer Rebellion, but their competition in subduing the Chinese would contribute to later tensions. When Russia still had not removed their troops from Manchuria following the resolution of conflicts with the Boxers and the Qing, Japan grew more anxious about the possibility of Russia undermining Japanese imperial interests.

Russia routinely underestimated Japanese military and political strength throughout the nineteenth century. Finance Minister Sergei Witte's commitment to the expansion of the Trans-Siberian Railway in the 1890s irritated the Japanese, who saw this expansion as a threat to their ambitions in northern China and Korea. Japan proposed a way to resolve the rivalry: the Man-Kan kōkan, or "exchanging Manchuria for Korea." This meant that Japan would recognize Russia's influence in Manchuria if Russia would recognize Japan had freedom to act in Korea. Russia repeatedly denied this initiative, although the Japanese would continue to float this idea until 1904.

Neither Russia nor Japan was prepared for a long war at the turn of the century; each country continued to build its army and navy while attempting to resolve the territorial disputes plaguing their diplomatic relations. Japan recognized the fearful prospect of other European countries becoming involved in the dispute, and so the Anglo-Japanese Alliance of 1902 was part of Japan's strategy to build support before attempting any offensive maneuver against the Russians. Pressure built in Japan to attack Russia while the Trans-Siberian Railroad was still incomplete and the fleet was not at full capacity; Russian policy toward the Japanese continued to be indecisive and Russian troops failed to withdraw in Manchuria by 1903. Finally, Japan had militarized enough by February 1904 to attack the Russian fleet at Port Arthur, although there was no guarantee of success.

As a result of half a century of territorial struggles, Japan had joined the old European powers in the "Great Game" of imperialism in East Asia, and yet, the Western countries vacillated as to whether Japan represented the "yellow peril," or the fear that the people of East Asia would threaten the interests of the predominately white West, or if Japan was the "yellow hope," a racial group that fell in between the yellow peril and white hegemony and would firmly assist Western ambitions in subduing China. By 1905, many European nations viewed Japan's victory positively; President Roosevelt began the negotiations at Portsmouth initially partial to Japan, perceived American allies at the time.

The Treaty of Portsmouth changed the status quo of territorial acquisitions in East Asia, particularly in Manchuria and Korea. Russia turned away from Asian expansion and toward domestic political issues; Japan solidified its power. Korea, which had been a major point of contention for the Japanese, was basically under martial rule; in 1910, Japan annexed Korea. Russia, Britain, and the United States recognized Japanese interests in Korean in return for Japan acknowledging British and American rights. Many in the global community, including President Roosevelt, hailed Japan's victory as a victory for more recently developed world powers like the United States.

However, in the short term, the treaty actually contributed to a renewed time of Russia and Japan cooperating with each other. In 1906 and 1917, the two countries composed agreements acknowledging the other country's spheres of influence in East Asia, especially in Manchuria. The two countries recognized the need to cooperate in the face of encroaching Anglo-American ambitions. In the long term, the Treaty of Portsmouth encouraged Japanese ambitions towards Manchuria. After so many casualties and no real gains in the region through the treaty, the Japanese felt the need to continue working towards separating Manchuria from China. The Japanese would eventually succeed when they invaded Manchuria in 1931 and controlled it until the end of World War II.

Finally, the division of Korea after World War II

could be seen to have roots in the Treaty of Portsmouth. Japan's surrender ended thirty five years of rule in Korea, but the ensuing struggle between the Soviet and American forces over spheres of influence on the peninsula in 1945 culminated in a similar compromise to the one Roosevelt proposed for Japan and Russia over Sakhalin: Korea was divided between Soviet and American control. Dividing the region was a quick solution to political issues. However, just as with Sakhalin, division was not a forward-thinking solution. Russia regained the southern Japanese half of Sakhalin following World War II, and the people of North Korea continue to suffer the repercussions of an arbitrary division of the peninsula.

———*Ashleigh Fata, MA*

Bibliography and Further Reading

Ericson, Steven and Allen Hockley, eds. *The Treaty of Portsmouth and Its Legacies.* Hanover, NH: Dartmouth College Press, 2008. Print.

Kowner, Rotem, ed. *The Impact of the Russo-Japanese War.* New York: Routledge, 2007. Print.

Nakanishi, Michiko. *Heroes and Friends: Behind the Scenes of the Treaty of Portsmouth.* Portsmouth, NH: Peter E. Randall Publisher, 2005. Print.

Steinberg, John W., et al., eds. *The Russo-Japanese War in Global Perspective: World War Zero.* Boston: Brill, 2005. Print.

Trani, Eugene P. *The Treaty of Portsmouth: An Adventure in American Diplomacy.* Lexington, KY: University of Kentucky Press, 1969. Print.

Wells, David and Sandra Wilson, eds. *The Russo-Japanese War in Cultural Perspective, 1904-5.* New York: St. Martin's Press, 1999. Print.

John Kenneth Turner: *Barbarous Mexico*

Date: 1909
Author: John Kenneth Turner
Genre: book excerpt

Summary Overview
Socialists, leftists, and progressives profoundly transformed American cities, political processes, and public policy at the dawn of the nineteenth century. These do-gooding reformers fought tirelessly to better the lives of the downtrodden in the hope of enacting lasting change that might transform the country, but only one among them forever reshaped the politics of an entire hemisphere. By grit and determination, through tireless and tenacious investigation culminating in his 1909 book, *Barbarous Mexico*, editor, muckraker, and one-time gun runner, John Kenneth Turner, helped rally support for an oppressed peoples living south of the American border, and, as many would come to argue, inspired the successful realization of a popular revolution that would last for over a decade. Putting his own life on the line, Turner spent years going undercover in towns and cities across Mexico to painstakingly document the terrible injustices suffered by the people at the hands of a corrupt state. Government should exist to better the lives of its citizens, he argued, not to rule over them as masters over slaves. Although not without problems, and certainly biased, Turner's writing galvanized the Mexican revolutionaries while also shifting American foreign policy toward intervention. The resulting revolution would reshape not just Mexico and its culture, but both Americas, and ultimately completely restructure political relationships in the region for the next hundred years.

Defining Moment
John Kenneth Turner was a professional journalist with socialist leanings who, in the muckraking tradition of the time, believed it was the responsibility of the press to expose the many ills of society. Muckrakers saw themselves as the defenders of the public good. Heroes with pens. Crusaders. Ida B. Wells shone the spotlight on Jim Crow across the south, Ambrose Bierce exposed the political corruption inside the railroads, Helen Hunt Jackson forced American readers to face their government's policies regarding native peoples, and countless others filled the pages of newspapers and magazines with clear accounts of a dark and unjust world. As for all muckrakers, Turner's main audience was the American public. By changing public opinion through detailed accounts of the Mexican government's brutality, Turner hoped to change policy, as naturally in the United States, public opinion was usually proved at the polls.

Author Biography
John Kenneth Turner was born on April 5, 1878 in Portland, Oregon. Already a self-described socialist at age 16, he committed early to speaking out against corrupt political interests. After graduating from the University of California, Turner married and began work as a journalist, first at the Portland Journal and then at the Los Angeles Herald. In 1907, Turner formally joined the Socialist Labor Party and became enamored of the plight of Mexican revolutionaries. Turner made his first trip to Mexico in 1908, working undercover he found evidence of corruption in the government of Porfirio Diaz, the accounts of which made it into newspapers across the United States. Several more undercover trips followed culminating in the 1909 book *Barbarous Mexico*, in which he laid out a detailed indictment of the Diaz regime. The book was a resounding success, and was translated into dozens of languages including Spanish, and soon was being widely circulated around Mexico, effectively helping to launch the Mexican Revolution. In 1913, writing less but increasingly more involved in Mexican affairs, Turner was arrested by the Mexican government, tortured, and nearly executed. After the United States managed to get him released, Turner spoke out about his treatment at the hands of the Mexican government, directly causing Woodrow Wilson's administration to change its policy toward one favoring in intervention. Turner continued to write, but a growing anti-socialist sentiment following World War I along with criticism that he took money from the Mexican government drove Turner into bitterness and disillusionment. Turner and his wife divorced in 1925,

and by the time of World War II had all but renounced socialism, going even so far as to write a repudiation of Karl Marx. He died largely forgotten in 1948.

HISTORICAL DOCUMENT

From *Barbarous Mexico*, Chapter VII: The Diaz System

The slavery and peonage of Mexico, the poverty and illiteracy, the general prostration of the people, are due, in my humble judgment, to the financial and political organization that at present rules that country—in a word, to what I shall call the "system" of General Porfirio Diaz.

That these conditions can be traced in a measure to the history of Mexico during past generations, is true. I do not wish to be unfair to General Diaz in the least degree. The Spanish Dons made slaves and peons of the Mexican people. Yet never did they grind the people as they are ground today. In Spanish times the peon at least had his own little patch of ground, his own humble shelter; today he has nothing. Moreover, the Declaration of Independence, proclaimed just one hundred years ago, in 1810, proclaimed also the abolition of chattel slavery. Slavery was abolished, though not entirely. Succeeding Mexican governments of class and of church and of the individual held the people in bondage little less severe. But finally came a democratic movement which broke the back of the church, which overthrew the rule of , which adopted a form of government as modern as our own, which freed the slave in fact as well as in name, which gave the lands of the people back to the people, which wiped the slate clean of the blood of the past.

It was at this juncture that General Porfirio Diaz, without any valid excuse and apparently for no other reason than personal ambition, stirred up a series of revolutions which finally ended in his capture of the governmental powers of the land. While professing to respect the progressive institutions which Juarez and Lerdo had established before him, he built up a system all his own, a system in which he personally was the central and all-controlling figure, in which his individual caprice was the constitution and the law, in which all circumstances and all men, big and little, were bent or broken at his will. Like Louis XIV, The State—Porfirio Diaz was The State!

It was under Porfirio Diaz that slavery and peonage were re-established in Mexico, and on a more merciless basis than they had existed even under the Spanish Dons. Therefore, I can see no injustice in charging at least a preponderance of the blame for these conditions upon the system of Diaz.

I say the "system of Diaz" rather than Diaz personally because, though he is the keystone of the arch, though he is the government of Mexico more completely than is any other individual the government of any large country on the planet, yet no one man can stand alone in his iniquity. Diaz is the central prop of the slavery, but there are other props without which the system could not continue upright for a single day. For example, there is the collection of commercial interests which profit by the Diaz system of slavery and autocracy, and which puts no insignificant part of its tremendous powers to holding the central prop upright in exchange for the special privileges that it receives. Not the least among these commercial interests are American, which, I blush to say, are quite as aggressive defenders of the Diaz citadel as any. Indeed, as I shall show in future chapters, these American interests undoubtedly form the determining force in the continuation of Mexican slavery. Thus does Mexican slavery come home to us in the full sense of the term. For the horrors of Yucatan and Valle Nacional, Diaz is to blame, but so are we; we are to blame insofar as governmental powers over which we are conceded to have some control are employed under our very eyes for the perpetuation of a regime of which slavery and peonage are an integral part.

In order that the reader may understand the Diaz system and its responsibility in the degradation of the Mexican people, it will be well to go back and trace briefly the beginnings of that system. Mexico is spoken of throughout the world as a Republic. That is because it was once a Republic and still pretends to be one. Mexico has a constitution which has never been repealed, a constitution said to be modeled after our own, and one which is, indeed, like ours in the main. Like ours, it provides for a national congress, state legislatures and municipal aldermen to make the laws, federal, state and local judges to interpret them, and a president, governors and local executives to administer them. Like ours, it provides for manhood suffrage, freedom of the press and of speech, equality before the law, and the other guarantees of life, liberty and the pursuit of happiness which we ourselves enjoy, in a degree, as a matter of course.

Such was Mexico forty years ago. Forty years ago Mexico was at peace with the world. She had just overthrown, after a heroic war, the foreign prince, Maximilian, who had been seated as emperor by the armies of Napoleon Third of France. Her president, Benito Juarez, is today recognized in Mexico and out of Mexico as one of the most able as well as unselfish patriots of Mexican history. Never since Cortez fired his ships there on the gulf coast had Mexico enjoyed such prospects of political freedom, industrial prosperity and general advancement.

But in spite of these facts and the additional fact that he was deeply indebted to Juarez, all his military promotions having been received at the hands of the latter. General Porfirio Diaz stirred up a series of rebellions for the purpose of securing for himself the supreme power of the land. Diaz not only led one armed rebellion against a peaceable, constitutional and popularly approved government, but he led three of them. For nine years he plotted as a common rebel. The support that he received came chiefly from bandits, criminals and professional soldiers who were disgruntled at the anti-militarist policy which Juarez had inaugurated and which, if he could have carried it out a little farther, would have been effective in preventing military revolutions in the future—and from the Catholic church.

Repeatedly it was proved that the people did not want Diaz at the head of their government. Three times during his first five years of plotting he was an unsuccessful candidate at the polls. In 1867 he received a little more than one-third the votes counted for Juarez. In 1871 he received about three-fifths as many votes as Juarez. In 1872, after the death of Juarez, he ran against Lerdo de Tejada and received only one-fifteenth as many votes as his opponent. While in arms he was looked upon as a common rebel at home and abroad and when he marched into the national capital at the head of a victorious army and proclaimed himself president hardly a European nation would at first recognize the upstart government, while the United States for a time threatened complications.

In defiance of the will of the majority of the people of Mexico, General Diaz, thirty-four years ago, came to the head of government. In defiance of the will of the majority of the people he has remained there ever since—except for four years, from 1880 to 1884, when he turned the palace over to an intimate friend, Manuel Gonzalez, on the distinct understanding that at the end of the four years Gonzalez would turn it back to him again.

Since no man can rule an unwilling people without taking away the liberties of that people, it can be very easily understood what sort of regime General Diaz found it necessary to establish in order to make his power secure. By the use of the army and the police powers generally, he controlled elections, the press and public speech and made of popular government a farce. By distributing the public offices among his generals and granting them free rein to plunder at will, he assured himself of the continued use of the army. By making political combinations with men high in the esteem of the Catholic church and permitting it to be whispered about that the church was to regain some of its former powers, he gained the silent support of the priests and the Pope. By promising full payment of all foreign debts and launching at once upon a policy of distributing favors among citizens of other countries, he made his peace with the world at large.

In other words, General Diaz, with a skill that none can deny, annexed to himself all the elements of power in the country except the nation at large. On the one hand, he had a military dictatorship. On the other, he had a financial camarilla. Himself was the center of the arch and he was compelled to pay the price. The price was the nation at large. He created a machine and oiled the machine with the flesh and blood of a people. He rewarded all except the people; the people were the sacrifice. Inevitable as the blackness of night, in contrast to the sun-glory of the dictator, came the degradation of the people—the slavery, the peonage and every misery that walks with poverty, the abolition of democracy and the personal security that breeds providence, self-respect and worthy ambition ; in a word, general demoralization, depravity.

Take, for example, Diaz's method of rewarding his military chiefs, the men who helped him overthrow the government of Lerdo. As quickly as possible after assuming the power, he installed his generals as governors of the various states and organized them and other influential figures in the nation into a national plunderbund. Thus he assured himself of the continued loyalty of the generals, on the one hand, and put them where he could most effectively use them for keeping down the people, on the other. One variety of rich plum which he handed out in those early days to his governors came in the form of charters giving- his governors the right, as individuals, to organize companies and build railroads, each charter carrying with it a huge sum as a railroad subsidy.

The national government paid for the road and then the governor and his most influential friends owned it. Usually the railroads were ridiculous affairs, were of narrow-gauge and of the very cheapest materials, but the subsidy was very large, sufficient to build the road and probably equip it besides. During his first term of four years in office Diaz passed sixty-one railroad subsidy acts containing appropriations aggregating $40,000,000, and all but two or three of these acts were in favor of governors of states. In a number of cases not a mile of railroad was actually built, but the subsidies are supposed to have been paid, anyhow. In nearly every case the subsidy was the same, $12,880 per mile in Mexican silver, and in those days Mexican silver was nearly on a par with gold.

This huge sum was taken out of the national treasury and was supposedly paid to the governors, although Mexican politicians of the old times have assured me that it was divided, a part going out as actual subsidies and a part going directly into the hands of Diaz to be used in building up his machine in other quarters.

Certainly something more than mere loyalty, however invaluable it was, was required of the governors in exchange for such rich financial plums. It is a well authenticated fact that governors were required to pay a fixed sum annually for the privilege of exploiting to the limit the graft possibilities of their offices. For a long, time Manuel Romero Rubio, father-in-law of Diaz, was the collector of these perquisites, the offices bringing in anywhere from $10,000 to $50,000 per year.

The largest single perquisite whereby Diaz enriched himself, the members of his immediate family, his friends, his governors, his financial ring and his foreign favorites, was found for a long time in the confiscation of the lands of the common people—a confiscation, in fact, which is going on to this day. Note that this land robbery was the first direct step in the path of the Mexican people back to their bondage as slaves and peons.

In a previous chapter I showed how the lands of the Yaquis of Sonora were taken from them and given to political favorites of the ruler. The lands of the Mayas of Yucatan, now enslaved by the henequen planters, were taken from them in almost the same manner. The final act in this confiscation was accomplished in the year 1904, when the national government set aside the last of their lands into a territory called Quintana Roo. This territory contains 43,000 square kilometers or 27,000 square miles. It is larger than the present state of Yucatan by 8,000 square kilometers, and moreover is the most promising land of the entire peninsula. Separated from the island of Cuba by a narrow strait, its soil and climate are strikingly similar to those of Cuba and experts have declared that there is no reason why Quintana Roo should not one day become as great a tobacco-growing country as Cuba. Further than that, its hillsides are thickly covered with the most valuable cabinet and dye-woods in the world. It is this magnificent country which, as the last chapter in the life of the Mayas as a nation, the Diaz government took and handed over to eight Mexican politicians.

In like manner have the Mayos of Sonora, the Papagos, the Tomosachics—in fact, practically all the native peoples of Mexico—been reduced to peonage, if not to slavery. Small holders of every tribe and nation have gradually been expropriated until today their number as property holders is almost down to zero. Their lands are in the hands of members of the governmental machine, or persons to whom the members of the machine have sold for profit—or in the hands of foreigners.

This is why the typical Mexican farm is the million-acre farm, why it has been so easy for such Americans as William Randolph Hearst, Harrison Gray Otis, E. H. Harriman, the Rockefellers, the Guggenheims and numerous others each to have obtained possession of millions of Mexican acres. This is why Secretary of Fomento Molina holds more than 15,000,000 acres of the soil of Mexico, why ex-Governor Terrazas, of Chihuahua, owns 15,000,000 acres of the soil of that state, why Finance Minister Limantour, Mrs. Porfirio Diaz, Vice-President Corral, Governor Pimentel, of Chiapas, Governor Landa y Escandon of the Federal District, Governor Pablo Escandon of Morelos, Governor Ahumada of Jalisco, Governor Cosio of Queretaro, Governor Mercado of Michoacan, Governor Canedo of Sinaloa, Governor Cahuantzi of Tlaxcala, and many other members of the Diaz machine are not only millionaires, but they are millionaires in Mexican real estate.

Chief among the methods used in getting the lands away from the people in general was through a land registration law which Diaz fathered. This law permitted any person to go out and claim any lands to which the possessor could not prove a recorded title. Since up to the time the law was enacted it was not the custom to record titles, this meant all the lands of Mexico. When a man possessed a home which his father had possessed before him, and which his grandfather had possessed, which his great-grandfather had possessed, and which had been in the family as far back as history knew, then he considered that he owned that home, all of his neighbors considered that he owned it, and all governments up to that of Diaz recognized his right to that home.

Supposing that a strict registration law became necessary in the course of evolution, had this law been enacted for the purpose of protecting the land owners instead of plundering them the government would, naturally, have sent agents through the country to apprise the people of the new law and to help them register their property and keep their homes. But this was not done and the conclusion is inevitable that the law was passed for the purpose of plundering.

At all events, the result of the law was a plundering. No sooner had it been passed than the aforesaid members of the governmental machine, headed by the father-in-law of Diaz, and Diaz himself, formed land companies and sent out agents, not to help the people keep their lands, but to select the most desirable lands in the country, register them, and evict the owners. This they did on a most tremendous scale. Thus hundreds of thousands of small farmers lost their property. Thus small farmers are still losing their property. In order to cite an example, I reprint a dispatch dated Merida, Yucatan, April 11, 1909, and published April 12 in the Mexican Herald, an American daily newspaper printed in Mexico City:

"Merida, April 11.—Minister Olegario Molina, of the Department of Fomento, Colonization and Industry, has made a denouncement before the agency here of extensive territory lying adjacent to his lands in Tizimin *partldo*. The denouncement was made through Esteban Re] on Garcia, his *administrador* at that place.

"The section was taken on the ground that those now occupying them have no documents or titles of ownership.

"They measure 2,700 hectares (about 6,000 acres, or over nine square miles), and *include perfectly organized towns*, some fine ranches, including those of Laureano Breseno and Rafael Aguilar, and other properties. The *jefe politico* of Tizimin has notified the population of the town, the owners and laborers on the ranches, and others on the lands, that they will be obliged to vacate within two months or *become subject to the new owner*.

"The present occupants have lived for years upon the land and have cultivated and improved much of it. Some have lived there from generation to generation, and have thought themselves the rightful owners, having inherited it from the original 'squatters.'

"*Mr. Rejon Garcia has also denounced other similar public lands in the Espita partido.*"

Another favorite means of confiscating the homes of small owners is found in the juggling of state taxes. State taxes in Mexico are fearfully and wonderfully made. Especially in the less populous districts owners are taxed inversely as they stand in favor with the personality who represents the government in their particular district. No court, board or other responsible body sits to review unjust assessments. The *jefe politico* may charge one farmer five times as much per acre as he charges the farmer across the fence, and yet Farmer No. 1 has no redress unless he is rich and powerful. He must pay, and if he cannot, the farm is a little later listed among the properties of the *jefe politico*, or one of the members of his family, or among the properties of the governor of the state or one of the members of his family.

But if he is rich and powerful he is often not taxed at all. American promoters in Mexico escape taxation so nearly invariably that the impression has got abroad in this country that land pays no taxes in Mexico. Even Frederick Palmer made a statement to this effect in his recent writings about that country.

Of course such bandit methods as were employed and are still employed were certain to meet with resistance, and so we find numerous instances of regiments of soldiers being called out to enforce collection of taxes or the eviction of time-honored land-holders. Mexican history of the past generation is blotched with stories of massacres having their cause in this thing. Among the most noted of these massacres are those of Papantla and Tomosachic. Manuel Romero Rubio, the late father-in-law of General Diaz, denounced the lands of several thousand farmers in the vicinity of Papantla, Veracruz. Diaz backed him up with several regiments of regulars and before the farmers were all evicted four hundred, or some such number, were killed. In the year 1892, General Lauro Carrillo, who was then governor of Chihuahua, laid a tax on the town of Tomosachic, center of the Tomosachic settlement, which it was impossible for the people to pay. The immediate cause of the exorbitant tax, so the story goes, was that the authorities of the town had refused Carrillo some paintings which adorned the walls of their church and which he desired for his own home. Carrillo carried away some leading men of the town as hostages, and when the people still refused to pay, he sent soldiers for more hostages. The soldiers were driven away, after which Carrillo laid siege to the town with eight regiments. In the end the town was burned and a churchful of women and children were burned, too. Accounts of the Tomosachic massacre place the number of killed variously at from 800 to 2,000.

Cases of more recent blood spillings in the same cause are numerous. Hardly a month passes today without there being one or more reports in Mexican papers of disturbances, the result of confiscation of homes, either through the denunciation method or the excuse of nonpayment of taxes. Notable among these was the case of San Andreas, State of Chihuahua, which was exploited in the Mexican press in April, 1909. According to those press reports, the state authorities confiscated lands of several score of farmers, the excuse being that the owners were delinquent in their taxes. The farmers resisted eviction in a body and two carloads of troops, hurried to the scene from the capital of the state, promptly cleaned them out, shooting some and chasing half a hundred of them into the mountains. Here they stayed until starved out, when they straggled back, begging for mercy. As they came they were thrown into jail, men, women and children. The government carefully concealed the truth as to the number killed in the skirmish with the troops, but reports place it at from five to twenty-five.

An incident of the same class was that of San Carlos, also in the State of Chihuahua, which occurred in August, 1909. At San Carlos, center of a farming district, the misuse of the taxing power became so unbearable that four hundred small farmers banded together, defied a force of fifty *rurales*, forcibly deposed the *jefe politico*, and elected another in his place, then went back to their plows. It was a little revolution which the newspaper reports of the time declared was the first of its kind to which the present government of Mexico ever yielded. Whether the popularly constituted local government was permitted to remain or whether it was later overthrown by a regiment of soldiers is not recorded, though the latter seems most likely.

Graft is an established institution in the public offices of Mexico. It is a right vested in the office itself, is recognized as such, and is respectable. There are two main functions attached to each public office, one a privilege, the other a duty. The privilege is that of using the special powers of the office for the amassing of a personal fortune; the duty is that of preventing the people from entering into any activities that may endanger the stability of the existing regime. Theoretically, the fulfillment of the duty is judged as balancing the harvest of the privilege, but with all offices and all places this is not so, and so we find offices of particularly rosy possibilities selling for a fixed price. Examples are those of the *jefes politicos* in districts where the slave trade is peculiarly remunerative, as at Pachuca, Oaxaca, Veracruz, Orizaba, Cordoba and Rio Blanco; of the districts in which the drafting of soldiers for the army is especially let to the *jefes politicos*; of the towns in which the gambling privileges are let as a monopoly to the mayors thereof; of the states in which there exist opportunities extraordinary for governors to graft off the army supply contracts.

Monopolies called "concessions," which are nothing more nor less than trusts created by governmental decree, are dealt in openly by the Mexican government. Some of these concessions are sold for cash, but the rule is to give them away gratis or for a nominal price, the real price being collected in political support. The public domain is sold in huge tracts for a nominal price or for nothing at all, the money price, when paid at all, averaging about fifty Mexican centavos an acre. But never does the government sell to any individual or company not of its own special choice; that is, the public domain is by no means open to all comers on equal terms. Public concessions worth millions of dollars—to use the water of a river for irrigation purposes, or for power, to engage in this or that monopoly, have been given away, but not indiscriminately. These things are the coin with which political support is bought and as such are grafts, pure and simple.

Public action of any sort is never taken for the sake of improving the condition of the common people. It is taken with a view to making the government more secure in its position. Mexico is a land of special privileges extraordinary, though frequently special privileges are provided for in the name of the common people. An instance is that of the "Agricultural Bank," which was created in 1908. To read the press reports concerning the purpose of this bank one would imagine that the government had launched into a gigantic and benevolent scheme to re-establish its expropriated people in agriculture. The purpose, it was said, was to loan money to needy farmers. But nothing could be farther from the truth, for the purpose is to help out the rich farmer, and only the richest in the land. The bank has now been loaning money for two years, but so far not a single case has been recorded in which aid was given to help a farm that comprised less than thousands of acres. Millions have been loaned on private irrigation projects, but never in lumps of less than several tens of thousands. In the United States the farmer class is an humble class indeed; in Mexico the typical farmer is the king of millionaires, a little potentate. In Mexico, because of the special privileges given by the government, medievalism still prevails outside the cities. The barons are richer and more powerful than were the landed aristocrats before the French Revolution, and the canaille poorer, more miserable.

And the special financial privileges centering in the cities are no less remarkable than the special privileges given to the exploiters of the *hacienda* slave. There is a financial ring consisting of members of the Diaz machine and their close associates, who pluck all the financial plums of the "republic," who get the contracts, the franchises and the concessions, and whom the large aggregations of foreign capital which secure a footing in the country find it necessary to take as coupon-clipping partners. The "Banco Nacional," an institution having some fifty-four branches and which has been compared flatteringly to the Bank of England, is the special financial vehicle of the government camarilla. It monopolizes the major portion of the banking business of the country and is a convenient cloak for the larger grafts, such as the railway merger, the true significance of which I shall present in a future chapter.

Diaz encourages foreign capital, for foreign capital means the support of foreign governments. American capital has a smoother time with Diaz than it has even with its own government, which is very fine from the point of view of American capital, but not so good from the point of view of the Mexican people. Diaz has even entered into direct partnership with certain aggregations of foreign capital, granting these aggregations special privileges in some lines which he has refused to his own millionaires. These foreign partnerships which Diaz has formed has made his government international insofar as the props which support his system are concerned. The certainty of foreign intervention in his favor has been one of the powerful forces which have prevented the Mexican people from using arms to remove a ruler who imposed himself upon them by the use of arms.

When I come to deal with the American partners of Diaz I mention those of no other nationality in the same breath, but it will be well to bear in mind that England, especially, is nearly as heavily as interested in Mexico as is the United States. While this country has $900,000,000 (these are the figures given by Consul General Shanklin about the first of the year 1910) invested in Mexico, England (according to the South American Journal) has $750,000,000. However, these figures by no means represent the ratio between the degree of political influence exerted by the two countries. There the United States bests all the other countries combined.

Yet there are two English corporations so closely identified with the Mexican financial ring as to deserve special mention. They are the combination represented by Dr. F. S. Pearson, of Canada and London, and the other corporation distinct from the first, S. Pearson & Son, Limited. Of Dr. F. S. Pearson it is boasted that he can get any concession that he wants in Mexico, barring alone such a one as would antagonize other foreign interests equally powerful. Dr. Pearson owns the electric railway system of the Federal District and furnishes the vast quantity of electric light and power used in that political division of Mexico. Among other things, he is also a strong power along the American border, where he and his associates own the Mexico Northwestern Railway and several smaller lines, as well as vast tracts of lands and huge lumber interests. In Chihuahua he is establishing a large steel plant and in El Paso, just across the line, he is building a half million dollar sawmill as a part of his Mexican projects.

S. Pearson & Son have been given so many valuable concessions in Mexico that they were responsible for the invention of the term, "the partners of Diaz." Through concessions given them by the government they are in possession of vast oil lands, most of which are unexploited, yet so many of which are producing that the company recently gave out a statement that it would hereafter be in a position to supply its entire trade with Mexican oil. Its distributing company, "El Aguila," contains on its directorate a number of Diaz's closest friends. Pearson & Son, also, have monopolized the contracts for deepening and improving the harbors of Mexico. Since their advent into the country some fourteen years ago the government treasury has paid to this concern $200,000,000 for work on the harbors of Salina Cruz and Coatzacoalcos, and the Isthmus railroad. This amount, a government engineer told me personally, is an even double the price that should have been paid for the work. In 1908 Diaz's congress appropriated $50,000,000 to install an extensive irrigation project on the Rio Nasus, for the benefit of the cotton barons of the Laguna district in the State of Durango. Immediately afterwards the Pearson company organized a subsidiary irrigation concern with a capital of one million. The new company drew up plans for a dam, whereupon the Diaz congress promptly voted $10,000,000 out of the $50,000,000 to be paid to the Pearsons for their dam.

In this chapter I have attempted to give the reader an idea of the means which General Diaz employed to attract support to his government. To sum up, by means of a careful placing of public offices, public contracts and special privileges of multitudinous sorts, Diaz absorbed all of the more powerful men and interests within his sphere and made them a part of his machine. Gradually the country passed into the hands of his officeholders, their friends, and foreigners. And for this the people paid, not only with their lands, but with their flesh and blood. They paid in peonage and slavery. For this they forfeited liberty, democracy and the blessings of progress. And because human beings do not forfeit these things without a struggle, there was necessarily another function of the Diaz machine than that of distributing gifts, another material that went into the structure of his government than favors. Privilege—repression; they go hand in hand. In this chapter I have attempted to sketch a picture of the privilege attached to the Diaz system; in the succeeding chapter I shall attempt to define its elements of repression.

GLOSSARY

camarilla: a small group of people, especially a group of advisers to a ruler or politician, with a shared, typically nefarious, purpose

hacienda: a large estate or plantation

jefe politico: political boss, chief

peonage: debts slavery, or debt servitude

plunderbund: a league of commercial, political, or financial interests that exploits the public

rurales: during the Mexican Revolution members of a mounted police force called the Rural Guard (Guardia Rural)

Document Analysis
In this chapter from *Barbarous Mexico*, Turner describes a corrupt system of graph, extortion, and outright thievery, perpetrated by the very men who had sworn an oath to protect the Mexican people. The main culprit in Turner's story is the President of Mexico himself, General Porfirio Diaz. Turner paints a picture of a vast corrupt web, or system, with Diaz at its center, and driven to keep Mexican workers and farmers in a perpetual state of debt slavery. For the muckraker, there is no difference between crippling rents and chattel slavery, as both had the effect of tying the poor to the heels of the rich.

Turner begins with describing a Mexico of peace and opportunity, ground in revolution and constitution, which is conquered from within by a self-serving, resentful traitor. Despite the objections of the people, Diaz consolidated power, and has ever since, for decades ruled over Mexico under the ruse that the country is in fact a republic. Turner describes a repressive regime that stifles free speech and descent through the heavy handed use of the military and police. A regime that bribes the church and robs the people to enrich friends and patrons.

Much like Tammany Hall in New York and countless entities before or since, the Mexico described by Turner is one of open plunder. Bribes are a matter of public record. "The national government paid for the road and then the governor and his most influential friends owned it," he writes. Money flowed in every direction but always, most strongly, toward the middle. Contracts were sold to the biggest payoff. Political favors were exchanged for money and real estate. Land was taken from the poor and resold by the rich. Friends, family, political allies all saw gains. Turner gives examples of nearly every accusation. Turner names names, even if those names are American. Of the land theft he writes: "Small holders of every tribe and nation have gradually been expropriated until today their number as property holders is almost down to zero. Their lands are in the hands of members of the governmental machine, or persons to whom the members of the machine have sold for profit—or in the hands of foreigners." Turner even describes how it is all done, through exploitation of poor people's lack of education and literacy, to outright con games involving dirty dealing with deeds and leases, even by the law itself. One of the favorite tools of political bosses are taxes, wherein they set tax rates ad hoc, on individual farms and families, while wealthy land owners, those who could afford the bribes, are usually never taxed at all.

Of course, Turner writes, when people eventually resist, soldiers are sent in to keep the peace and teach the agitators a lesson. In this way hundreds have been killed, slaughtered by their own government, in exercising their constitutional rights to speak. There is no easy inner solution, Turner warns, no fix from within, change must come from outside, in the guise of political, financial, even military pressure from the United States and Europe. In the end Turner calls out the Western corporations that have enabled Diaz, challenging the robber barons to do what's right. For one segment of the population to rise another must fall, the inevitable exploitation leads to resistance and finally culminates in the curbing of liberties and loss of freedom. He concludes: "Privilege—repression; they go hand in hand."

Essential Themes

With the rise of the middle class and a growing reform-minded movement in the United States progressive activists began to take to journalism to inform the public and spark change. At the turn of the century several magazines such as Collier's Weekly, Munskey's Magazine, and the renowned McClure's Magazine, started running stories exposing the dark underbelly of industrialized society. Through a combination of investigative and at times yellow, or sensationalist, journalism, these magazines and others aimed to do public service by informing the citizenry of their truth. The wind caught fire and the era of what Theodore Roosevelt coined muckraking, was born. Shaped by events such as the fall of Tammany Hall, muckrakers like Isa M. Tarbell, Lincoln Steffens, and Ray Stannard Baker saw their mission as that of David pitted against an infinitely larger Goliath. They aimed to pour light on what they saw as the worst problems facing modern America: inequality, racism, exploitation, and abuse, not only by individual men, but by the institutions they represented. The muckrakers raked mud at governments, corporations, and especially the robber barons who pulled the strings, and by way of years spent in the trench wars between Hearst and Pulitzer, knew that the bigger and bloodier the story, the bigger the circulation.

The efforts of muckrakers unseated corrupt politicians from coast to coast, allowed for the dismantling of Standard Oil, led to the passage of the Food and Drug Act, and permanently outlawed child labor in the United States. But for some muckrakers progressive reforms in the country, were only part of the prize. As modern nations lurched toward global crisis, muckrakers began to challenge despotic regimes across the world. Their aim was to promote American middle class values, favoring a mixture of absolute freedom and caretaking purity. Echoing in some instances the notes of Darwinian social theory and imperialism, at times moved toward left leaning political interests, above all muckrakers were motivated by a deep spirit of egalitarianism and fairness. Mexico, having suffered for decades under the repressive rule of General Porfirio Diaz was of special interest to crusading journalists such as John Kenneth Turner because its proximity echoed and magnified many of the same injustices thriving in America. The work of muckrakers in exposing the cruelties of the Diaz regime, all be they, as some have argued, at times exaggerated, helped spark revolution.

The later arrest and further petitioning by Turner, along with suspicions of subsequent regimes after the discovery of the Zimmermann Telegram, led to direct American intervention. For the muckrakers change could be made manifest through knowledge, the idea that an informed citizenry could transform the world by will of their demands, and to preserve that change as lasting, democracy had to be preserved and expanded, cruelty and repression had to be resisted at all costs.

The writing of John Kenneth Turner informed the people of the United States and in Europe about the crimes of the Mexican government perpetrated against its own citizenry. The book, *Barbarous Mexico*, was a sensation, no place more significantly than in Mexico itself, where it served to grow popular support for anti-Diaz forces and launched the revolution. The war lasted for a decade, resulting in the overthrow of the old guard, thousands dead, and a slow progression toward inclusiveness, but its effects continued to reverberate for the next fifty years, forever transforming Mexican culture and government. The revolution led to the Constitution of 1917, one of the most progressive minded in the Western Hemisphere, and the rise of the Institutional Revolutionary Party, one of the largest, and certainly longest ruling parties in Mexico. But with the good came the bad, and Mexico struggles with corruption and near-autocratic rule until this day. The revolutionary spirit, and tradition of rebellion, rooted in over a decade of conflict, forever romanticized the Zapatista, and made insurrection a cultural touchstone. Many of the biggest heroes of the rebellion, such as the Pancho Villa, were pressured to fall in line, and murdered when they threatened to stir popular resentments. Turner, in his dying days grew first bitter, then disillusioned. By the end of his life he had given up on revolution and even his passion for reform. By the time of his death in 1948, few cared to remember John Kenneth Turner or his role in the shaping in the political destiny of a nation. In fact, today, he is better remembered in Mexico than he is in his native United States. But the legacy of the muckrakers endures, as the investigate traditions they invented have become an integral part of modern journalism. Without the likes of John Kenneth Turner there would have never been a Woodward and Bernstein, no revelation of the Pentagon Papers, no knowledge of government eavesdropping by institutions like the National Security Agency. By rallying against the corruption of the powerful, and exposing their secrets, the muckrakers institutionalized in America a fundamental expectation for the full, uncensored, and at times ugly truth.

—K.P. Dawes, MA

Bibliography and Additional Reading

Bausum, Ann. *Muckrakers: How Ida Tarbell, Upton Sinclair, and Lincoln Steffens Helped Expose Scandal, Inspire Reform, and Invent Investigative Journalism.* National Geographic, 2007

Cook, Fred J. *The Muckrakers : Sinclair, Tarbell, Russell, Steffens, Phillips : Crusading Journalists Who Changed America.* Doubleday, 1971.

Gilly, Adolfo. *The Mexican Revolution.* The New Press, 2006.

Goodwin, Doris Kearns. *The Bully Pulpit: Theodore Roosevelt, William Howard Taft, and the Golden Age of Journalism.* Simon and Schuster, 2014.

Katz, Friedrich. *The Life and Times of Pancho Villa.* Stanford University Press, 1998.

McLynn, Frank. *Villa and Zapata: A History of the Mexican Revolution.* Basic Books, 2002.

African American Debates

Most African American communities—nearly 90 percent of them—were located in the South as the twentieth century began. The Great Migration, whereby hundreds of thousands of black families moved to northern cities, would not get going until the World War I era and after.

The person who most embodied the conservative stance of black southern leaders at the turn of the century was Booker T. Washington. He counseled accommodation to the segregationist attitudes of southern whites and the learning of practical skills on the part of blacks. Nevertheless, even a traditionalist like Washington became increasingly disenchanted with the policy of accommodation in light of continued discrimination and violence against African Americans—particularly violence in the form of lynching. Black men and black women alike faced lynch mobs for minor infractions, trumped up charges, or even just being relatively successful.

The writer and activist Ida B. Wells first brought national attention to lynching in 1895, with A Red Record. Other African American organizations contributed their voices to the protest, as well. Following race riots in Atlanta in 1906 and in Springfield, Illinois, in 1908, activists formed the Niagara Movement to discuss solutions, and that initiative led to the creation of the National Association for the Advancement of Colored People (NAACP) in 1909.

Undoubtedly the strongest and most eloquent voice of protest in the early twentieth century was W. E. B. Du Bois, a cofounder of the NAACP. Du Bois argued against accommodation and for African American self-help, cultural development, and protest with the aim of achieving racial and economic equality and social justice.

Ida B. Wells: "Lynch Law in America"

Date: 1900
Author: Ida B. Wells
Genre: article

Summary Overview
"Lynch Law in America" appeared in the January 1900 issue of *Arena*, a Boston-based magazine with a broad audience of white Progressives and former abolitionists. "Lynch Law in America" sums up the arguments of the nation's leading anti-lynching activist of the late nineteenth century, Ida B. Wells-Barnett. In this article, she discusses the misinformation about lynching that has deceived the public, and she provides counterevidence that reveals the real motivations and gruesome practices that lynching entails. Her article makes an urgent appeal for white Americans to reassess the wave of anti-black violence across the country and consider its implications for America's international standing and devotion to the rule of law.

Defining Moment
Wells-Barnett published "Lynch Law in America" in the January 1900 issue of *Arena*, a Progressive Boston-based magazine devoted to raising awareness of injustices against the poor and powerless. Through this magazine, she reached an influential white audience that was not likely to read her pamphlets or newspaper articles.

Author Biography
Ida B. Wells was born in 1862 in Holly Springs, Mississippi, to a carpenter, James Wells, and a cook, Elizabeth Wells. Her parents were active supporters of the Republican Party during Reconstruction in Mississippi. When she was sixteen, her parents and a younger sibling died in an epidemic of yellow fever that swept through the community. To prevent the breakup of her remaining family, Wells dropped out of school to obtain a teaching position and became the primary provider for her five younger siblings.

In 1880, Wells accepted an aunt's invitation and moved to Memphis, Tennessee, with two of her younger sisters. Continuing to work as a schoolteacher, she became involved in politics after she was forcibly removed from the "Ladies Car" on a Tennessee rail line and was ordered to move to the smoking car. She sued the company and wrote her first newspaper editorial, for the *Living Way*, about her case, which she won in the local court. The Tennessee Supreme Court later overturned the ruling. Wells soon published a regular column in the *Living Way* under the pen name "Iola." In 1889, she launched her own newspaper, which she edited and co-owned, titled the Memphis *Free Speech and Headlight*.

On March 9, 1892, Wells's life changed dramatically when three of her close friends were found murdered, rumored to be the victims of a lynch mob. Wells was shocked when she determined that the cause of their murder derived from the business rivalry between a white-owned grocery store and the store jointly owned by the three black murder victims. She began to publish investigative journalist articles about the causes of lynching. Her editorial of May 21, 1892, titled "Eight Men Lynched," prompted angry whites to attack her newspaper office and destroy her printing equipment. Wells learned of the attack and of a threat made on her life while she was out of town on business, and she determined never to return to Memphis.

In New York, Wells was hired to write editorials for T. Thomas Fortune's *New York Age*, the leading black newspaper of the day. Her sensational anti-lynching editorials led to a pamphlet, *Southern Horrors: Lynch Law in All Its Phases*, published later in 1892. A testimonial dinner was held in her honor in June, announcing her arrival as a leading national voice for civil rights.

In 1893, Wells joined with Frederick Douglass and other prominent leaders to protest the exclusion and demeaning portrayal of blacks at the Chicago World's Fair. Wells took the lead in preparing a pamphlet titled *Why the Colored American Is Not in the World's Columbian Exposition*, which discussed a variety of racial injustices facing black Americans, from lynching to convict labor. Two thousand copies of the pamphlet were distributed at the fair. That same year, Wells received an invitation from British activists to speak on the subject of lynching in Great Britain. Her first tour brought international pressure upon the white community of the South, particularly in Memphis, where white newspapers were forced to respond to Wells's accusations and disclaim the practice of lynching. A second tour of Great Britain in 1894 was sponsored by the *Chicago Daily Inter-Ocean*, a leading Republican newspaper, which published Wells's accounts of her stay in a regular column titled "Ida B. Wells Abroad." By enlisting the international community to condemn lynching, Wells helped bring about a more honest public discourse on lynching in America, and her claims began to be taken more seriously.

In 1895, Wells married the Chicago lawyer and newspaper editor Ferdinand L. Barnett. Wells made the bold and unusual decision to keep her maiden name but to hyphenate it with Barnett's. The newly rechristened "Wells-Barnett" and her husband had four children; like her decision about her name, her approach to motherhood was equally unusual for the time: She continued to work and often brought her children along on speaking engagements. Wells-Barnett also became deeply involved in editing and writing for Barnett's paper, the *Chicago Conservator*. Wells-Barnett published two more anti-lynching pamphlets: *A Red Record* (1895) and *Mob Rule in New Orleans* (1900). She was also active in many civil rights organizations and women's clubs. The Ida B. Wells Club, for women, was named in her honor in Chicago in 1893. In 1909, she became a founding member of the NAACP. Her anti-lynching work continued for the rest of her life. She left an autobiography incomplete at her death in 1931, although her daughter later edited and published it.

HISTORICAL DOCUMENT

Our country's national crime is *lynching*. It is not the creature of an hour, the sudden outburst of uncontrolled fury, or the unspeakable brutality of an insane mob. It represents the cool, calculating deliberation of intelligent people who openly avow that there is an "unwritten law" that justifies them in putting human beings to death without complaint under oath, without trial by jury, without opportunity to make defense, and without right of appeal. The "unwritten law" first found excuse with the rough, rugged, and determined man who left the civilized centers of eastern States to seek for quick returns in the gold-fields of the far West. Following in uncertain pursuit of continually eluding fortune, they dared the savagery of the Indians, the hardships of mountain travel, and the constant terror of border State outlaws. Naturally, they felt slight toleration for traitors in their own ranks. It was enough to fight the enemies from without; woe to the foe within! Far removed from and entirely without protection of the courts of civilized life, these fortune-seekers made laws to meet their varying emergencies. The thief who stole a horse, the bully who "jumped" a claim, was a common enemy. If caught he was promptly tried, and if found guilty was hanged to the tree under which the court convened.

Those were busy days of busy men. They had no time to give the prisoner a bill of exception or stay of execution. The only way a man had to secure a stay of execution was to behave himself. Judge Lynch was original in methods but exceedingly effective in procedure. He made the charge, impaneled the jurors, and directed the execution. When the court adjourned, the prisoner was dead. Thus lynch law held sway in the far West until civilization spread into the Territories and the orderly processes of law took its place. The emergency no longer existing, lynching gradually disappeared from the West.

But the spirit of mob procedure seemed to have fastened itself upon the lawless classes, and the grim process that at first was invoked to declare justice was made the excuse to wreak vengeance and cover crime. It next appeared in the South, where centuries of Anglo-Saxon civilization had made effective all the safeguards of court procedure. No emergency called for lynch law. It asserted its sway in defiance of law and in favor of anarchy. There it has flourished ever since, marking the thirty years of its existence with the inhuman butchery of more than ten thousand men, women, and children by assault.

It is considered a sufficient excuse and reasonable justification to put a prisoner to death under this "unwritten law" for the frequently repeated charge that these lynching horrors are necessary to prevent crimes against women. The sentiment of the country has been appealed to, in describing the isolated condition of white families in thickly populated negro districts; and the charge is made that these homes are in as great danger as if they were surrounded by wild beasts. And the world has accepted this theory without let or hindrance. In many cases there has been open expression that the fate meted out to the victim was only what he deserved. In many other instances there has been a silence that says more forcibly than words can proclaim it that it is right and proper that a human being should be seized by a mob and burned to death upon the unsworn and the uncorroborated charge of his accuser. No matter that our laws presume every man innocent until he is proved guilty; no matter that it leaves a certain class of individuals completely at the mercy of another class; no matter that it encourages those criminally disposed to blacken their faces and commit any crime in the calendar so long as they can throw suspicion on some negro, as is frequently done, and then lead a mob to take his life; no matter that mobs make a farce of the law and a mockery of justice; no matter that hundreds of boys are being hardened in crime and schooled in vice by the repetition of such scenes before their eyes—if a white woman declares herself insulted or assaulted, some life must pay the penalty, with all the horrors of the Spanish Inquisition and all the barbarism of the Middle Ages. The world looks on and says it is well.

Not only are two hundred men and women put to death annually, on the average, in this country by mobs, but these lives are taken with the greatest publicity. In many instances the leading citizens aid and abet by their presence when they do not participate, and the leading journals inflame the public mind to the lynching point with scare-head articles and offers of rewards. Whenever a burning is advertised to take place, the railroads run excursions, photographs are taken, and the same jubilee is indulged in that characterized the public hangings of one hundred years ago. There is, however, this difference: in those old days the multitude that stood by was permitted only to guy or jeer. The nineteenth century lynching mob cuts off ears, toes, and fingers, strips off flesh, and distributes portions of the body as souvenirs among the crowd. If the leaders of the mob are so minded, coal-oil is poured over the body and the victim is then roasted to death. This has been done in Texarkana and Paris, Tex., in Bardswell, Ky., and in Newman, Ga. In Paris the officers of the law delivered the prisoner to the mob. The mayor gave the school children a holiday and the railroads ran excursion trains so that the people might see a human being burned to death. In Texarkana, the year before, men and boys amused themselves by cutting off strips of flesh and thrusting knives into their helpless victim. At Newman, Ga., of the present year, the mob tried every conceivable torture to compel the victim to cry out and confess, before they set fire to the faggots that burned him. But their trouble was all in vain—he never uttered a cry, and they could not make him confess.

This condition of affairs were brutal enough and horrible enough if it were true that lynchings occurred only because of the commission of crimes against women—as is constantly declared by ministers, editors, lawyers, teachers, statesmen, and even by women themselves. It has been to the interest of those who did the lynching to blacken the good name of the helpless and defenseless victims of their hate. For this reason they publish at every possible opportunity this excuse for lynching, hoping thereby not only to palliate their own crime but at the same time to prove the negro a moral monster and unworthy of the respect and sympathy of the civilized world. But this alleged reason adds to the deliberate injustice of the mob's work. Instead of lynchings being caused by assaults upon women, the statistics show that not one-third of the victims of lynchings are even charged with such crimes. The Chicago Tribune, which publishes annually lynching statistics, is authority for the following:

In 1892, when lynching reached high-water

shooting, drowning, hanging, and burning them alive. Not only this, but so potent is the force of example that the lynching mania has spread throughout the North and middle West. It is now no uncommon thing to read of lynchings north of Mason and Dixon's line, and those most responsible for this fashion gleefully point to these instances and assert that the North is no better than the South.

This is the work of the "unwritten law" about which so much is said, and in whose behest butchery is made a pastime and national savagery condoned. The first statute of this "unwritten law" was written in the blood of thousands of brave men who thought that a government that was good enough to create a citizenship was strong enough to protect it. Under the authority of a national law that gave every citizen the right to vote, the newly-made citizens chose to exercise their suffrage. But the reign of the national law was short-lived and illusionary. Hardly had the sentences dried upon the statute-books before one Southern State after another raised the cry against "negro domination" and proclaimed there was an "unwritten law" that justified any means to resist it.

The method then inaugurated was the outrages by the "red-shirt" bands of Louisiana, South Carolina, and other Southern States, which were succeeded by the Ku-Klux Klans. These advocates of the "unwritten law" boldly avowed their purpose to intimidate, suppress, and nullify the negro's right to vote. In support of its plans the Ku-Klux Klans, the "red-shirt" and similar organizations proceeded to beat, exile, and kill negroes until the purpose of their organization was accomplished and the supremacy of the "unwritten law" was effected. Thus lynchings began in the South, rapidly spreading into the various States until the national law was nullified and the reign of the "unwritten law" was supreme. Men were taken from their homes by "red-shirt" bands and stripped, beaten, and exiled; others were assassinated when their political prominence made them obnoxious to their political opponents; while the Ku-Klux barbarism of election days, reveling in the butchery of thousands of colored voters, furnished records in Congressional investigations that are a disgrace to civilization

The alleged menace of unive been avoided by the absolute negro vote, the spirit of mob n been satisfied and the butchery have ceased. But men, women, the victims of murder by indiv by mobs, just as they had been demands of the "unwritten law' domination." Negroes were killed terms of contracts with their e barns were burned some colored stop it. If a colored man resented a white man and the two came to man had to die, either at the hand then and there or later at the ha speedily gathered. If he showed geous manhood he was hanged the killing was justified by the d was a "saucy nigger." Colored w murdered because they refused where relatives could be found fo Boys of fourteen years have been representatives of American civili all kinds of offenses—and, for n murders to misdemeanors, men ar to death without judge or jury; so t political excuse was no longer nece sale murder of human beings went A new name was given to the ki excuse was invented for so doing.

Again the aid of the "unwritten and again it comes to the rescue. ten years a new statute has been a written law." This statute proclaim crimes or alleged crimes no negro a trial; that no white woman shall charge an assault under oath or to charge to the investigation of a co result is that many men have bee whose innocence was afterward e to-day, under this reign of the "un colored man, no matter what his re from lynching if a white woman, no standing or motive, cares to charge mark, there were 241 persons lynched. The entire number is divided among the following States:

Alabama: 22
Arkansas: 25
California: 3
Florida: 11
Georgia: 17
Idaho: 8
Illinois: 1
Kansas: 3
Kentucky: 9
Louisiana: 29
Maryland: 1
Mississippi: 16
Missouri: 6
Montana: 4
New York: 1
North Carolina: 5
North Dakota: 1
Ohio: 3
South Carolina: 5
Tennessee: 28
Texas: 15
Virginia: 7
West Virginia: 5
Wyoming: 9
Arizona Ter[ritory]: 3
Oklahoma: 2

Of this number, 160 were of negro descent. Four of them were lynched in New York, Ohio, and Kansas; the remainder were murdered in the South. Five of this number were females. The charges for which they were lynched cover a wide range. They are as follows:

Rape: 46
Murder: 58
Rioting: 3
Race Prejudice: 6
No cause given: 4
Incendiarism: 6
Robbery: 6
Assault and battery: 1
Attempted rape: 11
Suspected robbery: 4
Larceny: 1
Self-defense: 1
Insulting women: 2
Desperadoes: 6
Fraud: 1
Attempted murder: 2
No offense stated, boy and girl: 4

In the case of the boy and girl above referred to, their father, named Hastings, was accused of the murder of a white man. His fourteen-year-old daughter and sixteen-year-old son were hanged and their bodies filled with bullets; then the father was also lynched. This occurred in November, 1892, at Jonesville, La.

Indeed, the record for the last twenty years shows exactly the same or a smaller proportion who have been charged with this horrible crime. Quite a number of the one-third alleged cases of assault that have been personally investigated by the writer have shown that there was no foundation in fact for the charges; yet the claim is not made that there were no real culprits among them. The negro has been too long associated with the white man not to have copied his vices as well as his virtues. But the negro resents and utterly repudiates the efforts to blacken his good name by asserting that assaults upon women are peculiar to his race. The negro has suffered far more from the commission of this crime against the women of his race by white men than the white race has ever suffered through his crimes. Very scant notice is taken of the matter when this is the condition of affairs. What becomes a crime deserving capital punishment when the tables are turned is a matter of small moment when the negro woman is the accusing party.

But since the world has accepted this false and unjust statement, and the burden of proof has been placed upon the negro to vindicate his race, he is taking steps to do so. The Anti-Lynching Bureau of the National Afro-American Council is arranging to have every lynching investigated and publish the facts to the world, as has been done in the case of Sam Hose, who was burned alive last April at Newman, Ga. The detective's report showed that Hose killed Cranford, his employer, in self-defense, and that, while a mob was organizing to hunt Hose to punish him for killing a white man, not till twenty-four hours after the murder was the charge of rape, embellished with psychological and physical impossibilities, circulated. That gave an impetus to the hunt, and the Atlanta Constitution's reward of $500 keyed the mob to the necessary burning and roasting pitch. Of five hundred newspaper clippings of that horrible affair, nine-tenths of them assumed Hose's guilt—simply because his murderers said so, and because it is the fashion to believe the negro peculiarly addicted to this species of crime. All the negro asks is justice—a fair and impartial trial in the courts of the country. That given, he will abide the result.

But this question affects the entire American nation, and from several points of view: First, on the ground of consistency. Our watchword has been "the land of the free and the home of the brave." Brave men do not gather by thousands to torture and murder a single individual, so gagged and bound he cannot make even feeble resistance or defense. Neither do brave men or women stand by and see such things done without compunction of conscience, nor read of them without protest. Our nation has been active and outspoken in its endeavors to right the wrongs of the Armenian Christian, the Russian Jew, the Irish Home Ruler, the native women of India, the Siberian exile, and the Cuban patriot. Surely it should be the nation's duty to correct its own evils!

Second, on the ground of economy. To those who fail to be convinced from any other point of view touching this momentous question, a consideration of the economic phase might not be amiss. It is generally known that mobs in Louisiana, Colorado, Wyoming, and other States have lynched subjects of other countries. When their different governments demanded satisfaction, our country was forced to confess her inability to protect said subjects in the several States because of our State-rights doctrines, or in turn demand punishment of the lynchers. This confession, while humiliating in the extreme, was not satisfactory; and, while the United States cannot protect, she can pay. This she has done, and it is certain will have to do again in the case of the recent lynching of Italians in Louisiana. The United States already has paid in indemnities for lynching nearly a half million dollars, as follows:

Paid China for Rock Springs (Wyo.) massacre: $147,748.74

Paid China for outrages on Pacific Coast: 276,619.75

Paid Italy for massacre of Italian prisoners at New Orleans: 24,330.90

Paid Italy for lynchings at Walsenburg, Col[orado]: 10,000.00

Paid Great Britain for outrages on James Bain and Frederick Dawson: 2,800.00

Third, for the honor of Anglo-Saxon civilization. No scoffer at our boasted American civilization could say anything more harsh of it than does the American white man himself who says he is unable to protect the honor of his women without resort to such brutal, inhuman, and degrading exhibitions as characterize "lynching bees." The cannibals of the South Sea Islands roast human beings alive to satisfy hunger. The red Indian of the Western plains tied his prisoner to the stake, tortured him, and danced in fiendish glee while his victim writhed in the flames. His savage, untutored mind suggested no better way than that of wreaking vengeance upon those who had wronged him. These people knew nothing about Christianity and did not profess to follow its teachings; but such primary laws as they had they lived up to. No nation, savage or civilized, save only the United States of America, has confessed its inability to protect its women save by hanging, shooting, and burning alleged offenders.

Finally, for love of country. No American travels abroad without blushing for shame for his country on this subject. And whatever the excuse that passes current in the United States, it avails nothing abroad. With all the powers of government in control; with all laws made by white men, administered by white judges, jurors, prosecuting attorneys, and sheriffs; with every office of the executive department filled by white men—no excuse can be offered for exchanging the orderly administration of justice for barbarous lynchings and "unwritten laws." Our country should be placed speedily above the plane of confessing herself a failure at self-government. This cannot be until Americans of every section, of broadest patriotism and best and wisest citizenship, not only see the defect in our country's armor but take the necessary steps to remedy it. Although lynchings have steadily increased in number and barbarity during the last twenty years, there has been no single effort put forth by the many moral and philanthropic forces of the country to put a stop to this wholesale slaughter. Indeed, the silence and seeming condonation grow more marked as the years go by.

A few months ago the conscience of this country was shocked because, after a two-weeks trial, a French judicial tribunal pronounced Captain Dreyfus guilty. And yet, in our own land and under our own flag, the writer can give day and detail of one thousand men, women, and children who during the last six years were put to death without trial before any tribunal on earth. Humiliating indeed, but altogether unanswerable, was the reply of the French press to our protest: "Stop your lynchings at home before you send your protests abroad."

GLOSSARY

Anglo-Saxon: a reference to the Germanic tribes that invaded and settled Great Britain; more generally, Anglo-American civilization

Captain Dreyfus: Alfred Dreyfus, a Jewish French military officer who was at the center of a scandal that divided France in the 1890s after he was falsely convicted of treason

Irish Home Ruler: an Irish person who wanted an Ireland independent from the United Kingdom

"jumped" a claim: the practice of stealing someone's mining property

Mason and Dixon's line: a line surveyed in the eighteenth century to settle border disputes in the American colonies, more generally referring to the boundary between the North and the South in the United States

Spanish Inquisition: a tribunal established in fifteenth-century Spain to enforce Catholic orthodoxy; used often as a symbol of cruelty because of its use of torture and extreme punishments

Document Analysis

In "Lynch Law in America," Wells-Barnett declares that lynching has become a national crime to which all sections of the country have contributed and must bear responsibility. She begins the article by discussing the origin and evolution of lynching in the United States and the transformation of the practice into a tool of racist terror in the South. She describes the current situation with respect to the widespread incidents of lynching and the various excuses offered for it. Finally, she urges Americans to take action against the crime of lynching.

Lynching, according to Wells-Barnett, began in the far West, where settlers had no access to courts or the legal system. She refers to the communal justice of the frontier as following the "unwritten law." This custom, as she describes it, was harsh and severe and usually resulted in immediate hanging from the nearest tree. Facing hardships of a rough existence, there was little time to give prisoners constitutionally guaranteed rights, such as trial by jury, sworn testimony, right to a defense, or the right of appeal. Verdicts were immediately carried out (for the lack of jails perhaps), and judgments were final. But as "civilization spread into the Territories" and the apparatus of administered law became available, the practice of lynching "gradually disappeared from the West."

In its next phase, Wells-Barnett argues, the practice of lynching arose in the southern states and reflected a spirit of lawlessness that infected southerners during Reconstruction. When the Fourteenth and Fifteenth

Amendments conferred equal citizenship and the right of suffrage on the former slaves in the South, many white southerners refused to accept those changes. In defiance of the law, and the constitutional rights of blacks, unreconstructed Confederates began to form into vigilante groups. Secret societies such as the Red Shirts and the Ku Klux Klan inaugurated a campaign of violence that aimed to "beat, exile, and kill negroes" in opposition to the Reconstruction laws. The excuse for this outbreak of racist violence was that black suffrage would result in "negro domination"—a term that southerners used to refer to a government in which blacks made up an important constituency of the majority party and thus possessed political power. During this time, the excuse for killing blacks derived from the assertion of their rights, whether voting rights or contract rights or the right of self-defense.

After Reconstruction collapsed in the face of white violence, a new excuse for anti-black violence in the South appeared: the protection of white women. Wells-Barnett calls this justification a new "statute in the unwritten law." Wells-Barnett argues that when a white women accuses a black man of improper behavior toward her, including a mere insult, it has become accepted that a white mob must be raised and the man put to death. Unlike the violence of the Ku Klux Klan during Reconstruction, the practice of lynching has achieved, as Wells-Barnett shows, universal acceptance and approval by whites throughout the country. The theory that white womanhood is in imminent danger from the uncontrollable urges of black men is an unproven accusation, in Wells-Barnett's estimation, since it has not been subjected to the rule of law or proper criminal investigation. By connecting the "justified" racist violence of lynching to the widely reviled, politically motivated violence of Reconstruction, Wells-Barnett not only shows the continuity of this behavior of white southerners but also casts suspicion on the new excuse for it.

Wells-Barnett goes on to describe the kinds of violence that have become ritually incorporated into the act of "lynching." Great publicity and offers of rewards usually precede the act itself. When the accused is caught, a public ceremony is held. A holiday is sometimes declared by local authorities so that schoolchildren can witness the event and onlookers from afar can be given time to travel by rail to it. Without any trial or testimony, the accused is tortured and often burned alive. Dismemberment of the body is common, with the mob taking home souvenirs in the form of fingers, toes, and ears. Wells-Barnett compares these barbarities to the tortures of the Middle Ages and the Spanish Inquisition. The word *lynching* hardly encompasses all of the kinds of violence perpetrated by white mobs in these brutal events.

In the next section of the article, Wells-Barnett discusses some of the misconceptions about lynching and points to facts about the accused that have been ignored. First, she says that lynching has not been confined to the southern states but that it has begun to spread into the North and West as well. Second, she remarks that the widespread belief that lynchings have been enacted only in cases of threats or assaults on white women is untrue. Less than one-third of all cases of lynching involved accusations by white women against black men. In many of those cases, the accusations were later recanted or shown to have no merit. Some cases involved the lynching of women and children, rather than men. Statistics also show that a wide variety of accused crimes have resulted in lynchings, and, in some cases, no accusation at all had been leveled at the victims. Wells-Barnett cites the case of Sam Hose, who was burned alive in Georgia. The charge of rape was falsely proclaimed in the press in the days leading up to the lynching, but afterward, it was shown to have been an unfounded rumor and that Hose's "crime" was, in fact, an act of self-defense against his employer.

Wells-Barnett concludes her article by offering four reasons to oppose the practice of lynching: consistency, economy, national honor, and patriotism. Her four reasons have a common theme: Each refers to America's reputation in the eyes of the world. First, she points out that the practice of lynching conflicts with the democratic traditions of the nation. Throughout the article, she has referred to the violation of the rule of law and the Constitution. She goes further and alludes to the fact that the United States has presented itself to the world as a beacon of freedom. Indeed, Americans have denounced the injustices of other nations around the world to their oppressed minorities. She cites Turkish oppression of the Armenian Christians, Russian oppression of the Jews, English oppression of the Irish, Indian oppression of women, and Spanish oppression of Cubans as examples of causes Americans have taken up. Unless Americans confront their own oppression of blacks in tolerating the practice of lynching, she suggests, their criticism of other nations will appear as rank hypocrisy to the rest of the world.

Second, she points out that several instances of foreign nationals being lynched have caused the United States to pay hefty indemnities to other nations. By admitting that the US government cannot protect "said subjects" of other nations or bring the participants of a mob to justice, these payments are "humiliating in the extreme." Third, and related to this point, America's inability to maintain the rule of law puts its government on a par with the least "civilized" and respected nations of the world. She compares the triumph of "savagery" in the American South with the cannibalism of the South Sea Islands and the brutality of American Indian warriors. Their acts, Wells-Barnett suggests, can be explained by the lack of familiarity of these nations with Christianity, but the United States cannot use that excuse. National honor, therefore, demands that America reject lynching so as to live up to its own laws and moral principles.

Finally, Wells-Barnett appeals to American patriotism. If the world does not respect the United States, no American citizen can expect to travel abroad or participate in discussions on international affairs without inviting ridicule. The pride of the country is at stake, she implies. She concludes by citing a French newspaper that scoffed at American criticism of the French judicial system (which had been criticized widely for anti-Semitism in the treason case of Captain Alfred Dreyfus) by suggesting that Americans attend to their own lynching problem before criticizing others.

Perhaps the most interesting aspect of Wells-Barnett's article is her use of the concept of "civilization" and her invocation of world opinion and America's international standing to support her case. In her use of "civilization," Wells-Barnett turns the tables on racists who insist upon the "savagery" of black men. Control of primal urges (sexual ones especially) were considered a mark of "civilized" people in the nineteenth century. White women were in peril, supposedly, because black men could not control their sexual urges. Wells-Barnett, however, points out that white men have sexually transgressed the color line far more often than black men. But the crime of rape or sexual assault against a black woman by a white man has never been punished. Furthermore, the orgy of blood and murder that she describes in the practice of lynching suggests that white men have given in to the most primal forms of bloodlust and revenge. By the standards of "civilization" southern whites have more to answer for than blacks, as they seem unable to control their basest passions.

In 1893 and 1894, Wells-Barnett had undertaken two speaking tours of the British Isles to publicize her investigations into the practice of lynching. These extremely successful tours managed to create greater international awareness of the situation for southern blacks and initiate an international dialogue about it. British criticism stung Americans and put apologists for lynching on the defensive in the United States. Wells-Barnett clearly intends to press this strategy in the conclusion of "Lynch Law in America." By emphasizing the negative consequences of lynching on America's reputation on the world stage, she hits upon an effective strategy that puts pressure on white Americans regardless of their sympathy for black victims of lynching. It is in America's best interest to curb these embarrassing episodes and to follow the rule of law for all citizens, regardless of race, she maintains. Wells-Barnett takes every opportunity to remind her readers that America's response to lynching is being observed from abroad.

Essential Themes

Organized white violence against African Americans has had a long history in the United States. Slavery involved systematic violence against blacks on many levels. During the era of slavery, nonslaveholding whites often belonged to "slave patrols" that were called out to track down fugitive slaves and put down slave revolts. Organized like militias, these patrols fostered white solidarity and maintained the institution of slavery through community action. Community participation in slave patrols was a precursor to the organized violence against blacks in the postslavery period.

At the same time, white mob violence was also common in northern cities, particularly in the form of anti-abolitionist riots. Mobs that attacked abolitionists and broke up abolitionist meetings, beginning in the 1830s, often targeted blacks individually. It was not uncommon for northern whites to lynch or beat an innocent African American to death. One of the worst incidents of US racial violence came during the Civil War, when draft riots broke out in 1863 in northern cities, including New York, and turned into race riots, with dozens of blacks being murdered in the streets.

With emancipation, a new era of racial violence was inaugurated. The congressional policy of Reconstruction of the former Confederate states instituted new constitutional rights for black Americans, including the guarantee of equality before the law and the rights to hold political office, to serve on juries, and to vote.

The majority of white southerners vigorously opposed these policies, and some resorted to organized violence and terrorism to prevent blacks from exercising them. White militias were formed—such as the Red Shirts of South Carolina or the White Leagues of Louisiana and Mississippi—and used force and intimidation to prevent blacks from voting or attending political meetings. These groups were often responsible for atrocities like the slaughter of between seventy and one hundred fifty black men, women, and children in Colfax, Louisiana, in 1873. Secret societies like the Ku Klux Klan and the Knights of the White Camellia pursued similar goals but operated in disguise and undertook a variety of misdeeds under the cover of darkness. Mutilation, torture, and sexual assault were common by such groups. Over four hundred lynchings of blacks in the South are estimated to have occurred between 1868 and 1871 alone.

With the collapse of the Reconstruction governments in the late 1870s, the political incentive for white violence diminished, but the violence itself persisted, taking on new forms. White supremacist governments were firmly entrenched in each of the former Confederate states, and relatively few blacks attempted to exercise political power in the post-Reconstruction period. Southern white violence against blacks began to fade as an issue of national concern, with major incidents becoming less frequent for a few years. Incidents of white mob lynchings of individual black victims, however, began to rise again steadily in the mid- to late 1880s. The word *lynching* itself, which once had no racial connotations, began to refer strictly to white mob actions directed against blacks. Prior to the late 1880s, lynching had been practiced as a form of vigilante justice against accused criminals of all races, usually in isolated, typically rural regions of the country. In these cases, victims most often stood accused of a serious crime, especially rape or murder, which had aroused the ire of the community. Community anger, coupled with isolation from legal institutions, overrode the constitutional rights of the accused to a fair trial. But 1885 was the last year in which more whites than blacks were executed by lynch mobs. After that, the "lynch law" came to apply primarily against blacks accused of a crime in the South, and these incidents occurred often with the approval and assistance of police and legal authorities.

The peak year for lynchings in the United States came in 1892, with over 230 incidents documented nationwide, 161 of which involved black victims. The lynching of blacks also took on increasingly ritualized, predictable forms. Once a lynch mob was raised, police authorities would hand the accused over to the mob and disclaim responsibility for the victim's fate. The victim would often be tortured and mutilated—castration was common—before being shot or hanged. The body was often burned, and pieces were taken as souvenirs. Authorities never brought charges against participants in lynch mobs, and these murders were invariably classified as having been carried out "by persons unknown."

At first, there was little outcry over these acts and scant press coverage. It was widely rumored that such acts were done exclusively in response to the crime of rape, or attempted rape, of white women by black men (although, in fact, these accusations were present in only one-quarter of all cases of lynching). Because of the sensitive nature of rape—euphemistically known as the "nameless" or "unspeakable" crime—few black leaders or newspaper editors were willing to defend the victims who had been accused of it. Beginning in 1889, however, a white novelist and Radical Republican, Albion W. Tourgée, began denouncing lynchings in his weekly column in the *Chicago Daily Inter-Ocean*, and he detailed incidents of lynchings in which rape was not an issue and the "crimes" of the accused were based on flimsy accusations. The journalist Ida B. Wells-Barnett became the first black writer to systematically address the issue of lynching, in her articles for the *New York Age* in 1892.

Led by Wells, the campaign against lynching grew in prominence in the 1890s. Anti-lynching activists demanded that due process and the right to a fair trial be respected, no matter what the nature of the crimes alleged. Beginning in 1896 in Ohio, a few states began to adopt anti-lynching laws that brought punishment to the perpetrators of lynchings and the communities in which they occurred. Nevertheless, lynching continued to occur with impunity, especially in the southern states, and this became a major factor in the "Great Migration" of blacks out of the South beginning in the 1890s.

After the *Plessy v. Ferguson* case of 1896, in which the US Supreme Court ruled segregation to be consistent with the Fourteenth Amendment and the US Constitution generally, the movement for protection of African American rights suffered a devastating setback. The decade that followed has been described by historians as the "nadir" of the black experience in America because of the sense of hopelessness and despair. In 1898, the whites of Wilmington, North Carolina, massacred black leaders and publicists in a violent overthrow of the local government that had previously respected black voting rights. Allegations that black leaders had encouraged the rape of white women served as the primary cause for the white violence. Everywhere in the South, whites moved to disenfranchise black voters by law or by force. Some black leaders, such as Booker T. Washington, appeared ready to give up on political protest in favor of equal rights, while others, such as Wells-Barnett, continued the struggle.

In 1908 a bloody race riot in Springfield, Illinois, began when a police sheriff refused to turn over two black prisoners to a lynch mob. The event became the catalyst for a new civil rights organization: An alliance of black and white radicals—including Wells-Barnett—formed the National Association for the Advancement of Colored People (NAACP) with a mission to reverse the spread of racism and anti-black violence in the country.

In 1919, the NAACP published *Thirty Years of Lynching in the United States, 1889–1918*, which publicized many incidents of lynching and investigated the truth behind them. The NAACP also sponsored a national anti-lynching law—the Dyer bill—that would make lynching a federal crime and allow federal investigation and prosecution of its perpetrators. Although the Dyer bill was blocked by filibuster in the Senate, its proposal marked the beginning of a sharp decline in lynching across the nation. Total national lynchings dropped into the single digits, with eight incidents in 1936, and remained at that level for the next thirty years. Effective publication and condemnation of the practice by the NAACP and other groups were a major factor in turning the tide.

Although she was one of the few black leaders who made lynching a top focus for concern in the 1890s—a decade in which blacks also faced the imposition of disenfranchisement and Jim Crow segregation—Wells-Barnett's anti-lynching campaign succeeded in bringing the issue to national attention. Heightened awareness outside the South about the pervasiveness of this practice and the dubiousness of the public excuses for it eventually flowered into broad public disapproval. The response to mob violence in Springfield, Illinois, in 1908 that launched the NAACP reflected a changed opinion among Progressive northerners, who saw the spread of lynching as a moral concern of the first order. No doubt Wells-Barnett's campaign deserves a great deal of credit for this change in opinion.

—Mark Elliott, PhD

Bibliography and Further Reading

Bay, Mia. *To Tell the Truth Freely: The Life of Ida B. Wells.* New York: Hill and Wang, 2009.

Behind the Veil: Documenting African American Life in the Jim Crow South. Duke University Libraries Digital Collection, 2016. Web. 2 Aug. 2016. <http://library.duke.edu/digitalcollections/behindtheveil/>.

Davidson, James West. *"They Say": Ida B. Wells and the Reconstruction of Race.* New York: Oxford UP, 2007.

Giddings, Paula J. *Ida: A Sword among Lions.* New York: HarperCollins/Amistad, 2008.

Hendricks, W. A. *Gender, Race, and Politics in the Midwest.* Bloomington: Indiana UP, 1998.

Karcher, Carolyn L. "Ida B. Wells and Her Allies against Lynching: A Transnational Perspective." *Comparative American Studies* 3.2 (June 2005): 131–151.

_____. "The White 'Bystander' and the Black Journalist 'Abroad'": Albion W. Tourgée and Ida B. Wells as Allies against Lynching." *Prospects* 29 (October 2005): 85–119.

McMurry, Linda O. *To Keep the Waters Troubled: The Life of Ida B. Wells.* New York: Oxford University Press, 1998.

The Rise and Fall of Jim Crow. PBS/Educational Broadcasting Corporation, 2002. Web. 2 Aug. 2016. <http://www.pbs.org/wnet/jimcrow/>.

Schechter, Patricia A. *Ida B. Wells-Barnett and American Reform, 1880–1930.* Chapel Hill: University of North Carolina Press, 2001.

Wells, Ida B. *Southern Horrors and Other Writings: The Anti-Lynching Campaign of Ida B. Wells, 1892–1900.* Ed. Jacqueline Jones Royster. New York: Bedford Books, 1997.

George H. White: Farewell Address to Congress

Date: 1901
Author: George H. White
Genre: address; speech

Summary Overview

George H. White's Farewell Address to Congress was delivered to the House of Representatives on January 29, 1901. White was a two-term Republican congressman from North Carolina's Second Congressional District (known as the Black Second because of its large African American majority). During his years in the Fifty-fifth and Fifty-sixth Congresses, he had been the only black man among 357 representatives and 84 senators from 42 states. On the day White spoke, his legislative service was drawing to a close because he had chosen not to run for a third term in the November 1900 election, a decision he had made known in a speech on June 30 of that year. In consequence, he would leave the House of Representatives on March 4, 1901, the last African American to serve in Congress in the three and a half decades following the Civil War. Because of changes in the southern political landscape, there was little likelihood that another African American would soon succeed him.

White was a proud and stubborn man, and his four years in the House had been contentious and far from satisfying. He was the twenty-second African American since 1870 to hold congressional office, and like most of his predecessors (nineteen of them in the House, two in the Senate, and all of them Republicans), he was subjected to the institutional bias of white representatives and senators, who openly denigrated African Americans as ignorant, inferior, and incompetent; mocked them with "darky stories"; and mimicked them with an affected "plantation" dialect. In the weeks before his farewell speech, White had attempted on several occasions to call his white colleagues to account for such behavior but had been denied the opportunity. His efforts, for example, to introduce legislation on behalf of African Americans who, in the late 1890s, faced disenfranchisement by state legislatures and mob violence from white supremacy groups, brought immediate objection from southern Democrats that effectively left his proposals stillborn. When he boldly proposed reducing southern representation in Congress proportionate to the number of African Americans denied the vote, Democratic newspapers in North Carolina accused him of inciting racial unrest. These were matters that weighed heavily on White's mind as he prepared his valedictory address.

Defining Moment

There were 357 congressmen from forty-five states in the Fifty-sixth Congress. The division of the House was 187 Republicans, 161 Democrats, 5 Populists, and 4 members of splinter parties. Since the measure before the House of Representatives was the annual agricultural appropriation bill—under the existing rules the House was sitting as a Committee of the Whole, and members could choose not to attend—it is likely that not all of the members were present. An unknown number of spectators were in the galleries, but because White was known to be speaking that day, a goodly number of African Americans were probably present. (A gifted and forceful speaker, White had drawn such an audience on past occasions.)

White's full speech was printed twice in 1901: in the *Congressional Record* (Fifty-sixth Congress, 2nd session, volume 34, part 2) and as a stand-alone fourteen-page booklet, entitled *Defense of the Negro Race—Charges Answered. Speech of Hon. George H. White, of North Carolina, in the House of Representatives, January 29, 1901*. According to White's biographer, Benjamin H. Jutesen, portions of the Farewell Address were reprinted in such contemporary African American newspapers as the Washington, DC, *Colored American*; the *Cleveland Gazette*; and the *New York Age*, the most widely read black paper in the country. The address later appeared in several anthologies of black writing, giving it wide circulation well into the twentieth century. Its closing words—particularly "Phoenix-like he will rise up some day and come again"—resonated among African Americans for the next fifty years.

Author Biography

George Henry White was born on December 18, 1852, in Rosindale, North Carolina, to Wiley F. White, a free African American farmer, and his wife, Mary, a slave. (Under North Carolina law, George White was free at birth because of his father's status.) Wiley White could read and write and apparently passed those skills on to his son, who, at the end of the Civil War, attended black public schools in nearby Columbus County. In 1873, he entered Howard University in Washington, DC, earning a normal school (teaching) certificate in 1877. White qualified for the North Carolina bar in 1879 and practiced law while serving as the principal of several public schools, including the New Bern normal school for training black teachers. He gradually assumed leadership roles in the communities where he taught and became in time a respected public official.

White entered politics in 1880 when he was elected as a Republican to the first of two terms in the lower house of the North Carolina General Assembly. As a member of the legislature's Education Committee, he proposed improvements in teacher training, mandatory schooling for the young, and increased funding for white and black public schools. He took on important duties in the county Republican Party, served in the upper house of the General Assembly, and was a delegate to several Republican National Conventions. In 1886, White was elected to the prestigious and politically powerful position of solicitor (public prosecutor) for the Second Judicial District, thereby setting the stage for his entrance onto the national scene. Possessing a shrewd political mind, he bided his time for a decade, building public support in the predominantly African American "Black Second" congressional district, which elected him to the House of Representatives in 1896—the lone African American in the Fifty-fifth Congress but a part of the Republican majority brought into office with the winning Republican presidential candidate, William McKinley.

White was assigned to the House Agriculture Committee. He supported most Republican-backed foreign policy measures. His major focus, however, during his four years in Congress was on civil rights for African Americans. He was unsuccessful in both terms in securing federal action against the southern states' continuing disenfranchisement of black voters. Reelected to the House in 1898, White continued on the Agriculture Committee and served as well on the District of Columbia Committee, which oversaw Washington's municipal government. In his second term, he repeatedly sought anti-lynching legislation that would make mob violence a potential capital offense, but found little support from either the president or his fellow Republicans.

Although White considered himself a national spokesperson for African Americans (and the black newspapers seemed to agree), his positions were increasingly viewed as too radical by his House colleagues and by Republicans in his home district, where changes in the election law in his second term denied the ballot to many of his black supporters. In 1900, he made it known he would not run for reelection. In interviews with northern newspapers, he said that he could not live in North Carolina and be treated as a man, and he urged his black constituents to emigrate to the North or to the West in search of a better life.

Following his dramatic and powerful Farewell Address and his retirement from Congress in March 1901, White opened a successful private law practice in Washington, DC, moving his office to Philadelphia four years later. As an entrepreneur, he developed Whitesboro, a town for African Americans on the New Jersey shore at Cape May, and established the People's Savings Bank in Philadelphia to provide banking services, including home and business loans, to the city's African Americans. In the summer of 1917, after the People's Savings Bank became insolvent and closed its doors, White was appointed assistant city solicitor, his first public position since his years in Congress. He died in his sleep on December 28, 1918, ten days after his sixty-sixth birthday.

HISTORICAL DOCUMENT

I want to enter a plea for the colored man, the colored woman, the colored boy, and the colored girl of this country. I would not thus digress from the question at issue and detain the House in a discussion of the interests of this particular people at this time but for the constant and the persistent efforts of certain gentlemen upon this floor to mold and rivet public sentiment against us as a people and to lose no opportunity to hold up the unfortunate few who commit crimes and depredations and lead lives of infamy and shame, as other races do, as fair specimens of representatives of the entire colored race. And at no time, perhaps, during the Fifty-sixth Congress were these charges and countercharges, containing, as they do, slanderous statements, more persistently magnified and pressed upon the attention of the nation than during the consideration of the recent reapportionment bill, which is now a law. As stated some days ago on this floor by me, I then sought diligently to obtain an opportunity to answer some of the statements made by gentlemen from different States, but the privilege was denied me; and I therefore must embrace this opportunity to say, out of season, perhaps, that which I was not permitted to say in season.

In the catalogue of members of Congress in this House perhaps none have been more persistent in their determination to bring the black man into disrepute and, with a labored effort, to show that he was unworthy of the right of citizenship than my colleague from North Carolina, Mr. Kitchin. During the first session of this Congress, while the Constitutional amendment was pending in North Carolina, he labored long and hard to show that the white race was at all times and under all circumstances superior to the Negro by inheritance if not otherwise, and the excuse for his party supporting that amendment, which has since been adopted, was that an illiterate Negro was unfit to participate in making the laws of a sovereign State and the administration and execution of them; but an illiterate white man living by his side, with no more or perhaps not as much property, with no more exalted character, no higher thoughts of civilization, no more knowledge of the handicraft of government, had by birth, because he was white, inherited some peculiar qualification, clear, I presume, only in the mind of the gentleman who endeavored to impress it upon others, that entitled him to vote, though he knew nothing whatever of letters. It is true, in my opinion, that men brood over things at times which they would have exist until they fool themselves and actually, sometimes honestly, believe that such things do exist....

I might state as a further general fact that the Democrats of North Carolina got possession of the state and local government since my last election in 1898, and that I bid adieu to these historic walls on the 4th day of next March, and that the brother of Mr. Kitchin will succeed me. Comment is unnecessary. In the town where this young gentleman was born, at the general election last August for . . . state and county officers, Scotland Neck had a registered white vote of 395, most of whom of course were Democrats, and a registered colored vote of 534, virtually if not all of whom were Republicans, and so voted. When the count was announced, however, there were 831 Democrats to 75 Republicans; but in the town of Halifax, same county, the result was much more pronounced.

In that town the registered Republican vote was 345, and the total registered vote of the township was 539, but when the count was announced it stood 990 Democrats to 41 Republicans, or 492 more Democratic votes counted than were registered votes in the township. Comment here is unnecessary....

It would be unfair, however, for me to leave the inference upon the minds of those who hear me that all of the white people of the State of North Carolina hold views with Mr. Kitchin and think as he does. Thank God there are many noble exceptions to the example he sets, that, too, in the Democratic party; men who have never been afraid that one uneducated, poor, depressed Negro could put to flight and chase into degradation two educated, wealthy, thrifty white men. There never has been, nor ever will be, any Negro domination in that state, and no one knows it any better than the Democratic party. It is a convenient howl, however, often resorted to in order to consummate a diabolical purpose by scaring the weak and gullible whites into support of measures and men suitable to the demagogue and the ambitious office seeker, whose crave for office overshadows and puts to flight all other considerations, fair or unfair. . . .

I trust I will be pardoned for making a passing reference to one more gentleman—Mr. Wilson of South Carolina—who, in the early part of this month, made a speech, some parts of which did great credit to him, showing, as it did, capacity for collating, arranging, and advancing thoughts of others and of making a pretty strong argument out of a very poor case.

If he had stopped there, while not agreeing with him, many of us would have been forced to admit that he had done well. But his purpose was incomplete until he dragged in the reconstruction days and held up to scorn and ridicule the few ignorant, gullible, and perhaps purchasable negroes who served in the State legislature of South Carolina over thirty years ago. Not a word did he say about the unscrupulous white men, in the main bummers who followed in the wake of the Federal Army and settled themselves in the Southern States, and preyed upon the ignorant and unskilled minds of the colored people, looted the States of their wealth, brought into lowest disrepute the ignorant colored people, then hied away to their Northern homes for ease and comfort the balance of their lives, or joined the Democratic party to obtain social recognition, and have greatly aided in depressing and further degrading those whom they had used as easy tools to accomplish a diabolical purpose.

These few ignorant men who chanced at that time to hold office are given as a reason why the black man should not be permitted to participate in the affairs of the government which he is forced to pay taxes to support. He insists that they, the Southern whites, are the black man's best friend, and that they are taking him by the hand and trying to lift him up; that they are educating him. For all that he and all Southern people have done in this regard, I wish in behalf of the colored people of the South to extend our thanks. We are not ungrateful to friends, but feel that our toil has made our friends able to contribute the stinty pittance which we have received at their hands.

I read in a Democratic paper a few days ago, the *Washington Times*, an extract taken from a South Carolina paper, which was intended to exhibit the eagerness with which the Negro is grasping every opportunity for educating himself. The clipping showed that the money for each white child in the State ranged from three to five times as much per capita as was given to each colored child. This is helping us some, but not to the extent that one would infer from the gentleman's speech.

If the gentleman to whom I have referred will pardon me, I would like to advance the statement that the musty records of 1868, filed away in the archives of Southern capitols, as to what the Negro was thirty-two years ago, is not a proper standard by which the Negro living on the threshold of the twentieth century should be measured. Since that time we have reduced the illiteracy of the race at least 45 percent. We have written and published nearly 500 books. We have nearly 800 newspapers, three of which are dailies. We have now in practice over 2,000 lawyers, and a corresponding number of doctors. We have accumulated over $12,000,000 worth of school property and about $40,000,000 worth of church property. We have about 140,000 farms and homes, valued in the neighborhood of $750,000,000, and personal property valued about $170,000,000. We have raised about $11,000,000 for educational purposes, and the property per-capita for every colored man, woman and child in the United States is estimated at $75.

We are operating successfully several banks, commercial enterprises among our people in the South land, including one silk mill and one cotton factory. We have 32,000 teachers in the schools of the country; we have built, with the aid of our friends, about 20,000 churches, and support 7 colleges, 17 academies, 50 high schools, 5 law schools,

5 medical schools and 25 theological seminaries. We have over 600,000 acres of land in the South alone. The cotton produced, mainly by black labor, has increased from 4,669,770 bales in 1860 to 11,235,000 in 1899. All this was done under the most adverse circumstances. We have done it in the face of lynching, burning at the stake, with the humiliation of "Jim Crow" laws, the disfranchisement of our male citizens, slander and degradation of our women, with the factories closed against us, no Negro permitted to be conductor on the railway cars, whether run through the streets of our cities or across the prairies of our great country, no Negro permitted to run as engineer on a locomotive, most of the mines closed against us. Labor unions—carpenters, painters, brick masons, machinists, hackmen and those supplying nearly every conceivable avocation for livelihood—have banded themselves together to better their condition, but, with few exceptions, the black face has been left out. The Negroes are seldom employed in our mercantile stores. At this we do not wonder. Some day we hope to have them employed in our own stores. With all these odds against us, we are forging our way ahead, slowly, perhaps, but surely, You may tie us and then taunt us for a lack of bravery, but one day we will break the bonds. You may use our labor for two and a half centuries and then taunt us for our poverty, but let me remind you we will not always remain poor! You may withhold even the knowledge of how to read God's word and learn the way from earth to glory and then taunt us for our ignorance, but we would remind you that there is plenty of room at the top, and we are climbing. . . .

Mr. Chairman, before concluding my remarks I want to submit a brief recipe for the solution of the so-called "American Negro problem." He asks no special favors, but simply demands that he be given the same chance for existence, for earning a livelihood, for raising himself in the scales of manhood and womanhood, that are accorded to kindred nationalities. Treat him as a man; go into his home and learn of his social conditions; learn of his cares, his troubles, and his hopes for the future; gain his confidence; open the doors of industry to him; let the word "Negro" "colored" and "black" be stricken from all the organizations enumerated in the federation of labor.

Help him to overcome his weaknesses, punish the crime-committing class by the courts of the land, measure the standard of the race by its best material, cease to mold prejudicial and unjust public sentiment against him, and . . . he will learn to support . . . and join in with that political party, that institution, whether secular or religious, in every community where he lives, which is destined to do the greatest good for the greatest number. Obliterate race hatred, party prejudice, and help us to achieve nobler ends, greater results and become satisfactory citizens to our brother in white.

This, Mr. Chairman, is perhaps the negroes' temporary farewell to the American Congress; but let me say, Phoenix-like he will rise up some day and come again. These parting words are in behalf of an outraged, heart-broken, bruised, and bleeding, but God-fearing people, faithful, industrious, loyal people—rising people, full of potential force.

Mr. Chairman, in the trial of Lord Bacon, when the court disturbed the counsel for the defendant, Sir Walter Raleigh raised himself up to his full height and, addressing the court, said:

Sir, I am pleading for the life of a human being.

The only apology that I have to make for the earnestness with which I have spoken is that I am pleading for the life, the liberty, the future happiness, and manhood suffrage for one-eighth of the entire population of the United States.

GLOSSARY

bummers: foragers or marauders during the Civil War

Fifty-sixth Congress: the congressional term from 1899 to 1901, following the practice of numbering two-year congressional terms

hackmen: the drivers of hacks, or cabs

Jim Crow: the informal term used to designate laws and social customs that deprived African Americans of their liberties and rights

Lord Bacon: Francis Bacon, seventeenth-century scientist, jurist, statesman, and philosopher, tried by Parliament for corruption

Mr. Kitchin: William W. Kitchin, White's political rival, whose younger brother, Claude, would succeed White in office

Mr. Wilson: Stanyarne Wilson, a US congressional representative from South Carolina

musty records of 1868: the records of the state constitutional conventions during Reconstruction

phoenix: a legendary Arabian bird that was said to burn itself to death and then rise from the ashes

Sir Walter Raleigh: an English aristocrat and courtier of the late sixteenth and early seventeenth centuries who was a favorite of Queen Elizabeth I

Document Analysis

The document reproduced here is the speech George H. White delivered on the floor of the US House of Representatives on January 29, 1901, now known as his Farewell Address. The topic before the House that day was the annual appropriation bill of the House Agriculture Committee, a bill that included the continuation of a free seed program to the nation's farmers and payment of the salaries of scientists and other experts in the Department of Agriculture. Given the complexity and importance of the bill (H.R. 13801), the House was sitting as a Committee of the Whole, which means, in parliamentary terms, that the usual rules of procedure for legislative action are suspended, allowing any member of the House, who chooses to attend, to speak freely. A chairman chosen from the majority presides (rather than the speaker), and any vote is by a simple majority (rather than a specified quorum). The House in regular session may vote to overturn any decisions made in this way.

Because the House was meeting on January 29, 1901, as a Committee of the Whole, White was free to ignore H.R. 13801 and turn, if he wished, to more personal concerns. In his opening remarks, which are not included here, White acknowledges the importance of the bill's contents and then boldly seizes the opportunity to deliver a strong defense of his African American constituents and offer a profoundly moving farewell to the Congress he has faithfully served for four years.

White's eloquent opening sentences in paragraph 1 are among the best-known lines in his address. They provide a powerful introduction to the reasons he is ignoring the bill before the House and introduce his indictment of his colleagues, who have consistently slandered his race by linking "the unfortunate few" who commit crimes or lead less than exemplary lives to the majority of hard-working, responsible African Americans. Their calumnies intensified during the last weeks of the Fifty-sixth Congress as the House took up the reapportionment bill, which would increase the size of the House in 1903 by twenty-nine seats, bringing the chamber's total membership to 386 from 357. The debate gave White an opportunity to urge Congress to overturn the disenfranchisement provisions that several southern states had added to their constitutions or their election laws, thereby removing African Americans from the voting roles. White points out that because of parliamentary rulings he was denied the opportunity during the debate to respond to his white southern colleagues' demeaning statements.

White in paragraph 2 singles out his fellow representative from North Carolina, William W. Kitchin, a Democrat and a long-time political rival, as a particular scourge of African Americans, whose right to vote has been stripped away through a state constitutional amendment in August 1900. White deplores the unfairness of the amendment, which permits illiterate white men to vote if they register before 1908 and their ancestors were qualified to vote in 1867 or earlier, a qualification that is denied to African Americans, who are subject to a literacy test (including an interpretation of the state constitution) and a poll tax.

In paragraphs 3 and 4, White announces that he will leave the House in the next five weeks. He explains that William Kitchin's younger brother, Claude, would succeed him as a result of questionable vote counts. White carefully avoids charging fraud and says only that the returns went unchallenged in North Carolina's general election in August 1900.

In paragraphs 6 through 10, White directs his audience's attention to Stanyarne Wilson, a Democrat from South Carolina, who earlier took a leading role in the debate on reapportionment and disenfranchisement in the southern states. An example of White's biting wit is in paragraph 6, where he neatly insults his colleague without openly breaking the House rule that requires the chamber's members to treat each other with courtesy and respect. The veiled insult continues in paragraph 7 as White seems to accept Wilson's assertions that the Reconstruction government in South Carolina was corrupt and ineffective because of its Republican, biracial composition. What White is saying, however, is that if corruption existed (he concedes there may have been a few ignorant and gullible blacks in the legislature), it was not due to the African Americans in the legislature but to the work of unscrupulous whites from the North (carpetbaggers) who exploited the unstable institutions of the postwar South and then retreated to their northern homes or, White says in a witty aside, remained in the South and became Democrats.

White continues his assault on Wilson's argument in paragraph 8. He suggests that Wilson is probably correct in saying that southern whites are working to lift southern blacks and that he is grateful, but he quickly points out that it is black laborers who make it possible for their white "friends" to contribute the "stinty [limited or meager] pittance" that supports black education. White adds in paragraph 9 that for all the self-congratulation implicit in the Democrats' asserting that they are aiding African Americans to help themselves, statistics show that far greater sums are spent per capita on white schools than on black schools in South Carolina.

As he continues to rebut Wilson in paragraph 10, White's initial reference to "the musty records of 1868" is to the records of the several state constitutional conventions that year called to organize new governments during Reconstruction. Most of those constitutions provided universal education, suffrage to all males over twenty-one, and the right to hold public office regardless of race. The opponents of such measures then and in subsequent years argued that African Americans were unprepared for such responsibilities. In their view, most blacks were and continued to be ignorant, illiterate, or indolent, a caricature White rejects out of hand. He pointedly suggests that the condition of the freed slaves and of African Americans generally has changed significantly in the thirty-two years since the state constitutions were written. In paragraphs 10 and 11, he catalogs the advances that the race, despite obstacles imposed by the white world, have achieved in every area of life. It should be noted that the property values and other monetary references are in line with American averages in the nineteenth century.

Paragraphs 12 and 13 provide a stirring challenge to Congress and to white America to understand who African Americans are by moving past skin color and race to see them as human beings like themselves. White's language and his argument here are crystal clear: African Americans want what all Americans want: freedom, equality, family, and work. (The federation of labor White refers to in the last line of paragraph 12 is the recently organized American Federation of Labor, which was a cooperative composed of many independent trades, some of them identified as black or colored unions of, say, carpenters or plumbers, that united in the federation to seek common wages, rights, and protections.) Paragraph 13 carries White's defense of his people into the social and civic world, arguing that African Americans are denied full participation there not because of their own indifference but rather because of white prejudice and race hatred.

Paragraph 14 is White's eloquent valedictory. His first sentence is a bold prediction that references the phoenix, the fabulous bird of ancient myth that is eternally renewed through death. The second offers in a dozen or so words his brilliant refutation of white America's hate-filled stereotypes of African Americans. Together they make up the most quoted passage from the speech in the twentieth century and, to many African Americans, the most memorable.

The anecdote that White relates in paragraphs 15 and 16—a transition to his concluding remark—never happened. The English philosopher Sir Francis Bacon's bribery trial took place in 1621; he was found guilty, removed from office as attorney general, and fined. The English courtier and navigator Sir Walter Raleigh was executed in 1618 for disobeying King James I's orders not to invade Spanish territory in North America. In his first trial for treason in 1603, Raleigh, defending himself, unsuccessfully pleaded with the court to have his accusers brought to face him because "I am here for my life!"

White's speech comes full circle in paragraph 17 in a single-sentence summary of his argument, echoing the opening lines and reiterating his term-long struggle to get the House to respond to both the white supremacy violence and the disenfranchisement of African Americans in the southern states.

Essential Themes

White was the last of twenty African Americans elected to the House of Representatives in the nineteenth century, who collectively served thirty-eight two-year terms between 1870 and 1901. (The two African Americans elected to the Senate in the 1870s served a total of seven years.) They were all among the most visible beneficiaries of Radical Reconstruction policies that extended the suffrage to black males and other civil rights to the African American population in the South in the aftermath of the Civil War. That extension of rights generated opposition from powerful forces in the defeated South, and by the end of the century the personal freedoms of African Americans had been reduced or replaced by Jim Crow laws that, in turn, created a harsh segregated world in the American South.

The Civil War ended with the question of how to return the southern states to the Union unresolved and a matter of some confusion as a result of President Abraham Lincoln's assassination. Lincoln in 1862 had used his executive authority to appoint provisional military governors for the southern states recaptured by the Union army. His plan for Reconstruction was simplicity itself: States would be readmitted when at least 10 percent of the voters in 1860 took an oath of allegiance to the United States. After Lincoln's death, a struggle emerged in Congress between those who urged a continuation of the 10 percent plan and the antislavery wing of the Republican Party, who demanded a program of black civil rights to protect African Americans throughout the South. The Radicals, as they came to be known, gained control of the Congress and immediately clashed with President Andrew Johnson, whose policies seemed to support white supremacy.

In the 1866 congressional elections, the Radical Republicans gained two-thirds of the seats in Congress and immediately passed, over President Johnson's veto, the Reconstruction Acts of 1867 that divided the old Confederacy into five military districts. To secure readmission, each state had to accept the Thirteenth Amendment to the Constitution, which outlawed slavery, and the Fourteenth Amendment, which extended a broad range of civil and political rights to African Americans. A key provision required the states to revise their constitutions to include extending the vote to black males. The Freedmen's Bureau was authorized to oversee the implementation of the new laws and ensure that the rights of African Americans were protected. In 1868, most of southern states revised their constitutions to include, among other rights, the franchise (the vote) for blacks. They eliminated the earlier legislatures' Black Codes, which restricted or denied the postwar civil rights of the newly freed African Americans and controlled a broad range of personal freedoms, including employment, education, housing, and the right to move about freely after dark. In the fall elections Republican-dominated legislatures comprising a loose coalition of African Americans and whites emerged. The whites from the North were called carpetbaggers, while those from the South were labeled scalawags by their Democratic opposition. In due course, they enacted major civil rights programs in their states, including universal public education and revisions to the judicial system that included placing blacks on trial juries.

Beginning in 1870, Congress passed the Enforcement Acts, a series of laws that protected black voting rights, office holding, and jury service and (in 1871) outlawed the Ku Klux Klan, which had waged a campaign of violence and death against African Americans in the rural South. (Although the Klan disbanded in 1872—to be revived in 1915—white violence in the form of lynchings continued against blacks through the remainder of the nineteenth century and into the next.) The Radical Republicans passed the Civil Rights Act of 1875, prohibiting discrimination in hotels, trains, and other public spaces. By then, there was a growing movement among southern whites opposed to racial equality that sought to restore southern white rule in the old Confederacy. Known as the "Redeemers," they enjoyed a major success with the election of Wade Hampton, a former Confederate general dedicated to white supremacy, to the governorship of South Carolina in 1876. Another victory came with the formal end of Reconstruction starting in April 1877 with the withdrawal of federal troops from South Carolina and Louisiana, fulfilling the terms of the Compromise of 1877 that settled the disputed presidential election of 1876. In that election, the winner of the popular vote, Samuel J. Tilden, a Democrat, fell one vote short of a majority in the Electoral College because of confusing ballot counts from three southern states. After days of wrangling, the Democrats in Congress (most of them southerners) agreed to make the Republican Rutherford B. Hayes president. In return, Hayes promised to restore civilian rule in the two states still under military control. Shortly after his swearing-in, Hayes ordered all remaining federal troops out of the South.

During the next two decades, the largely Democratic Redeemers replaced the biracial Republican governments throughout the South and gradually stripped away the hard-won rights of African Americans. In consequence, Jim Crow laws, which in time denied blacks access to transportation, housing, employment, recreation, and education, created a racially segregated society that lasted until the middle of the next century. The laws were given legal sanction by the US Supreme Court in 1883 when it declared the Civil Rights Act of 1875 unconstitutional on the ground that Congress did not have the power to regulate the conduct and transactions of individuals. In 1896, the Court gave racial segregation constitutional standing in *Plessy v. Ferguson*.

The final assault by southern whites on African American empowerment began with the Mississippi Plan in 1890. Developed in the state's constitutional convention, the plan was manifested in a "purity" clause that expressly stated in the constitution that "blacks must no longer be allowed to vote." The means of enforcement (in order to circumvent the Fifteenth Amendment) was to apply a property requirement and a poll tax or a literacy test or both as a basis for voting. The literacy test over time evolved into an "understanding" test, in which the would-be voter would be required to interpret a passage from the state's constitution. The Mississippi Plan spread through the South and by 1910 had been adopted in seven states. Its constitutionality was affirmed by the Supreme Court in 1898 in *Williams v. Mississippi*. That same year the Louisiana legislature provided the last refinement to eliminating the black vote by adding a grandfather clause to the state constitution specifically exempting from the property, poll tax, and literacy tests "any individuals whose fathers or grandfathers were legally entitled to vote prior to January 1, 1867." No African American, of course, could meet that requirement. With variations in the date, the clause was soon added to other state constitutions in the South.

Most of these limitations on African Americans were in place in North Carolina in time for the fall election in 1900. Added to them were the internal political conflicts that divided the Democratic majority in the state from the once-dominant Republicans. Examining the possibility of his winning a third term in Congress and well aware of the defeats he had met in the House—his anti-lynching bill had died in the Judiciary Committee—George White decided not to seek reelection.

Because White had already forgone the 1900 election and thus given up his seat in the House, his Farewell Address had little impact on Congress—not that day or in the years following. His words did nothing to lessen the institutional racism that he and his African American predecessors had experienced in the House and Senate, and Congress failed to halt the southern states' violations of the Fifteenth Amendment that denied the vote to generations of African Americans until the 1960s. As for White himself, the southern Democrats were happy to be rid of him, as were many Republicans, who had been uncomfortable with the North Carolinian's outspoken and unapologetic ways. Congressmen of both parties from the North and West well into the twentieth century remained indifferent to the second-class status of African Americans, 90 percent of whom lived in the South in 1901.

White continued in the House without incident for another month and quietly withdrew into his Washington home on March 3, 1901, in advance of the swearing-in of his successor from North Carolina, a white man who had been the beneficiary of the state's changed voting standards that barred most African Americans from voting. The next day, at noon on March 4, both houses of the North Carolina legislature marked the official end of White's term in office by passing resolutions of thanksgiving that heralded a new era in which no black man would be serving in the US Congress. The principal newspaper in the state hailed the departure of its "insolent negro" as a blessing not only to the state but to the nation as well.

For nearly three decades, there were no African Americans in Congress until, as a consequence of the Great Migration of thousands of black men and women out of the South to the North, Oscar Stanton De Priest, a Republican from the South Side of Chicago, entered the Seventy-first Congress in March 1929—the first African American elected to the House of Representatives in the twentieth century. Through the following years the number of black men and women in Congress increased, especially in the years after 1950. In the 1960s, as a result of peaceful demonstrations by black students and others throughout the South, the barriers that had prevented African Americans from voting (and that had discouraged George White from seeking reelection in 1890) were removed. In January 1964, the Twenty-fourth Amendment to the US Constitution barred the use of a poll tax as a prerequisite to voting in national elections. The use of a poll tax in state and local elections was declared unconstitutional by the US Supreme Court in March 1966 in *Harper v. Virginia State Board of Elections*. President Lyndon Johnson signed the historic Voting Rights Act in August 1965, outlawing the use of literacy tests in voter registration and providing the federal government with powers to enforce the Fifteenth Amendment.

Additional milestones are worth noting: In November 1968, Edward W. Brooke, a Republican from Massachusetts, was elected to the Ninetieth Congress and served two terms in the US Senate—the first African American elected to that chamber in eighty-five years. And in 1973, Andrew Young, Democrat of Georgia, and Barbara Jordan, Democrat of Texas, entered the Ninety-third Congress as the first African Americans from the Deep South to be elected to the House since White bid the chamber farewell in 1901. Since 1870, a total of 119 African Americans have been elected to the House, six to the Senate. When the 111th Congress convened in January 2009, there were forty-one African Americans in the House of Representatives and one in the Senate, and Barack Obama was president of the United States. Nine months later, speaking at the Congressional Black Caucus Foundation's annual Phoenix Awards Dinner in Washington, DC, President Obama saluted his audience, telling them that they were the fulfillment of White's prophecy that "Phoenix-like" African American men and women would "rise up and come again" to serve the nation in the national government.

———*Allan L. Damon, MA*

Bibliography and Additional Reading

Anderson, Eric. *Race and Politics in North Carolina, 1872–1901: The Black Second*. Baton Rouge: Louisiana State UP, 1981.

"Black Americans in Congress." *History, Art & Archives: United States House of Representatives*. Office of Art & Archives, Office of the Clerk, n.d. Web. 2 Aug. 2016. <http://baic.house.gov/>.

"Defense of the Negro Race—Charges Answered." *Documenting the American South*. University Library, UNC Chapel Hill, 2004. Web. 2 Aug. 2016. <http://docsouth.unc.edu/nc/whitegh/whitegh.html>.

Dray, Philip. *Capitol Men: The Epic Story of Reconstruction through the Lives of Black Congressmen*. Boston: Houghton Mifflin, 2008.

Hahn, Steven. *A Nation Under Our Feet: Black Political Struggles in the Rural South, from Slavery to the Great Migration*. Cambridge, MA: Belknap Press of Harvard UP, 2003.

Jutesen, Benjamin R. *George Henry White: An Even Chance in the Race of Life*. Baton Rouge: Louisiana State UP, 2001.

North Carolina History Project. John Locke Foundation, 2016. Web. 2 Aug. 2016. <http://www.northcarolinahistory.org/>.

"Southern Negro's Plaint." *New York Times*, 26 Aug. 1900.

White, George Henry. *In His Own Words: The Writings, Speeches, and Letters of George Henry White*. Ed. Benjamin R. Jutesen. Lincoln, NE.: iUniverse, Inc., 2004.

Booker T. Washington: "Statement on Suffrage"

Date: 1903
Author: Booker T. Washington
Genre: address; speech

Summary Overview

Following his success as principal of Tuskegee Institute, Booker T. Washington began to address the issues confronting African Americans in the South. Washington was an astute politician. He developed associations with northern business leaders and southern politicians that enabled him to operate Tuskegee as a black educational institution. As he addressed the concerns of his race, he balanced his attack on the injustice of segregation and racial violence with his need to survive in an increasingly racist and violent South. The significant point is that Washington was not silent. He spoke out about the injustice of discrimination and biased suffrage laws and the horror of lynching. But his language was more moderate than shrill. He retained the belief that logic would prevail and that if they were shown that it was in their interest to promote the development of blacks, the leadership of the South and educated and cultured southerners would support the cause of racial justice.

Washington used a variety of means to express his views. His most famous statements were public speeches, but he also published "letters to the editor" in southern and northern newspapers, gave interviews, and wrote articles and private letters to powerful and influential white men to express his political and racial views. His "Statement on Suffrage" was made in a letter published in the Philadelphia *North American*. In it, Washington takes the position that voting laws passed in the South were largely unjust and discriminatory but that blacks' right to vote should be part of an overall process of education.

Defining Moment

Booker T. Washington's "Statement on Suffrage" sought to speak to the interests of both white southerners and African Americans. He encouraged African Americans to seek an industrial education because he believed that both blacks and whites would benefit. A more academically focused education for blacks would give rise to controversy and a white backlash. By deemphasizing the importance of civil and political rights, Washington hoped to attract the support of southern whites who favored social segregation and black disenfranchisement, but who might be convinced to support African Americans learning a trade. Similarly, Washington's suggestion that blacks seek the advice of whites when voting was almost certainly intended to appease whites who were hostile to black political participation.

At the same time, Washington was addressing a black audience. He assured the black community that he, too, opposed voting laws that disenfranchised the majority of black voters on the basis of race. However, the attainment of voting rights would be a long process. African Americans should concentrate on gaining an industrial education, which would not only increase educational levels in the black community but would also lead to greater economic prosperity and self-sufficiency. When blacks had accumulated more wealth and property they would be better prepared to fight for civil and political equality. Black suffrage would then be more acceptable to whites.

Author Biography

Booker Taliaferro Washington was born on a farm near Hale's Ford in the foothills of the Blue Ridge Mountains in Franklin County, Virginia, most likely on April 5, 1856. Washington spent the first eight years of his childhood as a slave. Following emancipation, he moved with his mother, brother, and sister to join his stepfather, who had found employment in the saltworks in Malden, West Virginia. Emancipation did not significantly raise the economic well-being of the family. The young Washington alternated between working in the saltworks and attending school.

At the age of sixteen, Washington left home for Virginia to further his education at Hampton Institute, under the influence of General Samuel C. Armstrong and his theory of industrial education. Three years later, he graduated as one of the school's top students and a protégé of General Armstrong. After a short stint as a schoolteacher in Malden, Washington returned to Hampton as a member of the faculty and for additional education. In May 1881, Armstrong arranged for his prize student to be named principal of a recently authorized Alabama state normal and industrial school for black students.

When Washington arrived in Tuskegee, he discovered that the school existed only on paper. Despite his youth and inexperience, he managed to create the school—acquiring land, erecting the buildings, and recruiting the faculty. More impressively, he mastered the political, administrative, and financial skills that he needed to form a black institution in the inhospitable hills of northern Alabama. By the early 1890s, Tuskegee Institute was a success, and Washington was beginning to address the broader political and economic issues that confronted African Americans.

In 1895, Washington was asked to speak at the opening ceremonies of the Atlanta Exposition. This speech was a phenomenal success and transformed Washington from a southern educator to the most influential and powerful African American in the United States. He consulted with presidents and corporate leaders and headed a political machine that dispersed funds and political patronage throughout the black community. In 1901, his status brought him an invitation to lunch at the White House with President Theodore Roosevelt.

Washington confronted the task of devising a strategy for blacks to successfully move from slavery to citizenship, a process made more difficult by the rise in racism, discrimination, and violence characterizing the beginning of the twentieth century. Washington's strategy addressed the needs of the vast majority of African Americans who resided in the South. It focused on education, self-reliance, hard work, and economic success. While his critics accused him of accepting discrimination and white supremacy, Washington consistently spoke out against segregation, lynching, and the restrictions placed on black suffrage. Nevertheless, in the early twentieth century, W. E. B. Du Bois and other African American leaders, especially in the North, became increasingly dissatisfied with Washington's program and his political power. The Niagara Movement, founded in 1905, and later, the National Association for the Advancement of Colored People (NAACP), founded in 1909, challenged his leadership. Still, at the time of his death in November 1915, Washington was still the most widely known and respected African American leader in the United States.

HISTORICAL DOCUMENT

MR. PRESIDENT AND GENTLEMEN OF THE BOARD OF DIRECTORS AND CITIZENS.

One-third of the population of the South is of the Negro race. No enterprise seeking the material, civil, or moral welfare of this section can disregard this element of our population and reach the highest success. I but convey to you, Mr. President and Directors, the sentiment of the masses of my race when I say that in no way have the value and manhood of the American Negro been more fittingly and generously recognized than by the managers of this magnificent Exposition at every stage of its progress. It is a recognition that will do more to cement the friendship of the two races than any occurrence since the dawn of our freedom.

Not only this, but the opportunity here afforded will awaken among us a new era of industrial progress. Ignorant and inexperienced, it is not strange that in the first years of our new life we began at the top instead of at the bottom; that a seat in Congress or the state legislature was more sought than real estate or industrial skill; that the political convention of stump speaking had more attraction than starting a dairy farm or truck garden.

A ship lost at sea for many days suddenly sighted a friendly vessel. From the mast of the unfortunate vessel was seen a signal, "Water, water; we die of thirst!" The answer from the friendly vessel at once came back, "Cast down your bucket where you are." A second time the signal, "Water, water; send us water!" ran up from the distressed vessel, and was answered, "Cast down your bucket where you are." And a third and fourth signal for water was answered, "Cast down your bucket where you are." The captain of the distressed vessel, at last heeding the injunction, cast down his bucket, and it came up full of fresh, sparkling water from the mouth of the Amazon River. To those of my race who depend on bettering their condition in a foreign land or who underestimate the importance of cultivating friendly relations with the southern white man, who is their next-door neighbour, I would say: "Cast down your bucket where you are"—cast it down in making friends in every manly way of the people of all races by whom we are surrounded.

Cast it down in agriculture, mechanics, in commerce, in domestic service, and in the professions. And in this connection it is well to bear in mind that whatever other sins the South may be called to bear, when it comes to business, pure and simple, it is in the South that the Negro is given a man's chance in the commercial world, and in nothing is this Exposition more eloquent than in emphasizing this chance. Our greatest danger is that in the great leap from slavery to freedom we may overlook the fact that the masses of us are to live by the productions of our hands, and fail to keep in mind that we shall prosper in proportion as we learn to dignify and glorify common labor and put brains and skill into the common occupations of life; shall prosper in proportion as we learn to draw the line between the superficial and the substantial, the ornamental gewgaws of life and the useful. No race can prosper till it learns that there is as much dignity in tilling a field as in writing a poem. It is at the bottom of life we must begin, and not at the top. Nor should we permit our grievances to overshadow our opportunities.

To those of the white race who look to the incoming of those of foreign birth and strange tongue and habits for the prosperity of the South, were I permitted I would repeat what I say to my own race, "Cast down your bucket where you are." Cast it down among the eight millions of Negroes whose habits you know, whose fidelity and love you have tested in days when to have proved treacherous meant the ruin of your firesides. Cast down your bucket among these people who have, without strikes and labor wars, tilled your fields, cleared your forests, built your railroads and cities, and brought forth treasures from the bowels of the earth, and helped make possible this magnificent representation of the progress of the South. Casting down your bucket among my people, helping and encouraging them as you are doing on these grounds, and to education of head, hand, and heart, you will find that they will buy your surplus land, make blossom the waste places in your fields, and run your factories. While doing this, you can be sure in the future, as in the past, that you and your families will be surrounded by the most patient, faithful, law-abiding, and unresentful people that the world has seen. As we have proved our loyalty to you in the past, in nursing your children, watching by the sick-bed of your mothers and fathers, and often following them with tear-dimmed eyes to their graves, so in the future, in our humble way, we shall stand by you with a devotion that no foreigner can approach, ready to lay down our lives, if need be, in defense of yours, interlacing our industrial, commercial, civil, and religious life with yours in a way that shall make the interests of both races one. In all things that are purely social we can be as separate as the fingers, yet one as the hand in all things essential to mutual progress.

There is no defense or security for any of us except in the highest intelligence and development of all. If anywhere there are efforts tending to curtail the fullest growth of the Negro, let these efforts be turned into stimulating, encouraging, and making him the most useful and intelligent citizen. Effort or means so invested will pay a thousand per cent. interest. These efforts will be twice blessed—"blessing him that gives and him that takes."

There is no escape through law of man or God from the inevitable:—

The laws of changeless justice bind
Oppressor with oppressed;
And close as sin and suffering joined
We march to fate abreast.

Nearly sixteen millions of hands will aid you in pulling the load upward, or they will pull against you the load downward. We shall constitute one-third and more of the ignorance and crime of the South, or one-third its intelligence and progress; we shall contribute one-third to the business and industrial prosperity of the South, or we shall prove a veritable body of death, stagnating, depressing, retarding every effort to advance the body politic.

Gentlemen of the Exposition, as we present to you our humble effort at an exhibition of our progress, you must not expect overmuch. Starting thirty years ago with ownership here and there in a few quilts and pumpkins and chickens (gathered from miscellaneous sources), remember the path that has led from these to the inventions and production of agricultural implements, buggies, steam-engines, newspapers, books, statuary, carving, paintings, the management of drug-stores and banks, has not been trodden without contact with thorns and thistles. While we take pride in what we exhibit as a result of our independent efforts, we do not for a moment forget that our part in this exhibition would fall far short of your expectations but for the constant help that has come to our educational life, not only from the southern states, but especially from Northern philanthropists, who have made their gifts a constant stream of blessing and encouragement.

The wisest among my race understand that the agitation of questions of social equality is the extremest folly, and that progress in the enjoyment of all the privileges that will come to us must be the result of severe and constant struggle rather than of artificial forcing. No race that has anything to contribute to the markets of the world is long in any degree ostracized. It is important and right that all privileges of the law be ours, but it is vastly more important that we be prepared for the exercises of these privileges. The opportunity to earn a dollar in a factory just now is worth infinitely more than the opportunity to spend a dollar in an opera-house.

In conclusion, may I repeat that nothing in thirty years has given us more hope and encouragement, and drawn us so near to you of the white race, as this opportunity offered by the Exposition; and here bending, as it were, over the altar that represents the results of the struggles of your race and mine, both starting practically empty-handed three decades ago, I pledge that in your effort to work out the great and intricate problem which God has laid at the doors of the South, you shall have at all times the patient, sympathetic help of my race; only let this be constantly in mind, that, while from representations in these buildings of the product of field, of forest, of mine, of factory, letters, and art, much good will come, yet far above and beyond material benefits will be that higher good, that, let us pray God, will come, in a blotting out of sectional differences and racial animosities and suspicions, in a determination to administer absolute justice, in a willing obedience among all classes to the mandates of law. This, this, coupled with our material prosperity, will bring into our beloved South a new heaven and a new earth....

Negro and the White

I believe it is the duty of the negro—as the greater part of the race is already doing—to deport himself modestly in regard to political claims, depending on the slow but sure influences that proceed from the possession of property, intelligence and high character for the full recognition of his political rights.

I think that the according of the full exercise of political rights is going to be a matter of natural, slow growth, not an over-night, gourd-vine affair. I do not believe that the negro should cease voting, for a man cannot learn the exercise of self-government by ceasing to vote, any more than a boy can learn to swim by keeping out of the water; but I do believe that in his voting he should more and more be influenced by those of intelligence and character who are his next-door neighbors.

I know colored men who, through the encouragement, help and advice of southern white people, have accumulated thousands of dollars worth of property, but who, at the same time, would never think of going to those same persons for advice concerning the casting of their ballots. This, it seems to me, is unwise and unreasonable, and should cease.

In saying this, I do not mean that the negro should truckle, or not vote from principle, for the instant he ceases to vote from principle he loses the confidence and respect of the southern white man even.

Suffrage Laws Unjust

I do not believe that any State should make a law that permits an ignorant and poverty-stricken white man to vote and prevents a black man in the same condition from voting.

Such a law is not only unjust, but it will react, as all unjust laws do, in time; for the effect of such a law is to encourage the negro to secure education and property, and at the same time it encourages the white man to remain in ignorance and poverty. I believe that in time, through the operation of intelligence and friendly race relations, all cheating at the ballot-box in the South will cease.

It will become apparent that the white man who begins by cheating a negro out of his ballot soon learns to cheat a white man out of his, and that man who does this ends his career of dishonesty by the theft of property or by some equally serious crime.

In my opinion, the time will come when the South will encourage all of its citizens to vote. It will see that it pays better, from every standpoint, to have healthy, vigorous life than to have that political stagnation which always results when one-half the population has no share and no interest in the government.

As a rule, I believe in universal, free suffrage, but I believe that in the South we are confronted with peculiar conditions that justify the protection of the ballot in many of the States, for a while at least, either by an educational test, a property test, or by both combined; but whatever tests are required they should be made to apply with equal and exact justice to both races.

GLOSSARY

Gewgaws: trinkets, showy but worthless toys

The laws of changeless justice bind…: from "At Point Royal" (1862) by American poet John Greenleaf Whittier

Document Analysis

In the years that followed the Atlanta address, Washington's power grew. In 1901, he lunched with President Theodore Roosevelt at the White House. He counted many top industrialists, such as Andrew Carnegie, as his supporters. Nonetheless, racial conditions grew steadily worse as segregation became entrenched and southern states deprived black citizens of their right to vote. Washington's prestige allowed him access to the media to voice his concerns about these developments, and he did so repeatedly. In June 1903, he addressed the suffrage issue in a letter published in the Philadelphia *North American*.

Washington began his letter with a discussion of black political rights. He argued that African Americans had a "duty" to be "modest" in their desire for political equality and should instead concentrate on accumulating property, gaining an education, and behaving with "high character." The attainment of these goals would effectively prove to white southerners that African Americans were deserving of the rights and freedoms guaranteed to them in the Constitution. It was Washington's belief that the granting of political rights would occur naturally after African Americans were able to gain more education and property. Black behavior could play a significant role in determining how whites viewed African Americans. If African Americans behaved like whites and adopted white, middle-class values, they would be more likely to be accepted by whites. Political rights would not come overnight but as a "matter of natural, slow growth," that is, the acquisition of white, middle class values.

To Washington, this did not mean that blacks should forego suffrage; but that they should concentrate on other issues and not force that issue with whites. The fight for political rights would increase racial tensions and limit opportunities for African Americans to obtain an education at industrial and agricultural schools. Washington was essentially arguing that blacks should fight for rights they were most likely to receive and that would provoke the least amount of opposition from whites.

Washington suggested that blacks who were able to vote should seek the guidance and support of knowledgeable and trusted southern whites. Washington stated that he knew many African Americans "who, through the encouragement, help, and advice of southern white people, have accumulated thousands of dollars-worth of property," and yet these same people would never think to ask southern whites "for advice concerning the casting of their ballots," a situation that Washington labeled "unwise and unreasonable."

Washington raised the issue of the unjust suffrage laws that discriminated against blacks. These laws had proliferated across the South in the years between 1895 and 1903 and been upheld by the Supreme Court in *Williams v. Mississippi* in 1898. He noted that these laws were unjust, discriminatory, and clearly targeted at African Americans. They did not prevent "ignorant and poverty-stricken white men" from participating in elections. These laws should serve as a further motivation for African Americans to concentrate on gaining property and an education. Ironically, they encouraged whites to remain poor and uneducated since they had the vote anyway.

Washington argued that whites who were willing to deny blacks the right to vote would eventually decide to deny other whites their voting rights as well. The denial of black rights established a precedent. However, Washington expressed confidence that the South would eventually have universal suffrage.

While Washington expressed support for universal suffrage, he also acknowledged that states have the right to protect the ballot "for a while at least, either by educational test, a property test, or both combined." However, these tests should be applied equally to African Americans and whites. He seemed to support some restrictions on the right to vote, but not their application solely to African Americans.

As was his style, Washington here presents logical arguments appealing to both the reason and the self-interest of his white audience. He is not confrontational. While this approach displeased many of his black critics, it allowed him to make his arguments in a way that did not undermine his position among whites and protected the security of Tuskegee and his family in rural Alabama. As persuasive as his arguments were, they did not have any immediate impact on the movement to deny blacks their political rights. However, even more aggressive attacks on disfranchisement did not bear fruit for many years.

During his lifetime, Washington witnessed the widespread erosion of black rights and freedoms. While the Fifteenth Amendment officially guaranteed African Americans the right to vote, it wasn't long after its passage that white southern Democrats began trying to undermine its effects. In 1882, South Carolina passed the Eight Box Law, which required voters to deposit a series of ballots in the proper ballot boxes before voting. Illiterate voters proved unable to identify the "correct" boxes without the help of white officials. Not surprisingly, African American voters were the primary victims of this new law. In 1889, Mississippi altered its constitution by including a number of complex voting requirements. Without mentioning race, Mississippi required voters to provide proof of residency, payment of taxes, and a $2 poll tax. Literacy was required, but illiterate men could still vote if they were able to demonstrate an understanding of the Constitution to voting officials. Officials almost universally accepted all white applicants while rejecting the vast majority of black voters. Similarly, in 1895, South Carolina changed their constitution to include an "understanding clause," which disenfranchised the majority of black voters.

In 1898, Louisiana created a new method for disenfranchising black voters called the grandfather clause. This clause stipulated that only men who had been eligible to vote or whose fathers or grandfathers were eligible to vote before 1867 could vote. As the vast majority of blacks had only recently been freed from slavery in 1867 and the Fifteenth Amendment had not yet been passed, this disenfranchised hundreds of thousands of black voters. In 1896, 130,000 thousand African Americans voted, but by 1904, as a result of the grandfather clause, only 1,342 voted. By the end of the nineteenth century, every southern state except Kentucky and West Virginia had enacted a series of elaborate voting laws meant to disenfranchise black voters.

During this same period, southern states enacted laws requiring segregation of the races in public places. In 1891, Louisiana passed a law that required segregation of the races on trains. Homer A. Plessy, who was one-eighth black and who had been arrested for using a railcar reserved for whites, sought to have the law declared unconstitutional. In 1896, the case—*Plessy v. Ferguson*—reached the Supreme Court, which ruled 8 to 1 to uphold the Louisiana law. A legal precedent having been established, southern states rushed to pass hundreds of laws requiring segregation of the races in railroad stations, theatres, auditoriums, bathrooms, and drinking fountains. While *Plessy v. Ferguson* permitted separate facilities for African Americans and whites as long as facilities of equal quality were provided for both, black facilities were generally substandard and, in many cases, nonexistent. Almost all hotels, restaurants, libraries, public and private parks, swimming pools, golf and tennis courses, refused to admit black people altogether.

At the same time that black voting rights were being eroded and segregation laws were being enacted, African Americans also faced increasing levels of violence in the form of mob attacks and lynchings. In 1898, a white mob attacked a black-owned newspaper, *The Daily Record*, in Wilmington, North Carolina, murdering at least twelve black men and causing 1,500 black residents to flee. A similar riot occurred in New Orleans two years later, leading to the death of more than thirty African Americans. However, more often than not, violence against African Americans came in the form of lynchings. Beginning in 1889, an average of two to three people, the majority of them black men, were lynched every week for the next thirty years, often with the tacit approval of white officials. In 1900 alone, 100 African Americans were lynched.

Within this environment of disenfranchisement, segregation, and racial violence, Washington arose to a position of leadership. He believed wholeheartedly that his message of accommodation towards segregation and disenfranchisement in favor of industrial education would eventually lead blacks towards progress and success. He also hoped that his policies would ease tensions between blacks and whites and, most importantly, reduce the increasing levels of violence.

Essential Themes

Washington's efforts to attract black and white support by emphasizing his industrial program and downplaying political and social rights revealed a pragmatic approach. Industrial education was a far less controversial issue than civil and political rights for blacks and as a result much less likely to excite opposition or violence from whites. White philanthropists in both the North and South were willing to provide financial support for black colleges offering an industrial education. Few of these white supporters would not have supported Washington had he advocated more aggressively for black political and civil rights. By 1915, there were sixteen black land-grant colleges including Florida A&M, Alcorn A&M in Mississippi, Southern University in Louisiana, and Washington's Tuskegee Institute, which received both public and private funding. Without these schools, southern blacks would have had few opportunities to receive any sort of higher education.

Yet, despite his support for industrial education and his attempts to placate suspicious whites, racial tension and violence against blacks continued unabated. In fairness, there was likely nothing Washington or any other black leader could have done to prevent continued violence, but the advocacy of industrial education did little if anything to protect African Americans from discrimination or violence.

Washington's insistence that African Americans concentrate on industrial education, forego liberal arts education, and postpone demands for political or civil rights engendered significant criticism and opposition from such prominent black leaders as Harvard-trained scholar W. E. B. Du Bois, African Methodist Episcopal Bishop Henry M. Bishop, and journalist Ida B. Wells. They argued that African Americans should not limit themselves only to an industrial education. There was an inherent value to a liberal education which included the learning of mathematics, literature, science, and languages. A number of private black colleges like Fisk, Morris Brown, and Paul Quinn continued to emphasize a liberal arts education and resisted pressures to switch to an industrial and agricultural-based curriculum.

Leaders like Du Bois and Bishop also strongly resented Washington's seeming indifference to the loss of political and civil rights. These leaders linked their support for a liberal education to their support for black civil and political rights arguing that such an education would create leaders more capable of leading the black masses towards greater equality. While Washington sought to create greater educational opportunities for African Americans, his efforts were criticized by other African American leaders who argued that he sacrificed too much for too little.

—*Gerald F. Goodwin, PhD & Cary D. Wintz, PhD*

Bibliography and Further Reading

Brundage, W. Fitzhugh, ed. *Booker T. Washington and Black Progress: Up from Slavery 100 Years Later.* Gainesville: U P of Florida, 2003. Print.

Harlan, Louis R. *Booker T. Washington: the Making of a Black Leader, 1856–1901.* Oxford, UK: Oxford UP, 1972. Print.

Harlan, Louis R. *Booker T. Washington: the Wizard of Tuskegee, 1901–1915.* Vol. 2. Oxford, UK: Oxford University Press, 1983. Print.

Hine, Darlene Clark, William C. Hine, and Stanley C. Harrold. *African Americans: A Concise History, Combined Volume.* Boston: Pearson, 2011. Print.

Norrell, Robert J. *Up from History: The Life of Booker T. Washington.* Cambridge, MA: Harvard University Press, 2009. Print.

Smock, Raymond W. *Booker T. Washington: Black Leadership in the Age of Jim Crow.* Chicago: Ivan R. Dee, 2009. Print.

Washington, Booker T. *Up from Slavery.* Mineola, NY: Dover Publications, 1995. Print.

W. E. B. Du Bois: *The Souls of Black Folk*

Date: 1903
Author: W. E. B. Du Bois
Genre: book excerpt

Summary Overview

In 1903, W. E. B. Du Bois published the classic book for which he is most remembered, *The Souls of Black Folk: Essays and Sketches*. A groundbreaking study of the African American community from a sociological perspective, the book outlines for both black and white readers the position of African Americans at the turn of the twentieth century. *The Souls of Black Folk* was in large part a repudiation of the views of Booker T. Washington, the black leader who urged other blacks to pursue economic equality before trying to gain political and social equality. Du Bois, in contrast, urged African Americans to develop a "black consciousness" based on an appreciation of their own unique art, culture, religious views, and history and to continue to pursue civil rights. In Chapter III, "Of Mr. Booker T. Washington and Others," Du Bois takes on the rift between Washington's accommodationist views and a more assertive, militant view of African American aspirations. *The Souls of Black Folk* was a key early doctrine of the Harlem Renaissance, the flowering of black culture and art that centered on the Harlem district of Manhattan in New York City, and it remains a central document in the seismic shift of African American consciousness at the start of the twentieth century.

Defining Moment

The audience for *The Souls of Black Folk* was broad. Several of the essays had already appeared in *The Atlantic Monthly* magazine, one of the nation's leading mainstream publications. Accordingly, the book attracted attention from both the black and the white intelligentsia and went through several editions. The author's purposes were to convince white readers of the essential humanity of African Americans and to promote among black readers a new consciousness. Virtually any writer, white or black, writing on race issues during the early decades of the twentieth century would have read and paid tribute to Du Bois and his book, and even in the twenty-first century the book is still regarded as a classic—and its ideas are still debated.

About the Author

William Edward Burghardt Du Bois was born on February 23, 1868, in Great Barrington, Massachusetts, and raised by his mother. In spite of the poverty of his childhood, Du Bois excelled in school and achieved one of the most impressive educations of his generation. He received bachelor degrees from Fisk University and Harvard University, pursued graduate work at Harvard and Germany's University of Berlin, and earned his PhD in history from Harvard in 1895. He received a faculty appointment at Wilberforce University in 1894, worked for the University of Pennsylvania on a study of blacks in Philadelphia in 1896, and joined the faculty of Atlanta University in 1897. In 1910, he left Atlanta and took a paid position as the director of publishing and research for the newly founded National Association for the Advancement of Colored People (NAACP). He served in that position and also as the founding editor of the NAACP journal, *The Crisis*, subtitled *A Record of the Darker Races*, until 1934, when he resigned over a policy dispute.

Following his departure from the NAACP, Du Bois returned to Atlanta University and to academic scholarship for ten years. In 1943, at the age of seventy-six, he was forced to retire from the university, and he accepted a position back at the NAACP. By this time, Du Bois was clearly out of step with the civil rights organization; his increasingly leftist, pro-Soviet politics and his criticism both of US foreign policy and of the NAACP director Walter White cost him his job in 1948. In the late 1940s and early 1950s, Du Bois became involved in leftist organizations, continued condemning the United States and its foreign policy while praising the Soviet Union, and ran for public office as a nominee of the American Labor Party. These activities made him a target of the post–World War II "Red Scare" inspired by Senator Joseph McCarthy. Although he was acquitted of charges related to his involvement with radical antiwar organizations, his passport was suspended from 1951 to 1958. When he regained the right to travel abroad, he made a series of trips, including highly publicized visits to East Germany, the Soviet Union, and Communist China. Du Bois's continued pro-

Communist political radicalism isolated him from the emerging civil rights movement. In 1961, disillusioned with the United States, Du Bois formally joined the US Communist Party before relocating to the newly independent nation of Ghana. In 1963, he became a citizen of his adopted country; on August 27, 1963, he died at the age of ninety-five.

Du Bois was the leading African American intellectual of his day. He first established his credentials with his scholarly publications on the Atlanta slave trade and on Philadelphia's black community. In 1897, he began to define his political and racial views, moving from academic work to political and social activism; his publication of "Strivings of the Negro People" in *The Atlantic Monthly* brought him national attention. Six years later, his classic work *The Souls of Black Folk* cemented his intellectual credentials. His involvement with the Niagara Movement, beginning in 1905, and with the National Association for the Advancement of Colored People made him the most significant of Booker T. Washington's critics and the most prominent and most respected head of the early-twentieth-century campaign for civil rights. In his books and articles, especially those published in *The Crisis*, Du Bois developed ideas that were fundamental to his vision of race in America and to the long struggle against discrimination and for equality. While he found himself increasingly out of the mainstream civil rights movement following his departure from the NAACP in 1934, Du Bois remained one of the giants among twentieth-century American intellectuals.

HISTORICAL DOCUMENT

III. Of Mr. Booker T. Washington and Others

From birth till death enslaved; in word, in deed, unmanned!
* * * * * * * * *
Hereditary bondsmen! Know ye not
Who would be free themselves must strike the blow?
—Byron

Easily the most striking thing in the history of the American Negro since 1876 is the ascendancy of Mr. Booker T. Washington. It began at the time when war memories and ideals were rapidly passing; a day of astonishing commercial development was dawning; a sense of doubt and hesitation overtook the freedmen's sons,—then it was that his leading began. Mr. Washington came, with a simple definite programme, at the psychological moment when the nation was a little ashamed of having bestowed so much sentiment on Negroes, and was concentrating its energies on Dollars. His programme of industrial education, conciliation of the South, and submission and silence as to civil and political rights, was not wholly original; the Free Negroes from 1830 up to war-time had striven to build industrial schools, and the American Missionary Association had from the first taught various trades; and Price and others had sought a way of honorable alliance with the best of the Southerners. But Mr. Washington first indissolubly linked these things; he put enthusiasm, unlimited energy, and perfect faith into his programme, and changed it from a by-path into a veritable Way of Life. And the tale of the methods by which he did this is a fascinating study of human life.

It startled the nation to hear a Negro advocating such a programme after many decades of bitter complaint; it startled and won the applause of the South, it interested and won the admiration of the North; and after a confused murmur of protest, it silenced if it did not convert the Negroes themselves.

To gain the sympathy and cooperation of the various elements comprising the white South was Mr. Washington's first task; and this, at the time Tuskegee was founded, seemed, for a black man, well-nigh impossible. And yet ten years later it was done in the word spoken at Atlanta: "In all things purely social we can be as separate as the five fingers, and yet one as the hand in all things essential to mutual progress." This "Atlanta Compromise" is by all odds the most notable thing in Mr. Washington's career. The South interpreted it in different ways: the radicals received it as a complete surrender of the demand for civil and political equality; the conservatives, as a generously conceived working basis for mutual understanding. So both approved it, and to-day its author is certainly the most distinguished Southerner since Jefferson Davis, and the one with the largest personal following.

Next to this achievement comes Mr. Washington's work in gaining place and consideration in the North. Others less shrewd and tactful had formerly essayed to sit on these two stools and had fallen between them; but as Mr. Washington knew the heart of the South from birth and training, so by singular insight he intuitively grasped the spirit of the age which was dominating the North. And so thoroughly did he learn the speech and thought of triumphant commercialism, and the ideals of material prosperity, that the picture of a lone black boy poring over a French grammar amid the weeds and dirt of a neglected home soon seemed to him the acme of absurdities. One wonders what Socrates and St. Francis of Assisi would say to this.

And yet this very singleness of vision and thorough oneness with his age is a mark of the successful man. It is as though Nature must needs make men narrow in order to give them force. So Mr. Washington's cult has gained unquestioning followers, his work has wonderfully prospered, his friends are legion, and his enemies are confounded. To-day he stands as the one recognized spokesman of his ten million fellows, and one of the most notable figures in a nation of seventy millions. One hesitates, therefore, to criticise a life which, beginning with so little, has done so much. And yet the time is come when one may speak in all sincerity and utter courtesy of the mistakes and shortcomings of Mr. Washington's career, as well as of his triumphs, without being thought captious or envious, and without forgetting that it is easier to do ill than well in the world.

The criticism that has hitherto met Mr. Washington has not always been of this broad character. In the South especially has he had to walk warily to avoid the harshest judgments,—and naturally so, for he is dealing with the one subject of deepest sensitiveness to that section. Twice—once when at the Chicago celebration of the Spanish-American War he alluded to the color-prejudice that is "eating away the vitals of the South" and once when he dined with President Roosevelt—has the resulting Southern criticism been violent enough to threaten seriously his popularity. In the North the feeling has several times forced itself into words, that Mr. Washington's counsels of submission overlooked certain elements of true manhood, and that his educational programme was unnecessarily narrow. Usually, however, such criticism has not found open expression, although, too, the spiritual sons of the Abolitionists have not been prepared to acknowledge that the schools founded before Tuskegee, by men of broad ideals and self-sacrificing spirit, were wholly failures or worthy of ridicule. While, then, criticism has not failed to follow Mr. Washington, yet the prevailing public opinion of the land has been but too willing to deliver the solution of a wearisome problem into his hands, and say, "If that is all you and your race ask, take it."

Among his own people, however, Mr. Washington has encountered the strongest and most lasting opposition, amounting at times to bitterness, and even today continuing strong and insistent even though largely silenced in outward expression by the public opinion of the nation. Some of this opposition is, of course, mere envy; the disappointment of displaced demagogues and the spite of narrow minds. But aside from this, there is among educated and thoughtful colored men in all parts of the land a feeling of deep regret, sorrow, and apprehension at the wide currency and ascendancy which some of Mr. Washington's theories have gained. These same men admire his sincerity of purpose, and are willing to forgive much to honest endeavor which is doing something worth the doing. They cooperate with Mr. Washington as far as they conscientiously can; and, indeed, it is no ordinary tribute to this man's tact and power that, steering as he must between so many diverse interests and opinions, he so largely retains the respect of all.

But the hushing of the criticism of honest opponents is a dangerous thing. It leads some of the best of the critics to unfortunate silence and paralysis of effort, and others to burst into speech so passionately and intemperately as to lose listeners. Honest and earnest criticism from those whose interests are most nearly touched,—criticism of writers by readers,—this is the soul of democracy and the safeguard of modern society. If the best of the American Negroes receive by outer pressure a leader whom they had not recognized before, manifestly there is here a certain palpable gain. Yet there is also irreparable loss,—a loss of that peculiarly valuable education which a group receives when by search and criticism it finds and commissions its own leaders. The way in which this is done is at once the most elementary and the nicest problem of social growth. History is but the record of such group-leadership; and yet how infinitely changeful is its type and character! And of all types and kinds, what can be more instructive than the leadership of a group within a group?—that curious double movement where real progress may be negative and actual advance be relative retrogression. All this is the social student's inspiration and despair.

Now in the past the American Negro has had instructive experience in the choosing of group leaders, founding thus a peculiar dynasty which in the light of present conditions is worth while studying. When sticks and stones and beasts form the sole environment of a people, their attitude is largely one of determined opposition to and conquest of natural forces. But when to earth and brute is added an environment of men and ideas, then the attitude of the imprisoned group may take three main forms,—a feeling of revolt and revenge; an attempt to adjust all thought and action to the will of the greater group; or, finally, a determined effort at self-realization and self-development despite environing opinion. The influence of all of these attitudes at various times can be traced in the history of the American Negro, and in the evolution of his successive leaders.

Before 1750, while the fire of African freedom still burned in the veins of the slaves, there was in all leadership or attempted leadership but the one motive of revolt and revenge,—typified in the terrible Maroons, the Danish blacks, and Cato of Stono, and veiling all the Americas in fear of insurrection. The liberalizing tendencies of the latter half of the eighteenth century brought, along with kindlier relations between black and white, thoughts of ultimate adjustment and assimilation. Such aspiration was especially voiced in the earnest songs of Phyllis, in the martyrdom of Attucks, the fighting of Salem and Poor, the intellectual accomplishments of Banneker and Derham, and the political demands of the Cuffes.

Stern financial and social stress after the war cooled much of the previous humanitarian ardor. The disappointment and impatience of the Negroes at the persistence of slavery and serfdom voiced itself in two movements. The slaves in the South, aroused undoubtedly by vague rumors of the Haytian revolt, made three fierce attempts at insurrection,—in 1800 under Gabriel in Virginia, in 1822 under Vesey in Carolina, and in 1831 again in Virginia under the terrible Nat Turner. In the Free States, on the other hand, a new and curious attempt at self-development was made. In Philadelphia and New York color-prescription led to a withdrawal of Negro communicants from white churches and the formation of a peculiar socio-religious institution among the Negroes known as the African Church,—an organization still living and controlling in its various branches over a million of men.

Walker's wild appeal against the trend of the times showed how the world was changing after the coming of the cotton-gin. By 1830 slavery seemed hopelessly fastened on the South, and the slaves thoroughly cowed into submission. The free Negroes of the North, inspired by the mulatto immigrants from the West Indies, began to change the basis of their demands; they recognized the slavery of slaves, but insisted that they themselves were freemen, and sought assimilation and amalgamation with the nation on the same terms with other men. Thus, Forten and Purvis of Philadelphia, Shadd of Wilmington, Du Bois of New Haven, Barbadoes of Boston, and others, strove singly and together as men, they said, not as slaves; as "people of color" not as "Negroes." The trend of the times, however, refused them recognition save in individual and exceptional cases, considered them as one with all the despised blacks, and they soon found themselves striving to keep even the rights they formerly had of voting and working and moving as freemen. Schemes of migration and colonization arose among them; but these they refused to entertain, and they eventually turned to the Abolition movement as a final refuge.

Here, led by Remond, Nell, Wells Brown, and Douglass, a new period of self-assertion and self-development dawned. To be sure, ultimate freedom and assimilation was the ideal before the leaders, but the assertion of the manhood rights of the Negro by himself was the main reliance, and John Brown's raid was the extreme of its logic. After the war and emancipation, the great form of Frederick Douglass, the greatest of American Negro leaders, still led the host. Self-assertion, especially in political lines, was the main programme, and behind Douglass came Elliott, Bruce, and Langston, and the Reconstruction politicians, and, less conspicuous but of greater social significance, Alexander Crummell and Bishop Daniel Payne.

Then came the Revolution of 1876, the suppression of the Negro votes, the changing and shifting of ideals, and the seeking of new lights in the great night. Douglass, in his old age, still bravely stood for the ideals of his early manhood,—ultimate assimilation through self-assertion, and on no other terms. For a time Price arose as a new leader, destined, it seemed, not to give up, but to re-state the old ideals in a form less repugnant to the white South. But he passed away in his prime. Then came the new leader. Nearly all the former ones had become leaders by the silent suffrage of their fellows, had sought to lead their own people alone, and were usually, save Douglass, little known outside their race. But Booker T. Washington arose as essentially the leader not of one race but of two,—a compromiser between the South, the North, and the Negro. Naturally the Negroes resented, at first bitterly, signs of compromise which surrendered their civil and political rights, even though this was to be exchanged for larger chances of economic development. The rich and dominating North, however, was not only weary of the race problem, but was investing largely in Southern enterprises, and welcomed any method of peaceful cooperation. Thus, by national opinion, the Negroes began to recognize Mr. Washington's leadership; and the voice of criticism was hushed.

Mr. Washington represents in Negro thought the old attitude of adjustment and submission; but adjustment at such a peculiar time as to make his programme unique. This is an age of unusual economic development, and Mr. Washington's programme naturally takes an economic cast, becoming a gospel of Work and Money to such an extent as apparently almost completely to overshadow the higher aims of life. Moreover, this is an age when the more advanced races are coming in closer contact with the less developed races, and the race-feeling is therefore intensified; and Mr. Washington's programme practically accepts the alleged inferiority of the Negro races. Again, in our own land, the reaction from the sentiment of war time has given impetus to race-prejudice against Negroes, and Mr. Washington withdraws many of the high demands of Negroes as men and American citizens. In other periods of intensified prejudice all the Negro's tendency to self-assertion has been called forth; at this period a policy of submission is advocated. In the history of nearly all other races and peoples the doctrine preached at such crises has been that manly self-respect is worth more than lands and houses, and that a people who voluntarily surrender such respect, or cease striving for it, are not worth civilizing.

In answer to this, it has been claimed that the Negro can survive only through submission. Mr. Washington distinctly asks that black people give up, at least for the present, three things,—

First, political power,
Second, insistence on civil rights,
Third, higher education of Negro youth,—

and concentrate all their energies on industrial education, and accumulation of wealth, and the conciliation of the South. This policy has been courageously and insistently advocated for over fifteen years, and has been triumphant for perhaps ten years. As a result of this tender of the palm-branch, what has been the return? In these years there have occurred:

1. The disfranchisement of the Negro.
2. The legal creation of a distinct status of civil inferiority for the Negro.
3. The steady withdrawal of aid from institutions for the higher training of the Negro.

These movements are not, to be sure, direct results of Mr. Washington's teachings; but his propaganda has, without a shadow of doubt, helped their speedier accomplishment. The question then comes: Is it possible, and probable, that nine millions of men can make effective progress in economic lines if they are deprived of political rights, made a servile caste, and allowed only the most meagre chance for developing their exceptional men? If history and reason give any distinct answer to these questions, it is an emphatic *No*. And Mr. Washington thus faces the triple paradox of his career:

1. He is striving nobly to make Negro artisans business men and property-owners; but it is utterly impossible, under modern competitive methods, for workingmen and property-owners to defend their rights and exist without the right of suffrage.
2. He insists on thrift and self-respect, but at the same time counsels a silent submission to civic inferiority such as is bound to sap the manhood of any race in the long run.
3. He advocates common-school and industrial training, and depreciates institutions of higher learning; but neither the Negro common-schools, nor Tuskegee itself, could remain open a day were it not for teachers trained in Negro colleges, or trained by their graduates.

This triple paradox in Mr. Washington's position is the object of criticism by two classes of colored Americans. One class is spiritually descended from Toussaint the Savior, through Gabriel, Vesey, and Turner, and they represent the attitude of revolt and revenge; they hate the white South blindly and distrust the white race generally, and so far as they agree on definite action, think that the Negro's only hope lies in emigration beyond the borders of the United States. And yet, by the irony of fate, nothing has more effectually made this programme seem hopeless than the recent course of the United States toward weaker and darker peoples in the West Indies, Hawaii, and the Philippines,—for where in the world may we go and be safe from lying and brute force?

The other class of Negroes who cannot agree with Mr. Washington has hitherto said little aloud. They deprecate the sight of scattered counsels, of internal disagreement; and especially they dislike making their just criticism of a useful and earnest man an excuse for a general discharge of venom from small-minded opponents. Nevertheless, the questions involved are so fundamental and serious that it is difficult to see how men like the Grimkés, Kelly Miller, J. W. E. Bowen, and other representatives of this group, can much longer be silent. Such men feel in conscience bound to ask of this nation three things:

1. The right to vote.
2. Civic equality.
3. The education of youth according to ability.

They acknowledge Mr. Washington's invaluable service in counselling patience and courtesy in such demands; they do not ask that ignorant black men vote when ignorant whites are debarred, or that any reasonable restrictions in the suffrage should not be applied; they know that the low social level of the mass of the race is responsible for much discrimination against it, but they also know, and the nation knows, that relentless color-prejudice is more often a cause than a result of the Negro's degradation; they seek the abatement of this relic of barbarism, and not its systematic encouragement and pampering by all agencies of social power from the Associated Press to the Church of Christ. They advocate, with Mr. Washington, a broad system of Negro common schools supplemented by thorough industrial training; but they are surprised that a man of Mr. Washington's insight cannot see that no such educational system ever has rested or can rest on any other basis than that of the well-equipped college and university, and they insist that there is a demand for a few such institutions throughout the South to train the best of the Negro youth as teachers, professional men, and leaders.

This group of men honor Mr. Washington for his attitude of conciliation toward the white South; they accept the "Atlanta Compromise" in its broadest interpretation; they recognize, with him, many signs of promise, many men of high purpose and fair judgment, in this section; they know that no easy task has been laid upon a region already tottering under heavy burdens. But, nevertheless, they insist that the way to truth and right lies in straightforward honesty, not in indiscriminate flattery; in praising those of the South who do well and criticising uncompromisingly those who do ill; in taking advantage of the opportunities at hand and urging their fellows to do the same, but at the same time in remembering that only a firm adherence to their higher ideals and aspirations will ever keep those ideals within the realm of possibility. They do not expect that the free right to vote, to enjoy civic rights, and to be educated, will come in a moment; they do not expect to see the bias and prejudices of years disappear at the blast of a trumpet; but they are absolutely certain that the way for a people to gain their reasonable rights is not by voluntarily throwing them away and insisting that they do not want them; that the way for a people to gain respect is not by continually belittling and ridiculing themselves; that, on the contrary, Negroes must insist continually, in season and out of season, that voting is necessary to modern manhood, that color discrimination is barbarism, and that black boys need education as well as white boys.

In failing thus to state plainly and unequivocally the legitimate demands of their people, even at the cost of opposing an honored leader, the thinking classes of American Negroes would shirk a heavy responsibility,—a responsibility to themselves, a responsibility to the struggling masses, a responsibility to the darker races of men whose future depends so largely on this American experiment, but especially a responsibility to this nation,—this common Fatherland. It is wrong to encourage a man or a people in evil-doing; it is wrong to aid and abet a national crime simply because it is unpopular not to do so. The growing spirit of kindliness and reconciliation between the North and South after the frightful difference of a generation ago ought to be a source of deep congratulation to all, and especially to those whose mistreatment caused the war; but if that reconciliation is to be marked by the industrial slavery and civic death of those same black men, with permanent legislation into a position of inferiority, then those black men, if they are really men, are called upon by every consideration of patriotism and loyalty to oppose such a course by all civilized methods, even though such opposition involves disagreement with Mr. Booker T. Washington. We have no right to sit silently by while the inevitable seeds are sown for a harvest of disaster to our children, black and white.

First, it is the duty of black men to judge the South discriminatingly. The present generation of Southerners are not responsible for the past, and they should not be blindly hated or blamed for it. Furthermore, to no class is the indiscriminate endorsement of the recent course of the South toward Negroes more nauseating than to the best thought of the South. The South is not "solid"; it is a land in the ferment of social change, wherein forces of all kinds are fighting for supremacy; and to praise the ill the South is today perpetrating is just as wrong as to condemn the good. Discriminating and broadminded criticism is what the South needs,—needs it for the sake of her own white sons and daughters, and for the insurance of robust, healthy mental and moral development.

Today even the attitude of the Southern whites toward the blacks is not, as so many assume, in all cases the same; the ignorant Southerner hates the Negro, the workingmen fear his competition, the money-makers wish to use him as a laborer, some of the educated see a menace in his upward development, while others—usually the sons of the masters—wish to help him to rise. National opinion has enabled this last class to maintain the Negro common schools, and to protect the Negro partially in property, life, and limb. Through the pressure of the money-makers, the Negro is in danger of being reduced to semi-slavery, especially in the country districts; the workingmen, and those of the educated who fear the Negro, have united to disfranchise him, and some have urged his deportation; while the passions of the ignorant are easily aroused to lynch and abuse any black man. To praise this intricate whirl of thought and prejudice is nonsense; to inveigh indiscriminately against "the South" is unjust; but to use the same breath in praising Governor Aycock, exposing Senator Morgan, arguing with Mr. Thomas Nelson Page, and denouncing Senator Ben Tillman, is not only sane, but the imperative duty of thinking black men.

It would be unjust to Mr. Washington not to acknowledge that in several instances he has opposed movements in the South which were unjust to the Negro; he sent memorials to the Louisiana and Alabama constitutional conventions, he has spoken against lynching, and in other ways has openly or silently set his influence against sinister schemes and unfortunate happenings. Notwithstanding this, it is equally true to assert that on the whole the distinct impression left by Mr. Washington's propaganda is, first, that the South is justified in its present attitude toward the Negro because of the Negro's degradation; secondly, that the prime cause of the Negro's failure to rise more quickly is his wrong education in the past; and, thirdly, that his future rise depends primarily on his own efforts. Each of these propositions is a dangerous half-truth. The supplementary truths must never be lost sight of: first, slavery and race-prejudice are potent if not sufficient causes of the Negro's position; second, industrial and common-school training were necessarily slow in planting because they had to await the black teachers trained by higher institutions,—it being extremely doubtful if any essentially different development was possible, and certainly a Tuskegee was unthinkable before 1880; and, third, while it is a great truth to say that the Negro must strive and strive mightily to help himself, it is equally true that unless his striving be not simply seconded, but rather aroused and encouraged, by the initiative of the richer and wiser environing group, he cannot hope for great success.

In his failure to realize and impress this last point, Mr. Washington is especially to be criticised. His doctrine has tended to make the whites, North and South, shift the burden of the Negro problem to the Negro's shoulders and stand aside as critical and rather pessimistic spectators; when in fact the burden belongs to the nation, and the hands of none of us are clean if we bend not our energies to righting these great wrongs.

The South ought to be led, by candid and honest criticism, to assert her better self and do her full duty to the race she has cruelly wronged and is still wronging. The North—her co-partner in guilt—cannot salve her conscience by plastering it with gold. We cannot settle this problem by diplomacy and suaveness, by "policy" alone. If worse come to worst, can the moral fibre of this country survive the slow throttling and murder of nine millions of men?

The black men of America have a duty to perform, a duty stern and delicate,—a forward movement to oppose a part of the work of their greatest leader. So far as Mr. Washington preaches Thrift, Patience, and Industrial Training for the masses, we must hold up his hands and strive with him, rejoicing in his honors and glorying in the strength of this Joshua called of God and of man to lead the headless host. But so far as Mr. Washington apologizes for injustice, North or South, does not rightly value the privilege and duty of voting, belittles the emasculating effects of caste distinctions, and opposes the higher training and ambition of our brighter minds,—so far as he, the South, or the Nation, does this,—we must unceasingly and firmly oppose them. By every civilized and peaceful method we must strive for the rights which the world accords to men, clinging unwaveringly to those great words which the sons of the Fathers would fain forget: "We hold these truths to be self-evident: That all men are created equal; that they are endowed by their Creator with certain unalienable rights; that among these are life, liberty, and the pursuit of happiness."

GLOSSARY

"Atlanta Compromise": the informal name of a speech given by Booker T. Washington in 1895

Attucks, Salem, and Poor: African Americans Crispus Attucks, Peter Salem, and Salem Poor, who fought in the Revolutionary War

Aycock: North Carolina governor Charles Aycock, a white supremacist

Banneker: Benjamin Banneker, an accomplished African American scientist, mathematician, and surveyor who helped lay out Washington, DC

Barbadoes: James G. Barbadoes, one of the founders of the American Anti-Slavery Society

Ben Tillman: an open racist who fought Republican government in South Carolina as a member of a paramilitary group known as the Red Shirts

Bruce: Blanche Kelso Bruce, the first black US senator to serve a full term

Byron: George Gordon Lord Byron, a prominent British romantic poet of the early nineteenth century; the quotation is from his long narrative poem *Childe Harold's Pilgrimage*

Cato of Stono: a reference to the Stono Rebellion of 1739 (also called Cato's Rebellion), a slave revolt in South Carolina

Crummell: Alexander Crummell, a prominent abolitionist and pan-Africanist

Cuffes: a reference to Paul Cuffe and his followers, who wanted to establish a free colony in West Africa

Danish blacks: a group of slaves who, in 1723, gained control of Saint John in the Virgin Islands (then the Danish West Indies) for six months

Derham: James Derham, the first African American doctor in the colonies

Douglass: Frederick Douglass, the preeminent abolitionist of the nineteenth century

Du Bois of New Haven: probably a reference to Du Bois's ancestor, Alexander Du Bois, who was disowned by his family because his mother was a black Haitian

Elliott: Robert Brown Elliott, a black congressman

Forten: James Forten, an early abolitionist and businessman

Gabriel: Gabriel Prosser, who led a slave revolt in Virginia in 1800

Grimkés: a reference to the half-brothers of prominent white abolitionists Sarah and Angelina Grimké, born of their father's liaison with a slave woman

Haytian revolt: the revolution that led to a free Haiti in 1803

J. W. E. Bowen: John Wesley Edward Bowen, a Methodist clergyman, university educator, one of the first African Americans to earn a PhD degree in the United States, and the first African American to receive a PhD from Boston University

Jefferson Davis: the president of the Confederate States of America during the Civil War

Joshua: in the Old Testament, the leader of the Israelites after the death of Moses

Kelly Miller: a scientist, mathematician, essayist, and newspaper columnist; the first black admitted to The Johns Hopkins University

Langston: Charles Langston, a black activist and grandfather of the poet Langston Hughes

Maroons: escaped slaves in Haiti and throughout the Caribbean who formed gangs that lived in the forests and attacked French plantations

Nat Turner: leader of a slave rebellion in Virginia in 1831

Nell: William Cooper Nell, an abolitionist, author, journalist, and civil servant

Payne: Daniel Payne, a bishop in the African Methodist Episcopal Church and one of the founders of Wilberforce University

Phyllis: Phillis Wheatley, an eighteenth-century slave poet

President Roosevelt: Theodore Roosevelt, who earlier had led forces in the Spanish-American War

Price: William G. Price, an African American educator

Purvis: Robert Purvis, a nineteenth-century abolitionist who was three-quarters white but chose to identify with the black community

Remond: Charles Lenox Remond, an orator and abolitionist

Revolution of 1876: a reference to the disputed presidential election of 1876, which led to the end of the Reconstruction era

Senator Morgan: John Tyler Morgan, a segregationist Alabama senator after the Civil War

Shad: probably a reference to Abraham Shadd, a free black who opposed African colonization by US blacks

Socrates: an ancient Greek philosopher

St. Francis of Assisi: a Catholic saint who founded the Franciscan order of priests

Thomas Nelson Page: an author of sentimental novels idealizing pre–Civil War plantation life

Toussaint: Toussaint Louverture, the leader of the Haitian Revolution

Tuskegee: Tuskegee Institute, the educational institution, stressing occupational skills, founded by Booker T. Washington

Vesey: Denmark Vesey, who led a slave revolt in South Carolina in 1822

Walker's wild appeal: David Walker's influential *Appeal to the Coloured Citizens of the World*

Wells Brown: William Wells Brown, a prominent historian, lecturer, playwright, and novelist

Document Analysis

The Souls of Black Folk advances the thesis that "the problem of the Twentieth Century is the problem of the color-line." Du Bois traces what he calls the "double-consciousness" of African Americans, the "sense of always looking at one's self through the eyes of others." The book assesses the progress of blacks, the obstacles that blacks face, and the possibilities for progress in the future. Chapter III, "Of Mr. Booker T. Washington and Others" directly addresses Washington's assimilationist views. The cleavage between Washington and Du Bois is one that still reverberates in American race relations.

In the first eight paragraphs of Chapter III, Du Bois outlines the rise of Booker T. Washington to prominence. He points to the growth and industrial development of the United States, what other authors have called the "Gilded Age" when business was expanding and fortunes were being made in the decades following the Civil War. He notes that in the antebellum years, efforts to provide blacks with industrial training had taken place under the auspices of organizations such as the American Missionary Association and individuals such as William G. Price, an African American educator whose career mirrored that of Washington. Du Bois refers to these efforts at industrial education as a "by-path" that Washington was able to turn into a "Way of Life." Du Bois continues by noting that Washington's program won applause in the South and admiration in the North, though not necessarily among blacks.

Du Bois then goes into more detail about Washington and his program. He refers to Washington's efforts in creating Tuskegee Institute and cites the "Atlanta Compromise" speech of 1895, in which Washington advocated (to a largely white audience) that blacks abandon the quest for social and political equality until they have achieved economic equality. Many blacks saw the speech as a surrender, but many whites applauded it, making Washington—in the words of Du Bois—the "most distinguished Southerner since Jefferson Davis" the president of the Confederate States of America during the Civil War. In paragraph 4, Du Bois begins his critique of Washington by suggesting that he had "grasped the spirit of the age which was dominating the North" and that he had learned the speech of "triumphant commercialism," where manual skills were more important than something as presumably esoteric as French grammar. In paragraph 5, Du Bois ironically refers to Washington as a "successful man" in gathering a "cult" of followers, but he also indicates that the time has come to point out Washington's mistakes and shortcomings.

Du Bois hints at the nature of the criticism that Washington has encountered. In his position, Washington has had to "walk warily" to avoid offending his patrons and the South in general. Du Bois notes that at the National Peace Jubilee at the end of the Spanish-American War, Washington alluded to racial prejudice, and he appears to have done so at a White House dinner he had with President Theodore Roosevelt in 1901—a highly publicized and controversial event. These events attracted some criticism, but Washington has generally managed adroitly to avoid giving offense, says Du Bois. In paragraph 7, Du Bois asserts that Washington has encountered opposition, some of it bitter, among his own people, particularly "educated and thoughtful colored men." While these men might admire Washington's honest efforts to do something positive, they feel "deep regret, sorrow, and apprehension" because of the popularity of Washington's views. Paragraph 8 notes, however, that people are hesitant to criticize Washington openly. This, says Du Bois, is "dangerous" and he raises the question of whether African Americans are submitting to a leader who has been imposed on them by external pressure.

Paragraph 9 begins to examine the history of leadership in the African American community. Du Bois observes that these leaders emerge from the environment in which the people lived, and when that environment consists of "sticks and stones and beasts" people will oppose it. Thus, in paragraph 10, he discusses black leadership before 1750. He makes reference to the "Maroons" the name given to escaped slaves in Haiti and throughout the Caribbean who formed gangs that lived in the forests. These gangs, which were generally small but sometimes grew to thousands of men, repeatedly attacked French plantations. "Danish blacks" refers to a group of slaves who, in 1723, gained control of Saint John in the Virgin Islands (then the Danish West Indies) for six months. Cato of Stono is a reference to the Stono Rebellion of 1739 (also called Cato's Rebellion), a slave revolt in South Carolina. By the end of the century, however, it was thought that "kindlier relations" would replace rebellion, as exemplified in the poetry of "Phyllis" (that is, Phillis Wheatley) and the heroism of blacks such as Crispus Attucks, Peter Salem, and Salem Poor during the Revolutionary War. James Durham was the first African American doctor in the colonies, and Benjamin Banneker was an accomplished scientist, mathematician, and surveyor who helped lay out Washington, DC. "Cuffes" is a reference to Paul Cuffe and his followers, who wanted to establish a free colony in West Africa.

Du Bois then turns to the worsening condition of American slaves in the late eighteenth and early nineteenth century. Notable events included the revolt in Haiti led by Toussaint Louverture that resulted in an independent Haiti in 1803. Back in the United States, significant slave revolts were headed by Gabriel Prosser in Virginia in 1800, Denmark Vesey in South Carolina in 1822, and Nat Turner in Virginia in 1831. Meanwhile, in the North, African Americans were segregating themselves in black churches at a time when white mainstream churches were ignoring their needs. Paragraph 12 alludes to David Walker's highly influential *Appeal to the Coloured Citizens of the World*, written in 1829. Du Bois goes on to point out instances of prominent northern men who "sought assimilation and amalgamation with the nation on the same terms with other men" but says that they continued to be regarded as "despised blacks."

Accordingly, during the abolition era prior to the Civil War, numerous black leaders, including Charles Lenox Remond, William Cooper Nell, William Wells Brown, and Frederick Douglass, launched a new period of self-assertion. The logic of self-assertion reached its extreme with John Brown's raid on Harpers Ferry, Virginia, in 1859. After the Civil War, leadership in the African American community passed to Douglass and several others: Robert Brown Elliott, a black congressman; Blanche Kelso Bruce, the first black senator to serve a full term; Charles Langston, a black activist (and grandfather of the poet Langston Hughes); Alexander Crummell, an abolitionist and pan-Africanist; and Daniel Payne, a bishop in the African Methodist Episcopal Church and one of the founders of Wilberforce University, where he became the first African American college president in the nation's history.

In paragraph 14, Du Bois uses the term "Revolution" to refer to the disputed presidential election of 1876, which led to the end of the Reconstruction era. In the post-Reconstruction climate, Douglass and Bruce carried on, but Bruce died in 1898 and Douglass was aging. Booker T. Washington arose to fill the vacuum they left, becoming the leader not of one race but of two, both blacks and whites. Some blacks resented Washington's ascendancy, but their criticisms were hushed because of the potential of economic gains as northern businesses were investing in southern enterprises. All were weary of the race problem, and Washington's views seemed to provide a way out.

Beginning with paragraph 15, Du Bois takes on Washington directly. He describes Washington's program as one of "adjustment and submission" and one that "practically accepts the alleged inferiority of the Negro races." Washington "withdraws" the demands of African Americans for equality as citizens. He calls for African Americans to surrender political power, civil rights, and higher education and instead to "concentrate all their energies on industrial education, and accumulation of wealth, and the conciliation of the South." The result, however, has been the "disfranchisement" (usually spelled "disenfranchisement") of blacks, legalized civil inferiority, and loss of opportunities for higher education. In paragraph 17, Du Bois asks whether it is even possible for blacks to achieve economic equality when they have been denied political power, civil rights, and access to education. He then goes on to point out the paradoxes: that black artisans and workingmen cannot defend their rights without the vote, that submission will "sap" the manhood of any race, and that an institution like Tuskegee itself could not remain open without a class of African Americans who have pursued higher education. The result of these paradoxes has been the creation of two classes of blacks: those who "represent the attitude of revolt and revenge" and those who disagree with Washington but cannot say so. These people, according to Du Bois, are obligated to demand of the nation the right to vote, civic equality, and access to education. In paragraph 20, Du Bois acknowledges that the "low social level" of many African Americans leads to discrimination, but he also argues that "relentless color-prejudice is more often a cause than a result of the Negro's degradation." He insists that there is a demand for educational institutions to provide training for African American teachers, professionals, and leaders.

Du Bois continues in paragraph 21 by obliquely criticizing those, particularly blacks, who accept Washington and his views. He acknowledges that they see in Washington an effort to conciliate the South, no easy task. But he also insists that the issue is one that has to be approached honestly. They recognize that the right to vote, civic rights, and the right to be educated will not come easily, and that the prejudice of the past will not disappear overnight. But they also know that the path to progress will not open by throwing away rights; a people cannot gain respect by "continually belittling and ridiculing themselves."

With paragraph 22, Du Bois begins to build toward a conclusion. He insists that "the thinking classes of American Negroes" are obliged to oppose Washington. While acknowledging that there has been some progress in relations between North and South after the Civil War, he states that if reconciliation has to be bought at the price of "industrial slavery and civic death" or by "inferiority" then patriotism and loyalty demands disagreement with Washington. He maintains that it is necessary to judge the South with discrimination, to recognize that it is a place in ferment and undergoing social change. He concedes in paragraph 24 that the attitude toward blacks in the South is not uniform; ignorant people want to disenfranchise blacks, but not all southerners are ignorant. Among those who are ignorant, he mentions North Carolina governor Charles Aycock, a white supremacist; Thomas Nelson Page, who wrote sentimental novels idealizing pre-Civil War plantation life; and Ben Tillman, an open racist who fought Republican government in South Carolina as a member of a paramilitary group known as the Red Shirts.

Du Bois acknowledges that Washington has opposed injustice to people of color. Nevertheless, he calls Washington's views "propaganda" that justifies the South in its attitude toward African Americans, that blacks are responsible for their own degraded condition, and that only through their own efforts can blacks rise in the future. Du Bois counters these "half-truths" by arguing that race prejudice is still a potent force in the South, that earlier systems of education could not succeed without a class of educated blacks, and that blacks can rise only if the culture at large encourages and arouses this effort. The key mistake Washington makes is to impose the burden of the "Negro problem" on blacks without recognizing that it is a national problem, one that it will take the united efforts of North and South to solve. Indeed, says Du Bois, industrial training, along with virtues such as thrift and patience, are to the good, but without fighting for the right and duty to vote, eliminating the "emasculating effects of caste distinctions" and striving for higher education, the promise of the Founding Fathers that "all men are created equal" will never be realized.

Essential Themes

Du Bois came of age during the Reconstruction era that followed the Civil War, with "Reconstruction" referring to the political process of reintegrating the rebellious Confederate states into the Union. Confederate soldiers returning to ruined homes found themselves in tenuous financial and political circumstances. The defeated South entered a period of economic chaos. In the midst of this postwar turmoil, the US Congress, led by the Radical Republicans (the loose faction of the Republican Party that, before the war, opposed slavery and, after the war, defended the rights of African Americans and wanted to impose harsh terms on the rebellious South), enacted the Thirteenth Amendment, which abolished slavery and other forms of involuntary servitude throughout the United States.

What followed was a flood of legislation and constitutional amendments designed to reshape the racial landscape of the United States. The Civil Rights Act of 1866 gave blacks the right to buy and sell property and to make and enforce contracts to the same extent as white citizens. The Fourteenth Amendment, which was ratified in 1868, affirmed the citizenship rights of former slaves and guaranteed "due process" and "equal protection" to all citizens under the law. The four Reconstruction Acts (1867–1868) created military districts in the South to ensure order during the states' return to the Union, required congressional approval for new state constitutions (a requirement for Confederate states to rejoin the Union), gave voting rights to all men in the former Confederacy, and stipulated that Confederate states had to ratify the Fourteenth Amendment. The Fifteenth Amendment, which took effect in 1870, guaranteed the voting rights of all citizens. The Ku Klux Klan Act of 1871 gave the US president sweeping powers to combat the Klan and similar organizations in the South that were using violence and intimidation to deprive African Americans of their rights and that often directed their violence against white Republicans who supported equal rights for blacks. The Civil Rights Act of 1875 made it unlawful for inns, restaurants, theaters, and other public facilities to deny access to any individual based on race.

The Hayes-Tilden Compromise of 1877 represented the turning point in the fate of black Americans in the South. The most disputed presidential election in American history took place in 1876. After the votes were counted, Democrat Samuel Tilden held a narrow lead in both the popular vote and in the Electoral College over Republican Rutherford B. Hayes, but a number of electoral votes were in dispute. In the Compromise of 1877, Democrats (whose stronghold was in the South) agreed to recognize Hayes as president on the condition that he withdraw federal troops from Florida, South Carolina, and Louisiana, the only three southern states where postwar troops remained. This event marked the end of the Reconstruction era and allowed whites to reassert their dominance using violence, intimidation, and fraud.

Matters worsened in the years that followed. A series of US Supreme Court cases undermined the Fourteenth and Fifteenth Amendments. In the 1876 case *United States v. Reese*, the Court rejected an African American's challenge to a poll tax, holding that the Fifteenth Amendment did not affirmatively assure the right to vote and that the poll tax was racially neutral. *United States v. Cruikshank*, decided the same year, involved an action against a group of whites who used lethal force to break up a political rally that blacks had organized. The Court held that the blacks who brought the case had not established that they were denied any rights based on their color. In the Civil Rights Cases of 1883, which was a consolidation of several cases that presented similar issues, the Court declared that the 1875 Civil Rights Act was unconstitutional. The decision established the "state action" doctrine by holding that Congress did not have the authority to regulate private acts of discrimination. In 1896, segregation was affirmed when the Supreme Court ruled in *Plessy v. Ferguson* that laws requiring segregation in public transportation did not violate the Fourteenth Amendment as long as the separate facilities provided for blacks were equal to those available to whites. Yet another case upheld the outcome of Mississippi's 1890 state constitutional convention, which had the express purpose of disenfranchising black voters. In *Williams v. Mississippi*, the Supreme Court held in 1898 that because Mississippi's voter registration laws were not explicitly discriminatory, they did not violate the Fourteenth Amendment.

In *The Souls of Black Folk*, Du Bois reacted to the rising tide of segregation and racial subordination and established himself as one of the most prominent African American intellectuals and leaders of the early twentieth century. It also set off a heated debate that still reverberates in some circles. A few years before the book was published, the white South found what it believed would be a resolution of the still unsettled question of the status of the black population. The answer to the dilemma came from an unlikely source, a former slave who became perhaps the most powerful person of color in the history of the Republic. The bearer of this solution, Booker T. Washington, spent his childhood in Virginia assisting his family in a series of menial jobs. After he graduated from Hampton Normal and Agricultural Institute (now Hampton University), Washington received an offer to establish a school in rural Alabama. At what became the Tuskegee Institute, Washington developed a program emphasizing industrial education. He trained brick masons, carpenters, and other student artisans who constructed several of Tuskegee's buildings. Women were taught the domestic arts. Tuskegee's program was based on Washington's belief that black students would be served best by training for vocations in the industrial sphere rather than for professions.

In 1895, Washington delivered a historic speech in Atlanta, Georgia, before a large and mainly white audience—the so-called "Atlanta Compromise" speech. Invoking a metaphor that would be seen as the solution for race relations, Washington, in a statement Du Bois quotes in Chapter III of *The Souls of Black Folk*, held out one hand and said, "In all things purely social we can be as separate as the fingers, yet as one hand in all things essential to mutual progress." He then closed his fingers into a fist to buttress his point. The implication of Washington's words was clear: African Americans would be trained to be obedient and reliable workers who would not challenge white supremacy. The speech received national acclaim and made Washington the preeminent leader of black America, particularly among white Americans but among many black Americans as well.

Despite his success, there was much about Washington's philosophy that rankled many African Americans. In addition to preaching accommodation, Washington's speeches included numerous references to the shortcomings of blacks. These comments were often couched in humorous anecdotes that delighted his white audiences but were demeaning to blacks. Washington ridiculed classical education as "sheer folly" because it would not prepare African Americans for practical occupations.

The lines were drawn. Largely in response to Washington's popularity, Du Bois wrote *The Souls of Black Folk*, a collection of incisive essays, several of which had been previously published in *The Atlantic Monthly* magazine.

In *The Souls of Black Folk*, Du Bois boldly challenged Booker T. Washington and his accommodationist approach to race relations. Du Bois emphasized the need to develop a "Talented Tenth"—an educated vanguard that would serve as the teachers and leaders in the black community. Demanding political and civil rights for *all* Americans, in 1905, he organized the Niagara Movement, a group of black militants who were adamantly opposed to segregation. Regarded as a forerunner of the NAACP, the nation's oldest, most influential, and highly venerable civil rights organization, the Niagara Movement met annually in Buffalo, New York, through 1909. Around this time, the philosophical differences between Washington and Du Bois grew into a bitter personal animosity. Washington used his influence to block financial support for Atlanta University, and he intimated to the university's president that further support would not be forthcoming as long as Du Bois remained on the faculty. Consequently, Du Bois and Atlanta University parted company in 1910.

Du Bois went on to pursue a career as a distinguished activist, editor, and scholar. As one of the cofounders of the NAACP, he fought unceasingly for social change. The formation of the NAACP was fueled in part by a 1908 race riot in Springfield, Illinois. Violence of this sort was not new, as the lynching of African Americans had been increasing with alarming frequency throughout the late nineteenth century. The riot in Springfield was one of several episodes of brutality inflicted by white mobs against black communities. What was alarming about the Springfield riots was that they erupted outside the South in the birthplace of Abraham Lincoln. Many worried that the "race war" in the South would be transported to northern cities.

These events spurred Mary Ovington, a social worker who had been active in the Niagara Movement, to contact William English Walling, a socialist who supported progressive causes, and Dr. Henry Moskowitz, another well-known progressive. The group issued a call for the formation of a political movement that would develop a program aimed at securing racial equality. A conference of the newly formed NAACP was held on May 12–14, 1910, in New York City, where the organization outlined its goals. In *The Souls of Black Folk*, Du Bois had insisted on voting rights, civic equality, and access to higher education. These principles were incorporated into the fledgling organization's mission, which was to ensure the political, educational, social, and economic equality of people of color and to eliminate racial prejudice. Du Bois was appointed director of publicity and research for the NAACP.

By November 1911, a sixteen-page magazine under Du Bois's editorship was ready for distribution. For a title, Du Bois settled on *The Crisis: A Record of the Darker Races*. A thousand copies were printed, and the magazine was immediately successful. After *The Crisis* was established as the voice of the NAACP, Du Bois's stature rose rapidly. Within a short period of time, the magazine's circulation reached a thousand issues per month. As the periodical's reputation grew, Du Bois became the most well-known black intellectual of his time. When Booker T. Washington died in 1915, the power of the Tuskegee machine faded rapidly. Its influence was replaced by the NAACP, which by 1919 had more than 88,000 members.

Over the next decade, the NAACP continued its fight against segregation, using lobbying, public education, and demonstrations as its primary tools. Between 1918 and 1922, the NAACP campaigned for the adoption of anti-lynching laws by Congress. Such legislative measures failed to gain ground, however, even when argued on the basis of the fundamental Fourteenth Amendment right to due process. Du Bois viewed this and other barriers to equality for blacks as reprehensible, and he began to rethink the integrationist goals of the NAACP. In 1934, controversy erupted over an editorial Du Bois authored that argued that African Americans should adopt a program of self-segregation in which black-owned economic institutions would be encouraged and developed. Frustrated with the NAACP's inability to make progress toward eliminating segregation, Du Bois contended that integration would likely take a long time to achieve. During the interim, instead of focusing all of its energies on demands for integration, the black community would be better served by developing and relying on its own institutions.

Du Bois's editorial was perceived as acquiescing to continued segregation. A vigorous debate ensued. To many observers, Du Bois appeared to be advocating a return to Washington's philosophy. Du Bois's editorial independence was tolerated as long as *The Crisis* was self-supporting. But during the Great Depression years of 1930s, the publication lost money. In the wake of the controversy, the NAACP's board of directors took steps to rein in Du Bois by adopting a formal resolution requiring editorials to reflect the NAACP's institutional views and requiring advance approval by the board. This was more than Du Bois could take. In June 1934, he announced his resignation.

—Leland Ware, JD

Bibliography and Further Reading

"About the NAACP—History." *NAACP*. National Association for the Advancement of Colored People, 2016. Web. 2 Aug. 2016. <http://www.naacp.org/about/history>.

Crouch, Stanley, & Playthell Benjamin. *Reconsidering the Souls of Black Folk: Thoughts on the Groundbreaking Classic Work of W. E. B. Du Bois*. Philadelphia: Running Press, 2002.

Du Bois, W. E. B. *Dusk of Dawn: An Essay toward an Autobiography of a Race Concept*. New York: Harcourt, Brace, 1940.

_____. *The Autobiography of W. E. B. Du Bois: A Soliloquy on Viewing My Life from the Decade of Its First Century*. New York: International Publishers, 1969.

Lewis, David Levering. *W. E. B. Du Bois: Biography of a Race, 1868–1919*. New York: Henry Holt, 1993.

_____. *W. E. B. Du Bois: The Fight for Equality and the American Century: 1919–1963*. New York: Henry Holt, 2009.

Marable, Manning. *W. E. B. Du Bois: Black Radical Democrat*. Boston: Twayne, 1986.

Rampersad, Arnold. *The Art and Imagination of W. E. B. Du Bois*. New York: Schocken Books, 1990.

W. E. B. Du Bois: Online Resources. Library of Congress, 2016. Web. 2 Aug. 2016. <http://www.loc.gov/rr/program/bib/dubois>.

W. E. B. Du Bois: "The Parting of the Ways"

Date: 1904
Author: W. E. B. Du Bois
Genre: article; essay

Summary Overview

W. E. B. Du Bois came of age during the nadir of race relations in the United States. The gains that African Americans had achieved during Reconstruction were undone as segregation became the standard across the country, southern states denied blacks the right to vote or participate in the political process, and the nation was swept by an epidemic of racial violence, especially in the form of lynching. Du Bois himself, despite his superior education and record of scholarship, could not obtain a faculty position in a "white" college or university. This was the reality that Du Bois confronted as he began his career as a professor and intellectual, and he chose to address the era's racial injustice with his pen. Various documents trace the development and evolution of his political thought from the beginning of his career in the late nineteenth century to his resignation from the NAACP in 1934. In his essay "The Parting of the Ways," Du Bois details the distinctions between his vision for the future of African Americans and that of Booker T. Washington.

Defining Moment

Booker T. Washington was the most prominent leader in the early twentieth century. His policies on political and social issues were taken seriously by not only African Americans but also prominent whites. Whites regarded him as *the* representative of African Americans. However, W. E. B. Du Bois found many of Washington's positions troubling, especially his seeming acquiescence to segregation and black disenfranchisement. A prominent leader in the black community in his own right, who benefitted greatly from his liberal arts education at Fisk and Harvard Universities, Du Bois believed that he must challenge Washington's positions on black education and civil and political equality. Du Bois does not address Washington by name, but "The Parting of the Ways" was clearly aimed at his leadership and his policies. Du Bois was trying to convince Washington's supporters that his emphasis on industrial and agricultural education for blacks at the expense of a liberal arts education and the downplaying of civil and political equality was a grave error. Du Bois told African Americans that they should continue to fight for all their rights: educational, political, and civil. They should never remain complicit in the face of segregation or political disenfranchisement.

Author Biography

William Edward Burghardt Du Bois was born on February 23, 1868, in Great Barrington, Massachusetts, and raised by his mother. In spite of the poverty of his childhood, Du Bois excelled in school and achieved one of the most impressive educations of his generation. He received bachelor degrees from Fisk University and Harvard University, pursued graduate work at Harvard and Germany's University of Berlin, and earned his PhD in history from Harvard in 1895. He received a faculty appointment at Wilberforce University in 1894, worked for the University of Pennsylvania on a study of blacks in Philadelphia in 1896, and joined the faculty of Atlanta University in 1897. In 1910, he left Atlanta and took a paid position as the director of publishing and research for the newly founded National Association for the Advancement of Colored People (NAACP). He served in that position and also as the founding editor of the NAACP journal, *The Crisis*, subtitled *A Record of the Darker Races*, until 1934, when he resigned over a policy dispute.

Following his departure from the NAACP, Du Bois returned to Atlanta University and to academic scholarship for ten years. In 1943, at the age of seventy-six, he was forced to retire from the university, and he accepted a position back at the NAACP. By this time, Du Bois was clearly out of step with the civil rights organization; his increasingly leftist, pro-Soviet politics and his criticism both of US foreign policy and of the NAACP director Walter White cost him his job in 1948. In the late 1940s and early 1950s, Du Bois became involved in leftist organizations, continued condemning the United States and its foreign policy while praising the Soviet Union, and ran for public office as a nominee of the American Labor Party. These activities made him a target of the post–World War II "Red Scare" inspired by Senator Joseph McCarthy. Although he was acquitted of charges related to his involvement with radical antiwar organizations, his passport was suspended from 1951 to 1958. When he regained the right to travel abroad, he made a series of trips, including highly publicized visits to East Germany, the Soviet Union, and Communist China. Du Bois's continued pro-Communist political radicalism isolated him from the emerging civil rights movement. In 1961, disillusioned with the United States, Du Bois formally joined the US Communist Party before relocating to the newly independent nation of Ghana. In 1963, he became a citizen of his adopted country; on August 27, 1963, he died at the age of ninety-five.

Du Bois was the leading African American intellectual of his day. He first established his credentials with his scholarly publications on the Atlanta slave trade and on Philadelphia's black community. In 1897, he began to define his political and racial views, moving from academic work to political and social activism; his publication of "Strivings of the Negro People" in *The Atlantic Monthly* brought him national attention. Six years later, his classic work *The Souls of Black Folk* cemented his intellectual credentials. His involvement with the Niagara Movement beginning in 1905 and with the National Association for the Advancement of Colored People made him the most significant of Booker T. Washington's critics and the most prominent and most respected head of the early-twentieth-century campaign for civil rights. In his books and articles, especially those published in *The Crisis*, Du Bois developed ideas that were fundamental to his vision of race in America and to the long struggle against discrimination and for equality. While he found himself increasingly out of the mainstream civil rights movement following his departure from the NAACP in 1934, Du Bois remained one of the giants among twentieth-century American intellectuals.

HISTORICAL DOCUMENT

The points upon which American Negroes differ as to their course of action are the following: First, the scope of education; second, the necessity of the right of suffrage; third, the importance of civil rights; fourth, the conciliation of the South; fifth, the future of the race in this country.

The older opinion as built up under the leadership of our great dead, Payne, Crummell, Forten and Douglass, was that the broadest field of education should be opened to black children; that no free citizen of a republic could exist in peace and prosperity without the ballot; that self-respect and proper development of character can only take place under a system of equal civil rights; that every effort should be made to live in peace and harmony with all men, but that even for this great boon no people must willingly or passively surrender their essential rights of manhood; that in future the Negro is destined to become an American citizen with full political and civil rights, and that he must never rest contented until he has achieved this.

Since the death of the leaders of the past there have come mighty changes in the nation. The gospel of money has risen triumphant in church and state and university. The great question which Americans ask to-day is, "What is he worth?" or "What is it worth?" The ideals of human rights are obscured, and the nation has begun to swagger about the world in its useless battleships looking for helpless peoples whom it can force to buy its goods at high prices. This wave of materialism is temporary; it will pass and leave us all ashamed and surprised; but while it is here it strangely maddens and blinds us. Religious periodicals are found in the van yelling for war; peaceful ministers of Christ are leading lynchers; great universities are stuffing their pockets with greenbacks and kicking the little souls of students to make them "move faster" through the courses of study, the end of which is ever "*Etwas schaffen*" and seldom "*Etwas sein*." Yet there are signs of change. Souls long cramped and starved are stretching toward the light. Men are beginning to murmur against the lower tendencies and the sound of the Zeitgeist strikes sensitive ears with that harrowing discord which prefigures richer harmony to come.

Meantime an awakening race, seeing American civilization as it is, is strongly moved and naturally misled. They whisper: What is the greatness of the country? Is it not money? Well then, the one end of our education and striving should be moneymaking. The trimmings of life, smatterings of Latin and music and such stuff—let that wait till we are rich. Then as to voting, what is the good of it after all? Politics does not pay as well as the grocery business, and breeds trouble. Therefore get out of politics and let the ballot go. When we are rich we can dabble in politics along with the president of Yale. Then, again the thought arises: What is personal humiliation and the denial of ordinary civil rights compared with a chance to earn a living? Why quarrel with your bread and butter simply because of filthy Jim Crow cars? Earn a living; get rich, and all these things shall be added unto you. Moreover, conciliate your neighbors, because they are more powerful and wealthier, and the price you must pay to earn a living in America is that of humiliation and inferiority.

No one, of course, has voiced this argument quite so flatly and bluntly as I have indicated. It has been expressed rather by the emphasis given industrial and trade teaching, the decrying of suffrage as a manhood right or even necessity, the insistence on great advance among Negroes before there is any recognition of their aspirations, and a tendency to minimize the shortcomings of the South and to emphasize the mistakes and failures of black men. Now, in this there has been just that degree of truth and right which serves to make men forget its untruths. That the shiftless and poor need thrift and skill, that ignorance can not vote intelligently, that duties and rights go hand in hand, and that sympathy and understanding among neighbors is prerequisite to peace and concord, all this is true. Who has ever denied it, or ever will? But from all this does it follow that Negro colleges are not needed, that the right of suffrage is not essential for black men, that equality of civil rights is not the first of rights and that no self-respecting man can agree with the person who insists that he is a dog? Certainly not, all answer.

Yet the plain result of the attitude of mind of those who, in their advocacy of industrial schools, the unimportance of suffrage and civil rights and conciliation, have been significantly silent or evasive as to higher training and the great principle of free self-respecting manhood for black folk the plain result of this propaganda has been to help the cutting down of educational opportunity for Negro children, the legal disfranchisement of nearly 5,000,000 of Negroes and a state of public opinion which apologizes for lynching, listens complacently to any insult or detraction directed against an eighth of the population of the land, and silently allows a new slavery to rise and clutch the South and paralyze the moral sense of a great nation.

What do Negroes say to this? I speak advisedly when I say that the overwhelming majority of them declare that the tendencies to-day are wrong and that the propaganda that encouraged them was wrong. They say that industrial and trade teaching is needed among Negroes, sadly needed; but they unhesitatingly affirm that it is not needed as much as thorough common school training and the careful education of the gifted in higher institutions; that only in this way can a people rise by intelligence and social leadership to a plane of permanent efficiency and morality. . . .

Moreover, notwithstanding speeches and the editorials of a subsidized Negro press, black men in this land know that when they lose the ballot they lose all. They are no fools. They know it is impossible for free workingmen without a ballot to compete with free workingmen who have the ballot; they know there is no set of people so good and true as to be worth trusting with the political destiny of their fellows, and they know that it is just as true to-day as it was a century and a quarter ago "Taxation without representation is tyranny."

Finally, the Negro knows perfectly what freedom and equality mean—opportunity to make the best of oneself, unhandicapped by wanton restraint and unreasoning prejudice. For this the most of us propose to strive. We will not, by word or deed, for a moment admit the right of any man to discriminate against us simply on account of race or color. . . . We refuse to kiss the hands that smite us, but rather insist on striving by all civilized methods to keep wide educational opportunity, to keep the right to vote, to insist on equal civil rights and to gain every right and privilege open to a free American citizen.

But, answer some, you can not accomplish this. America will never spell opportunity for black men; it spelled slavery for them in 1619 and it will spell the same thing in other letters in 1919. To this I answer simply: I do not believe it. I believe that black men will become free American citizens if they have the courage and persistence to demand the rights and treatment of men, and cease to toady and apologize and belittle themselves. The rights of humanity are worth fighting for. Those that deserve them in the long run get them. The way for black men to-day to make these rights the heritage of their children is to struggle for them unceasingly, and if they fail, die trying.

GLOSSARY

Etwas schaffen: German for "accomplish something"

Etwas sein: German for "be something"

greenbacks: dollars, money

Jim Crow cars: late-nineteenth-century and early-twentieth-century laws and customs that kept African Americans segregated and in a subservient position; "cars" refers to railroad cars

Payne, Crummell, Forten and Douglass: Daniel A. Payne (1811–1893), an author, educator, and clergyman associated with the African Methodist Episcopal Church; Alexander Crummell (1819–1898), an African American clergyman and missionary; James Forten (1766–1842), an African American businessman and abolitionist; Frederick Douglass (1818–1895), a prominent African American author and abolitionist

Zeitgeist: a German word literally meaning "spirit of the time"

Document Analysis

By 1904, Du Bois had concluded that the path chosen by Booker T. Washington to lead African Americans to their destiny was flawed and that, both for his own career and for the well-being of his people, he needed to advocate the pursuit of a different direction. Through the first few years of the twentieth century, the young Du Bois and the well-established Washington had formed an alliance. The concepts Du Bois had presented in his *Atlantic Monthly* essay did not conflict with Washington's teachings. However, the deterioration of civil rights, the rise in racial violence, and the increasing political influence of Washington convinced Du Bois of the need to chart another path. He had voiced mild criticism in his review of Washington's autobiography *Up from Slavery*, and he included additional criticism in his chapter on Washington in *The Souls of Black Folk*. As the split became irrevocable, Du Bois addressed his position in his essay "The Parting of the Ways," published in April 1904 in *World Today*, a small journal of politics and culture.

Du Bois crafted this essay carefully; after all, he was challenging the authority of the most prominent African American, who had a great deal of respect among whites. Interestingly, Du Bois never mentions Booker T. Washington by name. However, he clearly separates himself from Washington and writes as though the reader knows, perhaps through the essay's title, that he is doing so.

Du Bois acknowledged the diversity of opinions among African Americans regarding the best strategy for gaining equal access to education, the right to vote, civil rights, and ending racial disharmony. He noted that the "older opinion" was based on the ideas and positions of such eminent black leaders as Frederick Douglass, Daniel Payne, and Alexander Crummell, who encouraged African Americans to fight unequivocally and unapologetically for equal access to all levels of education and the right to vote. These men understood that "self-respect and proper development of character can only take place under a system of equal civil rights," a clear rebuke of Washington's argument that African Americans needed to improve themselves before they demanded equal political rights. According to Du Bois, Washington's position was in direct contrast to the positions of Douglass, Payne, and Crummell, who maintained that black passivity was unacceptable and that the only way African Americans would ever obtain the political and civil rights enjoyed by other Americans was to fight for those rights.

By the time that Du Bois published the "Parting of the Ways" in 1904, Douglass, Payne, and Crummell were dead. Du Bois worried that the ideals that they stood for were slowly being eroded as well. He observed that "the gospel of money has risen triumphant in church and state and university," leading many Americans to become more concerned with money and financial success than human rights. This focus on financial gain had influenced foreign policy as well for "the nation has begun to swagger about the world in its useless battleships looking for helpless peoples whom it can force to buy its goods at high prices." This viewpoint had also influenced the churches. Christian ministers urged peace in their churches, but war abroad.

The desire for material wealth had influenced African Americans as well. He noted that many black leaders had decided that "politics does not pay as well as the grocery business, and breeds trouble. Therefore get out of politics and let the ballot go." Much to Du Bois's consternation, some black leaders took the position that the fight for political rights should come after blacks prosper. The emphasis on economic improvement identified with Washington was labelled by Du Bois as the "gospel of money."

Washington's emphasis on the gaining of an industrial education at the expense of other types of education had superseded the fight for political and civil equality. It was undoubtedly true that African Americans deserved access to trade schools, but there was no reason for this legitimate demand to come at the expense of the fight for other rights. In taking such a position, Washington and other black leaders unintentionally contributed to both the weakening of educational opportunities for black children, "the legal disenfranchisement of nearly 5,000,000 of Negroes," and the allowance of a "new slavery to rise and clutch the South and paralyze the moral sense of a great nation."

Du Bois believed that most blacks understood the importance of an industrial education; at the same time they also recognized that access to "common school training" and "gifted higher institutions" is even more important. Equally significant, "black men in this land know that when they lose the ballot they lose all" and that the inability to vote only made it harder for blacks to compete economically against whites who were able to vote. Whites would vote for politicians who represented their economic interests, leaving African Americans further behind.

Du Bois rejected the notion that many African Americans would accept discrimination of any sort and concentrate solely on gaining an industrial education and accumulating wealth. The majority of African Americans "insist on striving by all civilized methods to keep wide educational opportunity, to keep the right to vote, to insist on equal rights and to gain every right and privilege open to a free American citizen. He concluded that the only way for African Americans to gain the rights and freedoms owed to them as American citizens was to fight for those rights.

While the accuracy of some of Du Bois's charges against Washington can be debated, they struck a chord among northern blacks who were already disenchanted with Washington's southern-directed leadership. They also applauded the hint of militancy in Du Bois's criticism, especially his concluding exhortation to African Americans to struggle unceasingly for black rights, and even if they fail, to "die trying."

Essential Themes

Du Bois's "The Parting of the Ways" was written during a critical juncture in African American history. In the early twentieth century, there was considerable debate over the direction African Americans should take in their fight for equality and greater freedom. In the late 1870s the southern states had begun a concentrated effort to reverse the political rights gained by blacks during Reconstruction. Although the Fifteenth Amendment granted black males the right to vote, southern state and local governments utilized poll taxes, literacy tests, property qualifications, and the infamous grandfather clause, which stipulated that only men who had been eligible to vote or whose fathers or grandfathers were eligible to vote before 1867 were allowed to vote, in order to disenfranchise the vast majority of black voters.

The Supreme Court's *Plessy v. Ferguson* decision in 1896, which ruled that a law segregating blacks from whites on railroad cars was constitutional, contributed to the expansion of legally required segregation of the races throughout the South. Within a short period of time, racial segregation spread to hospitals, schools, churches, buses, bathrooms, and water fountains. Most private businesses like restaurants and hotels and public facilities like parks, libraries, and swimming pools refused to admit African Americans all together. The years following the end of Reconstruction also saw a dramatic increase in incidents of racial violence. Between 1889 and 1932, there were at least 3,745 lynchings. Most took place in the South, and most of the victims were black males.

It was within this context of black disenfranchisement, rising segregation, and growing racial violence that debates over the direction of the black movement for greater equality took place. By 1900, Booker T. Washington, a graduate of the Hampton Normal and Agricultural Institute and founder of the Tuskegee Institute, had emerged as the most influential black leader in the United States. Heavily influenced by his own education and his work at Tuskegee, he argued that African Americans should postpone their fight for political and civil rights and instead concentrate on obtaining an industrial-based education. He argued that blacks would only gain acceptance from whites once they learned a trade and gained a level of economic security. Soon more than a dozen industrial schools opened in the South, preparing African Americans for jobs in the trades, agriculture, and domestic work, while largely ignoring education in the liberal arts, mathematics, languages, and the sciences.

Many African Americans did not share Washington's enthusiasm for an industrial education, especially as a replacement for a more traditional liberal education. They certainly did not share his views regarding about agitation for civil and political rights. Du Bois was one of these critics who offered an opposing position. Du Bois would become the leader in the fight against Washington's views and policies.

Du Bois's criticisms of Washington reflected the division that existed among African Americans over whether accommodation or confrontation was the best method for overcoming segregation and obtaining greater rights and freedoms for African Americans. As "Parting of the Ways" makes clear, Du Bois believed that confrontation was the only suitable method for confronting prejudice and discrimination. He had little interest in accommodating to the interests or sensibilities of white southerners and vehemently disagreed with African Americans like Washington who he accused of acquiescing to discrimination.

Du Bois continued to criticize Washington's positions. Their relationship grew even more acrimonious over time. In 1905, Du Bois invited a select group of African Americans to Niagara Falls, Canada, to discuss the future of black activism in the United States. The group, known as the Niagara Movement, agreed on a series of principles that included opposition to segregation, the denial of black political rights, and the lack of proper schooling, health care, and housing provided to African Americans. Although they were never as powerful as the groups Washington represented, they did provide a strong and vocal alternative to his vision.

Although the Niagara Movement collapsed in 1908, the following year, the National Association for the Advancement of Colored People (NAACP) arose in its wake. The NAACP, which included Du Bois and a number of white progressives influenced by his ideas among its founders, adopted a similar platform to the Niagara Movement. As its most prominent black member, Du Bois was editor of the NAACP newspaper *The Crisis*, where he argued against Washington's accommodationist platform, segregation laws, and the denial of black suffrage, among other things. He would remain editor for another twenty-five years and an influential voice in the fight against injustice and discrimination until his death in 1963.

—Gerald F. Goodwin, PhD & Cary D. Wintz, PhD

Bibliography

Dorrien, Gary. *The New Abolition: W. E. B. Du Bois and the Black Social Gospel*. New Haven, CT: Yale UP, 2015.

Gates, Henry Louis, Jr. & Terri Hume Oliver, eds. *The Souls of Black Folk: Authoritative Text, Contexts, Criticism*. New York: W.W. Norton & Co, 1999.

Hine, Darlene Clark, William C. Hine, & Stanley C. Harrold. *African Americans: A Concise History, Combined Volume*. Boston: Pearson, 2011.

Horne, Gerald. *W. E. B. Du Bois: A Biography*. Westport, Connecticut: Greenwood Press, 2009.

Lewis, David Levering. *W. E. B. Du Bois, 1868–1919: Biography of a Race*. New York: Henry Holt & Company, 1994.

Marable, Manning. *W. E. B. Du Bois: Black Radical Democrat*. Boulder, Colorado: Paradigm, 2005.

Wolters, Raymond. *Du Bois and His Rivals*. Columbia, Missouri: University of Missouri Press, 2003.

Ida B. Wells: "Booker T. Washington and His Critics"

Date: 1904
Author: Ida B. Wells
Genre: article

Summary Overview

Ida Wells was deeply affected by racism and the violence inflicted by whites upon blacks in the United States in the late nineteenth and early twentieth centuries. In an attempt to arouse the nation to confront its racial prejudices and barbaric actions, she began to write articles and pamphlets and to lecture widely both in this country and in Great Britain. Her vivid depictions of the horrors of lynching and her statistically supported discussion of that practice began the slow, arduous process toward public rejection of those crimes. Pulling no punches in her comments, Wells criticized both blacks and whites. Black elites, shielded by their wealth from many of the indignities of discrimination, ignored the problems of others in their communities. Black clergymen did not speak out strongly enough against segregation. Black politicians betrayed their race to seek the favor of whites. Whites accepted social myths and cultural stereotypes that allowed them to excuse inexcusable crimes against humanity.

Wells took it upon herself to wage a public crusade against the sufferings, indignities, and wrongs of an oppressed race. In her article "Booker T. Washington and His Critics," published in the *World Today*, she contests Washington's accommodationist philosophy, refusing to accept his measured and deferential approach to black advancement.

Defining Moment

Wells's scathing critique of Washington in "Booker T. Washington and his Critics" was clearly directed at an African American audience. Wells was not only upholding Washington's critics, she was also trying to convince his African American supporters that his policies were dangerous and that there were alternatives that were more likely to achieve success. African Americans should fight for access to all types of education and continue the fight for full political equality.

By linking Washington's advocacy of industrial education and refusal to oppose disenfranchisement of African Americans to the wants and desires of white southerners, Wells sought to discredit Washington in the eyes of the black community. Similarly, by pointing out the negative effect Washington's promotion of industrial education over more traditional forms of education, Wells demonstrated that his policies had consequences—the reduction of opportunities for African Americans.

Author Biography

Ida B. Wells was born a slave in Holly Springs, Mississippi, on July 16, 1862. When her parents and a younger brother died in a yellow fever epidemic in 1878, she accepted the first of several jobs as a rural schoolteacher to help support her six younger brothers and sisters. Success as a freelance writer eventually led to a career as a newspaper journalist and editor. Through newspaper articles and lectures, she quickly gained fame as a crusader against lynching. In addition to numerous newspaper and magazine articles, Wells is known for two pamphlets published in the 1890s—*Southern Horrors* and *A Red Record*. After marrying Ferdinand Lee Barnett, a Chicago newspaperman and civil rights advocate in 1895, Wells devoted much of her time to civic reform work. She also gained notoriety as an investigator into the causes of race riots. Wells disagreed philosophically with the accommodationist program advocated by Booker T. Washington. Although she was a signer of "The Call," a document inviting prominent black and white Americans to a conference that led to the formation of the National Association for the Advancement of Colored People (NAACP), and was a founding member of that organization, she found it too accommodating to whites. Ida Wells-Barnett died in Chicago of uremia on March 25, 1931.

Wells confronted a racially divided South on numerous occasions. While traveling to her job as a schoolteacher, she experienced segregation firsthand when a railway conductor ordered her to move to a car reserved for "colored" passengers even though she had purchased a first-class ticket. She took her case to court and won, only to have the Tennessee Supreme Court overturn that decision. She lost her teaching job in 1891 because she wrote articles criticizing the poor quality of education given to black children in segregated schools. When three friends of hers were lynched in Memphis, Tennessee, in 1892 and Wells publicly denounced their murders, the newspaper office of the Memphis *Free Speech*, of which she was editor and part owner, was destroyed by an angry white mob.

After the Memphis incident, Wells began a lifelong crusade against lynching. Through newspaper articles in the *New York Age* and later in the Chicago *Conservator* and in lectures in the United States and Great Britain, she demanded that the United States confront lynching, which she termed "our national crime." Her two major pamphlets, *Southern Horrors* and *A Red Record*, offered detailed statistical information on lynching as well as her own controversial interpretation of the data presented. As Wells continued her public crusade against lynching, she began to investigate the causal factors behind race riots, which seemed to be on the rise in a number of the nation's major cities. She also began to devote much of her time to civic reform in Chicago and worked to persuade black women to become directly involved in organizational work for racial justice.

Defiant and confrontational throughout her life, Wells challenged the racial policies of both the Woman's Christian Temperance Union and the National American Woman Suffrage Association, openly debated Booker T. Washington on the proper course for black progress, and withdrew from the NAACP because she was not comfortable with its liberal white leadership. During the 1920s, a decade that saw a rebirth of the Ku Klux Klan, Wells became increasingly disillusioned with the state of race relations in America. Never a black separatist, she was drawn to Marcus Garvey's Universal Negro Improvement Association during the 1920s because of his call for black self-help and economic independence and for instilling a new racial consciousness among African Americans. Feeling that she had lost her influence as a spokesperson for racial issues, Wells began writing her *Autobiography*. She was at work on the project when she died.

HISTORICAL DOCUMENT

Industrial education for the Negro is Booker T. Washington's hobby. He believes that for the masses of the Negro race an elementary education of the brain and a continuation of the education of the hand is not only the best kind, but he knows it is the most popular with the white South. He knows also that the Negro is the butt of ridicule with the average white American, and that the aforesaid American enjoys nothing so much as a joke which portrays the Negro as illiterate and improvident; a petty thief or a happy-go-lucky inferior. . . .

[Booker T. Washington] knows, as do all students of sociology, that the representatives which stand as the type for any race, are chosen not from the worst but from the best specimens of that race; the achievements of the few rather than the poverty, vice and ignorance of the many, are the standards of any given race's ability. There is a Negro faculty at Tuskegee, some of whom came from the masses, yet have crossed lances with the best intellect of the dominant race at their best colleges. Mr. Washington knows intimately the ablest members of the race in all sections of the country and could bear testimony as to what they accomplished before the rage for industrial schools began. The Business League, of which he is founder and president, is composed of some men who were master tradesmen and business men before Tuskegee was born. He therefore knows better than any man before the public to-day that the prevailing idea of the typical Negro is false. . . .

The men and women of to-day . . . know that the leaders of the race, including Mr. Washington himself, are the direct product of schools of the Freedmen's Aid Society, the American Missionary Association and other such agencies which gave the Negro his first and only opportunity to secure any kind of education which his intellect and ambition craved. Without these schools our case would have been more hopeless indeed than it is; with their aid the race has made more remarkable intellectual and material progress in forty years than any other race in history. They have given us thousands of teachers for our schools in the South, physicians to heal our ailments, druggists, lawyers and ministers. . . .

That one of the most noted of their own race should join with the enemies to their highest progress in condemning the education they had received, has been to them a bitter pill. And so for a long while they keenly, though silently, resented the jibes against the college-bred youth which punctuate Mr. Washington's speeches. He proceeds to draw a moral therefrom for his entire race. The result is that the world which listens to him and which largely supports his educational institution, has almost unanimously decided that college education is a mistake for the Negro. They hail with acclaim the man who has made popular the unspoken thought of that part of the North which believes in the inherent inferiority of the Negro, and the always outspoken southern view to the same effect.

This gospel of work is no new one for the Negro. It is the South's old slavery practice in a new dress. It was the only education the South gave the Negro for two and a half centuries she had absolute control of his body and soul. The Negro knows that now, as then, the South is strongly opposed to his learning anything else but how to work.

No human agency can tell how many black diamonds lie buried in the black belt of the South, and the opportunities for discovering them become rarer every day as the schools for thorough training become more cramped and no more are being established. The presidents of Atlanta University and other such schools remain in the North the year round, using their personal influence to secure funds to keep these institutions running. Many are like the late Collis P. Huntington, who had given large amounts to Livingston College, Salisbury, North Carolina. Several years before his death he told the president of that institution that as he believed Booker Washington was educating Negroes in the only sensible way, henceforth his money for that purpose would go to Tuskegee. All the schools in the South have suffered as a consequence of this general attitude, and many of the oldest and best which have regarded themselves as fixtures now find it a struggle to maintain existence. . . .

Admitting for argument's sake that its system is the best, Tuskegee could not accommodate one-hundredth part of the Negro youth who need education. The Board of Education of New Orleans cut the curriculum in the public schools for Negro children down to the fifth grade, giving Mr. Washington's theory as an inspiration for so doing. Mr. Washington denied in a letter that he had ever advocated such a thing, but the main point is that this is the deduction the New Orleans school board made from his frequent statement that previous systems of education were a mistake and that the Negro should be taught to work. Governor Vardaman, of Mississippi, the other day in his inaugural address, after urging the legislature to abolish the Negro public school and substitute manual training therefor, concluded that address by saying that all other education was a curse to the Negro race.

This is the gospel Mr. Washington has preached for the past decade. The results from this teaching then would seem to be, first, a growing prejudice in northern institutions of learning against the admission of Negro students; second, a contracting of the number and influence of the schools of higher learning so judiciously scattered through all the southern states by the missionary associations, for the Negroes benefit; third, lack of a corresponding growth of industrial schools to take their places; and fourth, a cutting down of the curriculum for the Negro in the public schools of the large cities of the South, few of which ever have provided high schools for the race.

Mr. Washington's reply to his critics is that he does not oppose the higher education, and offers in proof of this statement his Negro faculty. But the critics observe that nowhere does he speak for it, and they can remember dozens of instances when he has condemned every system of education save that which teaches the Negro how to work. They feel that the educational opportunities of the masses, always limited enough, are being threatened by this retrogression. . . .

There are many who can never be made to feel that it was a mistake thirty years ago to give the unlettered freedmen the franchise, their only weapon of defense, any more than it is a mistake to have fire for cooking and heating purposes in the home, because ignorant or careless servants sometimes burn themselves. The thinking Negro knows it is still less a mistake to-day when the race has had thirty years of training for citizenship. It is indeed a bitter pill to feel that much of the unanimity with which the nation to-day agrees to Negro disfranchisement comes from the general acceptance of Mr. Washington's theories.

Does this mean that the Negro objects to industrial education? By no means. It simply means that he knows by sad experience that industrial education will not stand him in place of political, civil and intellectual liberty, and he objects to being deprived of fundamental rights of American citizenship to the end that one school for industrial training shall flourish. To him it seems like selling a race's birthright for a mess of pottage.

They believe it is possible for Mr. Washington to make Tuskegee all it should become without sacrificing or advocating the sacrifice of race manhood to do it. They know he has the ear of the American nation as no other Negro of our day has, and he is therefore molding public sentiment and securing funds for his educational theories as no other can. They know that the white South has labored ever since reconstruction to establish and maintain throughout the country a color line in politics, in civil rights and in education, and they feel that with Mr. Washington's aid the South has largely succeeded in her aim.

GLOSSARY

birthright: an inheritance one is entitled to by birth

mess of pottage: literally, a single meal ("mess") of soup; an allusion to the story of Esau, recounted in the biblical book of Genesis, who sold his inheritance in exchange for something of little value

Reconstruction: the period following the Civil War, when the states of the Confederacy were brought back under US control

Vardaman: James Kimble Vardaman, governor of Mississippi in the early twentieth century

Document Analysis

Wells's most significant public debate resulted from philosophical disagreements she had with Booker T. Washington. Washington had attracted attention for the success of his school, the Tuskegee Institute in Alabama. The educational program at Tuskegee stressed black self-reliance and taught skills in agriculture and the trades that would allow blacks to become economically independent. Emerging as the dominant black leader in America after the death of Frederick Douglass in 1895, Washington broadened his reputation as a forward-looking black educator in speeches in which he advanced his prescription for black progress. He strongly believed that black education should concentrate on teaching industrial skills as the primary means for black economic advancement. If southern whites would provide the jobs that would enable black opportunity, whites would be repaid with increased economic growth and greater prosperity. He also believed that if blacks would defer demands for social and political equality, whites could be assured that the mutual cooperation he proposed could take place in a climate of racial harmony. Such cooperation would, in time, prepare the way for broader civil rights.

Wells also wanted to see blacks advance economically but disagreed with Washington's program. Where Washington contended that black advancement would come through patient effort that would win white acceptance, Wells saw lynching as a white contrivance designed to prevent black progress. Where Washington tolerated inequality to foster racial cooperation and economic uplift, Wells demanded immediate equality as a fundamental right. Where Washington believed that economic power could be gained by conforming to the status quo, Wells thought blacks should use their economic potential against white control. As an untapped labor force, Wells thought blacks could be an industrial factor in an industrializing South. If blacks would recognize that reality, they could gain economic leverage with both southern employers and Northern investors. An understanding of that power and its judicious use in areas where lynching was prevalent could do much to halt that practice. Both Washington and Wells agreed that white elites held the key to social and economic change in the South. But unlike Washington, Wells was more concerned about redirecting their self-interest than appealing to their good graces.

Wells began by explaining Washington's program for industrial education for African Americans. She argued that Washington's support for "an elementary education of the brain and a continuation of the education of the hand" had wide support among white southerners who overwhelmingly viewed African Americans as "illiterate and improvident, a petty thief or a happy-go lucky inferior." That so many white southern racists, who clearly did not have the best interests of African Americans in mind, supported such a platform should give the entire black community pause. Even worse, Washington's advocacy for industrial education seemed designed to elicit white support and not improve the conditions for African Americans.

According to Wells, Washington had a responsibility as a well-known, influential black leader to encourage blacks to fight for all of their civil and political rights and not accept industrial education as their high achievement. She pointed out that Washington and many of his black supporters "are the direct product of schools of the Freedman's Aid Society, the American Missionary Association and other agencies which gave the negro his first and only opportunity to secure any kind of education which his intellect and ambition craved." During the forty years since the end of the Civil War, these schools had trained thousands of physicians, lawyers, druggists, and ministers benefitting the black community significantly. Sadly, in advising African Americans to seek only an industrial education, Washington had essentially ignored, if not dismissed, the positive impact these schools had already had on the lives of thousands of African Americans. Inadvertently, Washington was endorsing the position of many racist white southerners at the time—African Americans were intellectually inferior and only capable of physical labor. Wells pointed out that this perspective was not dissimilar to the one used to justify slavery.

Washington's influence had the undesirable effect of damaging support for black schools in the South and the North. Wells noted that "all the schools in the South have suffered as a consequence of this general attitude, and many of the oldest and best which have regarded themselves as fixtures now find it a struggle to maintain existence." In New Orleans, the Board of Education announced that they were only going to provide schooling for African Americans until the fifth grade, and the governor of Mississippi had announced his desire to end public schooling for African Americans all together. Wells maintained that in both cases, Washington's program was cited as a justification for these decisions, which was not surprising as "this is the gospel Mr. Washington has preached for the past decade."

Washington's refusal to fight for political and civil rights was as problematic as his steadfast support of industrial education. While African Americans should have the opportunity to gain an industrial education, it should not exclude a fight for access to other types of education or demands for political and civil equality. She concluded by noting that most African Americans recognized the fallacies in Washington's positions. They understand that white southerners wanted to deny African Americans their civil rights and education, but they could also see that Washington's policies had ultimately helped white racists accomplish their goals.

By the turn of the century, Washington had gained notice for the success of his school and for his ability to raise money from northern white philanthropists. But to Wells, Washington's success had exacted a cost. Because Washington had placed such a pronounced emphasis on vocational as opposed to higher education, those who listened to his speeches and financially supported his school had concluded that college education was unnecessary for blacks. The impact of that general assumption, argues Wells, had been detrimental to black education in general. Northern donations to support black colleges had dwindled, while Northern colleges had reduced the number of black students they admitted. Citing Washington's educational theory as its guide for doing so, the Board of Education of New Orleans had limited the curriculum in the public schools for black children to the fifth grade. By his avoidance of the broader aspects of the topic, Wells says, Washington had enhanced the image of blacks as being inferior, if not uneducable. To counter the Washington position, Wells states at the end of the document that the black man understands that industrial education alone "will not stand him in place of political, civil and intellectual liberty, and he objects to being deprived of fundamental rights of American citizenship to the end that one school for industrial training shall flourish. To him it seems like selling a race's birthright for a mess of pottage."

Essential Themes

By the time Wells published "Booker T. Washington and his Critics" in 1904, southern state governments had largely reversed the political gains made by African Americans during Reconstruction. Poll taxes and a vast array of voting requirement tests had largely disenfranchised African Americans in the South essentially denying black men the voting rights guaranteed to them in the Fifteenth Amendment. In 1896, the Supreme Court's landmark *Plessy v. Ferguson* decision ruled that legally required segregation of the races in public places was constitutional. Before long "Jim Crow" laws were passed in every southern state, effectively separating blacks from whites in nearly every sector of public and private life.

At the same time that African American political rights were being denied and segregation was becoming the legal standard in the South, incidents of racial violence against African Americans increased dramatically. In 1900 alone, more than 100 blacks were lynched and between 1901, and in 1914, another thousand African Americans were murdered by racist white mobs.

A prominent journalist, Wells published many articles about lynchings and brought the issue to the attention of a national audience. She had a very personal reason for doing so. In 1889, Thomas Moss and a group of other black men opened up People's Grocery in a black neighborhood in Memphis, Tennessee, where Wells then lived. While the store prospered, it did so apparently at the expense of a white-owned grocery store across the street. After a dispute occurred in front of People's Grocery, the owner of the competing store enlisted the help of the police, who issued an arrest warrant for three employees who worked at People's. Shortly thereafter, an armed mob of whites entered People's with the intention of either arresting or killing the employees inside. After the employees responded with gunfire, they were arrested by the police. A short time later, an even larger mob of whites raided the jail and lynched Moss and two other employees.

Moss was a close friend of Wells, and the incident affected her deeply. In the aftermath, she not only wrote articles denouncing the incident, she also urged African Americans to flee Memphis, believing that they were unsafe. Whites in Memphis responded by destroying the newspaper offices of *Free Speech*.

Soon after, Wells began researching other lynchings, eventually releasing her findings in the pamphlet *Southern Horrors: Lynch Law in All Its Phases* (1892) and *A Red Record: Tabulated Statistics and Alleged Causes of Lynching in the United States* (1895). Some of her findings directly contradicted Washington's claim that the accumulation of property and money by blacks would gain white respect. Moss and other victims of lynchings were prominent African Americans who had managed to accumulate wealth and property against considerable odds. Their murders convinced Wells that no amount of material success would protect African Americans from racial violence. Wells believed that successful, prominent blacks were more likely to be the target of racial violence, as lynchings were intended to serve as a warning to the black community that success would be punished. Thus, no hard working black man with an industrial education would earn the respect of racist whites.

In her 1904 article "Booker T. Washington and his Critics," Wells provided a thorough critique of Washington's advocacy of industrial education and seeming disinterest in political rights. She demonstrated a willingness to challenge Washington's leadership of blacks in much the same way that W.E.B. Du Bois and other black leaders had also done. She was especially critical of Washington's popularity among whites, many of whom were racist, and the fact that he seemed to be actively trying to gain their support. She believed that in many areas there was little distinction between Washington's positions and those held by racist white southerners. She believed that by ignoring the need of African Americans for different kinds of education and by downplaying the importance of black suffrage, Washington was essentially supporting the policies of white racists who wanted black disenfranchisement and segregation.

She knew what white racists were capable of. As a journalist, she had studied lynchings and other incidents of racial violence against blacks, and she understood as well as anyone that an industrial education and some economic success would not protect African Americans from violence. She was angry that Washington sought to appeal to same groups that at best ignored and at worst supported acts of violence against African Americans.

Wells was not the only prominent African American leader to criticize Washington. W.E.B. Du Bois and Henry M. Bishop, among others, had made similar criticisms, particularly of Washington's advocacy of an industrial education at the expense of other forms of education and his seeming disinterest in black disenfranchisement. Thus, in publishing "Booker T. Washington and his Critics," Wells stood alongside Du Bois and Bishop, who favored confrontation over Washington's accommodationist policies.

Wells would continue to criticize Washington in the years ahead, but she would also help to found a number of organizations to achieve her program. Wells was an early member of the Niagara Movement (1905–1908), which was organized by Du Bois to challenge more directly Washington's leadership and accommodationist approach. After the Niagara Movement collapsed, Wells joined Du Bois and others to form the National Association for the Advancement of Colored People (NAACP) in 1909.

—*Gerald F. Goodwin, PhD & Cary D. Wintz, PhD*

Bibliography and Further Reading

Bay, Mia. *To Tell the Truth Freely: the Life of Ida B. Wells*. New York Hill & Wang, 2009. Print.

Giddings, Paula. *A Sword among Lions: Ida B. Wells and the Campaign against Lynching*. New York: Harper Collins, 2008. Print.

Hine, Darlene Clark, William C. Hine, and Stanley C. Harrold. *African Americans: A Concise History, Combined Volume*. Boston: Pearson, 2011. Print.

McMurry, Linda O. *To Keep the Waters Troubled: The Life of Ida B. Wells*. New York: Oxford University Press, 1998. Print.

Schechter, Patricia. *Ida B. Wells-Barnett and American Reform, 1880–1930*. Chapel Hill: U of North Carolina P, 2001. Print.

Silkey, Sarah. *Black Woman Reformer: Ida B. Wells, Lynching, and Transatlantic Activism*. Athens: U of Georgia P, 2014. Print.

Wells, Ida B. *Crusade for Justice: The Autobiography of Ida B. Wells*. Ed. Alfreda M. Duster. Chicago: University of Chicago Press, 1991. Print.

_____. *Southern Horrors and Other Writings; The Anti-Lynching Campaign of Ida B. Wells, 1892–1900*. Ed. Jacqueline Jones Royster. New York: Bedford Books, 1996. Print.

■ Niagara Movement Declaration of Principles

Date: 1905
Authors: W. E. B. Du Bois and Monroe Trotter
Genre: political tract; charter

Summary Overview

The Niagara Movement Declaration of Principles outlined a philosophy and political program designed to address racial inequality in the United States. The document had its origin on July 11, 1905, when twenty-nine African American men began deliberations at the Erie Beach Hotel in Fort Erie, Ontario, just across the border from Buffalo and Niagara, New York. When they adjourned three days later, the Niagara Movement had been born. The Niagara Movement had a limited impact on race relations in the United States. Within five years, it would cease to exist, and in the history of the struggle for equal rights, it has long been overshadowed by the more successful, long-lived, biracial National Association for the Advancement of Colored People (NAACP). Nevertheless, the Niagara Movement was an important landmark in US and African American history.

Several factors distinguish the movement. First, it was a purely African American effort to address discrimination and racial inequality. No whites were involved in its creation, organization, or operation. Second, it enunciated a clearly defined philosophy and political program, embodied in the Declaration of Principles that was drafted and approved at the 1905 meeting. While rephrased and modified somewhat, the sentiments and tone of the Declaration of Principles would outlive the Niagara Movement and help define the agenda of the NAACP and the civil rights movement of the 1950s and early 1960s. Finally, the gathering in Fort Erie pointedly excluded the most prominent African American leader of the day, Booker T. Washington, as well as anyone perceived to be allied with him. In addition to confronting American racism, the Niagara Movement and its Declaration of Principles were also a challenge to Booker T. Washington's leadership and his program for the advancement of African Americans.

Defining Moment

The authors of the Declaration of Principles concluded by submitting the document to the American people. While this may have represented the wishes of the group assembled at Fort Erie, the actual audience was much more modest. The initial audience for the document was that group of twenty-nine men assembled at the inaugural meeting of the Niagara Movement. The secondary audience was the four hundred or so men and women who would join the Niagara Movement before its demise in 1909. Of course, the intended audience was much larger. It included the African American community, especially in the North, and the intention was that blacks from all parts of the United States would hear about and read the document and join the Niagara Movement. The document was also crafted for a white audience. The language and moderate tone, as well as the specific statement of appreciation to white friends and allies, was intended to attract financial and political support for the agenda or the movement and convince progressive whites that they offered a realistic and palatable alternative to the racial agenda of Booker T. Washington.

In the short term, the audience was quite small, as press coverage of the Fort Erie meeting and the Declaration of Principles was limited. It is not clear how much coverage a small meeting of African Americans in Ontario would receive in the white press in ordinary circumstances, but in July 1905, a very effective campaign by the Tuskegee machine kept press coverage to a minimum. News of the Fort Erie events was kept out of most of the white press when a Washington ally went to the Buffalo Associated Press office and persuaded it not to forward the news of the Fort Erie meeting. There was some reporting in the African American press, especially in Atlanta and Washington, where there was widespread support for the Niagarites, and, of course, in Boston, where Trotter's *Guardian* pushed the story. But, on the whole, the black press remained loyal to Washington and withheld news of the meeting. Eventually, the audience grew significantly. The Declaration of Principles and much of the agenda of the Niagara Movement were picked up by the NAACP and influenced its approach to civil rights.

Author Biography

Most people assume that W. E. B. Du Bois was the

author of the Declaration of Principles. Actually, the authorship is not that simple or clear. The final form of the document would be approved by the twenty-nine delegates at the Fort Erie meeting. The actual drafting of the declaration was a collaboration between Du Bois and William Monroe Trotter.

W. E. B. Du Bois was born February 23, 1868, in Great Barrington, Massachusetts, and raised by his mother in an environment characterized by varying degrees of poverty. In spite of this, Du Bois excelled in school and achieved one of the most impressive educations of his generation. He took bachelor degrees at Fisk and then Harvard, pursued graduate work at Harvard and the University of Berlin, and earned his PhD in history from Harvard in 1895. He held faculty positions at Wilberforce University and then Atlanta University and spent a year working for the University of Pennsylvania on a study of blacks in Philadelphia. In 1903, he published *The Souls of Black Folk*, his third book and the one that propelled him to the forefront of African American intellectuals; shortly thereafter, he emerged as the most respected critic of Booker T. Washington. In 1905, he made his first major foray into racial politics when he assumed a major role in the creation and operation of the Niagara Movement.

William Monroe Trotter was born on April 7, 1872, in Chillicothe, Ohio, but was raised in Boston among the city's black elite. He attended Harvard, where he met Du Bois. After graduating Phi Beta Kappa, he worked in insurance and real estate. In 1901, he co-founded and became editor of the *Guardian*, a Boston newspaper noted for its militant, uncompromising, and often intemperate support of African American civil rights and racial justice and for its criticism and attacks on Booker T. Washington. In July 1903, he was the principal organizer of the "Boston Riot" and was sentenced to thirty days in jail for provoking the incident. While Du Bois was the leading African American intellectual of his day, Trotter was the race's most outspoken polemicist.

Although they were of different temperaments, Du Bois and Trotter worked well together on the Declaration of Principles. The document combined Du Bois's more scholarly approach with Trotter's more polemical style. The partnership did not last long. The two clashed over leadership issues, especially the role that whites should play in the Niagara Movement. Trotter withdrew from the organization and founded the National Equal Rights League in 1908. Although he participated in the creation of the NAACP, he objected to the dominant roles whites played in the organization. He continued to agitate for racial equality and publish the *Guardian* until his death in 1934. Du Bois assumed a major role in the NAACP, especially as editor of *The Crisis* from its founding in 1910 until he returned to Atlanta University in 1934. Du Bois was the premier African American intellectual of the twentieth century, as well as a civil rights advocate and an advocate of pan-Africanism. He died in Ghana in 1963.

HISTORICAL DOCUMENT

Progress: The members of the conference, known as the Niagara Movement, assembled in annual meeting at Buffalo, July 11th, 12th and 13th, 1905, congratulate the Negro-Americans on certain undoubted evidences of progress in the last decade, particularly the increase of intelligence, the buying of property, the checking of crime, the uplift in home life, the advance in literature and art, and the demonstration of constructive and executive ability in the conduct of great religious, economic and educational institutions.

Suffrage: At the same time, we believe that this class of American citizens should protest emphatically and continually against the curtailment of their political rights. We believe in manhood suffrage; we believe that no man is so good, intelligent or wealthy as to be entrusted wholly with the welfare of his neighbor.

Civil Liberty: We believe also in protest against the curtailment of our civil rights. All American citizens have the right to equal treatment in places of public entertainment according to their behavior and deserts.

Economic Opportunity: We especially complain against the denial of equal opportunities to us in economic life; in the rural districts of the South this amounts to peonage and virtual slavery; all over the South it tends to crush labor and small business enterprises; and everywhere American prejudice, helped often by iniquitous laws, is making it more difficult for Negro-Americans to earn a decent living.

Education: Common school education should be free to all American children and compulsory. High school training should be adequately provided for all, and college training should be the monopoly of no class or race in any section of our common country. We believe that, in defense of our own institutions, the United States should aid common school education, particularly in the South, and we especially recommend concerted agitation to this end. We urge an increase in public high school facilities in the South, where the Negro-Americans are almost wholly without such provisions. We favor well-equipped trade and technical schools for the training of artisans, and the need of adequate and liberal endowment for a few institutions of higher education must be patent to sincere well-wishers of the race.

Courts: We demand upright judges in courts, juries selected without discrimination on account of color and the same measure of punishment and the same efforts at reformation for black as for white offenders. We need orphanages and farm schools for dependent children, juvenile reformatories for delinquents, and the abolition of the dehumanizing convict-lease system.

Public Opinion: We note with alarm the evident retrogression in this land of sound public opinion on the subject of manhood rights, republican government and human brotherhood, arid we pray God that this nation will not degenerate into a mob of boasters and oppressors, but rather will return to the faith of the fathers, that all men were created free and equal, with certain unalienable rights.

Health: We plead for health—for an opportunity to live in decent houses and localities, for a chance to rear our children in physical and moral cleanliness.

Employers and Labor Unions: We hold up for public execration the conduct of two opposite classes of men: The practice among employers of importing ignorant Negro-American laborers in emergencies, and then affording them neither protection nor permanent employment; and the practice of labor unions in proscribing and boycotting and oppressing thousands of their fellow-toilers, simply because they are black. These methods have accentuated and will accentuate the war of labor and capital, and they are disgraceful to both sides.

Protest: We refuse to allow the impression to remain that the Negro-American assents to inferiority, is submissive under oppression and apologetic before insults. Through helplessness we may submit, but the voice of protest of ten million Americans must never cease to assail the ears of their fellows, so long as America is unjust.

Color-Line: Any discrimination based simply on race or color is barbarous, we care not how hallowed it be by custom, expediency or prejudice. Differences made on account of ignorance, immorality, or disease are legitimate methods of fighting evil, and against them we have no word of protest; but discriminations based simply and solely on physical peculiarities, place of birth, color of skin, are relics of that unreasoning human savagery of which the world is and ought to be thoroughly ashamed.

"Jim Crow" Cars: We protest against the "Jim Crow" car, since its effect is and must be to make us pay first-class fare for third-class accommodations, render us open to insults and discomfort and to crucify wantonly our manhood, womanhood and self-respect.

Soldiers: We regret that this nation has never seen fit adequately to reward the black soldiers who, in its five wars, have defended their country with their blood, and yet have been systematically denied the promotions which their abilities deserve. And we regard as unjust, the exclusion of black boys from the military and naval training schools.

War Amendments: We urge upon Congress the enactment of appropriate legislation for securing the proper enforcement of those articles of freedom, the thirteenth, fourteenth and fifteenth amendments of the Constitution of the United States.

Oppression: We repudiate the monstrous doctrine that the oppressor should be the sole authority as to the rights of the oppressed. The Negro race in America stolen, ravished and degraded, struggling up through difficulties and oppression, needs sympathy and receives criticism; needs help and is given hindrance, needs protection and is given mob-violence, needs justice and is given charity, needs leadership and is given cowardice and apology, needs bread and is given a stone. This nation will never stand justified before God until these things are changed.

The Church: Especially are we surprised and astonished at the recent attitude of the church of Christ—of an increase of a desire to bow to racial prejudice, to narrow the bounds of human brotherhood, and to segregate black men to some outer sanctuary. This is wrong, unchristian and disgraceful to the twentieth century civilization.

Agitation: Of the above grievances we do not hesitate to complain, and to complain loudly and insistently. To ignore, overlook, or apologize for these wrongs is to prove ourselves unworthy of freedom. Persistent manly agitation is the way to liberty, and toward this goal the Niagara Movement has started and asks the cooperation of all men of all races.

Help: At the same time we want to acknowledge with deep thankfulness the help of our fellowmen from the Abolitionist down to those who today still stand for equal opportunity and who have given and still give of their wealth and of their poverty for our advancement.

Duties: And while we are demanding, and ought to demand, and will continue to demand the rights enumerated above, God forbid that we should ever forget to urge corresponding duties upon our people:

The duty to vote.
The duty to respect the rights of others.
The duty to work.
The duty to obey the laws.
The duty to be clean and orderly.
The duty to send our children to school.
The duty to respect ourselves, even as we respect others.

This statement, complaint and prayer we submit to the American people, and Almighty God.

GLOSSARY

abolitionist: a person who advocated the complete, immediate, and unconditional abolition of slavery, especially in the United States, prior to and during the Civil War

agitation: the persistent and sustained effort to create change or promote a cause through appeals, discussions, demonstrations, and other means

artisans: skilled craftsmen or workers

assents: agrees with; accepts, or admits as true

barbarous: uncivilized; savage; brutal; cruel

civil rights: rights guaranteed to all citizens by law or the Constitution regardless of such differences as race

common school: a free public elementary school

compulsory: required, usually by law or other authority

convict-lease system: a system of labor in which prisoners are leased to an employer by the court or the prison system

curtailment: the act of limiting or restricting; the act of taking away a right or privilege

deserts: that which is deserved; worthiness through good behavior

execration: vehement denunciation

hallowed: sacred; respected; venerated beyond question

iniquitous: unjust

"Jim Crow" car: a segregated railroad coach, usually of inferior quality, set aside for African Americans

orphanages: institutions that house and care for children who have no parents

peonage: a system of agricultural labor in which workers are bound to their job, often against their will, by economic debt or other means; virtual bondage

retrogression: a reversal in development of condition; moving backward or becoming worse

suffrage: the right to vote

upright: moral; honorable; fair and just

wantonly: cruelly; without mercy

Document Analysis

The Declaration of Principles was approved by the assembly of African American men who met July 11–13, 1905, in Fort Erie, Ontario. The document drafted by W. E. B. Du Bois and William Monroe Trotter contains eighteen short paragraphs, each raising and briefly addressing a specific issue. The style of the declaration is that of a list or an outline rather than an analytical discussion of the status of African Americans. The first seventeen paragraphs contain a manifesto of grievances and demands; the eighteenth is a list of duties. Together they summarize the issues confronting African Americans in the early twentieth century and define the purpose and agenda of the Niagara Movement.

The first section of the declaration, "Progress" comments on the gathering of the Niagara Movement and congratulates African Americans on progress they had achieved in the preceding ten years. These ten years essentially covered the time period since the death of Frederick Douglass and the rise to power of Booker T. Washington, and the Niagarites viewed this as a period of failed leadership and a decline in the rights of African Americans. The progress cited—the increase in intelligence and in the acquisition of property, and the creation of successful institutions—omits reference to the political and civil rights of African Americans.

The next three paragraphs address in sequence "Suffrage" "Civil Liberty" and "Economic Opportunity"—areas in which African Americans faced clear and increasing discrimination. Here the declaration lists grievances for the first time and evokes protest as an appropriate response to these grievances. The declaration asserts the importance of manhood suffrage and then notes that black political rights have been curtailed and that blacks cannot afford to place their political fate in the hands of others. This argument did not address the specifics of the strategies used to disenfranchise blacks—literacy tests, the grandfather clause, or similar practices. Instead, it asserted that all men deserve the right to vote. This approach distinguished the Niagarites from Booker T. Washington, who supported suffrage and attacked disenfranchisement on the basis that it treated blacks differently than whites. The declaration sees universal manhood suffrage as a fundamental right of all men and calls on blacks to protest "empathically and continually" as long as their political rights are violated. This introduces a theme that runs through the declaration: that discrimination is a violation of the rights of African Americans and that the response to these violations must be agitation and protest (not negotiation and patience).

The declaration continues this argument in its examination of civil liberty. It defines civil liberty as civil rights—rights shared equally by all citizens. It broadens the concept to include the right to "equal treatment in places of public entertainment" that is, restaurants, theaters, hotels, and other places of public accommodation. Exclusion from such places must not be based on race or color but on the individual's behavior and demeanor. The declaration demands equal access not to residences or other private spaces but to places open to the public, the same places blacks finally achieved access to in the Civil Rights Act of 1964. Furthermore, to gain their civil rights, blacks must be willing to protest.

As it turns to economic opportunity, the Declaration of Principles directly confronts the heart of Washington's program for African American advancement. Washington believed that the acquisition of property and prosperity would earn blacks the respect of whites and equal rights and that this prosperity could most easily be achieved in the South. The declaration rejects this, noting that African Americans are denied equal economic opportunity in the South and that prejudice and inequity in the law in that region undermine black economic efforts. Specifically, it protests the spread of peonage that has returned blacks to virtual slavery in large areas of the rural South and the practice of discrimination in hiring, wages, and credit that has "crushed" black labor and small businesses.

Education was a key issue for the Niagara Movement. Most of the delegates who attended the gathering were from the college-educated black elite, the group that Du Bois termed the "Talented Tenth" and the group that most Niagarites believed would provide the leadership for African American advancement. Generally this group denigrated Booker T. Washington and his Tuskegee Institute for their focus on job training and practical education. However, the section on education in the Declaration of Principles recognizes the need for all forms of education in the African American community. It focuses its complaints on the lack of equal access to education for blacks, especially in the South. Specifically, it calls for "common" schools (basically elementary schools) to be free and compulsory for all children, regardless of race. It also calls for blacks to have access to high schools, colleges and universities, and trade and technical schools, and it calls for the US government to aid common-school education, especially in the South.

What is striking about the statement on education is that it does not call for the desegregation of education. It specifically asks for an increase in the number of public high schools in the South, where blacks rarely had access to them, and it requests white philanthropists to provide adequate endowments for black institutions of higher education. The focus is clearly on improving black access to educational facilities of all types and at all levels. The language of this section is also much more conciliatory; agitation is suggested only to pressure the US government to provide aid to black common schools. To understand this, it is important to remember that public school systems did not appear in most southern states prior to the period of Reconstruction, and in 1905, schools throughout the South were very poorly funded. Educational facilities for African Americans received significantly less support than did those for white students.

The next three paragraphs address three seemingly unrelated topics. The statement on courts begins with a "demand" for fair and honest judges, the inclusion without discrimination of blacks on juries, and fair and equitable sentencing procedures. It then lists additional needed reforms, including the founding of additional social-service institutions, such as orphanages and reformatories, and an end to the convict-lease system. In contrast, the statement on health begins, "We plead for health—for an opportunity to live in decent houses and localities." There was a connection between the two issues, although it was somewhat tenuous. Bringing justice to the criminal justice system extended to providing a decent environment for orphans, dependent children, and children in the court system; health was extended to include a healthy environment, both physically and morally, in which to raise children. While these concerns were not always at the forefront of civil rights agitation, these issues, especially those that relate to child welfare, reflected the social agenda voiced by white progressive reformers in the early years of the century.

The paragraph on public opinion introduces a new concern, a perceived shift away from the ideals of democracy that were voiced in the eighteenth century by the Founding Fathers. The last sentence, with its reference to "all men . . . created free and equal" and "unalienable rights" echoes the language of the Declaration of Independence. The Niagara delegates were not ignorant of the slavery and racial prejudice that were central to the founding of the United States, but their alarm over the "retrogression" was justified. Racial violence was rampant; democracy seemed challenged by labor wars and fears of unrestricted immigration; and the arts, sciences, and social sciences embraced a new scientific racism that was based on the application of Charles Darwin's "survival of the fittest" to efforts to categorize and rank human races.

The declaration's earlier discussion of economic opportunity focuses completely on conditions in the South. Now it turns to economic opportunity in the North, especially the abuses blacks have suffered at the hands of racially prejudiced labor unions and the practice of white employers exploiting blacks by using them as strike breakers. This situation, and especially the restrictive behavior of white labor unions, characterized the African American experience with organized labor throughout much of the twentieth century. It ran counter to the belief of many progressives and socialists that class unity would defeat racial prejudice. The declaration denounces the practices of both employers and unions in strong terms and blames them for contributing to class warfare.

Protest, along with agitation, were central tenets of the Niagara Movement's strategy for achieving racial justice, and both terms appear frequently in the Declaration of Principles. In contrast to Booker T. Washington's Atlanta Exposition Address, with its ambiguity on the effectiveness of agitation, the Declaration of Principles is crystal clear—protest and agitation are necessary tools to combat injustice. However, the language and tone in the section specifically discussing protest are exceptionally mild. The term *agitation* is not used, and the word *protest* is used only once. The argument is that blacks must not "allow the impression to remain" that they assented to inferiority, were "submissive" to oppression, or were "apologetic" when faced with insults, and the argument is worded to suggest that Washington was both apologetic and submissive. But there is little power or threat in this language beyond the assurance that although blacks may of necessity submit to oppression, they must continue to raise their voices in protest.

Beginning with the paragraph concerning the "Color Line," the Declaration of Principles returns to the issue of discrimination and its impact on African Americans. "Color-Line" discusses legitimate and illegitimate discrimination. The former included discrimination based intelligence, immorality, and disease (for example, quarantining someone with a highly infectious disease to protect public health). In contrast, discrimination based on physical conditions such as place of birth (immigrants) and race was never justified. The color line—segregation and discrimination based on race or skin color or both—is described in harsh terms, as barbarous and as a relic of unreasoning human savagery. According to the Declaration of Principles, the fact that the color line is sanctioned by law, custom, or community standards does nothing to legitimize it or to diminish the evil and injustice that it manifests.

The paragraphs that briefly address "'Jim Crow' Cars," "Soldiers," and "War Amendments" are all related to discrimination. "'Jim Crow' cars" refers to the segregation of African Americans on railroads. This issue had both practical and symbolic importance. Railroads were, by far, the chief means of intercity transportation at the beginning of the twentieth century. Policies that restricted black passengers to overcrowded, rowdy Jim Crow cars affected all black passengers, especially women and the black elite. Virtually every black who traveled through the South suffered this indignity. Du Bois himself had been victimized by this practice and sought Washington's help in an unsuccessful effort to seek redress from the Southern Railway Company. The issue of Jim Crow segregation on railroads was the subject of the *Plessy v. Ferguson* case; the Supreme Court ruling legitimizing separate-but-equal segregation provided the legal basis for segregation in schools, parks, public accommodations, and almost all areas of life. The Declaration of Principles condemns Jim Crow cars as effectively crucifying "wantonly our manhood, womanhood and self-respect."

"Soldiers" puts the Niagara Movement on record

protesting the inequity experienced by African Americans serving in the armed forces. This issue took on additional meaning a year later as blacks reacted to the harsh treatment of the black soldiers following a racial clash with local civilians in the so-called Brownsville incident in Brownsville, Texas, and it was revived again during World War I as black troops suffered from systematic discrimination and mistreatment.

One of the most frustrating issues facing African Americans was that along with abolishing slavery, the three Civil War amendments wrote civil rights and voting rights into the US Constitution. The Fourteenth Amendment guaranteed all citizens, including blacks, equal protection under the law and equal rights and privileges; the Fifteenth Amendment provided that no citizen could be denied the right to vote "on account of race, color, or previous condition of servitude." What the declaration calls for is legislation from Congress to enforce these provisions.

In examining the broad issue of oppression, the declaration presents a broad litany of crimes perpetrated on African Americans, from their kidnapping in Africa to their ravishment and degradation in America; as they have struggled to advance themselves, again and again, they have encountered criticism, hindrance, and violence. In a thinly veiled attack on Booker T. Washington, the Niagarites also place blame on African American leadership for providing in the face of oppression only cowardice and apology, essentially leaving it to the oppressor to define the rights of the oppressed. Finally, in the brief paragraph "The Church," the declaration charges churches and organized religion with acquiescence to racial oppression and condemns them as "wrong, unchristian and disgraceful."

Following this litany of grievances, the Declaration of Principles reaffirms its commitment to protest and agitation. The delegates vow to voice their grievances "loudly and insistently" and note that "manly agitation is the way to liberty." As in the section on "Protest" the language is clear but measured and temperate rather than threatening.

The Declaration of Principles concludes with a section recognizing with gratitude the valuable assistance that African Americans had received throughout their history from their white friends and allies. It then lists eight duties that it expects blacks to follow as they pursue their rights. These duties include civic responsibilities, such as the duty to vote, work, and obey the law, as well as personal obligations, such as the duty to be clean and orderly and to educate their children. These last two sections softened the impact of the declaration and were intended to assure whites that the Niagara Movement was neither revolutionary nor anti-white. Ironically, the tone of these concluding paragraphs is more that of Booker T. Washington than W. E. B. Du Bois. The final sentence of the declaration notes that the document, characterized as a "statement, complaint and prayer" is being submitted to the American people and to God.

Taken as a whole, the Declaration of Principles is both an interesting and a compelling document. It is a comprehensive list of issues, concepts, grievances, and statements about the conditions confronting blacks at the beginning of the last century. What is compelling is that this was the most successful effort to date to express all of this in one place and do so in language that was pointed and uncompromising yet restrained. At the same time, the declaration is interesting for what it did not say. By the standards of the twenty-first century, it is not a particularly radical document. Although the Niagara Movement was an all-black organization, there is no hint of black nationalism or separatism in its Declaration of Principles. Rather, it serves as a restrained, moderate document outlining a program of desegregation, equal rights, and racial justice. It praises white friends and allies for their support, and it reminds blacks that they have the duty and responsibility to be hardworking and law-abiding citizens who embody the values and habits of middle-class America. Despite the anti-Booker T. Washington nature of the Niagara Movement and its members and Washington's open hostility to both the Niagara Movement and its Declaration of Principles, there is little in the document with which the Tuskegeean could take issue.

Essential Themes

There is no question that the racial situation in the United States in the first decade of the twentieth century called out for a strong and assertive civil rights organization. Race relations in the country had deteriorated steadily since the end of Reconstruction following the Civil War. By the turn of the century, the promise of equality incorporated in the Reconstruction amendments to the US Constitution and the Civil Rights Acts of 1866 and 1875 had been undone by state action and by the US Supreme Court. A series of state laws and local ordinances segregating blacks and whites received sanction in the Supreme Court, culminating with the

Plessy v. Ferguson decision in 1896. In this case, the Supreme Court legitimized "separate but equal facilities" and provided the legal basis for segregation for the next half-century. At the same time, southern states began to place limits on the right of African American to vote, using tactics such as the grandfather clause, white primaries, literacy tests, residency requirements, and poll taxes to prevent blacks from voting. In 1898, the Supreme Court upheld so-called race-neutral restrictions on black suffrage in *Williams v. Mississippi*. The effect was virtually to eliminate black voting in the states of the South. African Americans did not fare much better in the North, where segregation, if not disenfranchisement, grew increasingly common.

Accompanying segregation and disenfranchisement was a resurgence in racial violence. While the Reconstruction-era Ku Klux Klan had been effectively suppressed by the mid-1870s, the late nineteenth century and early twentieth century experienced an unprecedented wave of racially motivated lynchings and riots. During the first decade of the twentieth century, between fifty-seven and 105 African Americans were lynched by white mobs each year. Lynch mobs targeted blacks almost exclusively, and any pretense of legalism and due process vanished. Furthermore, blacks more and more became victims of the more generalized racial violence of race riots. Race riots during this period typically involved whites rioting against blacks. Some, such as the 1898 riot in Wilmington, North Carolina, were linked to political efforts to stir up racial hostility as part of a campaign to disenfranchise blacks; others, such as the New York race riot of 1900 and the Atlanta race riot of 1906, grew out of resentment of the presence of blacks. To the degree that the rage they unleashed had an objective, it was to destroy the black community and put blacks in "their place."

As the racial scene deteriorated, African Americans faced a transition in leadership. Frederick Douglass, who had symbolized the African American struggle against slavery and had been an outspoken advocate for equal rights in the post-Civil War period, died in 1895. That same year, Booker T. Washington rose to national prominence with his speech at the Cotton States and International Exposition in Atlanta. The southern-based Washington focused on the economic development of African Americans as the surest road to equality, and while he opposed segregation and black disenfranchisement, he eschewed militant rhetoric and direct confrontation. Washington essentially believed that rational argument and an appeal to southerners' self-interest would defeat prejudice. As time passed and the racial situation worsened, many blacks, especially college-educated Northerners, grew impatient with Washington's leadership. By the early twentieth century, such critics as the Boston newspaper editor William Monroe Trotter had become increasingly outspoken about Washington's failures. After 1903, W. E. B. Du Bois emerged as the most respected opponent of Washington and his Tuskegee political machine, the loose coalition of friends and allies through which Washington exercised his political influence on the African American community.

Much like its audience, the impact of the Declaration of Principles grew over time. Initially, the influence of the Niagara Movement and its Declaration of Principles was limited. Membership never exceeded about four hundred, and the dream of a vibrant organization with chapters nationwide was never realized. Feuding leadership and the failure to secure adequate funding doomed the organization, and membership and attendance at its annual meeting began to decline. The Niagara Movement shut down following its 1909 meeting. During its short life the declaration accomplished one thing: It defined the terms of the Du Bois-Washington debate. As the writer and civil rights activist James Weldon Johnson noted, the animosity between these two factions reached an intensity that is difficult to comprehend today.

The principal impact of the document followed the demise of the Niagara Movement, when it essentially set the agenda of the NAACP. The Declaration of Principle's focus on voting rights and discrimination and segregation were the focus of the NAACP for its first fifty years; protest and agitation were its tools. Perhaps the clearest example of this impact is the use of the declaration's statement on the Civil War amendments and its call for Congress to enforce the provisions of these amendments. This is exactly what the NAACP did, using the courts instead of Congress. In 1915, the NAACP scored one of its first major victories when it filed a brief in *Guinn v. United States*, the case in which the Supreme Court overturned Oklahoma's use of the grandfather clause to restrict black suffrage. In the 1930s, the NAACP launched its legal assault on the continuing restrictions on black suffrage, provisions that kept blacks from serving on juries, and segregation, especially in public and higher education. Ultimately, this campaign led to the reversal of *Plessy v. Ferguson* and separate-but-equal segregation. In the 1950s and 1960s, the civil rights movement used the declaration strategy by successfully lobbying for a series of civil rights acts, finally enforcing provisions of the Fourteenth Amendment to attack segregation and enacting the Voting Rights Act to enforce the Fifteenth Amendment.

——Cary D. Wintz, PhD

Bibliography and Further Reading

Du Bois, W. E. B. "The Talented Tenth." *The Negro Problem: A Series of Articles by Representative Negroes of To-day*. New York: J. Pott and Company, 1903. The Gilder Lehrman Center for the Study of Slavery, Resistance, and Abolition at Yale University, 2016. Web. 5 Feb. 2008. <http://www.yale.edu/glc/archive/1148.htm>.

Fox, Stephen R. *The Guardian of Boston: William Monroe Trotter*. New York: Atheneum, 1970.

Harlan, Louis R. *Booker T. Washington: The Wizard of Tuskegee, 1901–1915*. New York: Oxford UP, 1983.

Lewis, David Levering. *W. E. B. Du Bois: Biography of a Race, 1868–1919*. New York: Henry Holt, 1993.

Marable, Manning. *W. E. B. Du Bois: Black Radical Democrat*. Boston: Twayne, 1986.

Meier, August. *Negro Thought in America, 1880–1915*. Ann Arbor, MI: U of Michigan P, 1968.

Moore, Jacqueline M. *Booker T. Washington, W. E. B. Du Bois, and the Struggle for Racial Uplift*. Wilmington, DE: Scholarly Resources, 2003.

"The Niagara Movement." *African American History of Western New York*. University of Buffalo, Apr. 1996. Web. 2 Jan. 2008. <http://www.math.buffalo.edu/~sww/0history/hwny-niagara-movement.html>. Accessed on January 2, 2008.

Rampersad, Arnold. *The Art and Imagination of W. E. B. Du Bois*. Cambridge, MA: Harvard UP, 1976.

Rudwick, Elliott M. *W. E. B. Du Bois: Propagandist of the Negro Protest*. New York: Atheneum, 1969.

Wolters, Raymond. *Du Bois and His Rivals*. Columbia, MO: U of Missouri P, 2002.

Theodore Roosevelt: Brownsville Legacy Special Message to the Senate

Date: 1906
Author: Theodore Roosevelt
Genre: address; speech

Summary Overview

Theodore Roosevelt's Brownsville Legacy Special Message to the Senate of December 19, 1906, explained his summary dismissal of 167 members of the segregated Twenty-fifth Infantry Regiment from the US Army. The dismissals resulted from charges that the soldiers had engaged in a conspiracy of silence after some members of their regiment had attacked the Mexican-border city of Brownsville, Texas, on the night of August 13, 1906. Reported shootings by the military took the life of a civilian and seriously wounded a police officer. The message was a response to two Senate information-gathering resolutions that had been submitted to Secretary of War William Howard Taft, and it was presented together with several documents, including a letter from General A. B. Nettleton and memoranda demonstrating precedents for the summary discharges. The dismissals involved virtually all members of Companies B, C, and D (the only companies of the regiment that went to Brownsville); they also led to the expulsion of black troops from Texas and the heightening of racial tension in the United States.

The president's Special Message caused a heated controversy within the government and across the nation. Republican Senator Joseph B. Foraker of Ohio, who perhaps was eyeing a presidential campaign, argued the innocence of the accused on the chamber floor as well as in public speeches and magazine articles. A report released in March 1908 by the Senate Committee on Military Affairs, however, supported Roosevelt's action, although a supplementary report recommended a policy of leniency toward the men that would allow them to reenlist, which the president himself had also urged earlier. With respect to the possibility that certain townspeople might have staged the attack on Brownsville and framed the regiment, Senator Foraker was able to obtain the support of only Senator Morgan G. Bulkeley of Connecticut. The perceived image of black soldiers attacking a town embittered racial relations in many garrison towns. It would not be until 1970 that the regiment's innocence would be reconsidered in a scathing study by the historian John D. Weaver that condemned Roosevelt's handling of the Brownsville affray. That book prompted California Democratic Representative Augustus Hawkins to introduce legislation signed by President Richard M. Nixon in 1972 that granted honorable discharges, nearly all of them posthumous, to the 153 cashiered servicemen who had not been allowed to reenlist.

Defining Moment

Roosevelt's immediate audience was the US Senate, which had requested information supporting his decision of November 4, 1906, to summarily discharge 167 members of the First Battalion of the Twenty-fifth Infantry. However, because of the public controversy waged in the media, he was also addressing a national audience. Aside from African Americans and a few sympathetic whites, most of the nation plainly agreed with the president's position and explanation.

Author Biography

Theodore Roosevelt, the twenty-sixth president of the United States, was born October 27, 1858, to a wealthy family in Oyster Bay, New York. The second of four children, Roosevelt was a sickly child and required homeschooling. A voracious reader and experienced world traveler even as a boy, Roosevelt entered Harvard at age eighteen. He excelled with the Harvard boxing team, among other sporting endeavors, and graduated in 1880. He ranched for several years in the Dakota Territory, where he built up his physique and developed a lifelong passion for nature.

Roosevelt served two years in the New York State Assembly, unsuccessfully campaigned for mayor of New York City, served on the US Civil Service Commission, became president of the New York City Board of Police Commissioners, and accepted an appointment as assistant secretary of the US Navy. In all of these positions, he displayed a marked enthusiasm for efficiency and public service. Along the way, he wrote several books, including *The Naval War of 1812* (1882) and the four-volume series *The Winning of the West* (1889–1896).

The Spanish-American War of 1898 defined Roosevelt for many Americans. His war plan dispatched Commodore George Dewey to a victory over the Spanish navy in the Philippines. At the start of the war, Roosevelt accepted the commission of lieutenant colonel and led the flamboyant "Rough Riders," or the First US Volunteer Cavalry, to fame in Cuba. The forty-year-old Roosevelt emerged from the war as "the Hero of San Juan Hill," having fought alongside troops that had included African Americans from the Twenty-fourth Infantry Regiment. For his heroism, he was posthumously awarded the Congressional Medal of Honor in 2001. Roosevelt's popularity brought the governorship of New York within his grasp; he easily won election and instituted several policies of reform during his two-year term. In 1900, he received the Republican vice presidential nomination. The assassination of William McKinley only six months into his second term catapulted Roosevelt to the presidency. At the time, he was only forty-two, the youngest man ever to have become president of the United States.

Roosevelt's presidency brought Progressivism to the national scene. He articulated a philosophy of a strong presidency as he took the lead in conservation and labor-management relations. He signed into law many pieces of reform legislation, such as the Hepburn Act, which strengthened the Interstate Commerce Commission Act, the Meat Inspection Act, and the Pure Food and Drug Act. In an unusual display of racial tolerance for the period, the president hosted the African American leader Booker T. Washington at a White House luncheon. He pursued a strong foreign policy, including intervention in the Panamanian insurrection against Colombia, which facilitated the construction of the Panama Canal. In a more diplomatic fashion, he arranged debt payments by the Dominican Republic to European creditor nations and won the Nobel Peace Prize in 1906 for his moderation of the Portsmouth Peace Conference in 1905, which had brought the Russo-Japanese War to an end.

In 1908, Roosevelt denied himself re-nomination as the Republican presidential candidate and appeared to have left the political arena once his chosen successor, William Howard Taft, won the election. However, he grew impatient with Taft's apparent caution and mounted a third-party campaign against him in 1912, running on the Progressive Party ticket. The division of the vote between Taft and Roosevelt assured the victory of Democrat Woodrow Wilson. Roosevelt then devoted much of his time to travel and writing until World War I. Frustrated in his attempts to strengthen American policy against Germany and, later, to revive his military career, Roosevelt died in his sleep on January 6, 1919.

HISTORICAL DOCUMENT

To the Senate:

In response to Senate resolution of December 6 addressed to me, and to the two Senate resolutions addressed to him, the Secretary of War has, by my direction, submitted to me a report which I herewith send to the Senate, together with several documents, including a letter of General Nettleton and memoranda as to precedents for the summary discharge or mustering out of regiments or companies, some or all of the members of which had been guilty of misconduct.

I ordered the discharge of nearly all the members of Companies B, C, and D of the Twenty-fifth Infantry by name, in the exercise of my constitutional power and in pursuance of what, after full consideration, I found to be my constitutional duty as Commander in Chief of the United States Army. I am glad to avail myself of the opportunity afforded by these resolutions to lay before the Senate the following facts as to the murderous conduct of certain members of the companies in question and as to the conspiracy by which many of the other members of these companies saved the criminals from justice, to the disgrace of the United States uniform.

I call your attention to the accompanying reports of Maj. Augustus P. Blocksom, of Lieut. Col. Leonard A. Lovering, and of Brig. Gen. Ernest A. Garlington, the Inspector-General of the United

States Army, of their investigation into the conduct of the troops in question. An effort has been made to discredit the fairness of the investigation into the conduct of these colored troops by pointing out that General Garlington is a Southerner. Precisely the same action would have been taken had the troops been white—indeed, the discharge would probably have been made in more summary fashion. General Garlington is a native of South Carolina; Lieutenant-Colonel Lovering is a native of New Hampshire; Major Blocksom is a native of Ohio. As it happens, the disclosure of the guilt of the troops was made in the report of the officer who comes from Ohio, and the efforts of the officer who comes from South Carolina were confined to the endeavor to shield the innocent men of the companies in question, if any such there were, by securing information which would enable us adequately to punish the guilty. But I wish it distinctly understood that the fact of the birthplace of either officer is one which I absolutely refuse to consider. The standard of professional honor and of loyalty to the flag and the service is the same for all officers and all enlisted men of the United States Army, and I resent with the keenest indignation any effort to draw any line among them based upon birthplace, creed, or any other consideration of the kind. I should put the same entire faith in these reports if it had happened that they were all made by men coming from some one State, whether in the South or the North, the East or the West, as I now do, when, as it happens, they were made by officers born in different States.

Major Blocksom's report is most careful, is based upon the testimony of scores of eye-witnesses—testimony which conflicted only in non-essentials and which established the essential facts beyond chance of successful contradiction. Not only has no successful effort been made to traverse his findings in any essential particular, but, as a matter of fact, every trustworthy report from outsiders amply corroborates them, by far the best of these outside reports being that of Gen. A. B. Nettleton, made in a letter to the Secretary of War, which I herewith append; General Nettleton being an ex-Union soldier, a consistent friend of the colored man throughout his life, a lifelong Republican, a citizen of Illinois, and Assistant Secretary of the Treasury under President Harrison.

It appears that in Brownsville, the city immediately beside which Fort Brown is situated, there had been considerable feeling between the citizens and the colored troops of the garrison companies. Difficulties had occurred, there being a conflict of evidence as to whether the citizens or the colored troops were to blame. My impression is that, as a matter of fact, in these difficulties there was blame attached to both sides; but this is a wholly unimportant matter for our present purpose, as nothing that occurred offered in any shape or way an excuse or justification for the atrocious conduct of the troops when, in lawless and murderous spirit, and under cover of the night, they made their attack upon the citizens.

The attack was made near midnight on August 13. The following facts as to this attack are made clear by Major Blocksom's investigation and have not been, and, in my judgment, can not be, successfully controverted. From 9 to 15 or 20 of the colored soldiers took part in the attack. They leaped over the walls from the barracks and hurried through the town. They shot at whomever they saw moving, and they shot into houses where they saw lights. In some of these houses there were women and children, as the would-be murderers must have known. In one house in which there were two women and five children some ten shots went through at a height of about 4 1/2 feet above the floor, one putting out the lamp upon the table. The lieutenant of police of the town heard the firing and rode toward it. He met the raiders, who, as he stated, were about 15 colored soldiers. They instantly started firing upon him. He turned and rode off, and they continued firing upon him until they had killed his horse. They shot him in the right arm (it was afterwards amputated above the elbow). A number of shots were also fired at two other policemen. The raiders fired several times into a hotel, some of the shots being aimed at a guest sitting by a window. They shot into a saloon, killing the bartender and wounding another man. At the same time other raiders fired into another house in which women and children were sleeping, two of the shots going through the mosquito bar over the bed in which the mistress of the house and her two children were lying. Several other houses were struck by bullets. It was at night, and the streets of the town are poorly lighted, so that none of the individual raiders were recognized; but the evidence of many witnesses of all classes was conclusive to the effect that the raiders were negro soldiers. The shattered bullets, shells, and clips of the Government rifles, which were found on the ground, are merely corroborative. So are the bullet holes in the houses; some of which it appears must, from the direction, have been fired from the fort just at the moment when the soldiers left it. Not a bullet hole appears in any of the structures of the fort.

The townspeople were completely surprised by the unprovoked and murderous savagery of the attack. The soldiers were the aggressors from start to finish. They met with no substantial resistance, and one and all who took part in that raid stand as deliberate murderers, who did murder one man, who tried to murder others, and who tried to murder women and children. The act was one of horrible atrocity, and so far as I am aware, unparalleled for infamy in the annals of the United States Army.

The white officers of the companies were completely taken by surprise, and at first evidently believed that the firing meant that the townspeople were attacking the soldiers. It was not until 2 or 3 o'clock in the morning that any of them became aware of the truth. I have directed a careful investigation into the conduct of the officers, to see if any of them were blameworthy, and I have approved the recommendation of the War Department that two be brought before a court-martial.

As to the noncommissioned officers and enlisted men, there can be no doubt whatever that many were necessarily privy, after if not before the attack, to the conduct of those who took actual part in this murderous riot. I refer to Major Blocksom's report for proof of the fact that certainly some and probably all of the noncommissioned officers in charge of quarters who were responsible for the gun-racks and had keys thereto in their personal possession knew what men were engaged in the attack.

Major Penrose, in command of the post, in his letter gives the reasons why he was reluctantly convinced that some of the men under him—as he thinks, from 7 to 10—got their rifles, slipped out of quarters to do the shooting, and returned to the barracks without being discovered, the shooting all occurring within two and a half short blocks of the barracks. It was possible for the raiders to go from the fort to the farthest point of firing and return in less than ten minutes, for the distance did not exceed 350 yards.

Such are the facts of this case. General Nettleton, in his letter herewith appended, states that next door to where he is writing in Brownsville is a small cottage where a children's party had just broken up before the house was riddled by United States bullets, fired by United States troops, from United States Springfield rifles, at close range, with the purpose of killing or maiming the inmates, including the parents and children who were still in the well-lighted house, and whose escape from death under such circumstances was astonishing. He states that on another street he daily looks upon fresh bullet scars where a volley from similar Government rifles was fired into the side and windows of a hotel occupied at the time by sleeping or frightened guests from abroad who could not possibly have given any offense to the assailants. He writes that the chief of the Brownsville police is again on duty from hospital, and carries an empty sleeve because he was shot by Federal soldiers from the adjacent garrison in the course of their murderous foray; and not far away is the fresh grave of an unoffending citizen of the place, a boy in years, who was wantonly shot down by these United States soldiers while unarmed and attempting to escape.

The effort to confute this testimony so far has consisted in the assertion or implication that the townspeople shot one another in order to discredit the soldiers—an absurdity too gross to need discussion, and unsupported by a shred of evidence. There is no question as to the murder and the attempted murders; there is no question that some of the soldiers were guilty thereof; there is no question that many of their comrades privy to the deed have combined to shelter the criminals from justice.

These comrades of the murderers, by their own action, have rendered it necessary either to leave all the men, including the murderers, in the Army, or to turn them all out; and under such circumstances there was no alternative, for the usefulness of the Army would be at an end were we to permit such an outrage to be committed with impunity.

In short, the evidence proves conclusively that a number of the soldiers engaged in a deliberate and concerted attack, as cold blooded as it was cowardly; the purpose being to terrorize the community, and to kill or injure men, women, and children in their homes and beds or on the streets, and this at an hour of the night when concerted or effective resistance or defense was out of the question, and when detection by identification of the criminals in the United States uniform was well-nigh impossible. So much for the original crime. A blacker [crime] never stained the annals of our Army. It has been supplemented by another, only less black, in the shape of a successful conspiracy of silence for the purpose of shielding those who took part in the original conspiracy of murder. These soldiers were not school boys on a frolic. They were full-grown men, in the uniform of the United States Army, armed with deadly weapons, sworn to uphold the laws of the United States, and under every obligation of oath and honor not merely to refrain from criminality, but with the sturdiest rigor to hunt down criminality; and the crime they committed or connived at was murder. They perverted the power put into their hands to sustain the law into the most deadly violation of the law. The noncommissioned officers are primarily responsible for the discipline and good conduct of the men; they are appointed to their positions for the very purpose of preserving this discipline and good conduct, and of detecting and securing the punishment of every enlisted man who does what is wrong. They fill, with reference to the discipline, a part that the commissioned officers are of course unable to fill, although the ultimate responsibility for the discipline can never be shifted from the shoulders of the latter. Under any ordinary circumstances the first duty of the noncommissioned officers, as of the commissioned officers, is to train the private in the ranks so that he may be an efficient fighting man against a foreign foe. But there is an even higher duty, so obvious that it is not under ordinary circumstances necessary so much as to allude to it—the duty of training the soldier so that he shall be a protection and not a menace to his peaceful fellow-citizens, and above all to the women and children of the nation. Unless this duty is well performed, the Army becomes a mere dangerous mob; and if conduct such as that of the murderers in question is not, where possible, punished, and, where this is not possible, unless the chance of its repetition is guarded against in the most thoroughgoing fashion, it would be better that the entire Army should be disbanded. It is vital for the Army to be imbued with the spirit which will make every man in it, and above all, the officers and noncommissioned officers, feel it a matter of highest obligation to discover and punish, and not to shield, the criminal in uniform.

Yet some of the noncommissioned officers and many of the men of the three companies in question have banded together in a conspiracy to protect the assassins and would-be assassins who have disgraced their uniform by the conduct above related. Many of these non-commissioned officers and men must have known, and all of them may have known, circumstances which would have led to the conviction of those engaged in the murderous assault. They have stolidly and as one man broken their oaths of enlistment and refused to help discover the criminals.

By my direction every effort was made to persuade those innocent of murder among them to separate themselves from the guilty by helping bring the criminals to justice. They were warned that if they did not take advantage of the offer they would all be discharged from the service and forbidden again to enter the employ of the Government. They refused to profit by the warning. I accordingly had them discharged. If any organization of troops in the service, white or black, is guilty of similar conduct in the future I shall follow precisely the same course. Under no circumstances will I consent to keep in the service bodies of men whom the circumstances show to be a menace to the country. Incidentally I may add that the soldiers of longest service and highest position who suffered because of the order, so far from being those who deserve most sympathy, deserve least, for they are the very men upon whom we should be able especially to rely to prevent mutiny and murder.

People have spoken as if this discharge from the service was a punishment. I deny emphatically that such is the case, because as punishment it is utterly inadequate. The punishment meet for mutineers and murderers such as those guilty of the Brownsville assault is death; and a punishment only less severe ought to be meted out to those who have aided and abetted mutiny and murder and treason by refusing to help in their detection. I would that it were possible for me to have punished the guilty men. I regret most keenly that I have not been able to do so.

Be it remembered always that these men were all in the service of the United States under contracts of enlistment, which by their terms and by statute were terminable by my direction as Commander in Chief of the Army. It was my clear duty to terminate those contracts when the public interest demanded it; and it would have been a betrayal of the public interest on my part not to terminate the contracts which were keeping in the service of the United States a body of mutineers and murderers.

Any assertion that these men were dealt with harshly because they were colored men is utterly without foundation. Officers or enlisted men, white men or colored men, who were guilty of such conduct, would have been treated in precisely the same way; for there can be nothing more important than for the United States Army, in all its membership, to understand that its arms cannot be turned with impunity against the peace and order of the civil community.

There are plenty of precedents for the action taken. I call your attention to the memoranda herewith submitted from The Military Secretary's office of the War Department, and a memorandum from The Military Secretary enclosing a piece by ex-Corporal Hesse, now chief of division in The Military Secretary's office, together with a letter from District Attorney James Wilkinson, of New Orleans. The district attorney's letter recites several cases in which white United States soldiers, being arrested for crime, were tried, and every soldier and employee of the regiment, or in the fort at which the soldier was stationed, volunteered all they knew, both before and at the trial, so as to secure justice. In one case the soldier was acquitted. In another case the soldier was convicted of murder, the conviction resulting from the fact that every soldier, from the commanding officer to the humblest private, united in securing all the evidence in their power about the crime. In other cases, for less offense, soldiers were convicted purely because their comrades in arms, in a spirit of fine loyalty to the honor of the service, at once told the whole story of the troubles and declined to identify themselves with the criminals.

During the civil war numerous precedents for the action taken by me occurred in the shape of the summary discharge of regiments or companies because of misconduct on the part of some or all of their members. The Sixtieth Ohio was summarily discharged, on the ground that the regiment was disorganized, mutinous, and worthless. The Eleventh New York was discharged by reason of general demoralization and numerous desertions. Three companies of the Fifth Missouri Cavalry and one company of the Fourth Missouri Cavalry were mustered out of the service of the United States without trial by court-martial by reason of mutinous conduct and disaffection *of the majority of the members of these companies* (an almost exact parallel to my action). Another Missouri regiment was mustered out of service because it was in a state bordering closely on mutiny. Other examples, including New Jersey, Maryland, and other organizations, are given in the enclosed papers.

I call your particular attention to the special field order of Brig. Gen. U. S. Grant, issued from the headquarters of the Thirteenth Army Corps on November 16, 1862, in reference to the Twentieth Illinois. Members of this regiment had broken into a store and taken goods to the value of some $1,240, and the rest of the regiment, including especially two officers, failed, in the words of General Grant, to "exercise their authority to ferret out the men guilty of the offenses." General Grant accordingly mustered out of the service of the United States the two officers in question, and assessed the sum of $1,240 against the said regiment as a whole, officers and men to be assessed pro rata on their pay. In its essence this action is precisely similar to that I have taken; although the offense was of course trivial compared to the offense with which I had to deal.

Ex-Corporal Hesse recites what occurred in a United States regular regiment in the spring of 1860. (Corporal Hesse subsequently, when the regiment was surrendered to the Confederates by General Twiggs, saved the regimental colors by wrapping them about his body, under his clothing, and brought them north in safety, receiving a medal of honor for his action.) It appears that certain members of the regiment lynched a barkeeper who had killed one of the soldiers. Being unable to discover the culprits, Col. Robert E. Lee, then in command of the Department of Texas, ordered the company to be disbanded and the members transferred to other companies and discharged at the end of their enlistment, without honor. Owing to the outbreak of the Civil War, and the consequent loss of records and confusion, it is not possible to say what finally became of this case.

When General Lee was in command of the Army of Northern Virginia, as will appear from the enclosed clipping from the *Charlotte Observer*, he issued an order in October, 1864, disbanding a certain battalion for cowardly conduct, stating at the time his regret that there were some officers and men belonging to the organization who, although not deserving it, were obliged to share in the common disgrace because the good of the service demanded it.

In addition to the discharges of organizations, which are of course infrequent, there are continual cases of the discharge of individual enlisted men without honor and without trial by court-martial. The official record shows that during the fiscal year ending June 30, last, such discharges were issued by the War Department without trial by court-martial in the cases of 352 enlisted men of the Regular Army, 35 of them being on account of "having become disqualified for service through own misconduct." Moreover, in addition to the discharges without honor ordered by the War Department, there were a considerable number of discharges without honor issued by subordinate military authorities under paragraph 148 of the Army Regulations, "where the service has not been honest and faithful—that is, where the service does not warrant reenlistment."

So much for the military side of the case. But I wish to say something additional, from the standpoint of the race question. In my message at the opening of the Congress I discussed the matter of lynching. In it I gave utterance to the abhorrence which all decent citizens should feel for the deeds of the men (in almost all cases white men) who take part in lynchings and at the same time I condemned, as all decent men of any color should condemn, the action of those colored men who actively or passively shield the colored criminal from the law. In the case of these companies we had to deal with men who in the first place were guilty of what is practically the worst possible form of lynching—for a lynching is in its essence lawless and murderous vengeance taken by an armed mob for real or fancied wrongs—and who in the second place covered up the crime of lynching by standing with a vicious solidarity to protect the criminals.

It is of the utmost importance to all our people that we shall deal with each man on his merits as a man, and not deal with him merely as a member of a given race; that we shall judge each man by his conduct and not his color. This is important for the white man, and it is far more important for the colored man. More evil and sinister counsel never was given to any people than that given to colored men by those advisers, whether black or white, who, by apology and condonation, encourage conduct such as that of the three companies in question. If the colored men elect to stand by criminals of their own race because they are of their own race, they assuredly lay up for themselves the most dreadful day of reckoning. Every farsighted friend of the colored race in its efforts to strive onward and upward, should teach first, as the most important lesson, alike to the white man and the black, the duty of treating the individual man strictly on his worth as he shows it. Any conduct by colored people which tends to substitute for this rule the rule of standing by and shielding an evil doer because he is a member of their race, means the inevitable degradation of the colored race. It may and probably does mean damage to the white race, but it means ruin to the black race.

Throughout my term of service in the Presidency I have acted on the principle thus advocated. In the North as in the South I have appointed colored men of high character to office, utterly disregarding the protests of those who would have kept them out of office because they were colored men. So far as was in my power, I have sought to secure for the colored people all their rights under the law. I have done all I could to secure them equal school training when young, equal opportunity to earn their livelihood, and achieve their happiness when old. I have striven to break up peonage; I have upheld the hands of those who, like Judge Jones and Judge Speer, have warred against this peonage, because I would hold myself unfit to be President if I did not feel the same revolt at wrong done a colored man as I feel at wrong done a white man. I have condemned in unstinted terms the crime of lynching perpetrated by white men, and I should take instant advantage of any opportunity whereby I could bring to justice a mob of lynchers. In precisely the same spirit I have now acted with reference to these colored men who have been guilty of a black and dastardly crime. In one policy, as in the other, I do not claim as a favor, but I challenge as a right, the support of every citizen of this country, whatever his color, provided only he has in him the spirit of genuine and farsighted patriotism.

Theodore Roosevelt

GLOSSARY

Col. Robert E. Lee: later a general who commanded the Army of Northern Virginia during the Civil War

disaffection: disloyalty to the government

Judge Jones: US District Court Judge Thomas Goode Jones, who heard a number of peonage cases in 1903

Judge Speer: Emory Speer, a judge in Georgia who ruled against the use of chain gangs and upheld the constitutionality of laws against peonage

noncommissioned officers: those of the rank of sergeant who command troops but are not commissioned as lieutenants, captains, and the like

peonage: the practice of requiring a debtor to work for his creditor until the debt is discharged

Document Analysis

President Roosevelt addresses Senate inquiries to him and Secretary of War William Howard Taft in his Special Message of December 19, 1906. In addition to his defense of his summary dismissal of almost all members of Companies B, C, and D of the Twenty-fifth Infantry, Roosevelt also submitted a Department of War report, a letter from General A. B. Nettleton, a memorandum on precedents supporting the action, and other documents. In his message, the president calls attention to his constitutional power as commander in chief of the armed forces, evidence of the guilt of the unit members, and the existence of a conspiracy of silence among the men to protect the known guilty. Roosevelt denies color as having been a factor in his decision and cites precedents that upheld the dismissals.

Obviously sensitive to the allegation of racial discrimination, Roosevelt defends the record of his investigators in the opening paragraphs of his message and his own record in his conclusion. The president attacks the premise that General Garlington had acted as a southerner; he also emphasizes that Lieutenant Colonel Leonard A. Lovering was a native of New Hampshire, while Major Blocksom had been born in Ohio and General Nettleton in Illinois. He notes that Blocksom had judged the men guilty in his report, while Garlington had acted to protect the innocent from the guilty soldiers. (Garlington and Roosevelt's views were that the guilty soldiers would be named by the innocent soldiers and escape dismissal. The townspeople considered all the soldiers guilty. The soldiers considered none of them guilty.)

He dismisses the notion of birthplace as having played any role in the investigation; all those involved had displayed professional honor and loyalty to the flag and the service. On his own behalf, Roosevelt recalls his condemnation of lynching in his message to the opening session of Congress, his appointment of African Americans to federal offices in both the North and South, and a determined policy to treat people as individuals, regardless of race.

Roosevelt emphasizes that the evidence, reports of federal investigators, and sworn testimony determined his decision, which was corroborated by the discovery of ammunition and other items in the streets of Brownsville. In taking this position, the president skirts the observation that some of the discovered military equipment was not of the type used by the army at that time; he also appears to give more credence to testimony of the Brownsville residents than that of the soldiers. In Roosevelt's view, the most trustworthy reports, of course, came from his appointed investigators. He acknowledges previous incidents that had involved the members of the Twenty-fifth Infantry, ascribing blame to both the soldiers and Brownsville civilians, but he denies any possible justification for the attack on the town. Roosevelt considers the testimony of civilians as consistent except for minor details and dismisses the possibility of collusion on their part. He also rejects as absurd the claim that townsmen shot one another to frame the soldiers; later studies, however, would propose the likelihood of that scenario. In Roosevelt's view, nine to twenty soldiers climbed over the fort's walls, hurried through an area near the fort, and shot at whomever they saw entering lighted buildings or otherwise moving about. Policemen, the target of fire, identified the shooters as soldiers. The culprits returned the short distance to the barracks, which was not more than 350 yards, within less than ten minutes and thus escaped discovery. Officers, believing the fort was under siege, became aware of the situation only several hours later, which gave the shooters sufficient time to return to their routines. Roosevelt oversaw the War Department's investigation of the white officers, which recommended that two be court-martialed.

The president focuses his frustration and anger on the noncommissioned officers, all of them African Americans, whom he considered the leaders of the alleged cover-up. He saw them as responsible primarily for the discipline and good conduct of the men. They held the keys to the arms room and must have known the whereabouts of the soldiers and suspected their guilt. Roosevelt felt no sympathy for the dismissal of the most senior noncommissioned officers, since supposedly they should have acted to prevent mutiny and murder. He left no room for the possibility of ignorance on the part of any of the dismissed soldiers. They were warned to separate themselves from the guilty or face expulsion from the army with no opportunity for future government employment. Roosevelt denied, however, that dismissal constituted punishment, for the proper punishment for murder was death.

Almost one quarter of President Roosevelt's message is devoted to precedents supporting his action, and he repeatedly denies that race had been a factor in reaching his decision. He cites a district attorney's letter about cases that had involved misconduct by white soldiers; every member of those units had cooperated in the investigations, which ended in findings of guilt for some soldiers and innocence for others. The Civil War presented numerous instances of summary dismissals for misconduct or desertion. In one case, General Ulysses S. Grant mustered two officers out of the service and forced the other brigade members to repay the loss of money to the victim of an unsolved robbery. Roosevelt observes that, in the 1906 fiscal year, the War Department had discharged 352 enlisted men for misconduct without trial or court martial. He reserves the concluding paragraph to recount his record as an advocate of racial equality in matters of education, opportunity, and employment.

Essential Themes

The Twenty-fifth Infantry was one of six African American US Army regiments organized by Congress in July of 1866 (two cavalry and four infantry). These regiments served in Texas and other western frontier areas for much of the late nineteenth century. They were often assigned frontier duty because of the need for security in the West and the Great Plains; furthermore, many military towns in the East were reticent about welcoming black soldiers. In the West, African American regiments not only offered protection to often ungrateful civilians from attacks by outlaws and Native Americans but also performed more mundane operations, such as stringing and maintaining telegraph lines, building roads, aiding travelers, delivering federal mail, performing agricultural experiments, and compiling weather records. Black soldiers patrolled reservations to ensure that Native Americans stayed on them. They also protected reservation residents from white intruders, occasionally arrested white buffalo hunters, and acted as translators and even agents for some tribes. For these services, Native Americans gave them a respected name, "Buffalo Soldiers."

From the outset, African American soldiers had to confront racial prejudice along with other obstacles. Customary indignities and occasional violence directed toward troops seldom drew retaliation. Two incidents, however, broke the sullen calm of garrison towns in the 1880s. At San Angelo, Texas, white citizens shot to death two Tenth Cavalry soldiers stationed at Fort Concho within ten days. Irate troopers scattered handbills around the community, protesting the unpunished murders and threatening to mete out justice. Some soldiers unleashed a volley of gunfire toward a suspected culprit, an act that prompted intervention by the Texas Rangers, punishment of the soldiers, and removal of the companies from Fort Concho. A similar incident played out at Sturgis City, Dakota Territory, in August 1885. The lynching of a black soldier provoked members of the Twenty-fifth Infantry from Fort Meade to fire into a saloon, killing a customer. In this instance, the War Department resisted public demands to remove the troops after having charged four soldiers with the shooting.

Black troops faced both indifference from town officials toward enforcing their safety and swift reprisals from the military for alleged transgressions. White officers, frequently hoping for a fast track to promotion, commanded the soldiers; indeed, West Point graduated only three African Americans over the course of the nineteenth century. Post commanders keenly felt the obligation to maintain good relationships with the citizenry of garrison towns, and the army never considered itself a laboratory for social experimentation. Whether the military meted out harsher justice for black troops than white troops in similar circumstances is a matter of debate among historians, but African Americans clearly worked under more difficult conditions, often in areas such as Texas, which once had been part of the Confederacy.

The transfer of black troops to the South after the Spanish-American War in 1898 sparked more frequent racial clashes between forts and towns than in preceding years. The higher incidence of conflict derived from opposing movements that had gained momentum after the war: an attempt in the southern states to further isolate blacks and remove them entirely from political participation and a determination on the part of black soldiers, many of whom had received commendations for valor in the recent war, to validate their constitutional rights. Partly as a reaction to the Populist movement, which threatened the establishment and brought whites and blacks together tentatively during political campaigns of the 1890s, southern legislatures enacted laws that stipulated stricter property qualifications and literacy tests for African American voters. Many southern states, including Texas, also required poll taxes for black voters and established all-white Democratic primaries. After the Supreme Court's *Plessy v. Ferguson* ruling (1896), many communities began to enforce segregationist practices even more strictly, such as requiring separate seating on newly introduced electric streetcars. Incidents of lynching reached an all-time high in the South in the early 1900s, with Texas ranking third in frequency, and black community groups complained of excessive use of force by police.

Members of all the African American regiments encountered hostility from whites after the end of the Spanish-American War. A group of Floridians booed the soldiers while cheering their Spanish military prisoners. Snipers fired at troop trains passing through Alabama and departing from Houston, Texas. National Guardsmen scuffled with black soldiers at Huntsville, Alabama. A constable in Texarkana, Texas, almost provoked retaliation when he attempted to arrest a soldier on a troop train after a disturbance at a local brothel. Some of the soldier's comrades, unaware of the circumstances, silently drew weapons at the sight of an armed civilian accosting a member of their unit. Their reaction allowed the soldier to disappear aboard the train, escaping arrest and identification. The most serious clashes, however, awaited the troops' arrival at their Texas posts in 1899.

Prior to the Brownsville affray, Texas clashes between soldiers and townspeople, often law officers, had erupted at Laredo, Rio Grande City, and El Paso. The events preceding these conflicts bore a dismal similarity to conditions in Brownsville. Predominantly Hispanic populations, governed by a white political and business establishment, greeted the arriving troops with suspicion followed by minor disturbances. Soldiers complained of discrimination and price gouging from the business community as well as harassment by local police. Some civilians plainly hoped that the War Department could be persuaded to remove the black troops and replace them with white units—a virtual impossibility in light of the strained resources of the military command. At Fort McIntosh, Laredo, Company D of the Twenty-fifth Infantry felt victimized by a local peace officer. Mistaking another officer for the man, a number of enlisted men assaulted him with rifle butts and then fired their arms in the streets. The mayor protested to the governor, who strongly supported the stance of the local official. The War Department resolved the matter by evacuating the post.

Almost simultaneously, another incident broke the peace at Fort Ringgold, Rio Grande City, a hundred miles to the south. After a ruckus in a gambling hall involving the citizenry and members of Troop D, Ninth Cavalry, rumors reached the post of an impending attack from the town. The disabled post commander gave credence to his men's reports of snipers by allowing the firing of a Gatling gun toward Rio Grande City. Mercifully, there were no casualties, but a major row ensued between officials of the town and the fort over culpability, each claiming attack by the other. Texas governor Joseph D. Sayers involved himself in the controversy, engaging in a dispute with the army over legal jurisdiction. The matter dissipated when an angry grand jury failed to return indictments against any soldier.

In the most serious civilian-military rift before Brownsville, a sergeant from Company A of the Twenty-fifth Infantry was charged with murder in 1900 for having led a group of soldiers to the El Paso jail to release a jailed comrade, who they believed had been unjustly detained. In the scuffle, a popular lawman received fatal wounds. Because of heated emotions in El Paso, a change of venue was ordered for the ensuing trial. A Dallas court sentenced Sergeant John Kipper to fifty years at hard labor, further embittering race relations between the military and civilians in the state.

Only the magnitude of the controversy that surrounded the Brownsville incident separated it from its lesser-known predecessors. The Twenty-fifth Infantry passed a productive six years abroad and stateside after its partial involvement in the Rio Grande City imbroglio. After the outbreak of the Philippine insurrection in 1899, all of the regiment's companies were shipped to the islands within one year. The regiment demonstrated the same combat efficiency in the Pacific as it had in Cuba, drawing accolades from Brigadier General A. S. Burt. Filipinos themselves praised the troops' decorum. These same heroics failed to impress Brownsville residents, who, for whatever reasons, refused to accept the troops, regardless of their stellar military campaign record. Among those who objected to the troops' presence were outright bigots, residents with an antimilitary bias, Latinos challenged by a new minority group, and the lawless. The highly publicized murder at El Paso had also promoted a feeling of apprehension among some of the citizenry. Disappointing news from Austin, Texas, elicited resentment from the soldiers as well; the War Department rescinded the regiment's participation in maneuvers at Camp Mabry after Texas National Guardsmen threatened the black soldiers with violence if they were to appear.

Tensions at Brownsville quickly mounted. Some residents wired Washington, DC, to complain about the First Battalion even before it was garrisoned at Fort Brown on July 28. Departing white troops acknowledged that they had heard threats against the incoming blacks. Although the city administration sought to maintain a constructive relationship with the army for defensive and financial reasons, federal authorities showed no concern. Fred Tate, a customs inspector, clubbed Private James W. Newton for supposedly jostling Tate's wife and another white woman on a sidewalk. Another customs officer, A. Y. Baker, pushed Private Oscar W. Reed into the Rio Grande. Baker claimed that he was trying to quiet the soldier, who allegedly had returned from Matamoras, Mexico, drunk and boisterous. Locals voiced racial slurs at the soldiers on the streets. Payday, August 11, passed without the confrontation that some had feared, but the following night, a report of an attack on a white woman by a black soldier jolted the community. Mrs. Lon Evans, who lived near the red-light district, complained that a uniformed black man had grabbed her hair and thrown her to the ground. The incident had caused Mrs. Evans little physical pain, and she could not swear that her assailant had worn a military uniform. Nevertheless, claims of blacks assaulting white women were known to incite lynch mobs. Accordingly, Mayor Frederick J. Combe and post commander Major Charles W. Penrose hastily met to defuse the situation. Penrose subsequently imposed an eight o'clock curfew on his men.

Around midnight shots rang out near the garrison wall separating the town from the fort. Various Brownsville residents later testified that they saw a shadowy group of nine to twenty persons who divided into two groups and charged up an alley toward town, firing several hundred shots at random into lighted areas. The shooters killed the bartender, Frank Natus, and shattered the arm of M. Y. Dominguez, a police lieutenant, necessitating its amputation. Alleged witnesses never were able to identify the culprits and insisted that the raiders had worn military uniforms or that the shots had emanated from military rifles. Daylight searches located spent army-type cartridges in the streets. Soldiers, contrarily, protested their innocence until the death of the last surviving serviceman over seventy years later. Major Penrose echoed the sentinel's belief that the post had been under attack, particularly after a roll call found all servicemen present or accounted for and a weapons and ammunition inspection revealed none missing. A morning visit from Mayor Combe, brandishing empty cartridges from the streets, convinced the commanding officer of the garrison's guilt, a view quickly adopted by Brownsville residents, newspapers, Texas congressmen, and Governor S. W. T. Lanham, who demanded removal of all African American soldiers from the state.

After an initial investigation, the US government accepted the widely held conviction of the soldiers' guilt. President Roosevelt sent Major General Augustus P. Blocksom to Brownsville several days after the raid. Eleven days later he submitted a report to the White House that differed from the view of the black regiment's guilt only in his conclusion that both sides had exaggerated the facts, that Tate probably had overreacted in his beating of Private Newton, and that some of the citizenry were racially prejudiced. Stating that black soldiers had adopted an aggressive stance, Blocksom posited a scenario in which some soldiers began firing between barracks and the wall, others fired into the air to create an alarm, and nine to fifteen men scaled the wall and rushed through an alley into the streets. The attackers subsequently returned to camp to clean and reassemble their weapons while duping their officers into believing they had not left the garrison. Blocksom also noted that the men's motivation for the raid was questionable, since some bars had served the soldiers and Natus had never quarreled with the troops. Nevertheless, he considered the accusers' testimony as more reliable than that of the soldiers. Blocksom also declared that the discovery of the empty cartridges, which did not fit the recently assigned Springfield rifles, was not pertinent to his decision. He recommended the discharge of every man in the battalion. Each soldier would be granted the option to reenlist only if he identified the guilty by a date determined by the War Department. Roosevelt, adhering to the demands of Texas officials and press, ordered the transfer of the First Battalion to Fort Reno, Oklahoma, except for those held as suspects involved in the raid. Captain William J. "Bill" McDonald of the Texas Rangers and Major Penrose settled on a dozen defendants, based strictly on conjecture, who—for lack of evidence—were grudgingly not indicted by the Cameron County grand jury. The War Department scheduled Fort Brown for temporary closure.

Determined to uncover the guilty, Roosevelt sent Brigadier General Ernest A. Garlington, inspector general of the US Army, to Fort Reno and Fort Sam Houston in San Antonio, Texas, to interrogate the suspects. Following Blocksom's suggestion, the president instructed Garlington to threaten all members of the battalion with dismissal without honor. When the mere threat proved ineffective, Garlington urged Roosevelt to proceed with its execution. Roosevelt complied on November 4 with War Department Special Order No. 266, an edict that escalated the Texas controversy to national stature and sparked criticism from African Americans and some whites. The *Richmond Planet* and *Atlanta Independent* accused Roosevelt of having delayed until after the congressional elections to assure a black Republican vote in key northern states. Black ministers joined the fray, and the scholar-activist W. E. B. Du Bois urged his followers to vote Democratic in the 1908 elections. Booker T. Washington, the widely publicized White House guest and administration patron to the African American constituency, continued to support Roosevelt and took his own share of criticism together with the chief executive and Secretary of War Taft, the front-runner for the Republican presidential nomination in 1908. An interracial organization, the Constitutional League, raised the argument of the troops' innocence. The director of the league, John Milholland, a white Progressive, assailed the reports of Blocksom and Garlington for racism, haste, and inconsistencies. Republican senator Joseph B. Foraker took up the argument and carried it to a larger stage.

Ordinarily the most stalwart of conservatives, Foraker may have acted from principle, presidential ambitions, or personal dislike of Roosevelt. In any case, he became the cashiered soldiers' most celebrated advocate. His Senate resolution called for an investigation of the raid and summoned the War Department to provide the evidence it had used in its decision. On December 19, Roosevelt countered with a Special Message defending the summary dismissals.

Impact

The Senate Committee on Military Affairs, on which Joseph Foraker served, conducted hearings on the Brownsville incident between February 1907 and March 1908. The sessions followed speeches by Foraker, who denounced the absence of trials and suggested that outside forces had raided Brownsville. Despite popularizing the controversy, Foraker's crusade on behalf of the soldiers met the same dismal fate as his campaign for the Republican presidential nomination. By a vote of nine to four, the committee sustained Roosevelt's action, with all five Democrats and four Republican members affirming it. A supplementary report signed by four senators provided for the reenlistment of men who had proven their innocence, a motion supported by Roosevelt. Senator Nathan B. Scott of West Virginia wrote a report that was signed by three other Republican members, including Foraker, which stated that the government had not proved its case. Foraker, in turn, issued a report with Senator Morgan Bulkeley of Connecticut that maintained the men's innocence, since they lacked a motive for the crime.

On a note to be echoed six decades later, Foraker and Bulkeley asserted that members of the citizenry stood to gain from the soldiers' disgrace and removal. Foraker continued his assault on the decision in an article in the *North American Review* one year later.

The government investigations resulted in courts-martial of two officers of the First Battalion. Major Penrose and Captain Edgar Macklin were tried for dereliction of duty but found not guilty. The War Department permitted fourteen of the cashiered soldiers to reenlist in 1910 but never stated its criteria for that determination. Although no new evidence had come to light, the First Battalion was exonerated more than a half century later. President Richard Nixon, acting on the proposal of Democratic Representative August Hawkins of California, granted an honorable discharge and a pension of $25,000 to each of the 153 dismissed servicemen in 1972, without ascribing any blame for the Brownsville attack. Nixon's decision came two years after the publication of a history of the incident, *The Brownsville Raid* by John D. Weaver, which convincingly presented Foraker's argument of innocence. Only one member of the battalion, Dorsey Willis, had survived to receive the pardon. Willis had continued to maintain the innocence of all the soldiers and their lack of knowledge about the raid. Most historians today believe that justice was not served in Roosevelt's action—from the lack of due process, the absence of certain evidence, or the likelihood of a conspiracy against the black soldiers.

——*Garna L. Christian, PhD*

Bibliography and Additional Reading

Christian, Garna L. *Black Soldiers in Jim Crow Texas, 1899–1917*. College Station: Texas A&M University Press, 1995.

Hearings before the Committee on Military Affairs, United States Senate, concerning the Affair at Brownsville, Tex., on the Night of August 13 and 14, 1906. Washington, DC: Government Printing Office, 1907.

Lane, Ann J. *The Brownsville Affair: National Crisis and Black Reaction*. Port Washington, NY: Kennikat Press, 1971.

Tinsley, James A. "Roosevelt, Foraker, and the Brownsville Affray." *Journal of Negro History* 41 (Jan. 1956): 43–65.

Weaver, John D. *The Brownsville Raid*. New York: W. W. Norton, 1970.

Native American Life

Two of the most significant developments in American Indian affairs in the early years of the twentieth century were 1) the authorization of the Antiquities Act of 1906, and 2) the establishment of the state of Oklahoma in 1907. The 1906 congressional act declared, among other things, that Native American skeletal remains and cultural objects found on federal land were the property of the United States, not the tribes to which they might ancestrally be linked. The law was a blow, of course, to indigenous rights supporters. It would not be until the passage of the Native American Graves Protection and Repatriation Act of 1990 that this policy would be reversed. (See the section "Politics and Reform" in the present volume for an analysis of the Antiquities Act.)

The entry of Oklahoma into the union in 1907 was accomplished by the merger of Oklahoma Territory (made up largely of white settlers) and Indian Territory (made up of displaced indigenous populations). The latter territory, moreover, was made open to additional non-Indian settlement through creation of the state.

In this section we present two documents relating to Native American life near the turn of the century. The first is a chapter from Charles Eastman's (Santee Dakota) Memories of an Indian Boyhood, which although documenting an earlier time was published in 1902 and brought Eastman a measure of fame. The second document is the introduction to Edward Curtis' noted photographic series The North American Indian, which began publication in 1907. Although not widely remarked in Curtis' lifetime, the photographs in this series would later come to be regarded both as valuable historical documents and as significant works of art.

Charles Eastman: *Indian Boyhood*

Date: 1902
Author: Charles Eastman
Genre: memoir

Summary Overview

Charles Eastman wrote his first book, *Indian Boyhood*, in 1902, for a predominantly non-Indian audience. As a well-educated, highly assimilated Indian, Eastman wanted to describe his youth among his Santee Dakota tribe in positive terms. Throughout his adult life, Eastman was well-aware of his mediating position between Native American people and the general American society. He wanted to expose non-Indian people to some of the positive things about Indian culture, as he does in this excerpt. In some of his other writings, and in much of his work in a variety of positions throughout his career, he also encouraged Native Americans to embrace parts of the general American culture, especially to become American citizens and to pursue education. In this selection from *Indian Boyhood*, Eastman describes how young boys were educated among his people. They were well-educated, but not in formal schools like white Americans would have considered typical. They were taught by their families, and were taught by listening to stories told by their parents or other elders in the tribe. Much of this teaching was about their spiritual beliefs, and these spiritual beliefs were also connected to many aspects of everyday life. The Santee people believed that many of their customs and ways of life were based on teachings that had been revealed by the spirits that inhabit much of the natural world. Eastman notes that many non-Indians assume that Indian have instinctive or inherited skills as hunters or warriors, but he notes that these skills were taught through careful instruction. He details some of the ways in which his uncle sought to instill in him the habits and behavior that would produce the skills of a hunter and a warrior. Some of this training was somewhat frightening, or was arduous in other ways—but Eastman wanted to please his uncle and be thought to be making progress, so he never complained about the lessons he was being taught.

Defining Moment

Charles Eastman was writing primarily for non-Indian readers, and there was an eager audience among the American people for his books. In the late nineteenth and early twentieth centuries, while there was still much prejudice against Native Americans, there was also great interest in learning about their culture. Many people read "dime novels" and other types of popular literature that often did not portray a very realistic account of the lifestyle of the Native peoples—but this does demonstrate at least the interest the reading public had about Indian cultures and lifestyles. Eastman was writing during the era of the "Friends of the Indians" movement, and he himself was a significant figure in this movement, writing in many of the journals associated with the movement, and speaking at gatherings such as the Lake Mohonk conferences where the "Friends of the Indians" gathered to discuss ideas about reform of U.S. government Indian policy. Eastman was well-respected by those involved in this movement, and his writings were well received by the general reading public. It is difficult to know how many Indian people read Eastman's writing, but he was well-respected by native peoples as well, and many Indians who read his writings probably came from backgrounds similar to how own—well educated in white schools, and somewhat assimilated into the general American culture.

Author Biography

Charles Eastman was born in 1858 (exact date unknown) on the Santee Sioux reservation in southwestern Minnesota. His father was a Santee warrior named Many Lightnings. His mother was the child of a Santee mother and a white father, Seth Eastman, an army officer who later became a prominent artist and illustrator. Since his mother died shortly after he was born, Charles was named Hakadah, meaning "the Pitiful Last" in Dakota. Later, however, he was named him Ohiyesa, which is Dakota for "the Winner."

In 1862, the Santee tribe rebelled against their mistreatment by the U.S. government. During the fighting, Charles was separated from his family, but was reunited with his father several years later. Many Lightnings had taken the name Jacob Eastman, using the surname Eastman from his wife's family. He had converted to Christianity, and lived among some Santee homesteaders near Flandreau, South Dakota. When Charles was fifteen, he came to live in this community of somewhat assimilated Indians. Charles spent more than eighteen years attending a variety of schools. He graduated from Dartmouth College in 1887, and earned a medical degree at Boston University in 1890. Eastman became a government physician at the Pine Ridge Agency in South Dakota, and was there during the time of the Wounded Knee massacre in December 1890. While at Pine Ridge, Eastman married Elaine Goodale, a white teacher in the reservation schools. During his career, he worked in a variety of positions for the Bureau of Indian Affairs. Eastman wrote a total of eleven books, and lectured widely on Indian affairs. He was one of most prominent Indian intellectuals and advocates of the early twentieth century. While he had firmly advocated assimilation for the Native Americans in his early career, in his later years, he argued that Indians needed to maintain much of their unique spirituality and culture. Eastman retired from public life in 1925, and spent the rest of his life living in a cabin near Detroit, MI. He died of pneumonia in Detroit on January 8, 1939.

HISTORICAL DOCUMENT

II: An Indian Boy's Training

It is commonly supposed that there is no systematic education of their children among the aborigines of this country. Nothing could be farther from the truth. All the customs of this primitive people were held to be divinely instituted, and those in connection with the training of children were scrupulously adhered to and transmitted from one generation to another.

The expectant parents conjointly bent all their efforts to the task of giving the new-comer the best they could gather from a long line of ancestors. A pregnant Indian woman would often choose one of the greatest characters of her family and tribe as a model for her child. This hero was daily called to mind. She would gather from tradition all of his noted deeds and daring exploits, rehearsing them to herself when alone. In order that the impression might be more distinct, she avoided company. She isolated herself as much as possible, and wandered in solitude, not thoughtlessly, but with an eye to the impress given by grand and beautiful scenery.

The Indians believed, also, that certain kinds of animals would confer peculiar gifts upon the unborn, while others would leave so strong an adverse impression that the child might become a monstrosity. A case of hare-lip was commonly attributed to the rabbit. It was said that a rabbit had charmed the mother and given to the babe its own features. Even the meat of certain animals was denied the pregnant woman, because it was supposed to influence the disposition or features of the child.

Scarcely was the embyro warrior ushered into the world, when he was met by lullabies that speak of wonderful exploits in hunting and war. Those ideas which so fully occupied his mother's mind before his birth are now put into words by all about the child, who is as yet quite unresponsive to their appeals to his honor and ambition. He is called the future defender of his people, whose lives may depend upon his courage and skill. If the child is a girl, she is at once addressed as the future mother of a noble race.

In hunting songs, the leading animals are introduced; they come to the boy to offer their bodies for the sustenance of his tribe. The animals are regarded as his friends, and spoken of almost as tribes of people, or as his cousins, grandfathers and grandmothers. The songs of wooing, adapted as lullabies, were equally imaginative, and the suitors were often animals personified, while pretty maidens were represented by the mink and the doe.

Very early, the Indian boy assumed the task of preserving and transmitting the legends of his ancestors and his race. Almost every evening a myth, or a true story of some deed done in the past, was narrated by one of the parents or grandparents, while the boy listened with parted lips and glistening eyes. On the following evening, he was usually required to repeat it. If he was not an apt scholar, he struggled long with his task; but, as a rule, the Indian boy is a good listener and has a good memory, so that the stories were tolerably well mastered. The household became his audience, by which he was alternately criticized and applauded.

This sort of teaching at once enlightens the boy's mind and stimulates his ambition. His conception of his own future career becomes a vivid and irresistible force. Whatever there is for him to learn must be learned; whatever qualifications are necessary to a truly great man he must seek at any expense of danger and hardship. Such was the feeling of the imaginative and brave young Indian. It became apparent to him in early life that he must accustom himself to rove alone and not to fear or dislike the impression of solitude.

It seems to be a popular idea that all the characteristic skill of the Indian is instinctive and hereditary. This is a mistake. All the stoicism and patience of the Indian are acquired traits, and continual practice alone makes him master of the art of wood-craft. Physical training and dieting were not neglected. I remember that I was not allowed to have beef soup or any warm drink. The soup was for the old men. General rules for the young were never to take their food very hot, nor to drink much water.

My uncle, who educated me up to the age of fifteen years, was a strict disciplinarian and a good teacher. When I left the teepee in the morning, he would say: "Hakadah, look closely to everything you see"; and at evening, on my return, he used often to catechize me for an hour or so. "On which side of the trees is the lighter-colored bark? On which side do they have most regular branches?"

It was his custom to let me name all the new birds that I had seen during the day. I would name them according to the color or the shape of the bill or their song or the appearance and locality of the nest—in fact, anything about the bird that impressed me as characteristic. I made many ridiculous errors, I must admit. He then usually informed me of the correct name. Occasionally I made a hit and this he would warmly commend.

He went much deeper into this science when I was a little older, that is, about the age of eight or nine years. He would say, for instance: "How do you know that there are fish in yonder lake?"

"Because they jump out of the water for flies at mid-day."

He would smile at my prompt but superficial reply. "What do you think of the little pebbles grouped together under the shallow water? and what made the pretty curved marks in the sandy bottom and the little sand-banks? Where do you find the fish-eating birds? Have the inlet and the outlet of a lake anything to do with the question?"

He did not expect a correct reply at once to all the voluminous questions that he put to me on these occasions, but he meant to make me observant and a good student of nature.

"Hakadah" he would say to me, "you ought to follow the example of the *shunktokecha* (wolf). Even when he is surprised and runs for his life, he will pause to take one more look at you before he enters his final retreat. So you must take a second look at everything you see.

"It is better to view animals unobserved. I have been a witness to their courtships and their quarrels and have learned many of their secrets in this way. I was once the unseen spectator of a thrilling battle between a pair of grizzly bears and three buffaloes—a rash act for the bears, for it was in the moon of strawberries, when the buffaloes sharpen and polish their horns for bloody contests among themselves.

"I advise you, my boy, never to approach a grizzly's den from the front, but to steal up behind and throw your blanket or a stone in front of the hole. He does not usually rush for it, but first puts his head out and listens and then comes out very indifferently and sits on his haunches on the mound in front of the hole before he makes any attack. While he is exposing himself in this fashion, aim at his heart. Always be as cool as the animal himself." Thus he armed me against the cunning of savage beasts by teaching me how to outwit them.

"In hunting" he would resume, "you will be guided by the habits of the animal you seek. Remember that a moose stays in swampy or low land or between high mountains near a spring or lake, for thirty to sixty days at a time. Most large game moves about continually, except the doe in the spring; it is then a very easy matter to find her with the fawn. Conceal yourself in a convenient place as soon as you observe any signs of the presence of either, and then call with your birchen doe-caller.

"Whichever one hears you first will soon appear in your neighborhood. But you must be very watchful, or you may be made a fawn of by a large wild-cat. They understand the characteristic call of the doe perfectly well.

"When you have any difficulty with a bear or a wild-cat—that is, if the creature shows signs of attacking you—you must make him fully understand that you have seen him and are aware of his intentions. If you are not well equipped for a pitched battle, the only way to make him retreat is to take a long sharp-pointed pole for a spear and rush toward him. No wild beast will face this unless he is cornered and already wounded, These fierce beasts are generally afraid of the common weapon of the larger animals—the horns, and if these are very long and sharp, they dare not risk an open fight.

"There is one exception to this rule—the grey wolf will attack fiercely when very hungry. But their courage depends upon their numbers; in this they are like white men. One wolf or two will never attack a man. They will stampede a herd of buffaloes in order to get at the calves; they will rush upon a herd of antelopes, for these are helpless; but they are always careful about attacking man."

Of this nature were the instructions of my uncle, who was widely known at that time as among the greatest hunters of his tribe.

All boys were expected to endure hardship without complaint. In savage warfare, a young man must, of course, be an athlete and used to undergoing all sorts of privations. He must be able to go without food and water for two or three days without displaying any weakness, or to run for a day and a night without any rest. He must be able to traverse a pathless and wild country without losing his way either in the day or night time. He cannot refuse to do any of these things if he aspires to be a warrior.

Sometimes my uncle would waken me very early in the morning and challenge me to fast with him all day. I had to accept the challenge. We blackened our faces with charcoal, so that every boy in the village would know that I was fasting for the day. Then the little tempters would make my life a misery until the merciful sun hid behind the western hills.

I can scarcely recall the time when my stern teacher began to give sudden war-whoops over my head in the morning while I was sound asleep. He expected me to leap up with perfect presence of mind, always ready to grasp a weapon of some sort and to give a shrill whoop in reply. If I was sleepy or startled and hardly knew what I was about, he would ridicule me and say that I need never expect to sell my scalp dear. Often he would vary these tactics by shooting off his gun just outside of the lodge while I was yet asleep, at the same time giving blood-curdling yells. After a time I became used to this.

When Indians went upon the war-path, it was their custom to try the new warriors thoroughly before coming to an engagement. For instance, when they were near a hostile camp, they would select the novices to go after the water and make them do all sorts of things to prove their courage. In accordance with this idea, my uncle used to send me off after water when we camped after dark in a strange place. Perhaps the country was full of wild beasts, and, for aught I knew, there might be scouts from hostile bands of Indians lurking in that very neighborhood.

Yet I never objected, for that would show cowardice. I picked my way through the woods, dipped my pail in the water and hurried back, always careful to make as little noise as a cat. Being only a boy, my heart would leap at every crackling of a dry twig or distant hooting of an owl, until, at last, I reached our teepee. Then my uncle would perhaps say: "Ah, Hakadah, you are a thorough warrior" empty out the precious contents of the pail, and order me to go a second time.

Imagine how I felt! But I wished to be a brave man as much as a white boy desires to be a great lawyer or even President of the United States. Silently I would take the pail and endeavor to retrace my footsteps in the dark.

With all this, our manners and morals were not neglected. I was made to respect the adults and especially the aged. I was not allowed to join in their discussions, nor even to speak in their presence, unless requested to do so. Indian etiquette was very strict, and among the requirements was that of avoiding the direct address. A term of relationship or some title of courtesy was commonly used instead of the personal name by those who wished to show respect. We were taught generosity to the poor and reverence for the "Great Mystery." Religion was the basis of all Indian training.

I recall to the present day some of the kind warnings and reproofs that my good grandmother was wont to give me. "Be strong of heart—be patient!" she used to say. She told me of a young chief who was noted for his uncontrollable temper. While in one of his rages he attempted to kill a woman, for which he was slain by his own band and left unburied as a mark of disgrace—his body was simply covered with green grass. If I ever lost my temper, she would say: "Hakadah, control yourself, or you will be like that young man I told you of, and lie under a green blanket!"

In the old days, no young man was allowed to use tobacco in any form until he had become an acknowledged warrior and had achieved a record. If a youth should seek a wife before he had reached the age of twenty-two or twenty-three, and been recognized as a brave man, he was sneered at and considered an ill-bred Indian. He must also be a skillful hunter. An Indian cannot be a good husband unless he brings home plenty of game.

These precepts were in the line of our training for the wild life.

GLOSSARY

aborigines: the original inhabitants of a region; thus the American Indians were the aborigines of the Western Hemisphere

birchen doe-called: a call for luring deer, made of birch bark

"Great Mystery": a translation of the Dakota phrase "Wakan Tanka," which refers to the greatest spirit or the sum of all spiritual power in the spirit world; sometimes translated "The Great Holy"

Hakadah: Eastman's original Indian name, meaning "The Pitiful Last"; it was given to him because his mother died shortly after giving birth to him

stoicism: a word taken from the ancient Roman Stoic philosophers, who sought to be unmoved by external circumstances; thus stoicism means to meet problems or concerns with bravery and fortitude

Document Analysis

In his book *Indian Boyhood,* Charles Eastman wrote about his life from his early childhood until the time he was reunited with his father and moved with him to a homestead near Flandreau in what is now South Dakota. After the Santee uprising in 1862, Charles had become separated from his father, and many of his extended family believed his father and siblings had all been killed. Charles moved with some Santee families into Canada for a time, to escape the fighting and its aftermath. In what is now Manitoba, they were able to continue their traditional way of life for several more years. Charles lived with his grandmother, and he was taught many of the Santee customs by his uncle, a brother of his father. His uncle was named Mysterious Medicine, although he was also known as "Big Hunter" and "Long Rifle." Throughout this excerpt, his uncle and grandmother refer to Charles as Hakadah, a name meaning "the Pitiful Last," given to him because he mother died shortly after his birth. Later, when he was about four years old, Charles represented his band in a sporting contest against another band, and when he was victorious, he was given the name Ohiyesa, meaning "The Winner."

This excerpt is chapter six in the book, and the beginning of part two. Eastman wrote about his childhood with a note of nostalgia, for he realized that even Native American youth, at the time he was writing, no longer lived like his people did when he was a child. He wanted to describe the lifestyle of the Santee tribe for non-Indian readers, in order to promote understanding between Indians and whites. In explaining his life as an Indian child, he describes many things that would have been foreign to non-Indian readers, yet he also draws out some commonalities that would resonate with all readers. He also seeks to show how some of the lessons he was taught might have broader application, and were valuable for people of varied backgrounds.

Like most Native Americans, the Santee or Dakota people believed that the world around them was filled with many powerful spirits, and that these affected the lives and fortunes of humans in many ways. The spirits could affect a woman during pregnancy, which would also impact the child to be born. Some of these impacts could be negative and be a danger to the child, but spirits could also impart valuable gifts of insight and power that would benefit a person. Eastman's writing reflects the intimate connection that native peoples believed that humans have with the natural world. Animals are to be regarded as friends, even though hunting and killing some animals is necessary for the sustenance of the people. He notes that animals were thought of "almost as tribes of people." Even today, it is common among many Native Americans to hear references to "the buffalo people" or "the deer people."

The first part of this excerpt deals with traditions and practices related to caring for infants and young children. Of course, Charles did not remember these from his own experience, but he saw how children younger than he were raised. It was believed that what the mother thought about and experienced during pregnancy could impact the character of the child. The mother would sing lullabies about great hunters or warriors while the child was still in the womb. A baby boy would be greeted as a future defender and provider for the people, while a baby girl would be thought to be the future mother of a great people.

Eastman wrote that it was popularly believed, by non-Indians, that the skills that made an Indian boy into a good hunter or warrior were "instinctive and hereditary." He argues this is not true. Young men were taught these skills, and they mastered them by "continual practice." He describes many of the ways his uncle taught him. Each day, Charles would report about new birds he had seen—describing their appearance and behavior, and trying to give them the proper name. If he was correct, his uncle would commend him warmly, but would correct him when he was wrong. His uncle often taught him by asking questions—more questions that Charles could ever answer as a youngster—but his uncle did not expect answers, he simply wished for Charles to think about these questions as this would make him more observant. He should learn from the example of the wolf, his uncle said. Even when surprised and fleeing for safety, the wolf would pause and take one more look before entering some safe cover. Learning the habits and characteristic behavior of the animals that are hunted would make one a better hunter. Also, learning how to approach dangerous animals, such as a grizzly bear in its den, would keep the hunter safe.

Some of his uncle's lessons were arduous and might be fearsome to a young boy. Others were simply frustrating. To teach him to find his way in the woods at night, and not to be afraid of the dark or unfamiliar surroundings, his uncle would send him to a stream to fetch water. But when Charles came back with the water, his uncle would pour it out and send him again—teaching patience and stoicism as well. But Charles did not complain—he wanted to learn these skills, and to show stamina and to prove himself to be brave.

Some of the teachings Eastman describes in this excerpt are simply about proper behavior—to show respect to elders, and to listen to adults without speaking unless invited to reply. When addressing a person, a title or respect or a term of relationship would be used, because direct address was considered improper. Their religion—their reverence for what the Dakota and the related Lakota peoples called "The Great Mystery"—taught them these rules of behavior, and also to be generous in sharing with the poor within the tribe. A young man was not to marry until he had proven that he had the skill as a hunter to provide for his family.

Charles believed he was being prepared for the life of a warrior, and that someday he would be called upon to avenge the death of his father. But as he describes later in the book, when he was fifteen years old, he was reunited with his father. His father had converted to Christianity, and was living as a homesteader in a community with other Christian Indians. His father had taken the name Jacob Eastman (taking the surname Eastman from his mother's white family). Ohiyesa then became known as Charles Eastman. When Charles went to live with his father, his life was changed dramatically and he began to be more exposed to the lifestyles of non-Indian people.

Essential Themes
Charles Eastman wrote *Indian Boyhood* in the waning days of the "Friends of the Indian Movement," and he himself was a prominent part of this movement, speaking often at some of their meetings such as the Lake Mohonk Conferences held in upstate New York, and publishing in the journals sympathetic to the movement. The Friends of the Indians was not a single organization but rather a loose coalition of like-minded people; it began in the post-Civil War era and lasted into the early twentieth century. They were genuinely angered at what they believed was the precipitate violence that was waged against Native Americans in incidents such as the Sand Creek Massacre in Colorado in 1864, and at the Washita Massacre in western Oklahoma in 1868. They advocated what they believed were positive reforms in Indian policy, but they operated from a paternalistic perspective and tended to believe that they, and not the Indians, knew what was best for the native people. They sought three major reforms: more and better schools for Indian children, allotment of reservation land into individual homesteads for Indian families, and citizenship for the Indians. Many Indian parents did want their children to receive more education, but they did not understand that the goal of this education, in that era, was often to stamp out the Indian culture in the hearts and minds of the children. Very few Indians supported allotment, and many bitterly opposed it, and it generally was a disaster that ultimately led to many Indians losing their lands. In the long run, citizenship was a positive reform because Indians could then use the protections of the U.S. Constitution in fighting for their rights, but few Indians at the time saw it as a positive development. By the 1920s, the Friends of the Indians had largely ceased to exist as an identifiable movement, partly because World War I had caused the American people to focus on the war effort and distract them from reform movements in general.

Eastman was also writing in the early days of the Progressive movement. Progressivism was a reform-minded movement that sought to make the government more responsive to the needs of the people, and to protect the small businessman and the consumer from the monopolistic power of big business. Progressives in general, however, did not show much concern for racial or ethnic minorities. There was a small sub-set within the movement known as the "Red Progressives." This included many Native American people like Eastman himself, and also the Apache medical doctor Carlos Montezuma, and the Winnebago tribal leader and educator Henry Roe Cloud. Both of these men were involved with Eastman in the founding of the Society of American Indians. Some non-Indians among the "Red Progressives included Wisconsin Senator Robert La-Follette, the western writer Hamlin Garland, and John Collier, a social worker who later became the Commissioner of the Bureau of Indian Affairs under President Franklin D. Roosevelt. The "Red Progressives" generally believed that ultimately, Native Americans would have to largely assimilate and become a part of the overall American society. Early in his career as a writer and activist, Eastman believed in this goal also, and was himself an example of a highly assimilated, educated American Indian. One writer has called him a "poster child" for assimilation. In his later writings, however, Eastman showed more concern for native peoples maintaining some of their traditional ways of life and their spiritual beliefs and practices.

Because Eastman wrote eleven books, and many journal articles and encyclopedia entries, and made scores of speeches over the years, all dealing with Indian culture, government Indian policy, and seeking to better the relations between Indians and whites, it would be difficult to identify the precise impact of any one of his books. But his first book, *Indian Boyhood*, was an immediate publishing success. It has been republished many times, and over a century after its first appearance, it is still in print and is still the subject of critical analysis by scholars of Native American history and culture, and by communication scholars studying the genre of autobiography. The book was sometimes used in public schools in the United States, at a time when few white students ever encountered anything written by a Native American author. Eastman became one of, if not the most famous American Indians of his day. All of his books sold well, and several were translated into a few foreign languages and sold widely overseas.

Toward the end of his life, Eastman had doubts about the kind of assimilation and acculturation her had urged Indians to pursue in his earlier writings. Although this book about his childhood does not lend itself to that kind of advocacy, it is interesting to read this book in conjunction with his later memoir of his adult years, *From the Deep Woods to Civilization*, published in 1916. Eastman lived long enough to see some movement away from the government's policies that had put a heavy emphasis on assimilating the American Indians, and he played a role in bringing about these changes. In 1923, he was asked to be part of the Committee of 100, a body of influential Americans who were asked to investigate conditions among the Indians and to make recommendations to the government for reform. Many of the problems this group identified were also noted by the Meriam Report published in 1928. This was a report produced for the Secretary of the Interior (the Bureau of Indian Affairs is part of the Department of the Interior) by an independent group consultants led by the social scientist Lewis Meriam. During the tenure of John Collier as Commissioner of the Bureau of Indian Affairs, many positive reforms were put in place. Collier was a friend of Eastman's, and believed the Indian people brought many positive things to American society. The disastrous policy of allotment was ended, and Collier directed that efforts should be made to preserve Indian languages and traditional arts and crafts.

——Mark S. Joy, PhD

Bibliography and Additional Reading

Allred, Christine Edwards. " 'Real Indian Art': Charles Eastman's Search for an Authenticating Culture Concept." In William R. Handley and Nathaniel Lewis, True West: Authenticity and the American West. Lincoln: University of Nebraska Press, 2004. Pp. 117-139.

Fitgerald, Michael Oren. The Essential Charles Eastman (Ohiyesa). Bloomington, IN: World Wisdom, 2007.

Heflin, Ruth J. "I Remain Alive": The Sioux Literary Renaissance. Syracuse, NY: Syracuse University Press, 2000.

Hertzberg, Hazel W. The Search for an American Indian Identity: Modern Pan-Indian Movements. Syracuse, NY: Syracuse University Press, 1971.

Katanski, Amelia. Learning to Write "Indian": The Boarding School Experience and American Indian Literature. Norman: University of Oklahoma Press, 2005.

Martínez, David. Dakota Philosopher: Charles Eastman and American Indian Thought. St. Paul: Minnesota Historical Society, 2009.

Wilson, Raymond. Ohiyesa: Charles Eastman, Santee Sioux. Urbana: University of Illinois Press, 1983.

Edward S. Curtis: Introduction to *The North American Indian*

Date: 1907
Author: Edward S. Curtis
Genre: book excerpt; essay

Summary Overview

This document is the introduction to the first volume of Curtis's massive work, *The North American Indian*, which eventually ran to twenty volumes with twenty accompanying portfolios of high-quality photographs. The set was completed in 1930. When Curtis wrote this introduction to the first volume, it is doubtful he had any idea how long it would take to complete the project. Curtis notes that the preliminary work on this project began in 1898. He believed he was racing against time in this project—he wanted to preserve a record of tribes that still maintained some of their traditional ways of life, but he believed this customs and traditions, and the Indian people themselves, would soon disappear. He believed the Indians would eventually be totally assimilated into the general American culture, and would disappear as a distinct people. He notes toward the end of the introduction, that if this project was delayed, it would not have been possible at all, because the traditional ways of life he was trying to record would have disappeared. Curtis describes some of his approach in this document—he wanted to present accurate depictions of Indian life, but he believed this could be done with artistry and attention to the aesthetic character of the subject. He notes that many native peoples were initially reluctant to describe their traditional ways of life and religious ceremonies, but that with patient exhibition of his good intentions, he eventually got them to open up to him. Although Curtis saw much to be admired in the traditional ways of the Indians, he also exhibits some of the racist views that were common among white Americans in that day, such as when he says the Indians will eventually be absorbed into the "superior race."

Defining Moment

Although Curtis may have hoped that the great mass of data he incorporated into *The North American Indian* and the iconic photographs he produced might reach the general public, in reality he was writing for an audience of wealthy Americans who could afford the expensive set of books and photographic portfolios. The books were sold by subscription, and of the complete set, only 500 were printed, and less than 300 of these were bound and distributed. President Theodore Roosevelt was a friend and supporter of Curtis, and partly through Roosevelt's suggestion, Curtis was able to get the financial backing of the financier J. Pierpont Morgan for the project. Over the many years he worked on the project, Curtis occasionally wrote articles for popular magazines, incorporating some of his research, so some of what he produced did reach a wider audience. In more recent times, advances in printing has made it possible to produce lower cost reproductions of many of his photographs, and much of his work has been reprinted in brief collections and it also accessible through various Internet sites.

Author Biography

Edward S. Curtis rose from impoverished circumstances to become a major American photographer. He was born in Whitewater, WI on February 16, 1868. In 1874, the family moved to Minnesota, and in 1885 Curtis became an apprentice in a photography studio in St. Paul. His interest in photography began with a camera he built, using a set of plans from a book, and a lens his father had acquired during the Civil War. In 1887, the family moved to Seattle, and in 1891, Curtis bought into a photography studio there. A few months later he moved to another studio, and soon became one of the preeminent photographers in the city.

Curtis attracted national attention in the mid-1890s with an illustrated article in *Century* magazine, and by winning a grand prize in a national photography exhibition. In 1898, an encounter with several scientists climbing Mount Ranier led to him becoming an official photographer on the Harriman Expedition to the Bering Sea in 1899. In 1904, Curtis was invited to photograph President Theodore Roosevelt's children. With Roosevelt's encouragement, Curtis approached financier J. Pierpont Morgan for support of his American Indian project. Morgan promised $75,000 over five years to pay for field work expenses, with Curtis receiving no salary. The project took more than 20 years, and after Morgan died, one of his sons continued intermittently to support Curtis's project.

Curtis married Clara Phillips in 1892, and they had four children together. For many years, she ran the studio in Seattle while Curtis was doing field work. Curtis was largely an absentee father and husband when he was involved in these expeditions, and in 1916, Clara divorced him, citing abandonment.

In his later years, Curtis work with his daughter Beth in a photography studio in Los Angeles. He also did still photography for some Hollywood film studios. He died in relative obscurity and poverty at his daughter Beth's home in Los Angeles, on October 21, 1952.

HISTORICAL DOCUMENT

GENERAL INTRODUCTION

The task of recording the descriptive material embodied in these volumes, and of preparing the photographs which accompany them, had its inception in 1898. Since that time, during each year, months of arduous labor have been spent in accumulating the data necessary to form a comprehensive and permanent record of all the important tribes of the United States and Alaska that still retain to a considerable degree their primitive customs and traditions. The value of such a work, in great measure, will lie in the breadth of its treatment, in its wealth of illustration, and in the fact that it represents the result of personal study of a people who are rapidly losing the traces of their aboriginal character and who are destined ultimately to become assimilated with the "superior race."

It has been the aim to picture all features of the Indian life and environment—types of the young and the old, with their habitations, industries, ceremonies, games, and everyday customs. Rather than being designed for mere embellishment, the photographs are each an illustration of an Indian character or of some vital phase in his existence. Yet the fact that the Indian and his surroundings lend themselves to artistic treatment has not been lost sight of, for in his country one may treat limitless subjects of an æsthetic character without in any way doing injustice to scientific accuracy or neglecting the homelier phases of aboriginal life. Indeed, in a work of this sort, to overlook those marvellous touches that Nature has given to the Indian country, and for the origin of which the native ever has a wonder-tale to relate, would be to neglect a most important chapter in the story of an environment that made the Indian much of what he is. Therefore, being directly from Nature, the accompanying pictures show what actually exists or has recently existed (for many of the subjects have already passed forever), not what the artist in his studio may presume the Indian and his surroundings to be.

The task has not been an easy one, for although lightened at times by the readiness of the Indians to impart their knowledge, it more often required days and weeks of patient endeavor before my assistants and I succeeded in overcoming the deep-rooted superstition, conservatism, and secretiveness so characteristic of primitive people, who are ever loath to afford a glimpse of their inner life to those who are not of their own. Once the confidence of the Indians gained, the way led gradually through the difficulties, but long and serious study was necessary before knowledge of the esoteric rites and ceremonies could be gleaned.

At times the undertaking was made congenial by our surroundings in beautiful mountain wild, in the depths of primeval forest, in the refreshing shade of cañon wall, or in the homes and sacred places of the Indians themselves; while at others the broiling desert sun, the sand-storm, the flood, the biting blast of winter, lent anything but pleasure to the task.

The word-story of this primitive life, like the pictures, must be drawn direct from Nature. Nature tells the story, and in Nature's simple words I can but place it before the reader. In great measure it must be written as these lines are—while I am in close touch with the Indian life.

At the moment I am seated by a beautiful brook that bounds through the forests of Apacheland.

Numberless birds are singing their songs of life and love. Within my reach lies a tree, felled only last night by a beaver, which even now darts out into the light, scans his surroundings, and scampers back. A covey of mourning doves fly to the water's edge, slake their thirst in their dainty way, and flutter off. By the brookside path now and then wander prattling children; a youth and a maiden hand in hand wend their way along the cool stream's brink. The words of the children and the lovers are unknown to me, but the story of childhood and love needs no interpreter.

It is thus near to Nature that much of the life of the Indian still is; hence its story, rather than being replete with statistics of commercial conquests, is a record of the Indian's relations with and his dependence on the phenomena of the universe—the trees and shrubs, the sun and stars, the lightning and rain,—for these to him are animate creatures. Even more than that, they are deified, therefore are revered and propitiated, since upon them man must depend for his well-being. To the workaday man of our own race the life of the Indian is just as incomprehensible as are the complexities of civilization to the mind of the untutored savage.

While primarily a photographer, I do not see or think photographically; hence the story of Indian life will not be told in microscopic detail, but rather will be presented as a broad and luminous picture. And I hope that while our extended observations among these brown people have given no shallow insight into their life and thought, neither the pictures nor the descriptive matter will be found lacking in popular interest.

Though the treatment accorded the Indians by those who lay claim to civilization and Christianity has in many cases been worse than criminal, a rehearsal of these wrongs does not properly find a place here. Whenever it may be necessary to refer to some of the unfortunate relations that have existed between the Indians and the white race, it will be done in that unbiased manner becoming the student of history. As a body politic recognizing no individual ownership of lands, each Indian tribe naturally resented encroachment by another race, and found it impossible to relinquish without a struggle that which belonged to their people from time immemorial. On the other hand, the white man whose very own may have been killed or captured by a party of hostiles forced to the warpath by the machinations of some unscrupulous Government employé, can see nothing that is good in the Indian. There are thus two sides to the story, and in these volumes such questions must be treated with impartiality.

Nor is it our purpose to theorize on the origin of the Indians—a problem that has already resulted in the writing of a small library, and still with no satisfactory solution. The object of the work is to record by word and picture what the Indian is, not whence he came. Even with this in view the years of a single life are insufficient for the task of treating in minute detail all the intricacies of the social structure and the arts and beliefs of many tribes. Nevertheless, by reaching beneath the surface through a study of his creation myths, his legends and folklore, more than a fair impression of the mode of thought of the Indian can be gained. In each instance all such material has been gathered by the writer and his assistants from the Indians direct, and confirmed, so far as is possible, through repetition by other members of their tribe.

Ever since the days of Columbus the assertion has been made repeatedly that the Indian has no religion and no code of ethics, chiefly for the reason that in his primitive state he recognizes no supreme God. Yet the fact remains that no people have a more elaborate religious system than our aborigines, and none are more devout in the performance of the duties connected therewith. There is scarcely an act in the Indian's life that does not involve some ceremonial performance or is not in itself a religious act, sometimes so complicated that much time and study are required to grasp even a part of its real meaning, for his myriad deities must all be propitiated lest some dire disaster befall him.

Likewise with their arts, which casual observers have sometimes denied the Indians; yet, to note a single example, the so-called "Digger" Indians, who have been characterized as in most respects the lowest type of all our tribes, are makers of delicately woven baskets, embellished with symbolic designs and so beautiful in form as to be works of art in themselves.

The great changes in practically every phase of the Indian's life that have taken place, especially within recent years, have been such that had the time for collecting much of the material, both descriptive and illustrative, herein recorded, been delayed, it would have been lost forever. The passing of every old man or woman means the passing of some tradition, some knowledge of sacred rites possessed by no other; consequently the information that is to be gathered, for the benefit of future generations, respecting the mode of life of one of the great races of mankind, must be collected at once or the opportunity will be lost for all time. It is this need that has inspired the present task.

In treating the various tribes it has been deemed advisable that a geographic rather than an ethnologic grouping be presented, but without losing sight of tribal relationships, however remote the cognate tribes may be one from another. To simplify the study and to afford ready reference to the salient points respecting the several tribes, a summary of the information pertaining to each is given in the appendices.

In the spelling of the native terms throughout the text, as well as in the brief vocabularies appended to each volume, the simplest form possible, consistent with approximate accuracy, has been adopted. No attempt has been made to differentiate sounds so much alike that the average student fails to discern the distinction, for the words, where recorded, are designed for the general reader rather than the philologist, and it has been the endeavor to encourage their pronunciation rather than to make them repellent by inverted and other arbitrary characters.

I take this opportunity to express my deep appreciation to those who have so generously lent encouragement during these years of my labor, from the humblest dwellers in frontier cabins to the captains of industry in our great commercial centres, and from the representatives of the most modest institutions of learning to those whose fame is worldwide. Without this encouragement the work could not have been accomplished. When the last opportunity for study of the living tribes shall have passed with the Indians themselves, and the day cannot be far off, my generous friends may then feel that they have aided in a work the results of which, let it be hoped, will grow more valuable as time goes on.

GLOSSARY

aboriginal, aborigines: the original in habitants of a region; thus, the American Indians are the aboriginal peoples of North America

"Digger" Indians: a derogatory term applied to Indians who lived in the Great Basin area in parts of Utah, Nevada, and California; they lived in a very bleak environment and had very little technology, so they were often considered "backward"

ethnologic grouping: a grouping of peoples based on ethnology, which is the study of the characteristics of different people groups and the differences between them

philologist: one who practices philology, the study of written languages and their transmission

Document Analysis

This document is Curtis's brief introduction to the massive collection entitled *The North American Indian*, which eventually totaled 20 volumes, and was not completed until 1930. Over the course of the project, Curtis took more than 40,000 photographs, and wrote many accounts of Indian customs and traditions.

Curtis states that his goal was to produce a study of all the important tribes in North America that "still retain to a considerable degree their primitive customs and traditions." While this was his stated goal, in reality the book deals only with tribes west of the Mississippi River, and he does not mention any awareness that even for the western tribes, many of their customs and ways of life had already been impacted by centuries of contact with Europeans and Americans. In the late 1800s, the federal government's Indian policy was often aimed at detribalizatiton—trying to break down the tribal bonds that tied Indian people to their culture, in an attempt to hasten assimilation. In some cases, Curtis photographed Indian performing religious ceremonies that had been outlawed by federal regulations. When he made a motion picture of Navajo dancers doing the sacred Snake Dance, some of the Navajo participants were later arrested for breaking such laws.

Curtis believed that his massive project was a race against time. The Native Americans were rapidly losing the aspects of their culture that he wanted to preserve. He notes that in some cases, individual Indians that he had photographed or interviewed in the early stages of the project had already passed away. Whenever any Indian elder died, there was a chance that the knowledge of some traditional lifeways was dying with them.

Like many Americans of his time, Curtis had a great interest in the Indians, and a genuine concern for their welfare, but at the same time exhibited racist assumptions. He believed the Indians were a "vanishing race" that were going to be completely assimilated into what he unhesitatingly called the "superior race." Since this was thought to be inevitable, Curtis never concerned himself with suggesting reforms that might delay or stop this process. As some modern scholars have noted, viewing people as a "vanishing" people might actually encourage actions that hasten their disappearance. In reality, Curtis was working at a time when the long decline of Native American population was ending, and the number of Indians was beginning a slow growth which turned into a rapid growth toward the end of the twentieth century.

Curtis often photographed his subjects outdoors, and in their natural environment. He notes the close connection of the Indian people to nature, and how much of their life revolves around this connection to nature, and to the things that nature provides for the sustenance of the people. He also comments about the Indian religions. Many people in early America thought the Indians had no religion, since they had no sacred texts or idols, and many did not seem to worship a supreme creator. Yet Curtis notes that many aspects of their daily lives were connected to their spiritual beliefs, and he recorded both photographs and written descriptions of many Indian religious customs.

Curtis writes that he intended to present the various features of Indian life without embellishment. He claimed that he was photographing what actually existed. Scholars today debate whether or not this is true. Curtis posed photographs, and his Indian subjects are often in elaborate costumes that were not likely their usual everyday clothing. In several portraits of individual Indian men, from various tribes, taken over a long period of time, the men all appear to be wearing the same shirt—was it perhaps a shirt that Curtis owned and thought was a "typical" Indian shirt? In a picture

1906. A Tewa girl. (IMAGE: EDWARD S. CURTIS/LIBRARY OF CONGRESS)

he took of Lakota Indians on the Pine Ridge Reservation, he attempted to recreate what a Lakota war party might have looked like—but by the time that picture was taken, it is unlikely any Lakotas had been in a war party for thirty years or more.

One of the thousands of pictures included in *The North American Indian* is reproduced here as an example of Curtis's photography. The Tewa girl portrait was taken in 1906. The Tewa are a part of the Pueblo people, and lived in villages along the Rio Grande River north of Santa Fe in New Mexico. The young woman's hair is done in what the Tewa called a "squash blossom" fashion. While nothing appears to be inauthentic about the young woman's clothing or the setting of the portrait, it does exhibit the "pictorialist" style of photography which Curtis embraced. The focus is soft; Curtis was not seeking sharp detail. Light and shadows are used artistically to create a certain mood or feeling in the portrait. While he endeavored to photograph what really existed, Curtis did so with an eye to artistic treatment which had made him a renowned and highly collected photographer.

Essential Themes

Curtis began *The North American Indian* project at a time when there was much interest in Native Americans, even though there remained a considerable amount of prejudice against them. Some of the interest in native peoples was clearly connected to this prejudice—they were seen as a quaint, pre-industrial people whose ways of life were disappearing, and thus there was a kind of antiquarian interest in knowing about their cultures, and preserving some knowledge of these cultures before they disappeared. Many Americans shared Curtis's view that the Indians would eventually be totally assimilated into the general American society and would disappear as a distinct people group. When Curtis shared his ideas for the project with President Theodore Roosevelt, the president told him it was good he was already working on this project, because it would not be possible to carry out if delayed too long.

The racism exhibited toward Native Americans was fueled by arguments among scientists about the origins of the different races of humanity. In earlier times it was generally believed that all humans come from common ancestors. But in the late nineteenth and early twentieth centuries, some scientists were suggesting that different races might have had different origins, and might have evolved differently over time. If so, it might be natural to assume that there might be differences between these races, and that some might be more advanced and capable than others. This so-called "scientific" view, which had largely been rejected by modern science, seemed to justify the racist assumptions that some ethnic groups were superior to others.

Curtis's photographic work also needs to be seen in the context of the "pictorialist" school of photography, also known as the "photo-secession" movement. These photographers emphasized the use of artistic effects in photography—more like a painting than a simple mechanical reproduction of the subject. Lighting and shading were used to great effect, and a soft focus was preferred rather than sharp, crisp detail. Alfred Stieglitz and Frank Eugene were the leading practitioners of pictorialism in the United States at this time, and Curtis was clearly influenced by their work.

The reception of Curtis's *The North American Indian* is a complex story in itself. It is a work more famous than read, due to its sheer size, and until recently, its rarity. Few people have actually seen an entire set of the books, let alone read them. When Curtis first began the work, the press was fascinated with it. Publication of the first few volumes were met not only with positive reviews, but with news stories about the accomplishment. But as the interval between the appearance of new volumes grew longer, the press generally lost interest. When the final volume was published in 1930, press response was virtually non-existent. The 20 volume set sold by subscription, and the price was $3500. Few sets were ever sold. In 1928 Curtis turned over all rights to the project, and much of his unpublished material, to the J. P. Morgan family. It appears he got nothing from this transaction other than a commitment that the Morgan family would see that the remaining volumes were published. In 1935, the Morgan family sold most of this material, including 19 bound sets of *The North American Indian* and thousands of glass negatives, copper printing plates, and photographic prints, to a Boston rare book dealer, Charles Lauriat, Jr., for $1000. This material was largely forgotten until the 1970s, when art collectors began seeking more examples of Curtis's work. Today, original Curtis prints sell for thousands of dollars, and in the early 2000s, entire sets of *The North American Indian* have sold for over $1 million. Some scholars believe Curtis is the world's most widely collected art photographer.

In the 1980s, scholars also began to rediscover Curtis, and numerous books, journal articles, and films have appeared since then dealing with his body of work. Some scholars applaud his efforts to record ways of life that were disappearing. Others criticize him for posing photographs, dressing his subjects in non-authentic clothing, and charge him with many inaccuracies. Native Americans, likewise, have varying opinions about Curtis and his work. Some are thankful for what he preserved, and sometimes can even identify their ancestors in his photos. Others criticize his racist assumptions, and charge him with "cultural appropriation"—taking parts of Indian culture for his own use. Neither the interest of collectors and art critics nor the work of scholars investigating Curtis seem to show any signs of abating in the near future.

——*Mark S. Joy, PhD*

Bibliography and Additional Reading

Egan, Timothy. Short Nights of the Shadow Catcher. New York: Mariner, 2012.

Gidley, Mick. Edward S. Curtis and the North American Indian, Incorporated. New York: Cambridge University Press, 1998.

Gidley, Mick, ed., Edward S. Curtis and the North American Indian Project in the Field. Lincoln: University of Nebraska Press, 2003.

Hausman, Gerald and Bob Kapoun, eds., Prayer to the Great Mystery: The Uncollected Writings and Photography of Edward S. Curtis. New York: St. Martins, 1995.

Lawlor, Laurie. Shadow Catcher: The Life and Work of Edward S. Curtis. Lincoln, NE: Bison Books, 2005.

Lyman, Christopher M. The Vanishing Race and Other Illusions: Photographs of Indians by Edward S. Curtis. New York: Pantheon Books, in association with the Smithsonian Institution Press, 1982.

Makepeace, Anne. Edward S. Curtis: Coming to the Light. Washington, DC: National Geographic Society, 2001.

Vizenor, Gerald. "Edward Curtis: Pictorialist and Ethnographic Adventurer." In William R. Handley and Nathaniel Lewis, eds., True West: Authenticity and the American West. Lincoln: University of Nebraska Press, 2004. Pp. 179-193.

Philosophy and Religion

Although by no means a representative sampling of the variety of American religious experience at the start of the twentieth century, the two documents examined in this section do reveal a small slice of the religious (and philosophical) life of the time. The first is by Rufus Jones, a lauded Quaker historian and theologian who helped set up an organization that later became the American Friends Service Committee. The second document hails from the pen of Rudolf Steiner, an Austrian esoteric thinker whose "anthroposophical" writings enjoyed great popularity in the United States and elsewhere.

Rufus M. Jones: "Essential Truths"

Date: 1900
Genre: religious tract
Author: Rufus Matthew Jones (January 25, 1863–June 16, 1948)

Summary Overview

"Essential Truths" written by Rufus M. Jones, is a statement of belief of the Religious Society of Friends from the early twentieth century. It is an excerpt from a larger document known as the Uniform Discipline, which was completed in 1900 by Jones and another American Friend, James E. Wood (1839–1925). A discipline is a document that outlines the organizational structure, standards, and beliefs of the Religious Society of Friends and acts a guide for the gathered community of faith. The earliest discipline was written in 1668 by George Fox and served as the basis for later disciplines in England and America. The Uniform Discipline was adopted by a group of Quakers (the informal name for Friends) in 1902, the Five Years Meeting of the Friends in America. The "Essential Truths" section was one of three documents included in the Five Years Meeting's Authorized Declaration of Faith in 1922. The other two documents are George Fox's Letter to the Governor of Barbados, from 1671, and the Declaration of Faith (or Richmond Declaration) put forward at a conference held in Richmond, Indiana, in 1887, written by the English Quaker Joseph Bevan Braithwaite, with the help of two American Quakers, James E. Rhoads and James Carey Thomas.

The Religious Society of Friends was founded in the late 1640s in England by George Fox (1624–1691). Today most Quakers affirm that they are Christians like the Protestant denominations established during and after the Reformation era, including Lutherans, Baptists, Methodists, and the Reformed. Some Quakers do not affirm a strictly Christian identity, however, and have embraced a more universalist perspective about the role of Jesus in history. "Essential Truths" does not represent the beliefs of all Quakers. It applies chiefly to the yearly meetings that hold membership in the Five Years Meeting, known since 1960 as Friends United Meeting (FUM). (*Yearly meeting* is the Quaker term for both the annual sessions at which the business of a region is done and the name of that geographic region that contains the individual congregations or monthly meetings.) The Quakers of these yearly meetings were most influenced by the evangelical Protestantism of the nineteenth century. They are known as Orthodox Friends or Gurneyite Friends, after the influential English Quaker minister Joseph John Gurney (1788–1847). By the late nineteenth century there were, in fact, three distinct branches of Quakerism in America—Hicksite, Orthodox, and Conservative—all divided over Quaker beliefs and practices. Historically, "Essential Truths" represents an attempt by the Orthodox Quakers to carve out their own religious identity vis-à-vis the other branches of Quakerism and other Protestant denominations. It followed earlier efforts at Orthodox self-definition, most notably that of the Richmond Conference in 1887 and the Declaration of Faith that came out of that conference.

The member yearly meetings of FUM do not believe that the "Essential Truths" or the other statements in the Authorized Declaration of Faith are authoritative in the same manner as creeds in the Protestant and Catholic churches. The session of the Five Years Meeting in 1912 concluded that the Richmond Declaration and other statements of faith were "not to be regarded as constituting a creed." When the Five Years Meeting finally adopted the three statements into the Authorized Declaration of Faith in 1922, it again emphasized that the statements were not creeds. Further, a study done by the General Board of FUM in 1974 affirmed the decisions of the 1922 meeting of the Five Years Meeting, and it too pointed out the limitations of doctrinal statements.

The Five Years Meeting had recognized the Authorized Declaration of Faith as a statement of belief for over twenty years when a committee drafted a revision of the Uniform Discipline in 1945. The member yearly meetings could not agree on the doctrinal statements in the revised version, however, and the yearly meetings were left to use those statements as they saw fit. Despite the lack of unity with respect to the Uniform Discipline and the Authorized Declaration of Faith since that time, the "Essential Truths" remains an important statement of Quaker belief within FUM. Of the three documents that comprise the Authorized Declaration of Faith, Essential Truths has been the least controversial, characterized as it is by simplicity and brevity. FUM member yearly meetings still use it as a guide for understanding what they believe about God, Jesus Christ, the Holy Spirit, ministry, the Fall, the Resurrection, the Bible, and other matters of their faith.

Defining Moment

The context necessary for understanding "Essential Truths" extends back to the early nineteenth century in America, when the Religious Society of Friends was united by distinct beliefs and practices that separated it from its Protestant and Catholic neighbors. Quakers were quietists, which means that they sought to live a life of meditation and reflection. They focused on the workings of the Holy Spirit on the soul, not on liturgical forms of worship. Friends believed that scripted preaching, sacraments, and other external forms of the expression of grace were distractions in their quest for unity with and obedience to God, and they maintained silence in their worship where they listened for the Holy Spirit. When preaching did occur, it was to be under the direct inspiration of the Holy Spirit, as planning and preparation in the form of writing out the sermon in advance or memorizing it were frowned upon. Such spontaneous preaching could be offered by anyone sitting in the silent worship—man, woman, or child—in obedience to the prompting of the Holy Spirit.

The hallmark belief of the historical Quakers was George Fox's doctrine of the Light, the divine light of Christ within each soul that, if followed, could lead to salvation. This has come to be referred to as the Inward Light or, more commonly, Inner Light. Fox and other early Friends affirmed the Atonement, that is, the belief that Christ died for one's sins, but they subordinated it to their focus on following the Light through the trials and tribulations of life. Unlike the Protestant notion of justification by grace, which privileged the moment of salvation, Quakers rarely spoke of a decisive moment of conversion and instead focused on the process of obeying the Light. Moreover, Quakers did not speak of going to a "church" but gathered together with fellow believers to worship in silence at the "meeting for worship" which did not need a special building and might be held anywhere.

The concept of the Inner Light became controversial in the early nineteenth century as Quakers came into contact with evangelical preachers of the Second Great Awakening who used revivals to win converts to their faith. Evangelicalism is difficult to define, but the primary characteristic shared by most evangelicals is the emotional conversion experience through which the believer could claim a personal relationship with God. Many evangelicals of the day united justification (the moment of salvation) and sanctification (the process of becoming more holy) into the conversion experience, which meant that a new believer could claim a life of complete holiness and freedom from sin. This was incongruous with the Quaker ideal of gradually working out one's salvation by obeying the Inner Light.

The Great Separation of 1827–1828 at the sessions of Philadelphia Yearly Meeting divided Quakers sympathetic to the beliefs of the evangelicals from those who maintained the centrality of the Inner Light at the expense of traditional "orthodox" Christian doctrines. The latter group, called Hicksites after their leader Elias Hicks (1748–1830), a Long Island farmer, tended to spiritualize Jesus and did not believe in a moment of justification through the death and resurrection of Christ on the cross. Hicks argued that Jesus was the Son of God in the same sense that all people were. Jesus was an example to follow because he had perfectly obeyed his Inner Light. Hicks also claimed that the revelation of scripture was subordinate to the power of the Holy Spirit. In so doing, he did away with many of the doctrines central to traditional Christianity, most notably the atonement and original sin. This prompted the Orthodox group to denounce Hicks and his followers and to emphasize the divinity of Christ, the atonement, and the authority of the Bible over the authority of the Holy Spirit.

The Second Separation, between the Gurneyite Orthodox and the Wilburite Conservatives, happened at New England Yearly Meeting sessions in 1845–1846. The Orthodox Friends were led by Joseph John Gurney, a British biblical scholar, church historian, linguist, and preacher who traveled extensively as a missionary in Europe and America. Although he was a proponent of the Inner Light and the traditional Quaker form of silent worship, Gurney believed (with the evangelicals) that the Bible was the divinely inspired Word of God and that salvation depended on faith in the atoning death of Jesus Christ. His opponent, John Wilbur (1774–1856), was a Rhode Island farmer and land surveyor who traveled in the ministry among Friends in New England and New York yearly meetings during the years 1821–1827 and 1833–1837. Wilbur disagreed with Gurney's belief in the higher authority of the Bible over the Holy Spirit and therefore opposed the Gurneyite focus on Bible study. The Wilburites chose to separate themselves from the "world" that they believed had corrupted Gurney and his followers. Many Orthodox meetings in America were soon divided into Gurneyite and Wilburite factions.

The Orthodox Gurneyite Quakers found themselves divided yet again in the decades after the Civil War. During that period, some Orthodox meetings began implementing a system of planned "programmed" worship in imitation of their evangelical peers, even going so far as to hire pastors who brought prepared messages every Sunday, in direct opposition to George Fox's many injunctions against "the hireling ministry." Friends in Iowa, Indiana, and Kansas resisted these changes and established their own yearly meetings. These so-called Conservative Friends held to the older "unprogrammed" mode of Quaker worship shared by the Hicksites and by the Wilburites, from whom they became largely indistinguishable over time. The contrast between the pastoral and silent modes of Quaker worship is the most visible difference between the Orthodox and the Conservative and Hicksite Friends today, and it reflects the theological divide between those nineteenth-century Quakers who were more receptive to evangelical theology and those who held to Fox's notion of the Light as a gradual quietist means to salvation.

The late nineteenth century introduced new challenges to the Orthodox heirs of Gurney, including a crisis over the place of the ordinances of water baptism and physical communion shared by most evangelical Christians. The Orthodox grew increasingly concerned about the diversity of belief and practice in their yearly meetings. Many were sympathetic with the Conservatives, while others, known as "Waterites" were clearly in the evangelical camp; the latter supported the toleration of water baptism in their worship services. Some Orthodox Quakers, including David B. Updegraff (1830–1894) of Ohio Yearly Meeting, also believed in the evangelical "holiness" notion that once one was saved one could live a sanctified life free of all propensity or desire to sin. As early as 1870, one of the Orthodox yearly meetings, Western Yearly Meeting (of western Indiana), proposed a general council of all the yearly meetings to try to resolve this growing disunity. In 1887 the representatives from the Orthodox yearly meetings finally convened in Richmond, Indiana, to deal with the three major issues that had proved most divisive: the nature of sanctification through the Holy Spirit, the professional ministry, and the ordinances of baptism and Communion. The major players included those committed to evangelical theological principles of the wider Christian world such as Updegraff, conservatives like Joseph Bevan Braithwaite who valued the historic Quaker writings, and a middle party that sought to steer the Orthodox between the extremes of evangelical and Conservative Quakerism.

The Richmond Declaration's statements about God, the Holy Spirit, the Fall, the Bible, and conversion show the influence of evangelical Christianity. The Declaration devotes no attention to Fox's doctrine of the Light except to disavow it by claiming that there is no spiritual light inherent in human beings. On the other hand, it does not explicitly endorse an extreme evangelical "holiness" view on sanctification, as it affirms both justification and sanctification without claiming that one can live a life free from temptation. Nevertheless, its critics have argued that the language of the Declaration on sanctification strays too far from the historical Quaker focus on a life of quiet obedience to God. On the question of a professional ministry, the Declaration is rather vague, claiming that worship "stands neither in forms nor in the formal disuse of forms: it may be without words as well as with them, but it must be in spirit and in truth (John 4:24)." Finally, against the Waterites and those who tolerated the ordinances, the Declaration affirms the spiritual meaning of baptism and Communion as means of fellowship with Christ and the Holy Spirit.

The Richmond Conference did not resolve all the issues within Orthodox Quakerism, but it did manage to address pressing concerns for the Orthodox Quakers. The Richmond Declaration provided a statement of belief for the yearly meetings, although not all yearly meetings took identical actions toward it. Western (Indiana), Iowa, Kansas, and North Carolina yearly meetings adopted the Richmond Declaration into their books of discipline, while London, Ohio, and New England only noted it in their meeting minutes. New York, Baltimore, and Dublin yearly meetings approved the declaration but did not formally adopt it. Nonetheless, the Richmond Declaration set the Orthodox Quakers on the path to further self-definition, a path that led to the drafting of the Uniform Discipline a decade later. Indeed, William Nicholson (1826–1899), the clerk of Kansas Yearly Meeting, proposed forming a triennial conference of yearly meetings. His proposal led to quinquennial meetings, with the next meeting in 1892—hence the name Five Years Meeting adopted in

1902. It was at the meeting in 1897 that the delegates decided to draft the Uniform Discipline, which was completed in 1900 and from which "Essential Truths" is taken.

The original audience for the Uniform Discipline, from which "Essential Truths" is taken, was the Five Years Meeting of Friends in America, officially formed in 1902. The first yearly meeting to accept the Uniform Discipline was New England Yearly Meeting in 1900. The Orthodox yearly meetings in Baltimore, California, Indiana, Iowa, New York, North Carolina, Oregon, Western (Indiana), and Wilmington (Ohio) accepted it soon afterward, but Ohio Yearly Meeting did not. As the Five Years Meeting grew, so did the audience for the Uniform Discipline. For example, Canadian Yearly Meeting joined the Five Years Meeting in 1907, as did Nebraska Yearly Meeting in 1908.

Nevertheless, several yearly meetings were divided or left the Five Years Meeting because of further controversies over Orthodox Quaker identity. The decision of the Five Years Meeting to appoint the modernist Walter C. Woodward to the post of executive secretary in 1917 rankled those yearly meetings more sympathetic to fundamentalism. The inclusion of the Richmond Declaration in the Authorized Declaration of Faith in 1922 also proved controversial. Many meetings were divided between modernists like Rufus Jones and fundamentalist-friendly Quakers who wanted the Authorized Declaration to have the creedal authority to push the "unsound" modernists out of the Five Years Meeting. Oregon Yearly Meeting left in 1925, and many Friends sympathetic to fundamentalism in Indiana, Western, and California yearly meetings had left the Five Years Meeting by 1930.

The audience for the Uniform Discipline and "Essential Truths" has remained fluid to this day, as FUM has experienced both divisions and reunifications ever since. Moreover, the Orthodox failure to reach a consensus on the doctrinal statements in the 1945 revision of the Uniform Discipline has led to more diversity among the yearly meetings. The only fail-safe way to determine which FUM yearly meetings use the Essential Truths section is to read their individual disciplines.

About the Author

Rufus M. Jones was a scholar, peace activist, and mystic who emerged as a leading voice among Orthodox Quakers in the decade following the Richmond Conference in 1887. He was particularly influential for his role in the rise of modernist Quakerism, the attempt to reconcile Quaker beliefs with the conclusions of both modern science and historical criticism of the Bible (the application of scientific methods of study to the Bible not as a sacred text but as a historical document). Modernist Quakers hold the position that scientific and historical findings do not endanger their beliefs because, as many Friends contend, God progressively reveals new truths about the world and the Christian faith to humanity.

Jones was born in South China, Maine, in 1863 to a devout Gurneyite Quaker family and went to Quaker schools, including Providence Friends School in Rhode Island and Haverford College in Pennsylvania. While at Haverford, Jones encountered the founder of the Quakers, George Fox, through his reading of Ralph Waldo Emerson's *Essays*. He was especially impressed by Fox's focus on direct spiritual experience of the divine, and he regarded Fox as a mystic, that is, someone who seeks direct contact with the divine through religious experience.

Jones's work for the Orthodox Friends in America cannot be overstated, nor can his impact on American Quakerism. In the early 1890s he became deeply involved in the Religious Society of Friends, and in 1893 he became editor of the *Friends Review*, the most influential journal of Gurneyite Quakerism. One year later he was instrumental in the merger of the *Friends Review* with the *Christian Worker*, a Quaker publication based in Chicago. The result was a new journal published in Philadelphia called *American Friend*. Through *American Friend*, Jones became more popular and influential among Quakers of all persuasions and began moving toward a modernist theological position, especially after an extended trip to Europe in 1897. During this trip, Jones became close to a group of modernist Quakers in England who accepted the theory of evolution as well as historical critical study of the Bible. Among others, these Friends included John Wilhelm Rowntree and William Braithwaite.

Jones's work with James Woods on the Uniform Discipline, especially the "Essential Truths" section, is but one of many examples of his enduring influence on Orthodox Quakerism by his death in 1948. He lectured widely across the United States, Europe, and parts of Asia, and he was highly respected by Quakers around the world. He produced fifty-four books between 1889 and 1948 in addition to countless book chapters and introductions, journal and magazine articles, and book reviews. He trained volunteers at Haverford College for relief work in France during World War I, an effort that led to the formation of the American Friends Service Committee. Jones also helped establish the Friends World Committee for Consultation in 1937, an organization that grew out of a global All Friends Conference in London in the midst of World War I. In 1945, Jones managed to reunite New England Yearly Meeting, the setting of the original Gurneyite-Wilburite split; the Gurneyite yearly meeting, the Wilburite yearly meeting, and five independent Quaker monthly meetings came together to form one yearly meeting. Jones's influence was such that many Friends around the world regarded him as the preeminent spokesperson of Quakerism to non-Quakers. He died in 1948.

HISTORICAL DOCUMENT

The vital principle of the Christian faith is the truth that man's salvation and higher life are personal matters between the individual soul and God.

Salvation is deliverance from sin and the possession of spiritual life. This comes through a personal faith in Jesus Christ as the Savior, who, through his love and sacrifice draws us to Him.

Conviction for sin is awakened by the operation of the Holy Spirit causing the soul to feel its need of reconciliation with God. When Christ is seen as the only hope of Salvation, and a man yields to Him, he is brought into newness of life, and realizes that his sonship to God has become an actual reality. This transformation is wrought without the necessary agency of any human priest, or ordinance, or ceremony whatsoever. A changed nature and life bear witness to this new relation to Him.

The whole spiritual life grows out of the soul's relation to God and its co-operation with Him, not from any outward or traditional observances.

Christ Himself baptizes the surrendered soul with the Holy Spirit, enduing it with power, bestowing gifts for service. This is an efficient baptism, a direct incoming of divine power for the transformation and control of the whole man. Christ Himself is the Spiritual bread which nourishes the soul, and He thus enters into and becomes a part of the being of those who partake of Him. This participation with Christ and apprehension of Him become the goal of life for the Christian. Those who thus enter into oneness with Him become also joined in living union with each other as members of one body.

Both worship and Christian fellowship spring out of this immediate relation of believing souls with their Lord.

The Holy Scriptures were given by inspiration of God and are the divinely authorized record of the doctrines which Christians are bound to accept, and of the moral principles which are to regulate their lives and actions. In them, as interpreted and unfolded by the Holy Spirit, is an ever fresh and unfailing source of spiritual truth for the proper guidance of life and practice.

The doctrines of the apostolic days are held by the Friends as essentials of Christianity. The Fatherhood of God, the Deity and humanity of the Son; the gift of the Holy Spirit; the atonement through Jesus Christ by which men are reconciled to God; the Resurrection; the High priesthood of Christ, and the individual priesthood of believers, are most precious truths, to be held, not as traditional dogmas, but as vital, life-giving realities.

The sinful condition of man and his proneness to yield to temptation, the world's absolute need of a Saviour, and the cleansing from sin in forgiveness and sanctification through the blood of Jesus Christ, are unceasing incentives to all who believe to become laborers together with God in extending His kingdom. By this high calling the Friends are pledged to the proclamation of the truth wherever the Spirit leads, both in home and in foreign fields.

The indwelling Spirit guides and controls the surrendered life, and the Christian's constant and supreme business is obedience to Him. But while the importance of individual guidance and obedience is thus emphasized, this fact gives no ground for license; the sanctified conclusions of the Church are above the judgment of a single individual.

The Friends find no scriptural evidence or authority for any form or degree of sacerdotalism in the Christian Church, or for the establishment of any ordinance or ceremonial rite for perpetual observance. The teachings of Jesus Christ concerning the spiritual nature of religion, the impossibility of promoting the spiritual life by the ceremonial application of material things, the fact that faith in Jesus Christ Himself is all-sufficient, the purpose of His life, death, resurrection and ascension, and His presence in the believer's heart, virtually destroy every ceremonial system and point the soul to the only satisfying source of spiritual life and power.

With faith in the wisdom of Almighty God, the Father, the Son and the Holy Spirit, and believing that it is His purpose to make His Church on earth a power for righteousness and truth, the Friends labor for the alleviation of human suffering; for the intellectual, moral and spiritual elevation of mankind; and for purified and exalted citizenship. The Friends believe war to be incompatible with Christianity, and seek to promote peaceful methods for the settlement of all the differences between nations and between men.

It is an essential part of the faith that a man should be in truth what he professes in word, and the underlying principle of life and action for individuals, and also for society, is transformation through the power of God and implicit obedience to His revealed will.

GLOSSARY

apostolic days: New Testament times, when Christ's apostles preached and spread Christianity

sacerdotalism: a system of worship that requires priests to act as mediators between God and humans by engaging in religious ceremonies

Document Analysis

"Essential Truths" is rather short, being only thirteen paragraphs long and less than a thousand words in length. As such, it lends itself to detailed analysis. It portrays the Quaker faith as spiritualist, that is, unattached to the external ceremonies or ordinances of the Protestants and Catholics. Jones opposed the evangelicalism of some of the Orthodox yearly meetings, and "Essential Truths" reflects this point of view throughout the text. The evangelical tone of the Richmond Declaration is noticeably absent. In fact, Jones was opposed to the Declaration, calling it a "poor thin mediocre expression" of the Quaker faith, as quoted in Elizabeth Vining's biography. He used his influence at the formation of the Five Years Meeting in 1902 to prevent its inclusion in the Uniform Discipline.

Jones begins by focusing on the nature of the soul's relationship to God, claiming that the "vital principle of the Christian faith" is a personal relationship between the soul and God. This statement affirms the evangelical claim that the Christian faith is personal, yet it also includes Jones's vision of Quaker spirituality. Jones's use of the term *higher life* alongside *salvation* suggests that the Christian faith is about more than salvation, the final destination of the believer. It is also about the spiritual journey of the soul to God.

Jones makes the traditional claim that salvation is "deliverance from sin" through a "personal" faith in Christ and also notes that Christ's "love and sacrifice" draw the believer to God. It is noteworthy that the word *sacrifice* follows *love* and that there is no mention of the nature of this sacrifice. It is left to the reader to decide if Jones means the atonement (Christ's death and Resurrection) or some other kind of sacrifice, for he does not use the traditional evangelical code words such as *blood, cross,* or *propitiation*. Instead, Jones's focus is on how Jesus Christ "draws us to Him" which again suggests that the Christian life is a journey of the believer to God.

Jones introduces the role of the Holy Spirit in salvation. There is no mention of the Inner Light, as the historic Quaker doctrine was too controversial for the

Orthodox yearly meetings that preferred the Richmond Declaration. Although Jones would soon offer his thoughts on the Inner Light in his *Social Law and the Spiritual World* from 1904, "Essential Truths" is entirely silent on the matter. Instead, Jones writes a statement acceptable to the traditional position that there is no innate divine light or spark that allows a soul to move toward God on its own. The Holy Spirit must awaken a conviction for sin and act as the first mover, as it were, in the conversion experience. In addition, Jones denies the traditional Catholic notion of the priest as a go-between, or intercessor, between the believer and God. He also denies the notions of ordinances and ceremonies.

Jones comments here on the "whole spiritual life" of cooperation with God in contrast to the religious life of outward ceremonies and material aids. For Jones in "Essential Truths" these external forms are of no avail with respect to the spiritual life of the believer. Thus he reasserts the conclusions of the preceding paragraph: True Quaker Christianity looks inward to the soul, not outward to ceremonies used by Protestants and Catholics.

This is the section on the Quaker understanding of baptism and Communion. Unlike most Christians, who retained an actual water baptism for infants or adults, the Quakers affirmed a spiritual, inward baptism of the Holy Spirit. Jones does not stray from that historic Quaker position, noting that the spiritual baptism of the Holy Spirit empowers the believer's soul and bestows the believer with "gifts for service." He then addresses Holy Communion, which Protestants and Catholics usually celebrate with bread and wine or similar symbols of Christ's Last Supper. Jones again turns to the historic Quaker position that Christ is "Spiritual bread" that nourishes the soul of the believer. Using the Platonic language of "participation" that is, the idea that a physical, temporal being can somehow share or "participate" in an eternal spiritual being, he emphasizes that the goal of the Christian life for the believer is to unite with Christ. Moreover, those who unite with Christ are also united in a "living union with each other as members of one body."

Jones notes that Christian worship and fellowship are the fruits of the Quaker spiritualist belief in a personal relationship with God. For Jones, as well as for many other modernist Orthodox Quakers, a common fear was that too much emphasis on a personal, spiritualist faith would lead to isolated quietist spiritualism outside the gathering of the faithful. Thus Jones asserts that true spiritual religion is necessarily social, since it springs out of the relationship between believers and Christ.

Jones addresses the authority of holy scripture, and here "Essential Truths" departs from the Richmond Declaration. While Christians are "bound to accept" its doctrines and are to regulate their lives by its moral teachings, Jones does not privilege any one interpretation of the Bible over another, noting instead that scripture is to be "interpreted and unfolded" by the leadings of the Holy Spirit in the soul of the believer.

This is the first paragraph in which the Jones uses the word Friends to identify his audience. He confirms the importance of the traditional "apostolic" beliefs of Christianity: God understood as Father; the "Deity and humanity of the Son" both God and man; "the gift of the Holy Spirit"; the atonement; and the Resurrection. Jones also affirms the "High priesthood of Christ" and the "individual priesthood of believers" references to the traditional Protestant claim, against the Catholic Church, that believers do not require a priestly mediator between themselves and God for forgiveness of their sins and, ultimately, their salvation.

Jones turns to the missionary impulse of Christianity in this paragraph. He notes that because Christ died for the sins of humanity, it is the just calling of Quakers that they work together with God "in extending His kingdom" by going wherever they may be needed, whether at home or in foreign mission fields. They are to proclaim the truth of their beliefs through the leading of the Holy Spirit. This is the only place in "Essential Truths" where Jones uses traditional Atonement language, including the words blood and cleansing. He also affirms that the condition of humanity is sinful and "prone to temptation" which contradicts the "holiness" claims of evangelical Friends like David B. Updegraff. Jones addresses the issue of authority in this paragraph. He notes that surrender to the Holy Spirit and obedience to "Him" are what believers should strive for, but not at the expense of the judgments of the community as a whole. He argues that "the sanctified conclusions of the Church are above the judgment of a single individual." This is Jones's first use of the word Church in the document, and it is used in the traditional sense of the gathered community of faith, wherever it may be.

The Quaker spiritualist focus dominates this paragraph, as Jones affirms the historic Quaker conviction that there is no scriptural evidence for "sacerdotalism" that is, a system of worship that requires priests (the Latin sacerdos means "priest") to act as mediators between God and humans by engaging in religious ceremonies. For Jones, it is impossible to promote the spiritual life "through the ceremonial application of material things" since the presence of Jesus Christ in the believer's heart is sufficient for true religion. Jones writes that Christ's teaching, his life, his death, and his Resurrection "virtually destroy every ceremonial system and point the soul to the only satisfying source of spiritual life and power."

Jones here refers to the historic Quaker commitment to nonviolence, a commitment shared by certain other radical Christian groups from the sixteenth and seventeenth centuries, most notably the Anabaptists (the Mennonites, Amish, and Hutterite Brethren). Historically, the Anabaptists were those Christians during the Reformation era who rejected infant baptism; they believed that one must have faith in Christ before being baptized. From their reading of the New Testament, most Anabaptists also believed that that they should not bear arms and wage war and thus followed the example of Christ and his apostles. Jones again uses the word Church to describe the community of faith that is to work for justice, the alleviation of suffering, and the spiritual and moral improvement of humanity in general. For Quakers, war is "incompatible with Christianity."

Jones takes up the matter of oaths in this paragraph. Historically, the Quakers had always been opposed to swearing oaths. In this they were again like the Anabaptist groups. For the Quakers, telling the truth has always been a fundamental aspect of faith, and they believe that the taking of an oath (for example, an oath of loyalty or an oath to tell the truth) suggests that a person might otherwise not be truthful. Jones thus emphasizes the historic Quaker commitment to telling the truth by claiming that it is an essential part of faith that one's words match one's beliefs.

Essential Themes

"Essential Truths" is an important statement of faith for FUM and a testament to the influence of modernist thought within Orthodox Quakerism at the turn of the twentieth century. The moderate language used by Rufus Jones contrasts with the evangelical tone that characterizes the Richmond Declaration of Faith. Nevertheless, "Essential Truths" has clearly been overshadowed by the Richmond Declaration, which has become far more controversial within FUM and the Religious Society of Friends generally. For example, an evangelical splinter group from FUM formed in the mid-twentieth century, Evangelical Friends Alliance (now International), adapted its constitution from the Richmond Declaration of Faith. Moreover, in 1987, the FUM Triennial Meeting could not agree about the status of the Richmond Declaration and therefore did not reaffirm it, opting instead for a statement known among Friends as the Two o'Clock Minute. Twenty years later, however, the FUM General Board, meeting in Kenya, reaffirmed the Richmond Declaration as a statement of faith while not requiring adoption of it for membership, a development that has troubled some FUM Friends and prompted scholars to reflect on the future direction of FUM.

Ongoing Quaker debates about the status of the Richmond Declaration stand in full relief to the relative silence with respect to "Essential Truths." This silence speaks to the unifying character of "Essential Truths" which manages to assert Quaker distinctiveness with respect to its historical spiritualism and pacifism while also affirming "orthodox" Christian beliefs about God, Christ, the Holy Spirit, justification and sanctification, the Bible, and the church. With the Uniform Discipline and its "Essential Truths" the Orthodox Quakers were able to establish the Five Years Meeting in America in 1902. This group eventually became FUM, now headquartered in Richmond, Indiana. As of 2010 FUM is the largest organization of Quakers in the world, with eleven yearly meetings in North America in addition to yearly meetings in the Caribbean and East Africa. Kenya is particularly significant, with fifteen yearly meetings as of 2010 and the majority of FUM members.

——Adam W. Darlage, PhD

Bibliography and Further Reading

Abbott, Margery Post, et al., eds. *Historical Dictionary of the Friends (Quakers)*. Lanham, Md.: Scarecrow Press, 2003.

Fox, George. *The Works of George Fox*. 8 vols. Philadelphia: Marcus T. C. Gould, 1831.

Hamm, Thomas D. *The Transformation of American Quakerism: Orthodox Friends, 1800–1907*. Bloomington: Indiana University Press, 1988.

Jones, Rufus M. *Social Law in the Spiritual World: Studies in Human and Divine Inter-Relationship*. New York: Swarthmore Press, 1923.

Mekeel, Arthur J. *Quakerism and a Creed*. Philadelphia: Friends Book Store, 1936.

Minear, Mark. *Richmond 1887: A Quaker Drama Unfolds*. Richmond, Ind.: Friends United Press, 1987.

Minutes and Proceedings of the Five Years Meeting of the American Yearly Meetings Held in Indianapolis, Indiana, 1902. Philadelphia: J. C. Winston, 1903.

Proceedings, Including the Declaration of Christian Doctrine: Of the General Conference of Friends, Held in Richmond, Ind., U.S.A., 1887. Richmond, Ind.: Nicholson, 1887.

Vining, Elizabeth Gray. *Friend of Life: The Biography of Rufus M. Jones*. Philadelphia: Lippincott, 1958.

Hamm, Thomas D. "Friends United Meeting and Its Identity: An Interpretative History." *Quaker Life* (January–February 2009): 10–15. Available online at http://www.fum.org/QL/issues/0901/FUM_Identity_Hamm.htm

"Friends United Meeting: About FUM—Declaration of Faith." Friends United Meeting Web site. http://www.fum.org/about/declarationfaith.htm#Worship

Rudolf Steiner: *Theosophy*

Date: 1904
Author: Rudolf Joseph Lorenz Steiner (February 25, 1861—March 30, 1925)
Genre: book chapter

Summary Overview

Rudolf Steiner wrote *Theosophy: An Introduction to the Spiritual Processes in Human Life and in the Cosmos* (1904) as part of his lifelong project to reconcile the sensory and supersensory realms in the study of the nature of human beings. These two dimensions are clearly evident from the very subtitle of the book, in which spiritual processes are perceived to be part of human life. The book identifies three spheres of existence—body, soul, and spirit, which are interdependent and structure human life. At the heart of the book lies Steiner's reworking of the concepts of reincarnation of the spirit and karma, which the author elaborates differently from Oriental philosophies and identifies as a doctrine that could give purpose to human existence.

According to his autobiography, Steiner was aware from a very early age of the existence of the visible as well as an invisible world—the latter world with which he felt more at ease. He admits candidly to his difficulty in learning factual and measurable data about natural objects and phenomena. Accordingly, he states his preference for the spiritual realm, which, to him, always bore the genuine character of reality. Steiner thus set out to modify the prevailing materialist and positivist beliefs, rooted in sensory experience and empirical evidence, that marked philosophical thought at the turn of the twentieth century in favor of the spiritual science that he called Anthroposophy; he worked to create a connection between the physical and the spiritual worlds. The very term *Anthroposophy* identifies knowledge of the human condition that encompasses both its spirituality and its physicality (with *anthropo* referencing the human being and *sophia* meaning "wisdom"). Steiner's mode of thought entails the belief that to understand the world, knowledge of the physical must be complemented with the spiritual dimensions, as both are equally part of the human condition. A type of knowledge that rests merely on sensory impressions cannot lead to the satisfaction of the innate spiritual quest of the human soul.

Steiner intended *Theosophy* as an introduction to the knowledge of the spiritual world and the fate of the human being. The book grew out of his intense activity as a lecturer in the German and other European theosophical circles in which he was engaged at the turn of the century. Its genesis is also to be found in Steiner's reworking of the articles in *Lucifer* and *Lucifer-Gnosis*, two successive theosophical reviews that he founded and edited in Berlin. With *Theosophy*, Steiner gave his spiritual philosophy book-length treatment, dedicating it to the spirit of Giordano Bruno, the sixteenth-century Italian philosopher who was burned at the stake as a heretic by the Catholic Inquisition for his claim that the universal soul continuously reincarnates in different forms.

Defining Moment

The cultural seeds for the composition of *Theosophy* and the establishment of the discipline as a "spiritual science" date back to Steiner's scientific studies at Vienna's Technical University in the late 1870s. There Steiner studied mathematics, biology, physics, and chemistry as principal subjects, coming to understand the importance of scrupulous research. Significantly, Steiner's doctorate, which he would obtain in Germany in 1891 at Rostock University, would be on the relationship between truth and science in the thinking of the German philosopher Johann Gottlieb Fichte and would be published in 1892 as *Truth and Science*. Fichte's influence on Steiner would be lasting, and the German idealist is quoted at the beginning of *Theosophy*.

At the same time, Steiner developed a keen interest in the classics, the arts, and the humanities. As a result of his double focus on science and classics, Rudolf was fascinated by the German poet and intellectual Johann Wolfgang von Goethe's scientific writings, whose spiritual view on the world he came to share. At only twenty-two years of age, Steiner was appointed to edit Goethe's scientific writings for the Deutsche National Literatur, a scholarly series of German literary classics, and this task acquainted him with Goethe's notion of the "sensory-supersensory" form, which would be an important influence on *Theosophy*. This form represents an interposition between natural vision and spiritual perception, between a sensory and a spiritual apprehension. At this point, Steiner became clearly interested in overcoming the boundaries of single disciplines and to depart from received notions of what formed orthodox and acceptable fields of enquiry. Goethe showed Steiner that thinking could be an organ of perception just as a material organ like an ear or an eye. While these organs perceive material events, thinking recognizes ideas.

Goethe's "sensory-supersensory form" and Fichte's idealist philosophy were two unlikely models for a young researcher to observe, given the prevailing intellectual milieu at the turn of the century. This milieu was characterized by the fast dissemination of the French philosopher Auguste Comte's positivist beliefs. Comte's philosophy aimed at demonstrating how humankind had finally succeeded in throwing off all religious superstitions and was moving toward an understanding of the world in purely material terms without any recourse to spiritual realms. To Comte's optimistic teleology of human existence, based on belief in linear progress, philosophers like the Germans Arthur Schopenhauer and Friedrich Nietzsche, whom Steiner would meet in 1896, opposed a nihilistic vision of humankind, whose evolution they found ultimately meaningless. Such a pessimistic vision would receive impetus from the tragic historical events that took place during Steiner's life and which, culminating with World War I, brought to an end the Russian, German, Ottoman, and Austro-Hungarian empires. Theosophy rejects the positivist understanding of the world in mere material terms and its tenet that the visible and earthly world encompasses the entire reality that humans can experience. At the same time, Steiner could not share Nietzsche's skepticism and agnosticism because his awareness of the spiritual led him to believe that human life has a purpose.

Theosophy originated in Steiner's conviction that, in addition to his numerous lectures on the issue, he had to find a more inclusive mode of communication for his anthroposophical work. After the foundation of the German section of the Theosophical Society in 1901, the following year Steiner launched the monthly journal *Lucifer* with the help of Marie von Sivers, one of Steiner's closest collaborators and his second wife. The title refers to the doctrine found in the ancient mysteries that Christ is the true Lucifer, in its literal meaning as "bearer of light." (The mysteries were secret religious groups that flourished during the Hellenistic period and sought to initiate individuals into cults of deities, stressing private worship and a personal relationship with the god rather than a public expression of faith.) As the number of subscribers increased quickly, the journal absorbed the Viennese publication *Gnosis* and was renamed *Lucifer-Gnosis*. Steiner wrote most of the articles for the journal, and its reputation grew steadily.

Steiner did not initially conceive his lectures to be later published in volumes. His first cycles of lectures were given to the small audiences who attended the Theosophical Society and the Theosophical Library in Berlin. But Steiner's oratorical skills were rapidly appreciated by the most diverse audiences, as the author is estimated to have given over six thousand lectures throughout his career. In contrast to the simple language of the lectures, the written books, including *Theosophy*, may baffle the reader in several passages. Steiner reflects in the preface to the first edition of the book that the reader will have to figure out each and every page as well as many individual sentences. The author goes on to explain that this is intentional, so as to make the reader experience and live the truths that the book has to communicate. This reflection points to the tension and difficulty of describing phenomena belonging to an immaterial world with a means—language—usually employed to represent the physical world. Form and content, therefore, are closely interrelated, as the style in which the material is narrated leads the reader to pursue an active path of knowledge. Reading thus becomes a form of spiritual exercise.

Steiner found an initial forum for his ideas in European theosophical circles, but he also immediately marked the difference between his thought and the prevailing ideas in those circles formed by the Russian medium and Theosophical Society founder Helena Blavatsky and the Theosophist and political activist Annie Besant. While these thinkers looked at Oriental philosophies to substantiate Theosophy, Steiner identified the incarnation of Christ or, in his preferred designation, "the Mystery of Golgotha" (referring to the site where Jesus was crucified), as the central event in the history of humanity for his spiritual science. Although he was critical of religious dogmas, Steiner regarded as unique the appearance on earth of the Son of God as Jesus of Nazareth. Blavatsky and Besant did not accept this centrality and this uniqueness, as their goal was to reach a synthesis of all different religions, which they held to all contain equally valid truths. After a years-long process of separation, in 1911 a section of the Theosophical Society encouraged by Besant founded the Order of the Star in the East, a branch that believed that Christ had reincarnated in a Hindu boy, Jiddu Krishnamurti, in a new earthly existence. By 1913 it had become apparent to Steiner that the two branches could not remain together, and he decided to found an independent Anthroposophical Society.

Author Biography

Rudolf Steiner was born on February 25, 1861, in Kraljevic, in the eastern Slavic provinces of the Austrian Empire. At the time of Steiner's birth, the vast empire ruled by the Hapsburg monarchy was beginning to dissolve under the pressures for independence among its different populations. After its humiliating defeat against Prussia in the Austro-Prussian War of 1866, the Austrian Empire found that the only way to survive was to strengthen its links with its eastern Slavic provinces. While consenting to greater independence for the Hungarian provinces in internal matters, the central government disregarded appeals for the preservation of the linguistic and cultural heritage of these regions. It tried to force a unified Germanic identity, against which Hungarian patriots vehemently reacted. Steiner was to experience firsthand the cultural clashes that took place in Austria-Hungary, as both of his parents were German speakers from Lower Austria but worked in the eastern provinces for much of his childhood and adolescence. His father, Johann, was an employee of the Austrian Southern Railway. Rudolf was the eldest of the three children born to Johann and his wife, Franziska. Because of their father's job, the family often moved during Rudolf's early life, at a time when he had already begun to experience visions of a higher, spiritual world.

For a few years the family lived in the Lower Austrian town of Pottschach, near the Hungarian border, where Steiner received private instruction at his home, owing to disagreements between his father and the village teacher. However, in 1869, the family moved to the Hungarian village of Neudörfl, where patriots were trying to revive the traditional Magyar language and culture in opposition to what they considered the imperialist policies of the Austrian government. Meanwhile, because Steiner's father wanted him to become a railway civil engineer, his formal studies were mainly scientific and technical. From a very early age, however, he also developed a keen interest in philosophy and psychology. Because his family lived at a subsistence level, Steiner had to use his pocket money to buy secondhand philosophy books. He began reading the German philosopher Immanuel Kant's *Critique of Pure Reason* (1781) at age fourteen and became convinced that he could find the bridge between the material and spiritual worlds only by acquiring and mastering the philosophical method advocated by Kant, which postulates that knowledge is independent of experience. During his childhood and adolescence, Steiner also discovered that he had supersensory abilities. At the age of seven, he saw the form of one of his aunts asking for help; unknown to his family, the aunt had died in a distant town. His childhood visions initially contributed to a deep feeling of loneliness, as he understood that he could not communicate the visions to his friends. With adolescence and maturity, these supersensory perceptions developed in the author the persuasion that he should translate them into conceptual structures so that they could be communicated to others in words.

Steiner's experiences of ethnic tensions can account for his decision, once his studies at Vienna's Technical University were complete in 1883, not to live in Austria again. Indeed, the cultural conflicts and crumbling of the existing social and political order left a deep mark on Steiner, as reflected in the cosmopolitanism of Anthroposophy and its rejection of preconceived ideas. He would remark directly in *The Threefold Commonwealth* (1919) on the failure of Austria-Hungary to find a balance between its peoples that could have had historical significance. Through the 1880s, 1890s, and early twentieth century, Steiner lectured extensively throughout western Europe, with the German cities of Berlin, Munich, and Stuttgart proving particularly important in the development of anthroposophical circles. When World War I broke out, he settled in Dornach, Switzerland, where he supervised the building of the Goetheanum, "a school for spiritual science" that he himself had designed and which would be used to spread Anthroposophy.

The carnage that Steiner witnessed during World War I certainly stimulated his reflection on life after death, which became a major theme in his postwar works. After the conflict, Steiner continued lecturing to disseminate anthroposophical ideas through initiatives with an ever-widening scope, embracing pedagogy, medicine, and agriculture. The folly of the war had persuaded Steiner that cultural renewal was essential, and to such a process he devoted the last years of his life, continuing to lecture tirelessly and focusing, in particular, on education. His ideas in this area gave rise to the first Waldorf School in 1919. Despite disagreements within the Anthroposophical Society, the burning of the Goetheanum in 1922 (with arson suspected), and his weakening health, Steiner embarked on a major reformation of the society he had founded, a project he worked on until his death on March 30, 1925.

Steiner's mature conviction that he should find a way to communicate his supersensory experiences to large audiences accounts for the large number of written volumes and lectures on Anthroposophy, including *Theosophy*. The majority of Steiner's books were actually transcriptions of his lectures, which his followers helped collect and publish in order to disseminate Anthroposophy. Steiner had acquired a reputation as an editor, reviewer, and lecturer of philosophy, literature, and pedagogy in Berlin circles by the 1890s. At the turn of the century, he decided to devote his intellectual strengths to Theosophy and subsequently, after the 1913 break with the Theosophical Society, to Anthroposophy. His primary audience was therefore represented by those attending meetings and lectures of the Theosophical Society. Steiner's ambition was to increase the number of people interested in the subject and to produce a true change of direction in the minds of his contemporaries. He thought that the turn of the century represented the peak in the separation of human thinking and willing from the spirit. Theosophy was designed to contribute to that "turn or reversal of direction in human evolution" that seemed so necessary to the author. Anthroposophy is today a worldwide movement, and *Theosophy* remains an important point of reference for Steiner's followers. They are mostly concentrated in Germany, Britain, and the United States.

HISTORICAL DOCUMENT

Chapter 1: The Constitution of the Human Being

***

Man continually links himself in this threefold way with the things of the world. One should not for the time being read anything into this fact, but merely take it as it presents itself. It makes it evident that man has THREE SIDES TO HIS NATURE. This and nothing else will for the present be indicated here by the three words BODY, SOUL, and SPIRIT. He who connects any preconceived meanings, or even hypotheses, with these three words will necessarily misunderstand the following explanations. By BODY is here meant that by which the things in the environment of a man reveal themselves to him, as in the example just cited, the flowers of the meadow. By the word SOUL is signified that by which he links the things to his own being, through which he experiences pleasure and displeasure, desire and aversion, joy and sorrow. By SPIRIT is meant that which becomes manifest in him when, as Goethe expressed it, he looks at things as "a so-to-speak divine being." In this sense the human being consists of BODY, SOUL, and SPIRIT.

Through his body man is able to place himself for the time being in connection with the things; through his soul he retains in himself the impressions which they make on him; through his spirit there reveals itself to him what the things retain in themselves. Only when one observes man in these three aspects can one hope to gain light on his whole being. For these three aspects show him to be related in a threefold way to the rest of the world.

Through his body he is related to the objects which present themselves to his senses from without. The materials from the outer world compose this body of his; and the forces of the outer world work also in it. And just as he observes the things of the outer world with his senses, he can also observe his own bodily existence. But it is impossible to observe the soul existence in the same way. All occurrences connected with my body can be perceived with my bodily senses. My likes and dislikes, my joy and pain, neither I nor anyone else can perceive with bodily senses. The region of the soul is one which is inaccessible to bodily perception. The bodily existence of a man is manifest to all eyes; the soul existence he carries within himself as HIS world.

Through the SPIRIT, however, the outer world is revealed to him in a higher way. The mysteries of the outer world, indeed, unveil themselves in his inner being; but he steps in spirit out of himself and lets the things speak about themselves, about that which has significance not for him but for THEM. Man looks up at the starry heavens; the delight his soul experiences belongs to him; the eternal laws of the stars which he comprehends in thought, in spirit, belong not to him but to the stars themselves.

Thus man is citizen of THREE WORLDS. Through his BODY he belongs to the world which he perceives through his body; through his SOUL he constructs for himself his own world; through his SPIRIT a world reveals itself to him which is exalted above both the others.

It is evident that because of the essential differences of these three worlds, one can obtain a clear understanding of them and of man's share in them only by means of three different modes of observation....

***

Chapter 2: Re-embodiment of the Spirit and Destiny

Reincarnation and Karma

In the midst between body and spirit lives the SOUL. The impressions which come to it through the body are transitory. They are present only as long as the body opens its organs to the things of the outer world. My eye perceives the color of the rose only so long as the rose is opposite to it and my eye is itself open. The PRESENCE of the things of the outer world as well as of the bodily organs is necessary in order that an impression, a sensation, or a perception can take place. But what I have recognized in my spirit as TRUTH concerning the rose does not pass with the present moment. And, as regards its truth, it is not in the least dependent on me. It would be true even although I had never stood in front of the rose. What I know through the spirit is timeless or ETERNAL. The soul is placed between the present and eternity, in that it holds the middle place between body and spirit. But it is also the INTERMEDIARY between the present and eternity. It preserves the present for the REMEMBRANCE. It thereby rescues it from impermanence, and brings it nearer to the eternity of the spiritual. It stamps eternity on the temporal and impermanent by not merely yielding itself up to the transitory incitements, but by determining things from out its own initiative, and embodying its own nature in them by means of the actions it performs. By remembrance the soul preserves the yesterday, by action it prepares the to-morrow.

My soul would have to perceive the red of the rose always afresh if it could not store it up in remembrance. What remains after an external impression, what can be retained by the soul, is the CONCEPTION. Through the power of forming conceptions the soul makes the corporal outer world so far into its own inner world that it can then retain the latter in the memory for remembrance and, independent of the gained impressions, lead with it thereafter a life of its own. The soul-life thus becomes the enduring result of the transitory impressions of the external world.

But an action also receives permanence when once it is stamped on the outer world. If I cut a branch from a tree something has taken place by means of my soul which completely changes the course of events in the outer world. Something quite different would have happened to the branch of the tree if I had not interfered by my action. I have called forth into life a series of effects which, without my existence, would not have been present. What I have done TO-DAY endures for TO-MORROW; it becomes permanent through the deed, as my impressions of yesterday have become permanent for my soul through memory.

Let us first consider memory. How does it originate? Evidently in quite a different way from sensation or perception, because these are made possible by the corporality. Without the eye I cannot have the sensation "blue." But in no way do I have the remembrance of "blue" through the eye. If the eye is to give me this sensation now, a blue thing must come before it. The corporality would always allow impressions to sink back into nothingness if it alone existed. I remember; that is, I experience something which is itself no longer present. I unite a past experience with my present life. This is the case with every remembrance. Let us say, for instance, that I meet a man and recognize him again because I met him yesterday. He would be a complete stranger to me were I not able to unite the picture perception with my impression of him to-day. The picture of to-day is given me by the perception, that is to say, by my corporality. But who conjures that of yesterday into my soul? It is the same being in me that was present during my experience yesterday, and that is also present in that of to-day. In the previous explanations it has been called soul. Were it not for this faithful preserver of the past each external impression would be always new to a man.

As preserver of the past the soul continually gathers treasures for the spirit. That I can distinguish right from wrong follows because I, as a human being, am a thinking being, able to grasp the truth in my spirit. Truth is eternal; and it could always reveal itself to me again in things, even if I were always to lose sight of the past and each impression were to be a new one to me. But the spirit within me is not restricted to the impressions of the present alone; the soul extends its horizon over the past. And the more it is able to bring to the spirit out of the past, the richer does it make the spirit. In this way the soul transmits to the spirit what it has received from the body. The spirit of man therefore carries each moment of its life a twofold possession within itself, firstly, the eternal laws of the good and the true; secondly, the remembrance of the experiences of the past. What he does, he accomplishes under the influence of these two factors. If we wish to understand a human spirit we must therefore know two different things about him, first, how much of the eternal has revealed itself to him; second, how much treasure from the past is stored up within him.

The treasure by no means remains in the spirit in an unchanged shape. The conceptions which man extracts from his experiences fade gradually from the memory. Not so, however, their fruits. One does not remember all the experiences one had during childhood when acquiring the arts of reading and writing. But one could not read or write if one had not had the experiences, and if their fruits had not been preserved in the form of abilities. And that is the transmutation which the spirit effects on the treasures of memory. It consigns the pictures of the separate experiences to their fate, and only extracts from them the force necessary for enhancing and increasing its abilities. Thus not one experience passes by unused; the soul preserves each one as memory, and from each the spirit draws forth all that can enrich its abilities and the whole content of its life. The human spirit grows through assimilated experiences. And, although one cannot find the past experiences in the spirit preserved as if in a storeroom, one nevertheless finds their effects in the abilities which the man has acquired.

Thus far spirit and soul have been considered only within the period lying between life and death. One cannot rest there. Anyone wishing to do that would be like the man who observes the human body also within the same limits only. Much can certainly be discovered within these limits. But the HUMAN FORM can never be explained by what lies between birth and death. It cannot build itself up unaided out of mere physical matter and forces. It takes rise in a form like its own, which has been passed on to it by propagation. Physical materials and forces build up the body during life; the forces of propagation enable another body, inheriting its form, to proceed from it; that is to say, one which is able to be the bearer of the same life-body. Each life-body is a repetition of its forefathers. Only BECAUSE it is such does it appear, not in any chance form, but in that passed on to it. The forces which have given me human form lay in my forefathers. But the spirit also of a man appears in a definite form. And the forms of the spirit are the most varied imaginable in different persons. No two men have the same spiritual form. One ought to make investigations in this region in just as quiet and matter-of-fact a manner as in the physical world. It cannot be said that the differences in human beings in spiritual respects arise only from the differences in their environment, their upbringing, etc. No, this is by no means the case, for two people under similar influences as regards environments, upbringing, etc., develop in quite different ways. One is therefore forced to admit that they have entered on their path of life with quite different predispositions. Here one is brought face to face with an important fact which, when its full bearing is recognized, sheds light on the nature of man.

Human beings differ from their animal fellow-creatures on the earth as regards their physical form. But among each other human beings are, within certain limits, the same in regard to their physical form. There is only one human species. However great may be the differences between races, peoples, tribes, and personalities as regards the physical body, the resemblance between man and man is greater than between man and any brute species. All that expresses itself as human species passes on from forefather to descendants. And the human form is bound to this heredity. As the lion can inherit its physical form from lion forefathers only, so the human being inherits his physical body from human forefathers only.

Just as the physical similarity of men is quite evident to the eye, the DIFFERENCE of their spiritual forms reveals itself to the unprejudiced spiritual gaze. There is one very evident fact which shows this clearly. It consists in the existence of the biography of a human being. Were a human being merely a member of a species, no biography could exist. A lion, a dove, lay claim to interest in so far as they belong to the lion, the dove genus. One has understood the separate being in all its ESSENTIALS when one has described the genus. It matters little whether one has to do with father, son, or grandson. What is of interest in them, father, son, and grandson have in common. But what a human being signifies begins, not where he is a mere member of a genus, but only where he is a separate being. I have not in the least understood the nature of Mr. Smith of Crowcorner if I have described his son or his father. I must know his own biography. Anyone who reflects accurately on the essence of biography becomes aware that in regard to spiritual things EACH MAN IS A SPECIES BY HIMSELF. Those people, to be sure, who regard a biography merely as a collection of external incidents in the life of a person, may claim that they can write the biography of a dog in the same way as that of a man. But anyone who depicts in a biography the real individuality of a man, grasps the fact that he has in the biography of ONE human being something that corresponds to the description of a whole genus in the animal kingdom.

Now if genus or species in the physical sense becomes intelligible only when one understands it as the result of heredity, the spiritual being can be intelligible only through a similar SPIRITUAL HEREDITY. I have received my physical human form from my forefathers. Whence have I that which comes to expression in my biography? As physical man, I repeat the shape of my forefathers. What do I repeat as spiritual man? Anyone claiming that what is comprised in my biography requires no further explanation has to be regarded as having no other course open to him than to claim equally that he has seen, somewhere, an earth mound on which the lumps of matter have aggregated quite by themselves into a living man.

As physical man I spring from other physical men, for I have the same shape as the whole human species. The qualities of the species, accordingly, could be bequeathed to me within the genus. As spiritual man I have my own shape as I have my own biography. I therefore can have obtained this shape from no one but myself. Since I entered the world not with un-defined but with defined predispositions; and since the course of my life as it comes to expression in my biography is determined by these predispositions, my work on myself cannot have begun with my birth. I must, as spiritual man, have existed before my birth. In my forefathers I have certainly not been existent, for they as spiritual human beings are different from me. My biography is not explainable through theirs. On the contrary, I must, as spiritual being, be the repetition of one through whose biography mine can be explained. The physical form which Schiller bore he inherited from his forefathers. But just as little as Schiller's physical form can have grown out of the earth, so little can his spiritual being have done so. It must be the repetition of another spiritual being through whose biography his will be explainable as his physical human form is explainable through human propagation. In the same way, therefore, that the physical human form is ever again and again a repetition, a reincarnation of the distinctively human species, the spiritual human being must be a reincarnation of the SAME spiritual human being. For as spiritual human being, each one is in fact his own species.

It might be said in objection to what has been stated here that it is pure spinning of thoughts, and such external proof might be demanded as one is accustomed to in ordinary natural science. The reply to this is that the re-embodiment of the spiritual human being is, naturally, a process which does not belong to the region of external physical facts, but is one that takes place entirely in the spiritual region. And to this region no other of our ORDINARY powers of intelligence has entrance, save that of THINKING. He who is unwilling to trust to the power of thinking cannot, in fact, enlighten himself regarding higher spiritual facts. For him whose spiritual eye is opened the above train of thoughts acts with exactly the same force as does an event that takes place before his physical eyes. He who ascribes to a so-called "proof" constructed according to the methods of natural science, greater power to convince than the above observations concerning the significance of biography, may be in the ordinary sense of the word a great scientist, but from the paths of true SPIRITUAL investigation he is very far distant.

One of the gravest prejudices consists in trying to explain the spiritual qualities of a man by inheritance from father, mother, or other ancestors. He who contracts the prejudice, for example, that Goethe inherited what constitutes his essential being from father or mother will at first be hardly approachable with arguments, for there lies within him a deep antipathy to unprejudiced observation. A materialistic spell prevents him from seeing the relations of phenomena in the true light....

Now how does the interaction between body and soul proceed? During life the spirit is bound up with the soul in the way shown above. The soul receives from it the power of living in the Good and the True, and of thereby bringing in its own life, in its tendencies, impulses, and passions, the spirit itself to expression. The spirit-self brings to the I, from the world of the spirit, the eternal laws of the True and the Good. These link themselves through the consciousness-soul with the experiences of the soul's own life. These experiences themselves pass away, but their fruits remain. The spirit-self receives an abiding impression by having been linked with them. When the human spirit approaches an experience similar to one with which it has already been linked, it sees in it something familiar, and is able to take up a different attitude toward it than if it were facing it for the first time. This is the basis of all learning. And the fruits of learning are acquired capacities. The fruits of the transitory life are in this way graven on the eternal spirit....IN EACH LIFE THE HUMAN SPIRIT APPEARS AS A REPETITION OF ITSELF WITH THE FRUITS OF ITS FORMER EXPERIENCES IN PREVIOUS LIVES. This life is consequently the repetition of another, and brings with it what the spirit-self has, by work, acquired for itself in the previous life. When the spirit-self absorbs something that can develop into fruit, it penetrates itself with the life-spirit. Just as the life-body reproduces the form, from genus to genus, so does the life-spirit reproduce the soul from personal existence to personal existence.

Thus the experiences of the soul become enduring not only within the boundaries of birth and death, but out beyond death. But the soul does not stamp its experiences only on the spirit which flashes up in it, it stamps them, as has been shown, on the outer world, also, through the DEED. What a man did yesterday is to-day still present in its effects. A picture of the connection between cause and effect is given in the simile of sleep and death. Sleep has often been called the younger brother of death. I get up in the morning. Night has interrupted my consecutive activity. Now, under ordinary circumstances, it is not possible for me to begin my activity again just as I like. I must connect it with my doings of yesterday if there is to be order and coherence in my life. My actions of yesterday are the conditions predetermining those I have to do to-day. I have created my fate of to-day by what I did yesterday. I have separated myself for a while from my activity; but this activity belongs to me and draws me again to itself after I have withdrawn myself from it for a while. My past remains bound up with me; it lives on in my present, and will follow me into my future. If the effects of my deeds of yesterday were not to be my fate to-day, I should have had, not to AWAKE this morning, but to be newly created out of nothing. It would be absurd if under ordinary circumstances I were not to occupy a house that I have had built for me.

The human spirit is just as little newly created when it begins its earthly life as is a man newly created every morning. Let us try to make clear to ourselves what happens when an entrance into this life takes place. A physical body, receiving its form through the laws of heredity, comes upon the scene. This body becomes the bearer of a spirit which repeats a previous life in a new form. Between the two stands the soul, which leads a self-contained life of its own. Its inclinations and disinclinations, its wishes and desires minister to it; it takes thought into its service. As sentient-soul it receives the impressions of the outer world and carries them to the spirit, in order that the spirit may extract from them the fruits that are for eternity. It plays, as it were, the part of intermediary; and its task is fully accomplished when it is able to do this. The body forms impressions for the sentient-soul which transforms them into sensations, retains them in the memory as conceptions, and hands them over to the spirit to hold throughout eternity. The soul is really that through which man belongs to his earthly life. Through his body he belongs to the physical human species. Through it he is a member of this species. With his spirit he lives in a higher world. The soul binds the two worlds for a time together.

But the physical world on which the human spirit enters is no strange field of action to it. On it the traces of its actions are imprinted. Something in this field of action belongs to the spirit. It bears the impress of its being. It is related to it. As the soul formerly transmitted the impressions from the outer world to the spirit in order that they might become enduring in it, so now the soul, as the spirit's organ, converts the capacities bestowed by the spirit into deeds which are also enduring through their effects. Thus the soul has actually flowed into these actions. In the effects of his actions man's soul lives on in a second independent life. And it is inevitable that the human spirit should meet again the effect of these actions. For only the one part of my deed is in the outer world; the other is in myself....

By means of his actions, therefore, the human spirit has really carved his fate. In a new life he finds himself linked to what he did in a former one.... The human spirit CAN only live in the surroundings which by its acts it has created for itself. There can be no more appropriate comparison than that of sleep with death. That I find in the morning a state of affairs which I on the previous day created, is brought about by the immediate progress of the events themselves. That I, when I reincarnate myself, find surroundings which correspond with the results of my deeds in a previous life, is brought about by the relationship of my reincarnated spirit with the things in the world around. From this it stands out clearly how the SOUL forms a member of the constitution of man. The physical body is subject to the laws of heredity. The human spirit, on the contrary, has to incarnate over and over again, and its law consists in its bringing over the fruits of the former lives into the following ones. The soul lives in the present. But this life in the present is not independent of the previous lives. For the incarnating spirit brings its destiny with it from its previous incarnations, and this destiny decides the kind of life. Whatever impressions the soul will be able to have, with what wishes it will be able to be gratified, what sorrows and joys spring forth for it, depend on the nature of the actions in the past incarnations of the spirit. The life of the soul is therefore the result of the self-created destiny of the human spirit. The course of man's life between birth and death is therefore determined in a threefold way. And he is by these means dependent in a threefold way on factors which lie ON THE OTHER SIDE of birth and death. The body is subject to the laws of hered ity; the soul is subject to the self-created fate. One calls this fate created by the man himself his karma. The spirit is under the law of re-embodiment or reincarnation. One can accordingly express the relationship between spirit, soul, and body in the following way as well. The spirit is eternal; birth and death have dominion over the corporality according to the laws of the physical world; the soul-life, which is subject to destiny, links them together during an earthly life.

GLOSSARY

Goethe: Johann Wolfgang von Goethe, a late-eighteenth- and early-nineteenth-century German playwright, philosopher, theologian, and scientist

Schiller: Johann Christoph Friedrich von Schiller, a late-eighteenth-century German poet, playwright, historian, and philosopher

Document Analysis

The present excerpt from *Theosophy: An Introduction to the Spiritual Processes in Human Life and in the Cosmos* includes parts of chapter 1, "The Constitution of the Human Being" and chapter 2, "Re-embodiment of the Spirit and Destiny." The term Theosophy is a compound of the Greek words *theos* (God) and *sophia* (wisdom), standing for "divine wisdom." Steiner argues that because of the prevailing materialist conceptions of existence at the turn of the century, people are blind to their spiritual dimension and consider only the physical world of sensory perceptions. In the text, Steiner describes the threefold nature of human beings as body, soul, and spirit, which allows them to go beyond sensory impressions and discover the deeper and truer layers of experience. Steiner also recognizes the eternal nature of the spirit, thus introducing a Christian path to reincarnation that diverges from Eastern models. In the thirty-third chapter of his autobiography, Steiner states that his goal in writing *Theosophy* was to stimulate understanding in his readers through descriptions drawn from supersensory realms but using language taken from the world of sense perception and intellect.

In the first chapter, "The Constitution of the Human Being," Steiner argues that human beings have three means by which they experience the outside world. The body allows them to enter into sensory and physical contact with the external features of the objects that they perceive, like flowers and their colors. The soul allows the human to link perceived objects to one's own being and express the feelings that they provoke. For example, looking at flowers, one will have certain reactions of pleasure, making them one's own. Through the spirit, the human being discovers the inherent and eternal qualities of the surrounding world. In experiencing something repeatedly, the spirit allows humans to detect timeless characteristics and thus the laws and true being of what surrounds them.

The whole being of a person is revealed only when these three aspects are taken into account, because through each aspect, one is connected to the rest of the world in a different way. Through sensory perceptions, one is able to observe objects from without and gain an understanding of bodily existence. But the feelings that such objects stimulate represent the region of the soul; they cannot be understood through the senses and are not directly accessible to others. Through the soul, one creates one's own private world and establishes a bridge between the body and the spirit. The spirit connects with the surrounding world on a higher plane, revealing what is significant in it not merely for one's subjectivity but more universally for the world itself. Citing the observation of "the starry heavens" as an example, Steiner writes that while the delight experienced by virtue of the soul belongs to the human being, the eternal laws of the stars apprehended through the spirit belong to the stars themselves.

The second chapter, "Re-embodiment of the Spirit and Destiny," starts by considering the intermediary position of the soul, between body and spirit. The body sends to the soul impressions that are temporary and which require the activation of a sensory organ by the presence of an object. But the soul passes to the spirit the emotional reactions to sensory perceptions and thus preserves the present for remembrance, conferring timelessness upon it. What the soul retains after the initial impression becomes the conception that one has of the object. One does not need to see a red rose constantly to have an idea of it, because the soul reworks the outer world into its inner world and stores its remembrance. Steiner defines the soul as "the faithful preserver of the past" and argues that it is thanks to the soul that past external impressions are remembered. The spirit, in turn, filters these remembrances of the past, extracting what can effectively enrich human abilities and human life. Steiner takes as an example the process of acquiring reading and writing skills in childhood. One obviously cannot remember all the experiences one has had while learning but will remember "their fruits...in the form of abilities."

Steiner then broadens his argument to consider the spirit and soul beyond the period "between birth and death." In this section, the author introduces his own vision of reincarnation and karma. According to Steiner, physical matter and forces cannot account for the human form in its entirety, because the human form is passed on by propagation. While physical materials and forces constitute the body during life, it is the forces of propagation that enable the inheritance of the form by another body. Steiner calls this second body "the bearer of the same life-body" and defines it as "a repetition of its forefathers." The spirit of a person, too, appears to be the result of this process of propagation. The differences of human beings in their spiritual dimension cannot arise only from the differences in their environment and upbringing, because people who are reared in the same environment or receive the same upbringing develop in different ways. Steiner therefore concludes that humans' spirits enter their path of life with different attitudes. These differences in nature are what make each human being unique, a fact that becomes apparent when one looks at the different life stories that exist because of these differences. "In regard to spiritual things" Steiner concludes, "each man is a species by himself."

Just as the physical outlook of a person can be understood with reference to physical heredity, so can the spiritual dimension be understood with reference to what Steiner calls spiritual heredity. Yet this is not a mechanical or deterministic process, and it would be wrong to assume that the spiritual heritage of a given person comes from his family members. On the contrary, Steiner explains that a human being's spiritual dimension is the result of one's development of the predispositions with which one enters life. Such work begins before birth, and, in spiritual terms, each man or woman is "the repetition of one through whose biography [his or hers] can be explained." The process of reincarnation ("re-embodiment") of the spiritual human being does not concern external physical facts but occurs in the supersensory realm, where none of the human faculties can be applied except for thought. With this conceptual development, Steiner rescues his argument from irrationality, pointing out that thinking can shed light on higher spiritual facts. Still, one should not approach spiritual matters with the eyes, seeking material evidence as a natural scientist would. This is the attitude that Steiner finds predominant in his era and that he calls a "materialistic spell" preventing the human being from considering the relationships between different phenomena in a true light. The reembodiment of the spirit shows the importance of the soul beyond physical death.

Because the soul acts as a mediator between the body and the spirit, the latter is able to recognize when a particular experience has occurred and decide what attitude to adopt. This produces learning; so the spirit confers eternity to the results of transitory experience. These resulting attitudes and conceptions remain as the heritage of the spirit, which brings them within itself in its next reembodiment. Again, Steiner rejects a purely automatic model of transmission that would exclude human agency by arguing that the spirit acquires this heritage "by work." He also adds that a human's "deeds" are extremely important for this spiritual heritage, as the effects of yesterday's actions are present in today's being and will be relevant for a person's fate. To exemplify his theory, Steiner draws a parallel between sleep and death. Just as a person waking up in the morning brings along into the new day all of one's previous experiences in life, so does the human spirit begin earthly life with the eternal fruits of previous lives. The spirit holds throughout eternity the conceptions that the soul has elaborated from the sensations provoked by bodily organs. Therefore, the physical world that the spirit enters is not completely foreign ground, as the spirit encounters again the same situations that it has already encountered in previous lives.

The last part of the document introduces the concept of fate created by a person through actions—karma.

The human spirit decides its fate through its actions, because the results of its actions remain in its heritage and link its present life with its former one. The destiny of the present life is inscribed in the spirit's previous incarnations and past actions. Steiner emphasizes the influence of past actions in human fate and calls this destiny "self-created" because it is dependent on the conceptions that the soul has elaborated from sensory experiences. In conclusion, the text summarizes the threefold nature of the human being, stressing that the spirit is eternal and subject to the laws of reincarnation, while the body is subject to the laws of heredity. The soul links spirit and body during earthly life.

Impact

Theosophy, as well as the author's other writings and lectures, helped revise the religious philosophy that had been identified with the Theosophical Society, established by Helena Blavatsky and Henry Steel Olcott, an American military officer and journalist, in New York in 1875. The Theosophical Society emphasized the importance of mysticism by stressing that God must be experienced directly to be known. In addition, it refused to identify one supreme religion but claimed that all faiths shared universal values and that their teachings represented quests for truth. Steiner became the head of the German branch of the society in 1902 but, less than a decade after the publication of *Theosophy*, broke away from it in 1913, founding his own Anthroposophical Society.

One of the main reasons for the theosophical controversy was Steiner's interest in finding a Western spiritual path to knowledge that would not discount Christianity to privilege Oriental and Eastern philosophies. Steiner also did not accept what he perceived as the uncritical adoption of occult traditions as a tenet of Theosophy as formulated by Blavatsky and Annie Besant. Steiner, whose training as a scientist taught him to value rigorous standards of research, constantly argued for the application of such standards to all types of observations. Significantly, his biographer, A. P. Shepherd, describes him as a "scientist of the invisible" because, throughout his oeuvre, the philosopher suggests means for a scientific investigation of the spiritual world that would not transcend a rigorous methodology of observation. Steiner's oeuvre has not only contributed to the fields of religion and mysticism but has also had far-reaching effects on education, agriculture, and medicine.

—*Luca Prono PhD*

Bibliography and Further Reading

Childs, Gilbert. *Rudolf Steiner: His Life and Work*. Hudson, N.Y.: Anthroposophic Press, 1996.

Easton, Stewart C. *Rudolf Steiner: Herald of a New Epoch*. Spring Valley, N.Y.: Anthroposophic Press, 1980.

Hemleben, Johannes. *Rudolf Steiner: An Illustrated Biography*. London: Sophia Books, 2000.

Lachman, Gary. *Rudolf Steiner: An Introduction to His Life and Work*. New York: Jeremy P. Tarcher/Penguin, 2007.

Shepherd, A. P. *Scientist of the Invisible: Spiritual Science, the Life and Work of Rudolf Steiner*. Rochester, Vt.: Inner Traditions International, 1983.

Steiner, Rudolf. *Autobiography: Chapters in the Course of My Life, 1861–1907*, trans. Rita Stebbing. Great Barrington, Mass.: SteinerBooks, 2006.

Wilkinson, Roy. *Rudolf Steiner: An Introduction to His Spiritual World-View, Anthroposophy*. Forest Row, U.K.: Temple Lodge Publishing, 2001.

Wilson, Colin. *Rudolf Steiner: The Man and His Vision*. London: Aeon Books, 2005.

Lachman, Gary. "Rudolf Steiner." Fortean Times Web site. http://www.forteantimes.com/features/profiles/109/rudolf_steiner.html

Rudolf Steiner Archive Web site. http://www.rsarchive.org/index1.php

APPENDIXES

Chronological List

1900: Henry Cabot Lodge: Speech on the Retention of the Philippine Islands 73
1900: Ida B. Wells: "Lynch Law in America" 155
1900: Rufus M. Jones: "Essential Truths" 257
1901: William McKinley: Last Speech 3
1901: The Insular Cases: *Downes v. Bidwell* 79
1901: Boxer Protocol 94
1901: George H. White: Farewell Address to Congress 166
1902: Eugene V. Debs: "How I Became a Socialist" 8
1902: Vladimir Lenin: *What Is to Be Done?* 103
1902: Charles Eastman: *Indian Boyhood* 239
1903: Lincoln Steffens: "The Shame of Minneapolis" 13
1903: Panama Canal Treaty 117
1903: Booker T. Washington: "Statement on Suffrage" 176
1903: W. E. B. Du Bois: *The Souls of Black Folk* 184
1904: Roosevelt Corollary to the Monroe Doctrine 127
1904: W. E. B. Du Bois: "The Parting of the Ways" 200
1904: Ida B. Wells: "Booker T. Washington and His Critics" 206
1904: Rudolf Steiner: *Theosophy* 266
1905: Anna Howard Shaw: Address on the Place of Women in Society and Address on the Condition of Women in Industry 26
1905: Treaty of Portsmouth 134
1905: Niagara Movement Declaration of Principles 213
1906: American Antiquities Act 32
1906: Pure Food and Drug Act 35
1906: Theodore Roosevelt: Brownsville Legacy Special Message to the Senate 223
1907: Jane Addams: "Passing of the War Virtues" 43
1907: Edward Curtis: Introduction to *The North American Indian* 247
1908: *Muller v. Oregon* 49
1908: Robert La Follette: Speech on the Amendment of National Banking Laws 58
1908: Samuel Gompers: Editorial on the Supreme Court Ruling in the Danbury Hatters' Case 64
1909: John Kenneth Turner: *Barbarous Mexico* 142

Web Resources

http://www.dcte.udel.edu/hlp2/resources/summer09/progressive_era_media.pdf

A helpful list of websites and films concerning topics, people, and movements associated with the Progressive Era through the 1920s.

digitalhistory.uh.edu

Offers an online history textbook, Hypertext History, which chronicles the story of America, along with interactive timelines. This online source also contains handouts, lesson plans, e-lectures, movies, games, biographies, glossaries, maps, music, and much more.

docsouth.unc.edu

A digital publishing project that reflects the southern perspective of American history and culture. It offers a wide collection of titles that students, teachers, and researchers of all levels can utilize.

docsteach.org

Centered on teaching through the use of primary source documents. This online resource provides activities for many different historical eras dating to the American Revolution as well as thousands of primary source documents.

edsitement.neh.gov

An online resource for teachers, students, and parents seeking to further their understanding of the humanities. This site offers lesson plan searches, student resources, and interactive activities.

gilderlehrman.org

Offers many options in relation to the history of America. The History by Era section provides detailed explanations of specific time periods while the primary sources present firsthand accounts from a historical perspective.

havefunwithhistory.com

An online, interactive resource for students, teachers, and anybody who has an interest in American history.

history.com/topics/american-history

Tells the story of America through topics of interest such as the Declaration of Independence, major wars, and notable Americans. Features videos from The History Channel and other resources.

historymatters.gmu.edu

An online resource from George Mason University that provides links, teaching materials, primary documents, and guides for evaluating historical records.

http://memory.loc.gov/ammem/index.html

Covers the various eras and ages of American history in detail, including resources such as readings, interactive activities, multimedia, and more.

nwhm.org/online-exhibits/progressiveera/introprogressive.html

A useful collection of photographs and descriptions concerning women and reform in the Progressive Era.

pbs.org/wgbh/americanexperience

Offers an array of source materials linked to topics featured in the award winning American Experience history series.

publichistory.org/reviews/view_issue.asp?IssueNumber=9

A diverse collection of online resources relating to the people. places, politics, and social movements of the Progressive Era.

si.edu/encyclopedia_si/nmah/timeline.htm

Details the course of American history chronologically. Important dates and significant events link to other pages within the Smithsonian site that offer more details.

smithsonianeducation.org

An online resource for educators, families, and students offering lesson plans, interactive activities, and more.

teachingamericanhistory.org

Allows visitors to learn more about American history through original source documents detailing the broad spectrum of American history. The site contains document libraries, audio lectures, lesson plans, and more.

teachinghistory.org

A project funded by the US Department of Education that aims to assist teachers of all levels to augment their efforts in teaching American history. It strives to amplify student achievement through improving the knowledge of teachers.

ushistory.org/us

Contains an outline that details the entire record of American history. This resource offers historical insight and stories that demonstrate what truly an American truly is from a historical perspective.

Bibliography

Abbott, Margery Post, et al., eds. *Historical Dictionary of the Friends (Quakers)*. Lanham, Md.: Scarecrow Press, 2003.

"About the NAACP—History." *NAACP*. National Association for the Advancement of Colored People, 2016. Web. 2 Aug. 2016. <http://www.naacp.org/about/history>.

Allred, Christine Edwards. " 'Real Indian Art': Charles Eastman's Search for an Authenticating Culture Concept." In William R. Handley and Nathaniel Lewis, True West: Authenticity and the American West. Lincoln: University of Nebraska Press, 2004. Pp. 117-139.

American Antiquities Act of 1906. , n.d.. Internet resource.

Anderson, Eric. *Race and Politics in North Carolina, 1872–1901: The Black Second*. Baton Rouge: Louisiana State UP, 1981.

Anguizola, Gustave. *Philippe Bunau-Varilla: The Man behind the Panama Canal*. Chicago: Nelson-Hall, 1980.

———. "Antecedents of the Roosevelt Corollary of the Monroe Doctrine." *Pacific Historical Review* 9 (September 1940): 267–279.

Baer, Judith A. *The Chains of Protection: The Judicial Response to Women's Labor Legislation*. Westport, Conn.: Greenwood Press, 1978.

Baker, Jean H. *Sisters: The Lives of America's Suffragists*. Hill and Wang, 2005.

Barkan, I.D. 1985. "Industry Invites Regulation: The Passage of the Pure Food and Drug Act of 1906." *American Journal of Public Health*. Vol. 75, No. 1, pp. 18-26.

Bausum, Ann. *Muckrakers: How Ida Tarbell, Upton Sinclair, and Lincoln Steffens Helped Expose Scandal, Inspire Reform, and Invent Investigative Journalism*. National Geographic, 2007

———. *With Courage and Cloth: Winning the Fight for a Woman's Right to Vote*. National Geographic, 2004

Bay, Mia. *To Tell the Truth Freely: the Life of Ida B. Wells*. New York Hill & Wang, 2009. Print.

Beale, Howard K. *Theodore Roosevelt and the Rise of America to World Power*. Baltimore, Md.: Johns Hopkins University Press, 1959.

Bederman, Gail. *Manliness and Civilization: A Cultural History of Gender and Race in the United States, 1880-1917 (Women in Culture and Society)*. University of Chicago Press, 1995.

Behind the Veil: Documenting African American Life in the Jim Crow South. Duke University Libraries Digital Collection, 2016. Web. 2 Aug. 2016. <http://library.duke.edu/digitalcollections/behindtheveil/>.

Bickers, Robert and R. G. Tiedemann, eds. *The Boxers, China, and the World*. New York: Rowman & Littlefield, 2007. Print.

"Black Americans in Congress." *History, Art & Archives: United States House of Representatives*. Office of Art & Archives, Office of the Clerk, n.d. Web. 2 Aug. 2016. <http://baic.house.gov/>.

Brands, H. W. *T.R.: The Last Romantic*. New York: Basic Books, 1997.

Brasch, Walter M. *Forerunners of the Revolution: Muckrakers and the American Social Conscience*. Lanham, MD: University Press of America, 1990.

Brundage, W. Fitzhugh, ed. *Booker T. Washington and Black Progress: Up from Slavery 100 Years Later*. Gainesville: U P of Florida, 2003. Print.

Bunau-Varilla, Philippe. *From Panama to Verdun*. Philadelphia: Dorrance and Co., 1940; <http://www.columbia.edu/cu/lweb/digital/collections/cul/texts/ldpd_6345181_000/index.html>.

Burnett, Christina Duffy, and Burke Marshall, eds. *Foreign in a Domestic Sense: Puerto Rico, American Expansion, and the Constitution*. Durham: Duke University Press, 2001.

Burnett, Christina Duffy. "Untied States: American Expansion and Territorial Deannexation." *University of Chicago Law Review* 72, no. 3 (2005): 797–880.

Carlisle, J. M. *The Cowboy and the Canal: How Theodore Roosevelt Cheated Colombia, Stole Panama, and Bamboozled America*. Tucson, Ariz.: Tangent Publishers, 2014.

Centennial of the American Antiquities Act of 1906: 100 Years of Preservation. Salem, Or.: Oregon State Parks and Recreation Dept., Heritage Programs Division, State Historic Preservation Office, 2006. Internet resource.

Chace, James. *Wilson, Roosevelt, Taft and Debs -The Election that Changed the Country*. Simon and Schuster, 2009.

Childs, Gilbert. *Rudolf Steiner: His Life and Work*. Hudson, N.Y.: Anthroposophic Press, 1996.

Christian, Garna L. *Black Soldiers in Jim Crow Texas, 1899–1917*. College Station: Texas A&M University

Press, 1995.

Cohen, Paul A. *History in Three Keys: the Boxers as Event, Experience, and Myth*. New York: Columbia UP, 1997. Print.

Collin, Richard H. *Theodore Roosevelt's Caribbean: The Panama Canal, the Monroe Doctrine, and the Latin American Context*. Baton Rouge: Louisiana State University Press, 1990.

"Congress Profiles | US House of Representatives: History, Art & Archives." *Congressional Profiles*. N.p., n.d. Web. 25 July 2016.

Conway, Jill. 1964. "Jane Addams: An American Heroine." *Daedalus*. Vol. 93, No. 2, pp. 761-780.

Cook, Fred J. *The Muckrakers: Sinclair, Tarbell, Russell, Steffens, Phillips: Crusading Journalists Who Changed America*. Doubleday, 1971.

Crouch, Stanley, & Playthell Benjamin. *Reconsidering the Souls of Black Folk: Thoughts on the Groundbreaking Classic Work of W. E. B. Du Bois*. Philadelphia: Running Press, 2002.

———. *Cuba and the United States: Ties of Singular Intimacy*. Athens: University of Georgia Press, 1990.

Dalton, Kathleen. *Theodore Roosevelt: A Strenuous Life*. New York: Alfred A. Knopf, 2002.

Davidson, James West. *"They Say": Ida B. Wells and the Reconstruction of Race*. New York: Oxford UP, 2007.

Debs, Eugene V. *Gentle Rebel: Letters of Eugene V. Debs*. University of Illinois Press, 1995.

———. *Writings of Eugene V Debs: A Collection of Essays by America's Most Famous Socialist*. Red and Black Publishers, 2009.

"Defense of the Negro Race—Charges Answered." *Documenting the American South*. University Library, UNC Chapel Hill, 2004. Web. 2 Aug. 2016. <http://docsouth.unc.edu/nc/whitegh/whitegh.html>.

Dorrien, Gary. *The New Abolition: W. E. B. Du Bois and the Black Social Gospel*. New Haven, CT: Yale UP, 2015.

Dray, Philip. *Capitol Men: The Epic Story of Reconstruction through the Lives of Black Congressmen*. Boston: Houghton Mifflin, 2008.

Dubois, Ellen Carol. *Feminism and Suffrage: The Emergence of an Independent Women's Movement in America, 1848-1869*. Cornell University Press, 1999.

Du Bois, W. E. B. *Dusk of Dawn: An Essay toward an Autobiography of a Race Concept*. New York: Harcourt, Brace, 1940.

———. *The Autobiography of W. E. B. Du Bois: A Soliloquy on Viewing My Life from the Decade of Its First Century*. New York: International Publishers, 1969.

———. "The Talented Tenth." *The Negro Problem: A Series of Articles by Representative Negroes of To-day*. New York: J. Pott and Company, 1903. The Gilder Lehrman Center for the Study of Slavery, Resistance, and Abolition at Yale University, 2016. Web. 5 Feb. 2008. <http://www.yale.edu/glc/archive/1148.htm>.

Dunne, Finley Peter. *Mr. Dooley's Opinions*. New York: R. H. Russell, 1901.

Easton, Stewart C. *Rudolf Steiner: Herald of a New Epoch*. Spring Valley, N.Y.: Anthroposophic Press, 1980.

Egan, Timothy. *Short Nights of the Shadow Catcher*. New York: Mariner, 2012.

Erickson, Nancy S. "*Muller v. Oregon* Reconsidered: The Origins of a Sex-Based Doctrine of Liberty of Contract." *Labor History* 30, no. 2 (1989): 228–250.

Esherick, Joseph. *The Origins of the Boxer Uprising*. Berkeley: UC Press, 1987. Print.

Fiss, Owen M. *Troubled Beginnings of the Modern State, 1888–1910*. Vol. 8: *History of the Supreme Court of the United States*. New York: Macmillan, 1993.

Fiztgerald, Michael Oren. *The Essential Charles Eastman (Ohiyesa)*. Bloomington, IN: World Wisdom, 2007.

Foner, Philip S. *The Spanish-Cuban-American War and the Birth of American Imperialism, 1895–1902*. 2 vols. New York: Monthly Review Press, 1972.

Fox, George. *The Works of George Fox*. 8 vols. Philadelphia: Marcus T. C. Gould, 1831.

Fox, Stephen R. *The Guardian of Boston: William Monroe Trotter*. New York: Atheneum, 1970.

Francisco, Luzviminda Bartolome, and Jonathan Shepard Fast. *Conspiracy for Empire: Big Business, Corruption, and the Politics of Imperialism in America, 1876–1907*. Quezon City, Philippines: Foundation for Nationalist Studies, 1985.

Franzen, Trisha. *Anna Howard Shaw: The Work of Woman Suffrage (Women in American History)*. University of Illinois Press, 2014.

Freeberg, Ernest. *Democracy's Prisoner*. Harvard University Press, 2009.

Friedan, Betty. *The Feminine Mystique (50th Anniversary Edition)*. Norton Press, 2001.

"Friends United Meeting: About FUM—Declaration of Faith." Friends United Meeting Web site. http://www.fum.org/about/declarationfaith.htm#Worship

Garraty, John A. *Henry Cabot Lodge: A Biography*. New

York: Alfred A. Knopf, 1953.

Gates, Henry Louis, Jr. & Terri Hume Oliver, eds. *The Souls of Black Folk: Authoritative Text, Contexts, Criticism*. New York: W.W. Norton & Co, 1999.

Giddings, Paula. *A Sword among Lions: Ida B. Wells and the Campaign against Lynching*. New York: Amistad, 2008. Print.

Gidley, Mick, ed., Edward S. Curtis and the North American Indian Project in the Field. Lincoln: University of Nebraska Press, 2003.

Gilly, Adolfo. *The Mexican Revolution*. The New Press, 2006.

Ginger, Ray. *The Bending Cross: A Biography of Eugene Victor Debs*. Haymarket Books, 2007.

Goodwin, Doris Kearns. *The Bully Pulpit: Theodore Roosevelt, William Howard Taft, and the Golden Age of Journalism*. New York: Simon and Schuster, 2013.

Gould, Lewis L. *The Presidency of Theodore Roosevelt*. Lawrence: University Press of Kansas, 1991.

Graham, Jr., Otis L. *An Encore for Reform: The Old Progressives and the New Deal*. New York: Oxford University Press, 1967.

Hahn, Steven. *A Nation Under Our Feet: Black Political Struggles in the Rural South, from Slavery to the Great Migration*. Cambridge, MA: Belknap Press of Harvard UP, 2003.

Haimson, Leopold H. *The Russian Marxists and the Origins of Bolshevism*. Cambridge, Mass.: Harvard University Press, 1955.

———. "Russian Workers' Political and Social Identities: The Role of Social Representations in the Interaction between Members of the Labor Movement and the Social Democratic Intelligentsia." In *Workers and Intelligentsia in Late Imperial Russia: Realities, Representations, Reflections*, ed. Reginald Zelnik. Berkeley: University of California Press, 1999.

Hamm, Thomas D. "Friends United Meeting and Its Identity: An Interpretative History." *Quaker Life* (January–February 2009): 10–15. Available online at http://www.fum.org/QL/issues/0901/FUM_Identity_Hamm.htm

———. *The Transformation of American Quakerism: Orthodox Friends, 1800–1907*. Bloomington: Indiana University Press, 1988.

Harding, Neil. *Lenin's Political Thought: Theory and Practice in the Democratic Revolution*. London: Macmillan, 1977.

Harlan, Louis R. *Booker T. Washington: the Making of a Black Leader, 1856–1901*. Oxford, UK: Oxford UP, 1972. Print.

———. *Booker T. Washington: the Wizard of Tuskegee, 1901–1915*. Vol. 2. Oxford, UK: Oxford University Press, 1983. Print.

Harmon, David, Francis P. McManamon, and Dwight T. Pitcaithley. *The Antiquities Act: A Century of American Archaeology, Historic Preservation, and Nature Conservation*. Tucson: University of Arizona Press, 2006. Print.

Hartshorn, Peter. *I Have Seen the Future: A Life of Lincoln Steffens*. Berkeley, CA: Counterpoint, 2011.

Harvey, Rowland H. *Samuel Gompers: Champion of the Toiling Masses*. Stanford University, Calif: Stanford University Press, 1935. Print.

Hausman, Gerald, and Bob Kapoun, eds. *Prayer to the Great Mystery: The Uncollected Writings and Photography of Edward S. Curtis*. New York: St. Martins, 1995.

Hearings before the Committee on Military Affairs, United States Senate, concerning the Affair at Brownsville, Tex., on the Night of August 13 and 14, 1906. Washington, DC: Government Printing Office, 1907.

Heflin, Ruth J. *I Remain Alive: The Sioux Literary Renaissance*. Syracuse, NY: Syracuse University Press, 2000.

Hemleben, Johannes. *Rudolf Steiner: An Illustrated Biography*. London: Sophia Books, 2000.

Hendricks, W. A. *Gender, Race, and Politics in the Midwest*. Bloomington: Indiana UP, 1998.

Hertzberg, Hazel W. The Search for an American Indian Identity: Modern Pan-Indian Movements. Syracuse, NY: Syracuse University Press, 1971.

Hine, Darlene Clark, William C. Hine, and Stanley C. Harrold. *African Americans: A Concise History, Combined Volume*. Boston: Pearson, 2011. Print.

Hofstadter, Richard. *The Age of Reform; From Bryan to F.D.R.* New York: Vintage Books, 1955

Horne, Gerald. *W. E. B. Du Bois: A Biography*. Westport, Connecticut: Greenwood Press, 2009.

Howe, Albert H. *The Insular Cases, Comprising the Records, Briefs, and Arguments of Counsel in the Insular Cases of the October Term, 1900, in the Supreme Court of the United States, Including the Appendixes Thereto*. Washington, D.C.: Government Printing Office, 1901.

"'Insular Cases' Made Puerto Rican Status Unclear, Panel Says." University of Virginia School of Law Web site. http://www.law.virginia.edu/html/news/2007_spr/insular.htm. Accessed on January 28, 2008.

Johnson, Dennis R. 1982. "The History of the 1906 Pure Food and Drug Act and the Meat Inspection Act." *Food Drug Cosmetic Law Journal*. Vol. 37, pp. 5-9.

Jones, Gregg. *Honor in the Dust: Theodore Roosevelt, War in the Philippines, and the Rise and Fall of America's Imperial Dream*. New York: New American Library, 2012.

Jones, Rufus M. *Social Law in the Spiritual World: Studies in Human and Divine Inter-Relationship*. New York: Swarthmore Press, 1923.

Jutesen, Benjamin R. *George Henry White: An Even Chance in the Race of Life*. Baton Rouge: Louisiana State UP, 2001.

Karcher, Carolyn L. "Ida B. Wells and Her Allies against Lynching: A Transnational Perspective." *Comparative American Studies* 3.2 (June 2005): 131–151.

———. "The White 'Bystander' and the Black Journalist 'Abroad'": Albion W. Tourgée and Ida B. Wells as Allies against Lynching." *Prospects* 29 (October 2005): 85–119.

Katanski, Amelia. *Learning to Write "Indian": The Boarding School Experience and American Indian Literature*. Norman: University of Oklahoma Press, 2005.

Katz, Friedrich. *The Life and Times of Pancho Villa*. Stanford University Press, 1998.

Kerr, James Edward. *The Insular Cases: The Role of the Judiciary in American Expansionism*. Port Washington, N.Y.: Kennikat Press, 1982.

Kirp, David L., Mark G. Yudof, and Marlene Strong Franks. *Gender Justice*. Chicago: University of Chicago Press, 1986.

Lachman, Gary. *Rudolf Steiner: An Introduction to His Life and Work*. New York: Jeremy P. Tarcher/Penguin, 2007.

LaFeber, Walter. "The 'Lion in the Path': The U.S. Emergence as a World Power." *Political Science Quarterly* 101, no. 5 (1986): 705–718.

———. *The Panama Canal: The Crisis in Historical Perspective*, updated ed. New York: Oxford University Press, 1989.

La, Follette R. M., and Matthew Rothschild. *La Follette's Autobiography: A Personal Narrative of Political Experiences*. Madison, Wisconsin: University of Wisconsin Press, 2013. Print.

Lane, Ann J. *The Brownsville Affair: National Crisis and Black Reaction*. Port Washington, NY: Kennikat Press, 1971.

Lawlor, Laurie. *Shadow Catcher: The Life and Work of Edward S. Curtis*. Lincoln, NE: Bison Books, 2005.

Lawson, Gary, and Guy Seidman. *The Constitution of Empire: Territorial Expansion and American Legal History*. New Haven, Conn.: Yale University Press, 2004.

Leonard, Thomas M. *The United States and Central America: The Search for Stability*. Athens: University of Georgia Press, 1991.

Lewis, David Levering. *W. E. B. Du Bois, 1868–1919: Biography of a Race*. New York: Henry Holt and Co, 2009. Print..

Lih, Lars T. *Lenin Rediscovered: What Is to Be Done? in Context*. Boston: Brill Academic Publishers, 2005.

Linn, Brian McAllister. *The Philippine War, 1899–1902*. Lawrence: University Press of Kansas, 2000.

Lyman, Christopher M. *The Vanishing Race and Other Illusions: Photographs of Indians by Edward S. Curtis*. New York: Pantheon Books, in association with the Smithsonian

Makepeace, Anne. *Edward S. Curtis: Coming to the Light*. Washington, DC: National Geographic Society, 2001.

Marable, Manning. *W. E. B. Du Bois: Black Radical Democrat*. Boulder, Colorado: Paradigm, 2005.

Martínez, David. *Dakota Philosopher: Charles Eastman and American Indian Thought*. St. Paul: Minnesota Historical Society, 2009.

"Marxism and Workers' Organisation: Writings of Marxists on Trade Unions, the General Strike, Soviets and Working Class Organisation." Marxists Internet Archive Web site. http://marxists.org/subject/workers/index.htm.

Mason, Alpheus T. 1924. "The Labor Clauses of the Clayton Act." *The American Political Science Review* Vol. 18, No. 3 (Aug., 1924), pp. 489-512.

———. "The Case of the Overworked Laundress." In *Quarrels That Have Shaped the Constitution*, ed. John A. Garraty. New York: Harper & Row, 1964.

Mayer, Robert. "Lenin and the Concept of the Professional Revolutionary." *History of Political Thought* 14, no. 2 (1993): 249–263.

McCullough, David. *The Path between the Seas: The Creation of the Panama Canal, 1870–1914*. New York: Simon & Schuster, 1977.

McKinley, William, John S. Olgilvie, and Stewart L. Woodford. *Life and Speeches of William Mckinley:*

Containing a Sketch of His Eventful Life ... Proceedings of National Convention, St. Louis, Platform of the Republican Party, Sketch of the Candidate for Vice-President, and Other Valuable Information for Every Citizen. New York: J.S. Ogilvie Pub. Co, 1981. Print.

McKinley, William. *Speeches and Addresses of William Mckinley: From March 1, 1897 to May 30, 1900.* New York: Doubleday & McClure Co, 1900. Print.

McLynn, Frank. *Villa and Zapata: A History of the Mexican Revolution.* Basic Books, 2002.

McMurry, Linda O. *To Keep the Waters Troubled: The Life of Ida B. Wells.* New York: Oxford University Press, 1998.

Meier, August. *Negro Thought in America, 1880–1915.* Ann Arbor, MI: U of Michigan P, 1968.

Mekeel, Arthur J. *Quakerism and a Creed.* Philadelphia: Friends Book Store, 1936.

Merritt, Walter Gordon. 1910. "The Law of the Danbury Hatters' Case." *The Annals of the American Academy of Political and Social Science.* Vol. 36, No. 2, The Settlement of Labor Disputes (Sep., 1910), pp. 11-22.

Miller, Grant. 2008. "Women's Suffrage, Political Responsiveness, and Child Survival in American History." *The Quarterly Journal of Economics.* Vol. 123, No. 3, pp. 1287-1327.

Miller, Stuart Creighton. *Benevolent Assimilation: The American Conquest of the Philippines, 1899–1903.* New Haven, Conn.: Yale University Press, 1982.

Minear, Mark. *Richmond 1887: A Quaker Drama Unfolds.* Richmond, Ind.: Friends United Press, 1987.

Minutes and Proceedings of the Five Years Meeting of the American Yearly Meetings Held in Indianapolis, Indiana, 1902. Philadelphia: J. C. Winston, 1903.

Moore, Jacqueline M. *Booker T. Washington, W. E. B. Du Bois, and the Struggle for Racial Uplift.* Wilmington, DE: Scholarly Resources, 2003.

Morris, Edmund. *Theodore Rex.* New York: Random House, 2001.

"Muller v. Oregon (Supreme Court upholds maximum hour law), February 24, 1908." *Women Working, 1800–1930,* Harvard University Library Web site. http://ocp.hul.harvard.edu/ww/events_muller.html. Accessed on October 15, 2007.

Munro, Dana G. *Intervention and Dollar Diplomacy in the Caribbean, 1900–1921.* Princeton, N.J.: Princeton University Press, 1964.

Norrell, Robert J. *Up from History: The Life of Booker T. Washington.* Cambridge, MA: Harvard University Press, 2009. Print.

North Carolina History Project. John Locke Foundation, 2016. Web. 2 Aug. 2016. <http://www.northcarolinahistory.org/>.

O'Connor, Richard. *The Boxer Rebellion.* London: Robert Hale, 1973. Print.

Pérez, Louis A. *Cuba between Empires, 1878–1902.* Pittsburgh: University of Pittsburgh Press, 1982.

Proceedings, Including the Declaration of Christian Doctrine: Of the General Conference of Friends, Held in Richmond, Ind., U.S.A., 1887. Richmond, Ind.: Nicholson, 1887.

Rampersad, Arnold. *The Art and Imagination of W. E. B. Du Bois.* New York: Schocken Books, 1990.

Rhode, Deborah L. *Justice and Gender: Sex Discrimination and the Law.* Cambridge, Mass.: Harvard University Press, 1989.

Rippy, J. Fred. "The British Bondholders and the Roosevelt Corollary of the Monroe Doctrine." *Political Science Quarterly* 49 (June 1934): 195–206.

Rivera Ramos, Efrén. *The Legal Construction of Identity: The Judicial and Social Legacy of American Colonialism in Puerto Rico.* Washington, D.C.: American Psychological Association, 2001.

Roosevelt, Theodore. *Addresses and Presidential Addresses by Theodore Roosevelt, 1902–1904.* New York: G. P. Putnam's Sons, 1904.

Rosselló, Pedro. *The Unfinished Business of American Democracy.* San Juan, Puerto Rico: Public Policy Institute, Ana G. Méndez University System, 2005.

Rudolf Steiner Archive Web site. http://www.rsarchive.org/index1.php

Rudwick, Elliott M. *W. E. B. Du Bois: Propagandist of the Negro Protest.* New York: Atheneum, 1969.

Salvatore, Nick. *Eugene V. Debs: Citizen and Socialist.* University of Illinois Press, 1984.

Schapiro, Leonard. "Lenin's Intellectual Formation and the Russian Revolutionary Background." In his *Russian Studies.* New York: Viking, 1987.

Schechter, Patricia A. *Ida B. Wells-Barnett and American Reform, 1880–1930.* Chapel Hill: University of North Carolina Press, 2001.

Seigfried, Charlene Haddock. 2013. "The Social Self in Jane Addams' Prefaces and Introductions." *Transactions of the Charles S. Peirce Society: A Quarterly Journal in American Philosophy.* Vol. 49, No. 2, pp. 127-156.

Service, Robert. *Lenin: A Biography.* Cambridge, Mass.:

Harvard University Press, 2000.

Shepherd, A. P. *Scientist of the Invisible: Spiritual Science, the Life and Work of Rudolf Steiner.* Rochester, Vt.: Inner Traditions International, 1983.

Silbey, David J. *A War of Frontier and Empire: The Philippine-American War, 1899–1902.* New York: Hill and Wang, 2007.

———. *The Boxer Rebellion and the Great Game in China.* New York: Hill and Wang, 2012. Print.

Silkey, Sarah. *Black Woman Reformer: Ida B. Wells, Lynching, and Transatlantic Activism.* Athens: U of Georgia P, 2014. Print.

Sklar, Kathryn Kish. "Why Were Most Politically Active Women Opposed to the ERA in the 1920s?" In *Rights of Passage: The Past and Future of the ERA,* ed. Joan Hoff-Wilson. Bloomington: Indiana University Press, 1986.

Smith, Richard. *China's Cultural Heritage: the Qing Dynasty, 1644-1912.* Boulder, CO: Westview Press, 1994. Print.

Smock, Raymond W. *Booker T. Washington: Black Leadership in the Age of Jim Crow.* Chicago: Ivan R. Dee, 2009. Print.

Sparrow, Bartholomew H. *The Insular Cases and the Emergence of American Empire.* Lawrence: University Press of Kansas, 2006.

Steffens, Lincoln. *The Autobiography of Lincoln Steffens.* New York: Harcourt, Brace, and World, 1931.

Steiner, Rudolf. *Autobiography: Chapters in the Course of My Life, 1861–1907,* trans. Rita Stebbing. Great Barrington, Mass.: SteinerBooks, 2006.

Taliaferro, John. *All the Great Prizes: The Life of John Hay, from Lincoln to Roosevelt.* New York: Simon & Schuster, 2003.

"The Insular Cases." Island Law Web site. http://macmeekin.com/Library/Insular%20Cases.htm. Accessed on January 28, 2008.

"The Niagara Movement." *African American History of Western New York.* University of Buffalo, Apr. 1996. Web. 2 Jan. 2008. <http://www.math.buffalo.edu/~sww/0history/hwny-niagara-movement.html>. Accessed on January 2, 2008.

"Theodore Roosevelt Speeches: Fifth Annual Message (December 5, 1905)." Miller Center of Public Affairs Web site. http://www.millercenter.virginia.edu/scripps/digitalarchive/speeches/spe_1 905_1205_roosevelt. Accessed on February 11, 2008.

The Rise and Fall of Jim Crow. PBS/Educational Broadcasting Corporation, 2002. Web. 2 Aug. 2016. <http://www.pbs.org/wnet/jimcrow/>.

Tinsley, James A. "Roosevelt, Foraker, and the Brownsville Affray." *Journal of Negro History* 41 (Jan. 1956): 43–65.

Unger, Nancy C. *Fighting Bob La Follette: The Righteous Reformer.* Chapel Hill: University of North Carolina Press, 2000. Print.

University Press.

Urofsky, Melvin I. *Louis D. Brandeis and the Progressive Tradition.* Boston: Little, Brown, 1981.

Vesser, Cyrus. *A World Safe for Capitalism: Dollar Diplomacy and America's Rise to Global Power.* New York: Columbia University Press, 2002.

———. "Inventing Dollar Diplomacy: The Gilded Age Origins of the Roosevelt Corollary to the Monroe Doctrine." *Diplomatic History* 27 (June 2003): 301–326.

Vining, Elizabeth Gray. *Friend of Life: The Biography of Rufus M. Jones.* Philadelphia: Lippincott, 1958.

Vizenor, Gerald. "Edward Curtis: Pictorialist and Ethnographic Adventurer." In William R. Handley and Nathaniel Lewis, eds., True West: Authenticity and the American West. Lincoln: University of Nebraska Press, 2004. Pp. 179-193.

"Vladimir Lenin Works Index." Lenin Internet Archive Web site. http://marxists.org/archive/lenin/works/index.htm.

Washington, Booker T. *Up from Slavery.* Mineola, NY: Dover Publications, 1995. Print.

Weaver, John D. *The Brownsville Raid.* New York: W. W. Norton, 1970.

W. E. B. Du Bois: Online Resources. Library of Congress, 2016. Web. 2 Aug. 2016. <http://www.loc.gov/rr/program/bib/dubois>.

———. *W. E. B. Du Bois: The Fight for Equality and the American Century: 1919–1963.* New York: Henry Holt, 2009.

Wells, Ida B. *Crusade for Justice: The Autobiography of Ida B. Wells.* Ed. Alfreda M. Duster. Chicago: University of Chicago Press, 1991. Print.

———. *Southern Horrors and Other Writings; The Anti-Lynching Campaign of Ida B. Wells, 1892–1900.* Ed. Jacqueline Jones Royster. New York: Bedford Books, 1996. Print.

White, George Henry. *In His Own Words: The Writings, Speeches, and Letters of George Henry White.* Ed. Benjamin R. Jutesen. Lincoln, NE.: iUniverse, Inc., 2004.

Widenor, William C. *Henry Cabot Lodge and the Search*

for an American Foreign Policy. Berkeley: University of California Press, 1980.

Wilkinson, Roy. *Rudolf Steiner: An Introduction to His Spiritual World-View, Anthroposophy.* Forest Row, U.K.: Temple Lodge Publishing, 2001.

Wilson, Colin. *Rudolf Steiner: The Man and His Vision.* London: Aeon Books, 2005.

Wilson, Harold. *McClure's Magazine and the Muckrakers.* Princeton, NJ: Princeton University Press, 1970.

Wilson, Raymond. *Ohiyesa: Charles Eastman, Santee Sioux.* Urbana: University of Illinois Press, 1983.

Woloch, Nancy. Muller v. Oregon: *A Brief History with Documents.* Boston: Bedford Books of St. Martin's Press, 1996.

Wolters, Raymond. *Du Bois and His Rivals.* Columbia, Missouri: University of Missouri Press, 2003.

Yarbrough, Tinsley E. *Judicial Enigma: The First Justice Harlan.* New York: Oxford University Press, 1995.

Zimmerman, Joan G. "The Jurisprudence of Equality: The Women's Minimum Wage, the First Equal Rights Amendment, and *Adkins v. Children's Hospital,* 1905–1923." *Journal of American History* 78, no. 1 (1991): 188–225.

Zimmermann, Warren. *First Great Triumph: How Five Americans Made Their Country a World Power.* New York: Farrar, Straus, and Giroux, 2002

Index

Symbols
14th Amendment 50–302, 51–302
59th Congress, The 32–302, 35–302, 36–302
111th Congress 175–302

A
abolition 31–302, 45–302, 143–302, 145–302, 195–302, 215–302, 216–302
abolitionists 31–302, 155–302, 163–302, 192–302
accommodationist 184–302, 197–302, 205–302, 206–302, 212–302
acculturation 245–302
Adams, H.B. 50–302
Adams, John Quincy 130–302
Adams, Samuel Hopkins 35–302
Addams, Jane v–302, 43–302, 48–302, 279–302
adulterated food 35–302, 40–302
Affordable Care Act 31–302
African American press 213–302
African Church 187–302
African Methodist Episcopal Church 193–302, 195–302, 203–302
Agricultural Bank 148–302
Aguinaldo, Emilio 73–302, 76–302
All Friends Conference 261–302
Allgeyer v. Louisiana 51–302, 54–302
allotment 245–302, 246–302
All-Russian Work 110–302, 114–302
American Anti-Slavery Society 192–302
American Asiatic Squadron 73–302
American Federationist 65–302, 66–302, 67–302
American Federation of Labor 11–302, 64–302, 65–302, 66–302, 68–302, 172–302
American Friends Service Committee 255–302, 261–302
American Indian project 247–302, 252–302
American Labor Party 184–302, 200–302
American Missionary Association 185–302, 194–302, 207–302, 210–302
American Quakerism 260–302, 264–302
American Railway Union 8–302, 9–302, 10–302, 11–302, 65–302
American Woman Suffrage Association 26–302, 31–302, 207–302
Ames, Albert Alonzo "Doc" 13–302
Ames, Dr. Alfred Elisha 14–302
Ames gang 19–302, 20–302

Amish 264–302
Anglo-American 140–302, 161–302
Anglo-Saxon 77–302, 85–302, 86–302, 88–302, 156–302, 160–302, 161–302
Antebellum America 26–302
Anthony, Susan B. 26–302
Anthroposophical Society 268–302, 269–302, 277–302
Anthroposophy 266–302, 268–302, 269–302, 277–302
anti-black violence 155–302, 162–302, 165–302
anti-lynching bill 174–302
Anti-Lynching Bureau 159–302
Anti-Lynching Campaign 165–302, 212–302
anti-lynching legislation 167–302
Antiquities Act of 1906 34–302, 237–302
antitrust legislation 58–302, 65–302
Apache 245–302
Apacheland 248–302
apostolic days 261–302, 262–302
Appeal to the Coloured Citizens of the World 193–302, 195–302
A Red Record: Tabulated Statistics and Alleged Causes of Lynching in the United States 211–302
Armstrong, Samuel C. 176–302
Armstrong v. United States 89–302
assimilated Indians 240–302
assimilationist 194–302
Atlanta Compromise 186–302, 190–302, 192–302, 194–302, 197–302
Atlanta Exposition 177, 177–302, 219, 219–302
Atlanta Independent 235–302
Atlanta slave trade 185–302, 201–302
Attucks, Crispus 192–302, 194–302
Austro-Prussian War 268–302
Authorized Declaration of Faith 257–302, 260–302
Autumnal Court of Assize 95–302
Aycock, Charles 192–302, 196–302

B
Bacon, Sir Francis 172–302
Baer, Judith 56–302
Baker, A. Y. 234–302
Baker, Ray 13–302, 25–302
Banneker, Benjamin 192–302, 194–302
Barbadoes, James G. 192–302
Barbarous Mexico v–302, 142–302, 143–302, 150–

302, 152–302, 279–302
Barnett, Ferdinand L. 156–302
Besant, Annie 267–302, 277–302
Bierce, Ambrose 142–302
Big Hunter 243–302
Bill of Grievances 65–302
Bishop, Henry M. 182–302, 212–302
black activism 205–302
Black Codes 173–302
black consciousness 184–302
black press 213–302
black separatist 207–302
black suffrage 162–302, 177–302, 205–302, 211–302, 221–302
Blavatsky, Helena 267–302, 277–302
Blocksom, Major General Augustus P. 234–302
Bolshevik Party 103, 103–302, 115, 115–302, 115–302
Bontecou, Josephine 13–302
boodle town 14–302, 23–302
Boston Riot 214–302
Bowen, John Wesley Edward 192–302
Boxer Protocol v–302, 94–302, 99–302, 100–302, 101–302, 135–302, 279–302
Boxer Rebellion xi–302, 71–302, 94–302, 99–302, 100–302, 101–302, 102–302, 134–302, 140–302
boycott 8–302, 11–302, 12–302, 65–302, 67–302, 68–302
Braithwaite, Joseph Bevan 257–302, 259–302
Braithwaite, William 260–302
Brandeis brief 49–302, 54–302, 56–302
Brandeis, Louis 50–302, 53–302, 54–302
Brewer, David J. 49–302
Brooke, Edward W. 175–302
Brown, John 188–302, 195–302
Brownsville vi–302, 220–302, 223–302, 225–302, 226–302, 228–302, 231–302, 233–302, 234–302, 235–302, 279–302
Brownsville Legacy Special Message to the Senate vi–302, 223–302, 279–302
Brown, Tom 21–302, 22–302
Brown v. Board of Education 56–302
Brown, William Wells 193–302, 195–302
Bruce, Blanche Kelso 192–302, 195–302
Bruno, Giordano 266–302
Bryan, William Jennings ix–302, 6–302, 77–302
Buffalo Soldiers 232–302
Bulkeley, Morgan G. 223–302
bummers 169–302, 170–302

Bunau-Varilla, Philippe 117–302, 118–302, 126–302
Bunting v. Oregon 56–302
Bunyan, John 24–302, 35–302
Bureau of Chemistry 35–302, 41–302
Bureau of Indian Affairs 240–302, 245–302, 246–302
Burns, Lucy 27–302
Burt, General A. S. 233–302
Butler, Colonel Ed. 14–302
Butler, Nicholas Murray 44–302
Byron, George Gordon Lord 192–302

C
Camp Mabry 233–302
Canadian Yearly Meeting 260–302
capitalism ix–302, x–302, 43–302, 44–302, 101–302, 104–302, 112–302, 114–302
Captain Alexander 19–302
Carnegie, Andrew 180–302
carpetbaggers 172–302, 173–302
Carrill, General Lauro 147–302
caste 143–302, 189–302, 191–302, 196–302
Catholic Inquisition 266–302
Cato of Stono 187–302, 192–302, 194–302
Cato's Rebellion 192–302, 194–302
Charlotte Observer 229–302
Chernyshevsky, Nikolay Gavrilovich 115–302
Chicago Conservator 156–302, 207–302
Chicago Daily Inter-Ocean 156–302, 164–302
Chicago Tribune 158–302
Chicago World's Fair 155–302
Childe Harold's Pilgrimage 192–302
child labor ix–302, x–302, 24–302, 30–302, 35–302, 59–302, 151–302
Chinese Christians 100–302, 101–302
Christian Indians 245–302
Christian Worker 260–302
Cigar Makers' International Union 64–302
civic equality 195–302, 198–302
civic rights 190–302, 195–302
civil disobedience 31–302
Civil Rights Act of 1866 196–302
Civil Rights Act of 1875 173, 173–302, 174, 174–302, 196, 196–302
Civil Rights Act of 1964 218–302
Civil Rights Cases of 1883 197–302
civil rights movement 185–302, 201–302, 213–302, 222–302
Clarke, Hovey C. 13–302, 19–302, 24–302
class conflict 11–302, 26–302, 105–302

Claude 171–302, 172–302
Clayton Act 64–302, 65–302, 68–302, 69–302
Cleveland Gazette 166–302
Cloud, Henry Roe 245–302
Coffee John 16–302, 19–302, 21–302, 22–302
Cohen, "Reddy" 18–302
Coit, Dr. Stanton 43–302
collective bargaining 59–302, 64–302
Collier, John 245–302, 246–302
Collier's Weekly 35–302, 151–302
Colón 118–302, 119–302, 120–302, 124–302
Combe, Mayor Frederick J. 234–302
Committee of 100 246–302
Committee of the Whole 166–302, 171–302
Compromise of 1877 174–302, 196–302
Auguste Comte 267–302
Com. v. Beatty 51–302
Com. v. Hamilton Mfg. Co 51–302
Confederate soldiers 196–302
Confederate states 163–302, 164–302, 196–302
Congressional Black Caucus Foundation 175–302
Conservative Friends 259–302
Constitutional League 235–302
convict-lease system 215–302, 217–302, 218–302
cotton-gin 187–302
Cotton States and International Exposition 221–302
Council of National Defense 27–302
Crawford, A. M. 50–302
Crisis, The 126–302, 184–302, 185–302, 198–302, 200–302, 201–302, 205–302, 214–302
Critique of Pure Reason 268–302
Croly, Herbert 44–302
Crossman v. United States 89–302
Crow, Jim 142–302, 165–302, 170–302, 171–302, 173–302, 174–302, 183–302, 202–302, 203–302, 211–302, 215–302, 217–302, 219–302, 235–302
Alexander Crummell 188–302, 192–302, 195–302, 203–302
Cuffe, Paul 192–302, 195–302
curtailment 214–302, 217–302
Curtis, Edward S. vi–302, 247–302, 253–302

D

Daily Record, The 182–302
Danbury Hatters' Case v–302, 64–302, 65–302, 67–302, 69–302, 279–302
Danish blacks 187–302, 192–302, 194–302
Darwin, Charles 219–302
Daughters of the American Revolution 44–302

Davis, Jefferson 186–302, 193–302, 194–302
Debs, Eugene V. v–302, vii–302, 8–302, 12–302, 279–302
Declaration of Faith 257–302, 260–302, 264–302, 265–302
Declaration of Independence 143–302, 219–302, 280–302
Declaration of Principles vi–302, 213–302, 214–302, 217–302, 218–302, 219–302, 220–302, 221–302, 279–302
declaration of women's rights 31–302
Defense of the Negro Race 166–302, 175–302
DeLaittre 17–302
De Lima v. Bidwell 80–302, 81–302, 89–302
D. E. Loewe & Company 67–302
Derham, James 192–302
desegregation 218–302, 220–302
detribalizatiton 251–302
Detroit 79–302, 240–302
Dewey, Commodore George 73–302, 224–302
Dewey, John 44–302
Diaz, Porfirio 142–302, 143–302, 144–302, 146–302, 150–302, 151–302
Diaz system 143–302, 144–302, 150–302
"Digger" Indians 249–302, 250–302
dime novels 239–302
disorderly houses 16–302, 17–302, 18–302, 23–302
doctrine of the Light 258–302, 259–302
Dominguez, M. Y. 234–302
Dooley v. United States 89–302
double-consciousness 194–302
Douglass, Frederick 155–302, 188–302, 192–302, 195–302, 203–302, 209–302, 217–302, 221–302
Downes v. Bidwell v–302, 79–302, 80–302, 89–302, 90–302, 92–302, 93–302, 279–302
Dreyfus, Captain Alfred 163–302
Durham, James 194–302
Dyer bill 165–302

E

Eastman, Charles vi–302, 237–302, 239–302, 243–302, 245–302, 246–302, 279–302
Eastman, Jacob 239–302, 245–302
Eastman, Seth 239–302
Education and Welfare 41–302
Edwards, "Billy" 17–302, 19–302, 20–302
Eight Box Law 181–302
Eight Men Lynched 155–302
Eight-Nation Alliance 94–302, 99–302

Elliott, Robert Brown 192–302, 195–302
Elwood, Lester 20–302
emancipation 51–302, 115–302, 163–302, 176–302, 188–302
Emerson, Ralph Waldo 260–302
Empress Dowager Cixi 94–302
Enforcement Acts 173–302
English-American common law tradition 53–302
enlightened industrialism 46–302, 47–302
equal protection under the law 220–302
Essential Truths vi–302, 257–302, 258–302, 260–302, 262–302, 263–302, 264–302, 279–302
Evangelical Friends Alliance 264–302
Evangelicalism 258–302
Evans, Mrs. Lon 234–302
execration 215–302, 217–302

F

Farewell Address to Congress v–302, 166–302, 279–302
Federal Security Agency 41–302
Federation of Organized Trades and Labor Unions 65–302
feminist theory 26–302
Fenton, William D. 50–302, 53–302
Fichte, Johann Gottlieb 266–302
Field, Stephen J. 49–302
Fifteenth Amendment 174–302, 175–302, 181–302, 196–302, 197–302, 204–302, 211–302, 220–302, 222–302
Filipino insurrection 78–302
Filipinos 71–302, 74–302, 75–302, 76–302, 77–302, 78–302, 91–302, 233–302
First Battalion 223–302, 233–302, 234–302, 235–302
First Nat. Bank v. Leonard 50–302
First US Volunteer Cavalry 224–302
Fitchette, John 16–302
Five Years Meeting of the Friends in America 257–302
Food and Drug Act v–302, vii–302, 32–302, 35–302, 36–302, 40–302, 41–302, 42–302, 151–302, 224–302, 279–302
Food and Drug Administration 32–302, 36–302, 41–302
Foraker Act 89–302, 91–302, 92–302
Foraker, Joseph B. 223–302, 235–302
Fort Snelling reservation 14–302
Fourteen Diamond Rings v. United States 89–302
Fourteenth Amendment 53–302, 54–302, 56–302, 164–302, 173–302, 196–302, 197–302, 198–302, 220–302, 222–302
Fox, George 257–302, 258–302, 259–302, 260–302, 264–302
franchise 51–302, 52–302, 54–302, 173–302, 208–302
Franciscan order 193–302
Fred Malone 18–302
Freedman's Aid Society 210–302
freedmen 185–302, 208–302
Freedmen's Aid Society 207–302
Freedmen's Bureau, The 173–302
free-market economy 49–302
Free Negroes 185–302
Friends in America 257–302, 260–302
Friends of the Indian Movement 245–302
Friends United Meeting 257–302, 265–302
Friends World Committee for Consultation 261–302
From the Deep Woods to Civilization 246–302
fugitive slaves 163–302
Fuller, Margaret 31–302
Fuller, Melville Weston 80–302
fundamentalism 260–302

G

Gardner, A. L. 16–302
Garland, Hamlin 245–302
Garlington, General 225–302, 231–302
Garvey, Marcus 207–302
Gilded Age ix–302, 44–302, 47–302, 133–302, 194–302
Gilfry, Henry H. 50–302
Gilman, Charlotte Perkins 44–302
Gnosis 266–302, 267–302
Goetheanum 268–302, 269–302
Goethe, Johann Wolfgang von 266–302, 275–302
Goetze v. United States 89–302
Goldmark, Josephine 54–302
Gompers, Samuel v–302, vii–302, 11–302, 64–302, 69–302, 279–302
Goodale, Elaine 240–302
Gotcher, Emma 53–302
grandfather clause 174–302, 181–302, 204–302, 218–302, 221–302
Grand Laundry 50–302, 53–302
Grant, Brig. Gen. U. S. 228–302
Grant, Ulysses S. 232–302
Great Depression 198–302
Great Migration 153–302, 164–302, 174–302, 175–302

Great Mystery 243–302, 244–302, 253–302
Great Separation, The 258–302
Great Society 31–302
greenbacks 201–302, 203–302
Grimké, Sarah and Angelina 192–302
Guardian 213–302, 214–302, 222–302
Guinn v. United States 221–302
Gurneyite Friends 257–302
Gurneyite Orthodox 258–302
Gurneyite Quakers 259–302
Gurneyite-Wilburite split 261–302
Gurney, Joseph John 257–302, 258–302

H
hackmen 170–302, 171–302
Haikwan tael 96–302
Haitian Revolution 193–302
Hakadah 239–302, 241–302, 242–302, 243–302
hallowed 215–302, 217–302
Hampton, Wade 173–302
Haney, B. E. 50–302
Hapsburg monarchy 268–302
Harding, Warren G 66–302
Harlem Renaissance 184–302
Harpers Ferry 195–302
Harper v. Virginia State Board of Elections 175–302
Harriman Expedition 247–302
Harrison, Benjamin 49–302, 79–302
Harrison Narcotics Tax Act 41–302
Haselbock, Joe 50–302
Hastings 159–302
hatters' union 65–302, 68–302
Hawaii v. Mankichi 90–302
Hawkins, Augustus 223–302
Hay-Bunau-Varilla Treaty 124–302
Hayes, Rutherford B. 125–302, 174–302, 196–302
Hayes-Tilden Compromise of 1877 196–302
Hay-Pauncefote Treaty 125–302
Haytian revolt 187–302, 192–302
Hay, U.S. Secretary of State John 117–302
Hepburn Act 58–302, 224–302
Hero of San Juan Hill, the 224–302
Hesse, Ex-Corporal 229–302
Hicks, Elias 258–302
Hicksite 257–302, 259–302
Hield, Willard J. 20–302
Hill, Captain 16–302, 21–302
Holden v. Hardy 51–302, 54–302
Hongzhang, Li 94–302, 95–302

Hose, Sam 159–302, 162–302
Howard, "Cheerful Charlie" 19–302
Howard University 167–302
H.R. 13801 171–302
Hughes, Langston 193–302, 195–302
Hull House 43–302, 44–302
Huntington, Collis P. 208–302
Hutterite Brethren 264–302

I
Ida B. Wells Club, The 156–302
imperialists 139–302
incorporation doctrine 79–302, 90–302, 91–302, 92–302
Indian affairs 237–302, 240–302
Indian Boyhood vi–302, 237–302, 239–302, 243–302, 245–302, 279–302
Indian culture 239–302, 245–302, 253–302
Indian languages 246–302
Indian policy 239–302, 245–302, 251–302
Indian Territory 237–302
Inner Light 258–302, 262–302, 263–302
Insular Cases, the xi–302, 79–302, 90–302, 92–302, 93–302
insurrectos 73–302, 78–302
integrationist 198–302
International Association of Machinists 65–302
International Peace Conference 46–302, 47–302
international police power 128–302, 130–302
International Women's Congress for Peace and Freedom 44–302
Interstate Commerce Commission Act 224–302
Inward Light 258–302
Irish Home Ruler 160–302, 161–302

J
Jackson, Helen Hunt 142–302
James Forten 192–302, 203–302
jefe politico 147–302, 148–302, 150–302
John Milholland 235–302
Johnson, Andrew 173–302
Johnson, James Weldon 221–302
Johnson, Lyndon 175–302
Jones, Alderman D. Percy 21–302
Jones, Judge 230–302
Jones, Rufus M. vi–302, 257–302, 260–302, 265–302, 279–302
Jones, Thomas Goode 230–302
Jordan, Barbara 175–302

Joshua 9–302, 191–302, 193–302
"jumped" a claim 156–302, 161–302
Jungle, The x–302, 35–302, 41–302
Jutesen, Benjamin H. 166–302

K
Kansas Yearly Meeting 259–302
Kant, Immanuel 268–302
Ketteler, Baron von 95–302, 99–302, 101–302
King, Captain "Norm" 21–302
King James I 173–302
Kipper, Sergeant John 233–302
Kitchin, William W. 171–302
Knights of Labor 65–302
Knights of the White Camellia 164–302
Krishnamurti, Jiddu 268–302
Krumweide, Captain 21–302
Ku Klux Klan 162–302, 164–302, 173–302, 196–302, 207–302, 221–302

L
labor movement x–302, 11–302, 14–302, 64–302, 65–302, 67–302, 114–302
LaFollette, Robert 245–302
Lakota Indians 252–302
land-grant colleges 182–302
Langston, Charles 193–302, 195–302
Lanham, Governor S. W. T 234–302
Lassalle, Ferdinand 64–302
Lauriat, Charles 252–302
Lee, Robert E. 229–302, 230–302
Lenin, Vladimir Ilich 103–302
Letter to the Governor of Barbados 257–302
Lincoln, Abraham 117–302, 173–302, 198–302
Lippmann, Walter 44–302
literacy tests 174–302, 175–302, 204–302, 218–302, 221–302, 232–302
Living Way 155–302
Lochner v. New York 51–302, 52–302, 53–302, 54–302, 55–302, 80–302
Lodge, Henry Cabot v–302, 73–302, 74–302, 78–302, 279–302
Loewe, Dietrich 67–302
Loewe v. Lawlor 65–302, 67–302
Long Rifle 243–302
Louis Brandeis 53
Lowell, Abbott Lawrence 92–302
Lucifer-Gnosis 266–302, 267–302
Lutherans 257–302

lynching bees 157–302, 160–302
lynch law 156–302, 164–302
lynch mob 155–302, 164–302, 165–302

M
MacArthur, Brigadier General Arthur 73–302
Macklin, Edgar 235–302
Magna Carta 65–302
magnanimità 45–302, 46–302
Magyar language 268–302
Manifest Destiny 73–302, 77–302
Manning, John 50–302
Many Lightnings 239–302
Marxism 64–302, 65–302, 104–302, 114–302, 115–302
Marx, Karl 12–302, 64–302, 114–302, 143–302
Mason and Dixon's line 157–302, 161–302
materialistic spell 273–302, 276–302
May Fourth Movement 101–302
McCarthy, Senator Joseph 184–302, 200–302
McClure's Magazine 13–302, 25–302, 151–302
McClure, S. S. 13–302, 23–302
McDonald, Captain William J. "Bill" 234–302
McKinley, William v–302, ix–302, 1–302, 3–302, 76–302, 91–302, 117–302, 127–302, 131–302, 167–302, 224–302, 279–302
Meat Inspection Act 35–302, 42–302, 224–302
meatpacking industry 24–302, 35–302
Megaarden, Sheriff 18–302, 19–302
Meix, Roman 18–302
Memories of an Indian Boyhood 237–302
Mennonites 264–302
Meriam Report 246–302
Merritt, Major General Wesley 73–302
Methodists 257–302
Miller, Kelly 189–302, 193–302
Modernist Quakers 260–302
monopolies ix–302, 1–302, 6–302, 64–302, 67–302, 68–302
Monroe, James 127–302, 130–302
Montezuma, Carlos 245–302
Morgan, J. Pierpont 247–302
Moskowitz, Dr. Henry 198–302
Moss, Thomas 211–302
Mount Ranier 247–302
muckrakers x–302, 13–302, 24–302, 25–302, 35–302, 142–302, 151–302, 152–302
mulatto 187–302
Muller, Curt 50–302, 53–302

Muller v. Oregon v–302, 49–302, 57–302, 279–302
Mysterious Medicine 243–302

N

National Afro-American Council 159–302
National American Woman Suffrage Association 26–302, 31–302, 64, 207–302
National Association for the Advancement of Colored People 44–302, 153–302, 165–302, 177–302, 184–302, 185–302, 199–302, 200–302, 201–302, 205–302, 206–302, 212–302, 213–302
National Civic Federation 64–302, 65–302, 66–302
National Conference of Social Work 44–302
National Consumers League 49–302, 54–302
National Equal Rights League 214–302
National Formulary 38–302, 41–302
National Peace Jubilee 194–302
National War Labor Board 66–302
Native American Graves Protection and Repatriation Act of 1990 237–302
Native peoples 239–302
Natus, Frank 234–302
Navajo 251–302
The Naval War of 1812 223–302
Nebraska Yearly Meeting 260–302
Negro-American 215–302
Neighborhood Guild of New York City 43–302
Nettleton, General A. B. 223–302, 231–302
neutrality 65–302, 123–302
New Culture Movement 101–302
New Deal 12–302, 25–302, 31–302
New England Yearly Meeting 258–302, 260–302, 261–302
Newer Ideals of Peace 43–302, 47–302
New Panama Canal Company 120–302, 122–302, 123–302, 124–302
Newton, Private James W. 234–302
New York Age 155–302, 164–302, 166–302, 207–302
New York Commercial Advertiser 13–302
New York Evening Post 13–302
Niagarites 213–302, 217–302, 218–302, 220–302
Nicholson, William 259–302
Nietzsche, Friedrich 267–302
Nineteenth Amendment 26–302, 27–302, 31–302, 55–302
Ninetieth Congress 175–302
Ninety-third Congress 175–302
Nixon, Richard M. 223–302

North American Review 235–302

O

Obama, Barack 31–302, 175–302
Ohio Yearly Meeting 259–302, 260–302
Ohiyesa 239–302, 244–302, 245–302, 246–302
Olcott, Henry Steel 277–302
Old Testament 46–302, 193–302
Opium Wars 100–302
Order of the Star in the East 268–302
Oregon's maximum-hours law 55–302
Oregon Supreme Court 53–302
Oregon Yearly Meeting 260–302
orphanages 215–302, 217–302, 218–302
Orthodox Friends 257–302, 258–302, 260–302, 264–302
Orthodox Quakers 257–302, 259–302, 260–302, 263–302, 264–302

P

Pabst Brewing Company 18–302
pacifist ideology 48–302
Page, Thomas Nelson 191–302, 193–302, 196–302
pan-Africanism 214–302
Panama Canal v–302, xi–302, 71–302, 117–302, 120–302, 122–302, 123–302, 124–302, 126–302, 133–302, 135–302, 224–302, 279–302
Panama Railroad Company 120–302, 122–302, 123–302, 124–302
Pan-American Federation of Labor 66–302
Panic of 1873 64–302
Parting of the Ways vi–302, 200–302, 203–302, 204–302, 205–302, 279–302
Passing of the War Virtues v–302, 43–302, 47–302, 279–302
patent medicine industry 35–302
Paul, Alice 26–302, 27–302
Pearson, Dr. F. S. 149–302
Penrose, Major Charles W. 234–302
peonage 143–302, 145–302, 146–302, 150–302, 215–302, 217–302, 218–302, 230–302
People's Grocery 211–302
People's Savings Bank in Philadelphia 167–302
Philadelphia Yearly Meeting 258–302
Philippine insurrection 233–302
Phillips, Clara 248–302
philology 250–302
Phoenix Awards Dinner 175–302
Pilgrim's Progress 24–302, 35–302

Pine Ridge Agency 240–302
Pine Ridge Reservation 252–302
Platt Amendment 73–302, 91–302, 128–302, 129–302, 130–302
Platt, Orville H. 130–302
Plessy, Homer A. 181–302
Plessy v. Ferguson 79–302, 80–302, 164–302, 174–302, 182–302, 197–302, 204–302, 211–302, 219–302, 221–302, 232–302
political machine 23–302, 177–302, 221–302
poll tax 172–302, 174–302, 175–302, 181–302, 197–302
Populist 15–302, 65–302, 232–302
Populist-Democrat ticket 15–302
Portsmouth Peace Conference 224–302
post-Civil War era 245–302
Powers, Fred M. 21–302
Price, William G. 193–302, 194–302
Priest, Oscar Stanton De 174–302
professional revolutionaries 103–302, 108–302, 110–302, 113–302, 114–302
Progressive Era ix–302, x–302, xi–302, 1–302, 280–302
Progressive movement ix–302, 13–302, 43–302, 245–302
Progressive party 48–302
prohibition 31–302, 99–302
Prosser, Gabriel 192–302, 195–302
Pueblo people 252–302
Pullman, George 11–302, 65–302
Pullman Palace Car Company 8–302, 11–302, 65–302
Pure Food and Drug Act of 1906 41–302, 42–302
Puritan 14–302, 18–302, 79–302
Purvis, Robert 193–302

Q

Qing Dynasty 94–302, 99–302, 100–302, 101–302, 102–302
Quaker 43–302, 255–302, 257–302, 258–302, 259–302, 260–302, 261–302, 262–302, 263–302, 264–302, 265–302
Queen Elizabeth I 171–302
Quintana Roo 145–302

R

race relations 180–302, 194–302, 197–302, 200–302, 207–302, 213–302, 233–302
race riot 165–302, 198–302, 221–302
race-suicide 27–302, 29–302, 30–302
racial equality 173–302, 198–302, 214–302, 232–302
racial segregation 174–302, 205–302
Radical Reconstruction 173–302
Radical Republicans 173–302, 196–302
Raleigh, Sir Walter 170–302, 171–302, 173–302
Reconstruction Acts of 1867 173–302
Redeemers 173–302, 174–302
Red Progressives 245–302
Red Scare 184–302, 200–302
"red-shirt" bands 157–302
Red Shirts 162–302, 164–302, 192–302, 196–302
Reed, Private Oscar W. 234–302
Reformation era 257–302, 264–302
Reformed 257–302
Religious Society of Friends 257–302, 258–302, 260–302, 264–302
Remond, Charles Lenox 193–302, 195–302
Republican Motherhood 30–302
reservation schools 240–302
Revolution of 1876 188–302, 193–302
Rhoads, James E. 257–302
Richmond Conference 257–302, 259–302, 260–302
Richmond Declaration of Faith 264–302
Richmond Planet 235–302
Rio Grande River 252–302
Ritchie v. People 51–302
Roosevelt Corollary to the Monroe Doctrine v–302, 127–302, 132–302, 133–302, 279–302
Rough Riders 77–302, 127–302, 224–302
Roundhead 14–302
Russian Social Democratic Labor Party 103–302
Russo-Japanese War xi–302, 134–302, 139–302, 141–302, 224–302

S

sacerdotalism 262–302, 263–302
Saint Petersburg industrial war of 1896 104–302, 111–302
Salem, Peter 192–302, 194–302
Salem Poor 192–302, 194–302
Sand Creek Massacre 245–302
Santa Fe 63–302, 252–302
Santee Dakota 237–302, 239–302
Santee uprising 243–302
Sant, Governor Van 18–302
Sayers, Joseph D. 233–302
Schiller, Johann Christoph Friedrich von 275–302
Schopenhauer, Arthur 267–302
Scott, Nathan B. 235–302

Second Great Awakening 30–302, 258–302
Second Separation 258–302
segregated schools 206–302
Senate Committee on Military Affairs 223–302, 235–302
sensory-supersensory form 267–302
separate-but-equal 56–302, 219–302, 222–302
separatism 220–302
settlement house 43–302
Seventy-first Congress 175–302
sex discrimination vii–302, 56–302
Shadd, Abraham 193–302
Shame of the Cities, The 13–302, 25–302
Shaw, Anna Howard v–302, 26–302, 30–302, 31–302, 279–302
A. P. Shepherd 277–302
Sherman Antitrust Act ix–302, 64–302, 65–302, 67–302, 68–302
shunktokecha 241–302
Sino-Japanese War 100–302, 134–302, 135–302, 140–302
Sivers, Marie von 267–302
slave revolt 192–302, 193–302, 194–302
Snake Dance 251–302
Social Darwinism 29–302, 30–302
Social Democratic Party 107–302, 109–302, 114–302
Socialist Party of America 12–302, 65–302
Social Law and the Spiritual World 263–302
Society of American Indians 245–302
Socrates 186–302, 193–302
Southern Horrors 155–302, 165–302, 206–302, 207–302, 211–302, 212–302
Southern Railway Company 219–302
Spanish Inquisition 158–302, 161–302, 162–302
S. Pearson & Son 149–302
Speer, Judge 230–302
Spooner bill 76–302, 78–302
Spooner, John C. 74–302, 76–302
Springfield riots 198–302
Standard Oil 13–302, 25–302, 60–302, 61–302, 62–302, 63–302, 151–302
Starr, Ellen Gates 43–302
Statement on Suffrage v–302, 176–302, 279–302
State v. Buchanan 51–302
Steffens, Lincoln v–302, x–302, 13–302, 25–302, 151–302, 152–302, 279–302
Steiner, Rudolf vi–302, vii–302, 255–302, 266–302, 268–302, 277–302, 279–302
St. Francis of Assisi 186–302, 193–302

Stieglitz, Alfred 252–302
stoicism 241–302, 243–302, 244–302
Stoic philosophers 243–302
Stono Rebellion 192–302, 194–302
Stover, Charles B. 43–302
Strasser, Adolph 64–302
Strivings of the Negro People 185–302, 201–302
suffrage laws 176–302, 181–302
suffrage movement x–302, 26–302, 31–302

T

Taft, William H. x–302
Talented Tenth 197–302, 218–302, 222–302
Tammany Hall 14–302, 25–302, 151–302
Tarbell, Ida x–302, 13–302, 25–302, 152–302
Tarbell, Isa M. 151–302
Tate, Fred 234–302
Taylor, Bayard 14–302
tenement regulation 43–302
Tenth Cavalry 232–302
Tewa girl portrait 252–302
Texas Rangers 232–302, 234–302
Theosophical Library 267–302
Theosophical Society 267–302, 269–302, 277–302
Theosophy vi–302, 266–302, 267–302, 269–302, 275–302, 277–302, 279–302
Thirteenth Amendment 31–302, 173–302, 196–302
Thirty Years of Lynching in the United States, 1889–1918 165–302
Thomas, James Carey 257–302
Tilden, Samuel J. 174–302
Tillman, Ben 191–302, 192–302, 196–302
Albion W. Tourgée 164–302, 165–302
Tourgée, Albion W. 164–302, 165–302
Toussaint Louverture 193–302, 195–302
Toynbee Hall 43–302
Treaty of Paris 74–302, 76–302, 79–302, 89–302, 91–302, 92–302
Trotter, William Monroe 214–302, 217–302, 221–302, 222–302
truth and science 266–302
Turner, Nat 187–302, 193–302, 195–302
Tuskegee Institute 176–302, 177–302, 182–302, 193–302, 194–302, 197–302, 205–302, 209–302, 218–302
Tweed, William March "Boss" 25–302
Twenty-fifth Infantry Regiment 223–302
Twenty-fourth Amendment 175–302
Twenty-fourth Infantry Regiment 224–302

Two o'Clock Minute 264–302

U
understanding clause 181–302
Uniform Discipline 257–302, 259–302, 260–302, 262–302, 264–302
United Hatters of North America 66–302, 67–302, 68–302
United States Pharmacopoeia 38–302, 41–302
United States v. Cruikshank 197–302
United States v. Reese 197–302
Universal Negro Improvement Association 207–302
universal suffrage 30–302, 31–302, 157–302, 181–302
Updegraff, David B. 259–302, 263–302
Up from Slavery 183–302, 203–302
urbanization 30–302, 43–302, 55–302
US Communist Party 185–302, 201–302
US House of Representatives 42–302, 171–302

V
vanishing race 251–302
Vardaman, James Kimble 209–302
Versailles Treaty 66–302
voter registration laws 197–302
Voting Rights Act 175–302, 222–302

W
Wakan Tanka 243–302
Waldorf School 268–302
Walling, William English 198–302
War Department's Division of Insular Affairs 88–302
War Department Special Order No. 266 234–302
Washington Times 169–302
Washita Massacre 245–302
Waterites 259–302
Weaver, John D. 223–302, 235–302
Wells, Elizabeth 155–302
Wells, Ida B. v–302, vi–302, 142–302, 153–302, 155–302, 156–302, 164–302, 165–302, 182–302, 206–302, 212–302, 279–302
Wells, James 155–302
Wenham v. State 51–302
Western Yearly Meeting 259–302
Wheatley, Phillis 193–302, 194–302
Wheelock, Ernest 21–302
White, George 166–302, 174–302, 175–302
White, Justice Edward 79–302
White Leagues 164–302
Whitesboro 167–302

white supremacy groups 166–302
White, Walter 184–302, 200–302
White, Wiley 167–302
Whittier, John Greenleaf 180–302
Wilberforce University 184–302, 193–302, 195–302, 200–302, 214–302
Wilburite Conservatives 258–302
Wilbur, John 258–302
Wiley Act 35–302
Wiley, Harvey Washington 35–302
Wilhelm, Kaiser II 131–302
Wilkinson, District Attorney James 228–302
Williams v. Mississippi 174–302, 181–302, 197–302, 221–302
Wilson administration 65–302, 66–302
Wilson, Stanyarne 171–302, 172–302
Wilson, William B. 65–302
Wilson, Woodrow 12–302, 49–302, 58–302, 64–302, 65–302, 132–302, 142–302, 224–302
Winnebago 245–302
Winning of the West, The 224–302
Winter, Ella 14–302
Woloch, Nancy 56–302
Wolverton, Chief Justice 50–302
Woman's Christian Temperance Union 207–302
Woman's Peace Party 44–302
Women's Christian Temperance Union 26–302
Women's International League for Peace and Freedom 44–302
women's rights 31–302, 43–302, 49–302
Women's suffrage 55–302
Wood, James E. 257–302
Woods, James 260–302
Woodward, Walter C. 260–302
Wounded Knee massacre 240–302

Y
Young, Andrew 175–302

Z
Zedong, Mao 101–302
Zeitgeist 201–302, 203–302